Congratulations!

As a student purchasing Holt's *Markets, Games, and Strategic Behavior,* you are entitled to a prepaid subscription to a series of online economic experiments called *VeconLab.*

The duration of your subscription is 6 months.

To activate your prepaid subscription:

1. Launch your Web browser and go to www.aw-bc.com/holt.

2. Select VeconLab.

3. Click on the Register button.

4. Follow the instructions on the screen to register yourself as a new user. Your pre-assigned Access Code is located underneath the scratch-off area below:

5. During registration, you will choose a personal Login Name and Password for use in logging into the Website.

6. Once your personal Login Name and Password are confirmed, you can begin using *VeconLab.*

This Access Code can be used only once to establish a subscription. This subscription is not transferable.

If you did not purchase a new textbook, this Access Code may not be valid! Choose to buy a new textbook or visit **www.aw-bc.com/holt** for information on purchasing a subscription.

Is Something Missing?

If the tear-out card is missing from this book, then you're missing out on an important part of your learning package. Choose to buy a new textbook or visit www.aw-bc.com/holt for information on purchasing a subscription.

Markets, Games, & Strategic Behavior

THE ADDISON-WESLEY SERIES IN ECONOMICS

Markets, Games, & Strategic Behavior

CHARLES A. HOLT

University of Virginia

PEARSON

Addison
Wesley

Boston San Francisco New York
London Toronto Sydney Tokyo Singapore Madrid
Mexico City Munich Paris Cape Town Hong Kong Montreal

Publisher: Greg Tobin
Editor in Chief: Denise Clinton
Senior Acquisitions Editor: Adrienne D'Ambrosio
Editorial Assistant: Margaret Beste
Director of Development: Kay Ueno
Managing Editor: Nancy Fenton
Senior Production Supervisor: Meredith Gertz
Design Manager: Charles Spaulding
Cover Designer: Julia Boyles
Director of Media: Michelle Neil
Media Producer: Susan Schoenberg
Senior Marketing Manager: Roxanne Hoch
Marketing Assistant: Kate MacLean
Senior Prepress Supervisor: Caroline Fell
Rights and Permissions Advisor: Shannon Barbe
Senior Manufacturing Buyer: Carol Melville
Production Coordination, Composition, Text Design,
    and Illustrations: Gillian Hall, The Aardvark Group
Copy Editor: Kathleen Cantwell, C4 Technologies
Proofreader: Holly McLean-Aldis
Indexer: Jack Lewis
Cover photo: © 2007 Getty Images

Library of Congress Cataloging-in-Publication Data

Holt, Charles A., 1948-
  Markets, games, and strategic behavior / Charles A. Holt.
    p. cm.
  Includes bibliographical references and index.
  ISBN 0-321-41931-6 (alk. paper)
  1. Economics--Study and teaching--Simulation methods. 2. Markets. 3. Game theory. 4.
Negotiation in business. 5. Economics--Psychological aspects. I. Title.

  HB74.5.H65 2007
  330.01'51927--dc22
2006019685

2 3 4 5 6 7 8 9 10—CRW—10 09 08 07 06

Economics is enjoying a resurgence of interest in behavioral considerations—in the study of how people actually make decisions when rationality and foresight are not unlimited and when psychological and social considerations may play a role. As a result, economics experiments are increasingly used to study behavior in markets, games, and other strategic situations. The rising excitement about experimental results is reflected in the 2002 Nobel Prize, which was awarded to an experimental economist and an experimental psychologist. Whole new sub-disciplines are arising in the literature, including behavioral game theory, behavioral law and economics, behavioral finance, and neuroeconomics. Laboratory and field experiments provide key empirical guideposts for developments in these areas.

This book is designed to combine a behavioral approach with active classroom learning exercises. Each chapter uses an initial experiment as an organizing device to introduce the economic concepts and main results. The classroom games set up simple economic situations, such as a market or an auction, which highlight several related economic ideas. Each chapter provides a short reading (10–15 pages) for a particular class to use in a one-a-day approach. The reading can serve as a supplement to other material or (preferably) as an assignment in conjunction with an in-class "experiment" in which students play the game. Doing the experiments *before* the assigned reading enhances their teaching value. Many of the games can be run in class "by hand" with dice or playing cards. Large classes can be divided into teams of 3–6 students, which facilitates the collection and announcement of results. Such team decisions are the norm in many M.B.A. programs, since team discussions allow students to clarify strategic insights and learn from each other. The Class Experiments section contains instructions for 20 hand-run games that are adapted for classroom use.

For those with computer access, all games are available on the Companion Website for this book at http://www.aw-bc.com/holt

Many colleges and universities have wireless Internet access, so a handful of "team communicators" can bring laptops to class, and one of these can be assigned to each team. Even in a computer lab it is often most effective to have groups of 2–3 people at each computer, which helps with group learning and discussion. Such discussions are not as important for non-interactive individual decisions (for example, a choice between two gambles). In this case, the Web-based Veconlab programs can be accessed by students individually before class when it is convenient for them. Running experiments after hours is also easy for games like the ultimatum, battle of sexes, and guessing games that are only played once, since students can read instructions and enter a decision before their partners have logged in.

The Veconlab programs can be set up and run from any standard browser connected to the Internet (Internet Explorer or Mozilla) without loading any software. Full instructions for conducting the programs can be found at the Veconlab site previously mentioned. Student participants receive fully integrated instructions that conform automatically to the features selected by the instructor in the setup process. Web-based games are quicker to administer and the instructor data displays can provide records of decisions, earnings, round-by-round data averages, and in some cases, theoretical calculations. These displays can be printed or projected for post-experiment discussions. There is an extensive menu of setup options for each game that lets the instructor select parameters, such as the numbers of buyers, sellers, decision rounds, fixed payments, and payoffs. For example, the private-value auction setup menu allows one to choose the range of randomly determined private values, the number of bidders and rounds, and the pricing rule (first-price or second-price and "winner-pays" or "all-pay"). I have also taught classes where students design their own experiments and run them using other students in the class, followed by a formal (Power-Point) presentation of results in the next class.

The first several chapters of this book contain examples of markets with buyers and sellers, simple two-person games, and individual lottery choice decisions. These initial chapters raise a few methodological issues, such as if and when financial incentives are needed for research experiments. In addition, the central notions of decision making and equilibrium are introduced. The focus of these chapters is on the basics; discussion of anomalies and alternative theories is deferred until later. After these chapters are covered, there is a lot of flexibility in terms of the order of coverage of the remaining chapters, which are divided into parts: markets, bargaining, public choice, auctions, individual decisions, games, and asymmetric information. It is possible to pick and choose, based on the level and subject matter of the course.

This book can provide an organizing device for a course in experimental economics, behavioral game theory, and topics in microeconomics. Typically, each chapter is based on a key experiment that is presented with a carefully measured amount of theory and related examples. Much of the discussion pertains to laboratory experiments, but innovative field experiments are included when possible. Chapters are relatively self-contained, making it possible to select specific chapters tailored as a supplement for a particular course, such as public economics. The book can also be integrated into courses in microeconomics, managerial economics, or strategy at the M.B.A. level. Many of the experimental designs may be of interest to non-economists, such as students of political science, anthropology, and psychology, as well as anyone interested in behavioral finance or behavioral law and economics.

The modular nature of the book makes it easy to use as a supplement to add active learning and behavioral elements to upper-level classes. For an intermediate microeconomics course, recommended chapters include the introductory chapters (Chapters 2 and 3); markets (Chapters 6–10); bargaining (Chapter 12); and public goods and externalities (Chapters 14 and 16). For a course in public economics you could use Chapters 2, 3, and 12, and public choice and voting (Chapters 14, 16, 17, and 18). A game theory course could be supplemented with Chapters 1–5 and Cournot markets (Chapter 6); bargaining (Chapter 12); rent seeking (Chapter 17); behavioral game theory (Chapters 23–26); and signaling (Chapter 33). A course with a special focus on information and auctions could cover Chapters 1–5; collusion (Chapter 9); market failure and matching mechanisms (Chapter 10); auctions (Chapters 19–22); and information (Chapters 30–34). A behavioral finance course could include Chapters 1–3 and risk aversion (Chapter 4); asset markets (Chapter 11); lottery choice anomalies (Chapter 28); and Bayes' rule, cascades, signaling, and prediction markets (Chapters 30–34).

Mathematical arguments are simple, since experiments are typically based on parametric cases that distinguish alternative theories. The mathematical calculations are sometimes illustrated with spreadsheet programs that are constructed in a step-by-step process. Then, a process of copying blocks of cells results in iterative calculations that converge to equilibrium solutions. Calculus is generally avoided except in the chapters on auctions and Cournot markets. These optional sections are preceded by discrete examples and graphs that provide the intuition behind more general results.

I have tried to keep the text simple, therefore there are no footnotes. References to other papers are often confined to an Extensions section at the end of the chapter. The book does not contain extensive surveys of related literature on research experiments. Such surveys can be found in Kagel and Roth's (1995) *Handbook of Experimental Economics* and in Hey's (1994) *Experimental Economics*, which are pitched at a level appropriate for advanced undergraduates, graduate students, and researchers in the field. For more discussion of methodology see Friedman and Sunder's (1994) *Experimental Methods*. For an upper-level or graduate course in experimental economics, Davis and Holt's (1993) *Experimental Economics* has the advantage of being organized around the main classes of experiments, with presentations of the associated theory and methodological concepts. The topics and references in all of these books are somewhat incomplete, given the recent heightened interest in behavioral game theory, field experiments, and social norms. Moreover, the number of published economics papers using laboratory methods has approximately doubled since 1995, when the last of these books was published, and there are many more unpublished working papers (see Figure 1.1 in Chapter 1). These new publications are listed and categorized by keyword in the bibliography of experimental economics and social science, available online at http://www.people.virginia.edu/~cah2k/y2k.htm

A friend once asked me to name my intellectual hero, and without hesitation I mentioned Vernon Smith (who was then at the University of Arizona and is currently at George Mason University, or maybe somewhere in Alaska). His work with his colleagues and students has always been a personal inspiration. His 2002 Nobel Prize in Economics (together with Danny Kahneman) is richly deserved, and the effects of his work pervade many parts of this book. I have been strongly influenced by my thesis advisor and former University of Minnesota colleague, Ed Prescott (Arizona State University), who forced his students to stay focused on using theory to explain observed regularities in the data.

I would especially like to thank my coauthor Lisa Anderson and her College of William and Mary students for many helpful suggestions about this book and the associated software. Much of what I know about these topics is due to joint research projects with Jacob Goeree (California Institute of Technology) and with the following collaborators:

Lisa Anderson, College of William and Mary

Simon Anderson, University of Virginia

Sheryl Ball, Virginia Polytechnic Institute and State University

Jordi Brandts, Consejo Superior de Investigaciones Científicas, Barcelona, Spain

Monica Capra, Emory University

Doug Davis, Virginia Commonwealth University

Catherine Eckel, University of Texas, Dallas

Jean Ensminger, California Institute of Technology

Roland Fryer, Harvard University

Rosario Gomez, Malaga University, Spain

Susan Laury, Georgia State University

Tom Palfrey, California Institute of Technology

David Reiley, University of Arizona

Al Roth, Harvard University

Andy Schotter, New York University

Roger Sherman, University of Houston

Rick Wilson, Rice University

The insurance example in Chapter 21 was suggested by Ann Musser. I also received numerous suggestions from the Addison-Wesley staff—especially the acquisitions editor, Adrienne D'Ambrosio, who has been a strong supporter of this project for several years. Others who have offered comments on earlier versions include the following:

Mark Bykowsky, Federal Communications Commission

Juan Camilo Cardenas, Universidad de los Andes, Colombia

Jeff Carpenter and his undergraduate class, Middlebury College

Gary Charness, University of California, Santa Barbara

James Cox, Georgia State University

Rachel Croson, University of Pennlvania

Nick Feltovich, University of Houston

Dan Friedman, University of California, Santa Cruz

Brit Grosskopf, Texas A&M University

David Grether, California Institute of Technology

Phil Grossman, St. Cloud State University

Shachar Kariv, University of California, Berkeley

Howard Leatherman, University of Maryland

James Murphy, University of Massachusetts, Amherst

Charlie Plott, California Institute of Technology

Tom Rietz, The University of Iowa

Tim Salmon, Florida State University

Betsy Sinclair, California Institute of Technology

Vernon Smith, George Mason University

Annie Talman, an actress who played the role of Michael Douglas's secretary in the film *Wall Street*, suggested the relevance of that film to the material in Chapter 20. While I'm at it, I should thank the wonderful people at various coffee shops where I did a lot of writing— Java Java and Greenberries in Charlottesville, Aromas in Williamsburg, Pete's in Pasadena, and even Amtrak.

Finally, I was fortunate to have an unusually talented and enthusiastic group of University of Virginia students who read parts of the manuscript: Emily Beck, A. J. Bostian, Jeanna Composti, Kari Elasson, Erin Golub, Katie Johnson, Shelley Johnson, Kurt Mitman, Angela Smith, Mai Pham, Loren Pitt, Uliana Popova, and Stacy Roshan. Any errors should be attributed to my subsequent changes. Joe Monaco and A. J. Bostian set up the Linux servers and procedures for running the programs on a network of hand-held, wireless "pocket" PCs with color, touch-sensitive screens. Imagine a game theory class, outside on the University of Virginia lawn, with students competing in an auction via wireless pocket PCs!

Charles A. Holt
University of Virginia

Contents

■ Class Experiments

Basic Concepts:
Decisions, Game Theory,
and Market Equilibrium

Part 1, which includes Chapters 1 through 5, provides an introduction to the main types of experiments: individual decisions, games, and markets. Each chapter presents some key concepts, such as *expected value*, *risk aversion*, *Nash equilibrium*, and *market efficiency*. Knowledge of these concepts makes it possible to pick and choose among the remaining chapters based on your goals and knowledge level.

Chapter 1 begins with an introduction to experimental games used for teaching and research, which is followed by an overview of the topics covered in the book. The final two sections of the chapter contain a discussion of methodology and a brief history of the development of experimental economics. These sections are optional for students in most courses (other than experimental economics).

Chapter 2 introduces a "pit market" that corresponds to the trading of commodity contracts in a trading pit, with free intermingling of prospective buyers and sellers. The best procedure is to participate in a class pit market experiment *before* discussing the chapter material. Instructions for this are provided in Chapter 2's Pit Market experiment in the Class Experiments section.

Chapter 3 presents some simple games of competition and coordination that serve to introduce the notion of a Nash equilibrium. The prisoner's dilemma and coordination games can be used to highlight the properties and drawing power of various equilibrium configurations that arise in experiments. The guessing game, which is easily run by hand or with the Veconlab program (http://www.aw-bc.com/holt), can be used to organize a discussion of how behavior may converge to a Nash equilibrium.

Chapter 4 shifts attention to individual decisions in situations with random elements that affect money payoffs. This permits a discussion of expected money value for someone who is "neutral" toward risk. A non-neutral attitude (risk aversion or risk seeking) is the main topic.

The notions of decision making in the presence of random elements are used in Chapter 5 to analyze simple matrix games in which the equilibrium may involve randomization, i.e., games of chicken, battle-of-sexes, and matching pennies. The techniques used to find equilibria in these games will be applied in more complex situations encountered later, such as the choice of price when there is danger of being undercut slightly by competitors.

chapter 1

Introduction

1.1 Origins

Like other scientists, economists observe naturally occurring data patterns and then try to construct explanations. The resulting theories are evaluated in terms of factors like plausibility, generality, and predictive success. As with other sciences, it is often difficult to sort out cause and effect when many factors are changing simultaneously. Thus, there may be several reasonable theories that are roughly consistent with the same observations. Without a laboratory to control extraneous factors, economists often test their theories by gauging reactions of colleagues (Keynes 1936). In such an environment, theories may gain support on the basis of mathematical elegance, persuasion, and focal events in economic history like the Great Depression. Theories may fall from fashion, but the absence of sharp empirical tests leaves an unsettling clutter of plausible alternatives. For example, economists are fond of using the word equilibrium preceded by a juicy adjective (e.g., proper, perfect, divine, or universally divine). This clutter is often not apparent in refined textbook presentations.

The development of sophisticated econometric methods has added an important discipline to the process of devising and evaluating theoretical models. Nevertheless, any statistical analysis of naturally occurring economic data is typically based on a host of auxiliary assumptions. Economics has only recently moved in the direction of becoming an experimental science in the sense that key theories and policy recommendations are suspect if they cannot provide intended results in controlled laboratory and field experiments. This book provides an introduction to the study of economic behavior, organized around games and markets that can be implemented in class.

The first classroom market games were conducted at Harvard University by Edward Chamberlin (1948). He proposed a new theory of monopolistic competition, and he used experiments to highlight failures of the standard model of perfect competition. Students were given buyer and seller roles and instructions about how trades could be arranged. For example, a seller would be given a card with a cost in dollars. If the seller were to find a buyer who agreed to pay a price above this cost, the seller would earn the difference. Similarly, a buyer would be given a card with a resale value, and the buyer could earn the difference if a purchase was arranged at a price below this resale value. Different sellers could be given cards with different cost numbers, and likewise, buyers could receive different values. These values and costs are the key elements that any theory of market price determination would use to derive predictions, as explained in Chapter 2. Without going into detail, it should be clear that it is possible to set up a laboratory market and provide financial incentives by using value and cost numbers in dollar amounts and by paying subjects their earnings in cash.

Chamberlin's classroom markets produced some inefficiencies, which he attributed to the tendency for buyers and sellers in a market to break off and negotiate in small groups. Vernon Smith, who attended Chamberlin's class, later began running classroom markets with an enforced central clearinghouse for all offers to buy and sell. This trading institution is called a *double auction* since sellers' asking prices tend to decline and buyers' bid prices rise. A trade occurs when the bid-ask spread closes and someone accepts another's offer to buy or sell. Smith observed efficient competitive outcomes, even with as few as 6–10 traders. This result is significant, since the classical large numbers assumptions were not realistic approximations for most market settings. Smith's early work on the double auction market figured prominently in his winning the 2002 Nobel Prize in Economics.

A parallel development is based on game-theoretic models of strategic interactions. In a matching pennies game, for example, each player chooses heads or tails with the prior knowledge that one will win a sum of money when the coins match, and the other will win when the coins do not match. Each person's optimal decision in such a situation depends on what the other player is expected to do. The systematic study of such situations began with John von Neumann and Oscar Morgenstern's (1944) *Theory of Games and Economic Behavior*. They asserted that standard economic theory of competitive markets did not apply to the bilateral and small group interactions that make up a significant part of economic activity. Their solution was incomplete, except for the case of zero-sum games in which one person's loss is another's gain. While the zero-sum assumption may apply to some extremely competitive situations, like sports contests or matching pennies games, it does not apply to situations where both players might prefer some outcome to another.

Economists and mathematicians at the RAND Corporation in Santa Monica, California, began applying game-theoretic reasoning to military tactics at the dawn of the Cold War. In many nuclear scenarios, it is easy to imagine that the "winner" may be much worse off than would be the case in the absence of war, which results in a non-zero-sum game. At about this time, a young graduate student at Princeton entered von Neumann's office with a notion of equilibrium that applies to a wide class of games, including the special case of those that satisfy the zero-sum property. John Nash's notion of equilibrium and the half-page proof that it generally exists were recognized by the Nobel Prize committee about 50 years later. With the Nash equilibrium as its keystone, game theory has recently achieved the central role that von Neumann and Morgenstern envisioned. Indeed, with the exception of supply and demand, the Nash equilibrium is probably used as often today as any other construct in economics.

Intuitively speaking, a Nash equilibrium is a set of strategies, one for each player, with the property that nobody would wish to deviate from their planned action given the strategies being used by the other players. For example, consider a situation in which each person would prefer to go to work if the other person does, but would prefer to stay home otherwise, since working alone is less productive in this case. In this coordination game, there could be two equilibria, one in which both work and another in which both stay home. This game could be implemented in class by letting each player choose one of two playing cards, with each card corresponding to one of the two decisions.

These classroom markets and games can be quite useful because participants learn what an economic situation is like from the inside *before* seeing standard presentations of the relevant economic theory. A classroom game (followed by structured question-and-answer discussion) can let participants discover the relevant economic principle for themselves, which enhances the credibility of seemingly abstract economic models. Each of the chapters that follow is typically built around a game or market that can be run in class, either using the Veconlab Web-based software suite and/or simple props like dice, playing cards, and decision sheets provided in the Class Experiments section.

1.2   Overview

Game Theory

A careful analysis of a strategic situation typically involves more than just identifying an equilibrium. For example, an equilibrium may be a bad position from which deviations are not so costly for any individual. Alternatively, there may be multiple equilibria, so that standard equilibrium theory makes no prediction. Observed behavioral tendencies in experiments can provide important guideposts for the development of new theoretical approaches. Indeed, the mathematicians and economists at the RAND Corporation began running game experiments at about the same time as Chamberlin's classroom market experiments. Basic game-theoretic concepts are introduced in Chapters 3 and 5, and the behavioral game theory chapters in Part 6 provide a careful consideration of conditions under which behavior does or does not conform to equilibrium predictions.

Individual Decisions

A game or market may involve a relatively complex set of interactions among multiple players or traders. Sometimes it is useful to study key aspects of behavior of individuals in isolation. For example, stock markets involve major risks of gains and losses, and it is instructive to consider how individuals react to simple risks that are not generated by the behavior of others in complicated market settings. It is straightforward to set up a simple decision experiment by giving a person a choice between gambles or lotteries, e.g., between a sure $1 and a coin flip that yields $3 in the event of heads. Which would you choose in this case? What if the choice were between a sure $100,000 and a coin flip that provides a fifty-fifty chance of $0 and $300,000? These types of decisions are considered in Chapter 4, which introduces the notions of expected values and risk aversion. Basic notions of decision making under risk are useful in the analysis of interactive situations in subsequent chapters. In addition, the chapters in Part 7 focus on a series of specific decision-making situations, e.g., prediction, search, and information processing.

Markets

Part 2 covers several ways that economists have modeled market interactions, with firms choosing prices, production quantities, quality grades, or entry decisions. Some markets have distinct groups of buyers and sellers; others more closely resemble stock markets in which purchase and resale is common. Market experiments can be used to assess the antitrust implications of mergers, contracts, and other market conditions. One goal of such experiments is to identify factors that increase the extent to which markets achieve all possible gains from trade, i.e., the market efficiency. Laboratory markets with enough price flexibility and good information about going prices tend to be highly efficient. In some contexts, however, laboratory markets can fail to generate efficient outcomes, due to imperfections in information, market power, or collusion among sellers.

Bargaining

Economic decisions in small-group settings often raise issues of fairness, since earnings may be inequitable. In a simple ultimatum bargaining game, one person proposes a way to divide a fixed amount of money, say $100, and the other may either agree to the division, which is implemented, or may reject the division, which results in zero earnings for both. Attitudes about inequity are more difficult to model than the simpler selfish money seeking motives that may dominate impersonal market situations. In this case, research experiments can provide insights in areas where theory is silent or less developed. Many topics in law and economics, for example, involve bargaining (e.g., bankruptcy and pre-trial settlements). Bargaining experiments have also been used by anthropologists (Ensminger 2004; Henrich et al. 2001) to study attitudes about fairness in primitive societies in Africa and South America. Part 3 pertains to games where fairness, equity, and other interpersonal factors seem to matter.

Public Choice

Inefficiencies can occur when some costs and values are not reflected in prices. For example, it may be difficult to set up a market that allows public goods like national defense to be provided by decentralized contributions. Another source of potential inefficiency occurs when one person's activity has a negative impact on others' well being, as is the case with pollution or the over-use of a freely available, shared resource. Non-price allocation mechanisms often involve the dedication of real resources to lobbying. No individual contestant would want the value of their effort to exceed the value of the object being sought, but the aggregate lobbying costs for a number of individuals may be large relative to the value of the prize. The public choice chapters in Part 4 pertain to such situations; topics include voluntary contributions, the use of a common-pool resource, costly lobbying, and voting-based resource allocations.

Auctions

The advent of Web-based communications has greatly expanded the possibilities for setting up auctions that connect large numbers of geographically dispersed buyers and sellers. Auctions are used extensively, for example, to allocate local communications bandwidth licenses to competing firms, and experiments have been instrumental in the design and testing of such auctions in the United States and in many European countries. Experiments provide government officials with confidence that new procedures will function smoothly and efficiently. In Virginia, for example, officials decided to adopt an innovative clock auction with computer driven bid increases, after observing how the process worked in laboratory experiments conducted at George Mason University. Similarly, several experimental economists at Georgia State used experiments to devise a set of rules that were used in a Georgia auction to determine which farmers would be paid not to irrigate during a severe drought in 2001. State officials observed some of these experiments before drafting the actual auction procedures. A large-scale field trial with more than one hundred bidders at five southwest Georgia locations preceded the actual auction, which involved about 200 farmers and $5 million in irrigation reduction payments. The auction had much of the look and feel of a laboratory experiment, with the reading of instructions, a round-by-round collection of bids, and Web-based bid collection and processing. Part 5 pertains to such auctions, including an account of current FCC initiatives for auctioning off combinations or packages of broadcast licenses. These initiatives are being evaluated by laboratory experiments conducted at a number of universities in the United States and Europe.

Information

Markets may also fail to generate efficient results when prices do not convey private information. With limited information, individuals often rely on signals like educational credentials or ethnic background. Informational asymmetries can produce interesting patterns of conformity or "herding" that may have large effects on stock prices, hiring patterns, and other data series where decisions are made in sequence. Experiments are particularly useful in these cases, since the effect of informational disparities is to produce many Nash equilibria. In addition, laboratory and field markets can be used to aggregate information held by different individuals; these are popularly called *prediction markets*. The information chapters in Part 8 include experiments on *Bayesian learning, herding, signaling, information aggregation,* and *discrimination.*

1.3 Methodology

The behavioral insights and theoretical predictions presented in the following chapters are illustrated with results from experiments run in the laboratory and the field. In order to evaluate the resulting data with a careful, skeptical eye, it is essential to understand underlying methodological considerations.

Treatment Structure

A treatment is a completely specified set of procedures, which includes instructions, incentives, and rules of play. Just as scientific instruments need to be calibrated, it is useful to calibrate economics experiments. *Calibration* typically involves establishing a baseline treatment for comparisons. For example, suppose that individuals are given sums of money that can either be invested in an individual account or a group account, where investments in the group account have a lower return to the individual, but a higher return to all group members. If the typical pattern of behavior is to invest half in each account, then this might be attributed either to the particular investment return functions used or to "going fifty-fifty" in an unfamiliar situation. In this case, a pair of treatments with differing returns to the individual account may be used. Suppose that the investment rate for the individual account is 50 percent in one treatment, which could be due to confusion or uncertainty, as indicated above. The importance of the relevant economic incentives could be established if the investment rate in the individual account falls sharply when the return for investing in the individual account is reduced.

Next, consider a market example. High prices may be attributed to small numbers of sellers or to the way in which sellers are constrained from offering private discounts to particular targeted buyers. These issues could be investigated by changing the number of sellers, holding discount opportunities constant, or by changing the nature of allowed discounting while holding the number of sellers constant. Many economics experiments involve a *2×2 design* with treatments in each of the four cells, e.g., low numbers with discounting, low numbers without discounting, high numbers with discounting, and high numbers without discounting.

One common design flaw is to use a treatment structure that changes more than one factor at the same time, so that it is difficult to determine the cause of any observed change in behavior. For example, a well-known study of lottery choice compared the tendency of subjects to choose a sure amount of money over a lottery that may yield higher or lower payoffs. In one treatment, the payoffs were in the $0 to $10 range with real money, and in another treatment the payoffs were in thousands of (hypothetical) dollars. The author concluded that there were no incentive effects, since there was no observed difference in the tendency to choose the safe payoff. The trouble with this conclusion is that the high-payoff treatment was conducted under hypothetical conditions, so two factors were being changed: the scale of the payoffs, and whether or not they were real or hypothetical. This conclusion turns out to be questionable. For example, Holt and Laury (2002) report in their experiments that scaling up hypothetical choices has little effect on the tendency to select the safer option. Thus, choice patterns with low real payoffs look like choice patterns with both low and high hypothetical payoffs. However, scaling up the payoffs in the real (non-hypothetical) treatments to hundreds of dollars causes a sharp increase in the tendency to choose the safer option. It is interesting to note that Holt and Laury were (correctly) criticized for presenting each subject with a low-payoff lottery choice *before* they made high-payoff choices, which can confound payoff-scale and order effects. To address this issue, Holt and Laury (2005) report an experiment in which each person made decisions in a single payoff-scale treatment only, all done in the same order, which brings us to the next topic.

Between-Subjects versus Within-Subjects Designs

Many of the following chapters are based on a single experiment. In order to preserve time for discussion, classroom experiments typically involve a pair of treatments. One issue is whether half of the people are assigned to each treatment, which is called a *between-subjects design*. The alternative is to let each person make decisions in both treatments, which puts more people into each treatment but affords less time to complete multiple rounds of decision making in each treatment. This is called a *within-subjects design* or sequential design, since behavior for a group of subjects in one treatment is compared with behavior for the same group in the other treatment. The between subjects and within subjects terminology is commonly used in psychology, where the unit of observation is typically the individual subject. Subjects in economics experiments generally interact, so the unit of analysis is normally the group or market, where a "within" design usually involves running one treatment before another, with the same group of subjects.

Each type of design has its advantages. If behavior is slow to converge or if many observations are required to measure what is being investigated, then the parallel (between-subjects) design may be preferred since it will generate the most repeated observations per treatment in the limited time available. Moreover, subjects are only exposed to a single treatment, which avoids *sequence effects*. For example, a market experiment that lets sellers discuss prices may result in some successful collusive arrangements, with high prices that may carry over even if communication is not allowed in a second treatment. When students are asked to design a classroom experiment to be conducted on others, they often come up with sequences of treatments for the same group. The most common ex post self-assessment is that "I wish I had used a single treatment on each half of the class so that we would not have to wonder about whether the change in behavior between treatments was due to prior experience." (For example, Figure 6.4 in Chapter 6 shows a sequence of dots that seem to evolve continuously across a change in treatment, as they decline from one theoretical prediction to another.) Even in research experiments, it is annoying to have to report and analyze decisions differently depending on where they were observed in a sequence.

Sometimes sequence effects are themselves the focus of the experiment, e.g., the issue of whether the imposition of a minimum wage causes worker aspiration wage levels to increase (Fehr 2006). If sequence effects are not the focus, they may be avoided with the use of a between-subjects design by exposing each group of subjects to a single treatment, and comparisons can be made across groups by recruiting from the same subject pool for the different treatments.

The advantage of a sequential (within-subjects) design is that individual differences are controlled by letting each person serve as their own control. For example, suppose that you have a group of adults, and you want to determine how much running speed is increased if people are wearing running shorts instead of blue jeans. In any group of adults, running speeds may vary by factors of 2 or 3, depending on weight, age, health, and other factors. In this case, it would be desirable to time running speeds for each person under both conditions, with alternating treatment orders, unless the distance is so great that fatigue would cause major sequence effects. In general, a within-subjects design (two or more treatments for each group) is more appealing if there is high behavioral variability across individuals or groups, e.g., the runners, relative to the variability caused by sequencing. A between-subjects design (one treatment per group) is better when there is less variability across individuals or groups, and when there are sequence effects that cause behavior in one treatment to be influenced by what happened in an earlier treatment. Sometimes the best choice between sequential and parallel designs is not clear, and a *sequence of experiments*, one with each method, provides a better perspective on the behavior being studied, e.g., the Holt and Laury (2002, 2005) combination of within-subjects and between-subjects designs.

Incentives

Economics experiments typically involve monetary decisions like prices, investments, or costly efforts. Most economists are suspicious of results of experiments done with hypothetical incentives, and therefore real cash payments are almost always used in laboratory research. As we will see in later chapters, sometimes incentives matter a lot and sometimes they do not matter at all. For example, people are more generous in offers to others when such offers are hypothetical than when generosity has a real cost; and people are considerably more risk averse when the stakes are very high (hundreds of dollars for a single decision) than when the stakes are hypothetical or involve only several dollars. Conversely, it is hard to imagine that scaled money payments would help serious students raise their GRE scores, and there is even some psychological evidence that money payments interfere with a child's test performance. In economics experiments, the general consensus is that money payments or other non-hypothetical incentives are necessary, because the underlying theoretical models have agents who are assumed to be motivated by incentives. Nevertheless, there is some evidence that scaling up payoffs does not have much of an effect in many laboratory situations (Smith and Walker 1993). There are many documented situations in the economics and psychology literature where money incentives do not seem to have much effect, but in the absence of a widely accepted framework for identifying such situations with precision, it is usually advisable to use money incentives in laboratory economics experiments.

In the classroom, it is not possible or even desirable to use monetary payments. The results of class experiments can provide a useful learning experience as long as the effects of payments in research experiments are provided when important incentive effects have been documented. Therefore, the presentations in the chapters that follow are based on a mixture of class and research experiments. When the term "experiment" or "research experiment" is used, it means that all earnings were at reasonable levels and were paid in cash. The term "classroom experiment" indicates that payoffs were basically hypothetical. However, for non-market classroom experiments discussed in this book, the author picked one person at random ex post and paid a small fraction of earnings, usually several dollars. This procedure is not generally necessary, but it was followed to reduce unexpected differences between classroom and research data.

Replication

One of the main advantages of experimental analysis is the ability to repeat the same setup numerous times in order to determine average tendencies that are relatively insensitive to individual or group effects. Replication requires that instructions and procedures are carefully documented. It is essential that instructions to subjects are written as a script that is followed exactly with each cohort that is brought to the laboratory. Having a set of written instructions helps ensure that unintended biased terminology is avoided, and it permits other researchers to replicate the reported results. The general rule is that enough detail should be reported so that someone else could replicate the experiment in a manner that the original author(s) would accept as being valid, even if the results turned out to be different. For example, if the experimenters provide a number of examples of how prices determine payoffs in a market experiment, and if these examples are not contained in the written instructions, the different results in a replication may be due to differences in the way the problem is presented to the subjects.

Control

A second main advantage of experimentation is the ability to control the factors that may affect observed behavior, so that extraneous factors are held constant (controlled) as the treatment variable changes. Control can be reduced or lost when procedures make it difficult to determine the incentives that participants actually faced in an experiment. The use of biased terminology may allow participants to act on homegrown values that conflict with or override the induced money incentives. For example, experiments pertaining to markets for emissions permits typically do not use the word pollution. If people are trading physical objects like university sweatshirts, differences in individual valuations make it hard to reconstruct the nature of demand in a market experiment. There are, of course, situations where non-monetary rewards are desirable, such as experiments designed to test whether ownership of a physical object makes it more desired (the endowment effect). Thus, control should always be judged in the context of the purpose of the experiment.

Another factor that can disrupt control is the use of deception. If subjects suspect that announced procedures are not being followed, then the announced incentives may not operate as intended. This counter-productive incentive effect is probably the main reason that deceptive practices are much less common in incentive-based economics experiments than in social psychology experiments. Even if deception is successfully hidden during the experiment, subjects may learn the truth afterward by sharing their experiences with friends, so the careful adherence to non-deceptive practices provides a public good for those who run experiments in the same lab at a later time. Ironically, the perverse incentive effects of deception in social psychology experiments may be aggravated by an ex post confession or debriefing, which is sometimes required by human subjects committees.

Psychological Biases

There is a rich behavioral literature in economics and psychology that documents psychological aspects of decision making that may have strong effects on economic behavior. These effects are sometimes called *biases* or *anomalies*, and many of them are summarized in Kahneman, Slovic, and Tversky (1982), Laibson (1997), Samuelson and Zeckhauser (1988), Tversky and Thaler (1990), and in Richard Thaler's provocative publications (e.g., Thaler 1988, 1989, 1992). Anomalies and biases will be considered in detail in later chapters, but it is useful to mention some that are most relevant for experimental design now.

- ■ **Loss Aversion:** This is the tendency for losses to provide stronger stimuli than gains. It is not uncommon for subjects to react strongly and erratically to losses, and it would be a serious mistake to make losses more prevalent in one treatment than in another, unless this difference is the focus of the experiment or the necessary result of the treatment.
- ■ **Status Quo Bias:** This is the tendency for subjects to maintain a decision or condition that is established by others or by the experimenter. A closely related idea is the notion of *anchoring*, whereby options are evaluated with reference to an initial position or salient property. Examples used in instructions may suggest focal starting points that can be a problem if they seem to affect results. This can be avoided by using numbers that are quite different from those that will be encountered in the experiment, or by letting subjects provide their own examples and then having the experimenter check calculations for those examples.

- **Endowment Effect:** Often it seems to be the case that ownership of an item or option increases its value to the owner. In particular, the elicitation of a *willingness to accept* sale price by an owner will typically generate higher values than the elicitation of a *willingness to pay* by a prospective buyer. A low willingness to pay for a gamble that has randomly determined payoffs indicates risk aversion, but the same person if given the gamble may demand a high selling price or willingness to accept, which would indicate risk-loving behavior. It is essential that results of an experiment are not reached through biases induced by ownership, unless this is the purpose of the experiment.

Context in Laboratory and Field Experiments

An important design decision for any experiment pertains to the amount and richness of context to provide. A little economic context can be very useful. For example, it is possible to set up a market with a detailed and tedious description of earnings in abstract terminology that does not mention the word "price." But market terminology helps subjects figure out which way is up, i.e., that sellers want high prices and buyers want low prices. Nevertheless, it is an accepted practice in economics experiments to strip away a lot of social context that is not an essential part of the economic theories being tested. If the theories being tested do not depend on assumptions about social context, then often the best approach is to try to hold this context constant as the economic parameters are changed. This process of holding context constant may involve minimizing its unintended and unpredictable effects, e.g., by taking steps that increase anonymity during the experiment. Even then, a lot can be learned by re-introducing social context in a controlled manner, e.g., by comparing individual and group decisions.

Social context can sometimes be critically important, as in some politics experiments where it is not possible to re-create the "knock on the door" or phone campaign solicitation in the lab. In such cases, researchers use *field experiments* involving people in their natural environments, who may not know that they are participating in an experiment. For example, Gerber and Green (2000) targeted political messages to randomly selected voters, using phone, personal contact, or mail, in order to evaluate the effects of these messages on voter turnout, which was determined by looking at precinct records after the election. Field experiments can also provide more relevant groups of subjects and can be used to avoid *experimenter demand effects*, i.e., situations in which behavior in the lab may be influenced by subjects' perceptions of what the experimenter wants or expects. There are, of course, intermediate situations where the lab setup is taken to the field, to use traders from particular markets in a context that they are familiar with. For example, List and Lucking-Reiley (2000) set up auctions for sports cards at a collectors' convention. Another type of *enriched laboratory experiment* involves making the lab look and feel more like the field situation, as in voting experiments where subjects are seated in a comfortable room decorated like a living room and are shown alternative campaign ads that are interspersed with clips from a local news show.

Although field experiments can introduce a more realistic social context and environment, the cost is often a partial loss of control over incentives, over measurement of behavior, or over the ability to replicate under identical conditions. For example, the effects of alternative political ads on voting behavior in an enriched laboratory setting are typically measured indirectly by surveys of voters' intentions, since actual votes for one candidate or another are not public information. In addition, replication may be complicated by interactions between political ads used in the experiment and the positive or negative dynamics of an ongoing political campaign. In other cases, reasonably good controls are available; e.g., even though individual valuations for specific sports cards are not induced directly, they can be approximately controlled by using matched pairs of cards with identical book values.

To the extent that social context and target demographics are important in a field experiment, each field experiment is in some sense like a data point that is specific to that combination of subjects and context unless appropriate random selection of subjects is employed. Thus, the results from a series of field experiments become more persuasive, just as do the results from a series of laboratory experiments, which is a point made convincingly by Kagel and Roth (1995). There can also be important interactions between the two approaches, as when results from the lab are replicated in the field, or when a general, but noisy, pattern discovered in diverse field situations shows up in a laboratory setting that abstracts away from the diverse field conditions. Parallel laboratory and field experiments will be discussed in some of the following chapters.

Independent Observations

In order to reach conclusions supported by standard statistical arguments, it is necessary to have independent observations. For example, suppose you run a market with communication among sellers and get an average price of $10, and you run it again without communication and get an average price of $9. Even though this outcome is consistent with your original hypothesis that communication would facilitate price increases, a strong statistical argument cannot be made on the basis of the overall average prices for these two sessions alone (at least not without further statistical modeling of the economic processes within each session). This is because there is always some randomness in prices, and under the null hypothesis of no effect, it is just as likely that the price in the communication session yields a higher price as a lower price. On the other hand, if you ran three separate market sessions with communication and observed higher prices than with three other no-communication sessions, the chances of seeing this pattern under the null hypothesis are much lower. In particular, think of each communication session as a quarter and each no-communication session as a dime. There are 20 different ways that the quarters and dimes can be arrayed along a horizontal line that represents average prices (see Question 5 at the end of the chapter), and of these, the most extreme outcome (all three quarters on the high price side) was observed, so the chance is only 1/20 that this could happen under the null hypothesis in which all 20 outcomes are equally likely. Thus, the null hypothesis of no-communication effect could be rejected at the $1/20 = 5$ percent level (when the alternative hypothesis is that communication raises prices). (See Questions 3–5 at the end of the chapter for a mathematical formula that can be used to construct these counting arguments.) These arguments do not depend on specific distributions with parameters for the mean and variance (like the normal distribution), and hence, the resulting tests are called *nonparametric* tests. The clearest presentation of the kinds of nonparametric statistics commonly used by experimenters can be found in Siegel (1956) or Siegel and Castellan (1988), which contain many examples from economics and psychology. These types of statistical arguments will be encountered in later chapters, but the main idea at this point is that making a statistical claim depends on getting sufficiently strong results with enough independent observations.

Independence of observations can be lost due to contamination. For example, if you had four pairs of people negotiating over the division of $10 and if the first agreement reached was announced, then it might affect the remaining three agreements. A more subtle case of contamination may be with re-matching, so that people are dealing with different partners in the second round. Without announcements, there would be four independent bargaining outcomes in round one, but the round two results might depend on the subjects' experience in the first round, which could result in contamination and loss of independence. If random matching is desired in order to make each round more like a single-period game, then the standard approach is to treat each group of people who are being re-matched in a series of rounds as a single independent observation. In this case, the experimenter would need to bring in a number of separate groups for each of the treatments (or treatment orders) being investigated. If this seems like an unnecessarily conservative approach, remember that the experimenter is often trying to persuade skeptics about the importance of the results.

Finally, it is important to qualify this discussion by noting that a lot might be learned from even a very small number of market trading sessions, each with many (e.g., hundreds) of participants. The analysis requires careful econometric modeling of the dynamic interactions within a session, so that the un-modeled factors can reasonably be assumed to be independent shocks. Think of it this way, the U.S. macro-economy is a single observation with lots of interactions, but this does not paralyze macroeconomists or invalidate econometric models of macroeconomic phenomena where much of the interest is in the interactive dynamics. But if the process being studied does not require dynamic interactions of large numbers of participants, then a design with more independent observations allows the researcher to reach conclusions without relying on extra modeling assumptions. Replication is one of the main advantages of experimental methods.

Fatal Errors

Professional economists often look to experimental papers for data patterns that support existing theories or suggest desirable properties of new theories and public policies. Therefore, the researcher needs to be able to distinguish between results that are replicable from those that are artifacts of improper procedures. Even students in experimental sciences should be sensitive to procedural matters so that they can evaluate others' results critically. Moreover, experiments can provide a rich set of topics for papers and senior theses.

Those who are new to experimental methods in economics should be warned that there are some fatal errors that can render the results of economics experiments useless. As the above discussion indicates, these include the following:

- inadequate or inappropriate incentives
- non-standardized instructions and procedures
- inappropriate context
- uncontrolled effects of psychological biases
- an insufficient number of independent observations
- loss of control due to deception or biased terminology
- the failure to provide a calibrated baseline treatment
- the change in more than one design factor at the same time

1.4   A Brief History of Experimental Economics

Figure 1.1 shows the trends in published papers in experimental economics. The first papers by Chamberlin and some of the game theorists at RAND were written in the late 1940s and early 1950s. In addition, early interest in experimental methods was generated by

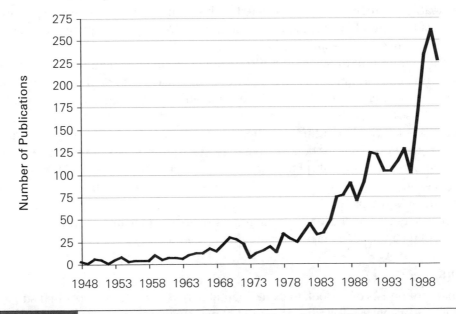

Figure 1.1   Number of Published Papers in Experimental Economics

the work of Fouraker and Siegel (1963). (Siegel was a psychologist with high methodological standards; some of his work on probability matching will be discussed in Chapter 27.) In the late 1950s, business school faculty at places like Carnegie-Mellon became interested in business games, for teaching and research. And Vernon Smith's early market experiments were published in 1962. Even so, there were fewer than 10 publications per year before 1965, and fewer than 30 per year before 1975. Much of the interesting work during this period was done by Reinhard Selten and other Germans; there was an international conference on experimental economics held in Germany in 1973. During the late 1970s, Vernon Smith was a visitor at Caltech, where he began working with Charles Plott, who had studied at Virginia under James Buchanan and was interested in public choice issues. Plott's (1979) first voting experiments stimulated work on voting and agendas by political scientists in the early 1980s. Other interesting work included the Battalio, Green, and Kagel (1981) experiments with rats and pigeons, and Al Roth's early bargaining experiments, e.g., Roth and Malouf (1979). There were still fewer than 50 experimental economics publications per year before 1985. At about that time, a thesis advisor and former colleague told me that "Experimental economics was dead end in the 1960s and it will be dead end in the 1980s."

In the 1970s and 1980s, Vernon Smith and his colleagues and students at the University of Arizona established the first large laboratory and began the process of developing computerized interfaces for experiments. In particular, Arlington Williams wrote the first double auction program in 1976. After a series of conferences in Tucson, the Economic Science Association was founded in 1986, and the subsequent presidents constitute a partial list of key contributors (Smith, Plott, Battalio, Hoffman, Holt, Forsythe, Palfrey, Cox, Schotter, Camerer, Fehr, and Kagel).

Vernon Smith and Mark Isaac began editing *Research in Experimental Economics*, a series of collected papers appearing about every other year since 1979. The first comprehensive books in this area were published in the 1990s, e.g., Davis and Holt (1993) and Hey (1994). The *Handbook of Experimental Economics*, edited by Kagel and Roth (1995), contains survey papers on key topics such as auctions, bargaining, public goods, and market experiments. These surveys have some "bite," and they are still remarkably good resources. The first specialty journal, *Experimental Economics*, was started in 1998. The strong interest among Europeans is indicated by the fact that one of the founding co-editors (Arthur Schram) was the University of Amsterdam, where there is a separate Department of Experimental Economics. The Economic Science Association now hosts an annual international meeting and additional regional meetings in the United States Europe, and Asia. These developments have resulted in more than one hundred publications every year since 1990, with highs of more than 200 per year since 1999. A searchable bibliography of more than 4,000 papers in experimental economics and related social sciences can be found in *Y2K Bibliography of Experimental Economics* (http://www.people.virginia.edu/~cah2k/y2k.htm).

There are lots of exciting developments in the field. Economics experiments are being integrated into introductory courses and the workbooks of some major texts. Theorists are looking at laboratory results for applications and tests of their ideas, and policymakers are increasingly willing to look at how proposed mechanisms perform in controlled tests before risking a full-scale implementation. Experimental methods have been used to design large auctions (e.g., the FCC spectrum auctions) and systems for matching people with jobs (e.g., medical residents and hospitals). Two of the recipients of the 1994 Nobel Prize in Economics, Nash and Selten, were game theorists who had run their own experiments. Most significantly, the 2002 Nobel Prize in Economics was awarded to an experimental economist (Smith) and to an experimental psychologist (Kahneman), who is widely cited in the economics literature. Economics is well on its way to becoming an experimental science!

QUESTIONS

One of the themes of this book is that learning by doing can help students discover and understand key concepts at a deeper level. In addition to participating in experiments, it is important to try out one's understanding by working through problems. Some of the questions that follow provide a brief introduction to the way non-parametric statistical arguments are used by experimentalists.

1. It has been observed that collusion on price may be hard to establish if it involves unequal sacrifices, but that once established, collusive agreements in experiments can be stable under some conditions, e.g., if mid-period changes in posted prices are not allowed. In an experiment to evaluate the effects of communication opportunities on price levels, would you prefer to have each group of sellers subjected to a single treatment, or would you prefer to have each group experience some periods with communication and some without, perhaps alternating the order? What considerations might be relevant?

2. A consulting firm conducted a random survey of community residents, describing a planned riverside park and then asking each respondent the question: "What is the most that you would be willing to pay to have this park built along the river?" Do you think that the monetary benefits estimated from the responses are likely to be an overestimate or an underestimate? What is the source of the bias?

3. Consider a between-subjects design with two treatments: dime and quarter. If there are just two separate sessions, one with each treatment, and if the one with the lowest price outcome is listed on the left, then the two possible ranking outcomes can be represented as DQ and QD. Suppose instead that there are two sessions with each treatment, so that one of the possible rankings is DDQQ. Find the other five rankings.

4. The setup in Question 3, with two sessions in each of two treatments, yields six possible rankings of the D and Q designators. Mathematically, this represents the number of

ways of ranking four things by type, when there are two things of each type. The mathematical formula for this is: (4*3*2*1) divided by (2*1)*(2*1), or (4!)/(2!)*(2!), which yields 24/4 = 6. Now consider a setup with a total of six sessions, with three sessions for each of two treatments, D and Q. Either calculate or count the number of rankings by type, and explain your answer. (It is not permissible to simply quote the number given in the chapter.)

5. Think about the intuition behind the ratio of factorial expressions in the previous question. With four items, there are four ways to pick the first element in a sequence, three ways to pick from the remaining three elements, two ways to pick the third element, and only one element left for the final position, so the number of possible orders is 4*3*2*1. Thus, the numerator of the formula (4!) is the total number of possible rankings for the sessions. Division by the factorial expressions in the denominator reduces the number in the numerator. This is done because all that is required in the statistical argument is that the sessions be identified by the treatment, e.g., Q or D, and not by the particular session done with that treatment. For example, if Q_1 is the first session done with the Q treatment, and Q_2 is the second session, then the two orderings, Q_1Q_2 and Q_2Q_1, are only counted once, since the theory does not make a prediction about order within the same treatment. Using this observation, explain why the denominator in the formula is the product of two factorial expressions.

6. Consider a within-subjects design in which each person (or group) is exposed to two treatments, e.g., two numerical decisions (D_1 and D_2) are made under differing conditions, with one decision to be chosen at random ex post to determine earnings. If $D_1 > D_2$, then code this as a heads for that person. A natural null hypothesis would be that the probability of heads is 1/2, so the chances of two heads in two trials is (1/2)(1/2) = 1/4. If there are five subjects and heads is observed in all cases, what are the chances that this could have occurred at random?

chapter 2

A Pit Market

When buyers and sellers can communicate freely and openly as in a trading pit, the price and quantity outcomes can be predictable and efficient. Deviations tend to be relatively small and may be due to informational imperfections. The discussion should be preceded by a class experiment, either using playing cards and the instructions provided in this chapter's Pit Market experiment in the Class Experiments section, or using the Double Auction program, which is listed under the Markets menu on the Veconlab site.

2.1 A Simple Example

Chamberlin (1948) set up the first market experiment by letting students with buyer or seller roles negotiate trading prices. The purpose was to illustrate systematic deviations from the standard theory of perfect competition. Ironically, this experiment is most useful today in terms of what factors it suggests are needed to promote efficient, competitive market outcomes.

In the experiment, each seller was given a card with a dollar amount or cost written on it. For example, one seller could have a cost of $2 and another could have a cost of $8. The seller earned the difference between the sale price and the cost, so the low-cost seller searched for a price above $2 and the high-cost seller searched for a price above $8. The cost was not incurred unless a sale was made, i.e., the product was "made to order." The seller would not want to sell below cost, since the resulting loss would be worse than the zero earnings from no sale.

Similarly, each buyer was given a card with a dollar amount or value written on it. A buyer with a value of $10, for example, earned the difference if a price below this amount was negotiated. A buyer with a lower value, say $4, would refuse prices above that level, since a purchase above value would result in negative earnings.

The market is composed of groups of buyers and sellers who can negotiate trades with each other, either bilaterally or in larger groups. For example, suppose that the market

Table 2.1	A Market Example			
Values			**Costs**	
Buyer 1	$10	Seller 9		$2
Buyer 2	$10	Seller 10		$2
Buyer 3	$10	Seller 11		$2
Buyer 4	$10	Seller 12		$2
Buyer 5	$4	Seller 13		$8
Buyer 6	$4	Seller 14		$8
Buyer 7	$4	Seller 15		$8
Buyer 8	$4	Seller 16		$8

structure is shown in Table 2.1. There are four buyers with values of $10 and four buyers with values of $4. Similarly, there are four sellers with costs of $2 and four sellers with costs of $8.

In addition to the "structural" elements of the market (numbers of buyers and sellers, and their values and costs), we must consider the nature of the market price negotiations. A *market institution* is a full specification of the rules of trade. For example, one might let sellers post catalogue prices and then let buyers contact sellers if they wish to purchase at a posted price, with discounts not permitted. This institution, known as a *posted-offer auction*, is sometimes used in laboratory studies of retail markets. The asymmetry, with one side posting and the other responding, is common when there are many people on the responding side and few on the posting side. Posting on the thin side may conserve information costs, and agents on the thin side may have the market power to impose prices on a "take-it-or-leave-it" basis. In contrast, Chamberlin used an institution that was symmetric and less structured; he let buyers and sellers mix together and negotiate bilaterally or in small groups, much as traders of futures contracts interact in a trading pit. Sometimes he announced transactions prices as they occurred, much as market officials watching over the trading pit would key in contract prices that are posted electronically and flashed to other markets around the world. At other times, Chamberlin did not announce prices as they occurred, which may have resulted in more decentralized trading negotiations.

2.2 A Classroom Experiment

Figure 2.1 shows the results of a classroom pit market experiment using the setup shown in Table 2.1. Participants were University of Virginia education school students who were interested in new approaches to teaching economics at the secondary school level. When a buyer and a seller agreed on a price, they came together to the recording desk,

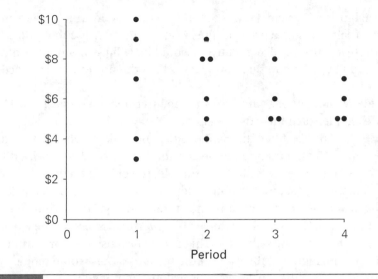

Figure 2.1 A Contract Price Sequence for the Design in Table 2.1

where the price was checked to ensure that it was no lower than the seller's cost and no higher than the buyer's value, as required by the instructions given in this chapter's Pit Market experiment in the Class Experiments section. (The prohibition of trading at a loss was used since the earnings in this classroom experiment were only hypothetical.) Each dot in Figure 2.1 corresponds to a trade. Notice that the quantity of trades began at five, went up to six, and then declined to 4. The prices were variable in the first two periods and then stabilized in the $5–$7 range.

Consider the question of why the prices converged to the $5–$7 range, with a transactions quantity of four units per period. Notice that the quantity could have been as high as eight. For example, suppose that the four high-value ($10) buyers negotiated with high-cost ($8) sellers and agreed on prices of $9. Similarly, suppose that the negotiated prices were $3 for sales from the low-cost ($2) sellers to the low-value ($4) buyers. In this scenario, all of the sellers' units sell, the quantity is eight, and each person earns $1 for the period. Prices, however, would be quite variable. These patterns are not observed in the price sequence of trades shown in Figure 2.1. There is high variability initially, as some of the high-cost units are sold at high prices, and some of the low-value units are purchased at low prices. By the third period, prices converge to the $5–$7 range, which prevents high-cost sellers from selling at a profit and low-value buyers from buying at a profit. The result is that only the four low-cost units are sold to the four high-value buyers.

The intuitive reason for the low price dispersion in later periods is fairly obvious. At a price of $9, all eight sellers would be willing (and perhaps eager) to sell, but only the four high-value buyers would be willing to buy, and perhaps not so eager given the low buyer earnings at that high price. This creates a competitive situation in which sellers may try to lower prices to get a sale, causing a price decline. Conversely, suppose that prices began in the $3 range. At these low prices, all eight buyers would be willing to buy, but only the four low-cost sellers would be willing to sell. This gives sellers the power to raise price without losing sales.

Finally, consider what happens with prices in the intermediate range, from $4 to $8. At a price of $6, for example, each low-cost seller earns $4 (= $6 − $2), and each high-value buyer earns $4 (= $10 − $6). Together, the eight people who make trades earn a total of $32. These earnings are much higher than $1 per person that was earned with price dispersion, for a total of $1 times 16 people = $16. In this example, the effect of reduced price dispersion is to reduce quantity by half and to double total earnings. The reduced price dispersion benefits buyers and sellers as a group, since total earnings go up, but the excluded high-cost sellers and low-value buyers are worse off. Nevertheless, economic efficiency has increased by these exclusions. The sellers have high costs because the opportunity costs of the resources they use are high, i.e., the value of the resources they would employ is higher in alternative uses. Moreover, the buyers with low values are not willing to pay an amount that covers the opportunity cost of the extra production needed to serve them.

One way to measure the efficiency of a market is to compare the actual earnings of all participants with the maximum possible earnings. It is a simple calculation to verify that $32 is the highest total earnings level that can be achieved by any combination of trades in this market. The efficiency was 100 percent for the final two periods shown in Figure 2.1, since the four units that traded in each of those periods involved low costs and high values. If a fifth unit had traded, as happened in the first period, the aggregate earnings must go down since the high cost ($8) for the fifth unit exceeds the low value ($4) for this unit. Thus the earnings total goes down by the difference ($4), reducing earnings from the maximum of $32 to $28. In this case, the outcome with price dispersion and five units traded only has an efficiency level of 28/32 = 87.5 percent. The trading of a sixth unit in the second period reduced efficiency even more, to 75 percent.

The operation of this market can be illustrated with a standard supply and demand graph. First, consider a seller with a cost of $2. This seller would be unwilling to supply any units at prices below this cost, and would offer the entire capacity (1 unit) at higher prices. Thus, the seller's individual supply function has a step at $2. The total quantity supplied by all sellers in the market is zero for prices below $2, but market supply jumps to four units at slightly higher prices as the four low-cost sellers offer their units. The supply function has another step at $8 when the four high-cost sellers offer their units at prices slightly above this high-cost step. This resulting market supply function, with steps at each of the two cost levels, is shown by the solid line in Figure 2.2. The market demand function is constructed analogously. At prices above $10, no buyer is willing to purchase, but the quantity demanded jumps to four units at prices slightly below this value. The demand function has another step at $4, as shown by the dashed line in Figure 2.2. Demand is vertical at prices below $4, since all buyers will wish to purchase at any lower price. The supply and demand

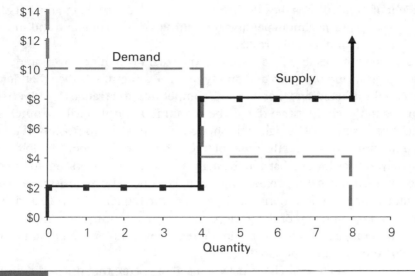

Figure 2.2   A Simple Market Design

functions overlap at a quantity of four in the range of prices from $4 to $8. At any price in this region, the quantity supplied equals the quantity demanded and the result is a competitive equilibrium. At lower prices, there is excess demand, which would tend to drive prices up. At prices above the region of overlap, there is excess supply, which would tend to drive prices back down.

The fact that the maximum aggregate earnings are $32 for this design can be seen directly from Figure 2.2. Suppose that the price is $6 for all trades. The value of the first unit on the left is $10, and since the buyer pays $6, the surplus value is the difference, or $4. The surplus on the second, third, and fourth units is also $4, so the consumers' surplus is the sum of the surpluses on individual consumers' units, or $16. Notice that consumers' surplus is the area under the demand curve and above the price paid. Since sellers earn the difference between price and cost, the producers' surplus is the area (also $16) above the supply curve and below the price. Thus, the total surplus is the sum of these areas, which equals the area under demand and above supply (to the left of the intersection). This total surplus area is four times the vertical distance ($10 − $2), or $32. The total surplus is actually independent of the particular price at which the units trade. For example, a higher price would reduce consumers' surplus and increase producers' surplus, but the total area would remain fixed at $32. Adding a fifth unit would reduce surplus since the cost ($8) is greater than the value ($4).

These types of surplus calculations do not depend on the particular forms of the demand and supply functions shown in Figure 2.2. Individual surplus amounts on each unit are the difference between the value of the unit (the height of demand) and the cost of the unit (the height of supply). Thus the area between demand and supply to the left of the intersection represents the maximum possible total surplus, even if demand and supply have more steps than the example in Figure 2.2.

Figure 2.3 shows the results of a classroom experiment with nine buyers and nine sellers, using a design with more steps and an asymmetric structure. Notice that demand is relatively flat on the left side, and therefore, the competitive price range ($7–$8) is relatively high. For prices in the competitive range, the consumers' surplus will be much smaller than the producers' surplus. The right side shows the results of two periods of pit market trading, with the prices plotted in the order of trade. Prices start at about $5, in the middle of the range between the lowest cost and the highest value. The prices seem to be converging to the competitive range from below, which could be due to buyer resistance to increasingly unequal earnings. In both periods, all seven of the higher value ($10 and $9) units were purchased, and all seven of the lower cost ($2 and $7) units were sold. As before, prices stayed in a range needed to exclude the high-cost and low-value units, and efficiency was 100 percent in both periods.

The asymmetric structure in Figure 2.3 was used to ensure that prices did not start in the equilibrium range, in order to illustrate some typical features of price adjustments. The first units that traded in each period were the ones with $10 values and $2 costs on the left side of the supply and demand figure. After these initial transactions in the $5–$7 range, the remaining traders were closer to the competitive margin. These marginal buyers were those with values of $9 and $4. The marginal sellers were those with costs of $7 and $8.

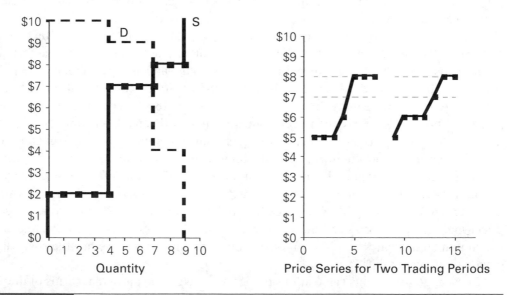

Figure 2.3   Demand (Solid Line), Supply (Dashed Line), and Transactions Prices (Connected Dots) for a Pit Market

Clearly, these units have to sell for prices above $7, which forces the prices closer to the competitive prediction at the end of the period. When sellers who sold early in the period see these higher prices, they may hold out for higher prices in the next period. Similarly, buyers will come to expect prices to rise later in the period, so they will scramble to buy early, which will tend to drive prices up earlier in each subsequent period. To summarize, the convergence process is influenced by the tendency for the highly profitable units (on the left side of demand and supply) to trade early, leaving traders at the margin where price negotiations tend to be near competitive levels. Price dispersion is narrowed in subsequent periods as traders come to expect the higher prices at the end of the period.

2.3 Chamberlin's Results and Vernon Smith's Reaction

The negotiations in the class experiments discussed above took place in a central area that served as the trading pit, although some participants broke off in pairs to finalize deals. Even so, the participants could hear the public offers being made by others, a process that is expected to reduce price dispersion. A high-value buyer, who is better off paying up to $10 instead of not trading, may not be willing to pay such high prices when some sellers are making lower offers. Similarly, a low-cost seller will be less willing to accept a low price when other buyers are paying more. In this manner, good market information about the going prices will tend to reduce price dispersion. A high dispersion is needed for high-cost sellers and low-value buyers to be able to find trading partners, so less dispersion will tend to exclude these extra-marginal traders.

Chamberlin did report some tendency for the markets to yield too many trades relative to competitive predictions, which he attributed to the dispersion that can result from small group negotiations. In order to evaluate this conjecture, he took the value and cost cards from his experiment and used them to simulate a *decentralized trading process*. These simulations were not laboratory experiments with student traders; they were mechanical, similar to today's computer simulations.

For groups of size two, Chamberlin would shuffle the cost cards and the value cards, and then match one cost with one value and make a trade at an intermediate price if the value exceeded the cost. Cards for trades that were not made were returned to the deck to be reshuffled and re-matched. It is useful to see how this random matching would work in a simple example with only four buyers and four sellers, as shown in Table 2.2. The random pairing process would result in only two trades if the two low-cost units were matched with the two high-value units. It would result in four trades if both low-cost units were matched with the low-value units, and high-cost units were matched with high-value units. The intermediate cases would result in three trades, for example when the value/cost combinations are: **$10/$2, $10/$8, $4/$2**, and $4/$8. The three value/cost pairs that result in a trade are shown in bold. To summarize, random matches in this example produce a quantity of trades of either two, three, or four, and some simulations should convince you that on average there will be three units traded.

Table 2.2	An Eight-Trader Example		
Values		**Costs**	
Buyer 1	$10	Seller 5	$2
Buyer 2	$10	Seller 6	$2
Buyer 3	$4	Seller 7	$8
Buyer 4	$4	Seller 8	$8

For groups larger than two traders, Chamberlin would shuffle and deal the cards into groups and would calculate the competitive equilibrium quantity for each group, as determined by the intersection of supply and demand for that group alone. In the four-buyer/four-seller example in Table 2.2, there is only one group of size eight (four buyers and four sellers), and the equilibrium for all eight is the competitive quantity of two units. This illustrates Chamberlin's general finding that quantity tended to decrease with larger group size in his simulations.

Notice the relationship between the use of simulations and laboratory experiments with human participants. The experiment provided the empirical regularity (excess quantity) that motivated a theoretical model (competitive equilibrium for subgroups), and the simulation confirmed that the same regularity would be produced by this model. In general, computer simulations can be used to derive properties of models that are too complex to solve analytically, which is often the case for models of out-of-equilibrium behavior and dynamic adjustment. The methodological order can, of course, be reversed, with computer simulations being used to derive predictions that can be tested with laboratory experiments using human participants.

The simulation analysis given above suggests that market efficiency will be higher when price information is centralized, so that all traders know the going levels of bid, ask, and transactions prices. Vernon Smith, who attended some of Chamberlin's experiments when he was a student at Harvard, used this intuition to design a trading institution that promoted efficiency. After some classroom experiments of his own, he began using a double auction in which buyers made bids, sellers made offers (or asks), and all could see the highest outstanding bid and the lowest outstanding ask. Buyers could raise the current best bid at any time, and sellers could undercut the current best ask at any time. In this manner, the bid/ask spread would typically diminish until someone closed a contract by accepting the terms from the other side of the market, i.e., until a seller accepted a buyer's bid or a buyer accepted a seller's ask. This is called a double auction because it involves buyers (bidding up, as in an auction for antiques) and sellers (bidding down, as would occur if contractors undercut each others' prices). A trade occurs when these processes meet, i.e., when a buyer accepts a seller's ask or when a seller accepts a buyer's bid.

Table 2.3 shows a typical sequence of bids and asks in a double auction. Buyer 2 bids $3.00, and Seller 5 offers to sell for $8.00. Seller 6 comes in with an ask price of $7.50, and

Table 2.3	A Price Negotiation Sequence		
	Bid	**Ask**	
Buyer 2	$3		
		$8	Seller 5
		$7	Seller 6
Buyer 1	$4		
Buyer 1	$4.50		
		$6	Seller 7
Buyer 2	Accepts $6		

Buyer 1 bids $4.00 and then $4.50. At this point Seller 7 offers to sell at $6.00, which Buyer 2 accepts.

In a double auction, there is always good public information about the bid/ask spread and about past contract prices. This information creates a large-group setting that tends to diminish price variability and increase efficiency. Smith (1962, 1964) reported that this double auction resulted in efficiency measures of more than 90 percent, even with relatively small numbers of traders (4–6) and with no information about others' values and costs. The double auction tends to be somewhat more centralized than a pit market, which does not close off the possibility of bilateral negotiations that are not observed by others. Double auction trading more closely resembles trading for securities on the New York Stock Exchange, where the specialist collects bids and asks, and all trades come across the ticker tape.

Besides introducing a centralized posting of all bids, asks, and trading prices, Smith introduced a second key feature into his early market experiments: the repetition of trading in successive market periods or trading days. The effects of repetition are apparent in Figure 2.4, which was done with the Veconlab Web-based interface in a classroom setting. The supply and demand curves for the first two periods are shown in bold on the left side; the values and costs that determine the locations of the steps were randomly generated. There were four trading periods, which are delineated by the vertical lines that separate the dots that show the transactions price sequence. The prices converge to near competitive levels in the second period. The demand and supply shift in the third period (higher light line on the left) causes a quick rise in prices, and convergence is observed by the end of the fourth period.

Figure 2.5 shows the results of a double auction market conducted under research conditions with a much more extreme configuration of values and costs that was used to provide a stress test of price convergence. The four buyers have a demand for four units each, for a total of 16 units, all with values of $6.80. The four sellers have a total of 11 units, all with costs of $5.70. In addition, each person received a commission of $.05 for each unit

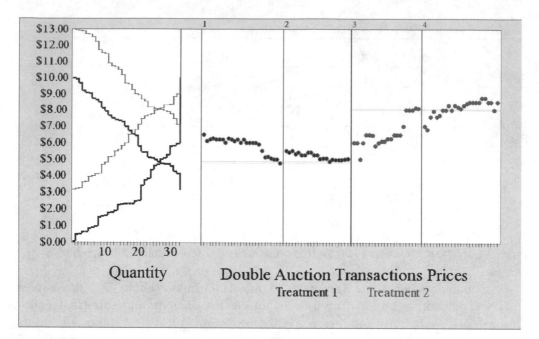

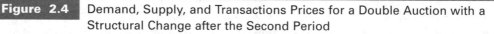

Figure 2.4   Demand, Supply, and Transactions Prices for a Double Auction with a Structural Change after the Second Period

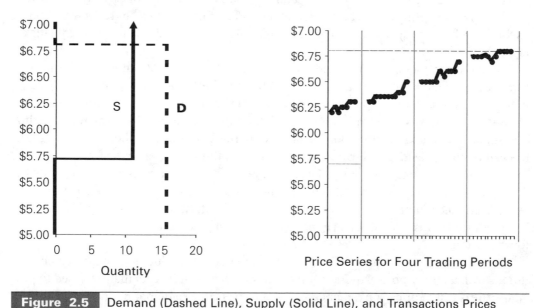

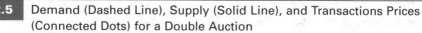

Figure 2.5   Demand (Dashed Line), Supply (Solid Line), and Transactions Prices (Connected Dots) for a Double Auction

that they bought or sold. The left side of the figure shows the resulting supply function, which is vertical at a quantity of 11 where it crosses demand. The intersection is at a price of $6.80, and at lower prices there is excess demand. The period-by-period price sequences are shown on the right side of the figure. Notice that first-period prices start in the middle of the range between values and costs, and then rise late in the period. Prices in the second period start higher and rise again. This upward trend continues until prices reach the competitive level of about $6.80 in the fourth period. At this point, buyers are earning pennies only (e.g., the commission) on each transaction. A second treatment, not shown, began in the sixth period with the total number of buyer units reduced to 11 and the number of seller units increased to 16. Buyers, who were already earning very little on each unit, were disappointed at having fewer units. But prices started to fall immediately; the very first trading price in the sixth period was only $6.65. Prices declined steadily, reaching the new competitive price of $5.70 by the tenth period. This session illustrates the strong convergence properties of the double auction, where excess demand or supply pressures can push prices to create severe earnings inequities that are unlikely to arise in bilateral bargaining situations.

2.4   Extensions

The simple experiments presented in this chapter can be varied in numerous useful directions. For example, an upward shift in demand, accomplished by increasing buyers' values should raise prices. An increase in the number of sellers would tend to shift supply outward, which has the effect of lowering prices. The imposition of a $1 per-unit tax on buyers would (in theory) shift demand down by $1. To see this, note that if one's value is $10, but a tax of $1 must be paid upon purchase, then the net value is only $9. All demand steps would shift down by $1 in this manner. Alternatively, a $1 tax per unit imposed on sellers would shift supply up by $1, since the tax is analogous to a $1 increase in cost. Some extensions will be considered in Chapter 8 on market power.

Of the market institutions that have been considered, Chamberlin's *pit market* corresponds most closely to trading of futures contracts in a trading pit, whereas Smith's double auction is more like the trading of securities on the New York Stock Exchange. A posted offer auction (where sellers set prices on a take-it-or-leave-it basis) is more like a retail market with many buyers and few sellers. These different trading institutions have different properties and applications, and outcomes need not match competitive predictions. Nevertheless, it is useful to consider outcomes in terms of market efficiency, measured as the percentage of maximum earnings achieved by the trades that are made. In evaluating alternative designs for ways to auction off some licenses, for example, one might want to consider the efficiency of the allocations along with the amounts of revenue generated for the seller.

The theoretical predictions discussed in this chapter are derived from an analysis of supply and demand. In the competitive model, all buyers and sellers take price as given.

This model may not provide good predictions when some traders perceive themselves as being price makers, with power to push prices in their favor. A single-seller monopolist will typically be able to raise prices above competitive levels, and a small group of sellers with enough of a concentration of market capacity may be able to raise prices as well. The exercise of this type of market power is discussed in the chapter on market institutions and power. The exercise of market power by price-setting sellers is a strategic decision, and the relevant theoretical models are those of *game theory*, which is the analysis of interrelated strategic decisions. The word "interrelated" is critical here, since the amount that one firm may wish to raise prices depends on how much others are expected to raise prices. We turn to a simple introduction of game theory in the next chapter. The discussion will be in terms of simple games with two players and two decisions, but the same principles will be applied later in the book in the analysis of more complex games with many sellers and many possible price levels.

QUESTIONS

1. Suppose that all of the numbered diamonds and spades from a deck of cards (excluding Ace, King, Queen, and Jack) are used to set up a market. The diamonds determine demand, e.g., a 10 represents a buyer with a redemption value of $10. Similarly, the spades determine supply. There are nine buyers and nine sellers, each with a single card.

   a. Graph supply and demand and derive the competitive price and quantity predictions.

   b. What is the predicted effect of removing the 3, 4, and 5 of spades?

2. When people are asked to come up with alternative theories about why prices in a pit market stabilize at a particular level observed in class, they sometimes suggest taking the average of all buyers' values and sellers' costs.

   a. Devise and graph two experimental designs (list all buyers' values and all sellers' costs) that have the same competitive price prediction, but different averages of values and costs.

   b. Devise and graph two experimental designs that have the same average of all values and costs, but different competitive price predictions.

3. Consider the following price-determination theory, which was suggested in a recent experimental economics class: "Rank all buyer values from high to low and find the median (middle) value. Then rank all seller costs from low to high and find the median cost. The price should be the average of the median value and the median cost." By giving buyers a lot more units than sellers, it is possible to create a design where the median cost and the median value are both equal to the lowest of all values and costs. Use

this idea to set up a supply and demand array where the competitive price prediction is considerably higher than the prediction based on medians. (If your design has a range of possible competitive prices, you may assume for purposes of discussion that the average price prediction is at the mid-point of this range.)

4. Large earnings asymmetries between buyers and sellers may slow convergence to theoretical predictions. This tendency will be especially pronounced if the traders on one side of the market are predicted to have zero earnings. If either of the experiment designs that you suggested in your answer to Question 3 involve zero earnings for traders on one side of the market, how could you alter the design to ensure that all trades made by those on the "disadvantaged" side of the market in each treatment generate earnings of about $.50 per unit?

chapter 3

Some Simple Games: Competition, Coordination, and Guessing

A game with two players and two decisions can be represented by a 2×2 payoff table or ma trix. Such games often highlight the conflict between incentives to compete or cooperate. This chapter introduces classic matrix games: prisoner's dilemma and coordination, with the purpose of developing the idea of a Nash equilibrium. This concept is a somewhat abstract and mathematical notion, and the guessing game, discussed last, serves to highlight the extent to which ordinary people might come to such an equilibrium. Both the matrix game and the guessing game can be run by hand (instructions are provided in this chapter's Push-Pull Game experiment in the Class Experiments section) and on the Veconlab site, where they are listed under the Games menu. (*Hint*: For an in-class card experiment, it sometimes helps to divide large classes into groups, e.g., rows, and to have pairs of groups reveal their decisions in sequence. For a remote-access Web experiment, use a one-round setup with the "go at your own pace" option, which lets participants read instructions and make a decision before their partners have logged in.)

3.1 Game Theory and the Prisoner's Dilemma

The Great Depression, which was the defining economic event of the 20th century, caused a major rethinking of existing economic theories that represented the economy as a system of self-correcting markets needing little in the way of active economic policy interventions. On the macroeconomic side, John Maynard Keynes' *The General Theory of Employment, Interest, and Money* focused on psychological elements ("animal spirits") that could cause a whole economy to become mired in a low-employment equilibrium, with no tendency for self-correction. An equilibrium is a state where there are no net forces causing further change, and Keynes' message implied that such a state may not necessarily be good. On the microeconomics side, as noted in Chapter 2, Chamberlin (1948) argued that markets may not yield efficient, competitive outcomes. At about the same time, von Neumann and Morgenstern (1944) published *Theory of Games and Economic Behavior*, which was motivated by the observation that a major part of economic activity involves bilateral and small-group interactions, where the classical assumption of non-strategic, price-taking behavior (used in Chapter 2) is not realistic. In light of the protracted Depression, these new theories generated considerable interest. Chamberlin's models of monopolistic competition were quickly incorporated into textbooks, and von Neumann and Morgenstern's book on game theory received front-page coverage in the *New York Times*.

A game is a mathematical model of a strategic situation in which players' payoffs depend on their own and others' decisions. A game is characterized by the players, their sets of feasible decisions, the information available at each decision point, and the payoffs (as functions of all decisions and random events). A key notion of a game involves a *strategy*, which is essentially a complete plan of action that covers all contingencies. For example, a strategy in an auction could be an amount to bid for each possible estimate of the value of the prize. Since a strategy covers all contingencies, even those that are unlikely to be faced, it could be given to a hired employee to be played out on behalf of the player in the game. An equilibrium is a set of strategies that is stable in some sense, i.e., with no inherent tendency for change. Economists are interested in notions of equilibrium that will provide good predictions after behavior has had a chance to settle down.

As noted in Chapter 1, a Princeton graduate student, John Nash, corrected a major shortcoming in the von Neumann and Morgenstern analysis by developing a notion of equilibrium for non-zero-sum games. Nash showed that this equilibrium existed under general conditions, and this proof caught the attention of researchers at the RAND Corporation headquarters in California. In fact, two RAND mathematicians immediately conducted a laboratory experiment designed to test Nash's theory. Nash's thesis advisor was in the same building and noticed the payoffs for the experiment written on a blackboard. He found the game interesting and made up a story of two prisoners facing a dilemma of whether or not to make a confession. This story was used in a presentation to the psychology department at Stanford University, and the prisoner's dilemma became the most commonly discussed paradigm in the new field of game theory.

In a prisoner's dilemma, two suspects are separated and offered a set of threats and rewards that make it best for each to confess and essentially rat on the other person, whether or not the other person confesses. For example, the prosecutor may say: "If you do not confess and the other person rats on you, then I can get a conviction and I will throw the book at you, so you are better off ratting on them." When the prisoner asks what happens if the other does not confess, the prosecutor replies: "Even without a confession, I can frame you both on a lesser charge, which I will do if nobody confesses. If you do confess and the other person does not, then I will reward you with immunity and book the holdout on the greater charge." Thus, each prisoner is better off implicating the other person even if the other remains silent. Both prisoners, aware of these incentives, decide to rat on the other, even though they would both be better off if they could somehow form a binding code of silence. This analysis suggests that two prisoners might be bullied into confessing to a crime that they did not commit, which is a scenario from *Murder at the Margin*, written by two mysterious economists under the pseudonym Marshall Jevons (1977).

A game with a prisoner's dilemma structure is shown in Table 3.1. The Row Player's Bottom decision corresponds to confession, as does the Column Player's Right decision. The Bottom/Right outcome, which yields payoffs of 3 for each, is worse than the Top/Left outcome, where both receive payoffs of 8. (A high payoff here corresponds to a light penalty.) The dilemma is that the "bad" confession outcome is an equilibrium in the following sense: if either person expects the other to talk, then their own best response to this belief is to confess as well. For example, consider the Row Player, whose payoffs are listed on the left side of each outcome cell in the table. If Column is going to choose Right, then Row either gets 0 for playing Top or 3 for playing Bottom, so Bottom is the best response to Right. Similarly, Column's Right decision is the best response to a belief that Row will play Bottom. There is no other cell in the table with this stability property. For example, if Row thinks Column will play Left, then Row would want to play Bottom, so Top/Left is not stable. It is straightforward to show that the diagonal elements, Bottom/Left and Top/Right are also unstable.

3.2 A Prisoner's Dilemma Experiment

The payoff numbers in the previous prisoner's dilemma experiment can be derived in the context of a simple example in which both players must choose between a low effort (0) and a higher effort (1). The cost of exerting the higher effort is $10, and the benefits to each person depend on the total effort for the two individuals combined. Since each person can choose an effort of 0 or 1, the total effort must be 0, 1, or 2. The benefit per person is shown in Table 3.2.

To see the connection between this production function and the prisoner's dilemma payoff matrix, let Bottom and Right correspond to 0 effort. Thus, the Bottom/Right out-

Table 3.1 | A Prisoner's Dilemma (Row's Payoff, Column's Payoff)

	Column Player	
Row Player	**Left**	**Right**
Top	8, 8	0, 10
Bottom	10, 0	3, 3

Table 3.2	An Example that Produces a Prisoner's Dilemma		
Total effort	0	1	2
Benefit per person	$3	$10	$18

come results in 0 total effort and payoffs of $3 for each person, as shown in the payoff matrix in Table 3.1. The Top/Left cell in the matrix is relevant when both choose efforts of 1 (at a cost of $10 each). The total effort is 2, so each earns $18 - 10 = 8$, as shown in the Top/Left cell of the matrix. The Top/Right and Bottom/Left parts of the payoff table pertain to the case where one person receives the benefit of 10 at no cost, the other receives the benefit of 10 at a cost of 10, for a payoff of $0. Notice that each person has an incentive to free ride on the other's effort, since one's own effort is more costly ($10) than the marginal benefit of effort, which is $7 (= 10 - 3)$ for the first unit of effort and $8 (= 18 - 10)$ for the second unit.

Cooper, DeJong, Forsythe, and Ross (1996) conducted an experiment using the prisoner's dilemma payoffs in the above matrix, with the only change being that the payoffs were (3.5, 3.5) at the Nash equilibrium. Their matching protocol prevented individuals from being matched with the same person twice, or from being matched with anyone who had been matched with them or one of their prior partners. This no-contagion protocol (meaning "not contagious like a disease") is analogous to going down a receiving line at a wedding and telling everyone the same bit of gossip about the bride and groom. Even if the story is so curious that everyone you meet in line repeats it to everyone they meet, you will never encounter anyone who has heard the story, since all of the people who have heard the story will be behind you in the line. In an experiment, the elimination of any type of repeated matching, either direct or indirect, means that nobody is able to send a message to future partners or to punish or reward others for cooperating. Even so, cooperative decisions (Top or Left) were fairly common in early rounds (43 percent), and the incidence of cooperation declined to about 20 percent in rounds 15–20. A recent classroom experiment using the Veconlab program with the Table 3.1 payoffs and random matching produced cooperation rates of about 33 percent, with no downward trend. A second experiment with a different class produced cooperation rates starting at about 33 percent and declining to zero by the fourth period. This latter group behaved quite differently when they were matched with the same partner for 5 periods; cooperation rates stayed level in the 33–50 percent range until the final period. The end-game effect is not surprising since cooperation in earlier periods may consist of an effort to signal good intentions and stimulate reciprocity. These forward-looking strategies are not available in the final round.

The results of these prisoner's dilemma experiments are representative. There is typically a mixture of cooperation and defection, with the mix being somewhat sensitive to payoffs and procedural factors, with some variation across groups. In general, cooperation rates are higher when individuals are matched with the same person in a series of repeated rounds. In fact, the first prisoner's dilemma experiment run at the RAND Corporation over 50 years ago lasted for 100 periods, and cooperative phases were interpreted as evidence against the Nash equilibrium.

A strict game-theoretic analysis would have people realizing that there is no reason to cooperate in the final round, and knowing this, nobody would try to cooperate in the next-to-last round with the hope of stimulating final-round cooperation. Thus, there should be no cooperation in the next-to-last round, and hence there is no reason to try to stimulate such cooperation. Reasoning backwards from the end in this manner, one might expect no cooperation even in the very first round, at least when the total number of rounds is finite and known. Nash responded to the RAND mathematicians with a letter maintaining that it is unreasonable to expect people to engage in this many levels of iterative reasoning in an experiment with many rounds. There is an extensive literature on related topics, e.g., the effects of punishments, rewards, adaptive behavior, and various tit-for-tat strategies in repeated prisoner's dilemma games.

Finally, it should be noted that there are many ways to present the payoffs for an experiment, even one as simple as the prisoner's dilemma. The Cooper et al. and the Veconlab experiments used a payoff matrix presentation. Alternatively, the instructions could be presented in terms of the cost of effort and the table showing the benefit per person for each possible level of total effort. This presentation is perhaps less neutral, but the economic context makes it less abstract and artificial than a matrix presentation. This chapter's Push-Pull Game in the Class Experiments section takes a different approach by setting up the prisoner's dilemma game as one where each person chooses which of two cards to play (Capra and Holt 2000). For example, suppose that each person has playing cards numbered 8 and 6. Playing the 6 pulls $6 (from the experimenter's reserve) into one's own earnings, and playing the 8 pushes $8 (from the experimenter's reserve) to the other person's earnings. If they both pull the $6, earnings are $6 each. Both would be better off if they played 8, yielding $8 for each. Pulling $6, however, is better from a selfish perspective, regardless of what the other person does. The best outcome from a selfish point of view is to pull $6 when the other person pushes $8, which yields a total of $14. A consideration of the resulting payoff matrix (see Question 2 at the end of the chapter) indicates that this is clearly a prisoner's dilemma. The card presentation is quick and easy to implement in class, where students hold the cards played against their chests, and the instructor picks people in pairs to reveal their cards. A Nash equilibrium survives an announcement test in that neither would wish they had played a different card given the card played by the other. In this case, the unique Nash equilibrium is for each to play 6.

3.3 A Coordination Game

Many production processes have the property that one person's effort increases the productivity of another's effort. For example, a mail order company must take orders by phone, produce the goods, and ship them. Each sale requires all three services, so if one process is slow, the efforts of those in other activities are to some extent wasted. In terms of our two-person production function, recall that one unit of effort produced a benefit of $10 per person and two units produced a benefit of $18. Suppose that the second unit of effort makes the first one more productive in the sense that the benefit is more than doubled when a second unit of effort is added. In Table 3.3, the per-person benefit is $30 for two units of effort.

If the cost of effort remains at $10 per unit, then each person earns $30 − $10 = $20 in the case where both supply a unit of effort, as shown in the revised payoff matrix shown in Table 3.4.

As before, the zero effort outcome (Bottom/Right) is a Nash equilibrium, since neither person would want to change from their decision unilaterally. For example, if Row knows that Column will choose Right, then Row can get $0 from Top and $3 from Bottom, so Row would want to choose Bottom, as indicated by the downward pointing arrow in the lower-right box. Similarly, Right is a best response to Row's decision to use Bottom, as indicated by the right arrow in the lower-right box.

There is a second Nash equilibrium in the Top/Left box of this modified game. To verify this, think of a situation in which we start in that box, and consider whether either person would want to deviate, so there are two things to check. Step 1: if Row is thought to choose Top, then Column would want to choose Left, as indicated by the left arrow in the Top/Left box. Step 2: if Row expects Column to choose Left, then Row would want to choose Top, as indicated by the up arrow. Thus, Top/Left survives an announcement test and would be stable. This second equilibrium yields payoffs of 20 for each, far better than the payoffs of 3 each in the Bottom/Right equilibrium outcome. This is called a coordination game, since

Table 3.3	An Example that Produces a Coordination Game		
Total Effort	0	1	2
Benefit per Person	$3	$10	$30

Table 3.4	A Coordination Game (Row's Payoff, Column's Payoff)	

	Column Player	
Row Player	**Left**	**Right**
Top	⇑ 20, 20 ⇐	0, 10
Bottom	10, 0	⇓ 3, ⇒ 3

the presence of multiple equilibria raises the issue of how players will guess which one will be relevant. (In fact, there is a third Nash equilibrium in which each player chooses randomly, but we will not discuss such strategies until Chapter 5.)

It used to be common for economists to assume that rational players would somehow coordinate on the best equilibrium, if all could agree which is the best equilibrium. While it is apparent that the Top/Left outcome is likely to be the most frequent outcome, one example does not justify a general assumption that players will always coordinate on an equilibrium that is better for all. This assumption can be tested with laboratory experiments, and it has been shown to be false. In fact, players sometimes get driven to an equilibrium that is worst for all concerned (Van Huyck, Battalio, and Beil 1990, 1991). Examples of data from such coordination games will be provided in a subsequent chapter on coordination problems. For now, consider the intuitive effect of increasing the cost of effort from $10 to $19. With this increase in the cost of effort, the payoffs in the high-effort Top/Left outcome are reduced to $30 − $19 = $11. Moreover, the person who exerts effort alone only receives a $10 benefit and incurs a $19 cost, so the payoffs for this person are −$9, as shown in Table 3.5.

Notice that Top/Left is still a Nash equilibrium: if Column is expected to play Left, then Row's best response is Top and vice versa, as indicated by the directional arrows in the upper-left corner. But Top and Left are very risky decisions, with possible payoffs of $11 and $9, as compared with the $10 and $3 payoffs associated with the Bottom and Right strategies that yield the other Nash equilibrium. While the absolute payoff is higher for each person in the Top/Left outcome, each person has to be very sure that the other one will not deviate. In fact, this is a game where behavior is likely to converge to the Nash equilibrium that is worst for all. These payoffs were used in a class experiment that lasted five periods with random matching of 12 participants. Participants were individuals or pairs of students at the same computer. By the fifth period, only a quarter of the decisions were Top or Left. The same people then played the less risky coordination game shown in Table 3.4, again with random matching. The results were quite different; all but one of the pairs ended up in the good (Top, Left) equilibrium outcome in all periods.

To summarize, it is not appropriate to assume that behavior will somehow converge to the best outcome for all, even when it is a Nash equilibrium as in the coordination games

Table 3.5	A Coordination Game with High Effort Cost (Row's Payoff, Column's Payoff)

	Column Player	
Row Player	**Left**	**Right**
Top	⇑ 11, 11 ⇐	−9, 10
Bottom	10, −9	⇓ 3, ⇒ 3

considered here. With multiple equilibria, the most attractive one may depend on payoff features (e.g., the effort cost) that determine which equilibrium is riskier. These issues will be revisited in Chapter 26 on coordination.

3.4   A Guessing Game

A key aspect of most games is the need for players to guess what others will do in order to determine their own best decision. This aspect is somewhat obscured in a 2×2 game since a wide range of beliefs may lead to the same decision; therefore, it is not possible to say much about the beliefs that stand behind any particular observed decision. In this section, we turn to a game with a continuum of decisions, from 0 to 100, and any number of players, N. Each player selects a number in this interval, with the advance knowledge that the person whose decision is closest to one-half of the average of all N decisions will win a money prize. (The prize is divided equally in the event of a tie.) Thus, each person's task is to make a guess about the average, and then submit a decision that is half that amount.

There is no way to learn from past decisions in the first round or if the game is only played once. In this case, each person must learn by thinking introspectively about what others might do, what others think they might do, and so on. The issue is how many levels of iterated reasoning are involved. The most naïve person would not think at all and might choose randomly between 0 and 100, with an average of 50; think of this low-rationality person as a level 0 type (Stahl and Wilson 1995). A slightly more forward-thinking person might reason that since the decisions must be between 0 and 100, without further knowledge it might be okay to guess that the average of others' decisions would be at the midpoint, 50. This person would submit a decision of 25 in order to be at about half of the anticipated average. Think of this person as a level 1 type, since they engaged in one level of iterated reasoning. A level 2 type would carry this one step further and choose half of 25, or 12.5. Even higher levels of iterated thinking will lead a person to choose a decision that is closer and closer to 0. So the best decision to make depends on one's beliefs about the extent to which others are thinking iteratively in this manner, i.e., on beliefs about the others' rationality. Since the best response to any common decision above 0 is to go down to one-half of that level, it follows that no common decision above 0 can be a Nash equilibrium. Clearly a common decision of 0 is a Nash equilibrium, since each person gets a positive share ($1/N$) of the prize, and to deviate and choose a higher decision would result in a $0 payoff. It turns out that this is the only Nash equilibrium for this game (see Question 5 at the end of the chapter).

Figure 3.1 shows data for a classroom guessing game run with the Veconlab software. There were five participants, who made first round decisions of 55, 29, 22, 21, and 6.25, which average to about 27. This result is roughly consistent with guessing game data first reported by Nagel (1995). Notice that the lowest person engaged in three levels of iterated rea-

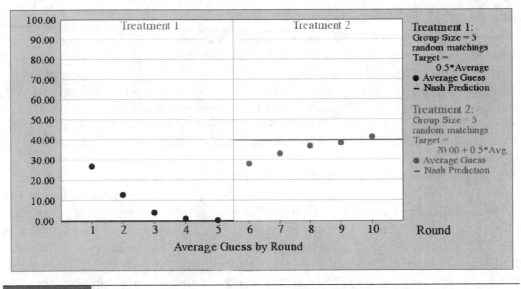

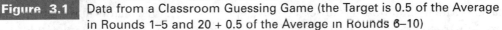

Average Guess by Round

| **Figure 3.1** | Data from a Classroom Guessing Game (the Target is 0.5 of the Average in Rounds 1–5 and 20 + 0.5 of the Average in Rounds 6–10) |

soning about what the others might do, and this person was closest to the target level of about 27/2 = 13.5. This person submitted the same decision in the second round and won again; the other decisions were 20, 15, 11.5, and 10. The other people did not seem to engage in any precise iterated reasoning, but it is clear that the person with the lowest decision was rewarded, which tended to pull decisions down in subsequent rounds. These decisions converge to near-Nash levels by the fifth round, although nobody selected 0 exactly.

The second treatment changes the calculation of the target from 0.5 of the average to 20 + 0.5 of the average. The instructor who ran this in class (the author) had selected the parameters quickly, with the conjecture that adding 20 to the target would raise the Nash equilibrium from 0 to 20. When the average came in at 28, the instructor thought that it would then decline toward 20, just as it had declined toward 0 in the first treatment. But the average rose to 33 in the next round, and continued to rise to a level that is near 40. Notice that if all choose 40, then the average is 40, half of the average is 20, and 20 + half of the average is 20 + 20 = 40, which is the Nash equilibrium for this treatment (see Question 6 at the end of the chapter).

This game illustrates a couple of things. Some people think iteratively about what others will do, but this is not uniform, and the effect of such introspection is not enough to move decisions to near-Nash levels in a single round of play. When people are able to learn from experience, behavior does converge to the Nash equilibrium in this game, even when the equilibrium is not apparent to the person who designed the experiment.

3.5 Extensions

The prisoner's dilemma game discussed in this chapter can be given an alternative interpretation, i.e., that of a public good. This is because each person's benefit depends on the total effort, including that of the other person. In effect, neither person can appropriate more than half of the benefit of their own effort, and in this sense the benefit is publicly available to both, just as national defense or police protection are freely available to all. We will consider the public goods provision problem in more detail in Chapter 14. The setup allows a large number of effort levels, and the effects of changes in costs and other incentives will be considered.

The prisoner's dilemma has a Nash equilibrium that is worse than the outcome that results when individuals cooperate and ignore their private incentives to defect. The dilemma is that the equilibrium is the bad outcome, and the good outcome is not an equilibrium. In contrast, the coordination game considered above has a good outcome that is also an equilibrium. Even so, there is no guarantee that the better equilibrium will be realized. A more formal analysis of the risk associated with alternative equilibria is presented in Chapter 26 on coordination. The main point is that there may be multiple Nash equilibria, and which equilibrium is observed may depend on intuitive factors like the cost of effort. In particular, a high effort cost may cause players to get stuck in a Nash equilibrium that is worse for all concerned, as compared with an alternative Nash equilibrium. The coordination game provides a paradigm in which an equilibrium may not be desirable. Such a possibility has concerned macroeconomists like Keynes, who worried that a market economy may become mired in a low-employment, low-effort state.

The guessing game is examined in Nagel (1995, 1999), who shows that there is a widespread failure of behavior to converge to the Nash equilibrium in a one-round experiment, regardless of subject pool. Nagel discusses the degree to which some of the people go through iterations of thinking that may lead them to choose lower and lower decisions (e.g., 50, 25, 12.5, . . .). The game was originally motivated by one of Keynes' remarks, that investors are typically in a position of trying to guess what stock others will find attractive (first iteration), or what stock others think other investors will find attractive (second iteration), and so on. Of course, the introspective thinking process is not going to be precise and may vary from one person to the next, depending on the degree to which they think strategically. Models of iterated introspection will be discussed and applied later in Part 6, the behavioral game theory part of the book (Chapter 25 in particular). By raising the lower limit of the range of guesses, it is possible to obtain more precise estimates of individuals' levels of iterated rationality in guessing games (Costa-Gomes and Crawford 2006).

In all of the equilibria considered so far, each person chooses a decision without any randomness. It is easy to think of games where it is not good to be perfectly predictable. For example, a soccer player in a penalty kick situation should sometimes kick to the left and sometimes to the right, and the goalie should also avoid a statistical preference for diving to one side or the other. Such behavior in a game is called a *randomized strategy*. Before considering randomized strategies (in Chapter 5), it is useful to introduce the notions of probability, expected value, and other aspects of decision making in uncertain situations. This is the topic of Chapter 4, where we consider the choice between simple lotteries over cash prizes.

For a brief, non-technical discussion of John Nash's original 1950 *Proceedings of the National Academy of Sciences* paper, its subsequent impact and policy applications, see Holt and Roth (2004).

QUESTIONS

1. Suppose that the cost of a unit of effort is raised from $10 to $25 for the example based on the table shown below. Is the resulting game a coordination game or a prisoner's dilemma? Explain, and find the Nash equilibrium (or equilibria) for the new game.

Total Effort	0	1	2
Benefit per Person	$3	$10	$30

2. What is the payoff table for the prisoner's dilemma game described in Section 3.2 based on pulling $6 or pushing $8?

3. Each player is given a 6 of hearts and an 8 of spades. The players select one of their cards to play. If the suit matches, then they each are paid $6 for the case of matching hearts and $8 for the case of matching spades. Earnings are zero in the event of a mismatch. Is this a coordination game or a prisoner's dilemma? Show the payoff table and find all Nash equilibria (that do not involve random play).

4. Suppose that the payoffs for the original prisoner's dilemma are altered as follows. The cost of effort remains at $10, but the per-person benefits are given in the table below. Recalculate the payoff matrix, find all Nash equilibria (that do not involve random play), and explain whether the game is a prisoner's dilemma or a coordination game.

Total Effort	0	1	2
Benefit per Person	3	5	18

5. Suppose that two people are playing a guessing game with a prize going to the person closest to one-half of the average. Guesses are required to be between 0 and 100. Show that none of the following are Nash equilibria:

   a. Both choose 1. (*Hint*: consider a deviation to 0 by one person, so that the average is 1/2, and half of the average is 1/4.)

   b. One person chooses 1 and the other chooses 0.

   c. One person chooses x and the other chooses y, where $x > y > 0$. (*Hint*: If they choose these decisions, what is the average, what is the target, and is the target less than the midpoint of the range of guesses between x and y? Then use these calculations to figure out which person would win, and whether the other person would have an incentive to deviate.)

6. Consider a guessing game with N people, and the person closest to 20 plus one-half of the average is awarded the prize, which is split in the event of a tie. The range of guesses is from 0 to 100. Show that 40 is a Nash equilibrium. (*Hint*: Suppose that $N-1$ people choose 40 and one person deviates to $x < 40$. Calculate the target as a function of the deviant's decision, x. The deviant will lose if the target is greater than the midpoint between x and 40, i.e., if the target is greater than $(40 + x)/2$. Check to see if this is the case.)

7. Consider a guessing game with N people, and the person closest to 10 plus two-thirds of the average is awarded the prize. Find the Nash equilibrium.

8. A more general formulation of the guessing game might be for the target level to be: $A + B*$(average decision), where $A > 0$ and $0 < B < 1$, and decisions must be between 0 and an upper limit $L > 0$. Find the Nash equilibrium. When is it equal to L?

9. For the guessing game in Question 6, a level 0 person would choose randomly on the interval from 0 to 100. What decision would be made by a level 1 person who simply makes a best response to a level 0 person? Do the decisions for those who engage in successively higher levels of reasoning converge?

chapter 4

Risk and Decision Making

In this chapter, we consider decision making in risky situations. Each decision has a set of money consequences or "prizes" and the associated probabilities. In such cases, it is straightforward to calculate the expected money value of each decision. A person who is neutral to risk will select the decision with the highest expected payoff. A risk-averse person is willing to accept a lower expected payoff in order to reduce risk. A simple lottery choice experiment is used to illustrate the concepts of expected value maximization and risk aversion. Variations on the experiment can be conducted prior to class discussions, either with the instructions included in this chapter's Lottery Choice experiment in the Class Experiments section or with the Veconlab software (select the Lottery Choice experiment listed under the Decisions menu). The Web-based version is recommended since it is a non-interactive individual decision problem that you can participate in by logging in after class.

4.1 Who Wants to Be a Millionaire?

Many decision situations involve consequences that cannot be predicted perfectly in advance. For example, suppose that you are a contestant on the television game show *Who Wants to Be a Millionaire?* You are at the $500,000 point and the question is on a topic that you know nothing about. Fortunately, you have saved the fifty-fifty option that rules out two answers, leaving two that turn out to be unfamiliar. At this point, you figure you only have a 50 percent chance of guessing correctly and becoming a millionaire. If you guess incorrectly, you receive the safety level of $32,000. Or you can fold and take the sure $500,000. In thinking about whether to take the $500,000 and fold, you decide to calculate the expected money value of the guess option. With 50 percent probability you earn $32,000, and with 50 percent probability you earn $1,000,000, so the expected value of a guess is as follows:

$$0.5(\$32,000) + 0.5(\$1,000,000) = \$16,000 + \$500,000 = \$516,000$$

This expected payoff is greater than the sure $500,000 one gets from stopping, but the trouble with guessing is that you either win $32,000 or $1 million, not the average. So the issue is whether the $16,000 increase in the average payoff is worth the risk, which is considerable if you guess. If you love risk, then there is no problem; make a guess. If you are neutral to risk, the extra $16,000 in the average payoff should cause you to take the risk. Alternatively, you might reason that the $32,000 would be gone in six months, and only a prize of $500,000 or greater would be large enough to bring about a change in your lifestyle (new SUV, tropical vacation, and so on), which may lead you to fold. To an economist, the person who folds would be classified as being *risk averse* in this case, because for this person the risk is sufficiently bad that it is not worth the extra $16,000 in average payoff associated with the guess.

Now consider an even more extreme case. You have the chance to secure a sure $1 million. The alternative is to take a coin flip, which provides a prize of $3 million for heads, and nothing for tails. If you believe that the coin is fair, then you are choosing between the following lotteries:

Safe Lottery: $1 million for sure
Risky Lottery: $3 million with 50 percent probability
                 $0 with 50 percent probability

As before, the expected money value for the risky lottery can be calculated by multiplying the probabilities with the associated payoffs, yielding an expected payoff of $1.5 million. When asked about this (hypothetical) choice, most people will select the safe million. Notice that for these people, the extra $500,000 in expected payoff is not worth the risk of ending up with nothing. An economist would call this risk aversion, but to a layman the reason is intuitive: the first million provides a major change in lifestyle. A second million is an equally large money amount, but it is hard for most of us to imagine how much *additional* benefit this would provide. Roughly speaking, the additional (marginal) utility of the second million dollars is much lower than the utility of the first million, and the marginal utility of the third million is likely to be even lower. A utility function with a diminishing marginal utility is one with a curved uphill shape, as shown in Figure 4.1.

This utility function is the familiar square root function, where utility (in millions) is the square root of the payoff (in millions). Thus, the utility of 0 is zero, the utility of $1 million is one, the utility of $4 million is two, the utility of $16 million is four, and so on. In fact, each time you multiply the payoff by four, the utility only increases by a factor of two, which is indicative of the diminishing marginal utility. This feature is also apparent from the fact that the slope of the utility function near the origin is high, and it diminishes as we move to the right. The more curved the utility function, the faster the utility of an additional million diminishes.

The diminishing-marginal-utility hypothesis was first suggested by Daniel Bernoulli (1738). There are many functions with this property. One is the class of power functions: $U(x) = x^{1-r}$, where x is money income and r is a measure of risk aversion that is less than 1.

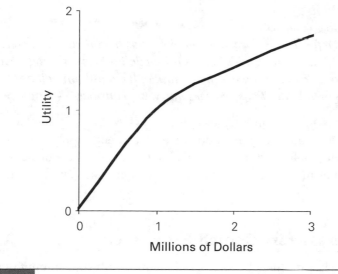

Figure 4.1   A Square Root Utility Function

Notice that when $r = 0$, the exponent in the utility function is 1, so we have the linear function: $U(x) = x^1 = x$. This function has no curvature, and hence no diminishing marginal utility for income. For a person whose choices are represented by this function, the second million is just as good as the first, so the person is neutral to risk. Alternatively, if the risk aversion measure r is increased from 0 to 0.5, we have $U(x) = x^{0.5}$, which is the square root function in the figure. Further increases in r result in more curvature, and in this sense r is a measure of the extent to which marginal utility of additional money income decreases. This measure is often called the coefficient of *relative risk aversion*.

In all of the examples considered up to this point, you have been asked to think about what you would do if you had to choose between gambles involving millions of dollars. The payoffs were (unfortunately) hypothetical. This raises the issue of whether what you say is what you would actually do if you faced the real situation, e.g., if you were really in the final stage of the series of questions on *Who Wants to Be a Millionaire?* It would be fortunate if we did not really have to pay large sums of money to find out how people would behave in high-payoff situations. The possibility of a *hypothetical bias*, i.e., the proposition that behavior might be dramatically different when high hypothetical stakes become real, is echoed in the film *An Indecent Proposal*:

> *John (a.k.a. Robert): Suppose I were to offer you one million dollars for one night with your wife.*
> *David (a.k.a. Woody): I'd assume you were kidding.*
> *John: Let's pretend I'm not. What would you say?*
> *Diana (a.k.a. Demi): He'd tell you to go to hell.*

John: I didn't hear him.

David: I'd tell you to go to hell.

John: That's just a reflex answer because you view it as hypothetical. But let's say there was real money behind it. I'm not kidding. A million dollars. Now, the night would come and go, but the money could last a lifetime. Think of it—a million dollars. A lifetime of security for one night. And don't answer right away. But consider it—seriously.

In the film, John's proposal was ultimately accepted, which is the Hollywood answer to the incentives question. On a more scientific note, incentive effects can be investigated with experimental techniques. Before returning to this issue, it is useful to consider the results of a lottery choice experiment designed to evaluate risk attitudes, which is the topic of Section 4.2.

4.2   A Simple Lottery-Choice Experiment

In all of the cases discussed above, the safe lottery is a sure amount of money. In this section we consider a case where both lotteries have random outcomes, but one is riskier than the other. In particular, suppose that Option A pays either $40 or $32, each with 50 percent probability, and that Option B pays either $77 or $2, each with 50 percent probability. First, we calculate the expected values as follows:

Option A: $0.5(\$40) + 0.5(\$32) = \$20 + \$16 = \$36.00$

Option B: $0.5(\$77) + 0.5(\$2) = \$38.50 + \$1 = \$39.50$

In this case, Option B has a higher expected value, by $3.50, but a lot more risk since the payoff spread from $77 to $2 is almost 10 times as large as the spread from $32 to $40.

This choice was on a menu of choices used in an experiment (Holt and Laury 2002). There were about 200 participants from several universities, including undergraduates, M.B.A. students, and business school faculty. Even though Option B had a higher expected payoff when each prize is equally likely, eighty-four percent of the participants selected the safe option, which indicates some risk aversion.

The payoff probabilities in the experiment were implemented by the throw of a ten-sided die. This allowed the researchers to alter the probability of the high payoff in one-tenth increments. A part of the menu of choices is shown in Table 4.1, where the probability of the high payoff ($40 or $77) is one-tenth in Decision 1, four-tenths in Decision 4, and so on. Notice that Decision 10 is a kind of rationality check, where the probability of the high payoff is 1, so it is a choice between $40 for sure and $77 for sure. The subjects indicated a preference for all ten decisions, and then one decision was selected at random, ex post, to determine earnings. In particular, after all decisions were made, a 10-sided die was thrown to determine the relevant decision, and then the ten-sided die was thrown again to determine the subject's earnings for the selected decision. This procedure has the advantage of providing data on all ten decisions without any wealth effects. Such wealth effects could

Table 4.1 | A Menu of Lottery Choices Used to Evaluate Risk Preferences

	Option A	Option B	Your Choice A or B
Decision 1	$40 if throw of die is 1 $32 if throw of die is 2–10	$77 if throw of die is 1 $2 if throw of die is 2–10	_____
. . .			
Decision 4	$40 if throw of die is 1–4 $32 if throw of die is 5–10	$77 if throw of die is 1–4 $2 if throw of die is 5–10	_____
Decision 5	$40 if throw of die is 1–5 $32 if throw of die is 6–10	$77 if throw of die is 1–5 $2 if throw of die is 6–10	_____
Decision 6	$40 if throw of die is 1–6 $32 if throw of die is 7–10	$77 if throw of die is 1–6 $2 if throw of die is 7–10	_____
. . .			
Decision 10	$40 if throw of die is 1–10	$77 if throw of die is 1–10	_____

come into play, for example, if a person wins $77 on one decision and this makes them more willing to take a risk on the subsequent decision. The disadvantage is that incentives are diluted, which was compensated for by raising payoffs.

The expected payoffs associated with each possible choice are shown under Risk Neutrality in the second and third columns of Table 4.2 (the other columns will be discussed later). First, look in the fifth row where the probabilities are 0.5. This is the choice previously discussed, with expected values of $36 and $39.50 as calculated above. The other expected values are calculated in the same manner, by multiplying probabilities by the associated payoffs, and adding up these products.

The best decision when the probability of the high payoff is only 0.1 (in the top row of Table 4.2) is obvious, since the safe decision also has a higher expected value, or $32.80, versus $9.50 for the risky lottery. In fact, 98 percent of the subjects selected the safe lottery (Option A) in this choice. Similarly, the last choice is between sure amounts of money, and all subjects chose Option B in this case. The expected payoffs are higher for the top four choices, as shown by the bold numbers in columns for risk neutrality. Thus, a risk-neutral person, who by definition only cares about expected values regardless of risk, would make four safe choices in this menu. In fact, the average number of safe choices was six, not four, which indicates some risk aversion. As can be seen from the 0.6 row of the table, the typical safe choice for this option involves giving up about $10 in expected value in order to reduce the risk. About two-thirds of the people made the safe choice for this decision, and 40 percent chose safe in Decision 7.

Table 4.2	Optimal Decisions for Risk Neutrality and Risk Aversion			
	Risk Neutrality Expected Payoffs for $U(x) = x$		Risk Aversion ($r = 0.5$) Expected Utilities for $U(x) = x^{1/2}$	
Probability of the High Payoff	**Safe** $40 or $32	**Risky** $77 or $2	**Safe** $40 or $32	**Risky** $77 or $2
0.1	**$32.80**	$9.50	**5.72**	2.15
0.2	**$33.60**	$17.00	**5.79**	2.89
0.3	**$34.40**	$24.50	**5.86**	3.62
0.4	**$35.20**	$32.00	**5.92**	4.36
0.5	$36.00	**$39.50**	**5.99**	5.09
0.6	$36.80	**$47.00**	**6.06**	5.83
0.7	$37.60	**$54.50**	6.12	**6.57**
0.8	$38.40	**$62.00**	6.19	**7.30**
0.9	$39.20	**$69.50**	6.26	**8.04**
1.0	$40.00	**$77.00**	6.32	**8.77**

The intuitive effect of risk aversion is to diminish the utility associated with higher earnings levels, as can be seen from the curvature for the square root utility function in Figure 4.1. With nonlinear utility, the calculation of a person's expected utility is analogous to the calculation of expected money value. For example, the safe Option A for Decision 5 is one-half of $40 and a one-half chance of $32. The expected payoff is found by adding up the products of money prize amounts and the associated probabilities as follows:

$$\text{Expected payoff (safe option)} = 0.5(\$40) + 0.5(\$32) = \$20 + \$16 = 36$$

The expected *utility* of this option is obtained by replacing the money amounts, $40 and $32, with the utilities of these amounts, which we will denote by $U(40)$ and $U(32)$. If the utility function is the square-root function, then $U(40) = (40)^{1/2} = 6.32$ and $U(32) = (32)^{1/2} = 5.66$. Since each prize is equally likely, we take the average of the two utilities as follows:

$$\text{Expected utility (safe option)} = 0.5\ U(40) + 0.5\ U(32)$$
$$= 0.5(6.32) + 0.5(5.66) = 5.99$$

This is the expected utility for the safe option when the probabilities are 0.5, as shown in the 0.5 row of Table 4.2 in the Safe column under Risk Aversion. Similarly, it can be shown that the expected utility for the risky option, with payoffs of $77 and $2, is 5.09. The other expected utilities for all ten decisions are shown in the two right-hand columns of Table 4.2. The safe option has the higher expected utility for the top six decisions, so the theoretical prediction for someone with this utility function is that they choose six safe options before crossing over to the risky option. Recall that the analogous prediction for risk neutrality (see the left side of the table) is four safe choices, and that the data for this treatment exhibit six safe choices on average. In this sense, the square-root utility function provides a better fit to the data than the linear utility function that corresponds to risk neutrality.

The percentages of safe choices are shown by the thick solid line in Figure 4.2, where the decision number is listed on the horizontal axis. The behavior predicted for a risk-neutral person is represented by the dashed line, which stays at the top (100 percent safe choices) for the first four decisions, and then shifts to the bottom (no safe choices) for the last six decisions. The thick line representing actual behavior is generally above this dashed line, which indicates the tendency to make more safe choices. There is some randomness in actual choices, however, so that choice percentages do not quite get to 100 percent on the left side of the figure.

This real-choice experiment was preceded by a hypothetical choice task, in which subjects made the same ten choices with the understanding that they would not be paid their earnings for that part. The data averages for the hypothetical choices are plotted as points on the thin line in the figure. Several differences between the real and hypothetical choice data are clear. The thin line lies below the thick line, indicating less risk aversion when choices have no real impact. The average number of safe choices was about six with real payments, and about five with hypothetical payments. Even without payments, subjects

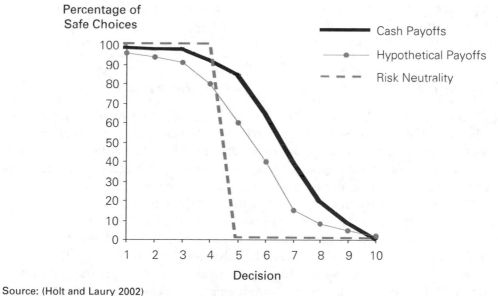

Source: (Holt and Laury 2002)

Figure 4.2   Percentages of Safe Choices with Real Incentives and Hypothetical Incentives

were a little risk averse as compared with the risk-neutral prediction of four safe choices, but they could not imagine how they really would behave when they had to face real consequences. Second, with hypothetical incentives, there may be a tendency for people to think less carefully, which may produce "noise" in the data. In particular, for Decision 10, the thin line is a little higher, corresponding to the fact that 2 percent of the people chose the sure $40 over the sure (but hypothetical) $77.

The question of whether or not to pay subjects is one of the key issues that divides research in experimental economics from some work on similar issues by psychologists. (See (Hertwig and Ortmann 2001) for a provocative survey on practices in psychology, with about 30 comments and an author's reply.) One justification for using high hypothetical payoffs is realism. Two prominent psychologists, Kahneman and Tversky (1979), justified the use of hypothetical incentives:

> *Experimental studies typically involve contrived gambles for small stakes, and a large number of repetitions of very similar problems. These features of laboratory gambling complicate the interpretation of the results and restrict their generality. By default, the method of hypothetical choices emerges as the simplest procedure by which a large number of theoretical questions can be investigated. The use of the method relies on the assumption that people often know how they would behave in actual situations of choice, and on the further assumption that the subjects have no special reason to disguise their true preferences.*

Of course, there are many documented cases where hypothetical and real-incentive choices coincide quite closely (one such example will be presented in Section 4.3). But in choices involving risk, it is dangerous to assume that real incentives are not needed.

4.3   Payoff Scale, Order, and Demographics Effects

A key aspect of the Holt and Laury design is that it permitted an examination of large changes in payoff scale. Since individuals have widely differing attitudes toward risk, each person was asked to make decisions for several different scales. After a trainer exercise to acquaint them with the dice and random selection procedures, all participants began by making 10 decisions for a low real-payoff choice menu, where all money amounts were 1/20 of the level shown in Table 4.1. Thus, the payoffs for the risky option were $3.85 and $0.10, and the possible payoffs for the safer option were $2.00 and $1.60. These low payoffs will be called the 1x treatment, and the payoffs in Table 4.1 will be called the 20x payoffs. Other treatments are designated similarly as multiples of the low payoff level. The initial low-payoff choice was followed by a choice menu with high hypothetical payoffs (20x, 40x, or 90x), followed by the same menu with high real payoffs (20x, 40x, or 90x), and ending with a second 1x real choice.

The average numbers of safe choices, shown in the top two rows of Table 4.3, indicate that the number of safe choices increases steadily as real payoffs are scaled up, but this

Table 4.3	Average Numbers of Safe Choices: Order and Incentive Effects					
Experiment	**Incentives**	**1x**	**10x**	**20x**	**50x**	**90x**
Holt and Laury (2002)	Real	5.2[a]		6.0[c]	6.8[c]	7.2
208 subjects		5.3[d]				
	Hypothetical			4.9[b]	5.1[b]	5.3[b]
Harrison et al. (2005)	Real	5.3[a]	6.4[b]			
178 subjects						
			6.0[a]			
Holt and Laury (2005)	Real	5.7[a]		6.7[a]		
168 subjects	Hypothetical	5.6[a]		5.7[a]		

Key: Superscripts indicate Order (a = 1st, b = 2nd, c = 3rd, d = 4th)

incentive effect is not observed as hypothetical payoffs are scaled up. Finally, note that the letter superscripts in the table indicate the order in which the decision was made (*a* first, *b* second, and so on). The 1x treatment done in the fourth position in the order yielded an average of 5.3 safe choices, as compared with 5.2 safe choices when this treatment was done first. This return to baseline suggests that risk aversion is not affected by the order in which the decision was made.

The dramatic effects of payoff scale are shown in Table 4.4, which presents the choice proportions for one of the high payoff (90x) paired lotteries made by 17 subjects. For this choice, 38 percent of the subjects selected the safe lottery even though its expected value was over $100 lower! These people were not willing to take any risk at these high payoffs. In all treatments, the experimenters had to go to each person's desk to throw the dice, and in the process it became apparent that making the high stakes decisions was stressful and exciting. For some, this manifested as changes in skin color around their necks.

Harrison et al. (2005) correctly point out this design mingles order and payoff scale effects, which might complicate the interpretation of the results. A comparison of the 1x

Table 4.4	Choice Percentages for a High Payoff Choice	
Lottery A		**Lottery B**
$200.00 if throw of die is 1–9		$336.50 if throw of die is 1–9
$160.00 if throw of die is 10		$9.00 if throw of die is 10
Chosen by 38 percent		Chosen by 62 percent

decisions (done first and last) with those of higher scales is complicated by the change in order, as are the comparisons of high hypothetical and high real payoffs (done in the second and third order respectively). The presence of order effects is supported by the Harrison et al. results summarized in the middle rows of the table, where inferred risk aversion is higher when the 10x scale treatment follows the 1x treatment than when the 10x treatment is done first. The order effect produces a difference of 0.4 safe choices. Such order effects call into question the real versus hypothetical comparisons, although it is still possible to make inferences about the scale effects from 20x to 40x to 90x in the Holt and Laury experiment, since these were made in the same order.

In response to these issues of interpretation, Holt and Laury (2005) ran a follow-up experiment with a 2×2 between-subjects design: real or hypothetical payoffs and 1x or 20x payoffs. Each participant began with a lottery choice trainer (again with choices between $3 and gambles involving $1 or $6. Then each person made a single menu of choices from one of the four treatment cells, so all decisions were made in the same order. Again, the scaling up of real payoffs caused a sharp increase in the average number of safe choices (from 5.7 to 6.7), whereas this incentive effect was not observed with a scaling up of hypothetical choices. Finally, the data from the lottery-choice trainers can be used to determine whether observed differences in the four treatments are somehow due to unanticipated demographic differences or other unobserved factors that may cause people in one cell to be intrinsically more risk averse than those in other cells. A check of data from the trainers shows virtually no differences across treatment cells, and if anything, the trainer data indicate slightly lower risk aversion for the group of people who were subsequently given the high real payoff menu.

The main conclusions are that participants are risk averse, the risk aversion increases with higher real payoffs, and that looking at high hypothetical payoffs may be very misleading. These conclusions are apparent from the graph of the distributions of the number of safe choices for each of the 10 decisions, as shown in Figure 4.3. In this context, it does not seem to matter much whether or not one used real money when the scale of payoffs is low, but observing no difference and then inferring that money payoffs do not matter in other contexts would be incorrect. Finally, note that payoff-scale effects may not be apparent in classroom experiments where payoffs are typically small or hypothetical.

Another interesting question is whether there are systematic demographic effects. The subjects in the original Holt and Laury (2002) experiment included about 60 M.B.A. students, about 30 business school faculty (and a Dean), and over a hundred undergraduates from three universities (University of Miami, University of Central Florida, and Georgia State University). There was a slight tendency for people with higher incomes to be less risk averse. The women were more risk averse than men in the low-payoff (1x) condition, as observed in some previous studies, but this gender effect disappeared for higher payoff scales. In other words, all of that bravado went away with high stakes (e.g., 20x scale). There was no white/non-white difference, but Hispanics in the sample were a little less risk

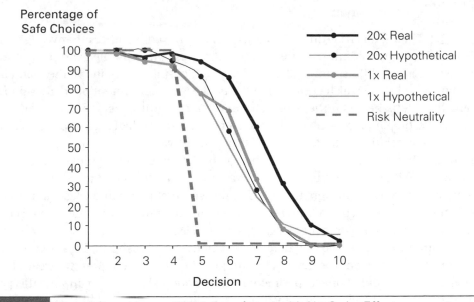

Figure 4.3   The Holt and Laury (2005) Experiment with No Order Effects

averse. It is not appropriate to make broad inferences about demographic effects from a single study using a sample of students and faculty at three universities. For example, the Hispanic effect could be due to the fact that most of the Hispanic participants were M.B.A. students in Miami, many of whose families emigrated from Cuba.

In contrast, Harrison, Lau, and Rutstrom (2005) used the Holt and Laury procedure to estimate risk preferences for a *representative sample* of 253 adults in Denmark, using high payoffs comparable to those in Table 4.1. (The payoffs were about eight times higher, but only one person in ten was actually paid.) One advantage of a field experiment with careful sampling is that it may be possible to make inferences about the effects of social policies for a whole country. The overall conclusion of this study is that the Danes are risk averse, with a relative risk aversion measure of about 0.67, which is similar to the value of 0.5 used to construct Table 4.2. Most demographic variables had no significant effect, with the exception that middle-aged and educated people tended to be less risk averse. There was no gender effect, which is consistent with the Holt and Laury high-payoff results. Most laboratory studies of risk aversion, however, do find a gender effect, with women being more risk averse, at least for small stakes and for survey-type questionnaires of a willingness to take risk. For example, Dohmen et al. (2005) conducted a large representative survey of Germans and found less risk aversion for men and for people who are younger, taller, and more educated.

4.4 Extensions

The menu structure in Table 4.1 has been used by others to investigate related issues with larger and more representative samples. One notable example is Andersen, Harrison, Lau, and Rutstrom (2005), who used a high-payoff version of the menu in Table 4.1 (converted into Danish currency) in the field experiment (mentioned above) involving Danish citizens between the ages of 18 and 75, excluding residents of several remote islands. Participants were generally risk averse, and individual measures of risk aversion tended to be relatively stable when the experiment was repeated with a sub-sample at a later date. Individual responses did change, but changes were typically small and non-systematic, with several exceptions. For example, students tended to exhibit less stability. Changes in risk aversion were unrelated to measured changes in background conditions, with one intuitive exception; those who were more favorable about their overall economic situation tended to become more willing to take risks.

Another issue that is being deferred is whether utility should be a function of final wealth or of gains from the current wealth position. In this chapter, we treat utility as a function of gains only. Some experimental and theoretical evidence supports this perspective, see Rabin and Thaler (2001) and Cox and Vjollca (2001).

QUESTIONS

1. For the square root utility function, find the expected utility of the risky lottery for Decision 6, and check your answer with the appropriate entry in Table 4.2.

2. Consider the quadratic utility function $U(x) = x^2$. Sketch the shape of this function in a figure analogous to Figure 4.1. Does this function exhibit increasing or decreasing marginal utility? Is this shape indicative of risk aversion? Calculate the expected utilities for the safe and risky options in Decision 4 for Table 4.1, i.e., when the probabilities are equal to 0.4 and 0.6.

3. Suppose that a deck with all the face cards (Ace, King, Queen, and Jack) removed, is used to determine a money payoff, e.g., a draw of a 2 of clubs would pay $2, a draw of a 10 of diamonds would pay $10, and so on. Write the nine possible money payoffs and the probability associated with each. What is the expected value of a single draw from the deck, assuming that it has been well shuffled? How much money would you pay to play this game?

4. Calculate the expected payoffs for the pair of lotteries in Table 4.4. Which lottery would be chosen by a risk-neutral person? Which would be chosen by someone with a square root utility function for income from the choice?

chapter 5

Randomized Strategies

In many situations there is a strategic advantage associated with being unpredictable, much as a tennis player does not always lob in response to an opponent's charge to the net. This chapter discusses randomized strategies in the context of simple matrix games (matching pennies and battle of sexes). The associated class experiments can be run using the instructions in this chapter's Battle of Colors Game experiment in the Class Experiments section. If a Web-based game with multiple rounds is to be run from remote locations, it is recommended that it be set up using the "go at your own pace" option and that the starting time be announced in advance. In this manner, the first person who logs in will be matched with the second, and so on, and delays will be minimal if people log in at about the same time.

5.1 Symmetric Matching Pennies Games

In a matching pennies game, each person uncovers a penny showing either heads or tails. By prior agreement, one person can take both coins if the pennies match (two heads or two tails), and the other can take the coins if the pennies do not match. A person cannot afford to have a reputation of always choosing heads, or of always choosing tails, because being predictable will result in a loss every time. Intuition suggests that each person will play heads half of the time.

A similar situation may arise in a soccer penalty kick, where the goalie has to dive to one side or the other, and the kicker has to kick to one side or the other. The goalie wants a match and the kicker wants a mismatch. Again, any tendency to go in one direction more often than another can be exploited by the other player. If there are no asymmetries in kicking and diving ability for one side versus the other, then each direction should be selected about half of the time.

It is easy to imagine economic situations where people would not like to be predictable. For example, a lazy manager only wants to prepare for an audit if such an audit is

Table 5.1	A Matching Pennies Game (Row's Payoff, Column's Payoff)	
	Column Player (auditor)	
Row Player (manager)	**Left (audit)**	**Right (not audit)**
Top (prepare)	1, −1 ⇒	⇓ −1, 1
Bottom (not prepare)	−1, 1 ⇑	⇐ 1, −1

likely. The auditor, who is rewarded for discovering problems, would only want to audit if it is likely that the manager is unprepared. The qualitative structure of the payoffs for these situations are represented in Table 5.1.

First, suppose that the manager expects an audit, so the payoffs on the left side of the table are more likely. Then the manager prefers to prepare for the anticipated audit to obtain the good outcome with a payoff of 1, which is greater than the payoff of −1 for getting caught unprepared. This preferred deviation is represented by the up arrow in the lower-left box. Alternatively, if the manager expects no audit (the right side of the table), then the manager prefers not to prepare, which again yields a payoff of 1 (notice the down arrow in the top-right box). Conversely, the auditor prefers to audit when the manager is not prepared, and to skip the audit otherwise.

Given the intuition about being unpredictable, it is not surprising that we typically observe a near-equal split on aggregate decisions for the symmetric matching pennies game in Table 5.1, although there can be considerable variation in the choice proportions from round to round. (In laboratory experiments, the payoffs are scaled up, and a fixed payment is added to eliminate the possibility of losses, but the essential structure of the game is unchanged, as shown in Chapter 24.) Despite the intuitive nature of fifty-fifty splits for the game in Table 5.1, it is useful to see what behavior is stable in the sense of being a Nash equilibrium. Up to now, we have only considered strategies without random elements, but such strategies will not constitute an equilibrium in this game. First, consider the Top/Left box in the table, which corresponds to audit/prepare. This would be a Nash equilibrium if neither player has an incentive to change unilaterally, which is not the case, since the auditor would not want to audit if the manager is going to prepare. In all cells, the player with the lower payoff would prefer to switch unilaterally.

As mentioned in Chapter 1, Nash (1950) proved that an equilibrium always exists (for games in which each person has a finite number of strategies). Since there is no equilibrium in non-random strategies in the matching pennies game, there must be an equilibrium that involves random play. The earlier discussion of matching pennies indicated that this equilibrium involves using each strategy half of the time. Think about the announcement test. If one person is playing heads half of the time, then playing tails will win half of the time; playing heads will win half of the time, and playing a fifty-fifty mix of heads and tails will win half of the time. In other words, when one player is playing randomly with probabilities of one half, the other person cannot do any better than using the same probabilities. If each person were to announce that they would use a coin flip to decide which side to play, the other could not do any better than using a coin flip. This is the Nash equilibrium for this game. It is called a *mixed equilibrium* since players use a probabilistic mix of each of their decisions. In contrast, an equilibrium in which no strategies are random is called a *pure strategy* equilibrium, since none of the strategies are probability mixes.

Another perspective on the mixed equilibrium is based on the observation that a person is only willing to choose randomly if no decision is any better than another. So the row player's choice probabilities must keep the column player indifferent, and vice versa. The only way one person will be indifferent is if the other is using equal probabilities of heads and tails, which is the equilibrium outcome.

Even though the answer is obvious, it is useful to introduce a graphical device that will help clarify matters in more complicated situations. This graph will show each person's best response to any given beliefs about the other's decisions. In Figure 5.1, the thick solid line shows the best response for the row player (manager). The horizontal axis represents what Row expects Column to do. These beliefs can be thought of as a probability of Right, going from 0 on the left to 1 on the right. If Column is expected to choose Left, then Row's best response is to choose Top, so the best response line starts at the top-left part of the fig-

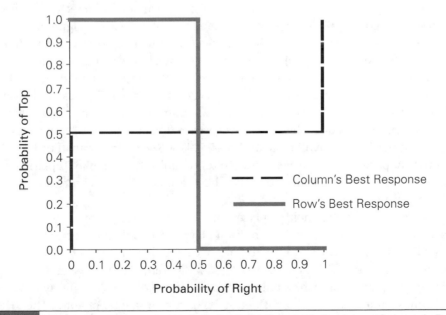

| Figure 5.1 | Row's Best Response to Beliefs about Column's Decision (Column's Best Response to Beliefs about Row's Decision) |

ure, as shown by the thick line. If Column is expected to choose Right, then Row should play Bottom, so the best response line ends up on the bottom-right side of the graph. The crossover point is where the Column's probability is exactly 0.5, since Row does better by playing Top whenever Column is more likely to choose Left.

A mathematical derivation of the crossover point (where Row is indifferent and willing to cross over) requires that we find the probability of Right for which Row's expected payoff is exactly equal for each decision. Let p denote Row's beliefs about the probability of Right, so $1 - p$ is the probability of Left. Recall from Chapter 4 that expected payoffs are found by adding up the products of payoffs and associated probabilities. From the top row of Table 5.1, we see that if Row chooses Top, then Row earns 1 with probability $1 - p$ and Row earns -1 with probability p, so the expected payoff is as follows:

$$\text{Row's expected payoff for Top} = 1(1 - p) - 1(p) = 1 - 2p$$

Similarly, by playing Bottom, Row earns -1 with probability $1 - p$ and 1 with probability p, so the expected payoff is as follows:

$$\text{Row's expected payoff for Bottom} = - (1 - p) + p = -1 + 2p$$

These expected payoffs are equal when $1 - 2p = -1 + 2p$. Solving, we see that $p = 2/4 = 0.5$, which confirms the earlier conclusion that Row is indifferent when Column is choosing each decision with equal probability.

A similar analysis shows that Column is indifferent when Row is using probabilities of one-half. Therefore, the best response line will cross over when Row's probability of Top is 0.5. To see this graphically, change the interpretation of the axes in Figure 5.1 to let the vertical axis represent Column's beliefs about what Row will do. And instead of interpreting the horizontal axis as a probability representing Row's beliefs about Column's action, now interpret it in terms of Column's actual best response. With this change, the dashed line that crosses at a height of one-half is Column's best response to beliefs on the vertical axis. If Column thinks Row will play Bottom, then Column wants to play Left, so this line starts in the bottom-left part of the figure. This is because the high payoff of 1 for Column is in the bottom-left part of the payoff table in Table 5.1. There is another payoff of 1 for Column in the top-right part of the table, i.e., when Column thinks Row will play Top, then Right is the best response. For this reason, the dashed best response line in Figure 5.1 ends up in the top-right corner.

In a Nash equilibrium, neither player can do better by deviating, so a Nash equilibrium must be on the best response lines for both players. The only intersection of the solid and dashed lines in Figure 5.1 is at probabilities of 0.5 for each player. If both players think the other's move is like a coin flip, they would be indifferent themselves, and hence willing to decide by a flip of a coin. This equilibrium prediction works well in the symmetric matching pennies game, but we will consider qualifications in a later chapter. The focus here is on calculating and interpreting the notion of an equilibrium in randomized strategies, not on summarizing all behavioral tendencies in these games.

5.2 Battle of the Sexes

Thus far, we have considered two types of games with unique Nash equilibria, the prisoner's dilemma (Chapter 3) and matching pennies. In contrast, the coordination game discussed in Chapter 3 had two equilibria in non-random strategies, one of which was preferred by both players. Next, consider another game with two equilibria in non-random strategies, the payoffs for which are shown in Table 5.2. This is a game where two friends who live on opposite sides of Central Park wish to meet at one of the entrances, i.e., on the East side or on the West side. It is obvious from the payoffs that Column wishes to meet on the West side, and Row prefers the East side. But notice the zero payoffs in the mismatched (West and East) outcomes, i.e., each person would rather be with the other than to be on the preferred side of the park alone. This in an example of a game generally known as a battle-of-sexes game.

Think of what you would do in a repeated situation. Clearly, most people would take turns. This is exactly what happens when two people play the game repeatedly in controlled experiments with the same partner. In fact, coordinated switching often arises even when explicit communication is not permitted. Table 5.3 shows a decision sequence for a pair who were matched with each other for six periods of a class experiment, using payoffs from Table 5.2. There is a match on East in the first period, and the Column player then switches to West in the second period, which results in a mismatch and earnings of $0 for each. Row switches to West in the third period, and they alternate in a coordinated manner in each subsequent period, which maximizes their joint earnings. Four of the six pairs alternated in this manner, and the other two pairs settled into a pattern where one earned $4 in all rounds.

Table 5.2	A Battle-of-Sexes Game (Row's Payoff, Column's Payoff)	

| | Column | |
Row	**West**	**East**
West	1, 4	0, 0
East	0, 0	4, 1

Table 5.3	Alternating Choices for a Pair of Subjects in a Battle-of-Sexes Game with Fixed Partners					

	Round 1	**Round 2**	**Round 3**	**Round 4**	**Round 5**	**Round 6**
Row Player	East ($4)	East ($0)	West ($1)	East ($4)	West ($1)	East ($4)
Column Player	East ($1)	West ($0)	West ($4)	East ($1)	West ($4)	East ($1)

The problem is harder if the battle-of-sexes game is played only once, without communication, or if there is repetition with random matchings. Consider the battle-of-sexes game shown in Table 5.4.

The payoffs in this table were used in a recent classroom experiment conducted at the College of William and Mary. There were 30 students located in several different computer labs, with random matchings between those designated as Row players and those designated as Column players. Table 5.5 shows the percentage of times that players chose the preferred location (Top for Row and Bottom for Column). Intuitively, one would expect that the percentage of preferred-location choices to be above one-half, and in fact this percentage converges to 67 percent. This mix of choices does not correspond to either equilibrium in pure strategies.

The remarkable feature of Table 5.5 is that both types seem to choose their preferred location about two-thirds of the time. It is not surprising that this fraction is above one-half, but why two-thirds? If you look at the payoff table, you will notice that Row gets either 2 or 0 for playing Top, and either 0 or 1 for playing Bottom, so in a loose sense Top is more attractive unless Column is expected to play Right with high probability. Similarly, from Column's point of view, Right (with payoffs of 0 or 2) is more attractive than Left (with payoffs of 1 and 0), unless Row is expected to play Top with high probability. This intuition only provides a qualitative prediction: that each person will choose their preferred decision

Table 5.4	A Battle-of-Sexes Game (Row's Payoff, Column's Payoff)

	Column	
Row	**Left**	**Right**
Top	2, 1	0, 0
Bottom	0, 0	1, 2

Table 5.5	Percentage of Preferred-Location Decisions for the Battle-of-Sexes Game in Table 5.4

Round	Row Players	Column Players	All Players
1	80	87	83.5
2	87	93	90
3	87	60	73.5
4	67	67	67
5	67	67	67
Nash	67	67	67

more often than not. The remarkable convergence of the frequency of preferred decisions to 2/3 cries out for some mathematical explanation, especially considering that each person's 2 and 1 payoffs add up to 3, and 2/3 of sum can only be obtained with the preferred decision.

Instead of looking for mathematical coincidences, let's calculate some expected payoff expressions as was done in the previous section. First, consider Row's perspective when Column is expected to play Right with probability p. Consider the top row of the payoff matrix in Table 5.4, where Row thinks the right column is relevant with probability p. If Row chooses Top, Row gets 2 when Column plays Left (expected with probability $1 - p$) and Row gets 0 when Column plays Right (expected with probability p). When Row chooses Bottom, these payoffs are replaced by 0 and 1. Thus, as shown in Equation (5.1), Row's expected payoffs are as follows:

$$\text{Row's expected payoff for Top} = 2(1 - p) + 0(p) = 2 - 2p$$
$$\text{Row's expected payoff for Bottom} = 0(1 - p) + 1(p) = 0 + p \tag{5.1}$$

The expected payoff for Top is higher when $2 - 2p > p$, or equivalently, when $p < 2/3$. Obviously, the expected payoffs are equal when $p = 2/3$, and Top provides a lower expected payoff when $p > 2/3$.

Since Row's expected payoffs are equal when Column's probability of choosing Right is 2/3, Row would not have a preference between the two decisions and would be willing to choose randomly. At this time, you might guess that since the game looks symmetric, the equilibrium involves each player choosing their preferred decision with probability 2/3. This guess would be correct, as shown in Figure 5.2. As before, the solid line represents Row's best response that we analyzed above. If the horizontal axis represents Row's beliefs about how likely it is that Column will play Right, then Row would want to "go to the top of the graph" (play Top) as long as Column's probability p is less than 2/3. Row is indifferent when $p = 2/3$, and row would want to "go to the bottom of the graph" when $p > 2/3$.

So far, we have been looking at things from Row's point of view, but an equilibrium involves both players, so let's think about Column's decision where the vertical axis now represents Column's belief about what Row will do. At the top, Row is expected to play Top, and Column's best response is to play Left in order to be in the same location as Row. Thus, Column's dashed best response line starts in the upper-left part of the figure. This line also ends up in the lower-right part, since when Row is expected to play Bottom (coming down the vertical axis), Column would want to switch to the preferred Right location. It can be verified by simple algebra that the switchover point is at 2/3, as shown by the horizontal segment of the dashed line.

Since a Nash equilibrium is a pair of strategies such that each player cannot do better by deviating, each player has to make a best response to the other's strategy. In Figure 5.2, a Nash equilibrium will be on both Row's (solid) best-response line and on Column's (dashed) best-response line. Thus, the final step is to look for equilibrium points at the intersections of the best response lines. There are three intersections. There is one in the

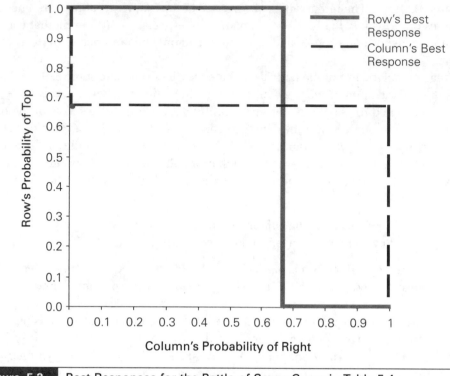

Figure 5.2 Best Responses for the Battle-of-Sexes Game in Table 5.4

upper-left corner of the figure where both coordinate on Row's preferred outcome (Row earns 2, Column earns 1). Similarly, the lower-right intersection is an equilibrium at Column's preferred outcome (Row earns 1, Column earns 2). We already found these equilibria by looking at the payoff matrix directly, but the third intersection point in the interior of the figure is new. At this point, players choose their preferred decisions (Top for Row and Right for Column) with probability 2/3, which is what we see in the data.

The graph shows the equilibria clearly, but it is useful to see how the random strategy equilibrium would be found with only simple algebra, since the graphical approach will not be possible with more players or more decisions.

Step 1. Summarize notation.

p = Probability that Column chooses Right.

q = Probability that Row chooses Top.

Step 2. Calculate expected payoffs for each decision.

Row's expected payoff for Top = $2(1 - p) + 0(p) = 2 - 2p$.

Row's expected payoff for Bottom = $0(1 - p) + 1(p) = 0 + p$.

Column's expected payoff for Right $= 0(q) + 2(1 - q) = 2 - 2q$.
Column's expected payoff for Left $= 1(q) + 0(1 - q) = q + 0$.

Step 3. Calculate the equilibrium probabilities.
Equate Row's expected payoffs to determine p.
Equate Column's expected payoffs to determine q.

We already showed that the first part yields $p = 2/3$, and it is easy to verify that $q = 2/3$.

The idea behind these calculations is that in order to randomize willingly, a person must be indifferent between the decisions, and indifference is found by equating expected payoffs. The tricky part is that equating Row's expected payoffs pins down Column's probability, and vice versa.

5.3   Extensions

The data in Table 5.5 is atypical in the sense that such sharp convergence to an equilibrium in randomized strategies is not always observed. Often there is a little more bouncing around the predictions, due to noise factors (see Question 6 at the end of the chapter). Remember that each person is seeing a series of other people, so people have different experiences, and hence different beliefs. This raises the issue of how people learn after observing others' decisions, a topic covered in later chapters. Second, the games discussed in this chapter are symmetric in some sense; payoff asymmetries may cause biases, as will be discussed in Chapter 24. Finally, the battle-of-sexes game discussed here was conducted under very low payoff conditions, with only one person out of 30 being selected ex post to be paid earnings in cash. High payoffs might cause other factors like risk aversion to become important, especially when there is a lot more variability in the payoffs associated with one decision than with another. If risk aversion is a factor, then the expected payoffs would have to be replaced with expected utility calculations.

QUESTIONS

1. Use the expected payoff calculations in Step 2 in Section 5.2 to solve for an equilibrium level of q for the battle-of-sexes game.

2. This chapter's Battle of Colors Game experiment in the Class Experiments section contains instructions for a game with playing cards.

   a. Write out the payoff matrix for round one of this game.
   b. Find all equilibria in non-random strategies and say what kind of game this is.
   c. Find expressions for Row's expected payoffs, one for each of Row's decisions.
   d. Find expressions for Column's expected payoffs.

    e. Find the equilibrium with randomized strategies, using algebra.

    f. Illustrate your answer with a graph.

3. Suppose that the payoffs in Table 5.4 are changed by raising payoff 2 to a 3, for both players. Next, answer Question 2, parts c, d, and e for this game.

4. Find the Nash equilibrium in mixed strategies for the coordination game in Table 3.2, and illustrate your answer with a graph.

5. Graph the best-response lines for the prisoner's dilemma game in Table 3.1, and indicate why there is a unique Nash equilibrium.

6. The data in the table below were for the battle-of-sexes game shown in Table 5.2. The 12 players were randomly matched, and the final 5 periods out of a 10-period sequence are shown. The game was run with an experimental economics class at the University of Virginia. Each player consisted of one or two people at the same PC, and one player was selected at random ex post to be paid a third of earnings. Calculate the percentage of times that Row players chose East in all 5 periods, the percentage of times that Column players chose West, and the average of these numbers. Then calculate the mixed-strategy Nash equilibrium.

Round	6	7	8	9	10
Row	6 East	3 East, 3 West	5 East, 1 West	5 East, 1 West	6 East
Column	2 East, 4 West	2 East, 4 West	1 East, 5 West	3 East, 3 West	2 East, 4 West

part 2

Market Experiments

♠

The games in Part 2 represent many of the standard market models that are used in economics. In a *monopoly*, there is a single seller, whose production decision determines the price at which the output can be sold. This model can be generalized by letting firms choose quantities independently, where the aggregate quantity determines the market price. This *Cournot* setup is widely used, and it has the intuitive property that an increase in the number of sellers will decrease the equilibrium price. The experiment discussed in Chapter 6 implements a setup with linear demand and constant cost, which permits an analysis of the effects of changing the number of competitors, including in a monopoly.

Many important aspects of a market economy pertain to sales of intermediate goods along a supply chain. Chapter 7 considers experiments based on a very simple case of a monopoly manufacturer selling to a monopoly retailer, with each firm equating marginal revenue to marginal cost. As verified by experiments, this process of *double marginalization* causes the industry output to be even lower than would be the case if the two firms merged into a single monopoly. Many industries are characterized by long supply chains, which link manufacturers, distributors, wholesalers, and retailers. Frictions and distortions (the bullwhip effect) that may arise along supply chains provide a rich source of topics for laboratory experiments.

The Cournot model may be appropriate when firms pre-commit to production decisions, but it is often more realistic to model firms as choosing prices independently. Chapters 8 and 9 pertain to price competition, imperfections, and the effects of alternative trading institutions when buyers are not simulated. Buyer and seller activities are essentially symmetric in the double auction, except that buyers tend to bid the price up, and sellers tend to undercut each other's prices. This strategic symmetry is not present in the *posted-offer auction*, where sellers post prices independently, and buyers are given a chance to purchase at the posted prices (further bargaining and discounting is not permitted). The posted-offer market resembles a retail market, with sellers producing to order and selling at catalogue or list prices. In contrast, the double auction more closely resembles a competitive open outcry market like that of the New York Stock Exchange. Collusion and the exercise of market power cause larger distortions in markets with posted prices, although these effects may be diminished if sellers are able to offer secret discounts.

The effects of asymmetric information about product quality are considered in Chapter 10. When sellers can select a quality grade and a price, the outcomes may be quite efficient under full information, but qualities may fall to low levels when buyers are unable to observe the quality grade prior to purchase. The unraveling of quality may eventually cause a market failure in which only low-quality units are traded. A different kind of unraveling has been observed in some labor markets, with students being recruited earlier and earlier by competing employers. In the market for medical school graduates, the costs of this unraveling caused the adoption of central clearinghouse mechanisms based on ranked preferences submitted by those on both sides of the market (medical students and hospitals). Experiments to evaluate alternative matching algorithms are also reviewed in Chapter 10.

Markets for economic assets are complicated by the fact that ownership provides two potential sources of value, i.e., the benefits obtained each period (services, dividends, and so on) and the capital gain (or loss) in the value of the asset. Asset values may be affected by market fundamentals like dividends and the opportunity cost of money (the interest that could be earned in a safe account). In addition, values can be affected by expectations about future value, and such expectations-driven values can cause trading prices to deviate from levels determined by market fundamentals. Chapter 11 summarizes some experimental work on such asset markets where price bubbles and crashes are often observed.

chapter 6

Monopoly and Cournot Markets

A monopolist can obtain a higher price by restricting production; profit maximization involves finding a balance between the desire to charge a high price and to maintain sales quantity. Subjects in experiments with simulated buyers are able to adjust quantity so that prices are at or near the monopoly level. This experiment can be done with the Veconlab Cournot program by setting the number of sellers to 1. The setup allows price to be subject to random shocks, which adds interest and realism. Then students, who may log in from remote locations, can use the price and quantity data to estimate demand and marginal revenue, and thereby derive the monopoly price that they already discovered through trial and error in the experiment.

The analysis of monopoly provides a natural bridge to the most widely used model of the interaction of several sellers (oligopoly). The key behavioral assumption of this model is that each seller takes the others' quantity choices as given, and then behaves as a monopolist maximizing profits for the resulting residual demand. The popularity of the Cournot model is, in part, due to the intuitive prediction that the market price will decrease from monopoly levels toward competitive levels as the number of sellers is increased. This tendency can be verified with the Veconlab Cournot program, or with the hand-run version found in this chapter's Quantity Choice Market experiment in the Class Experiments section.

6.1 Monopoly

A monopolist is defined as being a sole seller in a market, but the general model of monopoly is central to the analysis of antitrust issues because it can be applied more widely. For example, suppose that all sellers in a market are somehow able to collude and set a price that maximizes the total profit, which is then divided among them. In this case, the monopoly model would be relevant, either for providing a prediction of price and quantity, or as a benchmark from which to measure the success of the cartel.

In antitrust analysis, the monopoly model is also applied to the case of one large firm and a number of small fringe firms that behave competitively (expanding output as long as the price that they can obtain is above the cost of each additional unit of output). The behavior of the firms in the competitive fringe can be represented by a supply function, which shows the quantity provided by these firms in total as a function of the price. Let this fringe supply function be represented by $S(P)$, which is increasing in price if marginal costs are increasing for the fringe firms. Then the *residual demand* is the market demand, $D(P)$, minus the fringe supply, so the residual demand is $R(P) = D(P) - S(P)$. This function indicates a relationship between price and the sales quantity that is not taken by the fringe firms; this is the quantity that can be sold by the large dominant firm. In this situation, it may be appropriate to treat the dominant firm as a monopolist facing a residual demand function: $Q = R(P)$.

From the monopolist's point of view, the demand (or residual demand) function reveals the amount that can be sold for each possible price, with high prices generally resulting in lower sales quantities. It is useful to invert this demand relationship and think of price as a function of quantity, i.e., selling a larger quantity reduces price. For example, a linear inverse demand function would have the form: $P = A - BQ$, where A is the vertical intercept of demand in a graph with price on the vertical axis, and $-B$ is the slope, with $B > 0$. The experiments to be discussed in this chapter all have a linear inverse demand, which for simplicity, will be referred to as the *demand function*.

The left side of Figure 6.1 shows the results of a laboratory experiment in which each person was a monopolist in a market with a constant cost of $1 per unit and a linear demand curve: $P = 13 - Q$. Since the slope is minus one, each additional unit of output raises the cost by $1 and reduces the price by $1. The vertical axis in the figure is the average of the quantity choices made in each round. It is apparent that the participants quickly settle on a quantity of about 6, which is the profit-maximizing choice, as will be verified next.

The demand curve used in the experiment is also shown in the top two rows of Table 6.1. Notice that as price in the second row decreases from 12 to 11 to 10, the sales quantity increases from 1 to 2 to 3. The total revenue, PQ, is shown in the third row, and the total cost, which equals quantity, is given in the fourth row. Please take a minute to fill in the missing elements in these rows, and to subtract cost from revenue to obtain the profit numbers that should be entered in the fifth row. Doing this, you should be able to verify that profit is maximized with a quantity of 6 and a price of 7.

Even though the profit calculations are straightforward, it is instructive to consider the monopolist's decision as quantity is increased from 1 to 2, and then to 3, while keeping an eye on the effects of these increases on revenue and cost at the margin. The first unit of output produced yields a revenue of 12, so the marginal revenue of this unit is 12, as shown in the MR row at the left. An increase from $Q = 1$ to $Q = 2$ raises total revenue from 12 to 22, which is an increase of 10, as shown in the MR row. These additional revenues for the first and second units are greater than the cost increases of one dollar per unit, so the increases

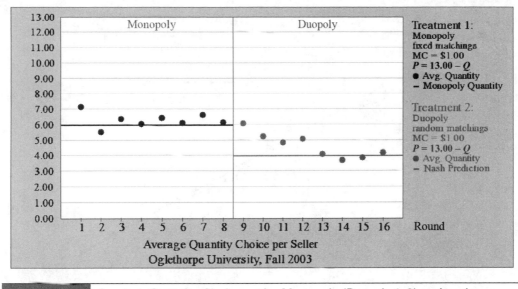

| Figure 6.1 | Average Quantity Choice under Monopoly (Rounds 1–8) and under Duopoly (Rounds 9–16) |

were justified. Now consider an increase to an output of 3. This raises revenue from 22 to 30, an increase of 8, and this marginal revenue is again greater than the marginal cost of 1. Profit increases as long as the marginal revenue is greater than the marginal cost, a process that continues until the output reaches the optimal level of 6, as you can verify.

One thing to notice about the MR row of Table 6.1 is that each unit increase in quantity, which reduces price by 1, will reduce marginal revenue by 2, since marginal revenue goes from 12 to 10 to 8, and so on. This fact is illustrated in Figure 6.2, where the demand line is the outer line, and the marginal revenue line is the thick dashed line. The marginal revenue

| Table 6.1 | Monopoly with Linear Demand and Constant Cost |

Quantity	1	2	3	4	5	6	7	8	9	10	11	12
Price	12	11	10	9	8	7	6	5	4	3	2	1
TR	12	22	30	36					36	30	22	12
TC	1	2	3	4					9	10	11	12
Profit	11	20	27	32					27	20	11	0
MR	12	10	8	6					−4	−6	−8	−10
MC		1	1	1	1					1	1	1	1

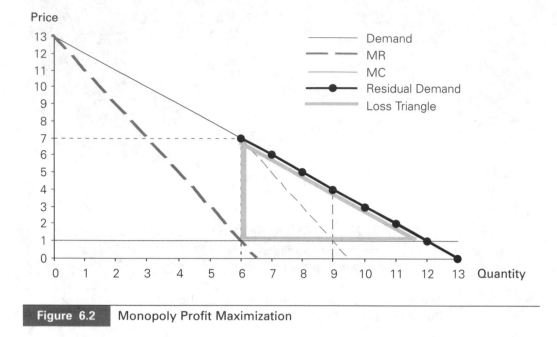

Figure 6.2   Monopoly Profit Maximization

line has a slope that is twice as negative as the demand line. The MR line intersects the horizontal marginal cost line at a quantity of 6. Thus, the graph illustrates what you will see when you fill out the table, i.e., that marginal revenue is greater than marginal cost for each additional unit, the first, second, third, fourth, fifth, and sixth, but the marginal revenue of the seventh unit is below marginal cost, so that unit should not be added. (The marginal revenues in the table will not match the numbers on the graph exactly, since the marginal revenues in the table are for going from one unit up to the next. For example, the marginal revenue in the sixth column of the table will be 2, which is the increase in revenue from going from five to six units. Think of this quantity as 5.5, and the marginal revenue for 5.5 in the figure is exactly 2.)

In addition to the table and the graph, it is useful to redo the same derivation of the monopoly quantity using simple calculus. (A brief review of the needed calculus formulas is provided in the Quick Calculus Review at the end of the chapter.) Since demand is: $P = 13 - Q$, it follows that total revenue, PQ, is $(13 - Q)Q$, which is a quadratic function of output: $13Q - Q^2$. Marginal revenue is the derivative of total revenue, $13 - 2Q$, which is a line that starts at a value of 13 when $Q = 0$ and declines by 2 for each unit increase in quantity, as shown in Figure 6.2. Since marginal cost is 1, it follows that marginal revenue equals marginal cost when $13 - 2Q = 1$, i.e., when $Q = 6$, the monopoly output for this market.

The case against monopoly can be illustrated in Figure 6.2, where the monopoly price is $7 and the marginal cost is only $1. Thus, buyers with valuations between $1 and $7 would be willing to pay amounts that cover cost, but the monopoly does not satisfy this demand, in order to keep price and earnings high. As shown in Chapter 2, the loss in buyers' value can be measured as the area under the demand curve, and the net loss is obtained by looking at the area below demand, to the right of 6 and above the marginal cost line in the figure. This triangular area, bounded by light gray lines, is a measure of the welfare cost of monopoly, as compared with the competitive outcome where price is equal to marginal cost ($1) and the quantity is 12.

The convergence of the quantity to the monopoly prediction on the left side of Figure 6.1 was observed in a context where the demand side of the market was simulated. This kind of experiment is probably appropriate if one is thinking of a market with a large number of consumers, none of whom have any significant size or power to bargain for reductions from the monopoly price.

6.2 Cournot Duopoly

Next, consider what would happen if a second firm were to enter the market. In particular, suppose that both firms have constant marginal costs of $1, and that they each select an output quantity, with the price then being determined by the sum of their quantities, using the top two rows of Table 6.1. This duopoly structure was the basis for the second part of the experiment summarized in Figure 6.1. Notice that the quantity per seller starts out at the monopoly level of 6 in round 9, which results in a total quantity of 12 and forces price down to $1 (= 13 − 12). When price is $1, which equals the cost per unit, it follows that earnings are zero. The average quantity is observed to fall in round 10, which is not surprising following a round with zero profit. The incentive to cut output can be seen from the graph in Figure 6.2. Suppose that one seller (the entrant) knew the other would produce a quantity of 6. If the entrant were to produce 0, the price would stay at the monopoly level of $7. If the entrant were to produce 1, the price would fall to $6, and so on. These price/quantity points for the entrant are shown as the dark line with dots, labeled Residual Demand in Figure 6.2. The marginal revenue for this residual demand curve has a slope that is twice as steep, as shown by the thin dotted line that crosses MC at a quantity of 9. This crossing determines an output of 3 for the entrant, since the incumbent seller is producing 6. In summary, when one firm produces 6, the best response of the other is to choose a quantity of 3. This suggests why the quantities, which start at an average of 6 for each firm in period 9, begin to decline in subsequent periods, as shown on the right side of Figure 6.1. The outputs fall to an average of 4 for each seller, which suggests that this is the equilibrium, in the sense that if one seller chooses 4, the best response of the other is to choose 4 also.

In order to show that the Cournot equilibrium is in fact 4 units per seller, we need to run through some other best response calculations, which are shown in Table 6.2. This table shows a firm's profit for the example under consideration for each if its own output decisions (listed in rows, increasing from bottom to top) and for each output decision of the other firm (listed in columns, increasing from left to right). Consider the column

| Table 6.2 | A Row Seller's Own Profit Matrix | | | | | | |

| | Column Firm's Output | | | | | | |
Row's Own Output	0	1	2	3	4	5	6
6	36*	30*	24	18	12	6	
5	35	30*	25*	20*	15	10	
4	32	28	24	20*	16**	12*	8
3	27	24	21	18***	15	12*	9*
2	20	18	16	14	12	10	8
1	11	10	9	8	7	6	5

* Indicates Row's best response
** Indicates a Cournot equilibrium
*** Indicates a joint-profit maximizing outcome

labeled 0 on the left side, i.e., the column that is relevant when the other firm's output is 0. If the Column firm produces nothing, then this is the monopoly case, and the Row firm's profits in this column are just copied from the monopoly profit row of Table 6.1: a profit of 11 for an output of 1, 20 for an output of 2, and so on. The highest profit in this column is 36 in the upper-left corner, at the monopoly output of 6. This profit has been indicated by a single asterisk. To test your understanding, fill in the two missing numbers in the right column. Some of the other best response payoffs are also indicated by a single asterisk. Recall that the firm's best response to another firm's output of 6 is to produce 3 (as seen in Figure 6.2), and this is the payoff in third row and far right column, 9*, that box is labeled with an asterisk.

A Nash equilibrium in this duopoly market is a pair of outputs, such that each seller's output is the best response to that of the other. Even though 3 is a best response to 6, the pair (6 for one, 3 for the other) is not a Nash equilibrium (see Question 1 at the end of the chapter). The payoff of 16, marked with a double asterisk in the table, is the location of a Nash equilibrium, since it indicates that an output of 4 is a best response to an output of 4, so if each firm were to produce at this level, there would be no incentive for either to change unilaterally. Of course, if they could coordinate on joint output reductions to 3 each, the total output would be 6 and the industry profit would be maximized at the monopoly level of 36, or 18 each. This joint maximum is indicated by the triple asterisk at the payoff of 18 in the table. This joint maximum is not a Nash equilibrium, since each seller has an incentive to expand output (see Question 2 at the end of the chapter).

The fact that the Nash equilibrium does not maximize joint profit raises an interesting behavioral question, i.e., why couldn't the subjects in the experiment somehow coordinate on quantity restrictions to raise their joint earnings? The answer is that the matchings were random for the duopoly phase. Thus, each seller was matched with another randomly selected seller in each round, and this switching made it difficult to coordinate quantity restrictions. In experiments with fixed matchings, such coordination is often observed, particularly with only two sellers. Holt (1985) reported patterns where sellers sometimes "walked" the quantity down in unison, e.g., both duopolists reducing quantity from 7 to 6 in one period, and then to 5 in the next, and so on. This kind of tacit collusion occurred even though sellers could not communicate explicitly. There were also cases where one seller produced a very large quantity, driving the price to 0, followed by a large quantity reduction in an effort to send a threat and then a conciliatory message, and thereby induce the other seller to cooperate. Such tacit collusion is less common with more than two sellers. Part of the problem is that when one seller cuts output, the other has a unilateral incentive to expand output, so when one shows restraint, the other has greater temptation. Also, an output expansion by one seller intended to punish another will lower the price and hurt all sellers, so these types of punishments cannot be targeted.

The Nash equilibrium just identified is also called a *Cournot equilibrium*, after the French mathematician who provided an analysis of duopoly and oligopoly models in 1838. Although the Cournot equilibrium is symmetric in this case, there can be asymmetric equilibria as well. A further analysis of Table 6.2 indicates that there is at least one other Nash equilibrium, also with a total quantity of 8, and hence an average of 4, even though the two firms' quantities are not equal. Can you find this asymmetric equilibrium? (See Question 3 at the end of the chapter.)

As was the case for monopoly, it is useful to illustrate the duopoly equilibrium with a graph. If one firm is producing an output of 4, then the other can produce an output of 1 (total quantity = 5) and obtain a price of 8 (= 13 − 5), as shown by one of the residual demand dots in Figure 6.3. Think of the vertical axis as having shifted to the right at the other firm's quantity of 4, as indicated by the vertical dotted line, and the residual demand dots yield a demand curve with a slope of minus 1. As before, marginal revenue will have a slope that is twice as negative, as indicated by the heavy dashed line in the figure. This line crosses marginal cost just above the quantity of 8, which represents a quantity of 4 for this firm, since the other is already producing 4. Thus, the quantity of 4 is a best response to the other's quantity of 4. As seen in the figure, the price in this duopoly equilibrium is $5, which is lower than the monopoly price of $7.

6.3   Cournot Oligopoly

The classroom experiment shown in Figure 6.4 was done with fixed matchings, for duopoly markets (left side) and then for three-firm markets (right side). Despite the fixed nature of the matchings, participants were unable to coordinate on output reductions below the duopoly prediction of 4 per seller. In the triopoly treatment, the outputs converge to 3 on average. Notice that outputs of 3 for each of three firms translates into an industry output of 9, as compared with 8 for the duopoly case (4 each) and 6 for the

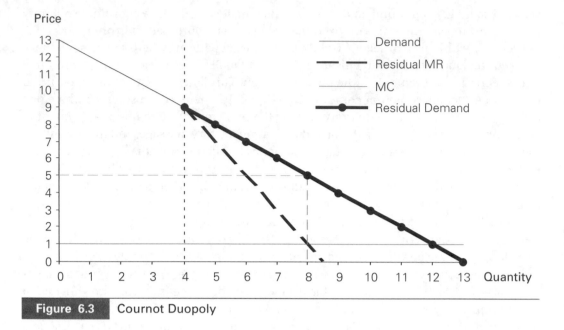

Figure 6.3   Cournot Duopoly

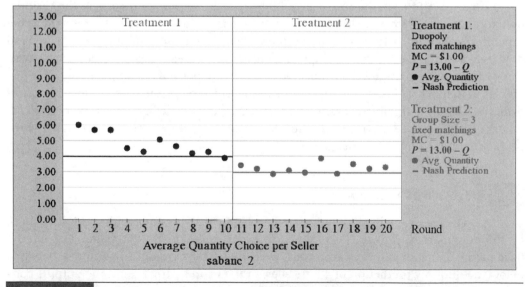

Figure 6.4   A Classroom Experiment with Duopoly (Rounds 1–10) and Triopoly (Rounds 11–20)

monopoly case. Thus, we see that increases in the number of sellers raise the total quantity and reduce price toward competitive levels.

It is possible to redraw Figure 6.3 to show that if two firms each produce 3 units each, then the remaining firm would also want to produce 3 units (see Question 4 at the end of the chapter). Instead, we will use a simple derivation based on the fact that when demand is linear, the marginal revenue has a slope that is twice as negative. It is also convenient to derive the equilibrium for the N-firm case, and come back to the triopoly calculation afterward.

First, suppose that the $N-1$ other firms each produce an output of X units, for a total of $(N-1)X$. If the firm we are considering chooses an output of Q, then the industry output is equal to the sum of $(N-1)X$ and Q, and the resulting price is equal to A minus B times this output, as shown in the top line of Equation (6.1). Then total revenue for the firm is found by multiplying this price times Q, to get the TR equation just below demand.

$$P = A - B(N-1)X - BQ$$
$$TR = AQ - B(N-1)XQ - BQ^2 \qquad (6.1)$$
$$MR = A - B(N-1)X - 2BQ$$

The marginal revenue is found by using the fact that its slope is twice as negative as that of the inverse demand, so replace the $-BQ$ term in the top line of (6.1) with $-2BQ$, as shown in the bottom line of Equation (6.1). (Alternatively, you could have taken the derivative of TR to obtain MR, as explained in the Quick Calculus Review at the end of the chapter; the 2 comes from the fact that the derivative of Q^2 is $2Q$.)

As was the case for a monopolist, the firm should expand output as long as the marginal revenue is greater than the marginal cost, C, and the optimal output is found by equating marginal revenue with marginal cost, as shown in the top line of Equation (6.2).

$$C = A - B(N-1)X - 2BQ \qquad (MC = MR)$$
$$C = A - B(N-1)Q^* - 2BQ^* \qquad (Using\ symmetry) \qquad (6.2)$$

Just as the duopoly outputs were equal at 4 for the example in Figure 6.3, there will be a symmetric equilibrium in which $Q = X = Q^*$, which denotes the common equilibrium output. This substitution produces the bottom line of Equation (6.2), which can be solved for the Cournot outputs as shown in Equation (6.3).

$$Q^* = \frac{A-C}{(N+1)B} \qquad (Cournot\ equilibrium) \qquad (6.3)$$

As N increases, the output per firm in (6.3) goes down, but the total industry output goes up. To see this, multiply the right side of (6.3) by N and consider what happens as N increases.

In research experiments with quantity choices, simulated demand, and fixed matchings, it is common for some tacit collusion to result in prices above those predicted in a Cournot equilibrium, at least with duopoly. But since the seller with the greatest output earns the most, rivalistic incentives can cause sellers to expand production above Cournot levels (Holt 1985). This effect is magnified when subjects can observe others' earnings levels, so imitation of those with the highest earnings would tend to expand outputs beyond the Cournot prediction (Hück, Normann, and Oechssler 1999).

6.4   Extensions

The Cournot model is perhaps the most widely used model in theoretical work in Industrial Organization. Its popularity is based on the prediction that the equilibrium price will be a decreasing function of the number of sellers. This prediction is supported by evidence from laboratory experiments that implement the Cournot assumption that firms select quantities independently.

The obvious shortcoming of the Cournot model is the specific way in which price is determined. The implicit assumption is that firms make quantity decisions independently, and then price is cut so that all production can be sold. For example, you might think of a situation in which the quantities have been produced, so the short run supply curve is vertical at the total quantity, and price is determined by the intersection of this vertical supply function with the market demand function. In other words, the price-competition phase is extremely competitive. There is some game-theoretic and experimental evidence to support this view. Even so, a Cournot equilibrium would not be appropriate if it is price, not quantity, that firms set independently, and then produce to fill the orders that arrive. Independent price choice may be an appropriate assumption if firms mail out catalogues or post "buy now" prices on the Internet, with the ability to produce quickly to fill orders. Some of the richer models of price competition with discounts will be discussed in the upcoming chapters.

Appendix: **Optional Quick Calculus Review**

The derivative of a linear function is just its slope. So for the demand function: $P = 13 - Q$ in Figure 6.2, the slope is -1 (each unit increase in quantity decreases price by \$1). To find the slope using calculus, we need a formula: the derivative of BQ with respect to Q is just B, for any value of the slope parameter B. Thus, the derivative of $(-1)Q$ is -1. The slope of the demand curve is the derivative of $13 - Q$ and we know that the derivative of the second part is -1, which is the correct answer, so the derivative of 13 must be 0. In fact, the derivative of any constant is 0. To see this, note that the derivative is the slope of a function, and if you graph a function with a constant height, then the function will have a slope of 0 in the same manner that a table top has no slope. For example, consider the derivative of a more general linear demand function: $A - BQ$. The intercept, A, is just a constant (it does not depend on Q, which is variable, but rather it stays the same). So the derivative of A is 0, and the derivative of $-BQ$ is $-B$, and therefore the derivative of $A - BQ$ is $0 - B = -B$. Here we have used the fact that the derivative of the sum of two functions is the sum of the derivatives. To summarize (ignore rules 4 and 5 for the moment):

1. **Constant Function:** $dA/dQ = 0$.

   The derivative of a constant like A is just 0.

2. **Linear Function:** $d(KQ)/dQ = K$.

   The derivative of a constant times a variable, which has a constant slope, is just the constant slope parameter, i.e., the derivative of KQ with respect of Q is just K.

3. **Sum of Functions:** The derivative of the sum of two functions is the sum of the derivatives.

4. **Quadratic Function:** $d(KQ^2)/dQ = 2KQ$.

   The derivative of a quadratic function is obtained by moving the 2 in the exponent down, so the derivative of KQ^2 is just $2KQ$.

5. **Power Function:** $d(KQ^x)/dQ = xKQ^{x-1}$.

   The derivative of a variable raised to the power x is obtained by moving the x down and reducing the power by 1, so the derivative of KQ^3 is just $3KQ^2$, the derivative of KQ^4 is $4KQ^3$, and in general, the derivative of KQ^x with respect to Q is xKQ^{x-1}.

For example, the monopolist being discussed has a constant marginal cost of $1 per unit, so the total cost of producing Q units is just Q dollars. Think of this total cost function as being the product of 1 and Q, so the derivative of $1Q$ is just 1 using rule 2 above. If there had been a fixed cost of F, then the total cost would be $F + Q$. Note that F is just a constant, so its derivative is 0 (rule 1), and the derivative of this total cost function is the derivative of the first part (0) plus the derivative of the second part (1), so marginal cost is again equal to 1.

Next, consider a case where demand is $P = A - BQ$, which has a vertical intercept of A and a slope of $-B$. The total revenue function is obtained by multiplying by Q to get the total revenue function: $AQ - BQ^2$, which has a linear term with slope of A and a quadratic term with a coefficient of $-B$. We know that the derivative of the linear part is just A (rule 2). The fourth rule indicates how to take the derivative of $-BQ^2$; you just move the 2 in the exponent down, so the derivative of this part is $-2BQ$. We add these two derivatives together to determine that the derivative of the total revenue function is: $A - 2BQ$, so marginal revenue has the same vertical intercept as demand, but the slope is twice as negative. This is consistent with the calculations in Table 6.1, where each unit increase in quantity reduces price by $1 and reduces marginal revenue by $2.

QUESTIONS

1. Use Table 6.2 to show that outputs of 6 and 3 do not constitute a Nash equilibrium for the duopoly model that is the basis for that table.

2. Use Table 6.2 to show that outputs of 3 for each firm do not constitute a Cournot/Nash equilibrium.

3. Find an asymmetric Cournot/Nash equilibrium in Table 6.2 with the property that the total quantity is 8 but one seller produces more than the other. Therefore, you must specify what the two outputs are, and you must show that neither seller has a unilateral incentive to deviate. (This asymmetric equilibrium is an artifact of the discrete nature of the quantity choices, which are constrained to be integers.)

4. Redraw Figure 6.3 for the triopoly case, putting the vertical dotted line at a quantity of 6 (three for each of two other firms) and show that the residual marginal revenue for the remaining firm would cross marginal cost in a manner that would make the output of 3 a best response for that firm.

5. Show that the price is a decreasing function of the number of firms, N, in the Cournot equilibrium for the linear model with the equilibrium quantity given in Equation (6.3).

6. It is useful to relate the formula in Equation (6.3) to the graph. If Figure 6.3 were to be redrawn for the general linear demand function, i.e., $P = A - BQ$, then the vertical intercept would be A, and the horizontal intercept would be obtained by setting $P = 0$ and solving to get $Q = A/B$. Notice the ratio $(A - C)/B$ in Equation (6.3). Now look at the horizontal line in Figure 6.3 that has a height equal to marginal cost; it has length $(A - C)/B$. This line is divided into three equal segments in the duopoly graph in the figure, just as the MR line divided it into two equal segments for the monopoly graph. In general, this line gets divided into $N + 1$ segments. Use geometric arguments to explain why this line has length $(A - C)/B$ and why it gets divided into $N + 1$ segments in a symmetric Cournot equilibrium.

chapter 7

Vertical Market Relationships

A complex economy is characterized by considerable specialization along the supply chain; with connections between manufacturers of intermediate products, manufacturers of final products, wholesalers, and retailers. There is some theoretical and empirical evidence that frictions and market imperfections may be induced by these vertical supply relationships. This chapter begins by considering the very specific case of a vertical monopoly, i.e., inter-action between an upstream monopoly wholesaler selling to a firm that has a local monopoly in a downstream retail market. In theory, the vertical alignment of two monopolists can generate retail prices that are even higher than those that would result with a single inte-grated firm, i.e., a merger of the upstream and downstream firms. These effects can be investigated with the Veconlab Vertical Monopoly program or with the instructions for a hand-run version that can be found in Badasyan et al. (2004). The addition of more layers in the supply chain raises the question of the extent to which demand shocks at the retail level may cause even larger swings in orders and inventories at the upstream levels of the supply chain, a phenomenon that is known as the *bullwhip effect*. The Veconlab Supply Chain pro-gram, listed under the Markets menu, can be used to implement a simple version of this setup, the Newsvendor Problem discussed in Section 7.2.

7.1 Double Marginalization

Since Adam Smith, economists have been known for their opposition to monop-oly. Monopolization (carefully defined) is a crime in U.S. antitrust law, and horizontal mergers are commonly challenged by the antitrust authorities if the effect is to create a monopoly. In contrast, there is much more leniency shown toward vertical mergers, i.e., between firms that do business with each other along a supply chain. One motivation for this relative tolerance of vertical mergers is that "two monopolies are better than one," at least when these two monopolies are arrayed vertically. The intuition is that each monopo-list restricts output to the point where marginal revenue equals marginal cost, a process that reduces production below competitive levels and results in higher prices. When this marginal restriction is made by one firm in the supply chain, it raises the price to a downstream firm, which in turn raises price again at the retail level. The resulting double marginalization may be worse than the output restriction caused by a merger of both firms into a vertically integrated monopolist.

The effects of double marginalization can be illustrated with a simple laboratory experiment based on a linear demand function: $P = 24 - Q$, which is the demand at the retail level. There is an upstream manufacturer with a constant marginal cost of production of \$4. The retailer purchases units and is, for simplicity, assumed to incur no cost, other than the wholesale price paid for each unit. Thus, there is a total production cost (manufacturing plus retail) of \$4 per unit. This would be the marginal cost of a single vertically integrated firm that manufactures and sells the product in a retail monopoly market.

First, consider the monopoly problem for this integrated firm, i.e., to find the output that equates the marginal cost of \$4 with the marginal revenue, as explained in Chapter 6. With a demand of $P = 24 - Q$, and an associated total revenue of $24Q - Q^2$, the marginal revenue will be $24 - 2Q$, since the marginal revenue is twice as steep as the demand curve. Equating this to the marginal cost of \$4 and solving for Q yields a monopoly output of 10 and an associated price of \$14. These calculations are illustrated by the thick lines in Figure 7.1. The demand curve has a vertical intercept of \$24, with a slope of –1, so it has a horizontal intercept of 24. The marginal revenue line (MR) also has a vertical intercept of \$24, but its slope is twice as steep, so the horizontal intercept is 12. This MR line intersects the hori-

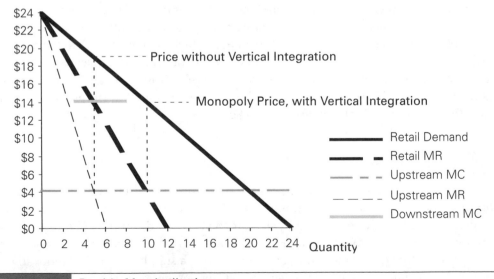

Figure 7.1   Double Marginalization

zontal MC line at a quantity of 10, which leads to a price of $14, as can be seen by moving from the intersection point vertically up to the demand curve along the light dotted line.

Next, consider the case in which the two firms are not vertically integrated. Each firm will equate marginal revenue and marginal cost. It turns out that in this kind of problem, it is easiest to start at the end of the supply chain (retail) and work backwards to consider the manufacturing level last. For any wholesale price, W, charged by the upstream manufacturer, the marginal cost to the downstream retailer will be W, since each unit sold at retail must be purchased at a wholesale price W, which is the only cost by assumption. Thus, the downstream firm is a monopolist who will equate this marginal cost, W, to the marginal revenue, $24 - 2Q$, to obtain a single equation: $W = 24 - 2Q$. This equation is also the inverse demand for the upstream firm, i.e., to sell each additional unit the wholesale price must be reduced by $2. This inverse wholesale demand function is exactly the same as the formula for marginal revenue ($24 - 2Q$) obtained in the previous paragraph. Thus, the *downstream market MR curve* (thick dashed line in Figure 7.1) is the *upstream demand function*. The upstream firm's marginal revenue line, shown by the thin dashed line, has the same vertical intercept, $24, but a slope that is twice as steep. The upstream firm will want to increase output until this marginal revenue is equal to the firm's marginal cost of 4, as shown in Figure 4.1, where the intersection occurs at a quantity of 5, which determines a wholesale price of: $W = 24 - 2Q = 24 - 10 = 14$. This upstream firm's ($14) then becomes the marginal cost to the downstream firm, as shown by the thick flat gray line segment at $14. This marginal cost line intersects the retail marginal revenue line at a quantity of 5, which determines a retail price of $24 - 5 = \$19$. To summarize, for the market in Figure 7.1 with a monopoly output of 10 and price of $14, the presence of two vertically stacked monopolists reduces the output to 5 and raises the retail price to $19. Thus, the output restriction is greater for two monopolists than it would be for one vertically integrated firm.

The market structure from Figure 7.1 was used in the first 5 rounds of the classroom market shown in Figure 7.2. These rounds involved pairs of students, with one retailer and one wholesaler in each pair. The wholesale and retail price predictions, $14 and $19 respectively, are indicated by the horizontal lines. The actual price averages by round are indicated by the dots converging to those lines. Notice that wholesale prices (large dots) are a little slow to converge to the theoretical prediction. This could be because the buyer (the retailer) is a participant in the experiment, not a simulated buyer as was the case for the retail demand in this experiment and in the monopoly experiments discussed in Chapter 6. In particular, the downstream buyer may respond to a wholesale price that is perceived to be unfairly high by cutting back on purchases, even if those purchases might result in more profit for the downstream seller.

The center part of Figure 7.2 shows 5 rounds in which each of the 12 participants from the first part was put into the market as a vertically integrated monopolist facing the retail demand determined by $P = 24 - Q$. The average prices converge to the monopoly level of $14 that is indicated by the horizontal line for periods 6–10. This reduction in retail price,

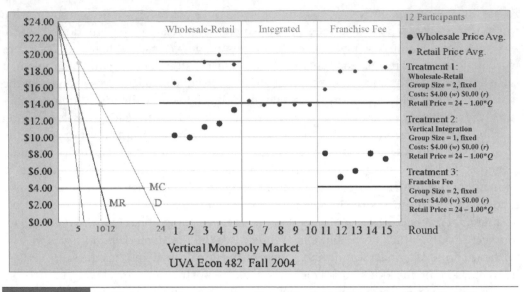

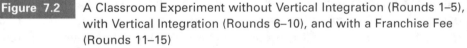

Figure 7.2   A Classroom Experiment without Vertical Integration (Rounds 1–5), with Vertical Integration (Rounds 6–10), and with a Franchise Fee (Rounds 11–15)

from about $19 to $14, resulted in an increase in sales quantity, and less of a monopoly output restriction, as predicted by theory. In addition, the profits of the integrated firm are larger, since by definition, profit is maximized at the monopoly level. This increase in profitability associated with vertical integration can be verified by calculating the profits for each firm separately (see Questions 1 and 2 and the end of the chapter).

Vertical integration may not be feasible or desirable, or even cost efficient in all cases. An alternative, which works in theory and is sometimes observed in practice, is for the upstream firm to require the retailer to pay a fixed franchise fee in order to be able to sell the product at all. In particular, the wholesale firm chooses a wholesale price and a franchise fee. The retailer may then reject the arrangement, in which case both earn 0, or accept and place an order for a specified number of units. The idea behind the franchise fee is to lower the wholesale price from the $14 charged when the firms are not integrated, to a level of $4 that reflects the true wholesale marginal cost, so that the retailer can maximize industry profit. When the retailer faces this marginal cost of $4, it will behave as an integrated monopolist, choosing an output of 10, charging the monopoly price of $14, and earning the monopoly profit of 10*14 – 10*4 = 100. If this were the whole story, the wholesaler would have zero profits, since the units were sold at a price that equals marginal cost. The wholesaler can recover some of this monopoly profit by charging a franchise fee. A fee of $50 would split the monopoly profit, leaving $50 for each. In theory, the wholesaler could demand $99.99 of the profit, leaving one penny for the retailer, under the assumption that the retailer would prefer a penny to a payoff of zero that results from rejecting the franchise contract. Intuition and other experimental evidence, however, suggest that such aggressive franchise fees would be rejected (see Chapter 12 on Bargaining). In effect, retailers will be likely to reject contract offers that are viewed as being unfair, and such rejections may even have the effect of inducing the wholesaler to make a more moderate demand in a subsequent period.

The far right side of Figure 7.2 shows average prices for periods 11–15 of the experiment, in which the participants were again divided into wholesaler/retailer pairs. The franchise fees, not shown, averaged about $40, nowhere near the $100 level that would capture all monopoly profit. Instead, it is apparent that the upstream sellers did not lower the wholesale price to their production cost of $4. Average prices do fall below the wholesale price levels in the first 5 rounds, but they only fall to a range from $6–$8. Thus, fairness considerations seem to be preventing the franchise fee treatment from solving the vertical monopoly problem.

7.2   The Newsvendor Problem

The double marginalization in the vertical monopoly model shows how monopoly power at each stage can magnify distortions. In this section, we consider a model in which there is no market power to manipulate prices, which are assumed to be fixed and exogenous. Thus, the firm buys units at a given wholesale price, W, and sells at a given retail price, $P > W$. The catch is that final demand at the retail level is random, and ordered units lose all value if they are unsold. This is called the *newsvendor problem*, since yesterday's newspaper does not have any commercial value. The point of this section is to determine whether the retail firm responds optimally to the randomness in demand and balances the costs of unsold units (when the order quantity is too high) with the foregone earnings on lost sales (when the order quantity is too low).

In the simplest version of this model, the retail demand is assumed to be any amount on the interval from 0 to 100 units, with an equal probability for each possible demand quantity. For example, if a 10-sided die (labeled 0, 1, . . . , 9) were thrown twice, with the first throw determining the tens digit, then the 100 possible outcomes would be the integers: 0, 1, . . . , 99, and each of these would have an equal chance (1/100) of being observed. This setup can be represented as shown in Figure 7.3, where the probability height of the dashed line is 0.01 on the vertical axis. If the order quantity is 60, for example, then there is a 0.6 chance that some units will remain unsold, since 60 of the 100 possible demand outcomes are to the left of 60. For simplicity, assume that demand can be any number between 0 and 100, with fractional demands allowed, so the area under the dashed line to the left of the order quantity is the probability that demand is less than the order. This situation is illustrated in Figure 7.3, where six-tenths of the area under the dashed line is to the

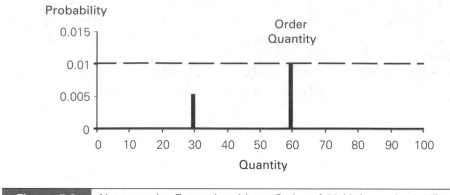

Figure 7.3 Newsvendor Example with an Order of 60 Units and a 0.6 Probability of Having Unsold Units

left of 60. The flat dashed line is called a *uniform distribution* since the probability (vertical height) is uniform over the interval. When demand turns out to be less than the order quantity in this example, the amount sold will be 30 on average, since each sales amount between 0 and 60 is equally likely.

In general, with this uniform demand distribution from 0 to 100, the probability that the random demand is less than X is $X/100$, and the probability that it is greater than or equal to X is $1 - X/100$. Thus, a firm that orders X units will sell all X units with probability $1 - X/100$. But there is a probability $X/100$ that not all units will be sold, and on average the sales in this case will be $X/2$, since each sales quantity in the interval from 0 to X is equally likely. Multiplying probabilities times sales quantities, we get: $X(1 - X/100) + (X/2)(X/100)$, where the first term is for the case where all X units sell and the second is for the case where (on average) only half of them sell. This expression for the expected sales quantity can be simplified to: $X - X^2/100 + X^2/200$, or equivalently, $X - X^2/200$. As shown in Equation (7.1), the firm's expected payoff is obtained by multiplying this expected sales quantity by the price, P, and then subtracting the cost of the order, XW, to obtain the following:

$$\text{Expected profit} = \left(X - \frac{X^2}{200} \right)P - XW = X(P-W) - \frac{X^2P}{200} \tag{7.1}$$

One way to find the profit-maximizing decision is to rewrite the right side of Equation (7.1) as a product of quantity, X, and a demand $P - (P/200)X$, which is linear in quantity and has a marginal function with a slope that is twice as negative: $P - 2(P/200)X$. This marginal function is then equated to marginal cost, W, to get Equation (7.2) as follows:

$$P - XP/100 = W, \tag{7.2}$$

or equivalently, as shown in Equation (7.3):

$$X = 100 \left(\frac{P-W}{P} \right) \tag{7.3}$$

An alternative derivation of Equation (7.3) is to take the derivative of the right side of Equation (7.1) with respect to X, and set this derivative equal to zero. Rules (2) and (3) from the Appendix at the end of Chapter 6 imply that the derivative of the linear (X) term is $P - W$, and the derivative of the quadratic term is: $-2XP/200$. Setting the resulting derivative equal to 0 yields Equation (7.2).

Thus, the optimal order quantity is the maximum demand, 100, times the ratio of the profit margin to the price of each unit. Since we used the expected value of profit, the implicit assumption is that the firm is risk neutral. For example, if the price is $4 and the wholesale cost is $2, then $(P - W)/P = 1/2$, and the optimal order quantity for a risk-neutral seller is 50. When the cost rises to $3, holding price constant, the optimal order falls to 25. Conversely, when the cost falls to $1, the optimal order quantity rises to 75. These parameters were used in a Web-based research experiment in which subjects made choices for 30 consecutive market periods. There were 36 subjects in the baseline ($W = 2$) treatment, and 24 subjects in each of the other treatments ($W = 1$, $W = 3$). The experiment was conducted at the University of Virginia using the Newsvendor option for the Veconlab Supply Chain program. The average order quantities are shown in Figure 7.4, along with the theoretical predictions (dashed lines). The separation of the data average lines indicates that order quantities do increase as the cost falls. There is, however, a tendency to order too much when the optimal order quantity is below 50 and to order too little when the optimal order

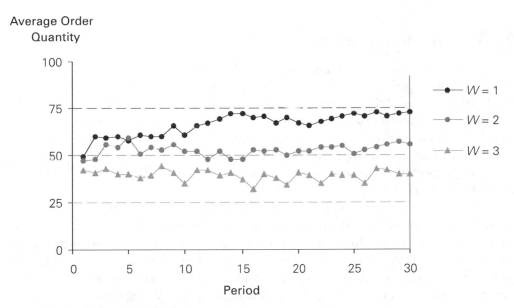

Source: (Bostian, Holt, and Smith 2005)

Figure 7.4   Newsvendor Average Order Quantities (Dots) and Predictions (Dashed Lines)

quantity is above 50. When the optimal order quantity is 50, there is a slight bias upward, which seems to carry over to the other treatments as well. Thus, one might characterize two biases relative to the theoretical predictions: an upward bias and a tendency for order quantities to respond sluggishly to wholesale price changes, i.e., a pull to the center. The sluggish adjustment effect is exactly the pattern reported by Schweitzer and Cachon (2000), who consider a number of explanations and end up rejecting them all.

One possible approach to explaining the pattern in Figure 7.4 might be to incorporate random noise in decision making, since randomness in decisions will tend to pull decisions up when the optimum is near the bottom and down when the optimum is near the top of the range of possible demand quantities. An alternative is provided by *direction learning theory*, proposed by Selten and Buchta (1999), which postulates that adjustments (if any) will tend to be in the direction of what would have been a best response in the previous period. For example, in the $W = 3$ treatment that produces an optimal order of 25, it will be the case that demand exceeds 25 three-fourths of the time, which will tend to pull the orders up. Conversely, in the $W = 1$ treatment that produces an optimal order of 75, demand will be less than 75 three-fourths of the time, which will tend to pull the orders down. Although this theory just predicts the directions of adjustments from period to period, not the magnitudes, it is easy to imagine how it might result in the observed pull to the center of the observed order decisions. Note that high order quantities are more likely to result in losses, especially in the high-cost ($W = 3$) treatment, so any upward bias in orders cannot be explained by loss aversion (see Question 8 at the end of the chapter).

7.3   The Bullwhip Effect

To summarize, the double marginalization problem associated with two monopolies may be alleviated to some extent by a vertical merger or by the introduction of competition downstream. Without these kinds of corrections, the analysis of Section 7.1 would apply to an even greater extent with a longer supply chain, e.g., with a monopoly manufacturer selling to a distributor, who sells to a wholesaler, who sells to a retailer, where the firms at each stage are monopolists. In this context, the effects of successive marginalizations are compounded, unless these effects are somehow diluted by competition between sellers at each level.

A second source of inefficiency in a long supply chain is the possibility that orders and inventories are not well coordinated, and that information is not transmitted efficiently from one level to the next. For example, Procter & Gamble found diaper orders by distributors to be too variable relative to consumer demand, and Hewlett-Packard found printer orders made by retail sellers to be much more variable than consumer demand itself. These and other examples are discussed in Lee, Padmanabhan, and Whang (1997a, 1997b).

There is a long tradition in business schools of putting M.B.A. students into a supply chain simulation known as the beer game. There are four vertical levels: manufacturing, distribution, wholesale, and retail (Forrester 1961). The participants in these classroom games must typically fill purchase orders from inventory, and then place new orders to the level above in the supply chain. There is a cost of carrying unsold inventory, and there is also a cost associated with not being able to fill an order from below, i.e., the lost profit per unit on sales. The setup sometimes involves having a stable retail demand for several rounds before it is subjected to an unexpected and unannounced increase that persists in later periods. The effect of this demand increase is to cause larger and larger fluctuations in orders placed upstream, which illustrates the bullwhip effect.

In classroom experiments with the beer game, the upstream sellers tend to attribute these large fluctuations to exogenous demand shifts, despite the fact that most of the fluctuation is due to the reactions of those lower in the supply chain (Sterman 1989). Subsequent experiments, however, have shown that the bullwhip effect cannot be attributed solely to demand shifts, since this effect has been observed even when the distribution of retail demand shocks is stationary and known (Croson and Donohue 2002, 2004, 2005).

Participants in a typical supply chain experiment are divided into teams of four participants, who are assigned to one of the four roles. Each person takes orders from below and submits orders to the person just upstream. Orders must be filled from inventory, and unfilled orders are recorded as a negative inventory number. There is a shipment delay of a couple of periods after an order is received; this delay is known and announced in advance. Subjects are given the incentive to minimize the sum of holding and backlog costs for the whole supply chain, as would be appropriate for an integrated firm.

Figure 7.5 shows the average variance of order quantities as one goes up the supply chain, from Retailer (on the left) to Wholesaler, Distributor, and Manufacturer (on the right). Notice the high variability of production orders at the manufacturing level, as com-

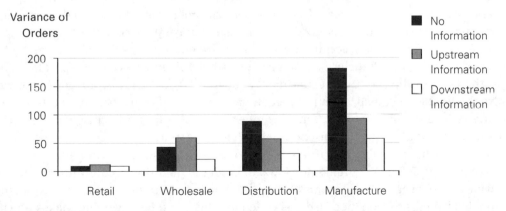

Source: (Croson and Donohue 2004)

Figure 7.5   The Bullwhip Effect and the Provision of Inventory Information

pared with wholesale purchase orders made by retailers on the left side. This is the essence of the bullwhip effect, where small variations at the retail level cause large swings in orders upstream. The issue addressed in the Croson and Donohue experiment is whether improved information might reduce this effect. In the baseline treatment (dark bars), participants were given no information about inventory levels at the other three positions in the supply chain. The two information treatments involved providing sellers with information about inventories (or unfilled orders for the case of negative inventories) of those who are either upstream in the supply chain or downstream, depending on the treatment. The downstream-information treatment resulted in a larger reduction in the bullwhip effect. Croson and Donohue (2003) also show that the effect is attenuated but not eliminated by providing point-of-sale information for others in the supply chain.

7.4   Extensions

Durham (2000) uses experiments to compare price-setting behavior by an upstream monopolist who selects a wholesale price and announces it to one or more downstream sellers. There are two treatments, one with a single downstream firm, and another with three downstream firms. Durham finds that the presence of downstream competition leads to outcomes similar to those under vertical integration. In effect, the competition at the downstream level takes out one of the sources of monopoly marginalization, so the price and quantity outcomes approach those that would result from a single monopolist. Another way of looking at this is to note that if there is enough competition downstream, then the price downstream will be driven down to marginal cost, and the total output will be a point on the retail demand curve, not a point on the retail marginal revenue curve. Then the upstream firm can essentially behave as an integrated monopolist who can select a point on the retail demand curve that maximizes total profit.

Ho and Zhang (2004) conducted a vertical monopoly experiment in which the upstream firm chose a franchise fee along with a wholesale price, i.e., a two-part tariff. As was the case for the classroom experiment shown in Figure 7.2, this procedure did not solve the double marginalization problem. In fact, market efficiencies were not improved relative to the baseline case of a single wholesale price with no franchise fee. A second treatment introduced quantity discounts, which in theory, provide an alternative solution to the double marginalization problem by giving the downstream firm an incentive to expand output. Efficiencies remained low, although the quantity discount procedure did provide a higher share of the surplus for the upstream firm. The authors concluded that the franchise fee fails to work because it is coded as a loss, and loss aversion makes downstream firms reluctant to accept high franchise fees. An alternative explanation is that a franchise fee will be rejected if it produces a division of the surplus that is viewed as being unfair (see the discussion on bargaining in Chapter 12).

QUESTIONS

1. Find the predicted profit for a monopoly seller in the market described in Section 7.1.

2. Find the profits for the wholesaler and retailer for the market described in Section 7.1 when the wholesale price is $14 and the retail price is $19, as predicted. Show that profits for these two firms are, in total, less than that of a vertically integrated monopolist, as calculated in Question 1.

3. Consider a market with an inverse demand function that is linear: $P = 46 - 2Q$. The cost at the wholesale level is 0 for each unit produced. At the retail level, there is a cost of $6 associated with retailing each unit purchased at wholesale. Thus, the average cost for both levels combined is also $6. Find the optimal output and retail price for a vertically integrated monopolist, either using a graph or calculus. In either case, you should illustrate your answer with a graph.

4. If you answered Question 3 correctly, your answers should imply that the firm's total revenue is $260, the total cost is $60, and the profit for the integrated monopolist is $200. Now consider the case in which the upstream and downstream firms are separate, and the upstream seller chooses a wholesale price, W, which is announced to the downstream firm on a take-it-or-leave-it basis (no further negotiation). Thus, the marginal cost downstream is $6 + W$. Equate this with marginal revenue (with a graph or with calculus) to determine the optimal quantity for the downstream firm, as a function of W. Then use this function to find the optimal level of W for the upstream seller (using a graph or calculus), and illustrate your answer with a graph in either case. (*Hint*: if you answered this correctly, the quantity should be half of the monopoly quantity that you found in your answer to Question 3.)

5. Suppose that the upstream monopolist for the setup in Question 4 can charge a franchise fee. If the downstream seller is perfectly rational and prefers a small profit to none at all, what is the highest fee that the upstream seller can charge? What is the best (profit-maximizing) combination of wholesale price and franchise fee from the point of view of the upstream seller?

6. Consider a retail firm with an exogenously given wholesale cost of $20 and an exogenously given retail price of $30. Demand is uniformly distributed from 0 to 300. What is the profit-maximizing order quantity for a risk-neutral firm?

7. Suppose that the firm described in Question 6 orders 100 units. Find the range of realized demand quantities for which this firm will end up losing money.

8. A firm is said to be loss averse if losses loom larger than gains in payoff calculations. Use your intuition to guess what the effect of loss aversion would be for the situation in Question 6, i.e., would loss aversion tend to raise or lower order quantities relative to the expected profit maximizing levels? Could loss aversion, by itself, explain the data patterns in Figure 7.4?

chapter 8

Market Institutions and Power

Traders in a double auction can see all transactions prices and the current bid/ask spread, as is the case with trading on the New York Stock Exchange. The double auction is an extremely competitive institution, given the temptation for traders to improve their offers over time in order to make trades at the margin. In contrast, markets with posted prices (Bertrand or posted-offer) allow sellers to pre-commit to fixed, take-it-or-leave-it prices that cannot be adjusted during a trading period. This chapter considers the price and efficiency outcomes of markets with posted prices, in particular when sellers possess *market power*, which is, roughly speaking, the ability of a firm to raise price profitably above competitive levels. In most cases, the market efficiency is higher in the double auction, since the price flexibility built into that institution tends to bring outcomes closer to a competitive (supply equals demand) outcome. These various market institutions can be implemented by hand with the instructions to Davis and Holt (1993) in this chapter's Appendix, or with the Veconlab double-auction, posted-offer, or Bertrand programs, which provide flexible setup options and automatic data and graphical summaries.

8.1 Introduction

The common perception that laboratory markets yield efficient competitive outcomes is surprising given the emphasis on market imperfections that pervade theoretical work in industrial organizations. This apparent contradiction is resolved by considering the effects of trading institutions. As discussed in Chapter 2, competitive outcomes are typical in double auction markets, with rules similar to those used in many centralized financial exchanges. But most markets of interest to industrial organization economists have different institutional characteristics; sellers post prices and buyers must either buy at those prices or engage in costly search and negotiation to obtain discounts. Unlike more competitive double auctions, the performance of markets with posted prices can be degraded by the presence of market power, price-fixing conspiracies, and cyclical demand shocks.

In many cases, it is common for prices to be set by the traders on the thin side of the market. Sellers, for example, typically post prices in retail markets. For this reason, theoretical (Bertrand) models are often structured around an assumption that prices are listed simultaneously at the beginning of each period. Using laboratory experiments, it is possible to make controlled comparisons between markets with posted prices and more symmetric institutions such as the double auction, where both buyers and sellers post bids and asks in an interactive setting that resembles a centralized stock market. Laboratory double auctions yield efficient, competitive outcomes in a surprisingly wide variety of settings, sometimes even in a monopoly (Smith 1962, 1981; Davis and Holt 1993). In contrast, prices in markets with posted prices are often above competitive levels (Plott 1989; Davis and Holt 1993).

Figures 8.1 and 8.2 show a matched pair of markets, one double auction and one posted-offer auction, which were run under research conditions with payments equaling one-fifth of earnings. The values and costs were arrayed in a manner such that predicted earnings per person were approximately equal. In each case, the buyer values were reduced after the fifth period by shifting demand down by $4, thereby lowering the com-

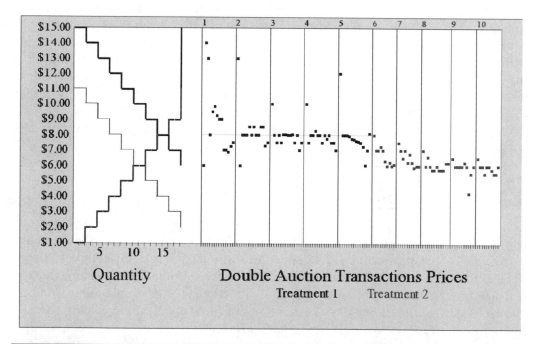

Figure 8.1   Price Sequence for a Double Auction with a Downward Shift in Demand after the Fifth Round

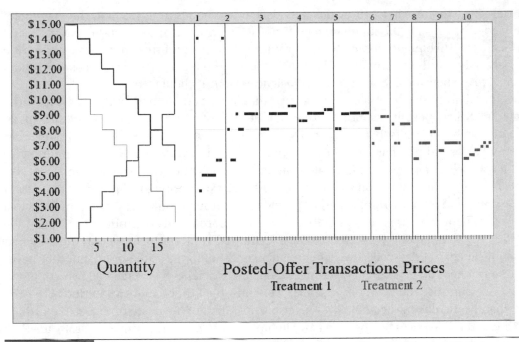

Figure 8.2 Price Sequence for a Posted-Offer Auction with a Downward Shift in Demand after the Fifth Round

petitive price prediction by $2, as shown on the left sides of each figure. For example, the two buyers with the highest-value units, at $15 in the fifth period, had these values reduced to $11 in the sixth period, whereas costs stayed the same in all periods.

First, consider the double auction, in Figure 8.1. The vertical lines to the right of the supply and demand curves indicate the starting point of each new trading period, and the dots represent transactions prices in the order in which they were observed. Recall that a trader in a double auction may make a price offer (bids for buyers and asks for sellers) or may accept the best offer on the other side of the market. Thus, traders typically see a sequence of declining ask prices and/or increasing bid prices, until the bid-ask spread narrows and one person accepts another's proposal.

Despite the considerable price variation in the first period, the double auction market achieved 99 percent of the maximum possible surplus, and this efficiency measure averaged 98 percent in the first five rounds, with quantities of 14 that equal the competitive prediction. All traders were told that some payoff parameters may have changed in the sixth round, but sellers who observed their own costs had not changed. However, sellers had no idea whether buyer values or others' costs had gone up or down. Transactions prices began in the sixth round at the old competitive level of $8, but fell to $6 by the end of the period. This is a typical pattern, where the high-value and low-cost units trade early in a period at levels close to those in the previous periods, but late trades for units near the margin are forced to be closer to the supply-demand intersection price. The transaction quantity was at the competitive prediction of 10 in all rounds of the second treatment. As early-period prices fell toward the competitive level after the sixth round, the price averages were about equal to the new prediction of $6, and efficiencies were at about 96 percent.

Recall from the discussion in Chapter 2 that buyers do not post bids in a posted-offer market. Sellers post prices independently at the start of each period, along with the maximum numbers of units that are offered for sale. Then buyers are selected in a random order to make desired purchases. The period ends when all buyers have finished shopping or when all sellers are out of stock. As shown in Figure 8.2, prices in the posted-offer market also began in the first period with considerable variation, although all prices were far from the competitive prediction. Prices in periods two through four seemed to converge to a level at about $1 above the competitive prediction. Both the average quantity (12) and the efficiency (86 percent) were well below the competitive levels observed in the matched double auction. Prices fell slowly after the demand shift in the sixth period, but they never quite reached the new competitive prediction, and efficiencies averaged 86 percent in the last five periods. The lowest efficiencies were observed in the first two periods after the demand shift, illustrating the more sluggish adjustment of the posted-offer market, which benefited sellers, as they were able to maintain prices above competitive levels. By the final period of each treatment, efficiencies had climbed above 90 percent, and the transactions quantity had reached the relevant competitive prediction.

The results shown in Figures 8.1 and 8.2 are fairly typical. Compared with double auctions, laboratory posted-offer markets converge to competitive predictions more slowly (Ketcham, Smith, and Williams 1984) and less completely (Plott 1986, 1989). Even in non-monopolized designs with stationary supply and demand functions, traders in a posted-offer market generally forego about 10 percent of the possible gains from trade, whereas traders in a double auction routinely obtain 95–98 percent of the total surplus in such designs.

The sluggish price responses shown in Figure 8.2 are even more apparent in markets with sequences of demand shifts that create a boom and bust cycle. First, consider a case where the supply curve stayed stationary as demand shifted up repeatedly in a sequence of periods, creating an upward momentum in expectations. This boom was followed by a sequence of unannounced downward demand shifts that reduced the competitive price prediction incrementally until it returned to the initial level. Prices determined by double auction trading tracked the predicted price increases and decreases fairly accurately, with high efficiencies. This is because the demand shifts are conveyed by the intensity of buyer bidding behavior during each period, so that sellers could learn about new market conditions as they started making sales. In contrast, prices in posted-price markets are selected before any shopping begins, so sellers cannot spot changes in market conditions, but rather, they must try to make inferences from sales quantities. When posted-offer markets were subjected to the same sequence of demand increases and decreases mentioned above, the actual trading prices lagged behind competitive predictions in the upswing, and prices continued to rise even after demand started shifting downward. Then prices fell too slowly, relative to the declining competitive predictions (where supply equals demand). The result was that prices stayed too high on the downswing part of the cycle, and these high prices caused transactions to fall dramatically, essentially drying up the market for several periods and causing severe profit reductions for sellers.

Davis and Holt (1996) replicated these sluggish adjustment patterns on posted-price markets subjected to a series of demand increases, followed by a series of demand decreases. Even in retail markets with posted prices, sellers may receive some useful information from buyer behavior. For example, sellers might be able to observe excess demand on the upswing, as buyers seek to make purchases but are not accommodated by the production quantities. There was a second treatment with the boom/bust cycle of demand shifts, with an added feature that let sellers observe excess demand by frustrated buyers at the prices that they set. This excess demand information improved price responsiveness and raised market efficiency, but not to the high levels observed in double auctions. Similar increases in efficiency were observed when sellers were allowed to offer a single mid-period price reduction ("clearance sale") after the posted prices had been submitted and some sales had been made at those prices.

8.2 The Exercise of Seller Market Power without Explicit Collusion

One of the major factors considered in the antitrust analysis of mergers between firms in the same market is the possibility that a merged firm may be able to raise price, to the detriment of buyers. Of course, any seller may raise a price unilaterally, and so the real issue is the extent to which price can be raised *profitably*. Such a price increase is more likely to boost profits if others in the market are not in a position to absorb increases in sales. Therefore, the capacities of other sellers may constrain a firm's market power, and a merger that reduces others' capacities may create market power. This raises the question of whether these high prices can be explained by game-theoretic calculations. It is straightforward to specify a game-theoretic definition of market power, based on the incentive of one seller to raise price above a common competitive level (Holt 1989). In other words, market power is said to exist when the competitive equilibrium is not a Nash equilibrium.

Although it is straightforward to check for the profitability of a unilateral deviation from a competitive outcome, it may be more difficult to identify the Nash equilibrium for a market with posted prices. The easiest case is where firms do not have constraints on what they can produce, a case commonly referred to as *Bertrand competition*. For example, if each firm has a common, constant marginal cost of C, then no common price above C would be a Nash equilibrium, since each firm would have an incentive to cut price slightly and capture all market sales. The Bertrand prediction for a price competition game played once is for a very harsh type of competition that drives price to marginal cost levels, even with only two or three firms.

Even with a repeated series of market periods, the one-shot Nash predictions may be relevant if random matchings are used to make the market interactions have a one-shot nature, where nobody can punish or reward other's pricing decisions in subsequent periods. Most market interactions are repeated, but if the number of market periods is fixed and known, then the one-shot Nash prediction applies in the final period, and a process of backward induction can be used to argue that prices in all periods would equal this one-shot Nash prediction. In most markets, however, there is no well-defined final period, and in this case, there is a possibility that a kind of tacit cooperation might develop. In particular, a seller's price restraint in one period might send a message that causes others to follow suit in subsequent periods, and sellers' price cuts might be deterred by the threat of retaliatory price cuts by others. There are many ways that such tacit cooperation might develop, as supported by punishment and reward strategies. A discussion of these is deferred for now while we focus on ways that market power might arise in single-period markets.

The Bertrand arguments in the above paragraphs depend on having a continuous set of price choices, so that "small" price cuts are possible. This observation suggests that a tacit agreement to stick with a discrete price grid may be anti-competitive. For example, Cason (2000) uses laboratory experiments to show that the NASDAQ dealers' convention of relying on "even eighths" may have facilitated collusion. Figure 8.3 shows results for a mar-

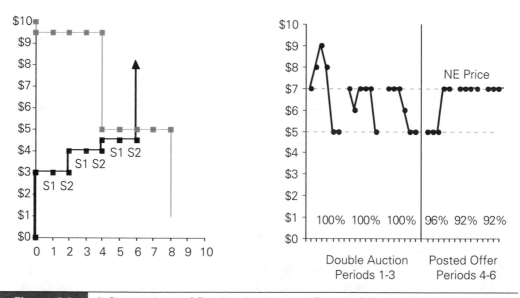

Figure 8.3   A Comparison of Double Auction and Posted-Offer Markets with Discrete Prices

ket in which prices were constrained to be in integer dollar amounts. The two sellers had three units each, with costs of $3, $4, and $4.50, as shown in the supply function on the left side of the figure. The competitive equilibrium price is $5 as determined by the intersection of supply and demand. This design was not selected for a research project, but rather, to illustrate the differences between double auction and posted-offer trading. The single session was run by hand with three periods of double auction trading, followed by three periods of posted-offer trading. Price sequences for each period are connected by a dark line, and the break in the line indicates the end of a period. The double auction prices on the left side fell to $5 at the end of all three trading periods, as sellers scrambled to sell their marginal units for a $0.50 profit. This competition resulted in six units being traded and an efficiency of 100 percent in all periods, as indicated by the percentages below the price sequences for each period. In the posted-offer periods that followed, sellers ended up raising prices to $7 and reducing sales to four units, which reduced efficiencies to 92 percent. With prices of $7, each seller would sell two units and earn $7 + $7 − $3 − $4 = $7. If one seller priced at $7 and the other cut price to $6, the one with the lower price would sell three units and earn $6 + $6 + $6 − $3 − $ 4 − $4.50 = $6.50, which indicates that there is a Nash equilibrium at $7. (You would have to check to see if a unilateral price increase is profitable, see Question 1 at the end of the chapter.) Thus, the prices in the posted offer periods rose to Nash equilibrium levels.

The effects of market power in a double auction were the focus of an experiment run by Holt, Langan, and Villamil (1986), using a five-seller design that is more complex than that shown in Figure 8.3, but with only a single unit of excess supply at prices just above the competitive level. Prices were not constrained to be in integer dollar amounts, and prices did exceed competitive levels in about half of the sessions. Even though the supply and demand design was selected to give sellers a strong incentive to exercise market power, prices in the other sessions did converge to competitive levels, which shows how competitive the double auction institution is. Davis and Williams (1991) replicated the Holt, Langan, and Villamil results for double auctions, and the resulting prices were slightly above competitive levels in most sessions. In addition, they ran a second series of sessions using posted-offer trading, which generated higher prices that resulted from sellers withholding their marginal units.

Vernon Smith (1981) investigated an extreme case of market power, with a single seller, and found that even monopolists in a double auction are sometimes unable to maintain prices above competitive levels, whereas posted-offer monopolists are typically able to find and enforce monopoly prices. The difference is that a seller in a posted-offer auction sets a single, take-it-or-leave-it price, so there is no temptation to cut price late in the period in order to sell marginal units. This temptation is present in a double auction. In particular, a monopolist who cuts price late in a trading period to sell marginal units will have a harder time selling units at near-monopoly levels at the start of the next period, and this buyer resistance may cause prices in a double auction monopoly to be lower than the monopoly prediction.

8.3 Edgeworth Cycles and Random Prices

When all sellers offer the same homogeneous product, buyers with good price information will flock to the seller with the lowest price. This can create a price instability, which may lead to randomized price choices. First, consider a specific example in which demand is inelastic at three units for all prices up to a limit price of $6, i.e., the demand curve is flat at a height of $6 for less than three units and becomes vertical at a quantity of three for prices below $6, as shown in Figure 8.4. There are two sellers, each with a capacity to produce two units at zero cost. Thus, the market supply is vertical at a quantity of four units, and supply and demand intersect at a price of $0 and a quantity of three. The sellers are identical, so each can expect to sell to half of the market only, one and one-half units on average, if they offer the same price. If the prices are different, the seller with the lower price sells two units and the other sells one unit only (as long as price is no greater than $6). If small price reductions are possible, there is no Nash equilibrium at any common price between 0 and $6, since each seller could increase expected sales from one and one-half to two units by decreasing price slightly. Nor is a common price of $0 a Nash equilibrium, since earnings are zero and either seller would have an incentive to raise price and earn a positive amount on the one-unit residual demand. Thus, there is no equilibrium in pure (non-random) strategies, and therefore, one would not expect to see stable prices.

One possibility is that prices would cycle, with each firm undercutting the other's price in a downward spiral. At some point, prices go so low that one seller may raise price, which creates a pattern known as an Edgeworth Cycle. In the example discussed above, suppose that one seller has a price that is a penny above a level p between 0 and $6. The other seller could cut price to p and sell two units, thereby earning $2p$, or raise price to $6, sell the single residual demand unit, and earn $6. Thus, cutting price would be better if $2p > 6$, or if $p > 3$.

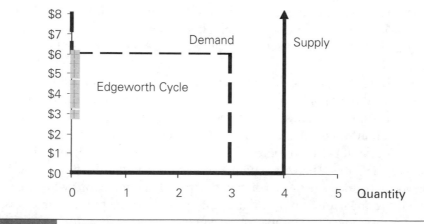

Figure 8.4   A "Box" Design with an Edgeworth Cycle

Raising price would be better if $p < \$3$. This reasoning suggests that prices might fall in the range from $6 down to $3, at which point one seller would raise price to $6 and the cycle would begin again. The problem with this argument is that if one seller knows that the other will cut price by $.01, then the best reaction is to cut by $.02, but then the other would want to cut by $.03, and so on. Thus, the declining phase of prices is likely to be sporadic and somewhat unpredictable in the range of the Edgeworth cycle. This raises the possibility that prices will be random, i.e., that there will be a Nash equilibrium in mixed strategies of the type considered in Chapter 5. Since sellers must be indifferent about all prices in the relevant range to be willing to randomize, the equilibrium price distribution must be such that the seller's expected earnings are constant for all prices in this range (see Calculation of a Mixed-Strategy Equilibrium in Prices at the end of the chapter for details of this calculation for the setup in Figure 8.4). As we will see, price cycles do arise over the Edgeworth cycle range, although the particular pattern predicted by a mixed-strategy Nash equilibrium is not observed.

8.4   The Effects of Market Power

There may be several reasons for observing prices that are above competitive levels in a design like that considered in Section 8.3. For example, with only two sellers, a type of tacit collusion may be possible, especially if the sellers interact repeatedly. Another possible reason is that demand is inelastic and the excess demand is only one unit at prices above the competitive level of $0 in this example. A final possible reason is that earnings would be zero at the competitive outcome, which might produce erratic behavior. These types of arguments led Davis and Holt (1994a) to consider a design with two treatments, each with the same aggregate supply and demand functions, but with a reallocation of units that creates market power. In particular, a reallocation of capacity from one seller to others changed the Nash equilibrium price from the competitive price (Bertrand result) to higher (randomized) prices over the range spanned by the Edgeworth cycle.

Consider the No-Power Design in Figure 8.5, where the market demand is shown by the dashed line. (A Power Design is created by reallocating seller S3's two high-cost units to S1 and S2.) The solid line supply curve has two steps, and the units are marked with seller ID numbers. Sellers S1, S2, and S3 each have three units, and S4 and S5 each have a single, low-cost unit. The demand curve has a vertical intercept of R and intersects supply at a range of prices from the highest competitive price, P_c, to the level of the highest cost step, C. The demand is simulated with the high-value units being purchased first. This demand process ensures that a unilateral price increase above a common price P_c would leave the eight high-value units to be purchased by the other sellers, whose capacity totals to eight units. Thus, a unilateral increase from a common competitive price will result in no sales, and hence, will be unprofitable. It follows that no seller has market power in this design.

Market power is created by giving seller S3's two high-cost units (shown in bold type) to S1 and S2. With this change, each of the large sellers, S1 and S2, would have four units,

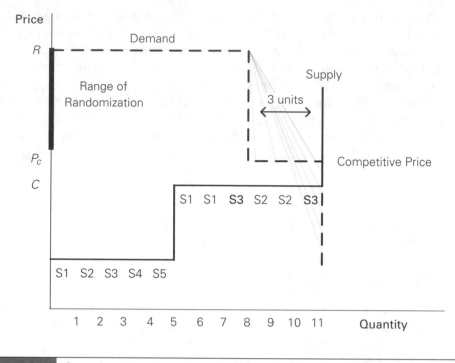

Figure 8.5   Capacity Allocations for a No-Power Design

which is more than the excess supply of three units for prices above the competitive level. If one of these sellers were to raise price unilaterally to the demand intercept, R, one of these four units would sell since the other four sellers have only enough capacity to sell seven of the eight units that are demanded at prices above the competitive level. By making the demand intercept high relative to the high-cost step, such deviations are profitable for the two large sellers, which creates market power. In this case, it is possible to calculate the price distributions in the mixed-strategy equilibrium, by equating sellers' expected payoffs to a constant (since a seller would only be willing to randomize if expected payoffs are independent of price on some range). These calculations parallel those in Calculation of a Mixed-Strategy Equilibrium in Prices at the end of the chapter, but the analysis is more tedious, given the asymmetries in sellers' cost structures (see Davis and Holt (1994a), for details). For market power design, the range of randomization is shown as the darkened region on the vertical axis. Note that this design change holds constant the number of sellers and the aggregate supply and demand arrays, so that price differences can be attributed to the creation of market power and not to other factors such as a small number of sellers or a low excess supply at supra-competitive prices.

Figure 8.6 shows the results of an experiment in which groups of five sellers chose prices for 60 market periods. Demand was determined by a passive, price-taking simulated buyer, and sellers were told the number of periods and all aspects of the demand and sup ply structure. In three of the sessions, the first 30 periods used the No-Power design in Figure 8.5, followed by 30 periods of the Power design obtained by giving S3's two high-cost units to the large sellers, S1 and S2. The price averages for these sessions are graphed by the thick black line in Figure 8.6, with the vertical line separating the two treatments. It is apparent that prices start high but fall to competitive levels by the 30th round. As soon as power is created, the prices jump to the high levels (black line) that had been achieved by the other three sessions that began with the market power treatment (thin gray line). In contrast, prices for the sessions that began with market power fell quickly after the power was taken away. Notice that prices did not fall all of the way to competitive levels, which indicates a sequence effect carryover from the earlier successful tacit collusion that had been established in the initial Power design.

Edgeworth cycles were observed in some of the sessions during periods with market power. A typical pattern was for one of the large sellers to raise price to a level near the demand intercept (R in Figure 8.5), and thereby carry the weight by only selling a single unit, although at a high price. As the other sellers were then able to sell all of their units, they would raise prices. When prices reached high levels, all sellers would generally try to

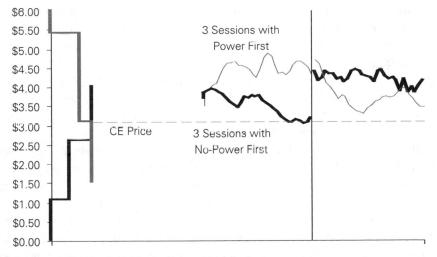

Key: Power/No-Power (thin line), No-Power/Power (thick line).

Source: (Davis and Holt 1994a)

Figure 8.6 Average Prices with and without Market Power

post prices that were high, but just below the highest of the other prices. This attempt to avoid being the one with the highest price would sometimes drive all prices down in an orderly decline. The cycle might restart with one of the large sellers signaling again with a price near the demand intercept. Such attempts to signal and hold price up by large sellers failed in the No-Power periods, since the seller with the highest price would make no sales in this treatment.

Market power resulted in large price increases in all six sessions, holding constant the number of sellers and the aggregate supply and demand structure. Note that this is a "within subjects" design, so each group of five sellers in a session serves as its own control. Under the null hypothesis of no effect, prices would have been just as likely to go up as down, so the chances of seeing higher prices in the power treatment are $1/2$ in a single session. But getting higher prices in all six sessions has a low probability under the null hypothesis: this would be like throwing a fair coin six times and getting six heads in a row, which has probability: $(1/2)(1/2)(1/2)(1/2)(1/2)(1/2) = 1/64 = 0.016$. Thus, the null hypothesis of no effect can be rejected at the 0.05 level, or even at the 0.02 level, but not at the "1 percent" level.

An alternative, less powerful, way of analyzing the data would be to use only the first 30 periods and use a between-subjects comparison of average prices for the sessions that began with Power and the three sessions that began with No Power. Here the null hypothesis is that the prices for each treatment are drawn from the same distribution, so there is a $1/2$ chance that the average price in one of the Power (first) sessions will be higher than the average price in one of the No-Power (first) sessions. The highest average prices are for the three sessions with power, and the probability of getting the three highest price averages for the three sessions with power under the null hypothesis is the same as the probability that a randomly arrayed set of three quarters and three dimes along a price line will end up with all three quarters at the high end. As noted in Chapter 1, there are 20 ways that the three quarters and three dimes can be arrayed along the line. So the probability of observing the most extreme case (all quarters to the right) is $1/20$, or 0.05. Thus, a test based on a between-subjects comparison for the first 30 periods would allow one to reject the null hypothesis at the 5 percent level of significance.

Even though the creation of market power resulted in price increases in this experiment, as predicted in a Nash equilibrium, the observed cyclic autocorrelation of prices is not consistent with randomization, a point that was also made by Kruse, Rassenti, Reynolds, and Smith (1994). In fact, the price-increasing effect of market power was considerably greater than the difference between the Nash/Bertrand price in the No-Power treatment and the mean of the Nash equilibrium distribution of prices in the Power treatment. Since explicit communications between sellers were not permitted, it is appropriate to use the term "tacit collusion" to describe this ability of sellers to raise prices above the levels determined by a Nash equilibrium. To summarize, market power has a double impact in this context: it raises the predicted mean price and it facilitates tacit collusion that raises prices above the Nash prediction.

8.5   Extensions

The recent literature on the effects of market power can be understood by reconsidering the narrowness of the vertical gap between demand and supply to the left of the supply/demand intersection (see Figure 8.5). This narrow gap implies that a seller who refuses to sell units with these relatively high costs will not forego much in the way of earnings. This seller might profit from such withholding if the price increase on low cost units sold would more than compensate for the lost earnings on these marginal units. Suppose that the demand/supply gap is large during a high-demand "boom" period, which makes marginal units more profitable and limits the exercise of market power. In contrast, the gap might fall during a contraction, thereby enabling sellers to raise prices profitably. Thus, the effects of market power in some markets may be counter-cyclical (Reynolds and Wilson 2005). A similar consideration may arise in the analysis of mergers that may create synergies, which lower costs. If these cost reductions occur on units near the margin, i.e., near the supply/demand intersection, then the cost reduction on the marginal unit may make the exercise of market power less profitable. Davis and Wilson (1998) discuss this case and also some contrary cases where cost-reducing synergies of a merger may create power where none previously existed.

A second aspect of market power is that unilateral price increases are more likely to be successful if competitors are not able to move in and expand their production. Godby (2002) explores the exercise of market power in situations where producers must acquire pollution permits to cover the byproducts of certain production activities. Then the acquisition of other sellers' permits may limit others' capacities, and hence enable a firm to raise price profitably.

Appendix: **Calculation of a Mixed-Strategy Equilibrium in Prices**

It is useful to begin with some more general discussion of price distributions before calculating the equilibrium distribution for the example from Section 8.3. With a continuous distribution of prices, the probability that another seller's price is less than or equal to any given amount p will be an increasing function of p, and we will denote this probability by $F(p)$. For example, suppose that price is equally likely to be any dollar amount between 0 and $10. This price distribution could be generated by the throw of a 10-sided die, with sides marked 1, 2, . . . , 10, and using the outcome to determine price. Then the probabilities would be given by the numbers in the second row of Table 8.1. For each value of p in the top row, the associated number in the second row is the probability that the other seller's price is less than or equal to p. For a price of $p = \$10$, all prices that might be chosen by the other seller are less than or equal to $10 by assumption, so the value of $F(p)$ in the second row of the far-right column is 1. Since all prices are equally likely, half of them will be less than or equal to the midpoint of $5, so $F(p) = 0.5$ when $p = \$5$. The other numbers in the table are calculated in a similar manner. A mathematical formula for this

Table 8.1	A Uniform Distribution of Prices									
p	$0	$1	$2	$3	$4	$5	$6	$7	$8	$9	$10
F(p)	0	0.1	0.2	0.3	0.4	0.5	0.6	0.7	0.8	0.9	1

uniform distribution of prices would be: $F(p) = p/10$, as can be verified by direct calculation (see Question 1 at the end of the chapter). Uniform price distributions, such as the one shown in Table 8.1, were used in the Newsvendor problem in Chapter 7 and will come up frequently in some of the subsequent chapters on auctions.

The function, $p/10$, shown in Table 8.1 is increasing in p, but it increases at a uniform rate, since all prices in the range from 0 to 10 are equally likely. Other distributions may not be uniform, e.g., some central ranges of prices may be more likely than extreme high or low prices. In such cases, $F(p)$ would still be an increasing function, but the rate of increase would be faster in a range where prices are more likely to be selected. In a mixed-strategy equilibrium, the distribution of prices, $F(p)$, must be determined in a manner to make each seller indifferent about the range of prices, since no seller would be willing to choose price randomly unless all prices in the range of randomization yield the same expected payoff. As was the case in Chapter 5, we will calculate the equilibrium under the assumption that players are risk neutral, so that indifference means equal expected payoffs.

Consider the duopoly example from Section 8.3, where the two sellers have zero costs and capacities of two units each (so costs are prohibitively high for a third unit). Thus, the market supply is vertical at a quantity of four. As before, assume that demand is inelastic at three units for all prices below some reservation price, which was $6 in the example. More generally, let the reservation price be denoted by V, which can be $6 or any other positive number. Since supply exceeds demand at all positive prices, the competitive price is $0, which is not a Nash equilibrium, as explained previously. Begin by considering a price, p, in the range from 0 to V. The probability that the other seller's price is less than or equal to p is $F(p)$, which is assumed to be increasing in p. When the other seller's price is lower, a firm sells a single unit, with earnings equal to p. When the other's price is higher, one's own sales are two units, with earnings of $2p$. Since prices are continuously distributed, we will ignore the possibility of a tie, and hence, $F(p)$ is the probability associated with having the high price and earning the payoff of p, and $1 - F(p)$ is the probability associated with having the low price and earning the payoff of $2p$. Thus, the expected earnings are: $F(p)p + [1 - F(p)]2p$. This expected payoff must be constant for each price in the range over which a firm randomizes, to ensure that the firm is indifferent among prices in this range. To determine this constant, note that setting the highest price, V, will result in sales of only one unit, since the other seller will have a lower price for sure. Thus, we set the expected payoff expression equal to the constant V, as shown in Equation (8.1).

$$F(p)p + [1 - F(p)]2p = V \qquad (8.1)$$

To summarize, Equation (8.1) ensures that the expected payoff for all prices is a constant and equals the earnings level for charging the buyer price limit of V. As shown in Equation (8.2), this equation can be solved for the equilibrium price distribution $F(p)$.

$$F(p) = \frac{2p-V}{p} \qquad (8.2)$$

for $V/2 \le p \le V$. Notice that Equation (8.2) implies that $F(p) = 1$ when $p = V$; the probability that the other seller's price is less than or equal to V is 1. The lower limit of the price distribution, $p = V/2$, is the value of p for which the right side of Equation (8.2) is 0. This is also the lower bound of the Edgeworth cycle discussed above (with $V = 6$, the lower bound of the cycle is 3). See Holt and Solis-Soberon (1992) for a more general approach to the calculation of mixed strategies in markets with capacity constraints; they also consider the effects of risk aversion.

QUESTIONS

1. Show that a unilateral price increase above a common price of $7 is not profitable in a posted-offer market.

2. Show that the formula, $F(p) = p/10$, produces the numbers shown in the second row of Table 8.1. How would the formula have to be changed if prices were uniform on the interval from $0 to $20, e.g., with one-half of the prices below $10, one-quarter below $5, and so on?

3. For the duopoly example in Section 8.3, show that prices of $0 for both sellers do not constitute a Nash equilibrium, i.e., show that a unilateral price increase by either seller will raise earnings.

4. Consider a modification of the duopoly example in Section 8.3, where demand is vertical at six units for all prices below $6, and each seller has a capacity of five units at zero cost. What is the range of prices over which an Edgeworth cycle would occur? Find the mixed-strategy Nash equilibrium distribution of prices, and compare the range of randomization with the range of the Edgeworth cycle.

5. Answer Question 4 for the case in which each seller's costs are constant at $1 per unit (with $V > 1$).

6. Construct an example with at least three sellers, in which a merger of two of the sellers reduces the costs of marginal units and makes the exercise of market power more profitable. Illustrate your answer with a graph that shows each seller's ID, and the way in which costs are reduced.

7. Construct an example (again with at least three sellers) of a merger that destroys market power by reducing costs on marginal units. Draw a graph that shows demand and seller costs and IDs for each unit, both before and after the treatment change.

chapter 9

Collusion and Price Competition

Ever since Adam Smith, economists have believed that sellers often conspire to raise price. Such collusion involves trust and coordination, and therefore, the plan may fall apart if some sellers defect. In fact, Smith's (1776) oft-quoted warning about the likelihood of price fixing is immediately qualified.

> *In a free trade an effectual combination cannot be established but by the unanimous consent of every single trader, and it cannot last longer than every single trader continues of the same mind. The majority of a corporation can enact a by-law with proper penalties, which will limit the competition more effectually and more durably than any voluntary combination whatever.*

Price-fixing is illegal in the United States and most other developed economies, and hence it is difficult to study. Moreover, conspirators will try to keep their activities secret from those who have to pay the high prices. There can be a selection bias, since data that does surface is more likely to come from disgruntled participants in failed conspiracies. Without good data on participants and their costs, it is difficult to evaluate the nature and success of collusion, and whether the breakdowns are caused by shifts in cost or demand conditions. Laboratory experiments are not hampered by these data problems, since controlled opportunities for price fixing can be allowed, holding constant other structural and institutional elements that may facilitate supra-competitive pricing. Another antitrust issue of interest is whether the observed patterns of bids and other market conditions can be used ex post to make inferences about the presence or absence of collusion.

9.1 Collusion in Posted-Offer Markets: "This *Is* Economics"

Given the difficulty of obtaining information about price-fixing conspiracies, it is not surprising to find differing opinions about the usefulness of prosecuting them. For example, Cohen and Scheffman (1989) argue that conspiracies are prone to failure and that enforcement costs incurred by antitrust authorities are, to a large extent, wasted. This point of view has been contested by other economists and by antitrust authorities (see (Werden 1989) and the discussion of the literature in (Davis and Wilson 2002)).

The results of early laboratory experiments indicate that the effectiveness of collusion depends critically on the nature of the market trading institution. Isaac and Plott (1981) report results from double auctions with trading rules that approximate those of organized asset markets, with a continuous flow of bids, asks, and trading prices. Sellers in these double auctions were allowed to go to a corner of the room and discuss prices between trading periods. These conspiracies were not very effective in actually raising transactions prices in the fast-paced competition of a double auction, where sellers are faced with the temptation to cut prices in order to sell marginal units late in the trading period. This observation suggests that conspiracies might be more effective if mid-period price reductions are precluded. Sellers only submit a single price in a posted-offer auction, so late price discounts in response to low trading volume are not permitted. A number of studies have documented the effectiveness of price collusion in posted-offer markets (Isaac, Ramey, and Williams 1984; Saijo, Une, and Yamaguchi, 1996; and Sherstyuk, 1999).

This section will be organized around a series of market experiments reported in Davis and Holt (1998), who replicated earlier results and then relaxed the price rigidity in posted-offer markets in a controlled manner by introducing discount opportunities. There were three buyers and three sellers in each session. At the beginning of each period, the buyers were taken from the room under the guise of assigning different redemption values to them. Then sellers were allowed to push their chairs back from their visually isolated cubicles so that they could see each other and discuss price. They were not permitted to discuss their own production costs or to divide earnings. Then they returned to their computers as the buyers came back into the room. At that time, sellers entered their posted prices independently, without further discussion. The buyers were unaware of the seller price discussions.

The supply and demand functions for all sessions are shown on the left side of Figure 9.1. The intersection of these functions determines a range of competitive prices, the highest of which is shown as a horizontal dashed line, labeled CE Price. Supply and demand were structured so that if all three sellers could set a price that maximized total earnings for the three of them, then they would each sell a single unit at a price indicated by the dashed horizontal line labeled M Price. (In all treatments, buyers were required to pay a \$.05 travel cost prior to approaching a seller, so this reduces the M-price line to a level that is \$.05 below the step on the demand curve at \$3.10.)

First, consider a session in which buyers were taken from the room for value assignments, as in all sessions, but sellers were *not* permitted to fix prices. The prices for this no-collusion session are shown in Figure 9.1 as boxes, and the units sold are shown as small black dashes in the lower part of the corresponding box. The dashes are stacked so that the thickness of these black marks is proportional to the seller's actual sales quantity at that price. The prices for each period are separated by vertical lines, and the prices for the three sellers are shown in order from left to middle to right, for sellers S1, S2, and S3 respectively.

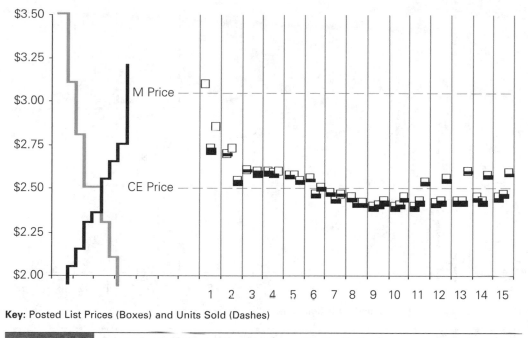

Key: Posted List Prices (Boxes) and Units Sold (Dashes)

Figure 9.1   Prices for a Posted-Offer Session with No Collusion

Notice that the low-price firm, S2, sells the most units in the first round, and that the other prices fall quickly. Prices are roughly centered around the competitive price in the later periods. The competitive nature of the market (without collusion) was an intentional design feature.

In contrast, Figure 9.2 shows the dramatic effects of collusion with the same market structure as before. The only procedural difference was that sellers were able to collude while buyers were out of the room. Attempts to fix a price resulted in high but variable prices in the early periods. Sellers agreed on a common price in the fourth round, but the failure of S2 to make a sale at this price forced them to deal with the allocation issue, which was solved more efficiently by an agreement that each will limit sales to one unit. This agreement broke down several periods later as S2 (whose price is always displayed in the center) listed a price below the others. A high price was reestablished in the final six periods, but prices remained slightly below the joint-profit-maximizing monopoly level. In two of these periods, 10 and 13, the sellers agreed to raise price slightly and hold sales to one unit each, but on both occasions S2 sold two units, leaving S3 with nothing. These defections were covered up by S2, who did not admit the extra sale, but claimed in the subsequent meeting that "this is economics," and that there is less sold at a higher price. The others went along with this explanation and agreed to lower price slightly.

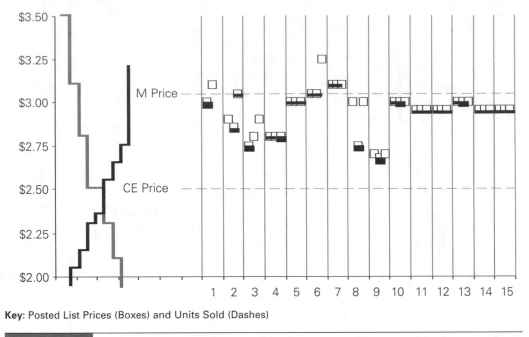

Key: Posted List Prices (Boxes) and Units Sold (Dashes)

Figure 9.2 Prices for a Posted-Offer Session with Collusion

Successful collusion was observed in all but one of the other sessions done with this treatment. In one session (not shown), sellers were not able to coordinate on a common price until the fifth round, but then all buyers made purchases from S1, which created an earnings disparity. S1 then suggested that they take turns having the low price, and that *he, S1, be allowed to go first!* This agreement was adopted, and S1 made all sales in the sixth period. The low price position was rotated from seller to seller in subsequent rounds, much like the famous 1960's "phases of the moon" price-fixing conspiracy involving electrical equipment. There was some experimentation with prices above and below the joint-profit-maximizing collusive level, but the prices stayed at approximately this level in most periods. Despite the high prices generated by this conspiracy, seller profits were not as high as they could have been. In particular, the rotation scheme was quite inefficient, since each seller had a low-cost unit that would not sell when it was not that seller's turn to have the low price (see Questions 1 and 2 at the end of this chapter for a related example).

9.2 Collusion with Secret Discounts

Most markets of interest to industrial organization economists cannot be classified as continuous double auctions (where all price activity is public) or as posted-offer markets (which do not permit discounts and sales). This raises the issue of how effective explicit collusion would be in markets with a richer array of pricing strategies and information conditions. In particular, markets for producer goods or major consumer purchases differ from the posted-offer institution in that sellers can offer private discounts from the list prices. The effectiveness of conspiracies in such markets is important for antitrust policy, since many of the famous price-fixing cases, like the electrical equipment bidding conspiracy discussed above, involve producer goods markets where discounts are often negotiated bilaterally.

Another treatment was used in order to evaluate the effects of discount opportunities for the market structure considered in Figures 9.1 and 9.2. For these sessions, sellers could collude as before, but when buyers returned and saw the sellers' posted prices, they could request discounts. A buyer whose turn it was to shop could either press a buy button for a particular seller or a "request discount" button. The seller would then type in a price, which could be equal to the list price (no discount) or lower. The seller's response was not observed by other sellers, so the discounts were given secretly. Sellers were free to discount selectively to some buyers and not others, and to hold discounts until later in a period.

Prices were much lower in the collusion sessions with opportunities for discounting than in the collusion sessions with no such opportunities. In fact, one of the sellers became so upset with the others that she refused to speak with them in the discussion period between periods. Even in groups that maintained an active price-fixing discussion, the results were often surprising. Consider, for example, the price sequence in Figure 9.3. As before, the small squares indicate list prices, and the black dashes indicate actual sales, often at levels well below posted list price. In the third period, for example, all sellers offered the same list price, but S1 (on the left) sold two units at deep discounts. In the sixth, seventh, and eighth periods, S2 began secret discounting, as indicated by the dashes below the middle price square. These discounts caused S1 to have no sales in two of these periods, and S1 responded with a sharp discount in the ninth period and a lower list price in the tenth period. After this point, discounts were pervasive, and the outcome was relatively competitive. *Notice that the sellers fixed a price, but the only price they succeeded in fixing in the end was essentially the competitive price.* This competitive outcome is similar to the results of several other sessions with discounting, and treatment effects are significant using nonparametric tests of the type discussed in Chapter 1.

One factor that hampered the ability of sellers to maintain high prices in the face of secret discounts was the inability to identify who was cheating on the agreement. Antitrust investigations have found that many successful price-fixing conspiracies, especially those with large numbers of participants, involved industries where a trade association reported reliable sales information for each seller (Hay and Kelly 1974). This observation motivated the trade association treatment where sellers were given reports of all sellers' sales quantities at the end of each round. All other procedures were identical, with both collusion and the possibility of secret discounts. Even with discounting, this ex post sales information permitted sellers to raise prices about half way between the competitive price and the collusive price. A typical session with trade association quantity reports is shown in Figure 9.4.

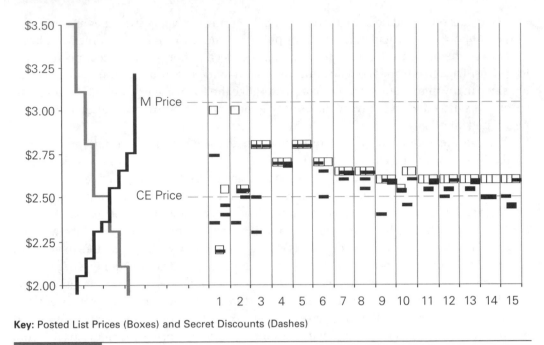

Key: Posted List Prices (Boxes) and Secret Discounts (Dashes)

Figure 9.3 Prices for a Session with Collusion and Secret Discounts

Notice that the explicit collusion resulted in high list prices, above even monopoly levels. There was not enough business to go around at these high prices, i.e., it was not possible for each seller to sell a unit at these prices. Perhaps as a result, virtually all units were sold at discount. The ex post quantity reports gave sellers something to talk about, and unequal sales quantities did have the effect of exposing discounters to disapproval, but all sellers were discounting, since they did not seem to trust each other. Nevertheless, the average transactions prices were closer to joint-profit-maximizing levels than to competitive levels, and earnings were much higher than in the sessions with no ex post quantity reporting.

List and Price (2005) report results for a field experiment in a market with multi-lateral decentralized bargaining. The participants were recruited at a sports card convention. Dealers were assigned seller roles, and non-dealer attendees were assigned buyer roles. The product was homogenous; a standard card was used for all trades. There were three treatments that parallel those of Davis and Holt: no communication among sellers, communication with publicly observed prices, and communication without publicly observed prices, which is roughly analogous to secret discounting. Prices were near competitive levels in the absence of opportunities for collusive discussions, and prices were much higher when collusion among sellers was allowed. For the intermediate treatment when collusion was allowed and prices were not perfectly observed by other sellers, the average prices

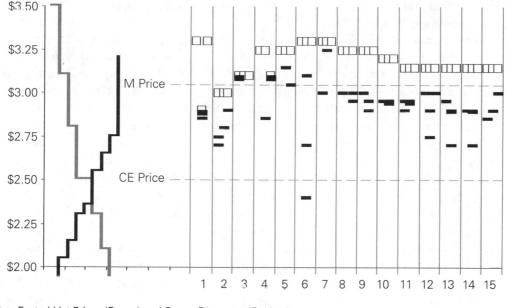

Key: Posted List Prices (Boxes) and Secret Discounts (Dashes)

| Figure 9.4 | A Session with Collusion, Secret Discounts, and Trade Association Reporting |

were in the middle of the averages for those of the other treatments. This was run like a laboratory experiment, but with more context and experienced participants. In this sense, the results add a new dimension to the results of earlier laboratory experiments.

9.3 Extensions: Cheap Talk, Mutual Forbearance, and the "V Word"

To summarize, the effects of market power and explicit collusion are much more severe in markets where sellers post prices on a take-it-or-leave-it basis. Opportunities to offer price reductions during the trading period make it difficult to coordinate collusive price increases and to exercise power in the absence of collusion. These results are consistent with the antitrust hostility to industry practices that are seen as limiting sellers' options to offer selective discounts. Sales contracts and business practices that deter discounts have been the target of antitrust litigation, as in the Federal Trade Commission's Ethyl case, where the FTC alleged that certain "best-price" policies deterred sellers from offering selective discounts. The best-price policies used by defendants in the Ethyl case had two components: most-favored-customer (MFC) and meet-or-release (MOR). A most-favored-customer provision in a contract ensured the buyer of obtaining the lowest price offered by that seller to any other buyer. Buyers with these contracts are typically permitted to inspect a seller's sales records, which prevents selective secret discounts. A meet-or-release contract forces the seller to meet a lower price offered by a competitor or release the buyer. Notice that a MOR contract lets the seller maintain sales quantity when a competitor cuts price, which in turn may result in a lower incentive to cut price unilaterally. The anti-competitive nature of these best-price practices is supported by results of an experiment run by Grether and Plott (1984), who used a market structure that was styled after the main characteristics of the market for lead-based anti-knock gasoline additives that was litigated in the Ethyl case. Roughly speaking, the experiments show that use of the best-price practices tended to raise prices from competitive levels (Bertrand competition) to the level that would result from sellers choosing quantities independently (Cournot competition). Holt and Scheffman (1987) provide a theoretical analysis of this price-increasing effect of best-price policies. (See Questions 3 and 4 for a related example.)

There have been a number of follow-up studies on the effects of price collusion. Isaac and Walker (1985) found that the effects of collusion in sealed bid auctions to be similar to those in posted price auctions. This is not surprising, since a sealed bid auction is similar to a posted-offer auction, except that only a single unit or prize is typically involved. Collusion in sealed bid auctions is an important topic, since many price-fixing conspiracies have occurred in such auctions, and since many companies rely more and more on auctions to procure supplies.

Another interesting issue is the extent to which the pattern of bids in a procurement auction might be used to infer collusion. Davis and Wilson (2002) investigate this issue with a pair of auction treatments. There were four bidders, each with a capacity to supply four units of a commodity, and a single buyer with a demand for four units. In the sessions with communication, the sellers were allowed to discuss price prior to the beginning of every fourth period, which implements the idea that illegal discussions may only occur infrequently. The supply and demand setup in one treatment was such that there was a Nash equilibrium in which all sellers choose the same competitive price. Here, the "suspicious" common pricing behavior is predicted in theory even when sellers do not communicate. In the experiment, prices tended to be lower and more variable when communication was not allowed, and common prices were *only* observed when communication was allowed. Thus, common pricing can be an indicator of collusion in this environment. Such collusion resulted in large price increases, especially toward the end of the session after sellers had established effective collusion.

Davis and Wilson (2002) also implemented a second market structure that was intended to mimic a market for construction contracts. In this setup, each of the four firms had a limited capacity in the sense that winning a contract in one period would raise their costs of taking on an additional project in the next several periods. The motivation for this cost increase is that a firm might have to pay overtime, incur delay penalties, or subcontract some of the work when it undertakes more than one project at a time. In this setting, it is natural to expect some bid rotation to develop, as companies with ongoing projects bid higher and allow others to take subsequent projects. Thus, the rotation of low bids, which is sometimes considered to be a suspicious pattern, would be expected to emerge even in the absence of collusion. Such rotations were observed in both the communication and the no-communication sessions, but Davis and Wilson concluded that collusion can often be inferred from the pattern of *losing* bids. In particular, there was less correlation between losing bids and costs when the losing bidders had agreed in advance to bid high and lose. This pattern was also observed in an empirical study of bidding for school milk programs (Porter and Zona 1993).

Finally, there is a separate series of papers on tacit collusion or a "meeting of the minds," which results in high prices, even in the absence of illegal direct communication. These papers identify market conditions and business practices that may facilitate such tacit collusion. In particular, there have been allegations that competitors who post prices on computer networks may be able to signal threats and cooperative intentions. Some bidders in early FCC bandwidth auctions used decimal places to attach zip codes to bids in an attempt to deter rivals by implicitly threatening to bid on licenses that rivals were trying to obtain. Similarly, some airlines attached aggressive letter combinations (e.g., FU) to ticket prices posted on the Airline Tariff Publishing (ATP) computerized price system. Cason (1995) reports that such nonbinding (cheap talk) communications can raise prices, but only temporarily. See Holt and Davis (1990) for a similar result in a market where sellers could post non-binding "intended prices" before posting actual prices. These non-binding price announcements would correspond to the posting of intended future prices on the ATP, which are visible to competitors before such prices are actually available for consumers. Cason and Davis (1995) find that price signaling opportunities had more of an effect in a multi-market setting, but even then the effects of purely nonbinding price announcements were quite limited.

For any kind of collusion (tacit or explicit) to be effective, it is important for the participants to be able to signal intentions and to identify and sanction violators. Even though explicit collusion is facilitated in sealed bid auctions, it can be the case that more open auction formats allow people to signal and punish others. Suppose that incumbency makes licenses being auctioned off more valuable to the current provider. For example, bidder A has a value of $10 for item A and $5 for item B, and conversely, bidder B has a value of $10 for B and $5 for A. Without collusion, the items might each sell for about $5. But imagine an ascending price auction in which both bidders can signal mutual forbearance by not raising bids on the other's preferred item. In this case, the bidding might stop at levels below $5. If this is not the case, each person could punish the other by bidding above $5 on the other's favored item, which would be a clear signal of displeasure if the values are known. A sealed bid auction takes away the possibilities for signaling of forbearance or punishment in incremental ways, and the result would likely be to break the tacit collusion. Plott and Li (2005) show how collusion can develop in ascending price auctions in a multi-bidder environment where each person has a preferred item, in a manner that generalizes the above example. They also show that a Dutch auction breaks this collusion. The Dutch auction, discussed in Chapter 19, has the property that the proposed bid price is decreased until the first person stops the auction by pressing the "buy button." The finality of the buy decision makes it harder to signal mutual forbearance. Also, see Brunner, Goeree, Holt, and Ledyard (2006), who report an experiment in which each bidder had a high value on a separate prize, which could be attributed to incumbency. Here mutual forbearance generated tacit collusion and low seller revenues in an ascending price "clock auction" (discussed in Chapter 22). This tacit collusion was broken if the ascending price phase was followed by the simultaneous submission of final sealed bids in a "shoot out." Here again, the finality of the sealed bids precludes collusion based on bid patterns that signal cooperation or punishment.

Goeree, Offerman, and Sloof (2005) also observe mutual forbearance (demand reduction) by incumbents in ascending price laboratory auctions, which generate lower sales revenues than a parallel series of sealed bid auctions. Their work was motivated by a widely discussed failure of the Dutch telecommunications auction to generate high revenues, as incumbents stopped bidding against each other. Given the spectacular success of such auctions in neighboring countries, the Dutch auction caused considerable embarrassment. The Dutch word for auction is "veiling," and at one point, economics consultants to a Dutch government agency were advised not to use the "V word."

QUESTIONS

1. Suppose that market demand is 0 at a price of $7, 1 at a price of $6, 2 at a price of $5, 3 at a price of $4, and so forth. There are three sellers in the market, each with costs of $1 for a first unit, $2 for a second unit, and $3 for a third unit. For example, these three sellers together could sell 3 units at costs of $1 each. If all three sellers collude and agree to sell equal amounts, what price would they choose and how much combined profit would they earn?

2. *Monopoly effectiveness* in an experiment is sometimes measured as the sum of all sellers' profits as a percentage of the maximum combined sellers' earnings. The monopoly effectiveness of the collusion described in the previous question would be 100 percent. Consider an alternative "phases of the moon" arrangement in which they take turns posting the low price and selling all units demanded at that price. Calculate the monopoly effectiveness of this arrangement.

3. Consider a duopoly with two sellers, each with constant marginal costs of $1 per unit. The market demand is provided by the top two rows of Table 6.1. Think of the demand as being generated by 12 buyers, each with a reservation price for a single unit that corresponds to one of the steps on the demand curve. As discussed in Chapter 6, perfect collusion would result in quantities of 3 for each seller, yielding the monopoly quantity

of 6 and a price of $7. Suppose that the market is initially at this collusive outcome, with six buyers making purchases, three for each seller. Each buyer has best-price contracts with their "own" sellers. The potential buyer with the next highest reservation value of $6 is not currently making a purchase. If Seller 1 wants to cut price from $7 to $6 in order to pick up this marginal buyer, the best-price clause requires that the price be cut to $6 for all three of the seller's other buyers. A price cut by Seller 1 would cause the other seller's customers to want to switch, but the best-price clause gives that other seller the option of meeting the lower price of $6, which is better than releasing them from the contract. Therefore a unilateral price cut by Seller 1 would result in a net increase in quantity of 1 unit, since the other seller would use the meet or release clause to maintain quantity. Show that Seller 1 would earn more money (at least initially) by making this unilateral price cut, and in this sense, that best-price policies would not sustain perfect collusion.

4. Now suppose that each seller (for the market described in Question 3) has best-price contracts with 4 buyers, and that the prices charged are $5 each. Show that a unilateral price cut by one seller to $4 would not be profitable. Explain the intuition for this result in terms of the Cournot equilibrium, which involves a quantity of 4 for each seller.

chapter 10

Market Failure Due to Unraveling: Lemons and Matching Markets

When buyers can observe price and product quality prior to purchase, there is pressure on sellers to provide good qualities at reasonable prices. In contrast, a seller may be tempted to cut quality when it is not observed by buyers in advance, and the result will be disappointed buyers who are hesitant to pay the high prices needed to cover the costs to the high-quality seller. As a consequence, sellers may be forced to cut both price and quality in an unraveling process. The "lemons market" terminology is attributed to George Akerlof (1970), who explained why there is no market for a new car that has just been purchased from the dealer and offered for resale, since prospective buyers will assume it is a lemon. Akerlof showed how asymmetric information can cause quality to deteriorate to such low levels that the market may fail to exist. Unraveling has also been observed in labor markets, but for a different reason. At certain times in the past, job offers to students in professional schools have been made earlier and earlier by competing employers, and this process caused problems when employment matches were made years in advance of graduation. This chapter reviews experiments that have been used to study the unraveling process and the types of market mechanisms that improve performance by stopping that process. The lemons market game can be administered using the instructions provided in this chapter's Price/Quality Market experiment in the Class Experiments section or with the Veconlab program. This is a game in which buyers shop in sequence, so in a large class, people should be divided into groups.

10.1 Endogenous Product Quality

The markets considered in this section have the feature that sellers can choose the qualities of their products. A high-quality good is more costly to produce, but it is worth more to buyers. These costs and benefits raise the issue of whether or not there is an optimal quality. Most markets have the property that buyers are diverse in their willingness to pay for quality increases, so there will be a variety of different quality levels being sold at different prices. Even in this case, sellers who offer high-cost, high-quality items may face a temptation to cut quality slightly, especially if buyers cannot observe quality prior to purchase. Quality might be maintained, even with asymmetric information about quality, if sellers can acquire and maintain reputations reported or signaled by warranties and return policies. Before considering the effects of such policies, it is useful to examine how markets might fail if buyers cannot observe quality in advance.

For simplicity, consider a case where all buyers demand at most one unit each and have the same preferences for quality, which is represented by a numerical grade, g. The maximum willingness to pay for a unit of the commodity will be an increasing function of the grade, $V(g)$. Similarly, let the cost per unit be an increasing function, $C(g)$, of the grade. The net value for each grade g is the difference: $V(g) - C(g)$. The optimal grade maximizes this difference. The optimal grade may not be the highest feasible grade. For example, it is often prohibitively expensive to remove all impurities or reduce the risk of product failure to zero. The important behavioral issue in this type of market is the extent to which competition will force quality to near-optimal levels.

The main features of the market can be illustrated with a simple classroom experiment with three quality grades. Each buyer demands only one unit of the commodity, and buyers have identical valuations. The value of the commodity depends on the quality grade: $4.00 for grade 1, $8.80 for grade 2, and $13.60 for grade 3. With four buyers and a grade of 2, for example, the market demand would be vertical at a quantity of four units for any price below $8.80, as shown by the grade 2 demand line in the middle part of Figure 10.1. The other demand lines are similar, with cutoff prices of $4.00 and $13.60 for grades 1 and 3 respectively.

Market supply is determined by the costs given to sellers. Each seller has a capacity to produce two units, with the cost of the second unit being $1 higher than the cost of the first unit. For a grade of 1, the costs for the first and second units produced are $1.40 and $2.40 respectively, so each individual seller's supply curve would have two steps, before becoming perfectly inelastic at two units for prices above $2.40. With three identical sellers, the market supply will also have two steps with three units on each step. The market supply for grade 1 is located in the lower part of Figure 10.1, and it crosses the demand for grade 1 at a price of $2.40. The supply and demand curves for the other grades are shown above those for grade 1. In particular, the costs for the first and second units are $4.60 and $5.60 for grade 2, and they are $10.80 and $11.80 for grade 3. The total surplus (for consumers and producers) corresponds to the area between the supply and demand curves for a given grade. It is apparent from Figure 10.1 that the sum of consumer and producer surplus is maximized at a grade of 2.

The results of a classroom experiment from Holt and Sherman (1999) are shown in Table 10.1. This was run with the instructions from the Class Experiments section, and students were divided into groups and given roles corresponding to four buyers and three

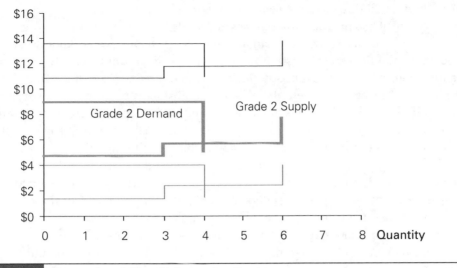

Figure 10.1 Demand and Supply Arrays by Grade

Table 10.1 Results from a Classroom Experiment

	Seller 1	**Seller 2**	**Seller 3**
Period 1	$11.50	$6.00	$12.00
(full information)	grade 3	grade 2	grade 3
	sold 1	sold 2	sold 1
Period 2	$5.75	$5.50	$1.90
(full information)	grade2	grade 2	grade 1
	sold 2	sold 1	sold 1
Period 3	$5.65	$5.60	$5.60
(full information)	grade2	grade 2	grade 2
	sold1	sold 2	sold 1
Period 4	$2.40	$5.60	$2.40
(only price information)	grade1	grade2	grade 1
	sold 1	sold 1	sold 2
Period 5	$2.40	$1.65	$5.50
(only price information)	grade 1	grade 1	grade 1
	sold 1	sold 1	sold 2

Source: (Holt and Sherman 1999)

sellers. In the first three rounds, sellers chose price and grade and wrote them on record sheets. When all had finished, these prices and grades were written on the blackboard, and buyers were selected one by one in random order to make purchases. Notice that two of the three quality choices in the first round were at the maximum level. Each of these high-quality sellers sold a single unit, but the seller who offered a grade of 2 sold two units and earned more. The buyers preferred the grade 2 good since it provided more surplus relative to the price charged. All three sellers had settled on the optimal grade of 2 by the third round, and the common price of $5.60 was approximately equal to the competitive level determined by the intersection of supply and demand at this grade.

The three "full-information" rounds were followed by two rounds in which sellers selected price and grade as before, but only the price was written on the board for buyers to see while shopping. Two of the sellers immediately cut grade to 1 in the fourth round, although they also cut the price, so buyers would be tipped off if they interpreted a low price as a signal of a low grade. In the final round, Seller 3 offered a low grade of 1 at a price of $5.50, which had been the going price for a grade of 2. The buyer who purchased from this seller must have anticipated a grade of 2, and this buyer lost money in the round. This pattern is similar to the quality unraveling observed by Holt and Sherman (1990) in a more complex market setting.

As noted by Akerlof (1970), market failure can occur even if sellers are not able to choose the quality grades of the products that they sell, as long as there is asymmetric information in the sense that buyers do not observe quality prior to purchase. This market failure with exogenous quality grades may happen in a process of adverse selection in which sellers with high-quality items drop out, since they do not expect to obtain high prices from buyers who cannot observe this quality. As the high-quality sellers drop out, the average quality in the market falls, and hence buyers' willingness to pay declines, which drives additional sellers with higher-than-average quality goods out of the market. The end result of this unraveling process may be a situation in which no trade occurs, or a complete market failure. The key characteristic of this process is that the quality is not observed by traders on one side of the market.

There have been a number of experimental studies of the effects of practices and institutions that alleviate the lemons market problem. Lynch et al. (1986) show that performance in double auctions with information asymmetries can be improved with certain types of warranties, requirements for truthful advertising, and so on. DeJong, Forsythe, and Lundholm (1985) allowed sellers to make price and quality representations, but the quality representation did not have to be accurate, and the buyer had imperfect information about quality even after using the product. In this experiment, the sellers could acquire reputations for providing higher quality based on buyer experience. This process of reputation building prevented the markets form collapsing to the lowest quality. Miller and Plott (1985) report experiments in which sellers can make costly decisions that "signal" high quality, which might prevent quality deterioration. Signaling games are discussed in Chapter 33.

10.2 Clearinghouse Mechanisms and Unraveling in Labor Markets

Just as firms might cut prices and quality grades, resulting in a low-grade outcome that is bad for all concerned, it is possible for a series of actions and reactions in labor markets to cause costly market failures. This kind of unraveling can occur when employers seek to beat the competition and congestion at graduation times for professional schools by making early offers, even though early offers entail some costs on both sides of the market. In the market for federal appellate court clerks in the United States, for example, judges who compete with each other for the best law students began to make earlier and earlier offers. This process continued until offers were being extended and accepted two years prior to graduation, on the basis of first-year law school grades (Avery, Jolls, Posner, and Roth 2001). An alternative, which is used in many medical labor markets, is to establish a centralized clearinghouse in which a computer-based job assignment is determined from ranked preferences submitted by both prospective employers and employees. Such a system was adopted in the United States in the 1950s for medical residents, and a modified version of this system is still in use (Roth 1984, 1990). The success of the U.S. National Resident Matching Program was noticed in the U.K., where unraveling and early offers were prevalent in the 1950s and early 1960s. The computer matching algorithms subsequently adopted in the U.K. varied from place to place. Some of these systems have survived and prospered, whereas others have failed as unraveling did not diminish. This section describes the Kagel and Roth (2000) clearinghouse experiment, which compares the performance of the two prominent types of matching mechanisms in use.

Both matching algorithms begin by having each prospective employee ("worker") submit a ranked list of employers ("firms"), with number 1 being the person's top preference, 2 next, and so on. Similarly, each firm submits a ranked list of available workers. Under one system, which will be called the *priority product* system, the attractiveness of a specific worker-firm match is the product of the rankings from each side for the other. This product is 4, for example, if the worker is the firm's second choice and the firm is the worker's second choice. The process begins by enacting the match with the lowest priority product. The worker and firm for this match are then removed from the pool, with the lowest priority product for the remaining workers and firms determining the next match, and so on. With equal numbers of workers and positions, this will result in no unmatched workers or firms.

The other matching method is known as the *deferred acceptance* system, since at each stage, workers keep their best offer on the table and reject others, which firms then send to workers lower on their lists. The computerized process is done mechanically on the basis of submitted rankings, but it is useful to think of it as beginning with firms sending an offer to the worker at the top of their lists. Some workers will get multiple offers, and in this case they will keep the offer that they have ranked the highest, rejecting the others. If a firm has a rejected offer, it can submit it in the next stage to the worker highest on its list who has not previously rejected its offer. A worker who keeps an offer on the table in one stage may reject it later if another offer arrives that is higher on the worker's preference list. Thus, each worker's satisfaction with the match on the table will not go down. The computer stops this process after a stage in which there are no rejections to be implemented on the basis of the submitted rankings.

The deferred acceptance process produces a stable outcome in the sense that it would be impossible to find a worker and firm who would prefer to be matched with each other instead of keeping their assigned partners. To see this, note that if a firm prefers a particular worker to the person with whom it is matched, then it must have previously proposed a match to that preferred worker. The worker who rejected that offer previously would reject it again since the value of the worker's match does not go down from one stage to the next. Thus, it is a Nash equilibrium for workers and firms to submit their true rankings under this deferred acceptance system. In contrast, the priority product system does not always produce a stable outcome, as will be shown next by looking at an example.

The setup in the experiment involved six workers and six firms. Three of the workers were of high productivity, and a match with them was worth about $15 to each firm, regardless of its own productivity. In contrast, a firm that was matched with a low productivity worker earned $5 on average. Similarly, three of the firms were high productivity firms in the sense that a worker matched with one of them would earn $15 on average; matches with one of the other three firms only provided the worker with $5 average earnings. The actual earnings for each match were equal to the average, plus or minus a small, privately observed, random deviation that was less than $1 in absolute value. These random deviations were meant to model idiosyncratic match values, e.g., that a medical student may have a small preference for a hospital that is located near friends and relatives. A simplified version of this setup, with only four workers and four firms, is shown in Table 10.2. For example, the high productivity firm F1 would earn $14.90 if it is matched with worker W2, who is preferred to W1, W3, and W4 in that order.

If the true rankings in the table are submitted under the deferred acceptance procedure, then firms 1 and 2 send initial offers to W2, who keeps F2 on the table and rejects F1. Firms 3 and 4 send offers to W1, who keeps F3 and rejects F4. The low-productivity workers get no offers in the first stage. The F1 offer that was rejected initially is resent to W1, who keeps it and rejects the offer it had (F3). At this stage, the high-productivity workers, W1 and W2, are provisionally matched with firms F1 and F2 respectively, and these pairings cannot be overturned by a low-productivity match. It can be shown that the process ends when W3 is matched with F3 and W4 is matched with F4 (see Question 5 at the end of the chapter). In the end, W4 would rather be matched with F3, but F3 would not want to switch, since W3 is preferred to W4 by this firm. A similar observation can be made for the high-productivity firms and workers, so the outcome is stable.

Next, consider the priority product method under the assumption that participants submit their true preference rankings. Since W2 and F2 are each other's first choice, the priority product is 1 for this match, which can be shown to be the lowest product. This match is then implemented, taking W2 and F2 out of the picture. Next, consider whether F1 will be matched with W1. They are each the other's second choice, so the priority product is 4. This

Table 10.2	Payoffs for Each Matching

High-Productivity Firms		Low-Productivity Firms	
F1	**F2**	**F3**	**F4**
W2 = 14.90	W2 = 15.50	W1 = 15.30	W1 = 14.90
W1 = 14.20	W1 = 14.60	W2 = 15.00	W2 = 14.50
W3 = 5.90	W3 = 5.30	W3 = 5.50	W4 = 5.50
W4 = 5.60	W4 = 4.60	W4 = 4.70	W3 = 5.10

High-Productivity Workers		Low-Productivity Workers	
W1	**W2**	**W3**	**W4**
F2 = 14.90	F2 = 15.50	F1 = 15.50	F1 = 15.50
F1 = 14.80	F1 = 14.60	F2 = 14.60	F2 = 15.10
F3 = 5.60	F3 = 5.00	F3 = 5.30	F3 = 4.90
F4 = 5.30	F4 = 4.60	F4 = 4.60	F4 = 4.50

is higher than the product for F1 and W3, which is 3 since F1 is W3's first choice and W3 is F1's third choice. The product for F3 and W1 is also 3, and these are the lowest priority products remaining after those in the initial match (W2, F2) were removed (see Questions 6 and 7 at the end of the chapter). Thus, the algorithm will match W1 and F3 in one pair, and W3 and F1 in another. This is unstable since both of the high-productivity agents (F1 and W1) would prefer to be matched with each other.

An unstable system will create regret and dissatisfaction after matchings are announced, so participation may decline as workers and firms seek to match with each other bilaterally. The way the process worked in the experiment was that each firm could send an offer to a single worker in each period. There were three periods in the process, –2, –1, and 0 (graduation day). Such bilateral matches incur a cost of $2 if accomplished at time –2, and they incur a cost of $1 if accomplished at time –1. There is no cost for making a match in time 0. Anyone who arranges a match must not make or accept subsequent offers. If there is a clearinghouse, it operates for unmatched people and firms in time 0. Anyone who remains unmatched after time 0 earns $0. Each session began with 10 rounds or repetitions of this three-period market process, with no clearinghouse. Match value profiles were shuffled randomly from round to round, but these profiles stayed the same for the periods –2, –1, and 0 of a round. After 10 rounds with no clearinghouse, one of the clearinghouse mechanisms was implemented at period 0 of round 11 and in all subsequent rounds.

One way to evaluate the outcomes is to look at the average costs associated with early matches, which are graphed in Figure 10.2. The first two sets of bars, on the left side, are for

Average Cost

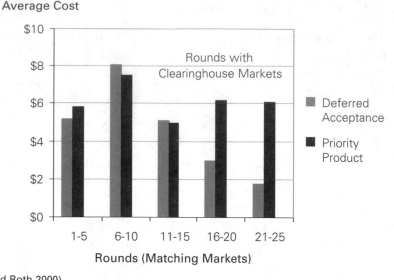

Rounds (Matching Markets)

Source: (Kagel and Roth 2000)

Figure 10.2   Average Costs of Early Matchings

the 10 rounds prior to the imposition of a clearinghouse in round 11. Notice that costs of early matching rise from the first five rounds to the second five rounds, which shows the unraveling as earlier matches generate higher costs. Then costs for both treatments fall in rounds 11–15, as each type of clearinghouse reduces costs for the sessions in which it is operative. But in the final rounds 16–25, costs increase for the sessions with the priority product algorithm, and costs fall for the deferred acceptance sessions. Although not shown in the graph, the most costly matches in time period –2 vanish completely for the deferred acceptance sessions in markets 21–25.

This experiment is quite innovative from a methodological perspective. First, note that the sequential (within-subjects) design is used because the clearinghouse mechanisms were implemented in a natural experiment in settings where unraveling had already occurred, so any sequence effects were a focus of attention, not a nuisance. The experiments enabled the authors to observe the patterns of behavior during the process of adjustment at a level of detail that was not available from field data. In the experiments, the sudden availability of a clearinghouse option did not deter firms from making early offers just as they had before. What happened, however, was that workers who were not matched in periods –2 and –1 ended up trying the clearinghouse and becoming satisfied with its results, especially for the deferred acceptance mechanism. The priority product mechanism did improve matching initially before unraveling re-emerged. In addition, the laboratory experiment, with only six agents on each side of the market, was able to reproduce both the unraveling patterns observed in the field and the superior performance of the mechanism that generated stable matches. Without a laboratory experiment, one might have wondered whether the survival of the deferred acceptance method in two locations in the U.K. and the demise of the priority product system in two other locations had been due to chance differences in demographics, social norms, or some other unobserved aspect of the field context. The laboratory used subjects selected from the same pool for both treatments, so the performance differences could be attributed to the incentive properties of the two mechanisms. Taken together, the laboratory experiment and the natural experiment provide a clearer picture of adjustment and behavior in these types of markets.

10.3 Extensions: Baseball, Dorm Rooms, School Choice, Deep Space, Sorority Rush, . . . but Marriage?

The matching mechanisms discussed in Section 10.2 involved both sides of the market. The deferred acceptance procedure was developed by Gale and Shapley (1962), who discussed applications to college admissions and marriage. Two-sided mechanisms are widely used in sorority rush, where unraveling might mean making a choice soon after arriving on campus, before having time to find a group of friends (Mongell and Roth 1991). Nalbanthian and Schotter (1995) report market-like experiments motivated by matching of free agents in professional baseball. In addition, there are many interesting experimental studies of one-sided matching problems, e.g., assigning students to dorm rooms when money-based allocations like auctions are precluded (Chen and Sönmez 2004). Olsen and Porter (1994) study both auction-like and non-price rankings-based mechanisms that are motivated by the Jet Propulsion Lab's allocation of time slots on its Deep Space Network of antennas. Chen and Sönmez (2005) used experiments to evaluate the "Boston system" of assigning students to schools on the basis of submitted rankings. They concluded that alternatives like the Gale-Shapley mechanism would improve performance. The Boston system looked good on paper because students tend to get assigned to the school that they rank the highest. Chen and Sonmez noted that students acted on incentives to misstate their preference rankings under this system, which made the assignments look better than they were in terms of actual preferences that were induced and known in their experiment. Economists were subsequently involved in redesigning the Boston school matching system, and the experimental evidence was useful in conveying the desirability of the change to a deferred acceptance procedure (Abdulkadiroglu, Pathak, Roth, and Sönmez 2005).

QUESTIONS

1. Use the unit costs and redemption values for the market design in Figure 10.1 to calculate the total surplus for each grade level.

2. In a competitive equilibrium for a given grade, the price is determined by the intersection of supply and demand for that grade. Compare the equilibrium profits for each grade for the market structure shown in Figure 10.1.

3. For the market structure shown in Figure 10.1, consider a small increase in the cost for each seller's first unit *for grade 2 only*. An increase of $0.25 in this cost would mean that the competitive equilibrium profits for each seller are lower for grade 2 than for the other grades. What effect do you think this cost increase would have on the tendency for grade choices by sellers to converge to the optimal grade (2)?

4. Groucho Marx once remarked: "Please accept my resignation, I don't want to belong to any club that will accept me as a member." How is this situation different from (or similar to) the exogenous quality model discussed in Section 10.1?

5. Assuming that the preference orderings implied by Table 10.2 are submitted under the deferred acceptance program, show that W3 is matched with F3 and that W4 is matched with F4.

6. Please fill out the table of priority products for the example from Section 10.2 of the chapter, assuming that the submitted preference orderings are those in Table 10.2. The second column and row of the priority product table have been completed for you, and this column and row can be crossed out since the top priority product (1) causes W2 and F2 to be matched first. Use the resulting table to determine all four matches.

	W1	W2	W3	W4
F1		2		
F2	2	1	6	8
F3		6		
F4		8		

7. Your answer to Question 6 should show F1 being matched with the low productivity worker W3. If F1 had foreseen this unfortunate outcome, how could F1 have changed the submitted ranking of workers to achieve a better match with a high-productivity worker? Explain.

8. Consider how you might modify one of the match value numbers in Table 10.2 to show that the deferred acceptance algorithm does not necessarily generate an efficient outcome in the sense of maximizing total earnings of all firms and workers. To do this, consider a very large change in a match value that does not alter the outcome of the deferred acceptance procedure, but that does cause a firm to miss out on an extremely productive match with a worker who does not rank that firm very high.

chapter **11**

Asset Markets and Price Bubbles

Many electronic markets for assets are run as call markets in which traders submit limit orders to buy or sell, and these orders are used to generate a single, market-clearing price when the market is called. Thus, all asset shares trade at the same price; the shares are purchased by those who submitted buy orders with a maximum willingness to pay limit at or above this price, and the shares are sold by those who submitted sell orders with a minimum willingness to accept limit at or below this price. The featured experiment in this chapter involves trading of shares that pay a randomly determined dividend. Traders are endowed with asset shares and cash that can either be used to purchase shares or earn interest in a safe account. The interest rate determines the value of the asset on the basis of fundamentals: dividends and associated probabilities, and the redemption value of each share after a pre-announced final round of trade. This fundamental value serves as a benchmark from which price bubbles can be measured. This setup is easy to implement using the Veconlab Limit Order Asset Market program. Large bubbles and crashes are typical for inexperienced traders, and the resulting discussion can be used to teach lessons about present value, backward induction, and so on.

11.1 Bubbles and Crashes

Despite the widespread belief that prices in equity markets rise steadily over the long term, these markets exhibit strong swings in price that do not seem to be justified by changes in the underlying economic fundamentals. Keynes' explanation for these swings was that many (or even most) investors are less concerned with the fundamentals that determine long-term future profitability of a company than with what the stock might sell for in several weeks or months. Such investors will try to identify stocks that they think other investors will flock to, and this herding may create its own self-confirming upward pressure on price. The psychology behind this process is described by Charles Mackay's (1841) account of the Dutch tulipmania in the 17th century:

> *Nobles, citizens, farmers, mechanics, seamen, footmen, maid-servants, even chimney-sweeps and old clotheswomen, dabbled in tulips. Houses and lands were offered for sale at ruinously low prices, or assigned in payment of bargains made at the tulip-mart. Foreigners became smitten with the same frenzy, and money poured into Holland from all directions.*

Of course, tulips are not scarce like diamonds. They can be produced, and it was only a matter of time until the correction, which in Mackay's words happened as follows:

> *At last, however, the more prudent began to see that this folly could not last forever. Rich people no longer bought the flowers to keep them in their gardens, but to sell them again at cent per cent profit. It was seen that somebody must lose fearfully in the end. As this conviction spread, prices fell, and never rose again. Confidence was destroyed, and a universal panic seized upon the dealers.*

Even if traders realize that prices are out of line with production costs and profit opportunities in the long run, a kind of overconfidence may lead traders to believe that they will be able to sell at a high level, or that they will be able to sell quickly enough in a crash to preserve most of the capital gains that they have accumulated. The problem is that there are no buyers at anything like previous price levels in the event of a crash, and often all it takes is slight decline, perhaps from an exogenous shock, to spook buyers and stimulate the subsequent free fall in price.

Price bubbles and crashes can be recreated in computer simulations by introducing a mix of trend-based and fundamentals-based traders. Then price surges can be stimulated by positive exogenous shocks, and such simulations can even produce negative bubbles that follow negative shocks (Steiglitz and Shapiro 1998). In a negative bubble, the trend traders are selling because they expect prior price decreases to continue and this sell pressure draws prices down if the fundamentals-based traders do not have the resources to correct the situation.

Computer simulations are suggestive, especially if they mimic the price and trading volume patterns that are observed in stock market booms and crashes. The obvious question, however, is how long human traders would stick to mechanical trading rules as conditions change. One problem with running a laboratory experiment with human subjects, however, is to decide how owners of unsold shares are compensated when the experiment ends.

Smith, Suchanek, and Williams (1988) addressed the endpoint problem by pre-specifying a redemption value for the asset after 20 periods. Traders were endowed with asset shares and cash, and they could buy and sell assets at the start of each period (via double auction trading). Assets owned at the end of a period paid a dividend that was randomly determined from a known distribution. Cash did not earn any interest, and all cash held at the end was converted to earnings at a pre-announced rate.

In most markets, the final redemption value was set to zero. To a risk-neutral person, each share would be worth the sum of the expected dividends for the periods remaining. For example, consider an asset that pays $0.50 or $1.50, each with 50 percent probability, so the expected dividend is $1.00. This asset would only be worth a number of dollars that equals the number of periods remaining, so the fundamental value of the asset declines linearly over time.

With this declining-value setup, price bubbles were observed in many (but not all) sessions. Figure 11.1 shows the results of a strong price bubble for a session where the final redemption value was $0.00 and the expected dividend was $0.16. Since there were rounds, the fundamental value line starts at $2.40 and declines by $0.16 per period, reaching $0.16 in the final round. The figure shows the average transactions prices for each round, as determined by double auction trading. The prices were below the fundamental value line in early rounds. Then prices increased steadily and rose above the declining value line. People who bought in one round and saw the price rise, would often try to buy again, and others wanting to join in on the gains would begin to buy as well. The price trajectory flattened out and then fell. As the final round approached, it became obvious that nobody would pay much more than the expected dividend in the final round. Such bubbles were observed with undergraduates, graduate students, business students, and even a group of commodity traders. Despite the lack of realism of having a fixed endpoint, the speculative bubbles could form, *even if* people knew that there was a fixed end point. These price patterns suggest that there might be even more frenzy in markets with no final period.

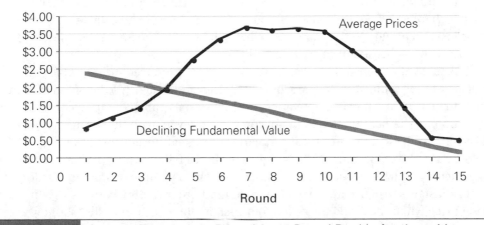

Figure 11.1 Average Transactions Prices in a 15-Round Double Auction with a Declining Fundamental Value

The observed bubbles are surprising given the obvious nature of the zero-value in the final round. Smith, Suchanek, and Williams did run some sessions with a non-zero final redemption value, which was set to be equal to the sum of the realized dividend payments for all rounds. Thus, the final redemption value would not be known in advance, but rather, would be determined by the random dividend realizations, and would generally decrease from period to period (see Question 1 at the end of the chapter).

Since most financial assets do not have predictable, declining fundamental values, it is instructive to set up experiments with constant or increasing values. Ball and Holt (1998) implemented this in a classroom experiment by using a fixed probability of breakage to induce a preference for the present (when the asset is not broken) over the future. In their setup, there was a 1/6 chance that each share would be destroyed, and they threw a six-sided die separately for each asset share at the end of each trading period (after trades were made via double auction and after dividends of $1 per share were paid). Any shares that remained at the end of a known final round could be redeemed for at a pre-announced rate of $6 per share.

One (incorrect) way to value this asset would be to take the final redemption value of $6 and add the total dividends of $1 per round, with some adjustment for the fact that an asset only has a 5/6 chance of surviving for another period, e.g., $6 + (5/6) + (5/6)(5/6) + ... The problem with this approach is that the $6 final payment is unlikely to be received. Even an asset that has survived up to the beginning of the final period has a 5/6 chance of producing the $6 redemption value. So at the start of the final round, the value of the asset is the dividend of $1 plus the 5/6 chance of getting $6, which for a risk-neutral person would be 1 + (5/6)6 = 1 + 5 = 6. Thus, an asset that is worth $6 at the end of the final round is also worth $6 at the beginning of the round. Working backwards, the next step is to think about the value of the asset at the beginning of the next-to-last round. This asset will pay $1 in that round and have a 5/6 chance of surviving to be worth $6 at the beginning of the last round, which for a risk-neutral person becomes: $1 + (5/6)6 = 6. Thus, the asset is valued at $6 in the last two rounds. In this manner, it can be shown that the fundamental value of the asset is $6 in all rounds, assuming risk neutrality.

This setup, with a constant fundamental value of $6, produced price bubbles in some, but not all, trading sequences. In one sequence, prices started at a little below $6 in round 1 and rose to near $9 in round 5, before prices fell as the final round (9) approached. An obvious question is whether bubbles would become more severe with more rounds, since the final round would seem more distant in early rounds, although the asset destruction process would choke off trade as the number of shares fell. Another problem is that the double auction trading used in this experiment is relatively time-consuming. Section 11.3 presents a faster alternative approach based on limit order trading with a single market-clearing price when the market is called. But first, it will be useful to discuss how assets with time streams of future dividends should be valued in the present.

11.2 A Digression on Present Value

Suppose that money can be invested in a safe account that earns interest at a rate of r per period. The simplest case to consider is an asset that only pays a dividend of D dollars once, at the end of the first period, and then the asset loses all value. Valuing the asset means deciding what to pay now for a dividend of D that arrives one period later. This asset is worth less than D now, since you could take D dollars, invest at an interest rate r, and earn $(1 + r)D$, by the end of the period, which is greater than D. Thus, it is better to have D dollars now than to have an asset that pays D dollars one period from now. This is the essence of the preference for present over future payments, which causes one to discount such future payments. To determine how much to discount, let's consider an amount that is less than D, and in particular consider $D/(1 + r)$ dollars now and invest at rate r, the amount obtained at the end of the period is the investment of $D/(1 + r)$ times $1 + r$, which equals D. To summarize, the present value of getting D dollars one period from now is $D/(1 + r)$. Similarly, the present value of any amount F to be received one period from now is $F/(1 + r)$. Conversely, an amount V invested today yields $V(1 + r)$ one period from now. These observations can be summarized as follows:

Present value of future payment F: $V = F/(1 + r)$
Future value of present investment V: $F = V(1 + r)$

Similarly, to find the future value of an amount V that is invested for one period and then reinvested at the same interest rate, we multiply the initial investment amount by $(1 + r)$ and then by $(1 + r)$ again. Thus, the future value of V dollars invested for two periods is $V(1 + r)^2$. Conversely, the present value of getting F dollars two periods from now is $F/(1 + r)^2$.

Present value of future payment F (2 periods later): $V = F/(1 + r)^2$
Future value (2 periods later) of present investment V: $F = V(1 + r)^2$

In general, the present value of an amount F received t periods into the future is $F/(1 + r)^t$. With this formula, one can value a series of dividend payments for any finite value of t. For example, the present value of an asset that pays a dividend D for two periods and then is redeemed for \$$R$ at the end of period 2 would be: $D/(1 + r) + D/(1 + r)^2 + R/(1 + r)^2$, where the final term is the present value of the redemption value.

The final issue to be addressed is how to value a series of dividend payments that has no terminal point. Equation (11.1) shows the main result.

$$V = \frac{D}{1 + r} + \frac{D}{(1 + r)^2} + \frac{D}{(1 + r)^3} + \ldots \frac{D}{(1 + r)^t} + \ldots = \frac{D}{r} \tag{11.1}$$

As indicated by the right-hand equality, this present value turns out to be D/r. One way to verify this is to use a mathematical formula for finding the sum of an infinite series, as shown in Equation (11.2).

$$1 + x + x^2 + x^3 + \ldots = \frac{1}{1 - x} \quad \text{if } x < 1 \tag{11.2}$$

To apply this formula, we need to regroup the terms in Equation (11.1) so that they begin with a 1, as shown in Equation (11.3).

$$V = \frac{D}{1 + r}\left[1 + \frac{1}{(1 + r)} + \frac{1}{(1 + r)^2} + \ldots\right] \tag{11.3}$$

Now we can apply the formula in (11.2) to evaluate the sum of terms in the square brackets in (11.3) by letting $x = 1/(1 + r)$, which is less than 1 as required. Since $1 - x = 1 - 1/(1 + r) = r/(1 + r)$, it follows that $1/(1 - x)$ is $(1 + r)/r$, which equals the sum of the terms in square brackets on the right side of (11.3). By making this substitution into (11.3) and letting the $(1 + r)$ terms cancel from the numerator and denominator, we obtain the resulting present value for the infinite series of dividends of D dollars per period is D/r.

It will be instructive to develop an alternative derivation of the result that the present value of an infinite sum of dividends, D per period, is D/r. First, since the future is infinite and the dividends do not change, it follows that the future always looks the same, even as time passes. Thus the present value of the future stream of dividends will be the same in each period. Let this present value be V. We can think of V as being the present value of getting a dividend at the end of the round, plus the present value of getting the asset (always worth V) back at the end of the round. Thus $V = D/(1 + r) + V/(1 + r)$, where the first term on the right is the effect of the end-of-period dividend, and the second term represents what the asset could be sold for at the end of the round after getting the dividend. This equation can be solved to obtain: $V = D/r$.

11.3   The Limit Order Market Experiment

In this section, we consider a simple asset pricing model with a safe asset that pays an interest rate of r per period (e.g., an insured savings account) and a risky asset that either pays a high amount, H, or a low amount, L, each with 50 percent probability. Let the expected value of the dividend be denoted by $D = (H + L)/2$. As shown in the previous section, the value of the asset would be D/r if the number of periods were infinite. In the first experiment to be discussed, $H = \$1.00$, $L = \$0.40$, so $D = \$0.70$. With an interest rate of 10 percent, $r = 0.1$, and hence the present value of an infinite-period asset would be $\$0.70/0.1 = \$7.00$. This is the present value of future dividends, and it does not change as time passes, since the future is always the same. The trick in setting up a finite-horizon experiment with an asset value that is constant over time is to have the final-period redemption value be equal to D/r, which would be the present value of the dividends if they were to continue forever. In this manner, the infinite future is incorporated into the redemption value per share in the final period, and the resulting asset value will be flat over time, even as the final round is approaching. Thus, the redemption value was set to be $\$7.00$.

Trades were arranged by letting people submit limit orders to buy and/or sell, and then using these orders to determine a single market-clearing price at which all trades are executed when the market is closed or "called." This setup is typically called a Call Market, since the process ends and trades are determined at a pre-specified time, e.g., at the end of the business day, or before the financial markets open in the morning. The experiment used the Veconlab LOM program, and the call occurred when all traders had submitted orders, or when the experimenter pressed the "Stop" button on the Admin Results page (whichever happened first).

A sell order involves specifying the maximum number of shares to be sold, and a *minimum* price that will be accepted. A buy order also stipulates a maximum number of shares, but the difference is that the price is the *maximum* amount that the person is willing to pay. Buy orders are ranked from high to low in a pseudo demand array, and the sell orders are ranked from low to high in a pseudo supply array. If more than one trader submits the same limit order price, then a randomly determined priority number is used to decide who gets listed first, i.e., who is highest in the bid queue or who is lowest in the offer queue. Then these supply and demand arrays are crossed to determine the market-clearing price and quantity. For example, if one buyer bids $5 for two shares and if another bids $4 for two shares, then the demand array would have steps at $5 and $4. Suppose that the only sell order involved three shares at a limit price of $3. Then three shares would trade at a price of $4, since there are four shares demanded at any price below $4 and only two shares demanded at any higher price.

For the first session to be discussed, there were 12 traders, each with an endowment of $50 in cash and six shares. The other parameters were as discussed above: an interest rate of 10 percent, dividends of either $0.40 or $1.00 per share, and a final-period redemption payment of $7 per share at the end period 20. Traders in this and all subsequent markets to be discussed were paid an amount that was 1/100 of total earnings. The trading activity for this session is shown in Figure 11.2. The first round results are to the left of the first vertical black line on the left side of the figure, at a price of $12. The dark line segments for subsequent periods show the market clearing prices for those periods, and the width of each segment is proportional to the number of shares traded. The bids and asks for traded shares are shown by the light dots that are above the clearing price for bids and below for asks. Thus, prices begin above fundamental value ($7), and rise steadily to about $28, followed by a sharp drop in rounds 17–19, and no trade in the final round.

Caginalp, Porter, and Smith (2001) report an experiment with a declining fundamental value, and they observe more price speculation when traders are endowed with higher amounts of initial cash, a factor that they label the "excess cash hypothesis." A similar effect can be induced in the Veconlab markets by increasing the interest rate and dividend payments, holding cash and share endowments constant. Thus, the fundamental value, D/r, would stay the same if the interest rate and expected dividends are doubled, leaving the final period redemption unchanged at $7.00. This observation motivated a second treatment with an interest rate of 0.2 and dividends that are equally likely to be $0.80 or $2.00.

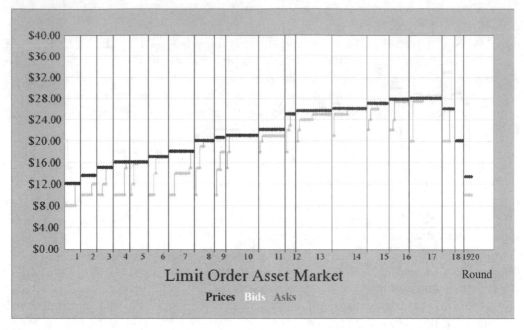

Limit Order Asset Market

Prices Bids Asks

Round

Source: (Bostian, Goeree, and Holt 2005)

Figure 11.2 A 20-Round Call Market with a Constant Fundamental Value of $7.00

Thus, the expected dividend was $1.40, and the fundamental value stayed at $7.00. This high-wealth treatment generated strong bubbles in all three sessions, as shown by the thick gray lines in Figure 11.3. In all three of these cases, the bubbles were followed by crashes back to the fundamental value of $7.00.

The tendency for prices to drop sharply in the final rounds of some markets provided the motivation for running long markets with 40-round horizons, but with the low wealth parameters (10 percent interest and an expected dividend of $0.70). These were, in a sense, high-wealth sessions since the accumulated effect of interest and dividends over the 40-period horizon was much larger than it is over the 20-period horizon. One of these 40-period markets resulted in dramatic surge after period 25, with prices peaking at $257 in round 31, which is over 30 times the fundamental value! The crash, when it came, started slowly and then accelerated with a $100 drop in round 34. Individual earnings were highly variable, with one person earning over $70 (after dividing final cash by 100), and with several people ending up with less than $5. This was the most extreme bubble observed, but other long sessions also generated strong bubbles.

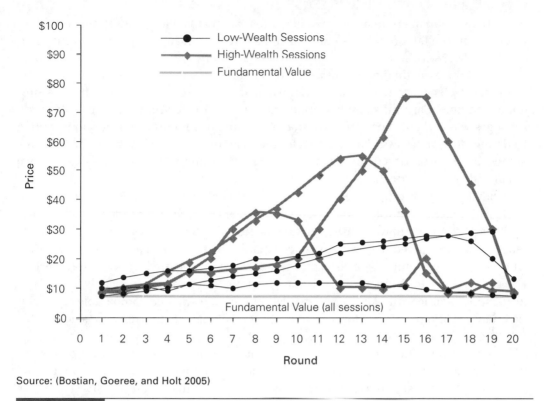

Source: (Bostian, Goeree, and Holt 2005)

Figure 11.3   Six Limit Order Markets with a Constant Fundamental Value of $7.00

11.4   Other Research on the Call Market Institution

All of the asset price bubbles shown so far have been for sessions with inexperienced participants, i.e., those who have not been in an asset trading experiment previously. In contrast, sessions with experienced subjects did not produce bubbles reliably (Smith, Suchanek, and Williams 1988; Van Boening, Williams, and LaMaster 1993). Peterson (1993) ran some asset market sessions with people who had been in two previous markets, and prices did not rise much above the declining fundamental value in this super-experience treatment. When discussing the implications of this difference, Vernon Smith once commented that crashes are relatively infrequent, sometimes decades apart, and many new investors enter the market in the meantime. Dufwenberg, Lindqvist, and Moore (2005) report that bubbles in their experiments are eliminated or largely abated when as few as a third of the traders are experienced. This suggests that bubbles are uncommon in mixed-experience settings, which may explain why severe surges and crashes are relatively few and far between in major financial markets. Other factors that can diminish the formation of bubbles in the lab are futures markets and short sales (King et al. 1993; Haruvy and Noussair 2006; Noussair and Tucker 2003; Porter and Smith 1995).

Most of the asset markets discussed in this chapter are called call markets because the final market-clearing price is calculated when the market is called, usually at a pre-announced time. Call market trading is commonly used for electronic trading of stocks on exchanges where there is not sufficient trading volume to support the continuous trading of a double auction process like that used for the New York Stock Exchange. And a call market mechanism is used to determine the opening prices on the New York Stock Exchange (Cason and Friedman 1997).

A classic study of computerized call markets is that of Smith et al. (1982), who provided buyers with redemption values for each unit and sellers with costs for each unit. (This kind of call market can be run with the Veconlab software using the CM program on the Markets menu.) Smith compared the outcomes of call markets with those of a double auction, in a stationary environment where costs and values stayed the same from period to period. Price convergence to competitive levels was generally faster and more reliable in the double auction, but one variant of the call market trading rules yielded comparable efficiency. Friedman (1993) reports price formation results for call markets that are almost as reliable as those of comparable double auctions.

Traders with multiple units in a call market may attempt to exercise market power. For example, a seller with a unit that has a cost close to the competitive price may wish to hold it back in an effort to shift the revealed supply curve up and thereby raise the price received on the seller's other (low-cost) units. Similarly, buyers may seek to hold back bids for marginal units in an effort to lower price. The McCabe, Rassenti, and Smith (1993) results revealed that traders on each side of the market sometimes tried to exercise market power in call markets. Despite these incentives, the markets that were run tended to be quite efficient, at levels comparable to those of double auctions.

Kagel and Vogt (1993) report results of two-sided call markets where buyer values and seller costs were determined randomly at the start of each trading period. The resulting prices are compared with predictions determined by a Nash equilibrium in which each person's bid or ask is a function of their realized value or cost (see Chapter 19 on private value auctions for this type of calculation). Call markets were slightly more efficient than the double auction. This result must be considered in light of the fact that call markets are easier to administer and can be run after hours, with traders who connect from remote locations and who do not need to monitor trading activity as carefully, since all included trades will be at the same price.

Cason and Friedman (1997) also compare call market prices to the Nash predictions. They find some persistent differences, and they use a model of learning to explain these differences.

QUESTIONS

1. Consider the setup discussed in Section 11.1, with no interest payments. Suppose that the experiment lasts for 15 periods, with dividends that are either $1 or $3, each with 50 percent probability, and with a final redemption value that equals the sum of the dividends realized in the 15 periods. There is no interest paid on cash balances held in each round. Thus, the actual final redemption value will depend on the random dividend realizations. Calculate the expected value of the asset at the start of the first period, before any dividends have been determined. On average, how fast will the expected value of the asset decline in each round? What is the highest amount the final redemption value could be, and what is the lowest amount?

2. Consider an asset that pays a dividend of $2 per period and has a 1/10 chance of being destroyed (after the dividend payment) in each round. The asset can be redeemed for $20 at the end of the fifth round. What is the fundamental value of the asset in each round?

part 3

Bargaining and Behavioral Labor Economics

Bilateral bargaining is pervasive, even in a developed economy, especially for large purchases like automobiles or specialty items like housing. Bargaining is also central in many legal and political disputes, and it is implicit in family relations, care of the elderly, and so on. The highly fluid give and take of face-to-face negotiations makes it difficult to specify convincing structured models that permit the calculation of Nash equilibria. Experimental research has responded in two ways. First, it is possible to look at behavior in unstructured bargaining situations to spot interesting patterns of behavior, like the well-known deadline effect, the tendency to delay agreements until the last moment. The second approach is to limit the timing and sequence of decisions, in order to learn something about fairness and equity considerations in a simplified setting. The ultimatum bargaining game discussed in Chapter 12 is an example of this latter approach. In an ultimatum game, one person makes a proposal about how to split a fixed amount of money, and the other either accepts or rejects, in which case both earn zero. Seemingly irrational rejections in such games have fascinated economists, and more recently, anthropologists.

The scenarios discussed in Chapter 13 also have alternating decision structures, but the focus is on manipulations that highlight issues of fairness, trust, and reciprocity. The trust game begins when one person is endowed with some cash, of which part or all may be passed to the other person. The money passed is augmented, e.g., tripled, and any part of the resulting amount may be passed back to the original person. A high level of trust would be indicated if the first person passed most of the initial cash stake, expecting the second person to reciprocate and pass back even more. The second setup that is considered, the reciprocity game, has more of a market context, but the underlying behavioral factors are similar. Here, the employer announces a wage, and seeing this, the worker chooses an effort level, which is costly for the worker but which benefits the employer. The issue is whether fairness considerations, which are clearly present in bilateral negotiations, will have an effect in more impersonal market settings.

Experiments with a focus on fairness issues are sometimes done only once, since repetition tends to smooth out payoff inequities. Therefore, these games may be run as single round versions, either with instructions provided or with the Veconlab setup, using the "go at your own pace" option, which makes it possible to run them after hours from remote locations.

chapter 12

Ultimatum Bargaining

The ultimatum bargaining game provides one person with the ability to propose a final offer that must be accepted or rejected, just as a monopolist may post a price on a take-it-or-leave it basis. The difference between the usual monopoly situation and ultimatum bargaining is that there is only one buyer of a single item in ultimatum bargaining, so a rejection results in zero earnings for both buyer and seller. Although rejections of positive amounts of money, however small, may surprise some, they will not surprise anyone who has participated in this type of bargaining, e.g., with the Veconlab Ultimatum Game or with the instructions provided in the Class Experiments section.

12.1 Strategic Advantage and Ultimatums

Many economic situations involve a final offer from one person to another, where rejection means zero earnings on the transaction for both. For example, suppose that a local monopolist can produce a unit of a commodity for $5. The sole buyer needs the product and is willing to pay any amount up to $15 but not a penny more, since $15 is what it would cost to buy the product elsewhere and pay to have it shipped into the local market. Then the surplus to be divided is $10, since this is the difference between the value and the cost. The buyer knows the seller's cost, and hence knows that a price of $10 would split the surplus. A higher price corresponds to offering a lower amount to the buyer. The seller has a strategic advantage if the seller can make a take-it-or-leave-it offer, which we assume to be the case. This setup is called an *ultimatum game* because the proposer (seller) makes a single offer to the responder (buyer), who must either accept the proposed split of the surplus (as determined by the price) or reject the proposal, which results in zero earnings for both.

The ultimatum game was introduced by Güth et al. (1982) because it highlights an extreme conflict between the dictates of selfish, strategic behavior and notions of *fairness*. If each person cares only about his or her own earnings, and if more money is preferred to less, then the proposer should be able to get away with offering a very small amount to the responder. The monopolist in the previous paragraph's example could offer a price of $14.99, knowing that the buyer would rather pay this price than a price of $15.00 (including shipping) from a seller in another market. The $14.99 price is unfair in the sense that $9.99 of the available surplus goes to the seller, and only a penny goes to the buyer. Even so, the buyer who only cares about getting the lowest possible price should accept any price offer below $15.00; and hence the seller should offer $14.99.

It is easy to think of situations in which a seller might hesitate to exploit a strong strategic advantage. Getting a reservation for dinner after graduation in a college town is the kind of thing one tries to do six months in advance. Restaurants seem to shy away from allocating the scarce table space on the basis of price, which is usually not raised on graduation day. Some moderate price increases may be hidden in the form of requiring the purchase of a special graduation meal, but this kind of price premium is nowhere near what would be needed to remove excess demand, as evidenced by the long lead time in accepting reservations. A possible explanation is that an exorbitant price might be widely discussed and reported, with a backlash that might harm future business. The higher the price, the lower the cost of rejecting the deal. In the monopoly example discussed above, a price of $14.99 would be rejected if the buyer is willing to incur a one-cent cost in order to punish the seller for charging such a price.

Several variants of the ultimatum game have been widely used in laboratory experiments because this game maximizes the tension between fairness considerations and the other extreme where people only care about their own earnings. Moreover, in the lab it is often possible to set up a one-shot situation with enough anonymity to eliminate any considerations of reputation, reward, and punishment. The next section describes an ultimatum experiment where laboratory control was a particularly difficult problem.

12.2 | Bargaining in the Bush

Jean Ensminger (2004) conducted an ultimatum experiment in a number of small villages in East Africa. All participants were members of the Orma clan. The Orma offer an interesting case where there is considerable variation in the extent of integration into a market economy, which may affect attitudes toward fairness. The more nomadic families raise cattle and live largely off the milk and other products, with very little being bought or sold in any market. Although some nomadic families have high wealth, which is kept in the herd, they typically have low incomes in terms of wage payments. Other Orma, in contrast, have chosen a more sedentary lifestyle for a variety of reasons, including the encroachment of grazing lands. Those who live sedentary lives in villages typically purchase food with money income obtained as wages or crop revenues. Thus exposure to a market economy is quite variable and is well measured as direct money income. Such income is not highly correlated with wealth, since some of the wealthiest are self-sufficient nomadic families with large herds. One can imagine at least two plausible conjectures about the effect of market integration on attitudes toward fairness. The first possibility is that interactions among nomadic people involve trust and reciprocity, whereas a market with more anonymous arrangements may make people more selfish. The opposite conclusion, however, could be reached by reasoning that many bargaining situations in a market context end up with individuals agreeing to split the difference, so that fair outcomes in an ultimatum game would be related to the degree of exposure to markets.

At least one adult was recruited from each household to play "fun games for real money." The experiments were conducted in grass houses, which enabled Ensminger to isolate groups of people during the course of the experiment. A grand master, who was known to all villagers, read the instructions. This person would turn away to avoid seeing decisions as they were made. The amount of money to be divided between the proposer and responder in each pair was set to be approximately equal to a typical day's wages (100 Kenyan shillings). The game was only played once. Each proposer would make an offer by moving some of the shillings to the other side of the table, before leaving the room while the responder was allowed to accept or reject this offer. Ensminger reports that the people enjoyed the game, despite some amusement at the "insanity" and "foolishness" of Western ways. She tried to move from one village to another before word of the results arrived.

The data for 56 bargaining pairs are shown in Figure 12.1. The average offer was 44 percent of the stake, with a clear mode at 50 percent. The lowest offer was 30 percent, and even these unequal splits were rarely rejected (as indicated by the light part at the bottom of the

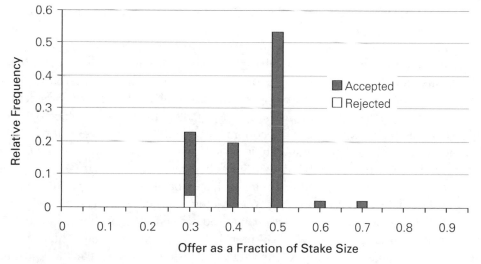

Source: (Ensminger 2004)

Figure 12.1   Distribution of Offers to Responders in an Ultimatum Game with the Orma (56 Pairs, One-Day Wage Stake)

bar). If people had foreseen that the 40 percent would all be accepted, then they might have lowered their offers. It is clear that the modal offer was not optimal in the sense of expected-payoff maximization against the actual ex post rejection pattern. People who made these generous offers almost always mentioned fairness as the justification in follow-up interviews. Ensminger was suspicious, however, and approached some reliable informants who revealed a different picture of the "talk of the village." The proposers were apparently obsessed with the possibility that low offers would be rejected, even though rejections were thought to be unlikely. Such obsessions suggest that expected-payoff maximization may not be an appropriate assumption for large amounts of money, e.g., a day's income. This conjecture is consistent with the payoff-scale effects on risk aversion discussed previously in Chapter 4.

In addition, it cannot be the case that individuals making relatively high offers were doing so *solely* out of fairness considerations, since offers were much lower in a second experiment in which the proposer's split of the same amount of money was automatically implemented. This game, without any possibility of rejection, is called a *dictator game*. The average offer fell from 44 percent in the ultimatum game to 31 percent when there was no possibility of rejection. Even though there seems to be some strategic reaction by proposers to their advantage in the dictator game, the modal offer was still at the fair or fifty-fifty division, and less than a tenth of the proposers kept all of the money.

Ensminger used a multiple regression to evaluate proposer offers in both the ultimatum and dictator games. In both cases, the presence of wage income is significantly related to offers; those with such market interactions tend to make higher offers. Her conjecture is that people exposed to face-to-face market transactions may be more used to the notion of splitting the difference. Variables such as age, gender, education, and wealth (in cattle equivalents) are not significant.

The unimportance of demographic effects relative to market organization measures is also evident in a cross-cultural study involving 15 small-scale societies on five continents (Henrich et al. 2001). This involved one-shot ultimatum games with comparable procedures that were conducted by anthropologists and economists. There was considerable variation, with the average offer ranging from 0.26 to 0.58 of the stake. The societies were ranked in two dimensions: the extent of economic cooperation and the extent of market integration. Both variables were highly significant in a regression, explaining about 61 percent of the variation, whereas individual variables like age, sex, and relative wealth were not. The lowest offers were observed in hunter-gatherer societies where very little production occurred outside of family units (e.g., the Machiguenga of Peru). The highest offers were observed in a society where production involved joint effort; offers above one-half for the Lamelara of Indonesia, who are whale hunters in large sea-going canoes. Thus, production requires assembling large groups of men and the division of whale meat after the hunt.

A one-shot ultimatum game, played for money, is a strange new experience for these people, and behavior seemed to be influenced by parallels with social institutions in some cases. The Ache of Paraguay, for example, made generous offers, above 0.5 on average. The proposed sharing in the ultimatum game has some parallels with a practice whereby Ache hunters with large kills will leave them at the edge of camp for others to find and divide.

12.3   Bargaining in the Lab

Ultimatum games have been conducted in more standard, student subject pools in many developed countries, and with stakes that are usually about $10. The mean offer, as a fraction of the stake, is typically about 0.4, and there seems to be less variation in the mean offer than was observed in the small-scale societies. Roth et al. (1991) report ultimatum game experiments that were run in four universities, each in a different country. The modal offer was 0.5 in the United States and Slovenia, as was the case for the Orma and for other studies in the United States (e.g., Forsythe et al. 1988). The modal offer was somewhat lower, 0.4, in Israel and Japan. Rejection rates in Israel and Japan were no higher than in the other two countries, despite the lower mean offers, which led the authors to conjecture that the differences in behavior across countries were due to different cultural norms about what is an acceptable division. These differences in behavior reported by Roth et al. (1991) were however, lower than the differences observed in the 15 small-scale societies, which are less homogeneous in the nature of their economic production activities.

Recall that the Orma made no offers below 0.3. In contrast, some student subjects in developed countries make offers of 0.2 or lower, and these low offers are rejected about half of the time. For example, consider the data in Figure 12.2, which is for a one-shot ultimatum game that was done in class, but with full money payments and a $10 stake. The mean offer was about 0.4 (as compared with 0.44 for the Orma), but about a quarter of the offers were 0.2 or below, and these were rejected one-third of the time.

Ultimatum bargaining behavior is relatively sensitive to various procedural details, and for that reason extreme care was taken in the Henrich et al. cross-cultural study. Hoffman et al. (1994) report that the *median* offer of 5 in an ultimatum game was reduced to 4 by putting the game into a market context. The market terminology had the proposer play the role of a seller who chose a take-it-or-leave-it price for a single unit. Interactions with posted prices are more anonymous than face-to-face negotiations, and market price terminology in the laboratory may stimulate less generous offers for this reason. The median offer fell again, to 3, when high scores on a trivia quiz were used to decide which person in each pair would play the role of the seller in the market. Presumably, this role-assignment effect is due to the fact that people may be more willing to accept an aggressive (low) offer from a person who earned the right make the offer.

Many business bargaining decisions are made by teams of managers or union officials, and several laboratory experiments have examined the offers made by groups of subjects in the laboratory. The general result is that groups tend to make lower offers to other groups, i.e., groups appear to be less fair-minded, or at least they expect other groups to be

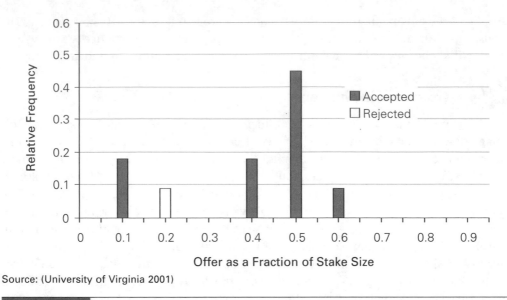

Source: (University of Virginia 2001)

| Figure 12.2 | Distribution of Offers to Responders in a One-Shot Ultimatum Game (11 Pairs, $10 Stake, Cash Payments) |

less fair-minded, as compared with individuals facing other individuals (Bornstein and Yaniv 1998). There is no clear consensus about what social dynamic is driving differences between individuals and groups, but experiments can shed some light on this process. Pallais (2005) reports an ultimatum experiment involving 220 subjects: 10 pairs of individuals, 10 paired groups of three, and 10 paired groups of seven. The pie size was $10 for the individuals, $30 for the three-person groups, and $70 for the seven-person groups. Each decision unit (group or individual) was placed in a separate classroom, and there was no imposed time limit for these one-shot ultimatum game decisions. Group discussions were not monitored, although all participants were asked to fill out ex post survey forms. The average offer made by the proposer was $4.40 for individuals, which was significantly higher than the average offers of $3.50 and $3.60 made by groups of three and seven respectively. In ex post surveys, the people in the individual treatment were much more likely to mention equity considerations. In addition, those in the individual treatment indicated more concern about the possible rejection of uneven offers than those in the group treatments did. This is a fine example of a research project done by a second-year undergraduate, with careful attention to procedural detail. For example, the decision was made not to use computers because of a fear that the person at the keyboard would control the discussion, and thereby diminish group size effects.

12.4   **Multi-Stage Bargaining**

Face-to-face negotiations are typically characterized by a series of offers and counter-offers. The ultimatum game can be transformed into a game with many stages by letting the players take turns making proposals about how to split an amount of money. If there is an agreement at any stage, then the agreed split is implemented. A penalty for delay can be inserted by letting the size of the stake shrink from one stage to the next. For example, the amount of money that could be divided in the first stage may be $5, but a failure to reach an agreement may reduce this stake to $2 in the second stage. If there is a pre-announced final stage and the responder in that stage does not agree, then both earn zero. Thus, the final stage is like an ultimatum game, and can be analyzed as such.

Consider a game with only two stages, with a money stake, $Y, in the first stage and a lower amount, $X, in the final stage. For simplicity, suppose that the initial stake is $15, which is reduced to $10 if no agreement is reached in the first round. *Warning: the analysis in this paragraph is based on the (questionable) assumption that people are perfectly rational and care only about their own payoffs.* Put yourself in the position of being the proposer in the first stage of this game, with the knowledge that both of you and the other player would always prefer the action with the highest payoff, even if that action only increases one's payoff by a penny. If you offer the other player too little in the first stage, then this offer will be rejected, since the other player becomes the proposer in the final (ultimatum game) stage. So you must figure out how much the other person would expect to earn in the final stage when they make a proposal to split the $10 that remains. In theory, the other person could make a second-stage offer of a penny, which you would accept under the assumption that you prefer more money (a penny) to less (zero). Hence, the other person would expect to earn $9.99 in the final stage, assuming perfect rationality and no concerns for fairness. If you offer less than $9.99 in the first stage, it will be rejected, and if you offer more it will be accepted. The least you could get away with offering in the first stage is, therefore, just a little more than $9.99, so you offer $10, leaving $5 for yourself, which is accepted.

In the previous example, the theoretical prediction is that the first-stage offer will equal the amount of the stake that would remain if bargaining were to proceed to the second stage. This result can be generalized. If the size of the money stake in the final stage is $X, then the person making the offer in that stage "should" offer the other a penny, which will be accepted. The person making the proposal in the final stage can obtain essentially the whole stake, i.e., $X − $0.01. Thus the person making an offer in the first stage can get away with offering a slightly higher amount, i.e., $X, which is accepted. In this two-stage game, the initial proposer earns the amount by which the pie shrinks, $Y − $X, and the other person earns the amount remaining in the second stage, $X.

An experiment with this two-stage structure is reported in Goeree and Holt (2001). The size of the stake in the initial stage was $5 in both cases. In one treatment, the pie was reduced to $2.00, so the first-stage offer should be $2.00, as shown in the middle column of

Table 12.1. The average first-stage offer was $2.17, quite close to this prediction. In a second treatment, shown on the right side of the table, the pie shrunk to $0.50, so the prediction is for the first-stage offer to be very inequitable ($0.50). The average offer was somewhat higher, at $1.62, as shown in the right column of the table. The reduction in the average offer was much less than predicted by the theory, and rejections were quite common in this second treatment. Notice that the cost of rejecting a low offer is low, and knowing this, the initial proposers were reluctant to exploit their advantage fully in this second treatment.

The effects of payoff inequities are even more dramatic in a second two-stage experiment reported by Goeree and Holt (2000). The initial proposers in this design made seven choices corresponding to seven different bargaining situations, with the understanding that only one of the situations would be selected afterward, at random, before the proposal for that situation was communicated to the other player. The initial pie size was $2.40 in all seven cases, but the second-stage pie size varied from $0.00 to $2.40, with five intermediate cases.

Two of the extreme treatments for this experiment are shown in Table 12.2. In the middle column, the pie shrinks from $2.40 to $0.00. This gives the initial proposer a large strategic advantage, so the initial offer would be a penny in a game between two selfish, rational players. This outcome would produce a sharp asymmetry in the payoffs in favor of the proposer. Adding insult to injury, the instructions for this case indicated (in a neutral manner) that the initial proposer would receive a fixed payment of $2.65 in addition to the earnings from the bargaining, whereas the initial responder would only receive $0.25. Only if the initial proposer were to offer the whole pie of $2.40 in the first stage would final earnings be equalized. This is listed as the "egalitarian first-stage offer" of $2.40 in the middle column. The average of the actual offers ($1.59) shown in the bottom row, is well above the Nash prediction ($0.01), and is closer to the egalitarian offer of $2.40.

A "low shrinkage" treatment is shown in the right-hand column of Table 12.2. Here the pie size only falls from $2.40 to $2.00 in the second stage, so the theoretical prediction is that the first-stage offer will be $2.00. The initial responder now has the strategic advantage, since the pie remains high in the final (ultimatum) stage when this person has the turn to

Table 12.1	A Two-Stage Bargaining Game Played Once	
	Treatment 1	**Treatment 2**
Size of Pie in First Stage	$5.00	$5.00
Size of Pie in Second Stage	$2.00	$0.50
Selfish Nash First-Stage Offer	$2.00	$0.50
Average First-Stage Offer	**$2.17**	**$1.62**

Source: (Goeree and Holt 2000)

Table 12.2	A Two-Stage Bargaining Game with Asymmetric Fixed Payments	
	Full Shrinkage	**Low Shrinkage**
Size of Pie in First Stage	$2.40	$2.40
Size of Pie in Second Stage	$0.00	$2.00
Proposer Fixed Payment	$2.65	$0.65
Responder Fixed Payment	$0.25	$2.25
Egalitarian First-Stage Offer	**$2.40**	**$0.40**
Selfish Nash First-Stage Offer	$0.01	$2.00
Average First-Stage Offer	**$1.59**	**$0.78**

Source: (Goeree and Holt 2000)

make the final offer. To make matters even more asymmetric, this strategic advantage is complemented with a high fixed payment to the initial responder. The only way for the disadvantaged initial proposer to obtain equal earnings would be to offer only $0.40 in the first stage, despite the fact that the theoretical prediction (assuming selfish behavior) is $2.00. The average of the observed offers, $0.78, is much closer to the egalitarian offer of $0.40.

To summarize, the first-stage offers in this experiment should be equal to the remaining pie size, but the asymmetric fixed payments were structured so that the egalitarian offers would be inversely related to the remaining pie size. This inverse relationship was generally present in the data for the seven treatments. The authors show that the data patterns are roughly consistent with an enriched model in which people care about relative earnings as well as their own earnings. For example, a person may be willing to give up some money to avoid having the other person earn more, which is an aversion to disadvantageous inequity. Roughly speaking, think of this as an "envy effect." It is also possible that people might wish to avoid making significantly more than the other person, which would be an aversion to advantageous inequity. Think of this as a kind of "guilt effect," which is likely to be weaker than the envy effect. These two effects are captured by a formal model of *inequity aversion* proposed by Fehr and Schmidt (1999). To get a feel for this model, let π_{self} denote a person's own payoff, and let π_{other} denote the other person's payoff. Then, as shown in Equation 12.1, the Fehr-Schmidt utility function can be represented as follows:

$$U(\pi_{self}, \pi_{other}) = \begin{cases} \pi_{self} - \alpha(\pi_{other} - \pi_{self}) & \text{if } \pi_{other} > \pi_{self} \quad \text{(Envy)} \\ \pi_{self} - \beta(\pi_{self} - \pi_{other}) & \text{if } \pi_{self} > \pi_{other} \quad \text{(Guilt)} \end{cases} \tag{12.1}$$

where α is an envy parameter, β is a guilt parameter, and $\alpha > \beta > 0$. Goeree and Holt (2000) use the two-stage bargaining game data to estimate these guilt and envy parameters, and they conclude that the envy effect is more pronounced.

Extensions: "I Will Be Spending Years Trying to Figure Out What This All Meant."

The first ultimatum experiment was reported by Güth et al. (1982), and the results were replicated by Forsythe et al. (1988), who introduced the dictator game. There have been many experiments in other, less-structured negotiations, where the order of proposal and response is not imposed by the experimenter. For example, Hoffman and Spitzer (1982, 1985) used an open, unstructured setting to evaluate the ability of bargainers to make binding agreements on efficient outcomes, irrespective of property rights (the Coase theorem). Similarly, generalizations of the ultimatum game have been used to study bargaining in legislatures in which the proposer is selected at random (see Chapter 18 on voting). Economists and others have been fascinated by behavior in these games where there is a high tension between notions of fairness and strategic, narrowly self-interested behavior. Ensminger (2004) reports that one of her African subjects jovially remarked: "I will be spending years trying to figure out what this all meant."

Many economists were initially skeptical of the high degree of seemly non-strategic play and costly rejections. Sefton (1992) found that allocations to the passive responder in dictator games fell by about a half when hypothetical payoffs were replaced by "normal" money payoffs. In ultimatum games, one possibility is that "irrational" rejections would diminish when the stakes of the game are increased, and that proposers would anticipate this and demand more. Hoffman et al. (1996) increased the stakes from $10 to $100, which did not have much effect on initial proposals. Carpenter, Verhoogen, and Burks (2005) assign subjects randomly to high and low stakes treatments, and they find no effect of going from $10 to $100 stakes with student subjects, for either proposals made in ultimatum games or demands made in dictator games. The effects of high stakes have also been studied by Slonim and Roth (1998) and List and Cherry (2000). For a field experiment, see Carpenter, Burks, and Verhoogen (2005). Falk and Fehr (2003) present a thoughtful analysis of the value of laboratory and field experiments that focus on labor market issues. See Eckel and Grossman (1998, 1999) for a discussion of gender effects in bargaining experiments.

Rejections are not, of course, irrational if individuals have preferences that depend on relative earnings. For example, a responder may prefer that both earn equal zero amounts to a situation with inequitable positive earnings. Bolton and Ockenfels (1998) proposed a model with preferences based on relative earnings, and Fehr and Schmidt (1999) developed a closely related model of inequity aversion that was mentioned above.

It is somewhat unusual for a seller to offer one unit only for sale to a buyer, and a multi-unit setup provides the buyer with an option for partial rejection. Suppose that there are 10 units for sale. Each costs $0 to produce, and each unit is worth $1 to the buyer. The seller posts a price for the 10 units as a group, but the buyer can decide to purchase a smaller number, which reduces each party's earnings proportionately. For example, suppose that the seller posts a price of $6, which would provide earnings of $6 for the seller and $4 for the buyer. By purchasing only half of the units, the buyer reduces these earnings to $3 for the seller and $2 for the buyer. This partial rejection option is implemented in the Veconlab software as a "squish" option (Andreoni, Castillo, and Petrie 2003). If this option is permitted, the responder can choose a fraction that indicates the extent of acceptance: with 0 being full rejection and 1 being full acceptance.

The importance of emotions in the rejection of unfair offers is reinforced by Xiao and Houser (2005), who report that such rejections are reduced in a laboratory experiment in which responders are allowed to express their emotional reactions to offers at the same time that the accept or reject decision is communicated to the proposer. Thus, cheap talk comments provide a substitute for costly rejections of unfair offers. Here is a case where taking the social context out of the original ultimatum game experiments produced perplexing outcomes, and putting some of the context back in led to data that are closer to game-theoretic predictions!

Another angle on the process of irrational rejections can be obtained by monitoring brain activity as people play ultimatum games. Sanfay et al. (2003) used functional magnetic resonance imaging (fMRI) to monitor blood flows to various parts of the participants' brains. Unfair offers stimulated activity in brain areas that are associated with both cognition (prefrontal cortex) and emotion (anterior insula). The heightened activity in the later areas when unfair offers were rejected indicates the importance of emotions in this process. This anterior insula activity was higher for offers that were more unequal, and it was higher when the offers were perceived as coming from other people, as opposed to offers that were computer generated. The particular area of anterior insula activity has been identified in other studies of "disgust" involving negative physical sensations of taste and odor. Thus, the results of the fMRI ultimatum study offer indirect evidence that unfair offers activate emotions similar to those resulting from a bad taste or smell.

QUESTIONS

1. Sometimes it is said that the person who makes the first move in a game has a strategic advantage, and this is the case for a simple ultimatum game. What game covered in this chapter does not necessarily provide a strategic advantage to the first mover? Explain.

2. Consider a two-stage alternating offer game with a pie of size $3 in the first stage, which shrinks to $2 in the second and final stage. Find the equilibrium first-stage offer, and explain whether it will be accepted, under the assumption that people are perfectly selfish and rational.

3. Consider a legislature composed of five voters, A, B, C, D, and E. There is a pot of money, $30, to be split, and if there is no agreement, most of this money is lost, since the earnings in the event of no agreement are $5 for A, $4 for B, $3 for C, $2 for D, and

$1 for E. Voter A is exogenously selected to make a single proposal for the division of the $30, which will then be considered in a vote, where each person votes yes or no. If at least three yes votes are obtained, then the proposed split is enacted, and if not, then the default payments are received. No amendments or further motions are allowed. What should voter A propose on the assumption that all voters are selfish and perfectly rational? After reading about the ultimatum game, would you advise voter A to propose something else? Explain.

4. A "disadvantageous counteroffer" is said to happen in a two-stage bargaining game when a person rejects an initial offer of $X and the pie then shrinks so that that person's counteroffer provides less money than the amount they just rejected. Give an example of this outcome, using specific numbers (make up your own game and the numbers for the initial offer and the counter offer). Would the Fehr-Schmidt utility function explained in Section 12.4 (with $1 > \alpha > \beta > 0$) be capable of explaining disadvantageous counteroffers?

chapter 13

Trust, Reciprocity, and Principal-Agent Games

Although increases in the size of the market may promote productive specialization and trade, the accompanying increase in anonymity raises the need to trust in trading relationships. The trust game sets up a stylized situation where one person can decide how much of an initial stake to keep and how much to pass to the other person. All money passed is augmented, and the responder then decides how much of this augmented amount to keep and how much to pass back to the initial decision maker. The trust game experiment puts participants into this situation so that they can experience the tension between private motives and the potential gains from trust and cooperation.

The gift-exchange view of wage setting is that employers set wages above market-clearing levels in an effort to elicit high effort responses, even though those responses are not explicitly rewarded ex post after wages have been set. The reciprocity game experiment is one where each employer is matched with a worker who first sees the wage that is offered and then decides on the level of costly effort to supply. The issue is whether notions of trust and reciprocity may have noticeable effects in a market context. The reciprocity game can be generalized by allowing the employer to choose a contract with penalty and/or ex post bonus provisions. All of the games considered can be run with the Veconlab software, by selecting the desired experiment under the Bargaining/Fairness menu.

13.1 The Trust Game

The *trust game* was examined in an experiment reported by Berg, Dickhaut, and McCabe (1995), with the objective of studying trust and reciprocity in a controlled setting. A standard version begins when one person in each pair is given $10. The first mover must decide how much (if any) of this money to pass to the other person, and how much to keep. Money that is passed is tripled before it is given to the second mover, who decides how much (if any) to return to the first person. The first mover earns the amount kept initially plus any money that is returned. The second mover earns the amount that is kept in the second stage. The game would typically be explained as an investment game, in order to avoid the suggestive "trust" terminology. If this game is only played once, as is often the case in experiments, then the subgame perfect Nash equilibrium for selfish players is for the second person to keep all that is passed, and hence for the first mover to pass nothing. The action of passing money initially would signal that the first mover trusts the second mover to return a reasonable amount of money, perhaps due to a feeling of reciprocity generated by the initial action.

Berg, Dickhaut, and McCabe ran this experiment with 32 pairs of participants in a single round interaction. Of these, almost all of the senders (30 of 32) passed a positive amount of money, and only about a third of the responders returned more than was sent. The average amount passed was $5.16 (out of $10), and after being tripled, the average amount returned was 18 percent. These behavior patterns are inconsistent with the prediction of a subgame-perfect Nash equilibrium for purely selfish players. (The idea of a subgame perfect equilibrium is discussed in Chapter 23, but what it means here is that the responder always maximizes the payoff in the final stage.)

Table 13.1 shows the amounts passed and returned for six pairs of individuals in a single-round demonstration experiment, which was run at the University of Virginia with full payment and with the standard parameters ($10 given to proposers, with the amount passed being tripled). Thus, in the aggregate, proposers were given $60. Based on the Berg, Dickhaut, and McCabe results, one would expect about half ($30) to be passed, which when tripled, would become $90, and about 18 percent of that ($16) to be returned. For the six pairs shown in the table, the aggregate amount passed was $33, which was tripled to $99, but only $10 was returned. In this experiment, the responders clearly did not live up to the expectations of the proposers, unless proposers were mainly trying to increase responder earnings.

Figure 13.1 shows the results of a classroom trust game run with random matchings and with amounts passed being tripled. This setting clearly induced a significant amount of money being passed (light bars), on average, and average return amounts (dark) that were just enough, on average, to reimburse the first movers.

Table 13.1	A Demonstration Trust Game Experiment					
	ID1	**ID2**	**ID3**	**ID4**	**ID5**	**ID6**
Amount Passed	$0	$10	$2	$10	$1	$10
Amount Returned	$0	$0	$0	$0	$0	$10
Proposer's Earnings	$10	$0	$8	$0	$9	$10
Responder's Earnings	$0	$30	$6	$30	$3	$20

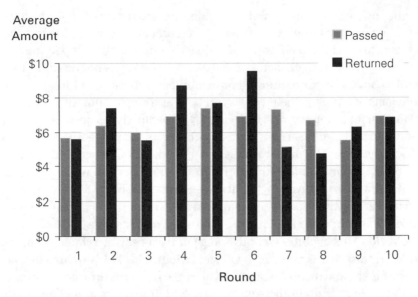

Source: (Veconlab Class Experiment at the University of Massachucetts)

Figure 13.1 A Classroom Trust Game

There has been considerable discussion of possible reasons for deviations of behavior from the Nash predictions for selfish players. Cox (1999) replicated the Berg, Dickhaut, and McCabe results, and compared the amounts passed with behavior in a second treatment where the responder did not have the opportunity to reciprocate. The amounts passed were not significantly different for the two treatments, which is evidence that the pass behavior may not be due to anticipated reciprocity. Cox suggested that the positive amounts typically passed and tripled were due to *altruism*, i.e., a kindness or other-regarding preference for increasing another person's earnings, even at some cost to oneself. Altruism is often mentioned as an explanation for voluntary contributions in public goods games discussed in Chapter 14. If altruism is driving these contributions, then it may not be the whole story, since responder behavior is not very cooperative. One difference, however, is that what is passed is tripled and what is returned is not altered, so the cost of altruism is lower for proposers. Cox argues that altruism is a factor in responder behavior, but he notes that reciprocity may also be involved, since responders tend to return more when the amount passed was decided on by a real proposer than in a second treatment where the amount passed was pre-set at a required level. Such reciprocity could arise if participants feel some social pressure to return a part of the gains from money passed by another person, despite the anonymity of the experimental procedures. A similar explanation would be that concern for the other's earnings goes up if the other person has shown some initial kindness.

Many economic interactions in market economies are repeated, and this repetition may enable trading partners to develop trust and reciprocal arrangements. For one thing, both people have the freedom to break out of a binary trading relationship in the event that the other's performance is not satisfactory. Even when a breakup is not possible, the repetition may increase levels of cooperation. For example, Cochard, Van Phu, and Willinger (2004) report results of a trust game that was run both as a single-shot interaction and as a repeated interaction for seven periods, but with payoff parameters scaled down to account for the higher number of periods. There were some other minor procedural differences that will not be discussed here. The main result is that the amounts passed and returned were higher in the repeated-interaction treatment. In the final period, which was known in advance, the amount passed stayed high, but the amount returned was very low.

Repeated interactions in market economies involve important elements of trust, and the mutual profitability of effective trust relationships suggests an evolutionary basis for this type of behavior. This evolutionary advantage of trust may be related to an apparent biological basis for trust that is reported by Kosfeld, Heinrichs, Zak, Fischbacher, and Fehr (2005). They ran a standard trust game in which participants in one treatment were exposed to a nasal spray containing oxytocin, a substance that is associated with social bonding behavior. In particular, oxytocin receptors are found in brain regions that are associated with pairing, maternal care, sexual approach, and monogamous relationships in non-human mammals. The (human) subjects in the oxytocin treatment passed 17 percent more on average, and they passed the maximum amount at twice the rate of the control group. The return rates were not significantly different.

13.2 A Labor Market Reciprocity Game

This game implements a setup where participants are matched in pairs, with one setting a wage and the other choosing an effort level. The person in the employer role is free to choose any wage between specified limits. This wage is paid irrespective of the worker's subsequent effort decision, which must be between zero and some upper limit. A higher level of worker effort is costly to the worker and beneficial to the employer. This is sometimes called a *reciprocity game*, since the employer may offer a high wage in the hope that the worker will reciprocate with high effort. In the experiment to be discussed, the wage was between $0 and $10, and the worker effort was required to be between 0 and 10. Each additional unit of effort reduced the worker's earnings by $0.25, and added $3.00 to the employer's earnings. Thus, economic efficiency would require an effort of 10 in this context. Employers did not know workers' costs, and workers did not know the value of effort to the employer.

The results of a classroom reciprocity game with these parameters are shown in Figure 13.2. The first 10 periods were done with random matchings, which gives workers little incentive to provide acceptable efforts. The average efforts, shown by the small dots, leveled off at about two in rounds 3–8, followed by a sharp fall at the end. The final period

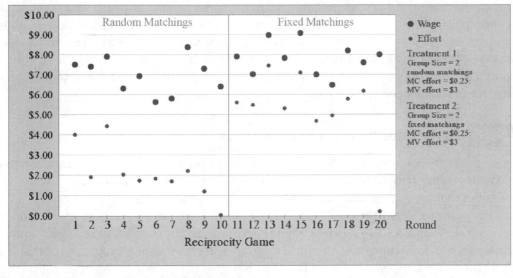

Key: Average Wage (Large Dot) and Effort (Small Dot)

| **Figure 13.2** | A Classroom Reciprocity Game Random Matchings (Rounds 1–10) and Fixed Matchings (Rounds 11–20) |

efforts of zero indicate that workers were aware that they had no incentive to be cooperative if employers had no opportunity to reciprocate. The second treatment was done with fixed matchings, and the increased incentive to cooperate resulted in much higher effort levels (until the final period) and higher earnings. For experimental evidence of reciprocity in a related context, see Fehr, Kirchsteiger, and Riedl (1993).

The reciprocity game can be given a richer structure by letting the employer propose a contract that has both a wage and some inducement for the worker to provide a specified goal level of effort. There are two likely directions that the employer might follow, the "stick" of stipulating a penalty if an effort goal is not achieved, and the "carrot" of stipulating an ex post bonus if the effort goal is reached. As in the reciprocity game, effort is costly for the worker and beneficial for the employer, and the worker always has the option of rejecting the contract, causing zero earnings for both. Fehr, Klein, and Schmidt (2001) ran an experiment of this type, where the ex post bonus mentioned in the contract was always purely optional, i.e., the employer could state a bonus amount if the goal effort is met and then not provide it. The penalty was a fine to be paid by the worker to the firm in the event of a low effort, but it could not always be collected, since collection required the verification of a third person, which only happened with one-third probability in the experiment. The penalty was constrained not to be too large. These were one-time games with random matching, so a selfish employer never had an incentive to keep a promise to pay a bonus, and therefore, a skeptical worker would not expect a bonus. When employers had to choose between bonus and penalty contracts, most of the contracts proposed and accepted were bonus contracts. This structure can be implemented with the Veconlab Principal Agent Game, and it was run with 24 students in a Contract Law Class at the University of Virginia (with hypothetical payments). As with the research experiment, bonus contracts were more commonly used (about three-fourths of the time). Moreover, efforts were lower for the penalty contracts.

13.4 Experiments: Field Experiments

As the surveys in Camerer (2003) and Fehr and Schmidt (2003) indicate, experiments involving trust and *reciprocity* are being widely used to obtain social preference measures that are comparable across cultures and to evaluate cultural differences.

For example, Fershtman and Gneezy (2001) used the trust game to measure attitudes between subjects from two different ethnic backgrounds. The subjects were Jewish undergraduates with last names that identified them as being from either Ashkenazic or Eastern backgrounds. Each person was told the last name of the person with whom they were matched, but not the person's identity. The data showed a significant distrust of those from Eastern backgrounds, with less money being passed in the standard trust game. This could be due to less concern for the earnings of those of Eastern origin, or it could be due to a belief that less will be returned. A parallel dictator game was used to distinguish these two explanations. The amounts given to the recipient in the dictator game were not affected by the recipient's ethnic origin. The authors concluded that the lower offers were driven by a fear that reciprocity would be less prevalent among those of Eastern origin.

Barr (2003) used the trust game experiment in a field study of 28 Zimbabwean villages in which transplanted farmers had to build new social relationships with strangers. Interestingly, the games themselves broke through villagers' reluctance to talk candidly and stimulated a lot of discussion, often initiated by the participants instead of the researchers. The villagers were fascinated by the metaphor of the trust game and what the results revealed about their own levels of trust and trustworthiness.

There is at least a public perception that business professionals are more selfish. Fehr and List (2004) investigated this issue by running a variant of a trust game experiment on parallel groups of students and CEOs. The students were from the University of Costa Rica, and the CEOs were attending the Costa Rica Coffee Institute's annual conference in 2001. The rules of the game were the same for both subject pools, except that payoffs for the CEOs were scaled up by a factor of 10 to equalize the importance of the incentives. The game was run as a trust game, with the proposer deciding how much to pass, and the responder deciding how much of the tripled pass amount to return. One change from the standard trust game was that the proposer had to stipulate a recommended payback amount in advance. The recommended payback was cheap talk, in the sense that it had no effect on the way that earnings were calculated from the pass and return decisions in this treatment. The results of the experiment contradicted the authors' conjecture that CEOs would be more selfish. The CEOs passed more than students, and for a given level of trans-fer, they tended to return more. The authors concluded that the CEOs were more trusting and more trustworthy. This result is fascinating, and it would be interesting to see it repli-cated with different subject pools and some other treatment variations.

Fehr and List ran a second treatment in which the proposer had an additional option of imposing a fixed penalty on responders who did not return the suggested payback amount. The size of the penalty was fixed, and the penalty was paid to the experimenter out of responder earnings. In this treatment, the proposer chose an amount to pass, a suggested give-back amount, and whether or not the penalty would be assessed if the responder did not meet the suggested give-back amount. Responders knew that the proposer had the option of imposing a penalty or not. Interestingly, having the option to impose a penalty and choosing *not* to impose it had a positive effect on pass-back amounts and on the pro-poser's earnings, both for students and for CEOs. The authors termed this a hidden benefit of incentives. In contrast, the imposition of the penalty option actually reduced the amount that responders tended to pass back, from 61 percent payback to 33 percent. This hidden cost of control is also documented in a parallel laboratory experiment (Falk and Fehr 2005).

The evidence of trusting behavior among CEOs in Costa Rica may be easier to under-stand in the context of a study by Karlin (2005), who used a laboratory trust game with bor-rowers in a non-profit village credit program in Peru. Both trusting and trustworthy behavior were generally correlated with geographic and social distance proximity. The inno-vative aspect of the experiment is the tie to field behavior. The experiment predicted pay-back behavior of the responders *over a year later*! Responders who returned more in the trust game experiment, and hence were more trustworthy, tended to pay back their credit union loans at a higher rate. In contrast, the savings and payback rates were lower for those who passed more in the trust game and would normally be classified as trusting. Since pay-back failures are subject primarily to informal sanctions, Karlin speculates that people who pass large amounts might simply be more willing to take a risk; and Schechter (2006) reaches similar conclusions on the basis of a trust game experiment conducted in Paraguay. In Karlin's experiment, the "trustworthy" people who return more in the trust game are often involved in one-on-one loans from acquaintances, whereas those who pass more in the experiment tend to borrow bilaterally less often, which could be because they are viewed as risk takers and bad credit risks. As Karlin notes, the act of passing money in the trust game is itself risky, as one of the people in the proposer role pointed out by remarking "Voy a jugar," which literally means "I'm going to play," but on the street means "I'm going to gamble."

QUESTIONS

1. Consider a trust game in which the Porposer has $10 that can be kept or passed, and what is passed gets tripled. If the Responder is expected to return nothing, then the Proposer is essentially choosing a pair of money payoffs. Represent the choices by a

straight "budget line" in a graph with the Proposer's payoff on the horizontal axis and the Responder's payoff on the vertical axis.

2. Suppose that the Proposer for the trust game in Question 1 decides to pass $10. Now the Responder gets to choose how much each person ends up earning. Represent the possible choices by a straight line in the graph for your answer to Question 1.

The following questions presume a knowledge of intermediate microeconomics.

3. What do the indifference curves for a perfectly selfish Proposer look like in the graph with the Proposer's payoff on the horizontal axis?

4. An "altruistic" Responder would be willing to give up some money to raise the Proposer's earnings. Would the indifference curves for an altruistic Responder have positive or negative slopes? Explain.

5. Think of "reciprocity" as a response to money passed by the Proposer that makes the Responder more altruistic, i.e. more willing to give up earnings to raise the Proposer's earnings. What is the effect of reciprocity on the Responder's indifference curves in a graph with Proposer earnings on the horizontal axis?

part 4

Public Choice

Many public programs and policies are designed to remedy situations where the actions taken by some people affect the well being of others. The classic example is the provision of a public good like national defense, which can be consumed freely by all without crowding and the possibility of exclusion. Chapter 14 introduces a model of voluntary contributions to a public good, where the private cost to each person is less than the social benefit. Non-selfish motives for giving are discussed in the context of laboratory experiments. A similar situation with external benefits arises when it takes only one volunteer to provide the good outcome preferred by all. The volunteer's dilemma (whether to incur the private cost to achieve this good outcome) is discussed in Chapter 15. This game is different from a standard public goods setup in that the private benefit to the volunteer exceeds the cost.

External effects on others' well being may arise in a negative sense as well, as is the case with pollution or overuse of a common resource. The common pool resource game in Chapter 16 is a setting where each person's efforts to secure benefits from a shared resource tend to diminish the value that others derive from their efforts, as might happen with excessive harvests from a fishery. The resource is like a public good in the sense that the problem arises from non-exclusion, but the difference is the presence of congestion effects, i.e., when one person's use reduces the value for others.

Chapter 17 introduces a problem of wasteful competition that may arise in non-market allocation procedures. In "beauty contest" competitions for a broadcast license, for example, the contenders may spend considerable amounts of real resources in the process of lobbying. Such lobbying expenses are examples of rent seeking, and the total cost of such activities may even exceed the value of the prize (full dissipation of rents). Factors that affect rent dissipation in theory are evaluated in the context of laboratory experiments.

Public expenditures are typically influenced by voting and other political processes, and the outcomes of such processes can be sensitive to the rules that govern voting. Chapter 18 provides an introduction to the results of voting in the laboratory and of related field experiments in political science.

chapter 14

Voluntary Contributions

This chapter is based on the standard voluntary contributions game, in which the private net benefit from making a contribution is negative unless others reciprocate later or the person receives satisfaction from the benefit provided to others. The setup makes it possible to investigate independent variations of the private internal benefit and the public external benefit to others. These and other treatment manipulations in experiments are used to evaluate alternative explanations for observed patterns of contributions. The Veconlab Public Goods game can be conducted prior to class discussion. Alternatively, a hand-run version using playing cards is easy to implement using the instructions provided in the Class Experiments section.

14.1 Social Norms and Public Goods

The selfish caricature of *homo economicus* implies that individuals will get a free ride from the public benefits provided by others' activities. Such free-riding may result in the under-provision of public goods. A pure public good, like national defense, has several key characteristics. It is *jointly provided* and *non-excludable* in the sense that the production required to make the good available to one person will ensure that it is available to all others in the group. In particular, access cannot be controlled. It is *non-rivaled* in the sense that one person's consumption of the good is not affected by another's, i.e., there is no congestion.

When a single individual provides a public good, like shoveling a sidewalk, the private provision cost may exceed the private benefit, even though the social benefit for all others exceeds the provision cost incurred by that person. The resulting misallocations have been recognized since Adam Smith's (1776) discussion of the provision of street lamps.

In many cases there is not a bright-line distinction between private and public goods. For example, parks are generally considered to be public goods, although they may become crowded and require some method of exclusion. A good that is rivaled but non-excludable is sometimes called a *common-pool resource*, which is the topic of Chapter 16. With common-pool resources like ground water resources, fisheries, or public grazing grounds, the problem is typically how to manage the resource to prevent overuse, since individuals may not take into account the negative effects that their own usage has on others. In contrast, most public goods are not provided by nature, and the major problems often pertain to provision of the appropriate amounts of the good.

Goods are often produced by those who receive the greatest benefit, but under-provision can be a problem if there are some public benefits to others that are not fully valued by the provider. Education, for example, offers clear economic advantages to the student, but the public at large also benefits from having a well-educated citizenry. A public goods problem remains when not all of the benefits are enjoyed by the provider, and this is one of the rationales for the heavy public involvement in school systems. The mere presence of public benefits does not necessarily justify public provision of such goods, given the inefficiencies and distortions due to the need to collect taxes. The political problems associated with public goods are complicated when the benefits are unequally distributed, e.g., public broadcasting of cultural materials.

In close-knit societies, public goods problems may be mitigated by the presence of social norms that dictate or reward other-regarding behavior. For example, Hawkes (1993) reports that large game hunters in primitive societies are expected to share a kill with all households in a village, and sometimes even with those of neighboring villages. Such wide-spread sharing seems desirable given the difficulty of meat storage and the diminishing marginal value of excess consumption in a short period of time. These social norms transform a good that would normally be thought of as private into a good that is jointly provided and non-excludable. This transformation is desirable since the private return from large-game hunting is lower than the private return from gathering and scavenging. For example, the "!Kung" of Botswana and Namibia are hunter-gatherer societies where large prey (e.g., warthogs) are widely shared, but small animals and plant food are typically kept within the household. Hawkes (1993) estimated that, at one point, male large-game hunters acquired an average of 28,000 calories per day, with only about one-tenth of that (2,500) going to an individual household. In contrast, the collection of plant foods yielded an estimated 5,000 calories per day, even after accounting for the extra processing required for the preparation of such food. Large-game hunting by males was more productive for the village as a whole, but had a return for individual households of about one-half of the level that could be obtained from unshared gathering activities. Nevertheless, many of the men continued to engage in hunting activities, perhaps due to the tendency for all to share the kills in a type of reciprocal arrangement. Hawkes, however, questioned the reciprocity hypothesis since some men were consistently much better hunters than others, and yet all were involved in the sharing arrangements. She stressed the importance of more private, fitness-related incentives, e.g., that successful large-game hunters have more allies and better opportunities for mating.

14.2   "Economists Free-Ride, Does Anyone Else?"

Economists are sometimes ridiculed for ignoring social norms and simply assuming that individuals will free-ride on the generosity of others. An early public goods experiment is reported by two sociologists, Marwell and Ames (1981). Their experiment involved groups of high school students who could either invest an initial endowment in a private exchange or a public exchange. Investment in the public exchange produced a net loss to the individual, even though the benefits to others were substantially above an individual's private cost. Nevertheless, the authors observed significant amounts of investment in the public exchange, with the major exception being when the experiment was done with a group of economics doctoral students. The resulting paper was titled: "Economists Free-Ride, Does Anyone Else?"

The Marwell and Ames paper initiated much literature on the extent to which subjects incur private costs in activities that benefit others. A typical experiment involves giving each person an endowment of tokens to be invested in a private exchange or account, with earnings per token that exceed the earnings per token obtained from investment in the public account. For example, each token might produce $.10 for the investor when invested in the private account, but only $.05 for the investor and for each of the others when invested in the public account. In this example, the social optimum would be to invest all tokens in the public account as long as the number of individuals in the group, N, is greater than 2, since the social benefit $5N$ would be greater than the private benefit of 10 for each token when $N > 2$. The $.10 private return can be thought of as the opportunity cost of investment in the public account. The ratio of the per capita benefit to the opportunity cost is sometimes called the *marginal per capita return (MPCR)*, which would be $5/10 = 0.5$ in this example. A higher MPCR reduces the net cost of making a contribution to the public account. For example, if the private account returns $.10 and the per-capita return on the public account is raised to $.09, there is only a $.01 private loss associated with the investment. Many of the experiments involved changes in the MPCR.

A second treatment variable of interest is the number of people involved, since a higher group size increases the social benefit of an investment in the public exchange when the MPCR is held constant. The social benefit in the example from the previous paragraph is $5N$, which is increasing in N. Alternatively, think about what you would do if you could give up $10 in order to return $1 to every member of the student body at your university, including yourself. Here, the MPCR is only 0.1, but the public benefit is extremely large. The motives for contribution to a public good are amplified if others are expected to reciprocate in the future. These considerations suggest that contributions might be sensitive to factors such as group size, the MPCR, and whether or not the public goods experiment involves repetition with the same group. In multi-round experiments, individuals are given new endowments of tokens at the start of each round, and groups can either be fixed or randomly reconfigured in subsequent rounds.

The upshot is that the extent of voluntary contributions to public goods depends on a wide variety of procedural factors, although there is considerable debate about whether contributions are primarily due to kindness, reciprocal reactions to others' kindness, or confusion. For example, there is likely to be more confusion in a one-time investment decision, and many people may initially divide their endowment of tokens equally between the two types of investment: public and private. This is analogous to the typical choice of dividing one's retirement fund contributions equally between stocks and bonds at the start of one's career. Some of the Marwell and Ames experiments involved a single decision, e.g., administered by a questionnaire that was mailed to high school students. Subsequent experiments by economists (that did *not* involve economics doctoral students) showed that repetition typically produced a declining pattern of contributions. People may stop contributing if others are observed to be getting a free ride. One motive for making contributions may be to prevent others from behaving in this manner, in the hope that contributions will be reciprocated in subsequent rounds. This reciprocity motive is obviously weaker in the final rounds. Although contributions tend to decline, some people even contribute in the final period. We begin with a summary of an experiment with a single round of decision making.

14.3 Single-Round Experiments

Ensminger (2004) reports the results of a public goods experiment involving young men of the Orma, a society from Kenya (see Chapter 12). Participants were divided into groups of four, and each person was given 50 shillings that could be kept or invested in a group project. Investments were made by placing tokens in envelopes, which were shuffled to preserve anonymity. The contents were emptied and publicly counted by a member of the group before being doubled by the experimenter and divided equally among the participants. For example, if one person contributed two shillings, they were doubled and the resulting four shillings were distributed, one per person. Thus, a contribution of two shillings yielded a private return of one, so the MPCR was 0.5.

The data for this single-round game is shown in Figure 14.1. The modal contribution is four-tenths of the endowment, with a fair amount of variation. In fact, one-quarter of the 24 participants contributed the entire 50 shillings. The average contribution was about 60 percent, which is at the high end of the 40–60 percent range observed in the first round of most public goods experiments done in the United States (Ledyard 1995). The absence of complete free-riding by anyone is notable in Figure 14.1. Ensminger conjectures that contributions were enhanced by familiarity with the Harambee institution used to arrange funding of public projects like schools. This practice involves the specification of suggested income-based voluntary contributions for each household, with social pressures for compliance. In fact, some of the participants commented on the similarity of the Harambee and the experimental setup, and a major Harambee solicitation was in progress at the time of the experiment.

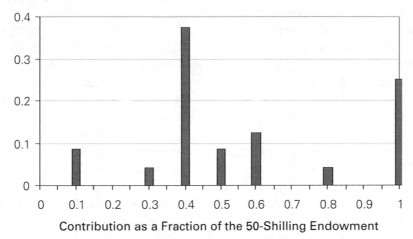

Relative
Frequency

Contribution as a Fraction of the 50-Shilling Endowment

Source: (Ensminger 2004)

Figure 14.1 Contributions to a Group Project for Young Orma Males, with Group Size = 4 and an MPCR = 0.5

MPCR Effects

The next topic is the extent to which contributions are affected by treatment variables like MPCR and group size. Goeree, Holt, and Laury (2002) report an experiment in which participants had to make decisions for 10 different treatments in which an endowment of 25 tokens was allocated to public and private uses. Subjects were paid $6 and were told that only one of the treatments would be selected ex post to determine additional earnings. This was a single-round experiment in the sense that there was no feedback obtained from decisions, and only one decision counted. A token kept was worth $.05 in all ten cases. In one treatment, a token contributed returned $.02 to each of the four participants. This yielded an MPCR of 0.4 since each $.05 foregone from the private return yielded $.02 from the public return, and 2/5 = 0.4. In another treatment, a token contributed returned $.04 to each of the four participants, so these treatments held the group size constant and increased the MPCR from 0.4 to 0.8. This doubling of the MPCR essentially doubled average contributions, from 4.9 to 10.6 tokens. Of the 32 participants, 25 increased their contributions, 3 decreased, and 4 showed no change. The null hypothesis, that increases are just as likely as decreases, can be rejected using any standard statistical test. Determining the significance level for such a test in this within-subjects design is analogous to computing the chances of getting 25 or more heads from 28 flips of a fair coin. This probability is less than 0.01, so the null hypothesis of equal probabilities (fair coin) can be rejected at the 1 percent significance level.

Internal and External Return Effects

In each of the treatments discussed, the benefit to oneself for contributing is exactly equal to the benefit that every other person receives. In many public goods settings, however, the person making a voluntary contribution may enjoy a greater personal benefit than others. For example, benefactors give money for projects that they particularly value for some reason. It is quite common for gifts to medical research teams to be related to illnesses that impact the donor's family. Even in Adam Smith's street lamp example, a person who erects a lamp over a street passes by that spot more often, and hence receives a greater benefit than any other randomly selected person in the town.

This difference between donor benefits and other public benefits can be examined by introducing the distinction between the internal return to the person making the contribution and the external return that is enjoyed by each of the other people in the group. Recall that one of the Goeree, Holt, and Laury treatments involved a return of $.02 for oneself and for each other person when a token worth $.05 was contributed. Thus, the internal return to oneself was $2/5 = 0.4$, and the external return to others was also $2/5 = 0.4$. There was another treatment in which the return to oneself was raised from $.02 to $.04, whereas the return to each of the three others was held constant at $.02. Thus, the internal return was increased from 0.4 to 0.8 ($=4/5$), with the external return constant at 0.4. This increase in the internal return essentially lowered the cost of contributing regardless of the motive for contributing (generosity, confusion, and so on). This doubling of the internal return essentially doubled the average observed contribution from 4.9 tokens to 10.7 tokens. Again, the effect was highly significant, with 25 people increasing their contributions, 3 decreasing, and 4 showing no change as the internal return increased holding the external return constant.

Next, consider the effects of changing the external return, holding the internal return constant at $.02 per token contributed (for an internal return of $R_I = 0.4$). The return to each of the other participants was raised from $.02 to $.06, which raised the external return from $R_E = 2/5 = 0.4$ to $R_E = 6/5 = 1.2$. This tripling of the external return approximately doubled the average observed contribution from 4.9 tokens to 10.5 tokens. (Contributions increased for 23 subjects, decreased for 2, and showed no change for the other 7.) The 10 treatments provide a number of other opportunities to observe external-return effects. Table 14.1 shows the average number of tokens contributed with group size fixed at 4, where the external return varies from 0.4 to 0.8 to 1.2. The top row is for a low internal return of 0.4, and the bottom row is for a high internal return of 0.8. With one exception, increases in the external return (moving from left to right) result in increases in the average contribution. A similar pattern (again with one exception) is observed in Table 14.2, which shows comparable averages for the treatments in which the group size was 2 instead of 4.

Finally, consider the vertical comparisons between two numbers in the same column of the same table, i.e., where the internal return is increased and the external return is held constant. The average contribution increases in all three cases. Overall, the lowest contributions are for the case of low internal and low external returns (upper-left corner of Table

Table 14.1	Average Number of Tokens Contributed with Group Size = 4			
External Return	**Low External** $R_E = 0.4$	**Medium External** $R_E = 0.8$	**High External** $R_E = 1.2$	**Very High External** $R_E = 2.4$
Low Internal Return: $R_I = 0.4$	4.9	—	10.5	—
High Internal Return: $R_I = 0.8$	10.7	10.6	14.3	—

Source: (Goeree, Holt, and Laury 2002)

Table 14.2	Average Number of Tokens Contributed with Group Size = 2			
External Return	**Low External** $R_E = 0.4$	**Medium External** $R_E = 0.8$	**High External** $R_E = 1.2$	**Very High External** $R_E = 2.4$
Low Internal Return: $R_I = 0.4$	—	—	7.7	—
High Internal Return: $R_I = 0.8$	6.7	12.4	11.7	14.5

Source: (Goeree, Holt, and Laury 2002)

14.1), and the highest contributions are for the case of a high internal return and a very high external return (bottom-right corner of Table 14.2).

Group-Size Effects

A comparison of the two tables affords some perspective on group-size effects. There are four cases where group size is changed, holding the returns constant, and the increase in group size (from Table 14.2 to Table 14.1) raises average contributions in all cases but one.

Economic Altruism

These comparisons (and some supporting statistical analysis) lead the authors to conclude that contributions respond positively to increases in internal return, external return, and group size, with the internal-return effect being strongest for the experiment being reported here. Despite the individual differences and the presence of some unexplained variations in individual decisions, the overall data patterns in these single-round experiments are roughly consistent with a model in which people tend to help others by contributing some of their tokens. Such contributions are more common when 1) the private cost of contributing is reduced, 2) the benefit to each other person is increased, and 3) the number of others who benefit is increased. Even a selfish free-rider may decide to contribute if it is thought that this might induce others to contribute in the future, but there is no opportunity for reciprocity in these one-round experiments. These results suggest that many individuals are not perfectly selfish free-riders. Moreover, any altruistic tendencies are not exclusively a warm-glow feeling from the mere act of contributing, but rather, altruism is in part economic in the sense that it depends on the costs to oneself and the benefits to others.

14.4 Multi-Round Experiments

Economists began running multi-round public goods experiments to determine whether free-riding behavior would emerge as subjects gained experience and began to understand the incentives more clearly. The typical setup involves 10 rounds with a fixed group of individuals. Figure 14.2 shows the fractions of endowment contributed for a classroom experiment with an internal return of 0.6 and an external return of 0.8. There is considerable variability across individuals. Player 1 (solid thin line) has relatively low contributions, with a spike upward in the fifth round. Player 2 contributes the full amount

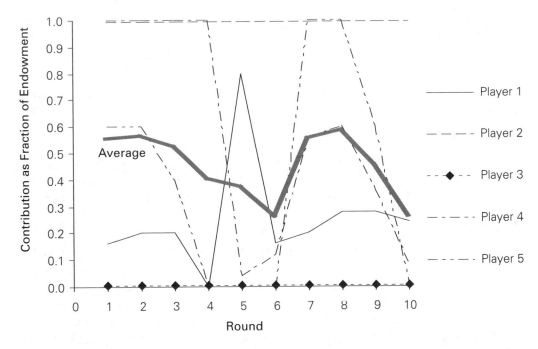

Source: (Class Experiment, University of Virginia 2001)

Figure 14.2   Data from a Five-Person Classroom Public Goods Game with an Internal Return of 0.6 and an External Return of 0.8

in all periods, and Player 3 contributes nothing in any period. Average contributions for all five individuals (the thick solid line) start at about 0.5 and decline slowly, with an upward surge in later periods caused largely by Player 5's change from no contributions to a full contribution of all 25 tokens. Average contributions fall in the final periods, but not to zero. The overall pattern shown here is somewhat typical of other 10-round public goods experiments; contributions tend to start in the 0.4–0.6 range and decline over time, with erratic movements as individuals become frustrated and try to signal (with high contributions) or punish (with low contributions). Contributions generally fall in the final period, when an attempt to signal others to contribute in the future is useless, but some people continue to contribute even in the final period.

As is the case with one-round public goods experiments, there is evidence that contributions in multi-round experiments respond to treatment variables that alter the benefits and costs of contributions. In a classic study, Isaac and Walker (1988b) used two different MPCR levels, 0.3 and 0.75, in a sequential design (two treatments per group), with the order being alternated in every other session. Six sessions were conducted with groups of 4, and six sessions were conducted with groups of 10. Group composition remained fixed for all 10 rounds. The average fractions of the endowment contributed are shown in the lower-left part of Table 14.3. The increase in MPCR approximately doubles contributions for both group sizes. The increase in group size raises contributions for the low MPCR, but not for the high MPCR.

These patterns are reinforced by the Isaac, Walker, and Williams (1994) results in the far-right column of Table 14.3. This column shows average contributions for three groups of 40, with an MPCR that goes from very low (0.03) to low (0.3) to high (0.75). Notice that both treatment variables have no effect when contributions go above about 40 percent of the endowment, as can be seen from the entries in the lower-right corner of the table.

The effects of varying the internal and external returns in multi-round public goods experiments are reported in Goeree, Holt, and Laury (2003). Subjects were paired in groups of 2, with new matchings in each round. Nobody was paired with the same person twice. With the internal return fixed at $R_I = 0.8$, the average number of tokens contributed (out of

Table 14.3	Average Fraction of Endowment Contributed for 10 Rounds		
	Group Size		
	N = 4	*N* = 10	*N* = 40
Very Low MPCR (0.03)	—	—	0.18
Low MPCR (0.3)	0.18	0.26	0.44
High MPCR (0.75)	0.43	0.44	0.39

Source: (Isaac and Walker 1988b; Isaac, Walker, and Williams 1994)

an endowment of 25) increased from 5 to 7.8 to 10 to 11.2 as the external return was increased from 0.4 to 0.8 to 1.2 to 2.4. Holding the external return fixed at $R_E = 1.2$, a reduction in the internal return from 0.8 to 0.4 caused average contributions to fall from 10 to 4.4. A (random-effects) regression based on individual data was used to evaluate the significance of these and other effects. The estimated regression (with standard errors shown in parentheses) is as follows:

$$Contribution = -1.37 - 0.37*Round + 9.7*R_I + 3.2*R_E + 0.16*Other_{t-1}$$
$$(3.1)\quad(0.1)\qquad\quad(3.6)\quad(1.2)\quad(0.02)\qquad\qquad(14.1)$$

The final "$Other_{t1}$" variable is the contribution made by the partner in the previous period. Notice that contributions tend to decline over time, and that the internal-return effect is stronger than the external return effect. The positive effect of the previous partner's contribution suggests that attitudes toward others may be influenced by their behavior. This is consistent with the results reported by van Dijk, Sonnemans, and van Winden (2002), who measured attitudes toward others before and after a multi-round public goods experiment. Changes in attitudes were apparent and depended on the results of the public goods game intuitively.

14.5   Extensions

There is considerable interest in the study of factors that influence voluntary contributions. An analysis based on economic theory only may be insufficient, since many of the relevant issues are behavioral and must be addressed with experiments. For example, List and Lucking-Reiley (2002) report a controlled field experiment in which different mail solicitations for donations mentioned different amounts of "seed money" gifts, i.e., pre-existing gifts that were announced in the solicitation mailing. The presence of seed money had a significant effect on contribution levels. A related issue is the extent to which the public provision of a public good will crowd out private voluntary donations (Andreoni 1993).

In a similar vein, Falk (2004) conducted a field reciprocity experiment in which about 10,000 people in the Zurich area received a mailing from an established charitable organization, asking for donations for street children living in Bangladesh. The recipients were taken from a "warm" list of possible potential donors. One-third of the recipients were randomly selected to receive a small gift of a postcard with children's art, and another third received a "large gift" of four postcards. The remaining third did not receive any gift. The letters were identical except that those with the gift stated that it could be used or given to someone else. The gifts had a surprisingly large effect on the numbers of donations, which went from 397 to 465 to 691 in the no-gift, small-gift, and large-gift treatments respectively. There was some tendency for the gifts to elicit extra small donations, but overall this effect was minor, and the size distributions of the gifts were similar. The author concluded that the inclusion of the gift was a profitable strategy for the charity.

There have been many public goods experiments that focus on the effects of factors like culture, gender, and age on contributions in public goods games, with somewhat mixed results. For example, there is no clear effect of gender (see the survey in (Ledyard 1995)). Goeree, Holt, and Laury (2002) found no gender differences on average, although men in their sample were more likely to make extremely low or high contributions.

A second strand of the literature consists of papers that examine changes in procedures, e.g., whether groups remain fixed or are randomly reconfigured each round (e.g., Croson 1996), and whether or not the experimenter or the participants can observe individual contribution levels. Letting people talk about contributions between rounds tends to raise the level of cooperation, an effect that persists to some extent even if communication is subsequently stopped (Isaac and Walker 1988a). Contributions are also increased in the presence of opportunities for individuals to levy punishments and rewards on those who did or did not contribute (Andreoni, Harbaugh, and Vesterlund 2003).

A third strand of the literature pertains to variations in the payoff structure, e.g., having the public benefits be nonlinear functions of the total contributions by group members. In the linear public goods games described in this chapter, it is optimal for a selfish person to contribute nothing, since the internal rate of return is less than *one*. In this case, the Nash equilibrium involves *zero* contributions by all, which is at the lower boundary of the range of possible contributions, so any noise or confusion would tend to raise contributions above the equilibrium prediction. This *boundary effect* can be avoided by devising a game with a Nash equilibrium somewhere in the middle of the range of possible contributions. One way to do this is to introduce a non-linearity in payoff functions, so that it is optimal to make some contributions when contribution levels are sufficiently low. See Laury and Holt (2000) for a survey of experiments with interior Nash equilibria. Alternatively, the payoff structure can be altered by requiring that total contributions exceed a specified threshold before any benefits are derived (Bagnoli and McKee 1991; Croson and Marks 2000). Such a *provision point* will introduce a coordination problem, since it is not optimal to contribute unless one expects that other contributions will be sufficient to reach the required threshold. Games with contribution thresholds can be implemented with the Veconlab Provision-Point Public Goods program.

Despite the large number of public goods experiments, there is still a lively debate about the primary motives for contribution. One approach is to model individuals' utility functions as depending on both the individual's own payoff and on payoffs received by others. Altruism, for example, can be introduced by having utility be an increasing function of the sum of others' payoffs. Anderson, Goeree, and Holt (1998) estimate that individuals in the Isaac and Walker (1988b) experiments were willing to give up at most about $.10 to give others $1, and similar estimates were obtained by Goeree, Holt, and Laury (2002). On the other hand, some people may not like to see others' earnings go above their own, which suggests that relative earnings matter, as discussed in Chapter 12. In multi-round experiments, individual attitudes toward others may change in response to others' behavior, and people may be willing to contribute as long as enough others do. Many of these alternative theories are surveyed in Holt and Laury (1998).

Up to this point, the discussion has pertained to voluntary contributions, but there are many mechanisms that have been designed to induce improved levels of provision. A critical problem is that people may not know how others value a public good, and people have an incentive to understate their values if tax shares or required efforts depend on reported values. In theory, there are some mechanisms that provide people with an incentive to report values truthfully, and these have been tested in the laboratory. For example, see Chen and Plott (1996) or the survey in Ledyard (1995). In practice, most public goods decisions are either directly or indirectly made on the basis of political considerations, e.g., lobbying and "log rolling" or vote trading. In particular, provision decisions may be sensitive to the preferences of the median voter with preferences that split others more or less equally. Moreover, the identity of the median voter may change as people move to locations that offer the mix of public goods that suits their own personal needs. See Hewett et al. (2005) for a classroom experiment in which the types and levels of public goods are determined by voting and relocation or "voting with feet." Voting experiments are discussed in Chapter 18.

QUESTIONS

1. What was the approximate MPCR for the large-game hunters in the !Kung example described in Section 14.1?

2. Suppose that Ensminger's experiment (discussed in Section 14.2) had used groups of eight instead of four, with all contributions being doubled and divided equally. What would the resulting MPCR have been?

3. How would it have been possible for Ensminger to double the group size and hold the MPCR constant? How could she have increased the MPCR from 0.5 to 0.75, keeping the group size fixed at four?

4. Ensminger wrote a small code number on the inside of each person's envelope, so that she could record who made each contribution. The others could not see the codes, so contributions were anonymous. What if she had wanted contributions to be double anonymous in the sense that nobody, not even the experimenter, could know who made each contribution? Can you think of a feasible way to implement this treatment and still be able to pay people based on the outcome of the game?

5. Suppose that Ensminger had calculated payoffs differently, by paying each of the four people in a group an amount that was one-third of the doubled total contributions of the other three participants. If contributions were 1, 2, 3, and 4 shillings for people with IDs 1, 2, 3, and 4, calculate each person's return from the group project.

6. What would the internal and external returns be for the example in Question 5?

7. The internal-return effects in Tables 14.1 and 14.2 are indicated by the vertical comparisons in the same table. The numbers effects are indicated by the comparisons from one table to the matched cell in the other. How many numbers-effect comparisons are there, and how many are in the predicted direction (more contributions with higher group size)?

8. The external-return comparisons in Tables 14.1 and 14.2 are found by looking at averages in the same row, with higher average contributions anticipated as one moves to the right. How many external-return comparisons are there in the two tables combined, and how many are in the predicted direction? (*Hint*: Do not restrict consideration to averages in adjacent columns.)

9. Which two entries in Table 14.1 illustrate the MPCR effect?

10. Calculate the MPCR for each of the two treatments described in the Play-or-Keep Game Instructions in the Class Experiments section.

chapter 15

The Volunteer's Dilemma

In some situations, it only takes a single volunteer to provide a public benefit. A dilemma arises if the per-capita value of this benefit exceeds the private cost of volunteering, but each person would prefer that someone else incur this cost. For example, each major country on the UN Security Council may prefer that a proposal by a small country is vetoed, but each would prefer to have another country incur the political cost of a veto that is unpopular with many small member nations. This dilemma raises interesting questions, such as whether volunteering is more or less likely in cases with large numbers of potential volunteers. The volunteer's dilemma game provides data that can be compared with both intuition and theoretical predictions. This setup is implemented by the relevant Veconlab game (under the Public Choice menu), or it can be run by hand with playing cards and the instructions provided in this chapter's Volunteer's Dilemma Game in the Class Experiments section.

15.1 Sometimes It Only Takes One Hero

After seeing the actress Teresa Saldana in the film *Raging Bull* in 1982, a crazed fan from Scotland came to Los Angeles and assaulted her as she was leaving home for an audition. Her screams for help attracted a group of people, but it was a man delivering bottled water who instinctively charged in and risked injury or worse by grabbing the assailant and holding him until the police and the ambulance arrived. Ms. Saldana survived her knife wounds; she has continued acting, and has been active with victims' support groups. This is an example of a common situation where many people may want to see a situation corrected, but all that is needed is for one person to incur a cost to correct it. Another example is a case where several politicians may each prefer that someone else propose a legislative pay increase. But if nobody else will make such a proposal, then each would rather take the political heat and make it. These are situations where it only takes one person's costly commitment to change an outcome for others, e.g., with a veto or the provision of information that can be used by all. This type of situation is called a *volunteer's dilemma*, since people would prefer that others volunteer, but they prefer to volunteer themselves if nobody else is going to.

15.2 Initial Experimental Evidence

This dilemma was first studied by Diekmann (1985, 1986) where the focus was on the effects of increasing the number of potential volunteers, which is denoted by N. Each person must decide whether or not to incur a cost of C and volunteer. Each receives a high payoff value of V if at least one person volunteers, and a lower payoff L if nobody in the group volunteers. Thus, there are three possible payoff outcomes, either you volunteer and earn a certain return of $V - C$, or you do not volunteer and earn either V or L, depending on whether or not at least one of the $N - 1$ others volunteers.

Consider a two-person setup, with $V - C > L$. This inequality ensures that it cannot be a Nash equilibrium for both people to refrain from volunteering. Nor can it be an equilibrium for both to volunteer, since each can save C by free-riding on the other's behavior. There are asymmetric equilibria in which one person volunteers and the other does not, since each would prefer to volunteer if the other is expected to refrain (see Question 6 at the end of the chapter). There is also a symmetric equilibrium in which each person volunteers with a probability p^*, which is a topic that we will consider subsequently. Intuitively, one would expect that the equilibrium probability of volunteering would be lower when there are more potential volunteers, since there is less risk in relying on the generosity of others in this case. This intuition is borne out in an experiment reported by Franzen (1995), with $V - L = 100$ and $C = 50$. The volunteer rates (middle column of Table 15.1) decline as group size is

Table 15.1	Group Size Effects in a Volunteer's Dilemma Experiment	
Group Size	**Individual Volunteer Rate**	**Rate of No-Volunteer Outcomes**
2	0.65	0.12
3	0.58	0.07
5	0.43	0.06
7	0.25	0.13
9	0.35	0.02
21	0.30	0.00
51	0.20	0.00
101	0.35	0.00

Source: (Franzen 1995)

increased from 2 to 7, and these rates level off after that point. The third column indicates that the probability of obtaining no volunteers is essentially 0 for larger groups.

The Franzen experiment was done as a one-time exercise, which raises the issue of what happens when subjects are able to learn and adjust. Figure 15.1 shows the results for a classroom experiment conducted with payoffs: $V = \$25$, $L = \$0$, and $C = \$5$. The setup involved 12 participants who were randomly paired in groups of two for each of eight rounds, followed by eight rounds of random matching in groups of four. (As with all classroom experiments reported in this book, participants were generally pairs of students at a single computer, and one participant pair was selected ex post at random to be paid a small fraction of earnings.) The round-by-round averages for the two-person treatment are generally in the 0.5 to 0.7 range, as shown on the left side of the figure. The increase in group size reduced the volunteer rate to about 0.4. The dashed lines in Figure 15.1 indicate the Nash mixed-strategy equilibrium volunteer rates for the two treatments; these predictions will be derived in the next section. In class, it is convenient to use a pair of treatments to make a point, but this figure also illustrates a disadvantage of using a within-subjects design, since the data points track more or less continuously across the treatment change

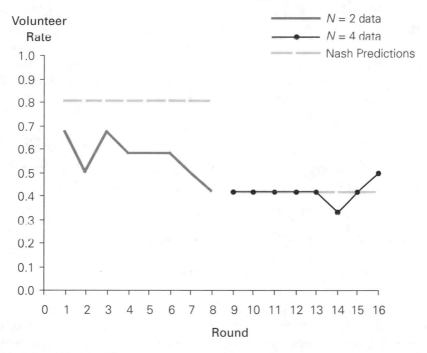

Source: (University of Virginia, Fall 2001)

Figure 15.1   Volunteer's Dilemma with Group Size Change

at round 10. (The group size effect will be revisited in a later discussion of a research experiment with a between-subjects design.)

The observation that the probability of volunteering is decreasing in group size is consistent with casual intuition and with results of social psychology experiments with staged emergencies, e.g., Darley and Latane (1968). The observed reluctance of individuals in large groups to intervene in such emergencies has been termed "diffusion of responsibility" in this literature. Public awareness of this tendency was heightened in the 1960s by the failure of over 30 onlookers to come to the aid of Kitty Genovese, who was raped and stabbed in the courtyard of her apartment complex in New York. Even though each individual may have a lower chance of volunteering in a large group, the chances of getting at least one volunteer from a large group may go up, as indicated by the third column of Table 15.1. The next section derives the game-theoretic predictions for these numbers effects.

15.3 The Mixed-Strategy Equilibrium

Most of the theoretical analysis of the volunteer's dilemma has focused on the symmetric Nash equilibrium with random strategies. Obviously, each person must be indifferent between volunteering and refraining, since otherwise it would be rational to choose the preferred action. In order to characterize this indifference, we need to calculate the expected payoffs for each decision and equate them. First, the expected payoff from volunteering is $V - C$ since this decision rules out the possibility of an L outcome. A decision not to volunteer has an expected payoff that depends on the others' volunteer rate, p. For simplicity, consider the case of only one other person (group size 2). In this case, the payoff for not volunteering is either V (with probability p) or L (with probability $1 - p$), so the expected payoff, as shown in Equation (15.1) is as follows:

$$\text{Expected payoff (not volunteer)} = pV + (1 - p)L \quad \text{(for } N = 2) \tag{15.1}$$

To characterize indifference, we must equate this expected payoff with the payoff from volunteering, $V - C$, to obtain an equation in p, as shown in Equation (15.2).

$$V - C = pV + (1 - p)L \quad \text{(for } N = 2) \tag{15.2}$$

which can be solved for the equilibrium level of p, as shown in Equation (15.3).

$$p = 1 - \left(\frac{C}{V - L}\right) \quad \text{(Equilibrium volunteer rate for } N = 2) \tag{15.3}$$

Recall that $V = \$25.00$, $L = \$0.00$, and $C = \$5.00$ for the parameters used in the first treatment in Figure 15.1. Thus, the Nash prediction for this treatment is 4/5, as indicated by the horizontal dashed line with a height of 0.8. The actual volunteer rates in this experiment are not this extreme, but rather are closer to 0.6.

The formulas derived above must be modified for larger group sizes, e.g., $N = 4$ for the second treatment. The payoff for a volunteer decision is independent of what others do, so this payoff is $V - C$ regardless of group size. If one does not volunteer, however, the payoff depends on what the $N - 1$ others do. The probability that one of them does not volunteer is $1 - p$, so the probability that none of the $N - 1$ others volunteer is $(1 - p)^{N-1}$. (This calculation is analogous to saying that if the probability of tails is $1/2$, then the probability of observing two tails outcomes is $(1/2)^2 = 1/4$, and the probability of having $N - 1$ flips all turn out tails is $(1/2)^{N-1}$.) To summarize, when one does not volunteer, the low payoff of L is obtained when none of the others volunteer, which occurs with probability $(1 - p)^{N-1}$. It follows that the high payoff V is obtained with a probability that is calculated: $1 - (1 - p)^{N-1}$. These observations permit us to express the expected payoff for not volunteering as the sum of terms on the right side of Equation (15.4).

$$V - C = V\left[1 - (1 - p)^{N-1}\right] + L(1 - p)^{N-1} \qquad (15.4)$$

The left side is the payoff for volunteering, so Equation (15.4) characterizes the indifference between expected payoffs for the two decisions that must hold if a person is willing to randomize. It is straightforward (see Question 7 at the end of the chapter) to solve this equation for the probability, $1 - p$, of not volunteering, as shown in Equation (15.5).

$$1 - p = \left(\frac{C}{V - L}\right)^{\frac{1}{N-1}} \qquad (15.5)$$

Therefore, the equilibrium volunteer rate, as shown in Equation (15.6) is as follows:

$$p = 1 - \left(\frac{C}{V - L}\right)^{\frac{1}{N-1}} \qquad \text{(Equilibrium volunteer rate)} \qquad (15.6)$$

Notice that Equation (15.6) reduces to Equation (15.3) when $N = 2$. It is easily verified that the volunteer rate is increasing in the value V obtained when there is a volunteer and decreasing in the value L obtained when there is no volunteer. As would be expected, the volunteer rate is also decreasing in the volunteer cost C. (These claims are fairly obvious from the positions of C, V, and L in the ratio on the right side of Equation (15.6) that is preceded by a minus sign, but they can be verified by changing the payoff parameters in the spreadsheet program used in Question 8 at the end of the chapter.)

Next, consider the effects of a change in the number of potential volunteers, N. For the setup in Figure 15.1, recall that $V = \$25.00$, $L = \$0.00$, $C = \$5.00$, and therefore, the volunteer rate is 0.8 when $N = 2$. When N is increased to 4, the formula in Equation (15.6) yields $1 - (1/5)^{1/3}$, which is about 0.41 (see Question 8), as shown by the dashed horizontal line on the right side of Figure 15.1. This increase in N reduces the predicted volunteer rate, which is consistent with the qualitative pattern in the data (although the $N = 2$ prediction is clearly too high relative to the actual data). It is straightforward to use algebra to show that the formula for the volunteer rate in Equation (15.6) is a decreasing function of N. This formula can also be used to calculate the Nash volunteer rates for the eight different group-size treatments shown in Table 15.1 (see Question 8).

Finally, we will evaluate the chances that none of the N participants volunteer. The probability that any one person does not volunteer, $1 - p$, is given in Equation (15.5). Since the N decisions are independent, like flips of a coin, the probability that all N participants decide not to volunteer is obtained by raising the right side of Equation (15.5) to the power N as shown in Equation (15.7) as follows:

$$\text{Probability that nobody volunteers} = (1 - p)^N = \left(\frac{C}{V - L} \right)^{\frac{N}{N-1}} \qquad (15.7)$$

The right side of Equation (15.7) is an increasing function of N (see Question 9 at the end of the chapter for a guide to making spreadsheet calculations). As N goes to infinity, the exponent of the expression on the far right side of Equation (15.7) goes to 1, and the probability of getting no volunteer goes to $C/(V-L)$. The resulting prediction (1/5) is inconsistent with the data from Table 15.1, where the probability of finding no volunteer is 0 for larger group sizes. What seems to be happening is that there is some randomness, which causes occasional volunteers to be observed in any large group.

One interesting feature of the equilibrium volunteer rate in Equation (15.6) is that the payoffs only matter to the extent that they affect the ratio, $C/(V - L)$. Thus, a treatment change that shifts both V and L down by the same amount will not affect the difference in the denominator of this ratio. This invariance was the basis for a treatment change designed by a University of Virginia student who ran an experiment on this topic using the Veconlab software. The student decided to lower these parameters by $15, from $V = \$25$ and $L = \$0$ to: $V = \$10$ and $L = -\$15$. The values of C and N were kept fixed at $5 and four participants per group. Table 15.2 summarizes these payoffs for alternative setups.

All payoffs are positive in the sure gain treatment, but a large loss is possible in the loss treatment. This pair of treatments was designed with the goal of detecting whether the possibility of large losses would result in a higher volunteer rate in the second treatment. Such an effect could be due to loss aversion.

The results for a single classroom experiment with these treatments are summarized in Figure 15.2. The observed volunteer rates closely approximate the common Nash prediction for both treatments, so loss aversion seems to have had no effect. This example was included to illustrate an invariance feature of the Nash prediction and to show how stu-

Table 15.2	Volunteer's Dilemma Payoffs for a Gain/Loss Design			
Own Decision	**Number of Other Volunteers**	**Own Payoff**	**Sure Gain Treatment**	**Loss Treatment**
Volunteer	Any number	$V - C$	$20	$5
Not Volunteer	None	L	$0	−$15
Not Volunteer	At least one	V	$25	$10

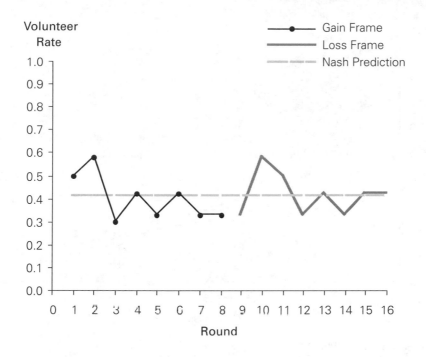

Source: (University of Virginia Class Experiment, Fall 2001)

Figure 15.2   Volunteer's Dilemma with Gain/Loss Change

dents can use theory to create clever experiment designs. The actual results are not defini-
tive however, because of the constraints imposed by the classroom setup: no replication,
very limited incentives, and no credible way of making a participant pay actual losses.

15.4   An Experiment on Group Size Effects

Goeree, Holt, and Smith (2005) ran an experiment designed to assess group size
effects. They use group sizes of 2, 3, 6, 9, and 12, with 36–48 subjects in each treatment. The
subjects participated in a series of 20 volunteer's dilemma games, with random matchings
and no change in group size (to avoid sequence effects). The total number of participants
in each session was scaled up so that it was at least four times the group size. The parameters, $V = \$1$, $C = \$0.20$, and $L = \$0.20$, were such that the Nash predictions declined from 0.5
to about 0.12 as the group size increased from 2 to 12. The Nash predictions and data averages are plotted in Figure 15.3. The observed volunteer rate is considerably lower than the
Nash prediction for the $N = 2$ treatment, as was the case with the classroom experiment in

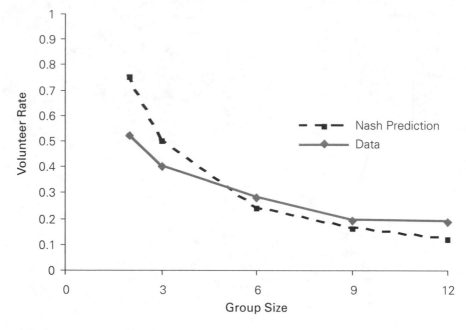

Source: (Goeree, Holt, and Smith 2005)

| **Figure 15.3** | The Effects of Group Size |

Figure 15.1. In contrast, the observed volunteer rates (solid line) are higher than predicted (dashed line) for large values of N, so that the data average line is flatter than the Nash prediction line.

When the group size is 2, the Nash volunteer rate is 0.75, and the probability of getting no volunteers is $(0.25)*(0.25) = 0.06$. When the group size is 3, the Nash volunteer rate is 0.5, and the probability of a no-volunteer outcome is $(0.5)*(0.5)*(0.5) = 0.125$, as shown in the top row of Table 15.3. Note that these predicted probabilities of no-volunteer outcomes increase for larger groups, which is the *opposite* of what is observed in the data (bottom

| **Table 15.3** | Group Size and the Rate of No-Volunteer Outcomes |

	N = 2	*N* = 3	*N* = 6	*N* = 9	*N* = 12
Predicted No-Volunteer Rate	0.06	0.125	0.19	0.21	0.22
Data Average	0.21	0.22	0.16	0.13	0.11

Source: (Goeree, Holt, and Smith 2005)

row). The higher-than-predicted volunteer rates for larger group sizes means that the probability of getting a no-volunteer outcome does not increase with group size.

15.5 Extensions

Goeree and Holt (2005b) discuss the volunteer's dilemma and other closely related games where individuals are faced with a binary decision, e.g., to enter a market or not or to vote or not. As they note, the volunteer's dilemma is a special case of a threshold public good in which each person has a binary decision of whether to contribute or not. The public benefit is not available unless the total number of contributors reaches a specified threshold, say M, and the volunteer's dilemma is a special case where $M = 1$. Goeree and Holt analyze the equilibria for these types of binary-choice games when individual decisions are determined by probabilistic choice rules of the type to be discussed in Chapters 23–26. Basically, the effect of introducing "noise" into behavior is to pull volunteer rates toward 0.5. This approach can explain why the probability of a no-volunteer outcome is *not* observed to be an increasing function of group size, as predicted in the Nash equilibrium. The intuition for why large numbers may decrease the chances of a no-volunteer outcome is that noise makes it more likely that at least one person in a large group will volunteer due to random causes. This intuition is consistent with the data from Franzen (1995) and is inconsistent with the Nash prediction that the probability of a no-volunteer outcome is an increasing function of group size. Goeree, Holt, and Smith (2005) estimate a probabilistic choice model for the data from the previous section's experiment. They also identify a downward bias in volunteer rates, which they attribute to inequity aversion.

Other aspects of the volunteer's dilemma are discussed in Diekmann and Mitter (1986) and Diekmann (1993), who reports experiments for an asymmetric setup.

QUESTIONS

1. Consider a volunteer's dilemma in which the payoff is 25 if at least one person volunteers, minus the cost (if any) of volunteering, the payoff for no volunteer is 0, and the cost of volunteering is 1. Consider a symmetric situation in which the group size is two and each decides to volunteer with a probability p. Find the equilibrium probability.

2. How does the answer to Question 1 change if the group size is three?

3. The Volunteer's Dilemma Game in Class Instructions part provides a setup for group sizes of two and four. Calculate the Nash equilibrium volunteer rate for each group size, using the payoff parameters in those instructions.

4. For the setup in Question 3, calculate the probability of obtaining no volunteer in a Nash equilibrium, and show that this probability is 16 times as large for groups of four as it is for groups of two.

5. In deciding whether or not to volunteer, which decision involves more risk? Do you think a group of risk-averse people would volunteer more often in a Nash (mixed-strategy) equilibrium for this game than a group of risk-neutral people? Explain your intuition.

6. The setup in Question 1 can be written as a 2×2 matrix game between a row and column player. Write the payoff table for this game, with the row payoff listed first in each cell. Explain why this volunteer's dilemma is not a prisoner's dilemma. Are there any Nash equilibria in pure (non-randomized) strategies for this game?

7. Derive Equation (15.5) from Equation (15.4) by showing all intermediate steps.

8. To calculate group-size effects for volunteer's dilemma experiments, set up a spreadsheet program. First, make column headings for the variables that you will be using. Put the column headings, N, V, L, C, $C/(V - L)$, and P in cells A1, B1, C1, D1, E1, and F1 respectively. Next, enter the following values for these variables (begin with the setup from the second treatment in Figure 15.1): 4 in cell A2, 25 in cell B2, 0 in cell C2, and 5 in cell D2. Then, enter a formula: =D2/(B2 − C2) in cell E2. Finally, enter the formula for the equilibrium probability from Equation (15.6) into cell F2; the Excel code for this formula is: =1−power(E2, 1/(A2 − 1)), which raises the ratio in cell E2 to the power $1/(N - 1)$, where N is taken from cell A2. If you have done this correctly, you should obtain the equilibrium volunteer rate mentioned in the chapter, which rounds off to 0.41. Experiment with some changes in V, L, and C to determine the effects of changes in these parameters on the volunteer rate. In order to obtain predictions from the Franzen model, enter the values 2, 100, 0, and 50 in cells A3, B3, C3, and D3 respectively, and copy the formulas in cells E2 and F2 into cells E3 and F3. The resulting volunteer rate prediction in cell F3 should be 0.5. Enter the other values for N vertically in the A column: these values are 3, 5, 7, 9, 21, 51, and 101. The predictions for these treatments can be obtained by copying the values and formulas for cells B3–F3 downward in the spreadsheet.

9. To obtain predictions for the probability of getting no volunteers at all, add a column heading in cell G1 ("No Vol.") and enter the formula from Equation (15.7) in Excel code into cell G2: =power(E2, A2/(A2 − 1)) and copy this formula down to the lower cells in the G column. What does this prediction converge to as the number of participants becomes large? (*Hint*: as N goes to infinity, the exponent in Equation (15.7) converges to 1.)

10. Explain the volunteer's dilemma to your roommates or friends and come up with at least one example of such a dilemma based on some common experience from class, dorm living, a recent film, and so on.

chapter 16

Externalities, Congestion, and Common Pool Resources

Many persistent urban and environmental problems result from excessive use or exploitation of a shared resource. For example, an increase in fishing activity may reduce the catch per hour for all fishermen, or a commuter's decision to enter a tunnel may slow down the progress of other commuters. Individuals tend to ignore the negative impact of their own activity on other's harvests or travel times. Indeed, people may not even be aware of the negative effects of their decisions if the effects are small and dispersed across many other users. This externality is typically not priced in a market, and overuse can result. This chapter considers two somewhat stylized paradigms of overuse or congestion.

In the common pool resource game, individual efforts to secure more benefits from the resource have the effect of reducing the benefits received by others. In technical terms, the average and marginal products of each person's effort are decreasing in the total effort of all participants. The Veconlab implementation of this game, listed under the Public Choice menu, may be used to compare behavior in alternate treatments.

In market entry games, participants decide independently whether or not to enter a market or activity for which the earnings per entrant are a decreasing function of the number of entrants. The outside option earnings from not entering are fixed. Kahneman (1988) once remarked on the tendency for payoffs to be equalized for the two decisions: "To a psychologist, it looks like magic." This impression should change for those who have participated in a classroom entry game experiment, run prior to the class discussion. Although entry rates are typically distributed around the equilibrium prediction, the rates are variable and too high since each person ignores the negative effects of their decisions on other entrants. The Veconlab congestion and market entry program, also listed under the Public Choice Menu, provides some policy options (tolls and "traffic report information") that correct these problems.

16.1   Water

Some of the most difficult resource management problems in both developing and advanced economies involve water. Consider a setup where there are upstream and downstream users, and in the absence of norms or rules, the downstream users are left with whatever is not taken upstream. This is an example of a common pool resource, where individual use may reduce the benefits obtained by others. Ostrom and Gardner (1993) describe such a situation involving farmers in Nepal. If upstream users tend to take most of the water, then their usage may be inefficiently high from a social point of view, e.g., if the downstream land is more fertile bottom land. Here the inefficiency is due to the fact that the upstream farmers draw water down until the value of its marginal product is very low, even though water may be used more productively downstream.

For example, the Thambesi system in Nepal is one where the headenders have established first-priority water rights over those downstream. The farmers located at the head of each rotation unit take all of the water they need before those lower in the system. In particular, the headenders grow water-intensive rice during the pre-monsoon season, and consequently, those lower in the system cannot grow irrigated crops at this time. If all farmers were to grow a less-water intensive crop (wheat), the area under cultivation during the pre-monsoon season could be expanded dramatically, nearly ten-fold. The irrigation decisions made by the headenders raise their incomes, but at a large cost in terms of lost crop value downstream. A commonly used solution to this problem is to limit usage, and such limits may be enforced by social norms or by explicit penalties. In either case, enforcement may be problematic. In areas where farmers own marketable shares of the water system, these farmers have an incentive to sell them so that water is diverted to its highest-value uses (Yoder 1986).

Besides overuse, there is another potential source of inefficiency if activities to increase water flow have joint benefits to both types of users. For example, irrigation canals may have to be maintained or renewed annually, and this work can be shared by all users, regardless of location. In this case, the benefit of additional work is shared by all users, so each person who contributes work will only obtain a part of the benefits, even though they incur the full cost of their own effort, unless their contribution is somehow reimbursed or otherwise rewarded. Note that the level of work on the joint production of water flow should be increased as long as the additional benefit, in terms of harvest value, is greater than the cost, in terms of lost earnings on other uses of the farmers' time. Thus, each person has an incentive to free-ride on others' efforts, and this perverse incentive may be stronger for downstream users if their share of the remaining water tends to be low.

To summarize, there are two main sources of inefficiency associated with common pool resources: overuse and under-provision. Overuse can occur if people do not consider the negative effects that their own use decisions have on the benefit of the resource that remains for others. Under-provision can occur if the benefits of providing the resource are shared by all users, but each person incurs the full cost of their own contribution to the group effort.

16.2   Ducks and Traffic

The pressures of free entry and congestion can be illustrated with the results of a famous animal foraging experiment done with a flock of ducks at the Cambridge University Botanical Garden (Harper 1982). The experiment was conducted by having two people go to opposite banks of the pond. Each person would simultaneously begin throwing out 5-gram bread balls at fixed intervals, every 10 seconds in one case and every 20 seconds in another. The 33 ducks quickly sorted themselves so that the expected food intake in grams per minute was equal for the groups of ducks in front of each person. A change in the time intervals resulted in a new equilibrium within about 90 seconds, in far less time than it would take for most ducks at either location to obtain a single bread ball.

Even after an equilibrium had been reached in an aggregate sense, individual ducks were always in motion in a stochastic and unpredictable pattern of movements. These are the same competitive pressures that force urban commuting times to equalize, but here the policy issue is whether it is possible to change the system to make everyone better off. Large investments to provide fast freeways, tunnels, and bridges often are negated with a seemingly endless supply of eager commuters during certain peak periods. The result may be that travel via the new freeways and tunnels is no faster than the older alternative routes via a maze of surface roads.

To illustrate this problem, consider a stylized setup in which there are *N* commuters who must choose between a slow, reliable surface route and a potentially faster route (freeway or tunnel). However, if large numbers decide to enter the faster route, the resulting congestion will cause traffic to slow to a crawl, so entry can be a risky decision. This setup was implemented in a laboratory experiment run by Anderson, Holt, and Reiley (2006). In each session, there were 12 participants who had to choose whether to enter a potentially congested activity or exit to a safe alternative. The payoffs for entrants were decreasing in the total number of entrants in a given round, as shown in Table 16.1.

You should think of the numbers in the table as the net monetary benefits from entry, which go down by $0.50 as each additional entrant increases the time cost associated with travel via the congested route. In contrast, the travel time associated with the alternative route (the non-entry decision) is less variable. For simplicity, the net benefit for each non-entrant is fixed at $0.50, regardless of the number who select this route. Obviously, entry is the better decision as long as the number of entrants is not higher than 8, and the equilibrium number of entrants that equalizes payoffs is, therefore, 8. In this case, each person earns $0.50, and the total earnings (net benefit) for the 12 people together is $6.00. In con-

Table 16.1	Individual Payoffs from Entry											
Entrants	1	2	3	4	5	6	7	8	9	10	11	12
Payoff	$4	$3.50	$3	$2.50	$2	$1.50	$1	$0.50	$0	−$0.50	−$1	−$1.50

trast, if only 4 enter, they each earn $2.50 and the other 8 earn $0.50, for total earnings of $14. It follows that an entry restriction will more than double the social net benefit.

The equilibrium described in the previous paragraph is one where non-random decisions equate payoffs for the two roads. There is another equilibrium in non-random strategies (see Question 6) in which payoffs are not exactly equalized. In addition, one might guess that there is a mixed-strategy equilibrium in which each of the 12 people enter with probability 2/3, since this yields (2/3)*12 = 8 entrants on average. This is a close guess, but not quite the case. For example, suppose that one person using a random device (e.g., throw of dice) obtains an outcome that indicates entry. Then that person would be indifferent between the two decisions if, on average, there are exactly 7 other entrants from the 11 other people, since in this case there would be a total of 8 entrants. Anderson, Holt, and Reiley (2006) show that the mixed-strategy equilibrium involves entry with probability 7/11 = 0.64, which is approximately two-thirds, but not quite.

The social benefit for this model of commuter choice is the sum of the earnings received by all players, including those who do not enter. It is straightforward to calculate the social benefit associated with alternative entry levels (see Question 1 at the end of the chapter), and the results are shown in Table 16.2. As noted above, it is reasonable to expect that uncontrolled entry decisions would lead to approximately 8 entrants, the number that equalizes earnings from the two alternative decisions. As a result, the total benefit to all participants is inefficiently low because each additional person who decides to enter lowers the net entry benefit by $0.50 for themselves *and for all other entrants*, and it is this external effect that may be ignored by each entrant. For example if there are currently 4 entrants, adding a fifth would reduce the earnings for the 4 existing entrants by $2 (4 × $0.50) and only increase the entrant's earnings by $1.50 (from the non-entry payoff of $0.50 to the entry payoff of $2), so total earnings decrease by $0.50. A sixth entrant would reduce total earnings by even more, $1.50 (a reduction of 5 × $0.50 that is only partly offset by the $1 increase in the entrant's earnings), since there are more people to suffer the consequences. As even more people enter, the earnings reductions caused by an additional entrant become higher, and therefore, the total payoff falls at an increasing rate. This is the intuition behind the very high costs associated with dramatic traffic delays during peak commuting periods. Any policy that pushes some of the traffic to non-peak periods will be welfare improving, since the cost of increased congestion in those periods is less than the benefit from reducing peak congestion.

Table 16.2	Social Benefit for 12 Participants Together										
Entrants	1	2	3	4	5	6	7	8	9	10	11	12
Total Payoff	$9.50	$12	$13.50	$14	$13.50	$12	$9.50	$6	$1.50	−$4	−$10.50	−$18

In laboratory experiments, as on the open road, people are like the ducks in that they ignore the negative external effects that their decisions have on others' payoffs. Figure 16.1 shows the data patterns for a group of 12 participants using the payoffs from Table 16.1. The average entry rate in the first 10 rounds is 0.69, which is quite close to the two-thirds (8 out of 12) rate that would occur in equilibrium. As was the case with the ducks, there is considerable variability, which in real traffic situations would be amplified by accidents and other unanticipated traffic events.

After 10 rounds, all entrants were required to pay an entry fee of $2, which reduces all numbers in the bottom row of Table 16.1 by $2. In this case, the equilibrium number of entrants is 4, i.e., an entry rate of 0.33, as shown by the dashed line on the right side of Figure 16.1. The average entry rate for these final 10 rounds was quite close to this level, at 0.38.

Even though the fee reduces entry to (nearly) socially optimal levels, the individuals do not enjoy any benefit. To see this, let's ignore the variability and assume that the fee reduces entry to the 0.33 rate. In equilibrium entrants earn $2.50 minus the $2 fee, and non-entrants earn $0.50, so everyone earns exactly the same amount, $0.50, as if they did not enter at all. Where did the increase in social benefit go? The answer is in the collected fees of $8 (4 × $2). This total fee revenue of $8 is available for other uses, e.g., tax reductions

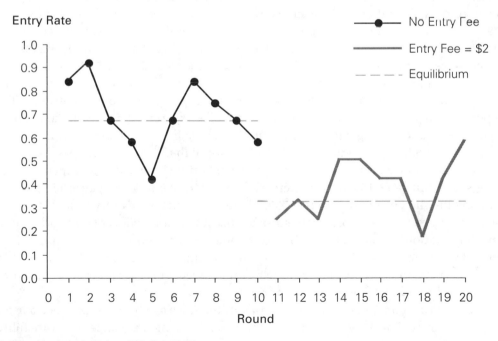

Source: (Anderson, Holt, and Reiley 2006)

Figure 16.1   Entry Game with Imposition of Entry Fee

and road construction. So if the commuters in this model are going to benefit from the reduction in congestion, then they must get a share of the benefits associated with the fee collections.

A second series of sessions was conducted using a redistribution of fee revenues, with each person receiving 1/12 of collections. After 10 rounds with no fee, participants were allowed to vote on the level of the fee for rounds 11–20, and then for each 10-round interval after that. The voting was carried out by majority rule after a group discussion, with ties being decided by the chair, who was selected at random from the 12 participants. In one session, the participants first voted on a fee of $1, which increased their total earnings, and hence was selected again after round 20 to hold in rounds 21–30. After round 30, they achieved a further reduction in entry and increase in total earnings by voting to raise the fee to $2 for the final 10 rounds. In a second session with voting, the group reached the optimal fee of $2 in round 20, but the chair of the meeting kept arguing for a lower fee, and these arguments resulted in reductions to $1.75, and then to $1.50, before it was raised to a near-optimal level of $1.75 for the final 10 rounds. Interestingly, the discussions in these meetings did not focus on maximizing total earnings. Instead, many of the arguments were based on making the situation better for entrants or for non-entrants (different people had different points of view, based on what they tended to do). In each of these two sessions, the imposition of the entry fees resulted in an approximate doubling of earnings by the final 10 rounds. Even though the average payoffs for entry (paying the fee) and exit are equal to $0.50 in equilibrium, for any fee, the fee of $2 maximized the amount collected, and hence maximized the total earnings when these included a share of the collections.

Regardless of average entry rate, there is considerable variation from round to round, as shown in Figure 16.1 and in the data graphs for the other sessions where fees were imposed, either by the experimenter or as the result of a vote. Similar persistent variability is reported by Selten et al. (2002) in a commuter choice experiment done with large numbers of rounds and varying information conditions. Variability is typically detrimental in this type of model. For the setup in Table 16.1, suppose that there is no fee, so that entry would tend to bounce up and down around the equilibrium level of 8 in an experiment. It can be seen from Table 16.2 that an increase in entry from 8 to 9 reduces total earnings (including the shared fee) from $6 to $1.50, whereas a reduction in entry from 8 to 7 only raises earnings from $6 to $9.50. In general, a bounce up in entry reduces earnings by more than a bounce down by an equal amount, so symmetric variation around the equilibrium level of 8 would reduce total earnings below the amount, $6, which could be expected in equilibrium with no variation. The intuition behind this asymmetry is that additional entry causes more harm with larger numbers of entrants.

Everyone who commutes by car knows that travel times can be variable, especially on routes that can become very congested. In this case, anything that can reduce variability will tend to be an improvement in terms of average benefits. In addition, most people dislike variability, and the resulting risk aversion, which has been ignored up to now, would make a reduction in variability more desirable. Sometimes variability can be reduced by better information. In many urban areas, there is a news-oriented radio station that issues traffic reports every 10 minutes, e.g., "on the eights" at WTOP in Washington, D.C. This information can help commuters avoid entry into already overcrowded roads and freeways. A stylized type of traffic information can be implemented in an experiment by letting each person find out the number of others who have already entered at any time up to the time that they decide to enter. In this case, the order of entry is determined by the participants themselves, with some people making a quick decision, and others waiting. The effect of this kind of information is to bring about a dramatic (but not total) reduction in variability, as can be seen for the experiment shown in Figure 16.2.

In a richer model, some commuters would have higher time values than others, and hence would place a higher value on the reduction in commuting time associated with reduced congestion. The fee would allow commuters to sort themselves out in the value-of-time dimension, with high-value commuters being willing to pay the fee. The resulting social benefit would be further enhanced by the effects of using price (the entry fee) to allocate the good (entry) to those who value it the most. This observation is similar to a result reported in Plott (1983), where the resale of licenses to trade, from those with low values to those with high values, raised both total earnings and market efficiency.

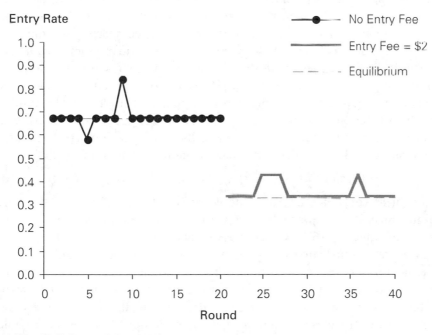

Source: (Anderson, Holt, and Reiley 2006)

Figure 16.2   Entry Game with Information about the Number of Prior Entrants

16.3 | Fish

Each person in the market entry game has two decisions: to enter or not to enter. In contrast, most common pool resource situations are characterized by a range of possible decisions, corresponding to the intensity of use. For example, a lobster fisherman not only decides whether to fish on any given day, but also (if permitted by regulations and weather) how many days a year to go out and how many hours to stay out each day. Let the fishing effort for each person be denoted by x_i, where the i subscript indicates the particular person. The total effort of all N fishermen is denoted by X, which is just the sum of the individual x_i for $i = 1 \ldots N$. For simplicity, assume that no person is more skilled than any other, so it is natural to assume that a person's fraction of the total harvest is equal to their fraction of the total effort, x_i/X.

In the experiment to be discussed, each person selected an effort level simultaneously, and the total harvest revenue, Y, was a quadratic function of the total effort, as shown in Equation (16.1):

$$Y = AX - BX^2 \qquad (16.1)$$

where $A > 0$, $B > 0$, and $X < A/B$ (to ensure that the harvest is not negative). This function has the property that the average revenue product, Y/X, is a decreasing function of the total effort. This average revenue product is calculated as the total revenue from the harvest, divided by the total effort: $(AX - BX^2)/X = A - BX$, which is decreasing in X since B is assumed to be positive. The fact that average revenue is decreasing in X means that an increase in one person's effort will reduce the average revenue product of effort for everyone else. This is the negative externality for this common pool resource problem.

Effort is costly, and this cost is assumed to be proportional to effort, so the cost for individual i would be Cx_i, where $C > 0$ represents the opportunity cost of the fisherman's time. Assuming that the harvest in Equation (16.1) is measured in dollar value, then the earnings for person i would be their share, x_i/X, of the total harvest in Equation (16.1) minus the cost of Cx_i that is associated with their effort choice, as shown in Equation (16.2):

$$\text{Earnings} = (AX - BX^2)(x_i / X) - Cx_i = (A - BX)x_i - Cx_i \qquad (16.2)$$

where the right side of Equation (16.2) is the average product of effort times the individual's effort, minus the cost of the person's effort decision. Note that this earnings expression on the right side of Equation (16.2) is analogous to that of a firm in a Cournot market, facing a demand (average revenue) curve of $A - BX$ and a constant cost of C per unit.

A rational, but selfish, person in this context would take into account the fact that an increase in their own effort reduces their own average revenue product, but they would not consider the negative effect of an increase in effort on the others' average revenue products. This is the intuitive reason that unregulated exploitation of the resource would result in too much production relative to what is best for the group in the aggregate (just as uncoordinated production choices by firms in a Cournot market results in a total output that is too high relative to the level that would maximize joint profits).

In particular, the Nash/Cournot equilibrium for this setup would involve each person choosing the activity level, x_i, that maximizes the earnings in Equation (16.2) taking the others' activities as given. Suppose that there are a total of N participants, and that the $N-1$ others choose a common level of y each. Thus, the total of the others' decisions is $(N-1)y$, and the total usage is: $X = x_i + (N-1)y$. With this substitution, the earnings in Equation (16.2) can be expressed as shown in Equation (16.3):

$$\begin{aligned} \text{Earnings} &= [A - B(N-1)y - Bx_i]x_i - Cx_i \\ &= Ax_i - B(N-1)yx_i - Bx_i^2 - Cx_i \end{aligned} \qquad (16.3)$$

which can be maximized by equating marginal revenue with marginal cost C. The marginal revenue is just the derivative of total revenue (as explained in Chapter 6 and its Appendix), and the marginal cost is the derivative of total cost, Cx_i. One way to find the best level of x_i is to note that the term in square brackets at the top of Equation (16.3) is like a demand function with slope $-B$, so the corresponding marginal function would have a slope of $-2B$, and equating this marginal revenue with marginal cost yields Equation (16.4). An equivalent derivation is to take the derivative of the earnings formula in Equation (16.3) with respect to x_i and then set it equal to zero.

$$A - B(N-1)y - 2Bx_i - C = 0 \qquad (16.4)$$

This equation can be used to determine a common decision, x^*, by replacing both y and x_i with x^* and solving to obtain Equation (16.5).

$$x^* = \frac{A - C}{(N + 1)B} \qquad (16.5)$$

The nature of this common pool resource problem can be illustrated in terms of the specific setup used in a research experiment run by Guzik (2004), who at the time was an undergraduate at Middlebury College. He ran experiments with groups of five participants with $A = 25$, $B = 1/2$, and $C = 1$. The cost was implemented by giving each person 12 tokens in a round. These could either be kept, with earnings of 1 each, or used to extract the common pool resource. Thus, the opportunity cost, C, is 1 for each unit increase in x_i. With these parameters and $N = 5$, Equation (16.5) yields a common equilibrium decision of $x = 8$. It can be shown that the socially optimal level of appropriation is 4.8 (see Question 5 at the end of the chapter).

The default setting for the Veconlab software presents the setup with a mild environmental interpretation to be used for teaching, i.e., in terms of a harvest from a fishery. Adjustments to the software and the use of supplemental instructions permitted Guzik to present the setup using either environmental terminology, workplace terminology, or a neutral "magic marbles" terminology. In each of these three treatments (environmental, workplace, and marbles) there were eight sessions, each with five participants. Each session was run for 10 rounds with fixed matchings. The purpose of the experiment was to see if the mode of presentation or "frame" would affect the degree to which people overused the common resource. There were no clear framing effects: the average decision was essentially the same for each treatment: 7.81 (environmental), 8.04 (marbles), and 7.8 (workplace). These small differences were not statistically significant, although there was a significant increase in variance for the non-neutral frames (workplace and environmental). The author was able to detect some small framing effects after controlling for demographic variables, but the main implication for experimental work is that if you are going to look at economic issues, then the frame may not matter much in these experiments, although one should still hold the frame constant and change the economic variables of interest.

The results reported by Guzik (2004) are fairly typical of those for common pool resource experiments; the average decisions are usually close to the Nash prediction, although there may be considerable variation across people and from one round to the next. However, if participants are allowed to communicate freely prior to making their decisions, then the decisions are reduced toward socially optimal levels (Ostrom and Walker 1991).

16.4 Extensions

Common pool resource problems with fisheries are discussed in Hardin (1968). For a wide-ranging coverage of issues related to the tragedy of the commons, see Ostrom, Gardner, and Walker (1994) and the special section of the Fall 1993 *Journal of Economic Perspectives* devoted to "Management of the Local Commons." The first common pool resource experiments are reported in Gardner, Ostrom, and Walker (1990), who evaluated the effects of subject experience, and by Walker, Gardner, and Ostrom (1990), who considered the effects of changing the endowment of tokens.

For results of a common pool resource experiment done in the field, see Cardenas, Stranlund, and Willis (2000), who conducted their experiment in rural villages in Colombia. The main finding is that the application of rules and regulations that are imperfectly monitored and outside of informal community institutions tends to increase the effect of individualistic motives and Nash-like results. They conclude ". . . modestly enforced government controls of local environmental quality and natural resource use may perform poorly, especially as compared to informal local management." In other words, the imperfectly enforced rules seemed to backfire by reducing the tacit cooperation that might otherwise help solve the commons problem. Regarding the self-governed institutions, Cardenas (2003) and Cardenas et al. (2002) report on a similar set of experiments in the field aimed at exploring the potential of non-binding face-to-face communication, which was effective in previous laboratory experiments with student subjects. Their findings suggest that actual inequalities observed in the field (regarding the social status and the wealth distances within and across groups) limited the effectiveness of communication. Groups of wealthier and more heterogeneous villagers found it more difficult to establish cooperation via communication. Although poorer participants had more experience with actual common dilemmas, the wealthier villagers' incomes were more dependent on their own assets, and they seemed to have had less frequent interactions in the past in these kinds of social exchange situations.

QUESTIONS

1. Calculate the social benefits associated with 4, 6, 8, 10, and 12 entrants for the setup in Tables 16.1 and 16.2 (show your work).

2. Use the numbers in Table 16.2 to explain why unpredictability in the number of entrants is bad, e.g., why a "fifty-fifty" of either 6 entrants or 10 entrants is not as good as the expected value (8 entrants for sure) in terms of expected earnings.

3. Explain in your own words why each increase in the number of entrants above 4 results in successively greater decreases in the social benefit in Table 16.2.

4. What would the equilibrium entry rate be for the game described in Section 16.3 if the entry fee were raised to $3 per entrant? How would the total amount collected in fees change by an increase from $2 to $3? How would the total amount in collected fees change as the result of a fee decrease from $2 to $1?

5. (Requires calculus) Derive a formula (in terms of A, B, C, and N) for the socially optimal level of appropriation of the common pool resource model in Section 16.3. What is the socially optimal level of appropriation per person for the parameters: $A = 25$, $B = 1/2$, $C = 1$, and $N = 5$?

6. For the payoffs in Table 16.1, show that there is another Nash equilibrium, without randomization, in which those who enter earn more than the $.50 payoff for those who do not.

chapter 17

Rent Seeking

Administrators and government officials often find themselves in a position of having to distribute a limited number of prized items (locations, licenses, and so on). Contenders for these prizes may engage in lobbying or other costly activities that increase their chances for success. No single person would spend more on lobbying than the prize is worth, but with a large number of contenders, expenditures on lobbying activities may be considerable. This raises the disturbing possibility that the total cost of lobbying by all contenders may dissipate a substantial fraction of the prize value. In economics jargon, the prize is an "economic rent," and the lobbying activity is referred to as *rent seeking*. This lobbying activity is thought to be more prevalent in developing countries, where some estimates are that such non-market competitions consume a significant fraction of national income (Krueger 1974). One only has to serve as a Department Chair in a U.S. university, however, to experience the frustrations of rent seeking. The game considered in this chapter is one in which the probability of obtaining the prize is equal to one's share of the total lobbying expenditures of all contenders. The game illustrates the potential costs of administrative (non-market) allocation procedures. It can be implemented with playing cards, as indicated in this chapter's Lobbying Game in the Class Experiments section, or it can be run on the Veconlab software.

17.1 Government with "a Smokestack on Its Back"

One of the most spectacular successes of recent government policy has been the auctioning off of bandwidth used to feed the exploding growth in the use of cell phones and pagers. The U.S. Federal Communications Commission (FCC) has allocated major licenses with a series of auctions that raised billions of dollars without adverse consequences. Several European countries have followed with similarly successful auctions, which have raised many more billions than expected in some cases. The use of auctions collects large numbers of potential competitors, and the commodities can be allocated quickly to those with the highest valuations. In the United States, this bandwidth was originally reserved for the armed forces, but it was underused at the end of the Cold War, and the transfer created a large increase in economic wealth, without significant administrative costs. It could have easily been otherwise. Radio and television broadcasting licenses were traditionally allocated via administrative proceedings, which are sometimes called beauty contests. The successful contender would have to convince the regulatory authority that service would be of high quality and that community social values would be protected. This often required establishing a technical expertise and an effective lobbying presence. The lure of extremely high potential profits was strong enough to induce large expenditures by aspiring providers. Those who had acquired licenses in this manner were opposed to market-based allocations that forced the recipients to pay for the licenses. Similar economic pressures may explain why beauty contest allocations continue to be prevalent in many other countries.

The first crack in the door appeared in the late 1980s, when the FCC decided to skip the administrative proceedings in the allocation of hundreds of regional cell phone licenses. The forces opposed to the pricing of licenses managed to block an auction, and the licenses were allocated by lottery instead. There were about 320,000 applications for 643 licenses. Each application involved significant paperwork (legal and accounting services), and firms specializing in providing completed applications began offering this service for about $600 per application. The resources used to provide this service have opportunity costs, and Hazlett and Michaels (1993) estimated the total cost of all submitted applications to be about $400,000. The lottery winners often sold their licenses to more efficient providers, and resales were used to estimate that the total market value of the licenses at that time was about a million dollars. Each individual lottery winner earned very large profits on the difference between the license value and the application cost, but the costs incurred by others were lost, and the total cost of the transfer of this property was estimated to be about 40 percent of the market value of the licenses. There are, of course, the indirect costs of subsequent transfers of licenses to more efficient providers, a process of consolidation that may take many years. In the meantime, inefficient provision of the cellular services may have created ripples of inefficiency in the economy. Episodes like this caused Milton and Rose Friedman (1989), in a discussion of the unintended side effects of government policies, to remark: "Every government measure bears, as it were, a smokestack on its back."

In a classic paper, Gordon Tullock (1967) pointed out that the real costs associated with competition for government granted rents may destroy or dissipate much of the value of those rents in the aggregate, even though the winners in such contests may earn large profits. This destruction of value is often invisible to those responsible, since the contestants participate willingly, and the administrators often enjoy the process of being lobbied. Moreover, some of the costs of activities like waiting in line and personal lobbying are not directly priced in the market. These costs can be quite apparent in a laboratory experiment of the type to be described next.

17.2 Rent Seeking in the Classroom Laboratory

In many administrative (non-market) allocation processes, the probability of obtaining a prize or monopoly rent is an increasing function of the amount spent in the competition. In the FCC lottery, the chances of winning a license were approximately equal to the applicant's efforts as a proportion of the total efforts of the other contestants. This provides a rationale for a standard mathematical model of rent seeking with N contestants. The effort for person i is denoted by x_i for $i = 1, \ldots, N$. The total cost of each effort is a cost c times the person's own effort, i.e., cx_i. In the simplest symmetric model, the value of the rent, V, is the same for all, and each person's probability of winning the prize is equal to their own effort as a fraction of the total effort of all contestants. Here the expected payoff is the probability of success, which is the fraction of total effort, times the prize value V, minus the cost of effort, as shown in Equation (17.1).

$$\text{Expected payoff} = \frac{x_i}{\displaystyle\sum_{j=1,\ldots,N} x_j} V - cx_i \qquad (17.1)$$

The effort cost on the right is not multiplied by any probability since it must be paid whether or not the prize is obtained.

Goeree and Holt (1999a) used the payoff function in Equation (17.1) in a classroom experiment with $V = \$16,000$, $c = \$3,000$, and $N = 4$. Each of the four competitors consisted of a team of two to three students. Efforts were required to be integer amounts. This requirement was enforced by giving 13 playing cards of the same suit to each team. Rent seeking effort was determined by the number of cards that the team placed in an envelope, as described in this chapter's Lobbying Game Instructions in the Class Experiments section. Each team incurred a cost of $3,000 for each card played, regardless of whether or not they obtained the prize. The cards played were collected, shuffled, and one was drawn to determine which contender would win the $16,000 prize. The number of cards played varied from team to team, but on average each team played about three cards. Thus a typical team incurred 3 × $3,000 in expenses, and the total lobbying cost for all four teams was over $36,000, all for a prize worth only $16,000!

Similar results were obtained in a separate classroom experiment using the Veconlab setup. The parameters were the same (four competitors, a $16,000 value, and a $3,000 cost per unit of effort), and the 12 teams were randomly put into groups of four competitors in a series of rounds. The average number of lobbying effort units was three in the first round, which was reduced to a little over two in the fourth and fifth rounds. Even with two units expended by each team, the total cost would be 2 (number of effort units) times 4 (teams) times $3,000 (cost of effort), for a total cost of $24,000. This again resulted in over-dissipation of the rent, which was only $16,000.

The Nash Equilibrium

A Nash equilibrium for this experiment is a lobbying effort for each competitor such that nobody would want to alter their expenditure given that of the other competitors. First, consider the case of four contenders, a $16,000 value, and a $3,000 effort cost. Note that efforts of 0 cannot constitute an equilibrium, since any person could deviate to an effort of 1 and obtain the $16,000 prize for sure at a cost of only $3,000. Next, suppose that each person is planning to choose an effort of 2 at a cost of $6,000. Since the total effort is 8, the chances of winning are 2/8 = 1/4 so the expected payoff is 16,000/4 – 6,000, which is *minus* $2,000. This cannot be a Nash equilibrium, since each person would have an incentive to deviate to 0 and earn nothing instead of losing $2,000. Next, consider the case where each person's strategy is to exert an effort of 1, which produces an expected payoff of 16,000/4 – 3,000 = 1,000. To verify that this is an equilibrium, we have to check to be sure that deviations are not profitable. A reduction to an effort of 0 with a payoff of 0 is obviously bad. A unilateral increase to an effort of 2, when the others maintain efforts of 1, will result in a 2/5 chance of winning, for an expected payoff of 16,000(2/5) – 6,000 = 400, which is also worse than the payoff of 1,000 obtained with an effort of 1.

In the symmetric equilibrium, the effort of 1 for each of the four contestants results in a total cost of 4(3,000) = 12,000, which dissipates three-fourths of the 16,000 rent. This raises the issue of whether a reduction in the cost of rent-seeking efforts might reduce the extent of wasted resources. In the context of the FCC lotteries, for example, this could correspond to a requirement of less paperwork for each separate application. Suppose that the resource cost of each application is reduced from $3,000 to $1,000. This cost reduction causes the Nash equilibrium level to rise from 1 to 3 (see Question 1 at the end of the chapter). Thus, cutting the cost to one-third of its original level is predicted to triple the amount of rent-seeking activity, so the social cost of this activity would be unchanged.

The Nash equilibrium calculations done so far were based on considering a particular level of rent-seeking activity, common to each person, and showing that a deviation by one person alone would not increase that person's expected payoff. This is a straightforward, but tedious, approach, and it has the additional disadvantage of not explaining how the candidate for a Nash equilibrium was found in the first place. The Mathematical Derivation of the Equilibrium at the end of this chapter contains a simple calculus derivation that uses the rules for derivatives encountered previously in the Optional Quick Calculus Review at the end of Chapter 6. It will be shown that the equilibrium amount of lobbying effort is given, as shown in Equation (17.2).

$$x^* = \frac{(N-1)}{N^2} \frac{V}{c} \qquad\qquad (17.2)$$

It is straightforward to verify that $x^* = 1$ when $V = \$16,000$, $c = \$3,000$, and $N = 4$. When the cost is reduced to $1,000, the equilibrium level of rent-seeking activity is raised to 3. Notice that the predicted effect of a cost reduction is that the total amount spent on rent-seeking activity is unchanged.

Finally, consider the total cost of all rent-seeking activity, which will be measured by the product of the number of contenders, the effort per contender, and the cost per unit of effort: Nx^*c. It follows from Equation (17.2) that this total cost is $(N - 1)/N$ times the prize value, V. Thus the amount of the rent that is dissipated is a fraction, $(N - 1)/N$, which is an increasing function of the number of contenders. With two contenders, half of the value is dissipated in a Nash equilibrium, and this fraction increases toward 1 as the number of contenders gets large. In general, *rent dissipation* is measured as the ratio of total expenditures on rent-seeking activity by all contenders to the value of the prize.

17.4 Comparative Statics for Changes in Cost and the Number of Competitors

At this point it is useful to summarize the results of Section 17.3, which will motivate the experiments to be discussed next. First, although an increase in the number of competitors is predicted to reduce the amount of lobbying effort for each one, the total social cost of lobbying is predicted to be higher with higher numbers of competitors. Second, a reduction in the cost of rent-seeking effort is predicted to generate an offsetting increase in this effort, so the fraction of rent dissipation is predicted to be independent of the cost of lobbying effort, c. For example, recall the previous example with four contenders, where the reduction in c from $3,000 to $1,000 raised the Nash equilibrium lobbying effort from 1 to 3, thereby maintaining a constant total level of expenditures.

These predictions were tested with a Veconlab experiment run on a single class with a 2×2 design with high and low lobbying costs, and with high and low numbers of competitors. There were 20 rounds (5 for each treatment). The prize value was $16,000 in all rounds, and each person began with an initial cash balance of $100,000. One person was selected at random ex post to receive a small percentage of earnings. The treatments involved a per-unit cost of either $500 or $1,000, and either two or four contenders. As predicted, a reduction in effort cost by a factor of one-half raised effort, from 6 to 10 ($N = 2$) and from 6 to 8 ($N = 4$), but the efforts did not double as predicted. All of the observed effort levels were higher than the Nash equilibrium predictions, and the total cost of the rent-seeking activity, as shown in Table 17.1 (rounded to the nearest $1,000), was a high fraction of the total prize value in all cases. With four competitors, the rent was either fully dissipated or over-dissipated, as can be seen from the numbers in the bottom row.

Several conclusions are apparent (see Questions 1 and 2 at the end of the chapter):

■ The total costs of rent-seeking activity are significant, and are greater than 50 percent of the prize value in all treatments.

Table 17.1	Total Rent-Seeking Costs (Rounded Off) in a Classroom Rent-Seeking Experiment with a Prize Value of $16,000	
	Low Effort Cost	**High Effort Cost**
N = 2	$10,000	$12,000
N = 4	$16,000	$24,000

- The total costs of rent-seeking activity are greater than the Nash predictions.
- An increase in the number of contenders tends to increase the total costs of rent seeking.
- A decrease in per-unit effort costs raises efforts, but not enough to offset the cost reduction.

The results of the classroom experiments are roughly consistent with data from an ongoing research experiment being run at the Univeristy of Virginia. The parameters are basically scaled down versions of those used above, with a prize value of $1.60 and an effort cost of $0.10. Participants were recruited in cohorts of 12, with random matchings for 20 rounds of play. Each cohort only participated in a single group size treatment, two or four, to avoid sequence effects. Figure 17.1 shows the average efforts for each treatment. Notice that both data sequences are above the Nash equilibrium prediction, shown by the relevant horizontal dashed line (at 4 for $N = 2$ and at 3 for $N = 4$). Again, we see over-dissipation in the 4-person design, since the average efforts of about 5 yield a total effort cost of about $4 \times 5 \times \$0.10 = \$2$, as compared with the $1.60 prize value.

17.5 Extensions

Rent-seeking models have been used in the study of political lobbying (Hillman and Samet 1987), which is a natural application because lobbying expenditures often involve real resources. In fact, any type of contest for a single prize may have similar strategic elements, e.g., political campaigns or research and development contests (Isaac and Reynolds 1988). There is a large and growing literature that uses the rent-seeking paradigm to study non-market allocation activities. Davis and Reilly (1998) use the fact that the rent-seeking model is equivalent to a lottery to compare revenue raised by lottery with revenue from an auction.

There have been a number of research experiments using the payoff structure in Equation (17.1), and over-dissipation is the typical result, e.g., Potters et al. (1998) and Millner and Pratt (1989). In a companion paper, Millner and Pratt (1991) used a lottery choice decision to separate people into groups according to their risk aversion. Groups with more risk-averse individuals tended to expend more on rent-seeking activity. Anderson and Stafford (2003) evaluated predictions of a generalization of the basic model, by giving different

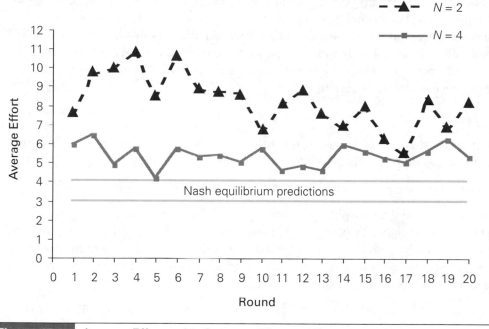

| Figure 17.1 | Average Efforts with Groups of Two and Four |

players different cost levels and allowing an initial decision of whether or not to compete at all. The total expenditures on rent seeking exceeded theoretical predictions in all treatments they considered, and the rent was over-dissipated in most treatments. The high effort levels reduced profitability for entrants, so the rate of participation in the rent-seeking contest was lower than predicted in theory.

Appendix: **Mathematical Derivation of the Equilibrium**

A calculus derivation is relatively simple, and is offered here as an option for those who are familiar with basic rules for taking derivatives (some of these rules are introduced in the Optional Quick Calculus Review at the end of Chapter 6). First, consider the expected payoff function in Equation (17.1), modified as shown in Equation (17.3) to let the decisions of the $N - 1$ others be equal to a common level, x^*.

$$\text{Expected payoff} = \frac{x_i}{x_i + (N - 1)x^*}V - cx_i \qquad (17.3)$$

This will be a "hill-shaped" (concave) function of the person's own rent-seeking activity, x_i, and the function is maximized at the top of the hill where the slope of the function is zero.

To find this point, the first step is to take the derivative and set it equal to zero. The resulting equation will determine player i's best response when the others are choosing x^*. In a symmetric equilibrium with equal rent-seeking activities, it must be the case that $x_i = x^*$, which will yield an equation that determines the equilibrium level of x^*. This analysis will consist of two steps: setting the derivative of player i's expected payoff equal to zero, and then using the symmetry condition that $x_i = x^*$.

Step 1

In order to use the rule for taking the derivative of a power function, it is convenient to express Equation (17.3) as a power function, as shown in Equation (17.4).

$$\text{Expected payoff} = x_i(x_i + (N - 1)x^*)^{-1}V - cx_i \qquad (17.4)$$

The final term on the right side of Equation (17.4) is linear in x_i, so its derivative is $-c$. The first term on the right side of Equation (17.4) is the product of x_i and a power function that contains x_i, so the derivative is found with the product rule (derivative of the first function times the second, plus the first function times the derivative of the second), which yields the first two terms on the left side of Equation (17.5).

$$(x_i + (N - 1)x^*)^{-1}V - x_i(x_i + (N - 1)x^*)^{-2}V - c = 0 \qquad (17.5)$$

Step 2

Next, we use the fact that $x_i = x^*$ in a symmetric equilibrium. Making this substitution into Equation (17.5) yields a single Equation (17.6) in the common equilibrium level, x^* as follows:

$$(x^* + (N - 1)x^*)^{-1}V - x^*(x^* + (N - 1)x^*)^{-2}V - c = 0 \qquad (17.6)$$

which can be simplified to Equation (17.7).

$$\frac{1}{Nx^*}V - \frac{1}{N^2x^*}V - c = 0 \qquad (17.7)$$

Finally, we can multiply both sides of Equation (17.7) by $N^2 x^*$, which yields an equation that is linear in x^* that reduces to the formula given previously in Equation (17.2).

QUESTIONS

1. Suppose that the cost per unit of effort is reduced from \$3,000 to \$1,000, with four competitors and a prize of \$16,000. Show that a common effort of 3 is a Nash equilibrium for the rent-seeking game with payoffs in Equation (17.1). (*Hint*: Check to be sure that a unilateral deviation to an effort of 2 or 4 would not be profitable, given that the

other three people keep choosing 3.) Of course, to be complete, all possible deviations would have to be considered, but you can get the idea by considering deviations to 2 and 4. An alternative is to use calculus.

2. Suppose that the effort cost is reduced to $500. Show that a common effort of 6 is a Nash equilibrium (consider unilateral deviations to 4 and 7).

3. Calculate the total amount of money spent in rent-seeking activities for the setup in Question 2. Did the reduction in the per-unit (marginal) cost of rent seeking from $1,000 to $500 reduce the predicted *total* cost of rent-seeking activity?

4. Suppose that the number of competitors for the setup in Question 1 is reduced from 4 to 2. The per-unit effort cost is $1,000 and the prize value is $16,000. Show that a common effort of 4 is a Nash equilibrium (for simplicity, only consider deviations to 3 and 5, or use calculus).

5. Did the reduction in competitors from 4 to 2 in Question 4 reduce the predicted extent of rent dissipation? (Rent dissipation is the total cost of all rent-seeking activity as a proportion of the prize value.)

chapter 18

Voting and Politics Experiments

Decentralized equilibrium outcomes are efficient in many economic markets, and as a consequence, economists sometimes fall into the trap of thinking that the outcomes of a political process necessarily have a high intrinsic value. In contrast, political scientists are well aware that the outcome of a vote may depend critically on factors like the structure of the agenda, whether straw votes are allowed, and the extent to which people vote strategically or naïvely. Voting experiments allow one to evaluate alternative political institutions, and to study how people actually behave in controlled laboratory conditions. These studies are complemented by clever field experiments that seek to create contexts with more external validity, e.g., having voters view media ads with differing formats. Some types of voting experiments can be run with the Veconlab Voting program, which allows simple agendas, runoffs, non-binding polls, approval voting, and randomly determined costs of voting for the study of turnout decisions. Hand-run instructions are available in Anderson and Holt (1999), for agenda effects, and in Wilson (2005), for candidate location along a line.

18.1 The Median Voter Theorem

Consider a simple classroom experiment in which each person has a constant marginal value for units of a public good, up to a limit determined by a numbered playing card that is dealt to that person. Thus, a person with an 8 would earn V dollars for each unit provided, up to 8 units, with additional units having no value. Each additional unit of the good costs an amount C, which is divided equally among the N committee members. Hewett et al. (2005) contains instructions for a classroom experiment with this setup, which induces single-peaked preferences for the level of the public good. If $V = 1$, $C = 1$, and $N = 5$, then the marginal cost per person is $C/N = \$0.20$, and the benefit of adding a unit up to one's maximum preferred level is $V - C/N = \$0.80$. Thus, the monetary preferences for a

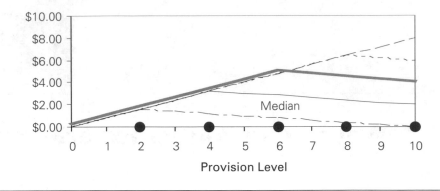

Figure 18.1 Single Peaked Preferences with a Median at 6

person with a card number X would have slope of $1 - 0.2 = 0.8$ up to X and a slope of -0.2 above X. The random allocation of playing cards would induce differing preference profiles, as shown in Figure 18.1 for draws of 2, 4, 6, 8, and 10. The person with a card of 10 has preferences that rise and peak at the right side. The middle person, with a card of 6, has preferences that peak at a level of 6, as shown by the gray thick line. The preferred points for each of the five voters are represented on the horizontal axis by solid dots.

With these preferences and majority rule voting, the standard prediction for the committee decision would be the preferred point of the median voter—in this case the person with a preferred point of 6. This is because there is no other outcome that would beat this point in a binary contest. For example, if the voter with a preferred point of 8 were to propose an alternative level of 8, then the three voters with preferred points of 2, 4, and 6 would vote against this alternative, which would fail on a 3 to 2 vote. This reasoning can be used to show that the level 6 would beat all alternatives in two-way contests under majority voting, which is the defining characteristic of a *Condorcet winner*.

A closely related notion is that of the *core*, which is the set of "unblocked" outcomes. Note that a level of 6 is the only outcome that cannot be blocked by another alternative, and therefore, 6 is the unique element in the core of this voting game. More generally, the core of a voting game is the set of outcomes that cannot be blocked by a coalition of voters who would all prefer an alternative outcome and who could implement it under the voting rules for the game by making a binding commitment among themselves to vote for the alternative. The example in Figure 18.1 illustrates another property of the core, i.e., that it need not be the outcome that maximizes total earnings, assuming that side payments are not permitted. This is because raising the provision level from 6 to 7, for example, only costs $1, but it provides an additional dollar benefit to each of the two voters with higher preferred levels. (In general, the earnings-maximizing level of the public good in this setup would be the largest integer X such that the number of voters with card numbers at or above X is greater than the cost C.)

To summarize, with single-peaked preferences along a single dimension, the preferred point of the middle person has strong drawing power, both in experiments and in theory. This pull to the center is referred to as the *median voter theorem*.

18.2 Experimental Tests of Spatial Voting Models

When voters have to make two related decisions, it is useful to model their preferences in a two-dimensional graph. For example, you could think of the horizontal dimension as expenditure on schools and the vertical dimension as expenditure on roads. Voters are assumed to prefer points closer to their own ideal points in the sense of Euclidian distance, so a voter's ideal point can be thought of as having concentric circular indifference points around a utility maximum at that point.

Figure 18.2 shows a special case where the median voter theorem generalizes to two dimensions. There are four large dots with connecting lines that intersect at a fifth dot in the center; these dots represent the ideal points of the five voters. Each dot has one or more concentric circles around it, indicating indifference curves composed of points equally distant from the voter's preferred point. A straight line connecting any two voters' ideal points is a contract curve of points that those two might agree to if they were bargaining, since from any point off of the line, a movement in a perpendicular direction to the line takes the outcome closer to the two endpoints of the line, and hence would make both voters better off. The special feature of the configuration in the figure is that the contract lines connecting four of the voters' ideal points intersect in the center at exactly the ideal point of the fifth voter. This central voter is the median voter along the horizontal dimension (with two others to the left and two to the right) and also along the vertical dimension (with two others above and two below). The central voter's ideal point in the figure is the core of this game; any other point can be blocked by a subset of the voters who would vote for the core point over the alternative.

Mckelvey and Ordeshook (1984) ran committee experiments with the setup in Figure 18.2. Preferences were induced by giving each voter a contour map of the issue space, with concentric circles labeled with probabilities that increased to 1 as the ideal point was approached. The final committee decision in the two-dimensional issue space determined the voter's probability of winning a high money prize in a lottery carried out after the meeting ended; this binary lottery payoff procedure was intended to minimize the chances of side payments. The meetings were run by a research assistant chair who was uninformed about the theoretical predictions. Discussion was governed by either a closed rule or an open rule. Under the closed rule, any person who wanted to speak or make a motion had to be recognized by the chair, all comments had to be directed to the chair, and only comments that pertained to a standing motion were allowed. Under the open rule, participants

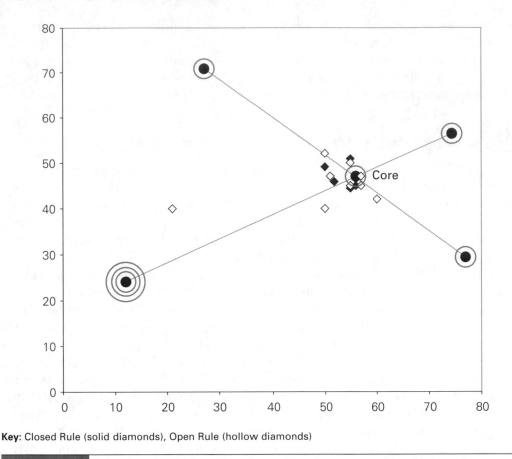

Key: Closed Rule (solid diamonds), Open Rule (hollow diamonds)

| **Figure 18.2** | McKelvey and Ordeshook Committee Outcomes with a Unique Core |

would speak directly with each other, without being recognized by the chair, and discussion was not limited to the motion on the floor. Under either rule, the initial position was the origin (0, 0), and any motion was required to represent a proposed movement in *only one direction*, i.e., a horizontal or a vertical movement. If a motion were seconded and passed, it would determine the new status quo. The experiment ended when a motion to adjourn was made and passed, and then final payoffs were determined by the lottery procedure.

The results of the committee decisions are shown in Figure 18.2 as solid diamonds for the closed rule meetings and as hollow diamonds for the open rule meetings. The core point has strong drawing power under either procedure, with the exception of one open rule meeting in which one of the voters consistently voted for the option that provided a lower payoff. These results confirm the earlier results of Fiorina and Plott (1978), that the core has a strong drawing power when it exists, a result that Palfrey (2005) has termed "core clustering" with "robustness" to procedural differences. Note that the closed rule points are somewhat closer than the open rule points, which is probably due to the stricter control over discussions under the closed rule.

Unfortunately, the core typically does not exist with multi-dimensional preferences, as the preference profile in Figure 18.3 indicates. Here, the fifth voter's ideal point does not lie on the intersection of lines connecting the other four. Instead, the lines connecting non-adjacent five ideal points form a pentagon, which frames most of the data points from both closed rule meetings (solid diamonds) and open rule meetings (hollow diamonds). But even the points inside of this pentagon are not in the core. To see this, begin with any point in the pentagon and consider an alternative that is in a direction perpendicular to one of the faces of the pentagon. The three voters with ideal points in that direction would favor the move, but the new point could then be blocked by a different coalition that prefers a movement toward a different face of the pentagon.

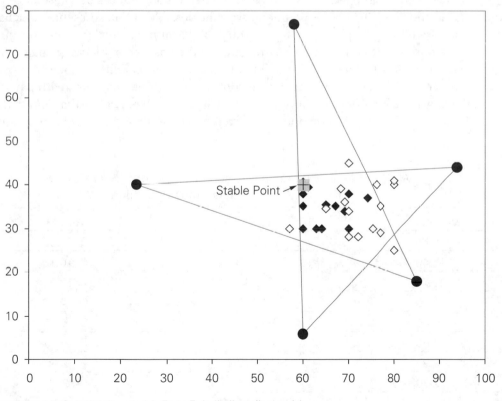

Key: Closed Rule (solid diamonds), Open Rule (hollow diamonds)

Figure 18.3   McKelvey and Ordeshook Committee Outcomes with No Core

The idea behind the McKelvey and Ordeshook experiments was that by limiting motions to movements in one direction only, the outcome might be driven to a stable point that lies at the intersection of the median of voters' ideal points in the horizontal direction and the median of voters' ideal points in the vertical direction. This stable point is the "+" sign in Figure 18.3. The committee outcomes do not cluster tightly around this stable point under either treatment, but the closed rule does draw the outcome points closer to the stable point. McKelvey and Ordeshook conclude that the closed rule provides a tighter reign on limiting consideration to movements in a single direction at a time, which would lead to a median outcome in each direction. This effect of political institutions on voting outcomes parallels earlier observations of the effects of market institutions on market outcomes.

18.3 Fairness and Deviations from Core Outcomes

There is a strand of the literature that is based on preferences over discrete outcomes. Isaac and Plot (1978) ran experiments with the possible options presented as a list. The results offered surprising support for the core, but the authors noted that the core outcome had a fairness attraction that was unrelated to the absence of blocking coalitions. Eavey and Miller (1984) altered the list of options in a manner that differentiated the core and fair outcomes. Each meeting involved a committee of three members, with payoffs determined by the committee decision as shown in Table 18.1. First, notice that option E is a Condorcet winner, since it is the most preferred outcome for Voter 1, and the options

Table 18.1	Voter Preferences for the Eavey and Miller Majority Rule Experiment with a Fair Outcome, G, that Differs from the Condorcet Winner, E		
	Voter 1	**Voter 2**	**Voter 3**
	E 19.60	I 22.00	B 23.50
	F 15.40	H 17.10	C 16.10
	G 12.20	J 13.15	A 13.20
	D 6.30	E 12.45	G 12.20
	A 5.40	G 12.20	D 5.70
	I 4.60	D 5.30	F 4.10
	J 3.35	F 3.70	E 2.65
	C 2.70	B 2.95	H 2.45
	H 2.10	A 1.20	J 1.50
	B 1.20	C 0.85	I 0.75

above E in the column for Voter 2 are below E for Voter 3, so E would always win by a 3 to 2 margin. Option G is identified as being "fair" since it is the only option that provides at least $10 for each player, i.e., it has something for everyone. Moreover, as compared with the Condorcet winner, E, the fair option G provides a large gain of almost $10 for Voter 3, at the cost of somewhat smaller sacrifices for Voters 1 and 2. In the experiment, each participant was only given information about their own payoff numbers, and discussions of the payoff numbers and side payments were prohibited. The fair outcome, G, was observed in 8 of 10 sessions, even though this outcome would be defeated in a binary contest against E if votes only depend on the voter's own payoffs.

18.4 Legislative Bargaining

Eavey and Miller (1984) also observed a strong bias toward the fair outcome over the unique core outcome in a different design where only one of the players, the agenda setter, could propose an alternative to an exogenously designated status quo. The setter model was generalized by Baron and Ferejohn (1989), who introduced a stylized model of legislative bargaining over a fixed sum of money. The bargaining process starts with one member of the legislature being selected at random to make a proposed division. If a proposal is accepted by majority vote, it will be implemented, and if not, another randomly selected member of the legislature is selected to make a new proposal. The theoretical prediction is that the first proposal will be structured to obtain the support of a bare majority, by offering each person in this coalition only slightly more than they can expect if the proposal is rejected and the game continues, i.e., their "continuation values." The proposer can maximize earnings by choosing the winning coalition to include those with the lowest continuation values (see Question 3 at the end of Chapter 12). Thus, the predictions are: 1) no delay, 2) full rent extraction, and 3) a minimal winning coalition. As results from ultimatum and setter game experiments suggest, experiments that implement the Baron and Ferejohn model result in delay, less-than-full rent extraction, and a tendency toward large winning coalitions.

The Frechette, Kagel, and Lehrer (2003) experiments implemented the Baron and Ferejohn model with groups of five voters and either an open rule or a closed rule. Under the closed rule, a proposal that is made must be voted on, whereas the open rule allows a second randomly selected person to either second or amend the proposal, with a runoff between the original and amended proposals in the event of an amendment. One difference from the earlier setter experiments is that Frechette, Kagel, and Lehrer let subjects participate in a series of committee bargaining games, which might tend to enhance learning and reduce fairness considerations if payoffs tend to equalize across games. The observed outcomes under the closed rule tended to approach the theoretical prediction of a minimal winning coalition in later meetings, although proposer earnings were lower than predicted. In contrast, the open rule sessions exhibited consistent super-majorities, with the share going to the proposer declining over time. An interesting and realistic extension of this research involves letting the "voters" in the experiment represent factions or voting blocks, with differing numbers of votes that they can deliver (Diermeier and Morton 2005).

18.5   Agendas and Strategic Voting

One type of agenda is to have one person be designated as a setter who unilaterally chooses a proposed alternative to the status quo. A more elaborate agenda would have initial votes determine the alternatives to be considered in the final vote. Agendas essentially put structure on the voting process, and interesting issues arise when voters at an early stage might wish to think strategically about which options will fare well at a later stage of the voting. Agendas can have dramatic effects on the voting outcome in cases where voters' preferences create a natural instability, with no Condorcet winner. For example, consider the preference profiles for three voter types, with the money payoffs given in parentheses as shown in Table 18.2.

These preferences generate a voting cycle. To see this, suppose that C is the status quo and A is proposed as an alternative. If people vote sincerely according to their preferences, A would beat C by a 6 to 3 vote, but then B would beat A, and then C would beat B, thus returning to the initial position. Anderson and Holt (1999) describe a simple card-based classroom experiment that typically results in a cycle: where voters increase school funding, and then increase highway funding, and then adopt a tax cut that scales back both types of funding.

The effect of a pre-set agenda is to provide a structure to the order in which options will be considered. The simplest agenda is one in which one option, say C, is the status quo that is run against the winner of an initial vote between A and B, as shown in Figure 18.4. In this first stage, the Type II and III voters might vote for B over A, since B provides higher payoffs for each of them. But then in the final stage, B would lose to C by a vote of 6 to 3. This result, which is shown by the dark arrows in the figure, would dismay the Type II voters who voted for their preferred option B initially but ended up with their least preferred option C and a payoff of only $0.50. If the Type II voters had voted strategically for the less preferred option, A, in the initial stage, then A would have won and would beat the status quo in the final stage. In this manner, strategic voting by the Type II voters would raise their payoffs from $0.50 to $2.00. The initial non-strategic voting by Type II voters for their pre-

Table 18.2	Preferences for a Voting Cycle

Type I (3 voters)	Type II (3 voters)	Type III (3 voters)
A ($3) > C ($2) > B ($0.50)	B ($3) > A ($2) > C ($0.50)	C ($3) > B ($2) > A ($0.50)

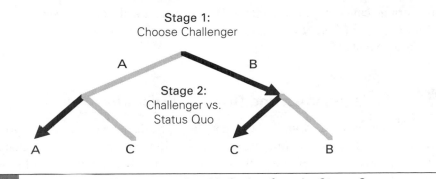

Figure 18.4   Sincere Voting for an Agenda with Option C as the Status Quo

ferred outcome in the first stage, without thinking ahead about the second stage, is called *sincere voting* in the political science literature, and it is sometimes called *myopic voting* in the economics literature.

This "C last agenda" was used in for a session reported in Holt and Smith (2006). The status quo, C, was selected in the initial vote, but then the Type II voters switched to strategic voting and option A won subsequently. Agenda changes that put another option last as the status quo resulted in that option being selected in the initial meeting, as predicted under sincere voting, and then the strategic outcome was observed after voters gained some experience. Thus, changes in the agenda changed the observed outcomes, even though voter preferences did not change. In addition, for a given agenda, the observed outcome changed as subjects learned to vote strategically.

These patterns are consistent with the agenda experiments of Herzberg and Wilson (1988) who observed a preponderance of sincere voting, and of Eckel and Holt (1989), who observed 100 percent sincere voting in the initial meeting, with strategic voting only emerging after several prior meetings. The lesson for agenda design is that sincere voting is probably a good assumption, unless the committee meets repeatedly, as with a university department faculty voting on hiring decisions, or unless the members have considerable experience with similar situations.

Plott and Levine (1978) identify several alternative types of non-strategic voting in somewhat more complicated agendas, and they used what they learned to manipulate the outcome of a meeting of a flying club (Levine and Plott 1977). The authors were members of an agenda committee for a club that was meeting to decide on a configuration for a fleet of general aviation planes. The authors preferred to have at least one larger plane, although a large faction of members preferred smaller, four-seat planes. The agenda was structured to defeat this option by pitting its supporters against a coalition of smaller groups with diverse interests. The club president was forced to follow the agenda, despite attempts to deviate, which included a proposed straw vote that might have helped club members vote more strategically. The club ended up selecting a fleet with some six-seat planes, and a subsequent poll indicated that this configuration was not a Condorcet winner. The authors were later expelled from the club.

18.6 Polls, Runoffs, and Other Coordinating Devices

In view of the dramatic agenda effects just discussed, it is not surprising that citizens might prefer more neutral methods of structuring the choice sequence from among multiple candidates or options. This section considers the effects of runoffs, opinion polls, and other devices that might be used by voters to coordinate their decisions. The type of coordination problem that can arise is illustrated in Table 18.3, which shows the basic payoffs used in a series of experiments conducted by Forsythe, Myerson, Rietz, and Weber (1993, 1996) and Morton and Rietz (2004).

Note that voters of Types I and II in this design have a strong preference for option A or B, but this majority is split in its preference for A or B. In binary contests, both A and B would defeat C. Therefore, C is, in this sense, a Condorcet loser. Under plurality voting, where all three options are on the ballot, option C would win if the majority splits between A and B, as would be the case with sincere voting. If a first stage vote is followed by a runoff between the top two contenders, however, the Condorcet loser would end up being matched with one of the other options, which would win. Thus, the runoff lets the split majority figure out which of the two preferred options has the best chance of winning in the runoff. Interestingly, Kousser (1984) argued that runoff elections might have been adopted in some parts of the United States in an effort to prevent minority candidates from winning. Forsythe, Myerson, Rietz, and Weber (1993) showed that a non-binding opinion poll held before a three-way contest will also serve to help the majority coordinate on one of its preferred options in committee voting experiments. Polls, however, were not as effective as runoffs in all cases, since poll results tend to show more randomness than actual votes.

One alternative to a simple plurality procedure is to let people vote for more than one candidate. This is called *approval voting*; voters receive a list of candidates or options and mark each with "approve" or "not approve." The option with the most approval votes wins.

Table 18.3	A Split Majority Profile	
Voter Type I (3 voters)	**Voter Type II (4 voters)**	**Voter Type III (5 voters)**
A 1.20	B 1.20	C 1.40
B 0.90	A 0.90	A 0.40
C 0.20	C 0.20	B 0.40

For the split-majority setup in Table 18.3, the use of approval voting might result in the selection of option A or B if enough Type I and II voters approve both of their top two options. In this manner, approval voting may not result in the selection of a Condorcet loser (option C in the table). Some non-Condorcet-winner results are reported in Holt and Smith (2006). Most controlled evaluations of approval voting, however, have used data from field experiments, with some mixed evaluations (Nagel 1984; Niemi and Bartels 1984). One interesting field experiment is reported in Brams and Fishburn (1988), who use data from elections of officers in two professional associations. In these elections, voters indicated their preferred candidate (plurality), but they also returned a preference ranking and an experimental approval voting ballot. The authors concluded that approval voting does not encourage the selection of a minimally approved candidate who offends the fewest people. Approval voting is used by a number of professional associations to select board members, including the Economic Science Association (for experimental economists).

18.7 Participation Games

One of the most perplexing problems for rational choice models of voting behavior is to explain why people vote at all in large elections. After all, the probability of altering the election outcome is small if there are many voters. Presumably, people vote anyway if the costs are low, or even negative for those who enjoy voting and telling family, friends, and coworkers about it. The high turnouts in recent Iraqi elections provide an example where the perceived benefits of voting outweigh high costs. There is some indirect evidence that costs matter, e.g., voter registration rates in the United States are lower in localities where jury selection lists are taken from lists of registered voters. Moreover, causal observation suggests that attendance rates at faculty meetings are higher when close issues need to be decided, i.e., when the potential benefit of affecting the outcome is likely to be larger. Laboratory experiments cannot address questions about the magnitudes of voting costs and benefits in the field, but experiments can test qualitative predictions about the effects of induced costs, benefits, and group sizes on turnout rates.

The basic voter turnout model is a *participation game*, first analyzed by Palfrey and Rosenthal (1983, 1985). Voters have costs of voting, which are either deterministic or randomly drawn from a cost distribution. For simplicity, consider a simple model with two voters of Type A and 2 voters of Type B, each of which has a cost of voting that is a common, known amount, c. If the committee chooses A, the voters of that type earn +1 and the voters of the other type earn −1, and vice versa. Ties are decided by the flip of a coin, so the expected payoff for a tie is 0 for each type. Thus, the gain from making or breaking a tie is +1. If $c > 1$, there is no reason to vote, so assume that $c < 1$. First, note that there is an equilibrium in which everyone votes, since a deviation to not voting would change a tie to a loss, which is worse than incurring the cost of voting. If costs are high enough, there can also be equilibria in which voters randomize, so let p denote the probability of voting for all four voters in a symmetric equilibrium with randomization. If $c = 13/16$, for example, there are mixed strategy equilibria at $p = 0.25$ and $p = 0.75$, as shown in the next paragraph (which can be skipped on a first reading).

Calculation of the Mixed-Strategy Equilibrium. To construct the mixed-strategy voting equilibrium for the four-person participation game in the previous paragraph, note that the expected gain is 1 for making a tie or breaking a tie. A decision to vote will always either make a tie or break a tie unless (1) your partner is not voting and the two voters of the other type are, which happens with probability $(1 - p)p^2$, or (2) your partner is voting and neither of the others are voting, which happens with probability $p(1 - p)^2$. Thus the probability that your vote will make a difference is: $1 - (1 - p)p^2 - p(1 - p)^2$. Recall that a voter must be indifferent to be willing to randomize, so the cost of voting, c, must equal to the probability that the vote makes a difference, multiplied by the difference of 1: $c = 1 - (1 - p)p^2 - p(1 - p)^2$. This equation can be expressed equivalently as: $p(1 - p) = 1 - c$, which can be solved for any given value of c. If $c = 13/16$, for example, it is straightforward to show that p will be either $1/4$ or $3/4$ as previously asserted. With higher numbers of voters of each type, the two mixed strategy probabilities move away from the center to become closer to the boundaries of 0 and 1.

Schram and Sonnemans (1996a, 1996b) ran participation game experiments with six voters of each type, a cost of 1, and a payoff difference of 2.5 if one's preferred outcome is selected. For this setup, the mixed strategy probabilities were near 0.1 and 0.9. The observed participation rate began in the middle and declined to the range from 0.2 to 0.3. Goeree and Holt (2005b) suggest that noisy behavior and bounded rationality may provide an explanation for participation rates that are not as extreme as predicted by theory (see the discussion of the incorporation of noise elements into game theory in Chapter 24). This approach is also used by Cason and Mui (2003) to explain data from another participation game experiment, and by Palfrey (2005) to explain less-than-predicted responses of data to treatment parameters in experiments with randomly determined voting costs, to be considered next.

All voters' costs have been assumed to be the same up to this point. A more realistic class of turnout models is obtained by letting voters' costs be randomly determined. In most cases, these models have similar qualitative predictions as those with randomization described above, and some of these predictions have been tested by Levine and Palfrey (2005) with large voting experiments involving groups of 3, 9, 27, and 51 voters. The theoretical predictions are quite intuitive: that turnout will be higher with small groups of voters and with close elections (more equal numbers of the two voter types). When there are more than three voters and unequal numbers of voters of each type, turnout is predicted to be larger for the minority group. The qualitative features of these predictions are supported by the experiments. The turnout rates are, however, less responsive to changes in treatment parameters than the theory would suggest.

Participation game experiments have shown that subjects in the lab respond to parameter changes qualitatively in ways that are predicted by theory, but the potentially strong effects of social interactions have been largely ignored, with the exception of Grober and Schram (2004), who add some realistic social context. As before, there are two types of voters with opposing preferences and known costs of voting. For each type, half are designated as senders who may decide to vote early or not. In one of the treatments, each of the senders is paired with a late voter of the same type, who is told whether or not the sender already voted. Senders who do not vote early are allowed to vote in the second stage, at the same time that the vote decisions of the late voters are made. This type of information exchange raised overall turnout rates dramatically, by about 50 percent as compared with a standard one-stage participation game control treatment.

18.8 Field Experiments

Many key elements in the political landscape involve social context. These elements involve such things as a knock on the door, a phone call, or an "attack ad," which may be difficult to replicate in a standard laboratory setting. Political scientists, therefore, have a long tradition of running clever field experiments, which can be roughly categorized as: 1) *enriched laboratory experiments* that may add a living room context or a randomly selected sample of voters, or 2) *pure field experiments* in which treatments are implemented in a natural setting so that the participants do not know they are in an experiment. This section contains an example of each type.

Ansolabehere, Iyengar, Simon, and Valentino (1994) used an enriched laboratory setting to study the effects of positive and negative campaign ads on turnout decisions. Subjects were recruited to come to a laboratory, which was furnished like a living room. They watched 15-minute tapes of a local news broadcast, which was interrupted by a commercial break with either a positive political ad, a negative political ad, or an ad for a commercial product (the control treatment). The positive and negative ads pertained to an actual upcoming election, and the substitution of positive and negative phrases was carefully done to maintain the same visuals, content, audio, and other features. In an ex post questionnaire, those exposed to a negative ad were 2.5 percent less likely to vote than those exposed to the neutral control, and they were 5 percent less likely to vote than those exposed to the positive ad. The authors concluded that the negative tone reduced the voter confidence in the responsiveness of the political institutions, thereby lowering intentions to vote. In a companion empirical study of 32 Senate races in the 1992 elections, the authors found evidence that negative ads tended to reduce voter turnout.

The control of running this experiment in the laboratory enabled the researchers to avoid possible biases, such as the tendency for people who remember an ad to be precisely those who were more likely to vote in the first place. On the other hand, the actual decision to vote was not directly observed, and participants' responses to survey questions about intentions to vote may be biased. This problem was cleverly addressed by Gerber and Green (2000), who used official voter records for New Haven precincts to determine whether specific participants actually voted in the election that followed the experiment. The field setting allowed them to deliver treatment stimuli in a realistic social context, without alerting recipients to the existence of a controlled experiment. The 29,380 participants were randomly assigned to treatments with messages urging them to vote. The treatments consisted of: no contact (control), direct mail, a phone call, face-to-face contact at home, or some combination. The messages were non-partisan, and urged people to vote on the basis of civic duty, neighborhood solidarity, or the closeness of the election. The main conclusion was that personal contact had a positive and substantial effect on turnout. There was a smaller direct mail effect, but phone contact did not seem to have an effect. This study attracted a lot of attention from political operatives, given the potentially large impacts of even small turnout increases in target districts where a particular candidate is known to be more popular.

18.9   Extensions

There have been some interesting experiments that focus on the competition between candidates for voters' support. When voter preferences are single peaked along a single dimension and candidates only care about winning, the arguments in Section 18.1 indicate that candidates will locate near the center, which is a common complaint sometimes made in the United States about the similarity of Democratic and Republican candidates. Wilson (2005) has developed a classroom experiment in which candidate convergence to the center is typical in a symmetric one-dimensional setting. Electoral contests are often asymmetric, with potentially large advantages for incumbents, film actors, relatives of popular presidents, and so on. There is some theoretical work predicting that disadvantaged candidates will tend to choose more extreme locations than candidates with an advantage; see Aragones and Plafrey (2004) for an experimental evaluation of these asymmetric contests.

Another interesting class of voting models pertains to situations where different voters obtain different information signals about some issue of common interest, much as bidders in common value auctions obtain independent estimates of the value of a prize (see Chapter 21). The analogue to the "winner's curse" in common value auctions is known as the *swing voter's curse*. For example, suppose that individuals on a jury form indepen-dent evaluations of whether or not a defendant is guilty. Under unanimity, it only takes one acquittal vote to block a conviction, so the only way that a juror's vote will be pivotal is if all other jurors vote to convict. If each juror votes sincerely, i.e., to acquit if their signal is "innocent" and to convict if their signal is "guilty," then would a juror really want to vote to acquit if they somehow knew that everyone else is voting to convict? As this question suggests, voting will not be sincere. In a Nash equilibrium, it can be shown that those who receive guilty signals will vote guilty, and those with innocent signals will vote guilty with positive probability. This type of deviation from sincere voting is observed in the jury voting experiments of Guarnaschelli, McKelvey, and Palfrey (2000).

The "signals" that voters perceive can be quite subtle, and one obvious source of asymmetry in actual campaigns arises from the personal appearances of the candidates. Todorov et al. (2005) showed subjects paired photos of candidates in U.S. congressional and Senate races, and asked them to judge the competence of the candidates. The competency judgments were based solely on 1-second exposures to black and white facial images. Responses for cases where the subject recognized one of the candidates were not used. The candidate who was considered to be more competent won in about two-thirds of the cases (significantly better than chance). The authors ruled out other factors such as assessments of age, attractiveness, and facial familiarity.

Recent surveys of political science experiments, organized around theoretical insights, can be found in Palfrey (2005) and Holt, Palfrey, and Smith (2005). See Holt and Smith (2006) for a longer survey, with data from selected experiments and a section on field experiments. Gerber and Green (2004) provide a thoughtful evaluation of the advantages of field experiments in politics.

QUESTIONS

1. Redraw the setup in Figure 18.2 with only three voters who have ideal points that differ. Under what conditions would a core exist, and under what conditions would it not exist? Explain.

2. For the setup in Table 18.1, explain why G is not a Condorcet winner.

3. Consider a situation in which there are equal numbers of high, middle, and low-income voters. The issue to be decided is the level of expenditures on public schools, to be financed by taxes. Public education is important to the middle-income voters, who prefer high expenditure, but their second choice is low expenditure since they will send their children to private schools if the public schools are not of top quality. The high-income voters will use private schools in any case, so to minimize taxes, they prefer low to medium to high expenditure levels. Finally, the low-income voters prefer medium to high to low expenditure levels. Show that there is not a Condorcet winner, and that these preferences induce a voting cycle.

4. Suppose that the status quo school spending level is low, and that preferences are as given in Question 3. An agenda pits medium and high levels, with the winner in the first stage being matched against the status quo in the final stage. What outcome would you expect if voting is sincere? Would the outcome change if voting is strategic? Explain.

5. Consider an asymmetric participation game in which there are two voters of Type A and only one voter of Type B, all of whom are risk neutral. The cost of voting is C for

each person. The payoffs for win, tie, and loss are +1, 0, and −1 respectively. In a mixed strategy equilibrium, let α denote the probability that each Type A person votes, and let β denote the probability that the Type B person votes. For a Type A person, a decision to vote will cost C and with generate a net gain of 1 (create a tie or break a tie) unless the other A person votes and the B person does not, which occurs with probability $\alpha(1 - \beta)$. Thus, the Type A person is indifferent between voting and not voting if: $1 - \alpha(1 - \beta) = C$. Using similar reasoning, show that the Type B person is indifferent between voting and not if: $1 - \alpha^2 = C$. Explain this reasoning or provide another derivation of this equation, and then calculate the equilibrium vote probabilities.

6. Have you had any experience attending a meeting (club, fraternity, student organization) and thinking that the agenda was rigged to generate a specific outcome? If so, describe the agenda and why it might have had an effect.

part 5

Auctions

Auctions can be very useful in the sale of perishable commodities like fish and flowers. The public nature of most auctions is also a desirable feature when equal treatment and "above-board" negotiations are important, as in the public procurement of milk, highway construction, and so on. Internet auctions can be particularly useful for a seller of a rare or specialty item who needs to connect with geographically dispersed buyers. And auctions are increasingly used to sell bandwidth licenses, as an alternative to administrative or "beauty contest" allocations, which can generate wasteful lobbying efforts.

Most participants find auctions to be exciting, given the win/lose nature of the competition. The two main classes of models are those where bidders know their own private values, and those where the underlying common value of the prize is not known. Private values may differ from person to person, even when the characteristics of the prize are perfectly known. For example, two prospective house buyers may have different family sizes or numbers of vehicles, and therefore, the same square footage may be much less useful to one than to the other, depending on how it is configured into common areas, bedrooms, and parking. An example of a common value auction is the bidding for an oil lease, where each bidder makes an independent geological study of the likely recovery rates for the tract of land being leased. Winning in such an auction can be stressful if it turns out that the bidder overestimated the prize value—a situation known as the "winner's curse."

Private value auctions are introduced in Chapter 19, where the focus is on comparisons of bidding strategies with Nash equilibrium predictions for different numbers of bidders. There is also a discussion of several interesting variations, e.g., an "all-pay" provision that forces all bidders to pay their own bids, whether or not they win, and a "second-price" rule that requires the high bidder to pay the second highest bid price.

Common value auctions are considered in Chapter 21, where the focus is on the effects of the numbers of bidders on the winner's curse. The "buyer's curse," discussed in Chapter 20, is a similar phenomenon that arises when a bidder seeks to purchase a firm of unknown profitability from the current owner. In each case, the curse effect arises because bidders may not realize that having a successful bid is an event that conveys useful information about others' valuations or estimates of value.

The Internet has opened up many exciting possibilities for new auction designs, and laboratory experiments can be used to test possible procedures prior to the final selection of the auction rules. For example, the Georgia Irrigation Reduction Auction, which was largely designed and run by experimental economists, was structured with no pre-announced final period and with some other features that were intended to defeat possible attempts at collusion by bidders (farmers). Another issue that arises when there are multiple prizes is the possibility of value complementarities. For example, a telecommunications company may place a high value on acquiring a combination or "network" of geographically adjacent broadcast licenses. In such cases, the companies may prefer to bid on packages of licenses, to avoid the exposure problem that arises when some of the desired licenses in the network are not obtained. The FCC is currently considering switching from simultaneous auctions for individual broadcast licenses to some form of package bidding, and experiments are being used to help evaluate the relative performance of alternative package bidding procedures. These (and other) public policy issues that arise from multi-unit auctions are discussed in Chapter 22.

chapter 19

Private Value Auctions

Internet newsgroups and online trading sites offer a fascinating glimpse into the various ways that collectibles can be sold at auction. Some people just post a price, and others announce a time period in which bids will be entertained, with the sale going to the person with the highest bid at the time of the close. These bids can be collected by email and held as sealed bids until the close, or the highest standing bid at any given moment can be announced in an ascending bid auction, which is a key feature of most eBay auctions. Trade is motivated by differences in individual values, e.g., as some people wish to complete a collection and others wish to get rid of duplicates. This chapter pertains to the case where individual valuations differ randomly, with each person knowing only their own "private" value. The simplest model of a private-value auction is one where bidders' values are independent draws from a distribution that is uniform in the sense that each money amount in a specified interval is equally likely. For example, one could throw a 10-sided die twice, with the first throw determining the tens digit and the second throw determining the ones digit. The chapter begins with the simplest case, where the bidder receives a value and must bid against a simulated opponent, whose bids are in turn determined by a draw from a uniform distribution. Next, we consider the case where the other bidder is another participant. In each case, the slope of the bid/value relationship is compared with the Nash prediction. These auctions can be done by hand with dice (see this chapter's Private Value Auction in the Class Experiments section), or with the Veconlab Private Value Auction program. This online auction has setup options that include an all-pay rule, a second price auction, and a revenue-sharing provision that returns a fraction of auction revenue to the bidders.

19.1 Introduction

The rapid development of e-commerce has opened up opportunities for creating new markets that coordinate buyers and sellers at diverse locations. The vast increase in the numbers of potential traders online also makes it possible for relatively thick markets to develop, even for highly specialized commodities and collectibles. These markets are structured as auctions, since an auction permits bids and asks to be collected 24 hours a day over an extended period. Gains from trade in such markets arise because different individuals have different values for a particular commodity. There are, of course, many ways to run an auction, and different sets of trading rules may have different performance properties. Sellers, naturally, would be concerned with selecting the type of auction that will enhance their sales revenues. From an economist's perspective, there is interest in finding auctions that promote the efficient allocation of items to those who value them the most. If an auction fails to find the highest-value buyer, this may be corrected by trading in an "after market," but such trading itself entails transactions costs, which may be 5 percent of the value of the item, and even more for low-value items where shipping and handling costs are significant.

Economists have typically relied on theoretical analysis to evaluate efficiency properties of alternative sets of auction rules. The seminal work on auction theory can be found in a *Journal of Finance* paper by William Vickrey (1961), who later received a Nobel Prize in economics. Prior to Vickrey, an analysis of auctions would likely be based on a Bertrand-type model in which prices are driven up to be essentially equal to the resale value of the item. It was Vickrey's insight that different people are likely to have different values for the same item, and he devised a mathematical model of competition in this context. The model is one where there is a probability distribution of values in the population, and the bidders are drawn at random from this population. For example, suppose that a buyer's value for a car with a large passenger area and low gas mileage is inversely related to the buyer's daily commuting time. There is a distribution of commuting distances in the population, so there will be a distribution of individual valuations for the car. Each person knows their own needs, and hence their own valuation, but they do not know for sure what other bidders' values are. Before discussing the Vickrey model, it is useful to begin with an overview of different types of auctions.

19.2   Auctions: Up, Down, and the "Little Magical Elf"

Suppose that you are a collector of cards from *Magic: The Gathering*. These cards are associated with a popular game in which the contestants play the role of wizards who duel with spells from playing cards. The cards are sold in random assortments, so it is natural for collectors to find themselves with some redundant cards. In addition, rare cards are more valuable, and some out-of-print cards sell for hundreds of dollars. Let's consider the thought process that may occur to you as you contemplate a selling strategy. Suppose that you log into the newsgroup site and offer a bundle of cards in exchange for a bundle that is proposed by someone else. You receive some responses, but the bundles offered in exchange contain cards that you do not want, so you decide to post a price for each of your cards. Several people seek to buy at your posted price, but suppose that someone makes a price offer that is a little above your initial price in anticipation of excess demand. This causes you to suspect that others are willing to pay more as well, so you post another note inviting bids on the cards, with a one-week deadline. The first bid you receive on a particularly nice card is $40, and then a second bid comes in at $45. You wonder whether the first bidder would be willing to go up a bit, say to $55. If you go ahead and post the highest current bid on the card each time a new high bid is received, then you are essentially conducting an *English auction* with ascending bids. On the other hand, if you do not announce the bids and sell to the high bidder at closing time, then you will have conducted a *first-price sealed-bid auction*. Lucking-Reiley (2000) reports that the most commonly used auction method for *Magic* cards is the English auction, although some first-price auctions are observed.

Reiley also found a case where cards were sold in a descending-bid *Dutch auction*. Here the price begins high and is lowered until someone agrees to the current proposed price. This type of descending-bid auction is used in Holland to sell flowers. Each auction room contains several clocks, marked with prices instead of hours. Carts of flowers are rolled into the auction room on tracks in rapid succession. When a particular cart is on deck, the quality grade and grower information are flashed on an electronic screen. Then the hand of the clock falls over the price scale, from higher to lower prices, until the first bidder presses a button to indicate acceptance. The process proceeds quickly, which results in a high sales volume that is nearly complete by late morning. The auction house is located next to the Amsterdam airport, so that flowers can be shipped by air to distant locations like New York and Tokyo.

If you know your own private value for the commodity being auctioned, then the Dutch auction is like the sealed-bid auction. This argument is based on the fact that you learn nothing of relevance as the clock hand falls in a Dutch auction. Consequently, you might as well choose your stopping point in advance, just as you would select a bid to submit in a sealed-bid auction. These two auction methods also share the property that the winning bidders pay a price that equals their own bid. In each case, a higher bid will raise the chances of winning, but the higher bid lowers the value of winning. In both auctions, it is never optimal to bid an amount that equals the full amount that you are willing to pay, since in this case you would be indifferent between winning and not winning. To summarize, the descending-bid Dutch auction is strategically equivalent to the first-price, sealed-bid auction in the case of known private prize values.

This equivalence raises the issue of whether there is a type of sealed-bid auction that is equivalent to the ascending-bid English auction. With a known prize value, the best strategy in an English auction is to stay in the bidding until the price just reaches your own value. For example, suppose that one person's value is $50, another's is $40, and a third person's value is $30. At a price of $20, all three are interested. When the auctioneer raises the price to $31, the third bidder drops out, but the first two continue to nod as the auctioneer raises the bid amount. At $41, however, the second bidder declines to nod. The first bidder, who is willing to pay more, will agree to $41 but should feel no pressure to express an interest at a higher price since nobody else will speak up. After the usual "going once, going twice . . ." warning, the prize will be sold to the first bidder at a price of $41. Notice that the person with the highest value purchases the item, but only pays an amount that is approximately equal to the second-highest value.

The observation that the bidding in an English auction stops at the second-highest value led Vickrey to devise a *second-price sealed-bid auction*. As in any sealed bid auction, the seller collects sealed bids and sells the item to the person with the highest bid. The winning bidder, however, only has to pay the second-highest bid. Vickrey noted that the optimal strategy in this auction is to bid an amount that just equals one's own value. To see why this is optimal, suppose that your value is $10. If you bid $10 in a second-price auction, then you will only win when all other bids are lower than your own. If you decide instead to raise your bid to $12, you increase your chances of winning, but the increase is *only* in those cases where the second-highest bid is above $10, causing you to lose money on the win. For example, if you bid $12 and the next bid is $11, you pay $11 for an item that is only worth $10 to you. Thus, it is never optimal to bid above value in this type of auction. Next, consider a reduction to a bid, say to $8. If the second-highest bid were below $8, then you would win anyway and pay the second bid with or without the bid reduction. But if the second bid were above $8, say at $9, then your bid reduction would cause you to lose the auction in a case where you would have won profitably. In summary, the best bid is your own value in a second-price auction. If everybody bids at value, then the high-value person will win, and will pay an amount that equals the second-highest value. But this is exactly what happens in an English auction where the bidding stops at the second-highest value. Thus, the second-price Vickrey auction is, in theory, equivalent to the English auction.

Lucking-Reiley (2000) points out that stamp collectors have long used Vickrey-like auctions as a way of including bidders who cannot attend an auction. For example, if two distant bidders mail in bids of $30 and $40, then the bidding starts at $31. If nobody enters a higher bid, then the person with the higher bid purchases at $31. If somebody else agrees to that price, the auctioneer raises the price to $32. The auctioneer continues to "go one up" on any bidder present until the higher mail-in bid of $40 is reached. This mixture of an English auction and a sealed-bid second-price auction is achieved by allowing proxy bidding, since it is the auctioneer who is entering bids based on the limit prices submitted by mail. It is a natural extension to entertain only mail-in bids and to simulate the English auction by awarding the prize to the high bidder at the second bid. Lucking-Reiley found records of a pure second-price stamp auction held in Northampton, Massachusetts, in 1893. He also notes that the most popular online auction, eBay, allows proxy bidding, which is explained as follows:

> *Instead of having everyone sit at their computers for days on end waiting for an auction to end, we do it a little differently. Everyone has a little magical elf (a.k.a. proxy) to bid for them and all you need to do is tell your elf the most that you want to spend, and he'll sit there and outbid the others for you, until his limit is reached.*

19.3   Bidding against a Uniform Distribution

This section describes an experiment conducted by Holt and Sherman (2000) in which bidders received private values, and others' bids were simulated by the throw of a 10-sided die. This experiment lets one study the tradeoffs involved in optimal bidding without having to do a full game-theoretic analysis of how others' bids are actually determined in a market with real (non-simulated) bidders. At the start of each round, the experimenter would go to each person's desk and throw a 10-sided die three times to determine a random number between $0.00 and $9.99. This would be the person's private value for the prize being auctioned. Since each penny amount in this interval is equally likely, the population distribution of values in this setup is uniform. After learning their value, each person would select a bid knowing that the "other person's" bid would be randomly determined by three throws of the 10-sided die. If the randomly determined other person's bid turned out to be lower than the bidder's own bid, then the bidder would earn the difference between their private value and their own bid. If the other's bid were higher, then the bidder would earn nothing.

Suppose that the first three throws of the die determine a value that will be denoted by v, where v is some known dollar amount between $0.00 and $9.99. The only way to win money is to bid below this value, but how much lower? The strategic dilemma in an auction of this type is that a higher bid will increase the chances of winning, but the value of winning with a higher bid is diminished because of the higher price that must be paid. Optimal bidding involves finding the right point in this tradeoff, given one's willingness to tolerate risk, which can be considerable since the low bidder in the auction earns nothing.

This strategic tradeoff can be understood better by considering the bidder's expected payoff under a simplifying assumption of risk neutrality. This expected payoff consists of two parts: the probability of winning and the payoff conditional on winning. A person with a value of v who wins with a bid of b will have to pay that bid amount, and hence will earn $v - b$. Thus, the expected payoff is the product of the winner's earnings and the probability of winning, as shown in Equation (19.1).

$$\text{Expected payoff} = (v - b)\,\Pr(\text{winning with } b) \tag{19.1}$$

The probability of winning with a bid of b is just the probability that this bid is above the simulated other bid, i.e., above the result of the throws of the 10-sided die. The other bid is equally likely to be any penny amount: $0.00, $0.01, \ldots, $9.99. For simplicity, we will ignore ties and assume that the other person will win in the event of a tie. Then, a bid of 0 would win with probability 0 and a bid of $10 would win with probability 1. This suggests that the probability of winning is $b/10$, which is 0 for a bid of 0 and 1 for a bid of 10. For a bid of $5, the probability of winning is exactly 1/2 according to this formula, which is correct since there are 500 ways that the other bid is below $5 ($0.00, $0.01, \ldots, $4.99), and there are 500 ways that the bid is greater than or equal to $5 ($5.00, $5.01, \ldots, $9.99). Using this formula ($b/10$) for the probability of winning, the expression for the bidder's expected payoff in Equation (19.1) can be expressed as shown in Equation (19.2).

$$\text{Expected payoff} = (v - b)(b/10) = vb/10 - b^2/10 \tag{19.2}$$

This expected payoff exhibits the strategic dilemma discussed earlier. The payoff conditional on winning, $v - b$, is decreasing in the bid amount, but the probability of winning, $b/10$, is increasing in b. The optimal bid involves finding the right balance between these two good things: high payoff and high probability of winning.

The bidder knows the value, v, at the time of bidding, so the function on the right side of Equation (19.2) can be graphed to find the highest point, as shown in Figure 19.1 for the case of $v = \$8$. The bid, b, is on the horizontal axis, and the function starts with a height of 0 when $b = 0$ since a 0 bid has no chance of winning. Thus, at the other end, a bid that equals the value v will also yield a 0 expected payoff, since the payoff for bidding the full value of the prize is 0 regardless of whether one wins or loses. Between these two points, the expected payoff function shows a hill-shaped graph, which rises and then falls as one moves to higher bids (from left to right).

One way to find the best bid is to use Equation (19.2) to create a spreadsheet to calculate the expected payoff for each possible bid and find the best one (see Question 1 at the end of the chapter). For example, if $v = \$4$, then the expected payoffs are: $0 for a bid of $0, $0.30 for a bid of $1, $0.40 for a bid of $2, $0.30 for a bid of $3, and $0.00 for a bid of $4. Filling in the payoffs for all possible bids in penny increments would confirm that the best bid is $2 when one's value is $4. Similarly, it is straightforward to show that the optimal bid is

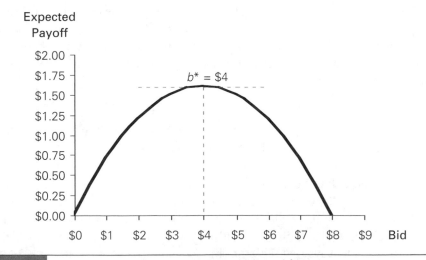

Figure 19.1   Expected Payoffs with a Private Value of $8

$2.50 when one's value is $5. These calculations suggest that the best strategy (for a risk-neutral person) is to bid one-half of one's value.

The graphical intuition behind bidding half of value is shown in Figure 19.1. When the value is $8, the expected payoff function starts at the origin of the graph, rises, and falls back to $0 when one's bid is equal to the value of $8. The expected payoff function is quadratic, and it forms a hill that is symmetric around the highest point. The symmetry is consistent with the fact that the maximum is located at $4, halfway between $0 and the value of $8.

At the point where the function is flat, the slope of a dashed tangent line is 0, and the tangency point is directly above a bid of $4 on the horizontal axis. This point could be found graphically for any specific private value. Alternatively, we can use calculus to derive a formula that applies to all possible values of v. (The rest of this paragraph can be skipped by those who are already familiar with calculus; those who need more review should see Optional Quick Calculus Review in Chapter 6.) A reader who is not familiar with calculus should read the discussion that follows; the only thing you will need besides a little intuition is a couple of rules for calculating derivatives (finding the slopes of tangent lines). First, consider a linear function of b, say $4b$. This is a straight line with a slope of 4, so the derivative is 4. This rule generalizes to any linear function with a constant slope of k: the derivative of kb with respect to b is just k. The second rule that will be used is that the derivative of a quadratic function like b^2 is linear: $2b$. The intuition is that the slopes of tangent lines to a graph of the function b^2 become steeper as b increases. The slope, $2b$, is an increasing function of b (the 2 is due to the number 2 in the exponent of b^2). This formula is easily modified to allow for multiplicative constants, e.g., the derivative of $3b^2$ is $3(2b)$, or the derivative of $-b^2$ is $-2b$.

The expected payoff in Equation (19.2) consists of two terms. The first one, can be written as $(v/10)b$, which is a linear function of b with a slope of $v/10$. Therefore, the derivative of the expected payoff will have a $v/10$ term in it, as can be seen on the right side of Equation (19.3).

$$\text{Derivative of expected payoff} = \frac{v}{10} - \frac{2b}{10} \tag{19.3}$$

The second term in the expected payoff expression Equation (19.2) is $-b^2/10$, and the derivative of this term is $-2b/10$ because the derivative of b^2 is $2b$. To summarize, the derivative on the right side of Equation (19.3) is the sum of two terms, each of which is the derivative of the corresponding term in the expected payoff in Equation (19.2).

The optimal bid is the value of b for which the slope of a tangent line is 0, so the next step is to equate the derivative in Equation (19.3) to 0, as shown in Equation (19.4).

$$\frac{v}{10} - \frac{2b}{10} = 0 \tag{19.4}$$

This equation is linear in b, and can be solved to obtain the optimal bidding strategy, as shown in Equation (19.5).

$$b^* = \frac{v}{2} \quad \text{(Optimal bid for risk-neutral person)} \tag{19.5}$$

The calculus method is general in the sense that it yields the optimal bid for all possible values of v, whereas the graphical and numerical methods have to be done separately for each value of v being considered.

To summarize, the predicted bid is a linear function of value, with a slope of 0.5. The actual bid data in the Holt and Sherman experiment formed a scatter plot with an approximately linear shape, but most bids were above the half-value prediction. A linear regression yielded the estimate, as shown in Equation (19.6):

$$b = 0.14 + 0.667v \quad (R^2 = 0.91) \tag{19.6}$$

where the intercept of \$0.14, with a standard error of 0.61, was not significantly different from 0. The slope, with a standard error of 0.017, was significantly different from 1/2.

By bidding above one-half of value, bidders obtain a higher chance of winning, but a lower payoff if they win. A willingness to take less money in order to reduce the risk of losing and getting a zero payoff may be due to risk aversion, as discussed in the next section. There could, of course, be other explanations for the over-bidding, but the setup with a simulated other bidder permits us to rule out some possibilities. Since the other bidder was just a roll of the die, the over-bidding cannot be due to issues of equity, fairness, or rivalistic desires to win or reduce the other's earnings.

19.4   Bidding Behavior in a Two-Person, First-Price Auction

The experiment described in the previous section with simulated other bids is essentially an individual decision problem. An analogous game can be set up by providing each of two bidders with randomly determined private values drawn from a distribution that is uniform from \$0 to \$10. As before, a high bid results in earnings of the difference between the person's private value and the person's own bid. A low bid results in earnings of 0. This is known as a *first-price auction* since the high bidder has to pay the highest (first) price.

Under risk neutrality, the Nash equilibrium for this game is to bid one-half of one's private value. The proof of this claim is essentially an application of the analysis given above, where the distribution of the other's bids is uniform on a range from \$0 to \$10. Now suppose that one person is bidding one-half of value. Since the values are uniformly distributed, the bid of one-half of value will be uniformly distributed from \$0 to a level of \$5, which is one-half of the maximum value. If this person's bids are uniformly distributed from \$0 to \$5, then a bid of \$0 will not win, a bid of \$5 will win with a probability that is essentially 1, and a bid of \$2.50 will win with a probability 1/2. So the probability of winning with a bid of b is $b/5$. Thus, the expected-payoff function is given in Equation (19.2) if the 10 in each denominator is replaced by a 5. Equations (19.3) and (19.4) are changed similarly. Then, multiplying both sides of the revised Equation (19.4) by 5 yields the $v/2$ bidding rule in Equation (19.5).

Recall that the predicted bidding strategy is linear, with a slope of 1/2 when bidders are risk neutral. Bids exceeded the $v/2$ line in an experiment with simulated other bids, and the same pattern emerges when the other bidder is a subject in the experiment. Figure 19.2 shows the bid/value combinations for 10 rounds of a Web-based classroom experiment. There were 10 bidding teams, each composed of one or two students on a networked PC. The teams were randomly matched in a series of rounds. The bidding pattern is approximately linear, except for a leveling off with high values, which is a pattern that has also been noted by Dorsey and Razzolini (2003). Only a small fraction of the bids are at or below the Nash prediction of $v/2$, which is graphed as the solid line. In fact, the majority of bids are above the dashed line with a slope of 0.67 obtained from a linear regression for the case discussed in the previous section; the bid-to-value ratio averaged over all bids in all rounds is about 0.7. This pattern of overbidding relative to the Nash prediction is typical, and the most commonly mentioned explanation is risk aversion. An auction model with risk-averse bidders is presented in the Risk Aversion Appendix at the end of this chapter. It is

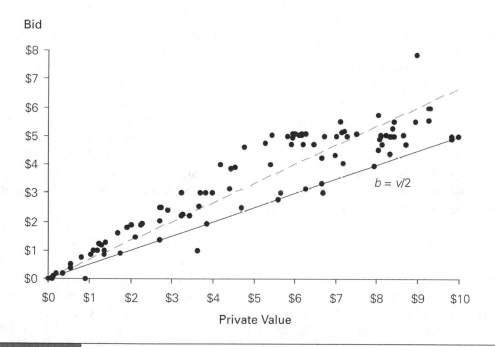

Figure 19.2 Observed Bidding Strategies for 10 Subjects in a Classroom Experiment

shown that bidding two-thirds of value is consistent with bidders having a square-root utility function, i.e., a coefficient of relative risk aversion of $1/2$. This amount of risk aversion is in the range of estimates previously discussed in Chapter 4.

19.5 Extensions

Some of the earliest experimental tests of the Vickrey model are reported by Coppinger, Smith, and Titus (1980). In particular, they observed overbidding relative to Nash predictions in a private-value, first-price auction, assuming risk neutrality. The effect of risk aversion on individual behavior was explored in a series of papers by Cox, Roberson, and Smith (1982), and Cox, Smith, and Walker (1985, 1988). See Kagel (1995) for a survey of auction experiments. Goeree, Holt, and Palfrey (2002) provide an analysis of risk aversion and noisy behavior in first-price auctions.

Up to now, we have only considered two-person auctions. Auctions with more bidders are more competitive, which causes bids to be closer to values. The formula in Equation (19.5) can be generalized to the case of N risk-neutral bidders drawing from the same uniform private value distribution, as shown in Equation (19.7):

$$b^* = \frac{(N-1)v}{N} \quad \text{(Optimal bid with risk neutrality)} \tag{19.7}$$

with a further upward adjustment for the case of risk aversion. Notice that Equation (19.7) specifies bidding one-half of value when $N = 2$, and that bids rise as a proportion of value for larger group sizes. As the number of bidders becomes very large, the ratio, $(N-1)/N$, becomes closer and closer to 1, and bids converge to values. This increase in competition causes expected payoffs to converge to 0 as bid/value differences shrink.

There are a number of other interesting variations of the basic first-price auction design. One option is to require all bidders to pay their own bids, with the prize still going to the highest bid. For example, if a bidder with a value of $4 bids $1 and if a second bidder with a value of $9 bids $5, then the first earns –$1 and the second earns $9 – $5 = $4. In this strategic setting, bidders with low values (and low chances of winning) will reduce their bids toward $0, to avoid having to pay in the event of a loss. But bidding exactly $0 will generate regret if another person wins a tied auction at that bid, so bids for those with lower values will rise slightly above $0. Those with a relatively high value will risk a higher bid, so that the bidding strategy will have a curved shape, only rising significantly above 0 at very high values. This curved pattern can be seen in the bids in Figure 19.3, which were observed in a research experiment conducted at the University of Virginia (with all payments made in cash). This all-pay auction is sometimes used to model lobbying competition or a patent race, where the contender with the highest effort will win, but even the losers incur the costs associated with their efforts.

A second variation provides for returning a fraction of the auction revenue to all bidders, divided equally among the bidders. This is analogous to using the revenue from the

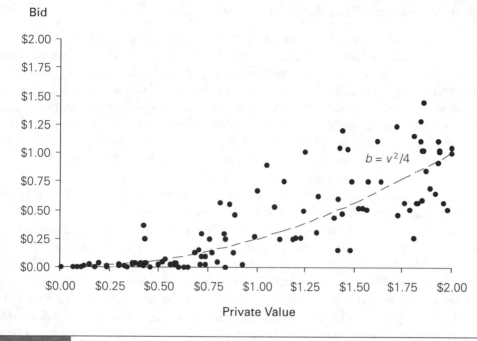

Bid

Figure 19.3   Observed Bids for 10 Subjects in an All-Pay Auction Experiment

sale of prize to reduce taxes for all bidders. Such revenue rebates tend to raise the bids.

   A third option in auction design is the specification of a minimum bid, or reserve price. There is literature on optimal reserve prices, and the Veconlab Seller Reserve Price Auction program puts subjects into the roles of sellers who choose reserve prices and buyers who choose bids. This program was used by Mitman (2004) in an analysis of the effects of the numbers of bidders on sellers' reserve price decisions.

   Laboratory tests can be complemented with field studies of people in naturally occurring markets. There is an interesting strand of research that uses online auctions to study the effects of changes in auction procedures. For example, Reiley (2005, 2006) uses auctions for collectible cards to study the effects of entry and seller reserve prices. While it is not possible to induce bidders' valuations in these field experiments, some effective control is achieved by using matched pairs of cards with identical assessed values. Reiley (2006) concludes that reserve prices reduce the number of bidders and the probability that an item will be sold, but the expected price conditional on a sale increases. Bidders with high valuations seem to raise their bids strategically in anticipation that others will bid higher in the presence of a seller reserve price. As Reiley notes, these results could be further studied with follow-up laboratory experiments. Another interesting implication of online auctions is that the bidding environments in the lab and the field are increasingly similar.

Appendix: **Risk Aversion**

The analysis in this section shows that a simple model of risk aversion can explain the general pattern of overbidding discussed above. The analysis uses simple calculus, i.e., the derivative of a power function like kx^p, where k is a constant and the variable x is raised to the power p. The derivative with respect to x of this power function is a new function where the power has been reduced by 1 and the original power enters multiplicatively. Thus, the derivative of kx^p is kpx^{p-1}, which is called the *power-function rule* of differentiation. A second rule that will be used is that the derivative of a product of two functions is the first function times the derivative of the second, plus the derivative of the first function times the second. This is analogous to calculating the change in room size (the product of length and width) as the length times the change in width plus the change in length times the width. This product rule is accurate for small changes.

Before using the power-function and the product rules, we must obtain an expression for a bidder's expected utility. The most convenient way to model risk aversion in an auction is to assume that utility is a nonlinear function, i.e., that the utility of a money amount $v - b$ is a power function $(v - b)^{1-r}$ for $0 \leq r < 1$. When $r = 0$, this function is linear, which corresponds to the case of risk neutrality. If $r = 1/2$, then the power $1 - r$ is also $1/2$, so the utility function is the square root function. A higher value of r corresponds to more risk aversion.

First, consider the simple case of bidding against a uniform distribution of other bids on the interval from 0 to 10. Thus, the probability of winning is $b/10$. With risk aversion, the expected payoff function in Equation (19.2) must be replaced with an expected utility function, which is the utility of the payoff times the probability of winning, as shown in Equation (19.8).

$$\text{Expected utility} = (v-b)^{1-r}\left(\frac{b}{10}\right) \tag{19.8}$$

As before, the optimal bid is found by equating the derivative of this function to 0. The expected utility on the right side of Equation (19.8) is a product of two functions of b, so we use the power-function rule to obtain the derivative (first function times the derivative of the second plus the derivative of the first times the second function). The derivative of $b/10$ is $1/10$, so the first function times the derivative of the second is the first term in Equation (19.9) below. Next, the power function rule implies that the derivative of $(v - b)^{1-r}$ is $-(1 - r)(v - b)^{-r}$, which yields the second term in Equation (19.9).

$$(v-b)^{1-r}\left(\frac{1}{10}\right) - (1-r)(v-b)^{-r}\left(\frac{b}{10}\right) \tag{19.9}$$

This derivative can be rewritten by putting parts common to each term in the parentheses, as shown on the left side of Equation (19.10).

$$(v-b)\left(\frac{(v-b)^{-r}}{10}\right) - (1-r)b\left(\frac{(v-b)^{-r}}{10}\right) = 0 \tag{19.10}$$

Multiplying both sides by $10/(v-b)^{-r}$, one obtains Equation (19.11).

$$v - b - (1-r)b = 0 \qquad (19.11)$$

This equation is linear in b, and can be solved to obtain the optimal bidding strategy, as shown in Equation (19.12).

$$b^* = \frac{v}{2-r} \quad \text{(Optimal bid with risk aversion)} \qquad (19.12)$$

This bidding rule reduces to the optimal bidding rule for risk neutrality (bidding one-half of value) when $r = 0$. Increases in r will raise the bids. When $r = 1/2$, the bids will be two-thirds of value, which is consistent with the results of the regression Equation (19.6).

Up to this point, we have only a risk-averse person's bid against a simulated bid that is uniform on the interval from 0 to 10 dollars. Now consider an auction with two bidders, and suppose that the equilibrium bidding strategy with risk aversion is linear: $b = \beta v$, where $0 < \beta < 1$. Then, the lowest bid will be 0, corresponding to a value of 0, and the highest bid will be 10β, corresponding to a value of 10. The distribution of bids is represented in Figure 19.4. For any particular value of β, the bids will be uniformly distributed from 0 to 10β, as indicated by the dashed line with a constant height representing a constant probability for each possible bid. The figure is drawn for the case of $\beta = 0.6$, so bids are uniform from \$0 to \$6. A bid of 0 will never win, a bid of $10\beta = 6$ will win with probability 1, and an intermediate bid will win with probability of $b/6$. In the general case, a bid of b will win with probability $b/10\beta$.

In a two-person auction when the other's bid is uniform from 0 to 10β, the probability of winning in the expected payoff function will be $b/10\beta$ instead of the ratio $b/10$ that was used earlier for the expected utility in Equation (19.8). The rest of the above analysis of optimal bidding in that section is unchanged, with the occurrences of 10 replaced by 10β, which cancels out of the denominator of Equation (19.10) just as the 10 did. The resulting

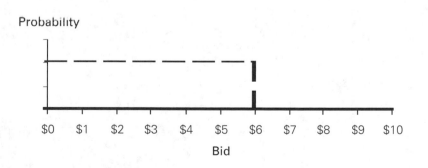

Probability

$0 $1 $2 $3 $4 $5 $6 $7 $8 $9 $10

Bid

Figure 19.4   A Uniform Distribution of Bids on [0, 6]

equilibrium bid is given in Equation (19.12) as before. This bidding strategy is again linear, with a slope that is greater than one-half when there is risk aversion ($r > 0$). Recall that a risk aversion coefficient of $r = 1/2$ will yield a bid line with slope 2/3, so the bids in Figure 19.2 are roughly consistent with a risk aversion coefficient of at least 1/2.

QUESTIONS

1. This question lets you create a simple spreadsheet to calculate the optimal bid. Begin by putting the text "V =" in cell A1 and any numerical value, e.g., 8, in cell B1. Then put the possible bids in the A column in $.50 increments: 0 in A3, 0.5 in A4, 1 in A5, and so on. (You can use penny amounts if you prefer.) The expected payoff formula in column B, beginning in cell B3, should contain a formula with terms involving B1 (the prize value) and $A3 (the bid). Use the expected payoff formula in Equation (19.2) to complete this formula, which is then copied down to the lower cells in column B. Verify the expected payoff numbers for a value of $4 that were reported in Section 19.2. By looking at the expected payoffs in column B, one can determine the bid with the highest expected payoff. If the value of 8 is in cell B1, then the optimal bid should be 4. Then change the value in cell B1 to 5 and show that the optimal bid is $2.50.

2. Recall that Equations (19.1) through (19.5) pertain to the case of a bidder who is bidding against a simulated other bidder. Write out the revised versions of Equations (19.2), (19.3), (19.4), and (19.5) for the two-person auction, assuming risk neutrality.

chapter 20

The Takeover Game

This chapter pertains to a situation in which a buyer cannot directly observe the underlying value of some object. A buyer's bid will only be accepted if it is higher than the value to the current owner. The danger is that a purchase is more likely to be made precisely when the owner's value is low, which may lead to a loss for the buyer. The tendency to purchase at a loss in such situations is called the "buyer's curse." The Veconlab Takeover Game sets up this situation, or alternatively, see Takeover Game Instructions in the Class Experiments section that use 10-sided dice.

20.1 *Wall Street* (the Film)

In the 1987 Hollywood film *Wall Street*, Michael Douglas plays the role of a corporate raider who acquires TELDAR Enterprises, with the intention of increasing its profitability by firing the union employees. After the acquisition, the new owners become aware of some previously hidden business problems (a defect in an aircraft model under development) that drastically reduce the firm's profit potential. As the stock is falling, Douglas turns and gives the order "Dump it." This event is representative of a wave of aggressive acquisitions that swept through Wall Street in the mid-1980s. Many of these takeovers were motivated by the belief that companies could be transformed by infusions of new capital and better management techniques. The mood later turned less optimistic as acquired companies did not achieve profit goals.

With the advantage of hindsight, some economists have attributed these failed mergers to a selection bias: it is the *less profitable* companies that are more likely to be sold by owners with inside information about problem areas that raiders may not detect. In a bidding process with a number of competitors, the bidder with over-optimistic expectations is likely to end up making the highest tender offer, and the result may be an acquisition price that is not justified by subsequent profit potential. The tendency for the winning bidder to lose money on a purchase is known as the winner's curse. Even with only a single potential buyer, a bid is more likely to be accepted if it is too high, and the resulting potential for losses is sometimes called the buyer's curse.

In a sense, winning in a bidding war can be an informative event. A bid that is accepted, at a minimum, indicates that the bid exceeds the current owner's valuation. Thus, there would be no incentive for trade if the value of the company were the same for the owner and the bidder. But even when the bidder has access to superior capital and management services, the bidder may end up paying too much if the intrinsic valuation cannot be determined in advance.

20.2 A Takeover Game Experiment

Some elements that affect a firm's intrinsic profitability are revealed by accounting data and can easily be observed by both current and prospective owners. Other aspects of a firm's operations are private, and internal problems are not likely to be revealed to outsiders. The model presented in this section is highly stylized in the sense that all profitability information is private and known only by the current owner. The "raider" or prospective buyer is unsure about the exact profitability and has only probabilistic information on which to make a bidding decision. The prospective buyer, however, has a productivity advantage that will be explained below.

The first scenario to be considered is one where the value of the firm to the current owner is equally likely to be any amount between 0 and 100. This current owner knows the exact value, V, and the prospective buyer only knows the range of possible equally likely values. In an experiment, one could throw a 10-sided die twice at the owner's desk to determine the value, with the throw being unobserved by the buyer. To provide a motivation for trade, the buyer has better management skills. In particular, the value to the buyer is 1.5 times the value to the current owner. For example, if a bidder offers 60 for a company that is only worth 50 to the current owner, then the sale will go though and the bidder will earn 1.5*50 minus the bid of 60, for a total of 15.

Table 20.1 shows the first round results from a classroom experiment. The proposer names (and their comments) have been removed. Notice that proposers in this round were particularly unfortunate. Except for proposer 6 (who knew "too much" as we will see below), the proposer bids averaged 49. All of these bids were accepted, and the owner values (21, 23, 31, 6, and 43 for Proposers 1 to 5 respectively) averaged 25. The first four proposers lost money, as shown by the bottom row of the table. The fifth proposer earned 1.5 times 43 on an accepted bid of 50, for earnings of 15 cents. This tendency for buyers to make losses is not surprising ex post, since a bid of about 50 will only be accepted if the seller value is lower than 50. The seller values averaged only 25, and 1.5 times this amount is 37.5, which is still below 50.

Table 20.1	First Round Results from a Classroom Experiment					
	Proposer 1	Proposer 2	Proposer 3	Proposer 4	Proposer 5	Proposer 6
Buyer Bid	60	49	50	36	50	0
Owner Value	21	23	31	6	43	57
Owner Response	accept	accept	accept	accept	accept	reject
Buyer Value	32	35	46	10	65	86
Buyer Earnings	–28	–14	–4	–26	15	0

Source: (University of Virginia, Spring 2002)

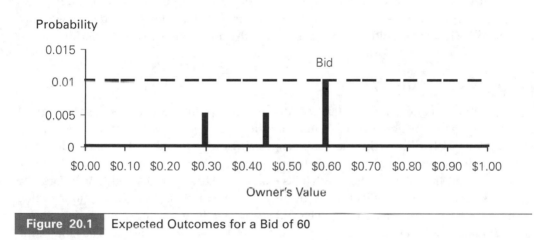

Figure 20.1	Expected Outcomes for a Bid of 60

The tendency for buyers to lose money is illustrated in Figure 20.1, where payoffs are in pennies. Owner values are uniformly distributed from 0 to 99, with a probability of 1/100 of each value, as indicated by the dashed line with a height of 0.01. A bid of 60 will only be accepted if the owner's value is lower, and since all lower bids are equally likely, the expected owner value is 30 for an accepted bid of 60. This average owner value of 30 translates into an average value of 1.5 times as high, as indicated by the vertical line at 45. So an accepted bid of 60 will only yield expected earnings of 45. This analysis is easily generalized. A bid of b will be accepted if the owner value is below b. Since owner values for accepted bids are equally likely to be anywhere between 0 and b, the average owner value for an accepted bid is $b/2$. This translates into a value of $1.5(b/2)$, or $(3/4)b$, which is less than the accepted bid, b. Thus, any positive bid of b will generate losses on average in this setup, and the optimal bid is 0.

The feedback received by bidders is somewhat variable, so it is difficult to learn this through experience. In five rounds of bidding in the classroom experiment, only 3 of the 13 accepted bids resulted in positive earnings, and losses resulted in lower bids in the subsequent round in all cases. But accepted bids with positive earnings were followed by bid increases, and rejections were followed by bid increases in about one-half of the cases (excluding the proposer who bid 0 and was rejected every time). The net effect of these reactions caused average bids to stay at about $.30 for rounds 2–5. The only person who did not finish the fifth round with a cumulative loss was the person who bid 0 in all rounds. This person, a second-year physics and economics major, had figured out the optimal bidding strategy on his own. The results of this experiment are typical of what is observed in research experiments summarized next.

The first buyer's curse experiment was reported in Bazerman and Samuelson (1983), who used a discrete set of equally likely owner values (0, 20, 40, 60, 80, and 100). Ball, Bazerman, and Caroll (1990) used a grid from 0 to 100 with M.B.A. subjects, and the bids did not decline to 0. The average bid stayed above 30, and the modal bid was around 50.

20.3 Quality Unraveling

Kirstein and Kirstein (2005) conducted an experiment with a generalization of the takeover game, which was reformulated as a market model with asymmetric quality information. Each seller in this market is given a single unit to sell, with a randomly determined quality, g, which is equally likely to be any penny amount between 0 and 1. Imagine a random draw from a bingo cage with balls marked 0, 0.01, ..., 0.99, and 1. As before, the quality is observed by the seller but not by buyers. In one of their designs, the money value to the seller for retaining a unit of grade g is $3g$, as shown by the seller's value line in Figure 20.2. Similarly, the value to a buyer is $4g$, as shown by the buyer's value line. Thus, the value to the buyer is above the value to the seller for each quality grade on the horizontal axis of the figure, so economic efficiency would require that a trade be made.

At the start of a round, each seller is matched with a buyer, who then makes a take-it-or-leave-it price bid, p. Since follow-up communications are not permitted, the seller who knows the grade, g, should accept the bid if the value to the seller is less than price. The buyer could maximize the chances of a purchase by offering a price of $3, which the seller would accept regardless of the grade. But the average grade is only 0.5 since each grade in the range from 0 to 1 is equally likely, and the value to the buyer for a grade of 0.5 is $4*(0.5) = 2. Thus, the buyer would be paying $3 for an item that is only worth $2 on average, so losses would tend to occur. What about a lower price, say of $1.50, as shown by the horizontal dashed line in the figure? This line intersects the seller value line at a grade of 0.5, so only sellers with grades at or below 0.5 would accept this lower price. The average grade in the range from 0 to 0.5 is the midpoint, 0.25, and the value of this average grade is only $1.00 to the buyer, who is paying a price of $1.50.

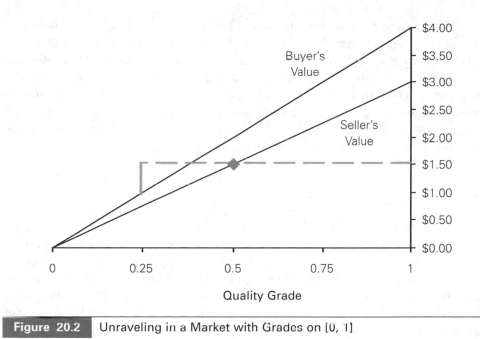

Figure 20.2   Unraveling in a Market with Grades on [0, 1]

As you might have guessed, these examples are easily generalized. Suppose the buyer offers a price, p, which the seller will accept if $3g < p$, or equivalently, if $g < p/3$. Thus, a price offer of p will generate a sale for any seller with a grade in the range from 0 to $p/3$. Since matchings are random, all grades in this acceptance region [0, $p/3$] are equally likely, so the average grade for an accepted bid of p is the midpoint: $(0 + p/3)/2 = p/6$. Recall that the value to the buyer is four times the grade, so four times the expected grade is $4p/6 = 2p/3$. Thus, a buyer with an accepted bid will end up paying p for a unit that is, on average, only worth $2p/3$, for an expected loss of $p/3$. Higher bids have higher expected losses, so bids should decline to 0, which would result in no sales.

In the Kirstein and Kirstein experiment, observed prices tended to fall from a high initial level toward a relatively stable level in the final periods. As the prices fell, the average quality of the items traded fell as well. The market did not collapse completely to a price of 0, which the authors attribute to a limited ability of the participants to think iteratively about what the optimal bid should be. The decline in bid prices in the experiment was slow and incomplete, with prices starting at about $1.70 in the first period, falling to about $1.00 in the tenth period, and leveling off in the range from $0.50 to $0.80 in periods 15–20. This pattern raises the issue of what is driving the dynamic adjustment process. In a market like this, the feedback for buyers will be somewhat noisy, since there will be times when a purchase turns out to be profitable, i.e., when the seller's grade is near the top of the acceptance region. There will also be periods when the buyer's bid is too low and is rejected. In either of these cases, buyers might be tempted to raise their bids in the next round, which will tend to offset bid reductions that might follow rounds where the buyer loses money. These observations suggest why learning that low bids are better might be a slow process. Feltovich (2005) uses computer simulations of the learning process to explain why price declines may be quite slow in this context. The particular learning process that he considers is one in which decisions that have earned more money in the past have a higher probability of being used, which is known as *reinforcement learning* and is discussed in Chapter 27.

20.4   Extensions: The Loser's Curse

In all of the setups described in this chapter, the optimal bid is 0. This is no longer the case when the lowest possible owner value is positive. When seller values range from 50 to 100 and buyer values are 1.5 times the seller value, for example, the optimal bid is at the upper end of the range, i.e., at 100 (see Questions 2–4 at the end of the chapter). Holt and Sherman (1994) ran experiments with this setup and found bids to be well below the optimal level. Similarly, this high-owner-value setup was used in periods 6–10 of the classroom experiment described above, and the average bids were 75, 76, 78, 83, and 83 in these rounds, well below the optimal level of 100. Holt and Sherman attributed the failure to raise bids to another type of error, i.e., *the failure to realize that an increase in the bid will pick up relatively high-value objects at the margin*. For example, a bid of 70 will pick up objects with seller values from 50 to 70, with an average of 60. But raising the bid from 70 to 71 will pick up a purchase if the seller value is at the upper end of this range, at 70. Failure to recognize this factor may lead to bids that are too low, which they termed the "loser's curse."

QUESTIONS

1. How would the analysis of optimal bidding in Section 20.2 change if the value to the bidder were a constant K times the value to the owner, where $0 < K < 2$ and the owner's value is equally likely to be any amount between 0 and 100? (Thus, an accepted bid yields a payoff for the bidder that is K times the owner's value, minus the amount of an accepted bid.) In particular, does the optimal bid depend on K?

2. Suppose that the owner values are equally likely to be any amount from 50 to 99, so that a bid of 100 will always be accepted. Assume that owners will not sell when they are indifferent, so a bid of 50 will be rejected and will produce 0 earnings. The value to the bidder is 1.5 times the value to the owner. Show that the lowest bid of 50 is not optimal. (*Hint*: compare the expected earnings for a bid of 50 with the expected earnings for a bid of 100.)

3. For the setup in Question 2, a bid of 90 will be accepted about four-fifths of the time. If 90 is accepted, the expected value to the owner is between 50 and 90, with an average of 70. Use this information to calculate the expected payoff for a bid of 90, and compare your answer with the expected payoff for a bid of 100 obtained earlier.

4. The analysis for your answers to Questions 2 and 3 (with owner values between 50 and 100) suggests that the best bid in this setup is 100. Let's model the probability of a bid of b being accepted as $(b - 50)/50$, which is 0 for a bid of 50 and 1 for a bid of 100. From the bidder's point of view, the expected value to the owner for an accepted bid of b is 50 plus one-half of the distance from 50 to b. The bidder value is 1.5 times the owner value, but an accepted bid must be paid. Use this information in a spreadsheet to calculate the expected payoff for all bids from 50 to 100, and thereby to find the optimal bid. The five columns of the spreadsheet should be labeled as follows:

   1. Bid b
   2. Acceptance Probability for a Bid b
   3. Expected Value to Owner (conditional on b being accepted)
   4. Expected Value to Bidder (conditional on b being accepted)
   5. Expected Payoff to Bidder for Making a Bid b (which is the product of columns 2 and 4)

   Alternatively, you may use this information to write the bidder's expected payoff as a quadratic function of b, and then use calculus by setting the derivative of this function to 0 and solving for b. (*Note*: A classroom experiment for the setup in Questions 2–4 resulted in average bids of about 80. This information will *not* help you find the optimal bid.)

5. Consider the random exogenous quality model in Section 20.3, with the modification that the value of a grade g item to the seller is $3g$ and the value to a buyer is $1 + 3g$. For a given bid of p, find the range of grades that will be accepted, and determine the probability that a bid of p will be accepted (remember that a probability cannot be greater than 1).

6. For the model in Question 5, discuss the optimal bid for a risk-neutral bidder. (*Hint*: use the midpoint of the acceptance range of grades for your answer to Question 5 to obtain the expected grade for an accepted bid of p. Then, one approach is to multiply the probability that a bid is accepted times the difference between the expected value *to the buyer* of the grade of an accepted item and the bid price paid for that item. The resulting expected payoff will be a quadratic function of the bid price, which can be maximized. If you have trouble with this, compare the buyer's expected payoff for a bid of 1 with the expected payoff for a bid of 0, to show that 0 is not the optimal bid.

chapter 21

Common-Value Auctions and the Winner's Curse

In many bidding situations, the value of the prize would be approximately the same for all bidders, although none of them can assess exactly what this "common value" will turn out to be. In such cases, each bidder may obtain an estimate of the prize value, and those with higher estimates are more likely to make higher bids. As a result, the winning bidder may overestimate the value of the prize and end up paying more than it is worth. This winner's curse is analogous to the buyer's curse discussed in Chapter 20. An auction where each bidder has partial information about an unknown prize value can be run using 10-sided dice to determine common value elements, as explained in the Common Value Auction instructions in the Class Experiments section. Alternatively, it can be run with the Veconlab Common Value Auction, which has default settings that permit an evaluation of increases in the number of bidders producing a more severe winner's curse.

21.1 "I Won the Auction but I Wish I Hadn't"

An interesting auction with common value elements occurs when the renters of self-storage units default on payments, and the owner sells the contents to the highest bidder. In California, prospective buyers are prohibited from entering the unit until the sale is completed, so the auctioneer opens the door and lets each bidder peek inside before the bidding begins. There are many stories about finding Rolex watches or hoards of cash in music cases, but these stories always involve "others" to avoid arousing the interest of the Internal Revenue Service. There is considerable downside uncertainty, as closed containers may contain only dirty dishes, or in some cases, bodies of murder victims. Bidders must make value estimates based on subtle observations, e.g., one person may bid high because the boxes appear to have been neatly stacked or sealed to protect valuables. In such cases, the high bidder may end up being the one with the most optimistic expectations, although experienced bidders should compensate for this risk.

Common value considerations also arise in markets for construction and home improvements. Once, the author asked several flooring companies to bid on replacing some kitchen floor tile. Each bidder would estimate the amounts of materials needed and the time required to remove the old tile and install the floor around the various odd-shaped doorways and pantry area. One of the bids was somewhat lower than the others. Instead of expressing happiness over getting the job, he exhibited considerable anxiety about whether he had miscalculated the cost, although in the end he did not withdraw his bid. This story illustrates the fact that winning an auction can be an informative event, or equivalently, the fact that your win produces new information about the unknown value of the prize. A rational bidder should anticipate this information in making the original bid. This is a subtle strategic consideration that is almost surely learned by (unhappy) experience.

The possibility of paying too much for an object of unknown value is particularly dangerous for one-time auctions in which bidders are not able to learn from experience. Suppose that two partners in an insurance business work out of separate offices and sell separate types of insurance, e.g., business insurance from one office and life insurance from the other. Each partner can observe the other's "bottom-line" earnings, but cannot determine whether the other one is really working. One of the partners is a single mother who works long hours, with good results despite a low earnings-per-hour ratio. The other, who enjoys somewhat of a lucky market niche, is able to obtain good earnings levels while spending a large fraction of each day socializing on the Internet. After several years of happy partnership, each decides to try to buy the whole business from the stockholders, who are current and former partners. When they make their bids, the one with the profitable niche market is likely to think that the other office is as profitable as his own, and hence to overestimate the value of the other office. As a result, this partner could end up acquiring the business for a price that exceeds its value.

The tendency for winners' value estimates to be biased has long been known in the oil industry, where drilling companies must make rather imperfect estimates of the likely amounts of oil that can be recovered on a given tract of land being leased. For example, Robert Wilson, a professor in the Stanford Business School, was once consulting with an oil company that was considering bidding at less than half of the estimated lease value. When he inquired about the possibility of a higher bid, he was told that firms that bid that aggressively on such a lease do not remain in business. (Source: personal communication at a conference on auction theory in the early 1980s.)

The intuition underlying the unprofitability of aggressive bidding is that the firm with the highest bid in an auction is likely to have overestimated the lease value. The resulting possibility of winning "at a loss" is more extreme when there are many bidders, since the highest estimate out of a large number of estimates is more likely to be biased upward, even though each individual estimate is ex ante unbiased. For example, suppose that a single value estimate is unbiased. Then the higher of two unbiased estimates will be biased upward. Analogously, the highest of three unbiased estimates will be even more biased, and the highest of 100 estimates may show an extreme bias toward the largest possible estimation error in the upward direction. Knowing this, bidders in an auction with many bidders should treat their own estimates as being inflated, which will likely turn out to be true if they win. This *numbers effect* can be particularly sinister, since the normal strategic reaction to increased numbers of bidders is to bid higher to stay competitive, as in a private value auction.

Wilson (1969) specified a model with this common-value structure and showed that the Nash equilibrium with fully rational bidders involved some downward adjustment of bids in anticipation of a winner's curse effect. Each bidder should realize that their bid is only relevant for payoffs if it is the highest bid, which means that they have the highest value estimate. The bidder should consider what they would want to bid, knowing that other estimates are likely to be lower than theirs in the event that they have the high bid, which is the only relevant event for estimating the payoff. The a priori correction of this overestimation produces bids that will earn positive payoffs on average.

Consider a simple situation where each of two bidders can essentially observe half of the value of the prize, as would be the case for two bidders who can drill test holes on different halves of a tract of land being leased for an oil well. Another example would be the case of the two insurance partners discussed in the previous section. In particular, let the observed value components or "signals" for bidders 1 and 2 be denoted by v_1 and v_2 respectively. The prize value is the average of the two signals, as shown in Equation (21.1):

$$\text{Prize value} = \frac{v_1 + v_2}{2} \tag{21.1}$$

Both bidders know their own estimates, but they only know that the other person's estimate is the realization of a random variable. In the experiment to be discussed, each person's value estimate is drawn from a distribution that is uniform on the interval from $0 to $10. Bidder 1, for example, knows v_1 and that v_2 is equally likely to be any amount between $0 and $10.

A classroom auction was run with these parameters, using five pairs of bidders in each round. One bidder had a relatively high value signal of $8.69 in the first round. This person submitted a bid of $5.03 (presumably the $.03 increase above $5 was intended to outguess anyone who might bid an even $5). The other person's signal was $0.60, so the prize was only worth the average of $8.69 and $0.60, which is $4.64. The high bidder won this prize, but paid a price of $5.03, which resulted in a loss. Three of the five winning bidders in that round ended up losing money, and about one out of five winners lost money in each of the remaining rounds.

The prize value function in Equation (21.1) can be generalized for the case of a larger number of bidders with independent signals, by taking an average, i.e., dividing the sum of all signals by the number of bidders. In a separate classroom experiment, conducted with 12 bidders, the sole winning bidder ended up losing money in three out of five rounds. As a result, aggregate earnings were 0 or negative for most bidders. A typical case was that of a bidder who submitted the high bid of $6.10 on a signal of $9.64 in the fifth and final round. The average of all 12 signals was $5.45, so this person lost $.65 for the round.

Despite some losses, earnings in the two-bidder classroom experiment discussed above averaged $3.20 per person for the first five rounds of bidding. In contrast, earnings per-person in the 12-bidder auctions averaged −$.30 for five rounds of bidding. These results show a tendency for the winner's curse effect to be more severe with large numbers of bidders. Think of it this way: the person with the highest signal often submits one of the highest bids. Since the maximum of 12 signals from a uniform distribution is likely to be much higher than the maximum of 2 signals, the person with the highest signal in the 12-person auction may be tempted to bid too high. Another way to think about this situation is that each signal is unbiased, since the value of the prize is the average of the two signals, but the maximum of a number of signals will be a biased estimate of the common value, and this bias is larger if there are more bidders.

A large telecommunications company was planning to bid in the first major U.S. auction for radio wave bandwidth to be used for personal communications services. The company was a major player, but it decided not to bid at the last minute. The company representative mentioned the danger of overpayment for the licenses at auction. This story illustrates the point that players who have an option of earning 0 with non-participation will never bid in a manner that yields negative expected earnings. The technical implication is that expected earnings in a Nash equilibrium for a game with an exit option cannot be negative. This raises the issue of how bidders rationally adjust their behavior to avoid losses in a Nash equilibrium, which is the next topic.

21.2 The Nash Equilibrium

As was the case in Chapter 19 on private-value auctions, the equilibrium bids will end up being linear functions of the signals, of the form shown in Equation (21.2).

$$b_i = \beta v_i, \quad \text{where } 0 < \beta < 1 \text{ and } i = 1,2 \tag{21.2}$$

Suppose that bidder 2 is using a special case of this linear bid function by bidding exactly one-half of the signal v_2. In the next several pages, we will use this assumed behavior to find the expected value of bidder 1's earnings for any given bid, and then we will show that this expected payoff is maximized when bidder 1 also bids one-half of the signal v_1, i.e., $\beta = 0.5$. Similarly, when bidder 1 is bidding one-half of their signal, the best response for the other bidder is to bid one-half of their signal too. Thus, the Nash equilibrium for two risk-neutral bidders is to bid one-half of one's signal.

Since the arguments that follow are a little more mathematical than most parts of the book, it is useful to break them down into a series of steps. We will assume for simplicity that bidders are risk neutral, so we will need to find bidder 1's expected payoff function before it can be maximized. (It turns out to be the case that risk aversion has no effect on the Nash equilibrium bidding strategy in this case, as noted later in the chapter.) In an auction where the payoff is 0 in the event of a loss, the expected payoff is the probability of winning times the expected payoff conditional on winning. So the first step is finding the probability of winning given that the other bidder is bidding one-half of their signal value. The second step is to find the expected payoff, *conditional on winning with a particular bid*. The third step is to multiply the probability of winning times the expected payoff conditional on winning, to obtain an expected payoff function, which will be maximized using simple calculus in the final step. The result will show that a bidder's best response is to bid one-half of the signal when the other one is bidding in the same manner, so that this strategy is a Nash equilibrium.

Before going through these steps, it may be useful to review how we will go about maximizing a function. Think of the graph of a function as a hill, which is increasing on the left and decreasing on the right, as shown in Figure 19.1 in Chapter 19 on private-value auctions. At the top of the hill, a tangent line will be horizontal, so to maximize the function, we need to find the point where the derivative of the function (slope of a tangent line) is 0. Both the probability of winning and the conditional expected payoff will turn out to be linear functions of the person's bid b, so the expected-payoff product to be maximized will be quadratic, with terms involving b and b^2. A linear term, like $b/2$, is a straight line through the origin with a slope of $1/2$, so the derivative is the slope, $1/2$. The quadratic term, b^2, also starts at the origin, and it increases to 1 when $b = 1$, to 4 when $b = 2$, to 9 when $b = 3$, and to 16 when $b = 4$. Notice that this type of function is increasing more rapidly as b increases, i.e., the slope is increasing in b. Here all you need to know is that the derivative of a quadratic expression like b^2 is $2b$, which is the slope of a straight line that is tangent to the curved function at any point. This slope is, naturally, increasing in b. Armed with this information, we are ready to find the expected payoff function and maximize it.

Step 1. Finding Bidder 1's Probability of Winning for a Given Bid

Suppose that the other person (bidder 2) is known to be bidding half of their signal. Since the signal is equally likely to be any value from $0 to $10, the second bidder's signal is equally likely to be any of the 1000 penny amounts between $0 to $10, as shown by the dashed line with height of 0.001 in Figure 21.1. When $b_2 = v_2/2$, then bidder 1 will win if $b_1 > v_2/2$, or equivalently, when the other's value is sufficiently low: $v_2 < 2b_1$. The probability of winning with a bid of b_1 is the probability that $v_2 < 2b_1$. This probability can be assessed with the help of Figure 21.1. Suppose that bidder 1 makes a bid of $2, as shown by the short vertical bar. We have just shown that this bid will win if the other's signal is less than $2b_1$, i.e., less than $4 in this example. Notice that four-tenths of the area under the dashed line is to the left of $4. Thus, the probability that the other's value is less than $4 is 0.4, calculated

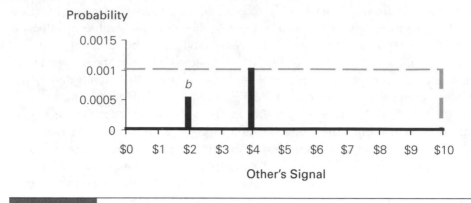

Probability

Other's Signal

Figure 21.1   A Uniform Distribution on the Interval [0, 10]

as $4/10 = 2b_1/10$. A bid of $0 will never win, and a bid of $5 will always win, and in general, we have the result shown in Equation (21.3).

$$\text{Probability of winning (with a bid of } b_1) \;=\; \frac{2b_1}{10} \tag{21.3}$$

Step 2. Finding the Expected Payoff Conditional on Winning

Suppose that bidder 1 bids b_1 and wins. This happens when $v_2 < 2b_1$. For example, when the bid is $2 as shown in Figure 21.1, winning would indicate that $v_2 < \$4$, i.e., to the left of the higher vertical bar in the figure. Since v_2 is uniformly distributed, it is equally likely to be any penny amount less than $4, so the expected value of v_2 would be $2 once we find out that the bid of $2 won. This generalizes easily; the expected value of v_2 conditional on winning with a bid of b_1 is just b_1 (see Question 1 at the end of the chapter). Bidder 1 knows the signal v_1 and expects the other signal to be equal to the bid b_1 if it wins, so the expected value of the prize is the average of v_1 and b_1, as shown in Equation (21.4):

$$\text{Conditional expected prize value (winning with a bid of } b_1) \;=\; \frac{v_1 + b_1}{2} \tag{21.4}$$

where v_1 is the bidder's own signal and b_1 is the bidder's expectation of what the other's signal is, conditional on winning.

Step 3. Finding the Expected Payoff Function

The expected payoff for a bid of b_1 is the product of the probability of winning in Equation (21.3) and the difference between the conditional expected prize value in Equation (21.4) and the bid shown in Equation (21.5).

$$\text{Expected payoff} \;=\; \frac{2b_1}{10}\left(\frac{v_1 + b_1}{2} - b_1\right) \;=\; \frac{b_1 v_1}{10} - \frac{b_1^{\,2}}{10} \tag{21.5}$$

Step 4. Maximizing the Expected Payoff Function

In order to maximize this expected payoff, we will set its derivative equal to 0. The expression on the far right side of Equation (21.5) contains two terms, one that is quadratic in b_1 and one that is linear. Recall that the derivative of $(b_1)^2$ is $2b_1$ and the derivative of a linear function is its slope coefficient, resulting in Equation (21.6).

$$\text{Expected payoff derivative} = \frac{v_1}{10} - \frac{2b_1}{10} \tag{21.6}$$

Setting this derivative equal to 0 and multiplying by 10 yields: $v_1 - 2b_1 = 0$, or equivalently, $b_1 = v_1/2$. To summarize, if bidder 2 is bidding half of value as assumed originally in Equation (21.2), then bidder 1's best response is to bid half of value as well, so the Nash equilibrium bidding strategy, shown in Equation (21.7) is for each person to behave in this manner.

$$b_i = \frac{v_i}{2} \quad i = 1,2. \quad \text{(Equilibrium bid)} \tag{21.7}$$

Normally, in a first-price auction one should bid below value, and it can be seen that the bid in Equation (21.7) is less than the conditional expected value in Equation (21.4). Finally, recall that this analysis began with an assumption that bidder 2 was using the strategy in Equation (21.2) with $\beta = 1/2$. This may seem like an arbitrary assumption, but it can be shown that the only linear bidding strategy for this auction must have a slope of $1/2$ (see Question 3 at the end of the chapter).

21.3 The Winner's Curse

When both bidders are bidding half of the value estimate, as in Equation (21.7), then the one who wins will be the one with the higher estimate, i.e., the one who overestimates the value of the prize. Another way to see this is to think about what a naïve calculation of the prize value would entail. One might reason that since the other's value estimate is equally likely to be any amount between $0 and $10, the expected value of the other's estimate is $5. Then knowing one's own estimate, say v_1, the expected prize value is $(v_1 + 5)/2$. This expected prize value, however, is not conditioned on winning the auction. Notice that this unconditional expected value is greater than the conditional expected value in Equation (21.4) whenever the person's bid is less than $5, which will be the case when bids are half of the value estimate. Except for this boundary case where the bid is exactly $5, the naïve value calculation will result in an overestimate of value, which can lead to an excessively high bid and negative earnings.

Holt and Sherman (2000) conducted a number of common-value auctions with a prize value that was the average of the signals. Subjects began with a cash balance of $15 to cover any losses. Figure 21.2 shows bids and signals for the final five rounds of a single session. One of the bidders can be distinguished from the others by the large square marks. Notice

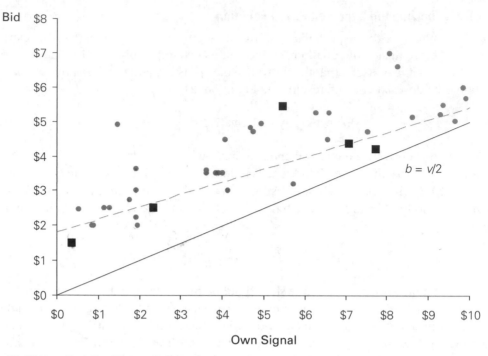

Key: Solid Line: Nash Equilibrium, Dashed Line: Regression for All Sessions

Source: (Holt and Sherman 2000)

Figure 21.2   Bids for Eight Subjects in the Final Five Rounds
of a Common-Value Auction

that this person is bidding in an approximately linear manner, but that this person's bids are above the $v/2$ line, which represents the Nash equilibrium. In fact, almost all bids are above the $v/2$ line, which indicates the earnings-reducing effects of the winner's curse in this session. The dashed line shows the regression line that was estimated using all bids over all sessions, so we see that this session was a little high but not atypical in the nature of the bid/value relationship.

21.4 Extensions

The winner's curse was first discussed in Wilson (1969), and applications to oil lease drilling were described in Capen, Clapp, and Campbell (1971). Kagel and Levine (1986) provided experimental evidence that the winner's curse could be reproduced in the laboratory, even with experienced subjects. The literature on common-value auctions is surveyed in Kagel (1995). A complete treatment of this and related topics can be found in Kagel and Levine (2002).

QUESTIONS

1. Sketch a version of Figure 21.1 for the case where bidder 1's bid is $1. Show the probability distribution for the other person's value, v_2, conditional on the event that the first person's bid is the high bid. Then calculate the expected value of v_2, conditional on bidder 1's winning with a bid of $1. Then explain in words why the expected value of v_2 conditional on the winning bid b_1 is equal to b_1.

2. (This question is somewhat mechanical, but it lets you test your knowledge of the bid derivations in the reading.) Suppose that the prize value in Equation (21.1) is altered to be the sum of the signals instead of the average. The signals are still uniformly distributed on the range from $0 to $10.

   a. What is the probability of winning with a bid of b_1 if the other person bids an amount that equals their signal, i.e., if $b_2 = v_2$.

   b. What is the expected prize value conditional on winning with a bid of b_1? (*Hint*: remember that the prize value is determined by the sum of the signals, not the average.)

   c. What is the expected payoff function for bidder 1? (*Hint*: please do not forget to subtract the bid from the expected prize value, since if you win you have to pay your bid. You should get a function that is quadratic in b_1.)

   d. (Calculus required.) Show that the bidder 1's expected payoff is maximized with a bid that is equal to the bidder's own signal.

3. The goal of this question is to show that the only linear strategy of the form in Equation (21.2) is one with a slope of $1/2$ when the prize value is the average of the signals.

   a. What is the probability of winning with a bid of b_1 if the other person bids: if $b_2 = \beta v_2$. (*Hint*: your answer should imply Equation (21.3) when $\beta = 1/2$.)

   b. What is the expected prize value conditional on bidding with a bid of b_1?

   c. What is the expected payoff function for bidder 1?

   d. (Calculus required.) Show that the bidder 1's expected payoff is maximized with a bid that equals one half of the bidder's own signal.

chapter 22

Multi-Unit and Combinatorial Auctions

This chapter pertains to situations where an auction is used to arrange multiple transactions at the same time. The chapter begins with a case study of the use of experiments to design an auction for multiple, identical prize units—in this case, irrigation permits. The auction was used to determine which tracts of land in drought-stricken southwest Georgia would not be irrigated during the 2001 growing season. The actual auction was conducted with a Web-based network of computers at eight different locations. A similar structure is used in the Veconlab Irrigation Reduction Auction.

The second part of the chapter contains a discussion of multi-round auctions for prizes that are related but not identical, e.g., the Federal Communications Commission (FCC) auctions for communications bandwidth at diverse locations. These auctions are run simultaneously for distinct bandwidth licenses, with bid-driven price increases. An alternative to the simultaneous ascending bid auctions of this type would be to have the proposed bid price increased automatically by a "clock," and to let bidders indicate whether they are still willing to buy after each upward click of the clock. Such a clock auction was used to sell Nitrous Oxide pollution allowances in Virginia in 2004. In multi-unit auctions, the seller may wish to consider letting bidders bid for combinations or packages of units in cases where bidders' values for such combinations may be worth more than the sum of individual unit valuations. Laboratory experiments are being used to help design and evaluate alternative multi-unit and package bidding procedures.

22.1 Dry 2K

In early 2000, just after the publicity associated with the new century and the Y2K computer bugs, a severe drought plagued much of the southeastern United States. Some of the hardest hit localities were in south Georgia, and one of the Atlanta newspapers ran a regular "Dry 2K" update on conditions and conservation measures. Of particular concern were the record low levels for the Flint River, which threatened wildlife and fish in the river and the oyster fishery in Florida. As a result, pressure was mounted to release water from a lake north of Atlanta into a parallel river to protect the oyster fishery downstream, and the threat to Atlanta drinking water was a factor in the final decision to take drastic action.

In April 2000, the Georgia legislature passed the Flint River Drought Protection Act, mandating the use of an auction-like process to restrict agricultural irrigation in certain areas if the Director of the Georgia Environmental Protection Department (EPD) called a drought emergency. The unspecified nature of the mandated auction made an ideal situation for laboratory testing of alternative auction mechanisms that might be recommended. This section summarizes the experiments and subsequent auction results, which are reported in Cummings, Holt, and Laury (2004).

The Flint River, which begins from a drainage pipe near the Atlanta Hartsfield Airport, grows to a size that supports some barge traffic by the time it reaches the Florida state line and later empties into the Gulf. About 70 percent of the water usage in this river basin is agricultural irrigation. Farmers have permits, which were obtained without charge, for particular circular irrigation systems that typically cover areas from 50 to 300 acres. Water is not metered, and therefore, it is liberally dumped into the fields during dry periods, creating the green circles visible from the air, which makes restrictions on irrigation easy to monitor.

The idea behind the law was to use the economic incentives of a bidding process to select relatively low-use-value land to retire from irrigation. Farmers would be compensated to reduce any negative political impacts. The state legislature set aside $10 million, taken from its share of the multi-state Tobacco industry settlement, to pay farmers not to use one or more permits for irrigation. Therefore, what was being purchased by the state was the right to irrigate, not the use of the land itself. Besides being non-coercive and sensitive to economic use value, the auction format was fair and easy to implement relative to administrative processes. Speed was also an important factor, given the limited time between the March 1 deadline for the declaration of a drought emergency and the optimal time for planting crops several weeks later. Finally, the scattered geographic locations of the farmers required that an auction collect bids from diverse locations, which suggested the use of Web-based communications between officials at a number of bidding sites.

Any auction would involve a single buyer, the state Environmental Protection Department (EPD), and many sellers—the farmers with permits. Permits varied in size in terms of the numbers of acres covered, and in terms of whether the water would come from the surface (river or creeks) or from wells. This was a multi-unit auction, since the state could "purchase" many permits, i.e., compensate the permit holders for not irrigating the covered areas for the specified growing season.

The people running the auction did not want the auction to be viewed as being arbitrary or unfair. The auction had to take out as much irrigation as possible (measured in acres covered by repurchased permits) given the budget available to be spent. Of course, economists would also be concerned with economic efficiency, i.e., that the auction would take less productive land out of irrigation.

A number of different types of auctions could be considered, and all involved bids being made on a per-acre basis so that bids for different sized tracks could be compared and ranked, with the low bids being accepted. One method, a discriminative auction, would have people submit sealed bids, with the winning low bidders each receiving the amounts that they bid. For example, if the bids were $100, $200, $300, and $400 per acre for four permits, and if the two lowest were accepted, then the low bidder would receive $100 per acre and the second low bidder would receive $200 per acre. This auction is discriminative since different people receive different amounts for approximately the same amount of irrigation reduction per acre. In contrast, a uniform-price auction would establish a cutoff price and pay all bidders at or below this level an amount that equals the cutoff price. If the cutoff price were $200 in the above example, then the two low bidders would each receive $200, despite the fact that one bidder was willing to accept a compensation of only $100 per acre. This uniform-price auction would have been a multi-unit, low-bidder-wins version of the second-price auction discussed in Chapter 19, whereas the discriminative auction is analogous to the first-price auction discussed in that chapter. Just as bidding behavior will differ between first- and second-price auctions, bidding behavior will differ between discriminative and uniform price multi-unit auctions, so it is not obvious which one will provide the greatest irrigation reduction for a given expenditure—this is why the experiments were used.

The initial experiments were run in May 2000 at Georgia State University, almost a year before the actual auction. Early discussions with state officials indicated that discriminative auctions were preferred, to avoid the apparent waste of paying someone more than they bid, which would happen in a uniform-price auction in which all bidders would be paid the same amount per acre. After some initial experiments, it became clear that a multi-round auction would remove a lot of the uncertainty that bidders face in such a new situation. In a multi-round auction, bids would be collected, ranked, and provisional winners would be posted, but the results would not implemented if the officials running the auction decided to accept revised bids in a subsequent round. Bids that were unchanged between rounds would be carried over, but bidders would have the option of lowering or raising their bids, based on the provisional results. This process was perceived as allowing farmers to find out approximately what the going price would be and then to compete at the margin to be included in the irrigation reduction. A decision was made not to announce the number of rounds in advance, to make it more difficult to collude and to maintain flexibility in terms of the required time.

Some of the early experiments were watched by state EPD officials, and a conscious decision was made to provide an amount of context and realism that is somewhat unusual for laboratory experiments. The feeling was that the notion of having low bids win was sufficiently confusing that it would be worthwhile to explain the setup in terms of the actual irrigation reduction situation. The money amounts used were in the range of $1 per acre, so the experimenters did not worry that participants would bring in homegrown values for what an acre would be worth. Participants were recruited in groups ranging in size from 8 to 42, and were told that they would play the role of farmers. Some of the participants were students from Atlanta, and others were farmers and locals from south Georgia. One final test involved more than 50 local participants and students bidding simultaneously at three different locations near Albany, to test the software and communication with officials in Atlanta. The final auction, conducted in March 2001, involved about 200 farmers in eight different locations.

Since most farmers had multiple tracts of differing sizes and productivities, each participant in the experiment was given three tracts of land. A tract was described by a specific number of acres and a use value, which is the amount of money that would be earned if that tract was irrigated and farmed for the current growing season. Participants were told that the land would not be farmed if the irrigation permits were sold.

For example, consider a person with three permits, with acreage and use values per acre as shown in the first two columns of Table 22.1. The first permit covers 100 acres, and has a use value of 100 per acre, so the bidder would require an amount above 100 per acre as compensation for not irrigating and using the land. In this example, the bid was 120 per acre on permit 1, and this bid was accepted, so the earnings are 120 (per acre) times 100 (acres) so the total shown in the right-hand column is 12,000. If this bid had been rejected, the farmer would have farmed the land and would have earned the use value of 100 per acre times the number of acres, for a total of 10,000. To be sure that you understand these calculations, please calculate the earnings for permit 2, with an accepted bid, and for permit 3, with a rejected bid. These calculations can be entered in the far-right column of Table 22.1.

After some experimentation with several sets of procedures and some consultation with EPD officials, discussions focused on two alternative setups. One proposed auction design involved a single-round, sealed-bid discriminative auction, and another involved a multi-round version of the same auction. In either case, all bids would be collected on bid sheets and ranked from low to high. Then starting with the low bids, the total expenditures would be calculated for adding permits with higher bids. A cutoff for inclusion was determined when the total expenditures reached the amount allotted by the auctioneer. For

Table 22.1		Sample Earnings Calculations for the Irrigation Reduction Auction			
	Total Acres	**Use Value (per acre)**	**Bid (per acre)**	**Auction Outcome**	**Earnings**
Permit 1	100	100	120	accepted	12,000
Permit 2	50	200	250	accepted	_____
Permit 3	100	300	400	rejected	_____

example, if the amount to be spent was set at 50,000, and if the lowest 20 bids yielded a total expenditure of 49,500, and a 21st bid would take the expenditure above this limit, then only 20 bids would be accepted. This cutoff would determine earnings in the single-round sessions, with earnings on permits with rejected bids being determined by their use values. In the sessions with a multi-round setup, the cutoff would be calculated, and the permits with bids below the cutoff would be announced as being provisionally accepted. Then new bids would be accepted and ranked, with a new announcement of which tracts had provisionally accepted bids. This process would continue until the experimenter decided to stop the auction, at which time the accepted bids would be used to determine earnings.

A typical session began with a "trainer" auction for colored writing pens (see the instructions in this chapter's Multi-Unit Auction in the Class Experiments section). This practice auction was intended to convey the main features of submitting different bids for different tracts, which would be ranked, with some low bids being accepted and others not, without providing practice with the actual payoff parameters to be used in the auction. The trainer auction lasted about 45 minutes, and it was followed with a single auction for real cash earnings. The decision not to run a series of repeated auctions was consciously made to mimic the field setting in which farmers would be participating in the auction for the first time. There was considerable concern that farmers who knew each other well would try to collude, so participants in the experiment were allowed to collude on bids in any manner, except that they were not permitted to block access to the bid submission area (which was discussed in one of the pilot sessions). Some people discussed price in small groups, and others made public suggestions.

Figure 22.1 shows the results of two sessions run with identical cost structures and a procedural (tie-breaking) difference to be explained subsequently. The line labeled "costs" shows the permit use values (opportunity costs) per acre, with each step having a width equal to the number of acres for the permit with a use value at that step. These opportunity costs, arrayed in this manner from low to high, constitute a supply function. In each of these sessions, there was a fixed total budget for purchasing permits. So a low total acreage could be purchased at a high price per acre, and a high total acreage could be purchased at a low price per acre. This fixed budget generates a curve that is analogous to a demand function. If B is the total budget available to purchase Q total acres at a price per acre of P, then all money is spent if $PQ = B$, or if $P = B/Q$, which generates the negative relationship between P and Q that is graphed on the left side of Figure 22.1. The connected lines on the right side of the figure show the average price per acre of the provisionally accepted bids, by round, for each of the sessions being compared. Notice that these price averages bracket the competitive predictions, despite the fact that participants could freely discuss the bidding process, announce suggested bids, and so on.

One advantage of laboratory experiments is that procedures can be tested so that unanticipated problems can be discovered and fixed before the real auction takes place. In one of the sessions shown in the figure, a participant asked what would happen if a number of bidders tied at the cutoff bid that exhausted the announced budget, and if there was

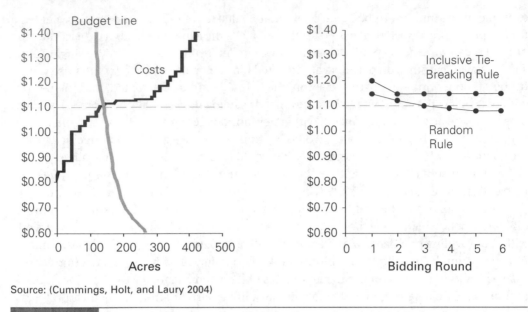

Source: (Cummings, Holt, and Laury 2004)

Figure 22.1   Results of Two Sessions with Different Tie-Breaking Rules

not enough money in the budget to cover all bids at the tie level. This possibility was not covered clearly in the instructions, and the experimenter in charge of the session announced that all of those tied would be included as provisional winners, or as final winners if this were the final round. In the second round of this session, a tie arose at a price about 5 percent above the competitive level, and all tied bids were provisionally included. In the subsequent round, more bids came in at the tie level from the previous round, and this accumulation of bids at the focal tie point continued. The resulting payments to subjects, which were needed to include all tied bids, ended up being twice the budgeted amount. This would have been analogous to spending $20 million in the actual auction instead of the $10 million budgeted by the legislature!

A second session was run with different people. The procedure was identical, except that it was announced that the bids to be included would be randomly determined in the event of a tie. The prices converged to the competitive level, as indicated by the lower price trajectory in Figure 22.1.

There were a number of other procedural changes that were implemented as a result of the experiments. For example, it became apparent that low bids tended to increase after the announcement of the cutoff bid, i.e., the highest provisionally accepted bid in each round. This pattern of increasing low bids was intuitive, since low bidders faced less risk with bid increases if they knew how high they could have gone in the previous round. In subsequent sessions, the list of provisional winners posted at the end of each round included the permit numbers, but not the actual bids. This reduction in information resulted in less of an upward creep of low bids in successive rounds, and as before, the high bids tended to fall as bidders scrambled to become included. These modifications in tie-breaking rules and the post-round announcement procedures were incorporated into the auction rules used by the EPD in the subsequent auction.

The final auction was conducted in April 2001, with the assistance of experimental economists from several universities. The results were collected and displayed to top EPD officials, who met in the Experimental Economics Laboratory at Georgia State, where the earlier experiments had been done. Almost 200 farmers turned up at eight locations at 8 A.M. on the designated Saturday morning, along with numerous television reporters and spectators. The procedures were quite close to those that had been implemented in the experiments, except that there were no redemption values and the EPD did not reveal what they intended to spend. Each bid was a signed contract, with one copy going to the bidder and another to the bid officials on-site. All bids were entered electronically by auction officials, as had been done in the experiments, and the resulting bids from the eight locations were ranked and projected in Atlanta, where officials then discussed whether to stop the auction, and if not, how much money to release to determine provisional winners for that round. This non-fixity of the budget differed from the procedures that had been used in the experiments, but it did not contradict any of the published auction rules. The changes in the provisionally released budget prevented significant drops in the cutoff bid, as falling bids in the relevant range allowed increasing numbers of acres to be provisionally included. The cutoff was $125 per acre in the fourth round. The director of the EPD then decided to release more money and raise the cutoff bid to $200 in the fifth round, when the auction was terminated.

If a fixed budget had been used, as in the experiments, then the cutoff bid would have fallen from round to round. The economists involved as advisers were concerned that the increasing budgets used from round to round may have discouraged some farmers from making bid reductions at the margin. In addition, the dramatic final-round increase in the budget expenditure and in the cutoff bid might have serious consequences for bidding in a future auction that used the same procedures.

The 2001 Irrigation Auction was considered to be a success. In particular, bids were received on about 60 percent of the acres that were eligible to be retired from irrigation. In total, about 33,000 acres were taken out of irrigation, at an average price of about $135 per acre.

In 2002, the state officials, in consultation with experimental economists (Laury and Cummings) decided to run the auction as a single-round discriminative auction, with sealed bids accepted by mail. This method was less expensive to administer, and attendance at the auction site was less important, since farmers were familiar with the compensation and low-bids-win features of the auction that had been implemented the previous year. In addition, the mail-in procedures may have enabled more people to participate, since attendance at the auction site was not required. (This participation effect could not have been inferred easily from laboratory experiments.) Results from the 2001 auction were used to select a reserve price (maximum bid) of $150 for the 2002 auction, which served as a substitute for the effects of multi-round competition. In this second auction, 41,000 more acres were removed from irrigation, at a slightly higher average cost of $143 per acre (McDowell 2002). In retrospect, these numbers represent an overall improvement relative to the 2001 auction (Petrie, Laury, and Hill 2004).

22.2   FCC Bandwidth Auctions and Package Bidding Alternatives

Government agencies in a number of countries have recently used simultaneous auctions to allocate portions of broadcast frequency bandwidth in different regional markets. These auctions generally involve a large number of licenses, which are defined by geographic region and adjacent frequency intervals. The rationale for conducting the auctions simultaneously is that there may be complementarities in valuation as bidders strive to obtain contiguous licenses that may allow them to enjoy economies of scale and to provide more valuable services to consumers. For example, a person who signs up for cell-phone service with a particular company would typically be willing to pay more if the company also provides service (free of roaming fees) in adjacent geographic areas.

With a few exceptions, these simultaneous auctions are run as English auctions, with simultaneous ascending bids for each license. Bids are collected in a sequence of rounds. At each round, bidders who are eligible to bid for a particular license but are not currently the high bidder, can maintain their active status by bidding above the current high bid by a specified increment. The activity rules can be complex, but the main idea is simple; they are intended to force bidders to keep bidding in order to be eligible to bid in later rounds. For example, a bidder who obtained two activity units via up-front payments at the start of the auction could bid for at most two units in a given round, although it is up to the bidder to decide which two units to bid on. A bidder who only bids on a single unit (and is not the current high bidder on any other) would lose a unit of activity. This bidder would only be able to bid on a single unit in subsequent rounds, unless one of a limited number of activity waivers is used to regain the second activity unit. The purpose of this forced bid activity is to keep the high bids moving upward, so that valuation information is revealed during the course of the auction, and not in sudden bid jumps in the final rounds. The auctions stop when no bids for any license are changed in a given round.

This type of simultaneous, multi-round (SMR) auction has been used by the U.S. Federal Communications Commission (FCC) to sell bandwidth for personal communications services, beginning in the 1990s. The amounts of money raised were surprisingly large, and similar auctions have been implemented in Europe and elsewhere. The auctions have proved to be fast, efficient, and lucrative as compared with the administrative "beauty-contest" allocations that were used previously (see Chapter 17 on rent seeking for more discussion of the potential inefficiencies of these administrative procedures).

There are, however, some reasons to question the efficiency of simultaneous auctions for individual licenses. A bidder's strategy in a single-unit, ascending-bid auction with a known private value is fairly simple—one must keep bidding actively until the high bid exceeds the bidder's private value. This way, the bidding will exclude the low value buyers and the prize will be awarded to the bidder with the highest value. The strategic environment is more interesting with common value elements, since information about the unknown common value might be inferred from observing when other bidders drop out of the bidding.

Even with private values, the strategic bidding environment can be complicated by valuation complementarities, as can be seen by considering a simple example. Suppose that there are two contiguous licenses being sold, A and B, with three competing bidders, 1, 2, and 3. Bidder 1 is a local provider in region A and has a private value of 10 for A and 0 for B. Conversely, Bidder 2 is a local provider in the other region and has a value of 0 for A and 10 for B. The Bidder 3 is a national provider, with values of 5 for A alone, 5 for B alone, and 30 for the AB combination. These valuations are shown in the left column of Table 22.2, where the subscripts indicate the license(s) obtained, A alone, B alone, and the AB combination.

Suppose that the bidding sequence for the first three rounds is as shown in Table 22.2. After the first round of bidding, Bidder 1 is the high bidder for A, and Bidder 2 is the high bidder for B. Suppose that the activity rule requires Bidder 3 to raise these bids to 5 to stay active in each region, as shown in the outcome for the second round. In response, Bidders 1 and 2 raise the bids for their preferred licenses to 6, to stay active, as shown in the third round column.

As the fourth round begins, Bidder 3 faces a dilemma if the private values of the first two bidders are not known. It makes no sense for Bidder 3 to compete for a single license, since the bidding has already topped the bidder's private value of 5 for each single license. But to bid above this value produces an exposure problem, since Bidder 2 does not know whether the other two bidders will push the individual bids for the two licenses up to a level where the sum is greater than 30, which is value of the AB combination to Bidder 3. Thus, it is dangerous for this bidder to compete for the AB combination and only end up winning one of them. If this exposure risk causes Bidder 3 to drop out, then the outcome is inefficient in the sense that the total value (10 for Bidder 1, who gets license A, and 10 for

Table 22.2	A Bid Sequence for a Simultaneous Ascending-Bid Auction: The Exposure Problem			
	Values	**Round 1**	**Round 2**	**Round 3**
Bidder 1	$V_A = 10$, $V_B = 0$, $V_{AB} = 10$	**4 for A**, 0 for B	no change	**6 for A**
Bidder 2	$V_A = 0$, $V_B = 10$, $V_{AB} = 10$	0 for A, **4 for B**	no change	**6 for B**
Bidder 3	$V_A = 5$, $V_B = 5$, $V_{AB} = 30$	3 for A, 3 for B	**5 for A, 5 for B**	no change

Bidder 2 who gets license B) is less than the value of the AB combination (30) to Bidder 3. The resulting efficiency would be 20/30 or 66 percent in this case. One way to reduce the severity of the exposure problem is to allow bidders to withdraw bids during the auction, and the FCC rules typically allow a limited number of such withdrawals. But opportunities for withdrawals are limited, and a bidder who defaults on a final winning bid is assessed a penalty, along with compensation to the FCC if the license is later sold below the default bid level. These withdrawal limits are intended to force bidders to make serious bids that convey real information about license valuations.

Since limited bid withdrawal options do not fully protect bidders who try to acquire combinations of units, the FCC is actively considering combinatorial auctions with package bidding. Such an auction, for example, would allow simultaneous bidding for A alone, for B alone, and for the AB package. When the bidding stops, the seller would then select the final allocation that maximizes the sales revenue, subject to some constraints, e.g., that no unit is sold twice. This is sometimes called *combinatorial bidding*, and with large numbers of licenses, it is complicated by the fact that it may be difficult to calculate the revenue-maximizing allocation of licenses, at least in a reasonable time. Economists and operations researchers have worked on algorithms to deal with the revenue-maximization problem in a timely manner, and as a result, the FCC has considered and tested the use of combinatorial bidding for bandwidth licenses. Combinatorial bidding was used in May 2006 in an FCC auction of spectrum for air-to-ground communications of commercial aircraft. Here the prior decision of how to configure different frequency bandwidth ranges was avoided by letting buyers submit bids on licenses in a limited number of pre-specified bandwidth combinations, a procedure known as "band plan."

Package bidding, of course, may introduce problems that are not merely due to computation. Consider the example shown in Table 22.3, where the valuations are as before, with the exception that the AB package for Bidder 3 has been reduced from 30 to 15. In this

Table 22.3	Bid Sequence for a Simultaneous Auction with Package Bidding: The Coordination or "Threshold" Problem

	Values	Round 1	Round 2	Round 3	Round 4
Bidder 1	$V_A = 10$, $V_B = 0$, $V_{AB} = 10$	**4 for A**, 0 for B	no change	**8 for A**	no change
Bidder 2	$V_A = 0$, $V_B = 10$, $V_{AB} = 10$	0 for A, **4 for B**	no change	**5 for B**	no change
Bidder 3	$V_A = 5$, $V_B = 5$, $V_{AB} = 15$	6 for AB	**10 for AB**	no change	**14 for AB**
Suggested Prices		$P_A = 4$, $P_B = 4$, $P_{AB} = 8$	$P_A = 5$, $P_B = 5$, $P_{AB} = 10$	$P_A = 8$, $P_B = 5$, $P_{AB} = 13$	$P_A = 8$, $P_B = 6$, $P_{AB} = 14$

example, the bidding in the first round is the same as before, except that Bidder 3 bids 6 for the AB package instead of bidding 3 for each license. Since Bidder 1 and Bidder 2 each submit bids of 4 for their preferred licenses, the revenue-maximizing allocation after the first round would be to award the licenses separately, for a total revenue of 8. Bidder 3 tops this in the second round by bidding 10 for the AB package, and the other bidders respond with bids of 8 for A and 5 for B in the third round, for a total of 13. To stay competitive, Bidder 3 responds with a bid of 14 for the AB package, which would be the revenue-maximizing allocation on the basis of bids up to the fourth round.

In order for Bidders 1 and 2 to obtain their preferred licenses, it would be necessary for them to raise the sum of their bids, but each would prefer that the other be the one to do so. For example, Bidder 1 would like to maintain a bid of 8 and have Bidder 2 come up to 7 to defeat the package bid of Bidder 3. But Bidder 2 would prefer to see some of the joint increase come from Bidder 1. This coordination problem is magnified if there are greater numbers of bidders involved and if they do not know one another's values. It is easy to imagine that a coordination failure might result, as some bidders try to free ride and let others bear the cost of raising the bid total. A coordination failure in this example would result in an allocation of the AB package to Bidder 3, for a total value of 15, which is below the sum of private values (10 + 10) if the licenses are awarded separately to Bidders 1 and 2. In this case, the efficiency would be 15/20 or 75 percent. The package bidding rules being considered by the FCC involve the provision of prices after each round, which would help bidders see how high they must go to get into the action on a particular license or package. See the bottom row of Table 22.3 for an example of how these prices might be computed.

One way that a large bidder could attempt to deter competition is to begin with a high jump bid on a package, e.g., going directly to a bid in the 10–14 range for the package AB for the setup in Table 22.3. In a more complicated design where Bidders 1 and 2 have other licenses that they pursue, the large jump bid on AB might cause these small bidders to focus their attention in a different direction, where the difference between their valuation and the current bid or suggested price is larger. Such behavior is sometimes called *straightforward bidding*, and it sometimes provides a good description of behavior in laboratory experiments.

McCabe, Rassenti, and Smith (1991) observed inefficiencies being created by occasional jump bids in laboratory experiments, and they devised a simple clock auction to alleviate this problem. As we discussed in Chapter 19, the idea behind a clock auction is that it provides prices on each item being auctioned, and these prices are increased in a mechanical manner in response to excess demand for an item. After prices are announced for a round, each bidder indicates which items or packages are of interest, where the package price is just the sum of the clock prices for the items in that package. The clock provides some incentives for bidders to truthfully reveal whether or not they are interested by not letting them come back in once they lose activity by withdrawing bids on an item or package.

The way a clock auction works is best explained by an example. For the valuation setup on the left side of Table 22.3, suppose that the clock prices start at 6 for each item. At these prices, Bidder 1 would indicate a willingness to buy A, Bidder 2 to buy B, and Bidder 3 to buy the AB package (for a price of $2 \times 6 = 12$). By bidding on the package, Bidder 3 avoids the exposure of bidding above 5 for either A or B singly, and the clock mechanism includes the package bid in the determination of excess demand for the items in this package. Thus, there would be excess demand for both items, with two bidders showing interest in each item. As a result, the clock would click up the price for each item to 7 and then 8, at which point Bidder 3 would withdraw, since that bidder would not be willing to pay $2 \times 8 = 16$ for the AB package. Thus, the two items would sell for 8 to the small bidders, which is the efficient outcome in this case. Notice that the gradual price increases in the clock auction preclude jump bids, and these increases force the small bidders to raise their bids together to stay in the auction, thereby solving the threshold problem in this case.

22.3 Experimental Tests of Package Bidding Alternatives

The discussion in the previous section does not begin to cover all of the alternative proposals that economists have put forth for running simultaneous multi-round auctions. Recently, some of the strongest interest has been in procedures that incorporate either computer-generated prices or clock-driven prices. In addition, there have also been proposals to follow the ascending price phase by a second phase, e.g., a sealed-bid proxy bidding phase with a second-price type of setup (Ausubel, Crampton, and Milgrom 2004). Most of the proposed approaches have not been evaluated with experiments, but for those that have, the focus has been on performance in two dimensions: sales revenue and economic efficiency. Government policymakers are also concerned that the selected auction format does not unfairly disadvantage small bidders, and high revenues are not considered beneficial per se if they result from losses incurred by winning bidders because of the exposure or other problems. The remainder of this section briefly summarizes the results of two evaluations of price-based mechanisms.

Porter, Rassenti, Roopnarine, and Smith (2003) report results of 55 laboratory auctions used to compare the combinatorial clock with other methods of selling off multiple units simultaneously, with and without package bidding. The combinatorial auction was uniformly more efficient than the alternative considered in the test environment; in fact, the combinatorial clock yielded 100 percent efficiency in all but two of the auctions in which it was used.

Since the clock raises prices until there is no excess demand, one can think of the combinatorial clock auction as a device for finding a competitive equilibrium set of prices. Nevertheless, value complementarities may preclude the existence of such prices (Bykowsky, Cull, and Ledyard 2000), as the example in Table 22.4 illustrates. Here there are three small bidders: Bidder 1 who is interested in licenses A and B, Bidder 2 who is interested in B and C, and Bidder 3 who is interested in A and C. Think of these bidders as being "regional" providers with partially overlapping interests. The large Bidder 4 is a "national" bidder who is interested in all three. This bidder's value of 36 for the ABC package produces the maxi-

Table 22.4	Bidder Value with Strong Complementarities: Non-existence of Competitive Equilibrium						
	Package						
Bidder	A	B	C	AB	BC	CA	ABC
1	3	3	0	30	3	3	30
2	0	3	3	3	30	3	30
3	3	0	3	3	3	30	30
4	3	3	3	24	24	24	**36**

mum efficiency in this example. Note that clock prices for A and B would have to equal at least 30 to keep Bidder 1 out of the action for the package AB. Similarly, the clock price sum for B and C and the sum for A and C would have to exceed 30. It follows that clock prices of at least 15 on all three licenses are needed to force the small bidders to withdraw, but at these prices the clock cost of the ABC package is 45, which exceeds Bidder 4's value of 36 for this package (as shown by the bold number in the lower-right corner of the table). It can be shown that there is no set of competitive prices for individual licenses in this example, i.e., prices for which there is only one interested bidder.

In contrast, non-clock based proposals for package bidding allow bids on combinations that are not the sum of the individual component prices. Note that by allowing prices for packages, we can ensure that demand equals supply, e.g., by putting a price of 35 on the ABC package and prices of 31 on the three paired packages, AB, BC, and AC. This example suggests that there may be cases where allowing bidders to submit bids on packages may yield better outcomes than having the prices determined by a clock mechanism.

The valuation structure in Table 22.4 is the basis for an experiment in Brunner, Goeree, and Holt (2005) that compared clock-driven and bid-driven package bidding mechanisms. Groups of four bidders competed in a series of 10 auctions, using randomly generated license valuations that were approximately centered around the numbers in the table. When the random realizations caused the ABC value for Bidder 4 to be large enough relative to the two-license packages for the regional bidders, a competitive equilibrium would typically exist. The realized valuation profiles were reordered and selected so that a competitive equilibrium set prices that did not exist in every other round. In the clock treatment, the price provided for each package at the start of each round was the sum of the clock prices for each license. In the non-clock package-bidding treatment, pseudo-competitive prices were provided so that bidders would know approximately how high they need to bid to get into the action in that round. (These prices were essentially those implied by the "RAD" pricing mechanism suggested in Kwasnica, Ledyard, Porter, and DiMartini (2005). For the final five auctions, the efficiencies were higher with package bidding (98 percent) and the combinatorial clock (98 percent) than with a simultaneous multi-round auction that did not allow package bidding (92 percent). While these two methods of package bidding were comparable in terms of efficiency, the combinatorial clock yielded higher revenues than the non-clock package bidding procedure.

The observation of relatively high efficiencies in this simple environment with three licenses raises the issue of which auction procedures would be better in more complex settings with more licenses and more bidders. This is the focus of current research by a number of experimentalists, including a consulting project for the FCC (Goeree, Holt, and Ledyard 2006). Brunner, Goeree, Holt, and Ledyard (2006) report that the combinatorial clock procedure yields significantly higher sales revenues than other auction mechanisms tested in environments with larger numbers of bidders and licenses. A good balance between efficiency and revenue outcomes is also provided by package bidding with RAD prices.

22.4 Extensions

See Klemperer (2002) for an authoritative discussion of the general considerations involved in designing multi-unit auctions, and see Noussair (2003) for a clear description of the exposure and threshold problems.

A clock auction was used in the 2004 Virginia NOx auction for tradable emissions permits. The prizes were thousands of one-ton permits, and bidders indicated their demand quantities as the clock price was raised, until demand fell to the available number of permits. This was a uniform-price auction in that all permits sold at the same market-clearing price. Separate auctions were run sequentially for two sets of permits in different years. The clearing prices were 3–6 percent above the current spot prices for those permits, which may be due to the values bidders placed on being able to bid for blocks of permits. This auction, which was considered a success in terms of transparency, speed, and revenue generation, was implemented after a series of laboratory experiments that demonstrated the feasibility of the clock format in this context (Porter, Rassenti, Shobe, Smith, and Winn 2005). Interestingly, the state government request for proposals (RFP) for administering the auction did not mention a clock format, since this format had never been used for selling permits, and there was less than three months between the date of the RFP and the end of the fiscal year when funding would evaporate. The successful brokerage firm was the only one to propose a clock auction, which it had learned about through an unpublished auction theory paper that turned up in a routine Internet search!

One issue that comes up with multi-unit uniform price auctions is the possibility that bidders will try to manipulate the market-clearing price. For example, suppose that two units are being auctioned, and the bids are 5 and 3 from one bidder, and the bids are 4 and 2 from the other. The ranked bids for the two units are, therefore, 5, 4, 3, 2, and the market-clearing price determined by the highest rejected bid would be 3. Using this uniform price rule, each bidder would purchase a unit for that price. By lowering the rejected bid of 3, the bidder who made that bid could reduce the amount paid for the winning bid. Of course, a bidder would not know ex ante whether a particular bid will end up being the highest rejected bid that determines price, but strategic bidding in this case often involves bidding lower for a second unit that has a lower marginal value to the bidder. Such strategic bidding has been observed in both laboratory and field settings. For example, List and Lucking-Reiley (2000) sold thousands of dollars of tradable sports cards in two-person, two-unit uniform-price auctions. These auctions were conducted at a sports card collectors' convention, with cards that had identical book values. In some auctions, the two bidders were sports card dealers, and in other auctions the bidders were collectors. By comparing bids, the authors concluded that bidding is typically below value on the second unit. In a follow-up field experiment, again with sports cards, this strategic demand reduction is less pronounced when there are larger numbers of bidders, as predicted in theory (Engelbrecht-Wiggans, List, and Reiley 2005). Even if there is some loss of control in field experiments like this where values are not induced directly, the increased external validity from using traders from the market being studied is very useful, and observations from a series of field experiments can add a valuable perspective. Moreover, such field experiments can be complemented with laboratory experiments. See Kagel and Levin (2004) for an analysis of the exposure problem and strategic demand reduction in a "clean" environment in which small bidders are simulated by computer.

As discussed in Chapter 9, a potential problem with sequential bidding procedures is that bidders with incumbency advantages in different locations may try to collude tacitly by signaling "I won't compete in your area if you don't compete in mine." Brunner, Goeree, Holt, and Ledyard (2006) report cases of this kind of tacit collusion in a clock auction. Collusion was never successful, however, when the clock auction was followed by a "final shootout" round of sealed combinatorial bids, where the winners were determined by maximizing the seller revenue using the entire "bid book" of all clock and final sealed bids for licenses and packages.

QUESTIONS

1. Consider the valuation setup in Table 22.4, with the only change being that the license C value for Bidder 3 is raised from 3 to 10. What is the efficient allocation in this case? Does a competitive equilibrium exist, and if so, what are the prices for A, B, and C that equate demand and supply (1 license)?

2. For the valuation setup in Question 1, what would the observed efficiency be if Bidder 4 were to win all three licenses?

3. The two-phase auctions alluded to at the beginning of Section 22.3 have the property that there is an initial auction followed by a second auction, a kind of "final shootout." For simplicity, suppose that there is a single prize and the second phase is a sealed-bid

first-price auction, with the prize going to the high bidder in the second stage. What can be done to keep the first phase from being ignored by bidders, i.e., what procedures could be adopted to induce bidders to compete seriously in the first phase?

4. Speculate on what types of auction procedures might be considered by a seller to counter possible bidder collusion, or to take advantage of strong bidder risk aversion.

Behavioral Game Theory: Treasures and Intuitive Contradictions

As one might expect, human behavior does not always conform tightly to simple mathematical models, especially in interactive situations. These models, however, can be extremely useful if deviations from the Nash equilibrium are systematic and predictable. Part 6 presents several games in which behavior is influenced by intuitive economic forces in ways that are not captured by basic game theory. Many of the applications are taken from Goeree and Holt (2001), "Ten Little Treasures of Game Theory and Ten Intuitive Contradictions." The treasures are treatments where data conform to theory, and the contradictions are produced by payoff changes with strong behavioral effects, even though these changes do not affect the Nash predictions. Since game theory is so widely used in the study of strategic situations like auctions, mergers, and legal disputes, it is fortunate that there is progress in understanding these anomalies.

Many games involve decisions by different players made in sequence. In these situations, players who make initial decisions must predict what those with subsequent decisions to make will do. These sequential games, which are represented by an extensive form or "decision tree" structure, will be considered in Chapter 23. Several matched pairs of extensive form games are used to show that the *magnitudes* of payoff differences may matter a lot, since one player may not trust another to respond reliably to small incentives. The generalized matching pennies game in Chapter 24 shows that behavioral deviations can be strongly influenced by payoff asymmetries. Existing data indicate that the Nash equilibrium only provides good, unbiased predictions by coincidence, i.e., when the payoffs for each decision exhibit a kind of balance or symmetry. Deviations from Nash predictions are even more dramatic in some versions of the traveler's dilemma game discussed in Chapter 25, where the data patterns and the Nash equilibrium may be on *opposite* ends of the range of possible decisions. Finally, the coordination game in Chapter 26 has a whole series of Nash equilibria, and the issue is which one will have more drawing power as determined by *risk and return*. This game is important in developing an understanding of how people may become stuck in an equilibrium that is bad for all concerned.

Many of the experiments to be considered have pairs of treatments with different data patterns, despite the equivalence of Nash predictions in both treatments. The issue is to explain how behavior in experiments might be responsive to payoff conditions that do not affect Nash predictions. The resulting models often relax the strong game-theoretic assumptions of perfect selfishness, perfect rationality, and perfect predictions of others' decisions.

Some of the earlier chapters on bargaining and voluntary contributions have already raised issues of fairness, reciprocity, and concern for others—factors that might bias behavior away from predictions based only on a person's own payoffs. Several other ways of explaining deviations from Nash predictions will be developed in Part 6. One approach is based on the idea that players are not able to predict perfectly what others will do, which may require a relaxation of the assumption that behavior is in equilibrium. As mentioned in Chapter 3, a level 0 person is someone who makes decisions randomly, with equal probabilities for each decision. Most players do better than this, and a level 1 person is someone who makes the best decision given beliefs that put equal probabilities on each decision.

Of course, higher levels of iterated rationality in this thought process are likely, and at each level the beliefs correspond to the decision probabilities for the next lower level. The resulting behavior is not an equilibrium if players' choice probabilities do not match other's beliefs about what they will do. It may not be reasonable to expect equilibrium predictions to be accurate in a game that is only played once, and iterated models of strategic thinking might help us understand behavior in one-shot games. For games with repetition and random matching, learning models may be used to explain the patterns of adjustment, e.g., whether prices converge from above or below, or if they converge at all. Both classes of models, learning and introspection, have the (useful) property that beliefs and choice probabilities may not coincide. Equilibrium models may be more appropriate after participants have had a chance to learn and adapt.

A second approach to explaining deviations from Nash predictions is to inject some randomness or "noise" into players' best response functions. The randomness is due to unmodeled effects of emotions, attention lapses, partial calculations, and other factors that may vary from person to person and from time to time for the same person. In a simple decision, such noise elements tend to spread decisions around the optimal choice, with the most likely choice being near the optimal level, but with some probability of error in either direction, which could create a bell curve pattern.

With strategic interaction, however, even small amounts of noise in one person's decisions may cause large biases in others' decisions. Imagine a person seeking the highest point on a hill, where the peak is on the edge of a steep cliff. The effect of this asymmetry in risk is that any slight chance of wind may cause the person to fall off of the peak. In a game, the payoff peaks depend on others' decisions, i.e., the peaks can *move*. In such cases, the effects of noise or small un-modeled factors may have a snowball effect, moving all decisions well away from the Nash predictions. Both of these approaches—iterated strategic thinking and noisy decision making—will be incorporated into the discussion in this part. The equilibrium with "noise" can be thought of as the limiting case of learning or of successively higher levels of iterated strategic thinking, with uncertainty about what others will do.

chapter 23

Multi-Stage Games

The games considered in Chapters 3 and 5 involve simultaneous decisions. Many interesting games, however, are sequential in nature, so that the first mover must try to anticipate how the subsequent decision-maker(s) will react. For example, the first person may make a take-it-or leave it proposal for how to split a sum of money, and the second person must either accept the proposed split or reject. This is a discrete example of an ultimatum bargaining game, which was considered in Chapter 12.

Another example is a labor market interaction, where the employer first chooses a wage or other set of contract terms, and the worker, seeing the wage, selects an effort level. There are several common principles that are used in the analysis of such games, and these will be covered here. Somewhat paradoxically, the first person's decision is sometimes more difficult, since the optimal decision may depend on a forecast of the second person's response, whereas the person who makes the final decision does not need to forecast the other's action if it has already been observed. In this case, we begin by considering the final decision-maker's choice, and then we typically work backward to consider the first person's decision, in a process known as *backward induction*. Of course, the extent to which this method of backward induction yields good predictions is a behavioral question, which will be evaluated in the context of laboratory experiments.

Several of the two-stage games discussed below are the default settings for the Veconlab Two-Stage Game program. There is a separate Centipede Game program, with setup options that allow any number of stages. A hand-run version of the Centipede game can be done easily with a roll of quarters and a tray (see Question 6 at the end of the chapter).

23.1 Extensive Forms and Strategies

This section will present a simple two-stage bargaining game, in which the first move is a proposal of how to divide $4, which must either be $3 for the proposer and $1 for the other, or $2 for each. The other player (responder) sees this proposal and either accepts, which implements the split, or rejects, which results in $0 for each. As defined in Chapter 3, a strategy for such a game is a complete plan of action that covers each possible contingency. In other words, a strategy tells the player what decision to make at each stage, and these instructions are so detailed that a strategy could be carried out by an employee or agent, who would never need to ask questions about what to do. In the two-stage bargaining game, a strategy for the first person is which proposal to offer, i.e., ($3, $1) or ($2, $2), where the proposer's payoff is listed on the left in each payoff pair. A responder's strategy must specify a reaction to each of these proposals. Thus, the responder has a number of options: a) accept both, b) reject both, c) accept ($3, $1) and reject ($2, $2), or d) reject ($3, $1) and accept ($2, $2). These strategies will be referred to as: AA, RR, AR, and RA respectively, where the first letter indicates the response, Accept or Reject, to the unequal proposal. Similarly, the proposer's strategies will be referred to as Equal (equal split) or Unequal (unequal, favoring the proposer). A Nash equilibrium is a pair of strategies, one for each player, with the property that neither can increase their own payoff by deviating to a different strategy under the assumption that the other player stays with the equilibrium strategy.

One Nash equilibrium for this game is (Equal, RA), where the proposer offers an equal split, and the responder rejects the unequal proposal and accepts the equal proposal. Deviations are not profitable, since the responder is already receiving the proposal that offers the higher of the two possible payoffs, and the proposer would not want to switch to the unequal proposal given that the responder's strategy requires that it be rejected. This Nash equilibrium, however, involves a threat by the responder to reject an unequal proposal ($3 for the proposer, $1 for the responder), thereby causing both to earn $0. Such a rejection would reduce the responder's payoff from $1 to $0, so it violates a notion of sequential rationality that requires play to be rational in all parts of the game (subgames).

The reader might wonder how this kind of irrationality can be part of a Nash equilibrium. The answer is that the simple notion of a Nash equilibrium only requires rationality in terms of considering unilateral deviations from the equilibrium by one player, under the assumption that the other player's strategy is unchanged. In the equilibrium being considered, (Equal, RA), the unequal proposal is not made, so the responder never has to carry out the threat to reject this proposal. Selten (1965) proposed that the rationality requirement be expanded to cover all parts of the game, which he defined as "subgames." He called the resulting equilibrium a *subgame perfect Nash equilibrium*. Obviously, not all Nash equilibria are subgame perfect; as the equilibrium (Equal, RA) demonstrates.

In order to find the (subgame perfect) equilibrium for this game, consider starting in the final stage, where the responder is considering a specific proposal. Each of the possible proposals involves strictly positive amounts of money for the responder, so a rational responder who only cares about his own payoff would accept either proposal. This analysis requires that the responder accept either proposal, so the only responder strategy that satisfies rationality in all subgames is AA. Next, consider the first stage. If the proposer predicts that the responder is rational and will accept either offer, then the proposer will demand the larger share, so the equilibrium will be (Unequal, AA). This is a Nash equilibrium, and from the way it was constructed, we know that it satisfies sequential rationality, i.e., it is subgame perfect.

The reasoning process that was used in the previous paragraph is an example of backward induction, which simply means analyzing a sequence of decisions by starting at the end and working backward toward the beginning. The concepts, backward induction, sequential rationality, and subgame perfection, can all be defined more precisely, but the goal here is for the reader to obtain an intuitive understanding of the principles involved, based on specific examples. This understanding is useful in constructing predictions for outcomes of simple multi-stage games, which can serve as benchmarks for evaluating observed behavior in experiments. As we shall see, these benchmarks do not always yield very good predictions, for a variety of reasons (discussed below).

Before proceeding with examples, it is instructive to show how the two-stage bargaining game would be represented as a decision tree, which is known as the extensive form of a game. In Figure 23.1, the game begins at the top, at the node that is labeled Proposer. This player either chooses an Equal proposal ($2, $2), or an Unequal proposal ($3, $1). The Responder has a decision node following each of these proposals. On the left, the Responder may either choose A (accept) or R (reject) in response to the Equal proposal. The same options are also available on the right. Notice that each decision node is labeled with the name of the player who makes a decision at that node, and each branch emanating from a node is labeled with the name of one of the feasible decisions. The branches end at the bottom (terminal nodes), which show the payoffs of the Proposer (on the left) and Responder (on the right).

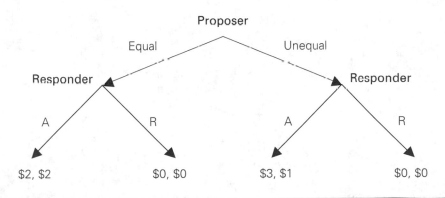

Figure 23.1 An Extensive Form Representation for the Bargaining Game

23.2 Two-Stage Trust Games

The first two experiments to be considered are based on the two games shown in Figure 23.2. Consider the top part, where the first player must begin by making a safe choice (S) or a risky choice (R). Decision S is safe in the sense that the payoffs are deterministic: 80 for the first player and 50 for the second (the first player's payoff will be listed on the left in each case). The payoffs that may result from choosing R depend on the second player's response, P or N. For the game shown in the top part of Figure 23.2, this is an easy choice, since the second player would earn 10 from choosing P and 70 from choosing N. The first player should make the risky choice R as long as the first player trusts the second player to be rational. This game was played only once, without repetition, by pairs of subjects. Payoffs were in pennies. As indicated in the top part of the figure, 84 percent of the first movers were confident enough to choose R, and all of these received the anticipated N response. Note that the second movers would have reduced their earnings by 60 if any of them had selected P in response to R.

The game shown in the bottom part of Figure 23.2 is almost identical, except that the second mover only loses 2 by making a P response, which generates a payoff of 68 for the

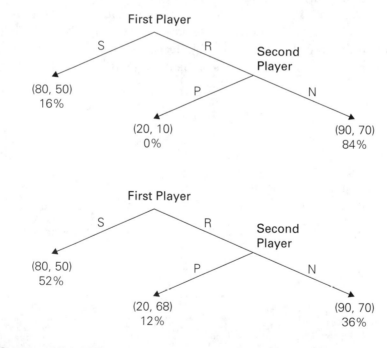

Source: (Goeree and Holt 2001)

Figure 23.2 A Two-Stage Game Where Mistakes Matter

second mover instead of 70. In this case, more than half of the first movers were sufficiently concerned about the possibility of a P response that they chose the safe decision, S. This fear was well founded, since a fourth of the first movers who chose R encountered the P response in the second stage. In fact, the first players who chose S in the bottom game in Figure 23.2 earned more on average than those who chose R (see Question 1 at the end of the chapter).

The standard game-theoretic analysis of the two games in Figure 23.2 would yield the same prediction for each game, since this analysis is based on the assumption that both players are rational and are concerned with maximizing their own payoffs. This assumption implies that the second player will choose N, regardless of whether it increases earnings by 60, as in the top game, or by only 2, as in the bottom game. In each of these games, we begin by analyzing the second player's best choice (choose N), and knowing this, we can calculate the best choice for the first player (choose R). The pair of choices, N and R, constitutes a Nash equilibrium, since neither player can increase earnings by deviating.

The Nash outcome (R and N) that was identified for the games in Figure 23.2 involves little tension in the sense that it maximizes the payoffs for each player. There is another Nash outcome, (S and P), which can be verified by showing that neither person has an incentive to deviate unilaterally (see Question 2 at the end of the chapter). In particular, the second player earns 50 in this equilibrium, and a unilateral deviation from P to N would not change the outcome, since the outcome is fully determined by the first player's S decision. This second equilibrium is typically ruled out because it implies a type of behavior for the second player that is not rational in a sequential sense. Despite these arguments, S is the most commonly observed outcome for the bottom game in Figure 23.2.

There is more tension for the games shown in Figure 23.3. As before, there are two Nash equilibria: (S and P) and (R and N). First consider the (R and N) outcome, which yields 90 for the first player and 50 for the second. If the second player were to deviate to P, then the outcome would be (R and P) with lower payoffs for the second player, since we are considering a unilateral deviation, i.e., a deviation by one player given that the other continues to use the equilibrium decision. Similarly, given that the second player is using N, the first player cannot deviate and increase the payoff above 90, which is the maximum for the first player in any case. This equilibrium (R and N) is the one preferred by the first player.

There is another equilibrium (S and P) (see Question 3 at the end of the chapter). Here, you can think of P as indicating "punishment," since a P decision in the second stage reduces the first player's payoff from 90 to 60. The reason that such a punishment might be enacted is that the second player actually prefers the outcome on the left side of the figure for each of the two games in Figure 23.3. The difference between the two games in the figure is that the cost of punishment is 40 for the top game, and only 2 for the bottom game.

The standard game-theoretic analysis of the games in Figure 23.3 would be the same, i.e., that the (S and P) equilibrium is implausible since it implies that the second mover is ready to use a punishment that is costly, and hence not credible. So the predicted outcome

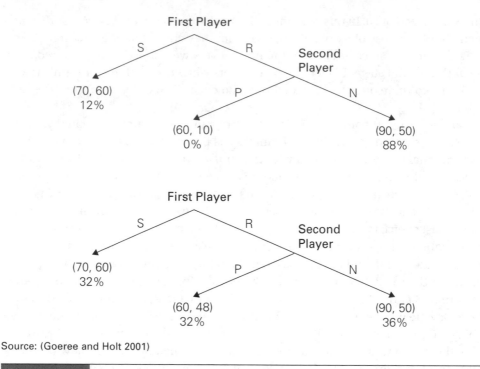

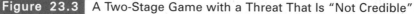

Source: (Goeree and Holt 2001)

Figure 23.3 A Two-Stage Game with a Threat That Is "Not Credible"

would be the equilibrium (R and N) in each case. This prediction is accurate for the game shown in the top part of the figure, where 88 percent of the outcomes are as predicted. The outcomes deviate sharply from this prediction for the game shown in the bottom part of the figure, since only about one-third of the observed outcomes are at the (R and N) node.

To summarize, the notion of sequential rationality rules out the possibility that the second mover will make a mistake in either of the games in Figure 23.2, or that the second mover will carry out a costly (and hence non-credible) threat for either of the games in Figure 23.3. Thus, the predicted outcome would be the same (R and N) in all four games. This prediction works well for only one of the games in each figure, but not for the other one. The problem with the assumption of perfect sequential rationality is that it does not allow room for random deviations or mistakes, which are more likely if the cost of the mistake is small (2 for each of the bottom games in the figures). Such deviations may be due to actual calculation and recording errors, or to un-modeled payoff variations caused by emotions, concerns about fairness, and so on. A more systematic analysis of the costs of deviations and their effects on behavior will be undertaken in Chapters 24 through 26.

23.3 The Centipede Game

In the two-stage games considered thus far, the first mover has to consider how the second mover will react to the initial decision. This may involve the first mover thinking introspectively: "What would I do in the second stage, having just seen this particular initial decision?" This process of seeing a future situation through the eyes of someone else may not be easy or natural, and the difficulty will increase greatly if there are more than two stages, so an initial decision-maker might have to think about reactions several stages later. In such cases, it is still often straightforward, but tedious, to begin with the last decision-maker, consider what is rational for that person, and work backward to the second-to-last decision-maker, and then to the third-to-last decision-maker, and so on in a process of backward induction. The noise observed in some of the two-stage games already considered in this chapter makes it plausible that players in multi-stage games may not be very predictable, at least in terms of their ability to reason via backward induction. Rosenthal (1982) proposed a sequential game with 100 stages, which serves as an extreme stress test of the backward induction reasoning process. Each of the 100 stages has a terminal node in the extensive form that hangs down, so the extensive form looks like an insect with 100 legs, which is why this game is known as the centipede game.

Figure 23.4 shows a truncated version of this game, with only four legs. At each node, the player (Red or Blue) can either move down, which stops the game, or continue to the right, which passes the move to the other player, except in the final stage. The play begins on the left side, where the Red player must decide whether to stop the game (the downward arrow) or continue (the right arrow). A stop/down move in this first stage results in payoffs of 40 for Red and 10 for the other player, Blue. Note that the payoffs for this first terminal node are listed as (40, 10), with payoffs for the Red player shown on the left. If Red decides to continue to the right, then the next move is made by Blue, who can either continue or stop, yielding payoffs of (20, 80), where the left payoff is for Red, as before. Blue might reason that stopping gives 80 for sure, whereas a decision to continue will either yield payoffs of 40 (if Red stops in the next stage), 320 (if Blue stops by moving down in the final stage), or 160 (if

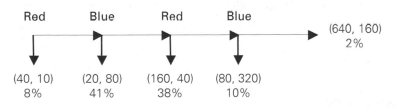

Source: (McKelvey and Palfrey 1992)

Figure 23.4   A Centipede Game

Blue moves right in the final stage). Obviously, it is better for Blue to move down in the final stage, getting 320 instead of 160. Having figured out the best decision in the final stage, we can begin the process of backward induction. If Blue is expected to go down in the final stage, then Red will expect a payoff of 80 if play reaches the final stage, instead of 160 if play stops in the previous stage. Thus, is would be better for Red to take the 160 and stop the game in the third stage, rather than pass to Blue and end up with only 80 in the final stage.

To summarize, we have concluded that Blue will stop in the final stage, and that Red, anticipating this, will stop in the third stage. Similar reasoning can be used to show that Blue will want to stop in the second stage, if play reaches this point, and hence that Red will want to stop in the first stage, yielding payoffs of 40 for Red and only 10 for Blue. Thus, the process of backward induction yields a very specific prediction, i.e., that the game will stop in the initial stage, with relatively low payoffs for both.

McKelvey and Palfrey (1992) used this setup in an experiment, which involved groups of 20 participants divided into Red and Blue player roles. Each participant was matched with all 10 people in the other role, in a series of 10 games, each game being the centipede game shown in Figure 23.4. The aggregate percentages for each outcome are shown in the figure, below the payoffs at each node. Only 8 percent of the Red players stopped in the first stage, so the experiment provides a sharp rejection of predictions based on backward induction. Rates of continuation were somewhat lower toward the end of the session, but the incidence of stopping in the initial stage remained relatively low throughout. Most of the games ended in the second and third stages, but 2 percent of the games went on until the final stage.

The failure of backward induction predictions in this game is probably due to the fact that even a small amount of unpredictability of others' decisions in later stages may make it optimal to continue in early stages, since the high payoffs are concentrated at the terminal nodes on the right side of the figure. The authors suggested that a small proportion of people ("altruists") were somewhat concerned with others' payoffs and that even if these types are not predominant, it would be optimal for selfish individuals to continue in early stages. In fact, any type of noise or unpredictability, regardless of its source, would have similar effects. Notice that about one in six Blue players continue in the final stage, which cuts their payoff in half but raises the Red player's payoff by a factor of 8, from 80 to 640. Whether this is due to altruism, to randomness from another cause, or to miscalculation is an open question. For an analysis of the effects of randomness in centipede games, see Zauner (1999).

23.4 Extensions

One possible explanation of the data pattern in the centipede game experiment is that the failure of backward induction may be due to low incentives, and that behavior would be more rational in high stakes experiments. Recent experiments with potential stakes of thousands of dollars indicate that this is not the case. High payoffs will cause quicker exits from the centipede game, but exits in the first stage are still not the norm (Parco, Rapoport, and Stein 2002). Other work has considered how subjects in experiments learn and adjust in centipede games (Nagel and Tang 1998) and (Ponti 2002). Bornstein, Kugler, and Ziegelmeyer (2004) compare behavior of individuals and groups in centipede games. When each of the two players corresponds to a group of three subjects, the result is more competitive. In particular, three-person groups exited the centipede game sooner than individuals (groups of size 1), and in this sense, groups were more "rational." Fey, McKelvey, and Palfrey (1996) report results of a variation of the centipede game, where the payoffs sum to a constant.

QUESTIONS

1. Show that the first players who chose S earned less on average than those who chose R in the game shown in the bottom part of Figure 23.2. (*Hint*: you have to use the response percentages shown below each outcome.)

2. Show that (S for the first player, P for the second player) is a Nash equilibrium for the games in Figure 23.2. To do this, you have to check to see whether a unilateral deviation by either player will increase that players' payoff, under the assumption that the other player stays with the equilibrium decision.

3. Show that (S for the first player, P for the second player) is a Nash equilibrium for each of the games in Figure 23.3; i.e., check the profitability of unilateral deviations for each player.

4. Consider a game in which there is $4 to be divided, and the first mover is only permitted to make one of the three following proposals:
   a. $3 for the first mover and $1 for the second mover
   b. $2 for each
   c. $1 for the first mover and $3 for the second mover

   The second mover is shown the proposal and can either accept, in which case it is implemented, or reject and cause each to earn $0. Show this game in extensive form. (*Hint*: the decision node for the first mover has three arrows, one for each decision, and each of these arrows leads to a node with two arrows.) Be sure to show the payoffs for each person, with the first mover listed on the left, for each of the six terminal nodes.

5. Show that the proposal in Question 4c is a part of a Nash equilibrium for the game in Question 4. To finish specifying the decisions for this equilibrium, you have to say what the second mover's response is to each of the three proposals. Does behavior in this equilibrium satisfy sequential rationality?

6. Consider a game in which the instructor has a $10 roll of quarters and divides the class into two groups. The instructor then puts a quarter into a collection tray and allows those on one side of the room to take the quarter (and somehow divide or allocate it among themselves) or to pass. A pass results in doubling the money (to two quarters) and giving those on the other side of the room the option to take or pass. This process of doubling the number of quarters in the tray continues until one side takes the quarters, or until one side's pass forces the instructor to put all remaining coins into the plate, which are then given to the side of the room whose decision would be the next one. Draw a figure that shows the extensive form for this game. Label the players A and B, and show payoffs for each terminal node as an ordered pair: ($ for A, $ for B). What is the predicted outcome of the game, on the basis of backward induction, perfect rationality, and selfish behavior?

chapter 24

Generalized Matching Pennies

There are many situations in which a person does not want to be predictable. The equilibrium in such cases involves randomization, but to be willing to randomize, each player must be indifferent about the decisions over which they are randomizing. In particular, each player's decision probabilities have to keep the *other* player indifferent. For this reason, changes in a player's own payoffs are not predicted to affect the player's own decisions. This counter-intuitive feature is contradicted by data from matching games with payoff imbalances, where own-payoff effects are systematic. These games can be run with minor modifications to Chapter 5's Battle of Colors Game instructions in the Class Experiments section, or with the Veconlab 2×2 Matrix Game program.

24.1 The Case of Balanced Payoffs

In a classic game of matching pennies, each person places a coin on a table, covering it so that the other person cannot see which side is up. By prior agreement, one person takes the pennies if the pennies match, and the other takes the pennies if they do not match. This is analogous to a soccer penalty kick, where the goalie must dive to one side or another before it is clear which way the kick will go, and the kicker cannot see which way the goalie will dive at the time of the kick. In this case, the goalie wants a match and the kicker wants a mismatch. Table 24.1 shows a game where the Row player prefers a match.

It can be shown that this game is equivalent to a matching pennies game in which there is always one player with a penny gain and another player with a penny loss (see Question 1 at the end of the chapter). In each of the cells of the payoff table, there is one person who would gain by altering the placement of their penny unilaterally, as indicated by the arrows. For example, if they were both going to choose heads, then the Column player would prefer to switch to tails, as indicated by the arrow pointing to the right in the

Table 24.1	A Modified Matching Pennies Game (Row's Payoff, Column's Payoff)	
	Column Player	
Row Player	**Left (heads)**	**Right (tails)**
Top (heads)	72, 36 $\Rightarrow$	$\Downarrow$ 36, 72
Bottom (tails)	36, 72 $\Uparrow$	$\Leftarrow$ 72, 36

upper-left box of the payoff table. The arrows in each box indicate the direction of a unilateral payoff-increasing move, so there is no equilibrium in non-random strategies. (Non-random strategies are commonly called "pure strategies" because they are not probability-weighted mixtures of other strategies.)

The game in Table 24.1 is balanced in the sense that each possible decision for each player has the same set of possible payoffs, i.e., 36 and 72. In games with this type of balance, the typical result is for subjects to play each decision with an approximately equal probability (Ochs 1994; Goeree and Holt 2001). This tendency to choose each decision with probability one-half is not surprising given the simple intuition that one must not be predictable in this game. Nevertheless, it is useful to review the representation of the Nash equilibrium as an intersection of the players' best response functions, as explained in Chapter 5. First, consider the Row player, who will choose Top if Column is expected to choose Left. Since Row's payoffs are 72 and 36 in the top part of Table 24.1 and are 36 and 72 in the bottom part, it is apparent that Row would choose Top as long as Left is thought to be more likely than Right. This best-response behavior is represented by the solid line in Figure 24.1 that begins in the top-left corner, continuing along the top until there is an abrupt drop to the bottom when the probability of Right is 0.5. (Please ignore the curved line for now.)

The column player's best response line is derived analogously and is shown by the thick dashed line that starts in the lower-left corner, rises to 0.5, and then crosses over horizontally to the right side, because Column would want to play Right whenever the probability of Top is greater than 0.5. The intersection of these two lines is in the center of the graph, at the point where each probability is 0.5, which is the Nash equilibrium in mixed strategies.

24.2   Noisy Best Responses

The previous analysis is not altered if we allow a little noise in the players' responses to their beliefs. Noisy behavior of this type was noticed by psychologists who would show subjects two lights and ask which was brighter, or let them hear two sounds and ask which was louder. When the signals (lights or sounds) were not close in intensity, almost everybody would indicate the correct answer, with any errors being caused by mis-

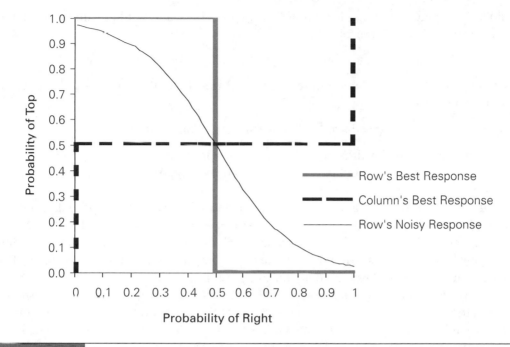

Figure 24.1 Best Response Functions for a Symmetric Matching Pennies Game: The Effect of Noisy Behavior

takes in recording decisions. As the two signals became close in intensity, then some people would guess incorrectly, e.g., because of bad hearing, random variations in ambient noise, or distraction and boredom. As the intensity of the signals approached equality, the proportions of guesses for each signal would approach 1/2 in the absence of measurement bias. In other words, there was not a sharp break where the stronger signal was selected with certainty, but rather a smooth tendency to guess the stronger signal more as its intensity increased. The probabilistic nature of this behavior is captured in the phrase "probabilistic choice" or "noisy best response."

This probabilistic-choice perspective can be applied to the matching pennies game. The intuitive idea is that Row will choose Top with high probability when the expected payoff for Top is a lot larger than the expected payoff for Bottom, but that some randomness will start to become apparent when the expected payoffs for the two decisions are not that far apart. To proceed with this argument, we begin by calculating these expected payoffs. Let p denote Row's beliefs about the probability of Right, so $1 - p$ is the probability of Left. From the top row of Table 24.1, we see that if Row chooses Top, then Row earns 72 with probability $1 - p$ and 36 with probability p, so the expected payoff is as follows:

$$\text{Row's expected payoff for Top} = 72(1 - p) + 36(p) = 72 - 36p$$

Similarly, by playing Bottom, Row earns 36 with probability $1 - p$ and 72 with probability p, so the expected payoff is as follows:

$$\text{Row's expected payoff for Bottom} = 36(1 - p) + 72(p) = 36 + 36p$$

It follows that the difference in these expected payoffs is $(72 - 36p) - (36 + 36p)$, or equivalently as follows:

$$\text{Row's expected payoff difference (for Top minus Bottom)} = 36 - 72p$$

When p is near zero, this difference is 36, but as p approaches $1/2$, this difference goes to zero, in which case Row is indifferent and would be willing to choose either decision or to flip a coin.

   If Row were perfectly rational (and responded to arbitrarily small expected payoff differences), then Top would be played whenever p is even a little less than $1/2$. The curved line in Figure 24.1 shows some departure from this rationality. Notice that the probability that Row plays Top is close to 1 but not quite there when p is small, and that the curved line deviates more from the best-response line as p approaches $1/2$.

   The curved noisy best-response line for Row intersects Column's dashed best-response line in the center of Figure 24.1, so a relaxation of the perfect rationality assumption for Row will not affect the equilibrium prediction. Similarly, suppose that we allow some noise in Column's best response, which will smooth off the sharp corners for Column's best response line, as shown by the upward sloping dashed line on the right side of Figure 24.2. This starts in the lower-left corner, rises with a smooth arc as it levels off at 0.5 in the center of the graph before curving upward along the upper-right boundary of the graph. Since this

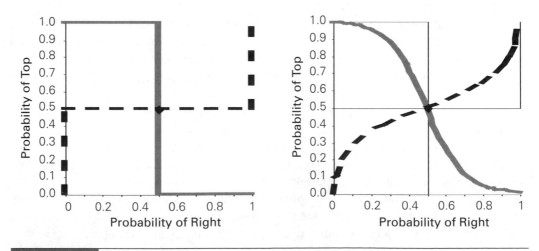

Figure 24.2   Best Responses (Left Side) and Noisy Best Responses (Right Side)

line will intersect Row's downward sloping noisy response line in the center of the graph, we see that the fifty-fifty prediction is not affected if we let each player's decision be somewhat noisy.

Finally, you should think about what would happen if the amount of randomness in behavior were somehow reduced. This would correspond to a situation where each person takes full advantage of even a slight tendency for the other to choose one decision even slightly more often than the other. These sharp responses to small probability differences would cause the curved lines on the right to become more like the straight-line best response functions, i.e., the "corners" on the curved lines would become sharper. In any case, the intersection would remain in the center, so adding noise has no effect on predictions in the symmetric matching pennies game.

24.3 The Effects of Payoff Imbalances

As one would expect, the fact that the noisy best response lines always intersect in the center of Figure 24.2 is due to the balanced nature of the payoffs for this game (Table 24.1). An unbalanced payoff structure is shown in Table 24.2, where the Row player's payoff of 72 in the Top/Left box has been increased to 360. Recall that the game was balanced before this change, and the choice proportions should be 1/2 for each player. The increase in Row's Top/Left payoff from 72 to 360 would make Top a more attractive choice for a wide range of beliefs, i.e., Row will choose Top unless Column is almost sure to choose Right. Intuitively, one would expect that this change would move Row's choice proportion for Top up from the 1/2 level that is observed in the balanced game. This intuition is apparent in the choice data for an experiment done with Veconlab software, where the payoffs were in pennies. Each of the three sessions involved 10–12 players, with 25 periods of random matching. The proportion of Top choices was 67 percent for the "360 treatment" game in Table 24.2.

This intuitive "own payoff effect" of increasing Row's Top/Left payoff is not consistent with the Nash equilibrium prediction. First, notice that there is no equilibrium in non-random strategies, as can be seen from the arrows in Table 24.2, which go in a clockwise

Table 24.2	An Asymmetric Matching Pennies Game (Row's Payoff, Column's Payoff)

	Column Player	
Row Player	**Left**	**Right**
Top	360, 36 $\Rightarrow$	$\Downarrow$ 36, 72
Bottom	36, 72 $\Uparrow$	$\Leftarrow$ 72, 36

circle. To derive the mixed equilibrium prediction, let p denote Row's beliefs about the probability of Right, so $1 - p$ is the probability of Left. Thus, Row's expected payoffs are as follows:

$$\text{Row's expected payoff for Top} = 360(1 - p) + 36(p) = 360 - 324p$$
$$\text{Row's expected payoff for Bottom} = 36(1 - p) + 72(p) = 36 + 36p$$

It follows that the difference in these expected payoffs is $(360 - 324p) - (36 + 36p)$, or equivalently, $324 - 360p$. Row is indifferent if the expected payoff difference is 0, i.e., if $\underline{p} = 324/360 = 0.9$. Therefore, Row's best response line stays at the top of the left panel in Figure 24.3 as long as the probability of Right is less than 0.9. The striking thing about this figure is that Column's best response line has not changed from the symmetric case; it rises from the Bottom/Left corner and crosses over when the probability of Top is 1/2. This is because Column's payoffs are exactly reflected (36 and 72 on the Left side, 72 and 36 on the Right side). In other words, the only way that Column would be willing to randomize is if Row chooses Top and Bottom with equal probability. In other words, the Nash equilibrium for the asymmetric game in Table 24.2 requires that Top and Bottom be played with exactly the same probabilities (1/2 each) as was the case for the case of balanced payoffs in Table 24.1. The reason is that Column's payoffs are the same in both games, and Row must essentially use a coin flip in order to keep Column indifferent.

The previous treatment change made Top more attractive for Row by raising Row's Top/Left payoff from 72 to 360. In order to produce an imbalance that makes Top *less* attractive, we reduce Row's Top/Left payoff in Table 24.1 from 72 to 40. Thus, Row's expected payoff for Top is $40(1 - p) + 36(p) = 40 - 4p$, and the expected payoff for Bottom is

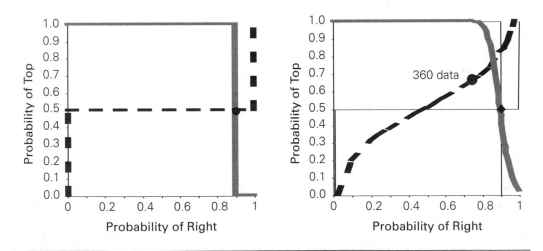

Figure 24.3   The 360 Treatment: Best Responses (Left Side) and Noisy Best Responses (Right Side)

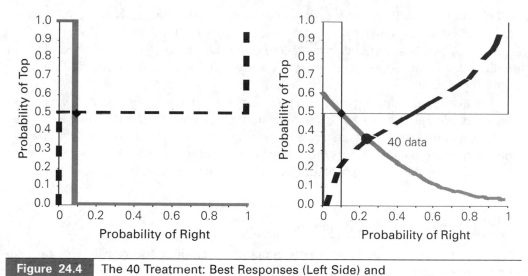

Figure 24.4   The 40 Treatment: Best Responses (Left Side) and
Noisy Best Responses (Right Side)

$36(1 - p) + 72(p) = 36 + 36p$. These are equal when $p = 4/40$, or 0.1. What has happened in
Figure 24.4 is that the reduction in Row's Top/Left payoff has pushed Row's best response
line to the bottom of the figure, unless Column is expected to play Right with a probability
that is less than 0.1. This downward shift in Row's best response line is shown on the left
side of Figure 24.4. The result is that the best response lines intersect where the probability
of Top is 1/2, which was the same prediction obtained from the left sides of Figures 24.2
and 24.3. Thus, a change in Row's Top/Left payoff from 40 to 72 to 360 does not change the
Nash equilibrium prediction for the probability of Top. The mathematical reason for this
result is that Column's payoffs do not change, and Row must choose each decision with
equal probability or Column would *not* want to choose randomly.

These invariance predictions are not borne out in the data from the experiments
reported here. Each of the three sessions involved 25 periods for each treatment, with the
order of treatments being alternated. The percentage of Top choices increased from 36 percent to 67 percent when the Row's Top/Left payoff was increased from 40 to 360. The Column players reacted to this change by choosing Right only 24 percent of the time in the 40
treatment, and 74 percent of the time in the 360 treatment.

The qualitative effect of Row's own-payoff effect is captured by a noisy-response model
where the sharp-cornered best response functions on the left sides of Figures 24.3 and 24.4
are rounded off, as shown on the right sides of the figures. Notice that the intersection of
the curved lines implies that Row's proportion of Top choices will be below 1/2 in the 40
treatment and above 1/2 in the 360 treatment, and the predicted change in the proportion

of Right decisions will not be as extreme as the movement from 0.1 to 0.9 implied by the Nash prediction. The actual data averages are shown by the black dots on the right sides of Figures 24.3 and 24.4. These data averages exhibit the strong own-payoff effects that are predicted by the curved best-response lines, and the prediction is fairly accurate, especially for the 40 treatment.

The quantitative accuracy of these predictions is affected by the amount of curvature that is put into the noisy response functions, and is ultimately a matter of estimation. Standard estimation techniques are based on writing down a mathematical function with a noise parameter that determines the amount of curvature and then choosing the parameter that provides the best fit. The nature of such a function is discussed next.

24.4   Probabilistic Choice

Anyone who has taken an introductory psychology course will remember the stimulus-response diagrams. Stochastic or noisy response models were developed after researchers noticed that responses could not always be predicted with certainty. The work of a mathematical psychologist, Duncan Luce (1959), suggested a way to model noisy choices, i.e., by assuming that response probabilities are increasing functions of the strength of the stimulus. For example, suppose that a person must judge which of two very faint sounds is loudest. The probability associated with one sound should be an increasing function of the decibel level of that sound. Since probabilities must sum to 1, the choice probability associated with one sound should also be a *decreasing* function of the intensity of the *other* sound.

In economics, the stimulus intensity associated with a given response (decision) might be thought of as the expected payoff of that decision. Suppose that there are two decisions, D_1 and D_2, with expected payoffs that we will represent by π_1 and π_2. For example, the decisions could be Row's choice of Top or Bottom, and the expected payoffs would be calculated using the equations given earlier, e.g., $\pi_1 = 360(1 - p) + 36p$, where p represents the probability with which the Row player thinks Column will choose Right. (Think of π as shorthand for payoff.)

Using Luce's suggestion, the next step is to find an increasing function, i.e., one with a graph that "goes uphill." (Mathematically, a function, f, is increasing if a $f(\pi_1) > f(\pi_2)$ whenever $\pi_1 > \pi_2$, but the intuitive idea is that the slope in a graph is from lower-left to upper-right.) Several examples of increasing functions are the linear function, $f(\pi_1) = \pi_1$, or the exponential function, $f(\pi_1) = \exp(\pi_1)$. The linear function obviously has an uphill slope; its graph is just the 45-degree line. The exponential function has a curved shape, like a hill that keeps getting steeper, like a snow-capped Mt. Fuji in a Japanese woodblock print.

Once we have found an increasing function, we might be tempted to assume that the probability of the decision is determined by the function itself, $\Pr(D_1) = f(\pi_1)$ and $\Pr(D_2) = f(\pi_2)$. The problem with this approach is that it does not ensure that the two probabilities sum to 1. This is easily fixed by a simple trick with a fancy name, normalization. Just divide each function by the sum of the functions as shown in Equation (24.1):

$$\Pr(D_1) = \frac{f(\pi_1)}{f(\pi_1) + f(\pi_2)} \text{ and } \Pr(D_2) = \frac{f(\pi_2)}{f(\pi_1) + f(\pi_2)} \tag{24.1}$$

If you are feeling a little unsure, try adding the two ratios in Equation (24.1) to show that $\Pr(D_1) + \Pr(D_2) = 1$. Now let's see what this gives us for the linear case, as shown in Equation (24.2):

$$\Pr(D_1) = \frac{\pi_1}{\pi_1 + \pi_2} \text{ and } \Pr(D_2) = \frac{\pi_2}{\pi_1 + \pi_2} \tag{24.2}$$

Suppose $\pi_1 = \pi_2 = 1$. Then each of the probabilities in Equation (24.2) will equal $1/(1 + 1) = 1/2$. This result holds as long as the expected payoffs are equal, even if they are not both equal to 1. This makes sense; if each decision is equally profitable, then there is no reason to prefer one over the other, and the choice probabilities should be 1/2 each. Next, notice that if $\pi_1 = 2$ and $\pi_2 = 1$, the probability of choosing decision D_1 is higher (2/3), and this will be the case whenever $\pi_1 > \pi_2$.

One potential limitation to the usefulness of the payoff ratios in Equation (24.2) is that expected payoffs may be negative if losses are possible. This problem can be avoided if we choose a function in Equation (24.1) that cannot have negative values, i.e., $f(\pi_1) > 0$ even if $\pi_1 < 0$. This non-negativity is characteristic of the exponential function, which can be used in Equation (24.1) to obtain Equation (24.3):

$$\Pr(D_1) = \frac{\exp(\pi_1)}{\exp(\pi_1) + \exp(\pi_2)}, \ \Pr(D_2) = \frac{\exp(\pi_2)}{\exp(\pi_1) + \exp(\pi_2)} \tag{24.3}$$

This avoids the possibility of negative probabilities, and all of the other useful properties of Equation (24.2) are preserved. The probabilities in Equation (24.3) will sum to one, they will be equal when the expected payoffs are equal, and the decision with the higher expected payoff will have a higher choice probability. The probabilistic choice model that is based on exponential functions is known as the *logit model*.

The curved lines in the right parts of the figures in this chapter were constructed using logit choice functions, but not quite the ones in Equation (24.3). It is true that Equation (24.3) applied to the expected payoffs for the matching pennies games will produce curved response functions, but the lines will not have as much curvature as those in the figures in this chapter. The lines drawn with Equation (24.3) have corners that are too sharp to explain the payoff effects that we are seeing in the matching pennies games. Just as we could make it harder to distinguish between the width of two pins by making them each half as thick, we can add more noise or randomness into the choice probabilities in Equation (24.3) by reducing all expected payoffs by one-half or more. Intuitively speaking, dividing all expected payoffs by 100 may inject more randomness, since dollars become pennies, and non-monetary factors (boredom, indifference, playfulness) may have more influence. The right panels of the figures in this chapter were obtained by using the logit model with all payoffs (expressed in pennies) being divided by 10, as shown in Equation (24.4).

$$\Pr(D_1) = \frac{\exp(\pi_1/10)}{\exp(\pi_1/10) \ + \ \exp(\pi_2/10)}, \ \Pr(D_2) = \frac{\exp(\pi_2/10)}{\exp(\pi_1/10) \ + \ \exp(\pi_2/10)} \tag{24.4}$$

At this point, you are probably wondering, why 10, why not 100? The degree to which payoffs are diluted by dividing by larger and larger numbers will determine the degree of curvature in the noisy response functions. Thus, we can think of the number in the denominator of the expected payoff expressions as being an error parameter that determines the amount of randomness in the predicted behavior. The *logit error parameter* will be called μ, and it is used in the logit choice probabilities, as shown in Equation (24.5):

$$\Pr(D_1) = \frac{\exp(\pi_1/\mu)}{\exp(\pi_1/\mu) \ + \ \exp(\pi_2/\mu)}, \ \Pr(D_2) = \frac{\exp(\pi_2/\mu)}{\exp(\pi_1/\mu) \ + \ \exp(\pi_2/\mu)} \tag{24.5}$$

The logit form in Equation (24.5) is flexible, since the degree of curvature is captured by a parameter that can be estimated. It also has the intuitive property that an increase in the payoffs will reduce the noise, i.e., will reduce the curvature of the noisy best response curves in the figures (see Question 4 at the end of the chapter).

24.5   Extensions

The use of probabilistic choice functions in the analysis of games was pioneered by McKelvey and Palfrey (1995), and the intersections of noisy best response lines in Figures 24.2 through 24.4 correspond to the predictions of a *quantal response equilibrium*. (A "quantal response" is essentially the same thing as a noisy best response.) Goeree, Holt, and Palfrey (2005, 2006) introduce the idea of a *regular quantal response equilibrium*, and discuss its empirical content and numerous applications. Goeree, Holt, and Palfrey (2003) use this approach to explain behavior patterns in a number of matching pennies games. Their analysis also includes the effects of risk aversion, which can explain the over-prediction of own-payoff effects for high payoffs that is seen on the right side of Figure 24.3. Risk aversion introduces diminishing marginal utility that reduces the attractiveness of the large 360 payoff for the Row player, and this shifts that person's best response line down so that the intersection is closer to the data average point.

All of the games considered in this chapter involve two decisions, but the same principles can be applied to games with more decisions (see (Goeree and Holt 1999b) and (Capra, Goeree, Gomez, and Holt 1999, 2002)), which will be discussed in Chapters 25 and 26.

QUESTIONS

1. In a matching pennies game, one person loses a penny and the other wins a penny, so the payoffs are 1 and –1. Show that there is a simple way to transform the game in Table 24.1 (with payoffs of 36 and 72) into this form. (*Hint*: first divide all payoffs by 36, and then subtract a constant from all payoffs.)

2. Consider a soccer penalty kick situation where the kicker is equally skillful at kicking to either side, but the goalie is better diving at to one side. In particular, the kicker will always score if the goalie dives away from the kick. If the goalie dives to the side of the kick, the kick is always blocked on the goalie's right but is only blocked with one-half probability on the goalie's left. Represent this as a simple game, in which the goalie earns a payoff of +1 for each blocked kick and –1 for each goal, and the kicker earns –1 for each blocked kick and +1 for each goal. A 0.5 chance of either outcome results in an expected payoff of 0. Determine the equilibrium probabilities used in the Nash equilibrium.

3. Show that the two choice probabilities in Equation (24.5) sum to 1.

4. Show that doubling all payoffs, i.e., both π_1 and π_2, has the same effect as reducing the noise parameter μ in Equation (24.5) by one-half.

5. Show that multiplying all payoffs in Equation (24.2) by 2 will not affect choice probabilities.

6. Show that adding a constant amount, say x, to all payoffs in Equation (24.5) will have no effect on the choice probabilities. (*Hint*: Even if you are not familiar with exponential functions, you can answer this question by using the fact that an exponential function of the sum is the product of the exponential functions of the two components: $\exp(\pi + x) = \exp(\pi)\exp(x)$.

chapter 25

The Traveler's Dilemma

Each player's best decision in a (single play) prisoner's dilemma is to defect, regardless of what the other person is expected to do. The dilemma is that both could be better off if they resist these incentives and cooperate. The traveler's dilemma game has a richer set of decisions; each person must claim a money amount, and the payment is the minimum of the claims, plus a (possibly small) payment incentive for the low claimant. Both would be better off making identical high claims, but each has an incentive to undercut the other to obtain the reward for having the lower claim. This game is similar to a prisoner's dilemma in that the unique equilibrium involves payoffs that are lower than can be achieved with cooperation. But here there is a more interesting dimension, since the optimal decision in the traveler's dilemma *does* depend on what the other person is expected to do. Thus, the game is more sensitive to interactions of imprecise beliefs and small variations in decisions. These interactions can cause data patterns to be quite far from Nash predictions, as will be illustrated with a set of iterated spreadsheet calculations.

This is a great game! It can be played with this chapter's Claim Game Instructions in the Class Experiments sesction or with the Traveler's Dilemma program on the Games menu of the Veconlab site. In addition, it is possible for students to play an online demonstration version of the Traveler's Dilemma, where the "other decision" is taken from a database of decisions made by University of Virginia law students in a behavioral game theory class. This online simulation can be accessed from: http://www.veconlab.com/tddemo.htm

25.1 | A Vacation with an Unhappy Ending?

Two travelers were returning from a tropical vacation where they had purchased identical antiques that were packed in identical suitcases. When both bags were lost in transit, the passengers were asked to produce receipts, an impossible task since the antiques were purchased with cash. The airline representative calmly informed the travelers that they should go into separate rooms and fill out claim sheets for the contents of the suitcases. He assured them that both claims would be honored if a) they are equal, and b) they are no greater than the liability limit of $200 per bag in the absence of proof of purchase. There was also a minimum allowed claim of $80 to cover the cost of the luggage and inconvenience. One of the travelers expressed some frustration, since the value of the suitcase and antique combined was somewhat above $200. The other traveler, who was even more pessimistic, asked what would happen if the claims differed. The reply was: "If the claims are unequal, then we will assume that the higher claim is unjustly inflated, and we will reimburse you both at an amount that equals the minimum of the two claims. In addition, there will be a $5 penalty assessed against the higher claimant and a $5 reward added to the compensation of the lower claimant." The dilemma was that each could obtain reasonable compensation if they made matching high claims of $200, and resisted the temptation to come down to $199 to capture the $5 reward for being low. If one person expects the other one to ask for $199, the best response is $198, but what if the other person is thinking similarly? This line of reasoning leads to an unfortunate possibility that a cycle of anticipated moves and counter-moves may cause each traveler to submit very low claims. Unfortunately, there was no way for the two travelers to communicate between rooms, and the stress of the trip led each to believe that there would be no sharing of any unequal compensation amounts received. The unhappy ending has both making low claims, and the alternative happy ending has both making high claims. The actual outcome is an empirical question that we will consider below.

This game was introduced by Basu (1994), who viewed it as a dilemma for the game theorist. With a very low penalty rate, there is little risk in making a high claim, and yet each person has an incentive to undercut any common claim level. For example, suppose that both are considering claims of $200; perhaps they whispered this to each other on the way to the separate rooms. Once alone, each might reason that a deviation to $199 would reduce the minimum by $1, which is more than compensated for by the $5 reward for being low. In fact, there is no possible belief about the other's claim that would make one want to claim the upper limit of $200. If one expects any lower claim, then it is better to undercut that lower claim as well. Reasoning in this manner, we can rule out all common claims as candidates for equilibrium, except for the lowest possible claim of $80. Similar reasoning shows that no configuration with unequal claims can be an equilibrium (see Question 1 at the end of the chapter).

The unique Nash equilibrium for the traveler's dilemma has another interesting property: it can be derived from an assumption that each person knows that the other is perfectly rational. Recall that there is no belief about the other's claim that would justify a claim of $200. Since they each know that the other will never claim $200, then the upper bound has shifted to $199, and there is no belief that justifies a claim of $199. To see this, suppose that claims must be in integer dollar amounts and note that $199 is a best response to the other's claim of $200 but it is not a best response to any lower claim. Since

$200 will not be claimed by any rational person, it follows that $199 is not a best response to any belief about the other's decision. Reasoning in this manner, we can rule out all successively lower claims except for the very lowest feasible claim. This argument, based on common knowledge of rationality, is called "*rationalizability*," and the minimum possible claim in this game is the unique *rationalizable equilibrium*. Economists often place persuasive adjectives in front of the word equilibrium, sometimes to no avail. This will turn out to be one of those times.

The dilemma for the theorist is that the Nash equilibrium is not sensitive to the size of the penalty/reward level, as long as this level is larger than the smallest possible amount by which a claim can be reduced. For example, the unilateral incentive to deviate from any common claim in the traveler's dilemma is not affected if the penalty/reward rate is changed from $5 to $4. If both were planning to choose a claim of $200, then one person's deviation to $199 would reduce the minimum to $199, but would result in a reward of $4 for the deviator. Thus, the person deviating would earn $199 + $4 instead of the $200 that would be obtained if they both claim $200. The same argument can be used to show that there is an incentive to undercut any common claim, whether the penalty/reward rate is $2 or $200. Thus, the Nash equilibrium is not sensitive to this penalty/reward rate as long as it exceeds $1, whereas one might expect observed claims to be responsive to large changes in this payoff parameter.

25.2   Data

The traveler's dilemma was analyzed by Capra et al. (1999), and it was an exciting experiment. The penalty/reward parameter was expected to have a strong effect on actual claim choices, even though the unique Nash prediction would be independent of changes in this parameter. Each session involved 10–12 subjects, who were randomly paired at the start of each round, for a series of 10 rounds with the same penalty-reward parameter. Claims were required to be between $0.80 and $2.00. Six sessions were run, each with a different penalty-reward parameter. The data averages for four of the treatments are plotted in Figure 25.1, where the horizontal axis shows the round number. The penalty-reward parameter is denoted by R.

With a high penalty/reward parameter of $0.80, the claims average about $1.20 in round 1 and fall to levels approaching $0.80 in the final four rounds, as shown by the thick solid line at the bottom of the figure. The data for the $0.50 treatment start somewhat higher but also approach the Nash prediction in the final rounds. In contrast, the first round averages for the $0.10 and $0.05 treatments, plotted as dashed lines, start at about $1 above the Nash prediction and actually rise slightly, moving *away* from the Nash prediction. The data for the intermediate treatments ($0.20 and $0.25) are not shown, but they stay in the middle range ($1.00 to $1.50) below the dashed lines and above the solid lines, with some more variation and crossover between the two intermediate treatments.

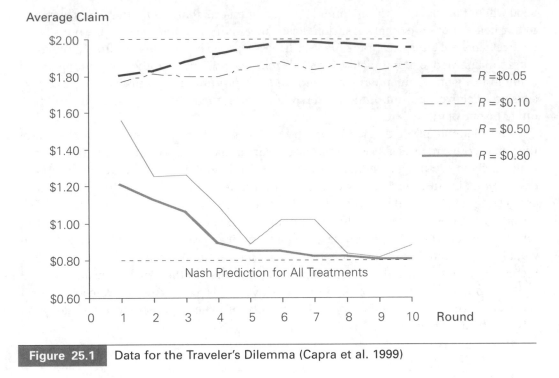

Figure 25.1   Data for the Traveler's Dilemma (Capra et al. 1999)

25.3   Learning and Experience

Notice that the most salient feature of the traveler's dilemma data, the strong effect of the penalty/reward parameter, is not predicted by the Nash equilibrium. One might dismiss this game on the grounds that it is somewhat artificial. There is some truth to this, although many standard economic games involve payoffs that depend on the mini-mum price, as is the case with Bertrand price competition (see Chapter 8) or Chapter 26's minimum-effort coordination game. An alternative perspective is that the traveler's dilemma game involves an intentionally abstract setting, which serves as a paradigm for particular types of strategic interactions. The traveler's dilemma is no more about lost lug-gage than the prisoner's dilemma is about actual prisoners. If standard game theory cannot predict well in such simple situations, then some rethinking is necessary. At a minimum, it would be nice to have an idea of when the Nash equilibrium will be useful and when it will not. Even better would be a theoretical apparatus that explains the convergence to Nash predictions in some treatments and the divergence in others. The rest of this chapter per-tains to several possible approaches to this problem. We begin with an intuitive discussion of learning.

Table 25.1

Traveler's Dilemma Data for a Classroom Experiment with $R = 10$

Round	Average (10 claims)	SuzSio	K Squared	Kurt/Bruce	JessEd	Stacy/Naomi
1	137	100 (133)	80 (195)	139 (140)	133 (100)	150 (135)
2	131	95 (191)	98 (117)	135 (140)	80 (130)	127 (200)
3	144	125 (135)	96 (117)	135 (100)	199 (199)	134 (200)
4	142	115 (125)	130 (100)	125 (115)	198 (115)	150 (134)

Key: Own Claim (Other's Claim)

Behavior in an experiment with repeated random pairings may evolve from round to round as people learn what to expect. For example, consider the data in Table 25.1 from a classroom experiment conducted at the University of Virginia. Claims were required to be between 80 and 200, and the penalty/reward parameter was 10. There were 20 participants, who were divided into 10 pairs. Each 2-person team had a handheld wireless PDA with a touch-sensitive color screen that showed the HTML displays from the Veconlab software. The table shows the decisions for five of the teams during the first four rounds. The round is listed on the left, and the average of all 10 claims is shown in the second column. The remaining columns show some of the team's own decisions, which are listed next to the decision of the other team for that round (shown in parentheses).

First, consider the first round decision for Stacy/Naomi, who claimed 150. The other team was lower, at 135, so the earnings for Stacy/Naomi were the minimum, 135, minus the penalty of 10, or 125. SuzSio began lower, at 100, and encountered a claim of 133. This team then cut their claim to 95, and encountered an even higher claim of 191 in round 2. This caused them to raise their claim to 125, and they finished round 10 (not shown) with a claim of 160.

K Squared began the first round with a decision of 80, which is the Nash equilibrium. They had the lower claim and earned the minimum, 80, plus 10 for being low. After observing the other's claim of 195 for that round, they raised their claim to 98 in the second round, and eventually to 120 in the tenth round. The point of this example is that the best decision in a game is not necessarily the equilibrium decision; it makes sense to respond to and anticipate the way that the others are actually playing. If K Squared had played the Nash equilibrium decision of 80 in the first four rounds, they would have earned 90 in each round, for a total of 360. They actually earned 409 by adapting to observed behavior and taking more risk. A claim of 200 in all rounds would have been even more profitable (see Question 4 at the end of the chapter).

Teams who were low relative to the other's claim tended to raise their claims, and teams that were high tended to lower them. This qualitative adjustment rule, however, does not explain why SuzSio's claim was lowered even after it had the lower claim in the first round. This reduction seems to be in anticipation of the possibility that other claims might fall. In the final round, the claims ranged from 110 to 200, with an average of 146 and a lot of dispersion.

One way to describe the outcome is that people have different beliefs based on different experiences, but by the tenth round, most expect claims to be about 150 on average, with a lot of variability. If claims had converged to a narrow band, say with all at 150, then the undercutting logic of game theory might have caused them to decline, as all seek to get below 150. But the variability in claims did not go away, perhaps because people had different experiences and different reactions to those experiences. This variability made it harder to figure out the best response to others' claims. In fact, claims did not diminish over time; if anything, there was a slight upward trend. The highest earnings were obtained by the JessEd team, which had a relatively high average claim of 177.

The first 10 rounds of this classroom experiment were followed by 10 more rounds with a higher payoff parameter (50). This created a strong incentive to be the low claimant, and claims did decline to the Nash equilibrium level of 80 after the first several rounds. Thus, we see that convergence to a Nash equilibrium seems to depend on the *magnitudes* of incentives, not just on whether one decision is slightly better than another. At an intuitive level, this is all you need to know. For a more scientific approach, Bounded Rationality in the Traveler's Dilemma: A Spreadsheet-Based Analysis at the end of the chapter contains an analysis that is sensitive to the magnitudes of payoff differences. The goal is to develop a theoretical explanation of the observed convergence to the Nash prediction in the high-R treatments and the divergence in the low-R treatments. The calculations in the Bounded Rationality in the Traveler's Dilemma are set up in terms of a spreadsheet, which is then used to generate the table and graph in the next section.

25.4   Iterated Rationality and Quantal Response Equilibrium

The analysis of the matching pennies game in Chapter 24 involved looking at the intersection of the curved stochastic best response lines. These intersections have the property that probabilities corresponding to Row and Column player beliefs are equal to the choice probabilities of the other player. This is a stochastic (quantal response) equilibrium in the sense that Row's beliefs about Column's decisions match Column's choice probabilities and vice versa. Instead of having just two decisions like Top or Bottom, the travelers' dilemma has many possible claim choices. In this section, for simplicity, only the 13 even dime amounts will be considered, i.e., $.80, $.90, and so on. A quantal response equilibrium will be a set of 13 probabilities with an equilibrium property that beliefs match choice probabilities. The process of finding the equilibrium used here will be iterative; we start with a set of beliefs and generate choice probabilities. If the choice probabilities differ from the original set of belief probabilities, then this is not an equilibrium. This iterative approach has the added advantage of being related to the discussion in Chapter 3 of iterated rationality for the guessing game. As was the case there, an analysis of the process of iterated strategic thinking may also shed some light on play in a game that is only played once.

The traveler's dilemma experiments discussed in this chapter have involved repeated random matching, so that people can learn from experience, even though they are not interacting with the same person in each round. In such situations, behavior might converge to some kind of equilibrium as people learn what to expect and react to it. In contrast, there is no opportunity to learn from past experience in a game that is only played once, and one-shot games are very important in many situations, e.g., military and political contests, special auctions, legal disputes, and so on. In games played only once, each person must base their claim decision on introspection about what the other is likely to do, about what the other thinks they will do, and so on. The observed average claims in the one-shot traveler's dilemma are strongly influenced by the size of the penalty/reward, even though changes in this parameter have no effect on the unique Nash equilibrium (Goeree and Holt 2001). Of course, it is not reasonable to expect data to conform to a Nash equilibrium in a one-shot game with no past experience, since this equilibrium (in pure strategies) implies that the other's claim is somehow known.

The development of models of introspection for one-shot games is an important and relatively new topic in game theory. A promising approach is to use the probabilistic choice functions that were introduced in Chapter 24 to add noise to the model of iterated thinking. To see how this process works without noise, recall the discussion of the guessing game in Chapter 3, where each person makes a guess between 0 and 100, and the person closest to half of the average wins a prize. In that case, the most naïve person is termed a level 0 person, who just chooses each number between 0 and 100 with equal probability, for an average guess of 50. A level 1 person expects others' guesses to be 50 on average and chooses 25, and a level 2 person chooses 12.5, and so on. The spreadsheet that will be constructed in the Appendix at the end of this chapter will let you do the same thing with the Traveler's Dilemma, using the logit probabilistic choice function introduced in Chapter 24. For the traveler's dilemma game, the level 0 person is assumed to choose each possible claim with equal probability, so the average claim in the 80–200 range would be 140. A level 1 person is assumed to make a noisy (logit) best response to the totally random level 0 person. The claim distribution for the level 1 type determines the beliefs of the level 2 type, and so on.

The spreadsheet constructed in the Appendix for this chapter uses the noisy claim distribution for each level to calculate predicted choices for someone who thinks with that level of iterated reasoning. Basically, the prediction for each higher level is obtained by copying a block of cells in the spreadsheet and pasting it to the right, to get a repetition of the calculations from beliefs that are determined by the next lower level. The spreadsheet is set up for a game with 13 possible claims: 80, 90, . . . , 200 (although it could be adapted to allow all 121 penny amounts between 80 and 200). Using an error parameter of 10, the spreadsheet can be used to calculate the probabilities for each claim in the $.10 penalty-reward treatment, as shown in Table 25.2 (see Question 6 at the end of the chapter). For the level 0 type, the probabilities of 0.08 for all possible claims in the top row are just the probabilities (rounded off) that make each decision equally likely, and the resulting average claim is 140. A person who behaves as if the others are level 0 players will have the noisy response probabilities in the second row. These probabilities for this level 1 type are already massed in the 170–190 range of claims that are common for the final rounds of this treatment ($R = 10$). The average claim in the level 1 row of the table is 168, which rises to 176 for level 2 and stays at 178 for levels 3 and 4.

In Table 25.2, the beliefs for each level type are shown in the row above that level, e.g., the beliefs for a level 1 type are shown in the level 0 row. A comparison of adjacent rows shows that introspection models with low levels of strategic thinking have beliefs that do not match the actual claim probabilities, and in this sense, are not equilibrium models. This disequilibrium property is desirable, since there is no reason to expect an equilibrium matching up of beliefs and decisions in a one-shot game. Note, however, that the beliefs for the level 4 type, shown in the level 3 row, are all within 0.01 of the choice probabilities in the bottom row that result from applying the logit probabilistic response function to those beliefs. Thus, these choice probabilities are essentially in equilibrium. This is an example of the quantal response equilibrium introduced in Chapter 24.

The average claim is 186 for the final five rounds of the data with the $R = 10$ treatment shown in Figure 25.1, and this sharp deviation from the Nash prediction of 80 is largely captured by the predictions in Table 25.2. The salient feature of the experiment, however is that the claims converge to near-Nash levels in some treatments (e.g., $R = 50$) and not in others. The spreadsheet in Bounded Rationality in the Traveler's Dilemma at the end of the chapter can be used to generate predictions for other treatments as well (by changing the

Table 25.2	Iterated Introspection Claim Distributions for a Traveler's Dilemma ($R = 10$ and $\mu = 10$)

	Claims												
	80	**90**	**100**	**110**	**120**	**130**	**140**	**150**	**160**	**170**	**180**	**190**	**200**
Level 0	.08	.08	.08	.08	.08	.08	.08	.08	.08	.08	.08	.08	.08
Level 1	0	0	.01	.02	.03	.05	.07	.10	.12	.14	.15	1.5	1.4
Level 2	0	0	0	0	.01	.02	.04	.08	.12	.17	.20	.20	.17
Level 3	0	0	0	0	0	.01	.03	.06	.12	.18	.22	.21	.18
Level 4	0	0	0	0	0	.01	.02	.05	.11	.18	.23	.22	.17

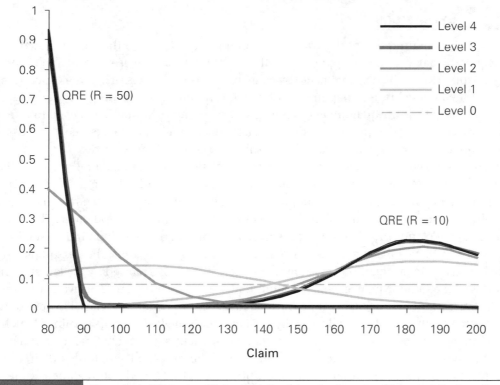

Figure 25.2   Traveler's Dilemma Claim Distributions for Levels of Iterated Rationality

number in the cell used for the penalty parameter). The resulting claim distributions for penalty-reward rates of 10 and 50 are shown in Figure 25.2. For each treatment, the level 0 probabilities are the same for all claims, as indicated by the horizontal dashed line in the figure. The claim distributions for successively higher levels of iterated rationality are shown by the successively darker solid lines, with the black line representing the level 4 case. The lines on the right side are for the low penalty-reward rate of 10, and the lines on the left side are for the high penalty-reward rate of 50. The same error rate ($\mu = 10$) is used for both sets of lines, so the same theory that predicts high claims in one treatment also predicts low claims in the other. The black line on each side overlaps the level 3 line, i.e., the level 3 and level 4 lines are virtually identical. Thus, these are claim distributions that get mapped into the same distributions, i.e., they each represent a quantal response equilibrium. Therefore, the black lines are given QRE labels for each treatment.

25.5 Extensions

The main result of the traveler's dilemma experiment is that the most salient aspect of the data, sensitivity to the size of the penalty-reward rate, is not explained by the Nash equilibrium, which is unaffected by changes in this rate. Decisions in the experiment seem to be affected by the magnitudes of payoff differences, even though these magnitudes do not affect the qualitative (greater than or less than) comparisons used to find a Nash equilibrium. An important lesson to be learned is that it may be very costly to use a Nash equilibrium strategy if others are not using their equilibrium strategies.

This lesson can be illustrated with an outcome observed from the online version of the traveler's dilemma mentioned in the introductory paragraph of this chapter, which has been played by more than 2,000 people to date. This demo involves five rounds with a penalty/reward rate of 10, and with claims required to be in the 80 to 200 range. The other decisions are claims saved in a database from an experiment involving Virginia law students from a behavioral game theory class. After finishing five rounds, the person playing the demo is told how their total earnings compare with the total earned by the law student who faced the same sequence of other claims that they themselves saw. The average claims from this law class were fairly high, in the 180 range, so someone who stays low (closer to the Nash equilibrium of 80) will typically earn less than the law student earnings benchmark. In fact, this was the case when a leading game theorist played the game and maintained claims near 130 in the lower-middle part of the range; although he did alter his claims in response to the others' observed claim levels. He earned about 25 percent less than the law student who had faced the same sequence of other claims.

An interesting one-shot traveler's dilemma experiment is reported by Becker, Carter, and Naeve (2005), who invited members of the Game Theory Society to submit claims or mixed strategies. The range of allowed claims was the interval [2, 100], and the penalty/reward rate was 2. Participants were also required to submit a probability distribution on this interval representing their beliefs about other decisions. Two of the entrants in the contest were selected at random, and were paid a money prize. One person was paid 20 times their earnings as determined by playing against other submitted strategies, and another person was paid a prize that was related to the accuracy of that person's submitted beliefs. In total, 26 of the 45 pure strategies submitted were above 90, and only 3 corresponded to the unique Nash equilibrium, 2. The modal decision was 100 (10 cases). The submitted belief distributions looked somewhat like the actual distributions of decisions. These results indicate the experts in game theory recognize a situation where the Nash equilibrium prediction will not be a good guide for what to expect.

There are several other games with a similar payoff that depend on the minimum of all decisions. One such game, discussed in Chapter 26, has the weakest-link property that the output is determined by the minimum of the individual effort levels. Similarly, the shopping behavior of uninformed consumers may make firms' profits sensitive to whether or not their price is the minimum in the market. Capra et al. (2002) provide experimental data for a price competition game with meet-or-release clauses, which release the buyer from the contract if a lower price offer is found and the original seller refuses to match. If all consumers are informed and all sellers are producing the same product, then each would rather match the other instead of losing all business as informed consumers switch. A unilateral price cut, however, may fail to pick up some business for a group of uninformed consumers. In any case, if one firm sets a lower price than the other, then it will obtain the larger market share, and the high-price firm will have to match the other's price to get any sales at all. This is like the traveler's dilemma in that earnings are determined by the minimum price, with a penalty for having a higher price. In particular, each firm earns an amount that equals the minimum price times their sales quantity, but the firm that had the lower price initially will have the larger market share by virtue of picking up sales to the informed shoppers.

The Capra et al. (2002) price-competition game also has a unique Nash equilibrium price at marginal cost, since at any higher price there is a unilateral incentive to cut price by a very small amount and pick up the informed shoppers. The Nash equilibrium is independent of the number of informed buyers who respond to even small price differences. Despite this independence property, it is intuitively plausible that a large fraction of buyers who are uninformed about price differences would provide sellers with some power to raise prices. This intuition was confirmed by the results of the experiments reported by the authors. As with the traveler's dilemma, data averages were strongly affected by a parameter that determines the payoff differential for being low, even though this parameter does not affect the unique Nash equilibrium at the lowest possible decision.

The iterated introspection approach in Section 25.4 is based on a small literature on how to model games played only once. As mentioned, in Chapter 3, Stahl and Wilson (1995) and Nagel (1995) were influenced by one-shot guessing game data to consider one or more levels of iterated strategic thinking. Goeree and Holt (1999b, 2001) introduce noise into the iterated introspection process and use the resulting model to explain data from a variety of games played once. Camerer and Ho (2004) incorporate heterogeneity by allowing different people to have different levels of strategic thinking, with a one-parameter distribution that determines the probability that a person will be of each different level. When confronted with the data, this approach suggests that people engage in about 1.5 steps of this reasoning process. Goeree and Holt (1999b) take a different approach, by letting the amount of noise be higher for higher levels of iterated reasoning in the sequence from "he thinks" to "he thinks I think" to "he thinks I think he thinks," and so on. The idea here is that one person may have some idea about what the other will do, but has a more dispersed idea about what the other thinks the first person will do, and an even more dispersed idea about what the second person thinks the first person thinks, and so on. The parameterizations suggested by Goeree and Holt essentially truncate this process after several iterations. Goeree and Holt (2001, 2004) use this model to explain data in a variety of one-shot games where deviations from Nash predictions are observed, including the Traveler's Dilemma. For a related model with two different error parameters, see Weizsäcker (2003) and Kübler and Weizsäcker (2004).

Appendix: **Bounded Rationality in the Traveler's Dilemma—A Spreadsheet-Based Analysis**

Recall from Chapter 24 that stochastic response functions can be used to capture the idea that the magnitudes of payoff differences matter. The form of these functions is based on the intuitive idea that a person is much more likely to be able to determine which of two sounds is louder when the decibel levels are not close together. In these games, the expected payoff is the stimulus analogous to the decibel level, so let's begin by calculating expected payoffs for each decision. To keep the calculations from becoming tedious, suppose that there are only 13 possible decisions in even increments: 80, 90, 100, . . . , 200. A person's beliefs will be represented by 13 probabilities that sum to 1.

These belief probabilities can be used to calculate expected payoffs for each decision, and the logit functions introduced in Chapter 24 can then be used to determine the choice probabilities that result from the initial beliefs. The intuitive idea is that a decision is more likely if its expected payoff is higher. In particular, choice probabilities are assumed to be increasing (exponential) functions of expected payoffs, normalized so that all probabilities sum to 1.

Some notation will be useful for the calculation of expected payoffs. Let P_i be the probability associated with claim i, so beliefs are characterized by $P_{80}, P_{90}, \ldots, P_{200}$. First, consider a claim of 80, which will tie with probability P_{80} and will be low with probability $1 - P_{80}$. The expected payoff is:

$$\text{Expected payoff for } 80 = 80P_{80} + (80 + R)(1 - P_{80})$$

Notice that the first term covers the case of a tie and the second covers the case of having the low claim. For a claim of 90, we have to consider the chance of having the higher claim and incurring the penalty of R, so the expected payoff is:

$$\text{Expected payoff for } 90 = 90P_{90} + (90 + R)(1 - P_{80} - P_{90}) + (80 - R)P_{80}$$

As before, the first term is for the possibility of a tie at 90, and the second is for the possibility that the other claim is above 90, which occurs with probability $1 - P_{80} - P_{90}$. The third term now reflects the possibility of having the higher claim. The payoff structure can be clarified, as shown in Equation (25.1) by considering a higher claim, say 150.

$$\begin{aligned} \text{Expected payoff for } 150 = {} & 150P + (150 + R)[1 - P_{80} - P_{90} - \ldots - P_{150}] \\ & + (80 - R)P_{80} + (90 - R)P_{90} + \ldots (140 - R)P_{140} \end{aligned} \quad (25.1)$$

In order from top to bottom, the parts on the right side of Equation (25.1) correspond to the cases of a tie, of having the lower claim, and of having the higher claim.

This section shows you how to do these calculations in an Excel spreadsheet that makes it possible to repeat the calculations iteratively in order to obtain predictions for how people might actually behave in a traveler's dilemma game when we do not assume perfect rationality. The logic of this spreadsheet is to begin with a column of probabilities for each claim (80, 90, . . . , 200). Given these probabilities, the spreadsheet will calculate a column of expected payoffs, one for each claim. Let the expected payoff for claim i be denoted by π_i^e, where $i = 80, 90, 100$, and so on. Then there is a column of exponential functions of expected payoffs, $\exp(\pi_i^e/\mu)$, where the expected payoffs have been divided by an error parameter μ. We want choice probabilities to be increasing in expected payoffs, but these exponential functions cannot be used as probabilities unless they are normalized to ensure that they sum to 1. Thus, the column of exponential functions is summed to get the normalizing element in the denominator of the logit probability formula: $\exp(\pi^e/\mu)/\Sigma_i$ $(\exp(\pi^e_i/\mu))$, which corresponds to Equation (24.5) from Chapter 24.

The best way to read this section is to create a spreadsheet. The instructions are provided for Excel, but analogous instructions will work in other spreadsheet programs. Table 25.3 is laid out like a spreadsheet, with columns labeled A, B, . . . , and rows labeled 1, 2, ...

Step 1: Parameter Specification

It is convenient to have the error parameter, μ, be at a focal location in the upper-left corner, along with the penalty/reward parameter. Put a value of **10** for the error parameter in cell **B1**, and put **10** for the penalty/reward parameter in cell **B2**. These numbers can later be changed to experiment with different amounts of noise for different treatments.

Step 2: Claim Values

Put a **70** in cell **A7**, so that the formula in **A8** can be: **=sum(A7 + 10)**, which will yield a value of 80. Then this formula can be copied to cells A9 to A20 by clicking on the lower-right corner of the A8 box and dragging it down. (You can go back and expand the table to allow for all penny amounts from 80 to 200, but the smaller table will do for now.)

Step 3: Initial Values

Before beginning to fill in the other cells, put values of 0 in cells F7 and H7; these are used to start cumulative sums, in a manner that will be explained below.

Step 4: Formulas

Notice that the formula that you used in Step 2 is shown at the top of the far-right column of Table 25.4. The formulas for row 8 cells of other columns are also shown in the right column. Enter these in cells **B8**, **C8**, . . . , **K8**, making sure to place the $ symbols in the places indicated. The $ symbol forces the reference to stay fixed even when the formula is copied to another location. For example, the references to the error parameter will be B1, with two $ signs, since both the row and column locations of the reference to this parameter must stay fixed. A reference to cell $B8, however, would keep the column fixed at B and allow one to copy the formula from row 8 to other rows. Use the $ symbols only where indicated, and not elsewhere. Finally, copy all of these formulas down from row 8 to rows 9–20, except in column **D** where rows 9–20 should be filled with zeros as shown in Table 25.3.

Table 25.3		Excel Spreadsheet for Traveler's Dilemma Logit Responses								

	A	B	C	D	E	F	G	H	I	J	K
1	$\mu =$	10									
2	$R =$	10									
3											
4											
5											
6	X	$X - R$	$X + R$	P	PX	$F(X)$	$P(X - R)$		π^e	$Exp(\pi^e/\mu)$	P
7	70					0		0			
8	80	70	90	1	80	1	70	70	80	2980	0.184
9	90	80	100	0	0	1	0	70	70	1096	0.067
10	100	90	110	0	0	1	0	70	70	1096	0.067
11	110	100	120	0	0	1	0	70	70	1096	0.067
12	120	110	130	0	0	1	0	70	70	1096	0.067
13	130	120	140	0	0	1	0	70	70	1096	0.067
14	140	130	150	0	0	1	0	70	70	1096	0.067
15	150	140	160	0	0	1	0	70	70	1096	0.067
16	160	150	170	0	0	1	0	70	70	1096	0.067
17	170	160	180	0	0	1	0	70	70	1096	0.067
18	180	170	190	0	0	1	0	70	70	1096	0.067
19	190	180	200	0	0	1	0	70	70	1096	0.067
20	200	190	210	0	0	1	0	70	70	1096	0.067
21				1	80					16140	1

Step 5: Sums

The numbers in column K will not make sense until you put the formula for the sum of exponentials into cell **J21**; this formula is given in the next-to-last row of Table 25.4. Add a formula to sum the probabilities and payoffs by copying the formula in cell **J21** to cells **D21**, **E21**, and **K21**.

At this point, the numbers in your spreadsheet should match those in Table 25.3. The initial probability column reflects a belief that the other person would choose 80 with certainty. Therefore, the expected payoff in column I is 80 if one matches this claim. Given these beliefs, any higher claim will result in a $.10 penalty, and the payoff will be other's claim of 80, which is the minimum, minus 10, or 70 as shown in column I. This column will

Table 25.4	Column Key for Spreadsheet in Table 25.3 (Formulas for Row 8 Should Be Copied Down to Row 20)		
Column	**Variable**	**Notation**	**Formula for Row 8**
A	Claim	X	= A7 + 10
B	Payoff if Lower	$X - R$	= A8 − B2
C	Payoff if Higher	$X + R$	= A8 + B2
D	Probability	P	1
E	Product	PX	= D8*$A8
F	Cumulative P	$F(X)$	= F7+D8
G	Product 2	$P(X - R)$	= D8*$B8
H	Cumulative Product 2		= H7 + G8
I	Expected Payoff	π^e	= E8 + (1 − F8)*$C8 + H7
J	Exponential of Payoff	$\exp(\pi^e/\mu)$	= exp(I8/B1)
Cell J21	Sum of Exponentials	$\Sigma_i(\exp(\pi^e_i/\mu)$	= sum(J8..J20)
K	Probability	$\exp(\pi^e/\mu)/\Sigma_i(\exp(\pi^e_i/\mu))$	= J8/J$21

provide expected payoffs for each decision as the initial belief column D is changed, so let's look at the structure of the formula in column I, as shown in Equation 25.2.

$$\text{Expected payoff for claim of } 80 = E8 + (1 - F8) \times C8 + H7 \qquad (25.2)$$

This formula has three parts that correspond to the three parts of Equation (25.1), i.e., depending on whether the other's claim is equal to, higher, or lower than one's own claim. We will discuss the three elements in turn.

- **Case of a Tie.** In Equation (25.2), the first term, **E8**, was calculated as the probability in **D8** that the other chooses 80 times the claim itself in **A8**. Thus, this first term covers the case of a tie.
- **Case of Having the Lower Claim.** The second term in Equation (25.2) involves **C8**, which is the claim plus the reward, R, so this term pertains to the case where one's claim is the lower one. The (1 − **F8**) term is the probability that the other's claim is higher, so **F8** is the probability that the other's claim is less than or equal to one's own claim of 80. Since there is no chance that the other is less than 80, **F8** is calculated as **F7**, which has been set to 0, plus the probability that the other's claim is exactly 80, i.e., **C8**. As this formula is copied down the column, we get a sum of probabilities, which can be thought of as the cumulative less-than-or-equal-to probabilities. Retracing our steps, 1 minus the less-than-or-equal-to probabilities in

column F will be the probability that the other's claim is higher, so the second term in Equation (25.1) has the (1 − **F8**) being multiplied by the claim plus the reward.

- **Case of Having the Higher Claim**. Here we have to consider each of the claims that are lower than one's own claim. Column B has claims with the penalty subtracted, and these payoffs are multiplied by the probability of that claim to yield the numbers in column G. Then column H calculates a cumulative less-than-or-equal-to sum of the elements in G. This sum is necessary since, for any given claim, there may be many lower claims that the other can make, with associated payoffs that must be multiplied by probabilities and summed to get an expected payoff.

Now that the expected payoffs are calculated in column I, they are put into exponential functions in column J after dividing by the error parameter in cell **B2**. These are then summed in cell **J21**, and the exponentials are divided by the sum to get the choice probabilities in column K. For example, in Table 25.3 the probability associated with a claim of 80 is about 0.184, as shown in cell **K8**. The other probabilities are about one-third as high. These other probabilities are all equal, since the other person is expected to choose a claim of 80 for sure, and therefore all higher claims lead to earnings of 70, as compared with the 80 that could be earned by matching the other's expected claim. This reduction in expected payoff is not so severe as to prevent deviations from happening, at least for the error parameter of 10 in cell B1 that is being used here. Try a lower error parameter, say 5, to be sure that it results in a higher probability for the claim of 80, with less chance of an "error" in terms of making a claim that is higher than 80.

Next, consider cell **E21**, which shows the expected value of the other person's claim for the initial beliefs. If you still have a probability of 1 in cell **D8** for the lowest claim, then the number in **E21** should be 80. As you change the probabilities in column D (making sure that they sum to 1), the expected claim in **E21** will change.

Finally, we can use the choice probabilities in column K to calculate the resulting expected claims. To make this calculation, we essentially need to get the formula in **E21** over to the right of the K column. At this point, you should save your spreadsheet (in case something goes wrong) and then perform the final two steps.

Step 6

Highlight the shaded block of cells in Table 25.3, i.e., from **E6** to **K21**. Then copy and paste this block with the cursor in cell **L6**, which will essentially replicate columns E to K, putting them in columns L to R. Now you should see that the average claim in cell **L21** is about 133, far above the average claim of 80 based on the initial beliefs.

Step 7

The next step is to perform another iteration. You could mark the shaded block in Table 25.3 again (or skip this step if it is still on the clipboard) and then place the cursor in cell **S6** and copy the block. The new average claim in cell **S21** should be 166. In two more iterations this average will converge to 178 (in cell **AG21**), and this average will not change in subsequent iterations.

At this point, there will be a vector of probabilities in column AG with the following interesting property: if these represent initial beliefs, then the stochastic best responses to these beliefs will yield essentially the same probabilities, i.e., the beliefs will be confirmed. This is the notion of equilibrium that was introduced in Chapter 24. Even more interesting is the fact that the level of convergence, 178, is approximately equal to the average claim for the $R = 10$ treatment in Figure 25.1. Now try changing the payoff parameter from 10 to 50 to be sure that the average claims converge to 80, and check to be sure that these convergence levels are not too sensitive to changes in initial beliefs, e.g., if you put a 1 in the bottom (**D20**) element of column D instead of in the **D8** element. In this sense, the model of logit stochastic responses can explain why behavior converges to the Nash prediction in some treatments (50 and 80), and why data goes to the other side of the set of feasible decisions in other treatments (5 and 10).

In equilibrium, beliefs are confirmed, and the result is called a logit equilibrium, which was used by Capra et al. (1999) to evaluate data from the experiment. Our spreadsheet calculations in this section have been based on an error rate of 10, which is close to the value of 8.3 that was estimated from the actual data, with a standard error of 0.5.

QUESTIONS

1. Show that unequal claims cannot constitute a Nash equilibrium in a traveler's dilemma.

2. What is the Nash equilibrium for the traveler's dilemma game where there is a $5 penalty and a $5 reward, and claims must be between −$50 and $50? (A negative claim means that the traveler pays the airline, not the reverse.)

3. Consider a traveler's dilemma with N players who each lose identical items, and the airline requests claim forms to be filled out with the understanding that claims will be between $80 and $200. If all claims are not equal, there is a $5 penalty if one's claim is not the lowest and a $5 reward for the person with the lowest claim. Speculate on the effect on average claims of increasing N from two to four players in a setup with repeated random matchings.

4. Calculate what the earnings would have been for the K squared team if they had chosen a claim of 200 in each of the first four rounds of the game summarized in Table 25.1.

5. Use the spreadsheet constructed in the Appendix for this chapter to show that the choices converge to the Nash level of 80 when the error rate is reduced to 1 for the $R = 10$ treatment.

6. (Introspection and Cognitive Hierarchy Models) Insert initial beliefs of 1/13 in column D of the spreadsheet, using $R = 10$ and $R = 50$ and an error rate of 10. Think of these initial beliefs as level 0 beliefs that give equal probability to each decision. The noisy level 1 beliefs are then those in column K, and the expected claim for these beliefs is found in cell L21. In this manner, find the level 2 beliefs and the average claim that results, and similarly for several higher levels. At what level does the expected claim stop changing by more than 10 percent?

chapter 26

Coordination Games

A major role of management is to coordinate decisions so that better outcomes can be achieved. The game considered in this chapter highlights the need for such external management, since otherwise players may get stuck in a situation where nobody exerts much effort because others are not expected to work hard either. In these games, the productivity of each person's effort depends on that of others, and there can be multiple Nash equilibria, each at a different common effort level. Behavior is sensitive to factors like changes in the effort cost or the size of the group, even though these have no effect on the set of Nash equilibria. The experiment can be run with the Veconlab Coordination Game. Alternatively, the matrix game with seven possible effort decisions discussed below is implemented by the default parameters for the large matrix game program, the $N \times N$ Matrix Game program. The instructions in this chapter's Effort Game in the Appendix are for the matrix-game version with seven decisions.

26.1 "The Minimum Effort Game? That's One I Can Play!"

Most productive processes involve specialized activities, where distinct individuals or teams assemble separate components that are later combined into a final product. If this product requires one of the components, then the number of units finally sold is sensitive to bottlenecks in production. For example, a marine products company that produces 100 hulls and 80 engines will only be able to market 80 boats. Thus, there is a bottleneck caused by the division with the lowest output. Students (and professors too) have little trouble understanding the incentives of this type of minimum-effort game, as one student's comment in the section title indicates.

The minimum-effort game was originally discussed by Rousseau in the context of a stag hunt, where a group of hunters form a large circle and wait for the stag to try to escape. The chances of killing the stag depend on the watchfulness and effort exerted by the encircling hunters. If the stag observes a hunter to be napping or hunting for smaller game instead, then the stag will attempt an escape through that sector. If the stag is able to judge the weakest link in the circle, then the chances of escape depend on the minimum of the hunters' efforts. The other aspect of the payoff is that effort is individually costly, e.g., in terms of giving up the chance of bagging a hare or taking a rest.

The game in Table 26.1 is a 2×2 version of a minimum effort game. First, consider the lower-left corner where each person has a low effort, and payoffs are 70 each. If the Row player increases effort, while the Column player maintains low efforts, then the relevant Row payoff is reduced to 60, as can be seen from the top-left box. Think of it this way: the unilateral increase in effort will not increase the minimum, but the extra cost reduces Row's payoff from 70 to 60, so the cost of this extra unit of effort is 10.

Now suppose that the initial situation is a high effort for Row and a low effort for Column, as in the upper-left box. An increase in Column's effort will raise the minimum, which raises Row's payoff from 60 to 80. Thus, a unit increase in the minimum effort will raise payoffs by 20, holding one's own effort constant. This one-unit increase in effort did not raise the Column player's payoff by 20 because effort is costly, and the fact that the Column player's payoff only went up by 10 suggests that the cost of the extra unit of effort is 10. These observations can be used to devise a mathematical formula for payoffs that will be useful in devising more complex games. Let the low effort be 1 and the high effort be 2, as indicated by the numbers in parentheses next to the Row and Column labels in the payoff table. Then the payoffs in this table are determined by the formula: 60 + (20 times the minimum effort) − (10 times one's own effort). Let M denote the minimum effort and E denote one's own effort, so that this formula, shown in Equation (26.1) is

$$\text{Own payoff} = 60 + 20M - 10E \qquad (26.1)$$

For example, the upper-right payoffs are determined by noting that both efforts are 2, so the minimum (M) is 2, and the formula yields: 60 + (20)*2 − (10)*2 = 80.

The formula in Equation (26.1) was used to construct the payoffs in Table 26.2, for the case of efforts that can range from 1 to 7. Notice that the four numbers in the bottom-left corner of the table correspond to the Row payoffs in Table 26.1. With a larger number of possible effort levels, we see the dramatic nature of the potential gains from coordination on high-effort outcomes. At a common effort of 7, each person earns 130, which is almost

Table 26.1 A Minimum Effort Game (Row's Payoff, Column's Payoff)

	Column Player	
Row Player	**Low Effort (1)**	**High Effort (2)**
High Effort (2)	60, 70 ⇓	⇒ 80, 80
Low Effort (1)	70, 70 ⇐	⇑ 70, 60

Table 26.2	The Van Huyck et al. (1990) Minimum Effort Game with Row Player's Payoffs Determined by the Minimum of Others' Efforts

	Column's Effort (or Minimum of Other Efforts)						
Row's Effort	1	2	3	4	5	6	7
7	10	30	50	70	90	110	**130**
6	20	40	60	80	100	**120**	120
5	30	50	70	90	**110**	110	110
4	40	60	80	**100**	100	100	100
3	50	70	**90**	90	90	90	90
2	60	**80**	80	80	80	80	80
1	**70**	70	70	70	70	70	70

twice the amount earned at the lowest effort level. Movements along the diagonal from the lower-left to the upper-right corner show the benefits from coordinated increases in effort; a one-unit increase in the minimum effort raises payoff by 20, minus the cost of 10 for the increased effort, so each diagonal payoff is 10 larger than the one lower on the diagonal.

Besides the gains from coordination, there is an additional feature of Table 26.2 that is related to risk. When the Row player chooses the lowest effort (in the bottom row), the payoff is 70 for sure, but the highest effort may yield payoffs that range from 10 to 130, depending on the Column player's choice. This is the strategic dilemma in this coordination game: there is a large incentive to coordinate on high efforts, but the higher effort decisions are risky.

An additional element of risk is introduced when more than two people are involved. Suppose that payoffs are still determined by the formula in Equation (26.1), where M is the minimum of all players' efforts. The result is still the payoff shown in Table 26.2, where the payoff numbers pertain to the Row player as before, but where the columns correspond to the minimum of the other players' efforts. For example, the payoffs are all 70 in the bottom row because Row's effort of 1 is the minimum regardless of which column is determined by the minimum of the others' efforts. Notice that the incorporation of larger numbers of players into this minimum-effort game does not alter the essential strategic dilemma, i.e., that high efforts involve high potential gains but more risk. At a deeper level, however, there is more risk with more players, since the minimum of a large number of independently selected efforts is likely to be small when there is some variation from one person to another. This is analogous to having a large number of hunters spread out in a large circle, which gives the stag more of a chance to find a sector where one of the hunters is absent or napping.

26.2   Nash Equilibria, Numbers Effects, and Experimental Evidence

These intuitive considerations (the gains from coordination and the risks of un-matched high efforts) are not factors in the structure of the Nash equilibria in this game. Consider Table 26.1, for example. If the other person is going to exert a low effort, the best response is a low effort that saves on effort cost. Thus, the lower-left outcome, low efforts for each, is a Nash equilibrium. But if the other player is expected to choose a high effort, then the best response is a high effort, since the gain of 20 for the increased minimum exceeds the cost of 10 for the additional unit of effort. Thus, the high-effort outcome in the upper-right corner of Table 26.1 is also a Nash equilibrium. This is an important feature of the coordination game: there are multiple equilibria, with one that is preferred to the other(s).

The presence of multiple equilibria is a feature that differentiates this game from a prisoner's dilemma, where all players may prefer the high-payoff outcome that results from cooperative behavior. This high-payoff outcome is not a Nash equilbrium in a prisoner's dilemma since each person has a unilateral incentive to defect. The equilibrium structure for the coordination game in Table 26.1 is not affected by adding additional players, each choosing between efforts of 1 and 2, and with the Row player's payoffs determined by the column that corresponds to the minimum of the others' efforts. In this case, adding more players does not alter the fact that there are two equilibria (in non-random strategies): all choose low efforts or all choose high efforts. Just restricting attention to the Nash equilibria would mean ignoring the intuition that adding more players would seem to make the choice of a high effort riskier, since it is more likely that one of the others will choose low effort and pull the minimum down.

The problem of multiple equilibria is more dramatic with more possible efforts, since any common effort is a Nash equilibrium, as shown in Table 26.2. To see this, pick any column and notice that the Row player's payoffs are highest on the diagonal of payoffs in bold. As before, this structure is independent of changes in the number of players, since such changes do not alter the payoff table. These considerations were the basis of an experiment conducted by Van Huyck et al. (1990), who used the payoffs from Table 26.2 for small groups (size 2) and large groups (sizes 14–16). The large groups played the same game 10 consecutive times with the same group, and the lowest effort was announced after each round to enable all to calculate their payoffs (in pennies). Even though a majority of individuals selected high efforts of 6 or 7 in the first round, the minimum effort was no higher than 4 in the first round for any large group. With a minimum of 4, higher efforts were wasted, and effort reductions followed in subsequent rounds. The minimum fell to the lowest level of 1 in all of the large groups, and almost all decisions in the final round were at the lowest level.

This experiment is important since previously it had been a common practice in theoretical analysis to assume that individuals could coordinate on the best Nash equilibrium when there was general agreement about which one is best, as is the case for Table 26.2. In contrast, the subjects in the experiment managed to end up in the equilibrium that is worst for all concerned. With groups of size 2, individuals were able to coordinate on the highest effort, except when pairings were randomly reconfigured in each round. With random matching, the outcomes were variable, with average efforts in the middle range. In any case, it is clear that group size had a large impact on the outcomes, even though changes in the numbers of players had no effect on the set of equilibria.

The coordination failures for large groups captured the attention of macroeconomists, who had long speculated about the possibility that whole economies could become mired in low-productivity states, where people do not engage in high levels of market activity because no one else does. The macroeconomic implications of coordination games are discussed in Bryant (1983), Cooper and John (1998), and Romer (1996), for example.

26.3   Effort-Cost Effects

Next, consider what happens when the cost of effort is altered. For example, suppose that the effort cost of 10 used to construct Table 26.1 is raised to 19, so that the payoffs (for an effort of E and a minimum effort of M) will be determined by: $60 + 20M - 19E$. In this case, a one-unit increase in each person's effort raises payoffs by 20 minus the cost of 19, so the payoffs in the upper right box of Table 26.3 are only 1 unit higher than the payoffs in the lower-left box. Notice that this increase in effort cost did not change the fact that there are two Nash equilibria, and that both players prefer the high-effort equilibrium. However, simple intuition suggests that effort levels in this game may be affected by effort costs. From the Row player's perspective, the top row offers a possible gain of only 1 and a possible loss of 19, as compared with the bottom row.

Goeree and Holt (2005a) report experiments in which the cost of effort is varied between treatments, using the payoff formula shown in Equation (26.2):

$$\text{Own payoff} = M - cE \qquad (26.2)$$

where M is the minimum of the efforts, E is one's own effort, and c is a cost parameter that is varied between treatments. Effort decisions were restricted to be any amount between

Table 26.3	A Minimum-Effort Game with High Effort Cost (Row's Payoff, Column's Payoff)	
	Column Player	
Row Player	**Low Effort (1)**	**High Effort (2)**
High Effort (2)	42, 61	62, 62
Low Effort (1)	61, 61	61, 42

(and including) $1.10 and $1.70. As before, any common effort is a Nash equilibrium in this game, as long as the cost parameter, c, is between 0 and 1, because a unilateral decrease in effort by one unit will reduce the minimum by 1, but it will only reduce the cost by an amount that is less than 1. Therefore, a unit decrease in effort will reduce one's payoff by $1 - c$. Conversely, a unilateral increase in effort by one unit above some common level will not raise the minimum, but the payoff will fall by c. Even though deviations from a common effort are unprofitable when c is greater than 0 and less than 1, the magnitude of c determines the relative cost of "errors" in either direction. A large value of c, say 0.9, makes increases in effort more costly, and a small value of c makes decreases more costly.

Figure 26.1 shows the results for sessions that consisted of 10–12 subjects who were randomly paired for a series of 10 rounds. There were three sessions with a low effort cost parameter of 0.25; the averages by round for these sessions are plotted as thin dashed lines. The thick dashed line is the average over all three sessions of this treatment. Similarly, the thin solid lines plot round-by-round averages for the three sessions with a high effort cost parameter of 0.75; the thick solid line shows the average for this treatment.

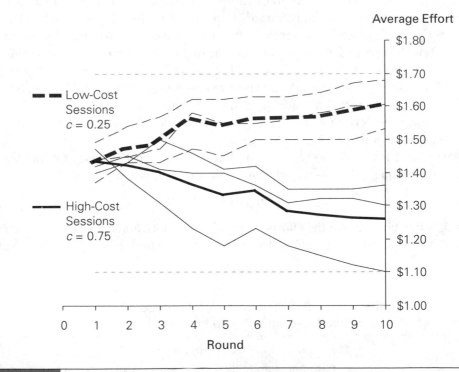

| Figure 26.1 | Average Efforts for the Goeree and Holt (2005a) Coordination Experiment: Thick Lines Are Averages over Three Sessions for Each Cost Treatment |

Efforts in the first round are in the range from $1.35 to $1.50, with no separation between treatments. Such separation arises after several rounds, and average efforts in the final round are $1.60 for the low-cost treatment, versus $1.25 for the high-cost treatment. Thus, we see a strong cost effect, even though any common effort is a Nash equilibrium.

One session in each treatment seemed to approach the boundary, which raises the issue of whether behavior will lock on one of the extremes. This pattern was observed in a Veconlab classroom experiment in which efforts went to $1.70 by the 10th period. This kind of extreme behavior is not universal, however. Goeree and Holt (2005a) report a pair of sessions that were run for 20 rounds. With an effort cost of $.25, the decisions converged to about $1.55, and with an effort cost of $.75 the decisions leveled off at about $1.38. Both of these outcomes seem to fit the pattern seen in Figure 26.1.

26.4 Equilibrium with Noisy Behavior

The spreadsheet-based analysis of noisy behavior for the travelers' dilemma, presented in the Class Experiments section in the Appendix to Chapter 25, can be adapted for the coordination game. The steps for constructing this new spreadsheet are provided later in this chapter (An Analysis of Noisy Behavior in the Coordination Game). The purpose of this analysis is to show how some randomness in individual decisions can result in data patterns (for numbers and effort-cost effects) that are roughly consistent with those observed in the experiments, even though these data patterns are not predicted on the basis of an analysis of the Nash equilibria for the game.

As before, we begin by considering successive levels of iterated strategic thinking. A level 0 person chooses each decision with equal probability, so the average decision is in the middle of the range, at 140, as shown in the Level 0 column on the left side of Table 26.4. A level 1 person believes that each decision is equally likely, and that person makes a noisy best response calculated with the logit probabilistic choice function (ratio of exponential functions). The resulting average effort increases to 147 for the low-cost treatment and decreases to 132 for the high-cost treatment, as can be seen from the Level 1 column. It is apparent from Table 26.4 that the average claims converge by about the fifth round, to levels that are reasonably close to the data averages shown in the far-right column of the table.

As explained in Chapter 25, the process of copying blocks of the spreadsheet cells to adjacent locations causes the choice probabilities for one level to become the initial beliefs of a person at the next highest level of iterated rationality. At successively higher levels of iterated rationality, the belief and choice distributions get closer and closer. When the belief and choice distributions converge, the result is a quantal response equilibrium for the particular error parameter used ($\mu = 10$). The series of choice distributions for the first five levels of iterated rationality are graphed in Figure 26.2, beginning with a flat dashed line (level 0). For each treatment, the equilibrium is reached by about level 5 (the dark line with the QRE label).

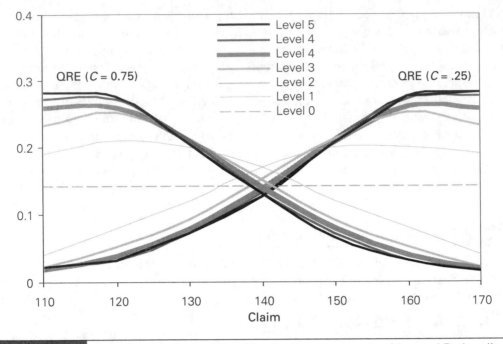

Figure 26.2   Coordination Game Effort Distributions for Levels of Iterated Rationality

Finally, the pattern of average claims in Table 26.4 can be thought of as a crude learning model, which begins in time 1 (level 1) with each person thinking that others will choose efforts randomly over the whole range. Then the stochastic responses in time 1 have averages of 147 in the low-cost treatment and 132 in the high-cost treatment. If people could see the whole distribution of efforts made at time 1, then their stochastic best responses at time 2 would be the effort distributions for level 2, with averages of 151 for the low-cost treatment and 129 for the high-cost treatment. This pattern of adjustment is qualitatively similar to that observed in the data in Figure 26.1, but the data shows a somewhat slower divergence away from the starting point of about 145. The slower divergence in the

Table 26.4   Average Effort Predictions with Iterated Rationality ($\mu = 10$)

	Level 0	Level 1	Level 2	Level 3	Level 4	Level 5	Data Average (Last 5 Rounds)
Low Cost C = 0.25	140	147	151	153	154	154	159
High Cost C = 0.75	140	132	129	127	126	126	126

data may be due to the fact that people in the experiment did not see the whole distribution of others' effort decisions, so they could not learn as quickly, and they tended to respond more strongly to the particular decision that they just encountered. Although it is possible to construct richer learning models that are based on limited individual observations, it is interesting to note that even a crude learning model can explain the main qualitative feature of the patterns of adjustment in the data. The importance of the "noisy" part of the noisy best response calculations in Table 26.4 is indicated by the fact that a perfect best response to 140 is to choose exactly 140. Thus the predictions for higher levels of iterated rationality would not diverge from the midpoint of the effort range if there is no randomness in the model.

Goeree and Holt (2005a) also considered the effects of raising the number of players per group from two to three, holding effort cost constant, which resulted in a sharp reduction of effort levels. Effort-cost effects were observed as well in games in which payoffs were determined by the median of the three efforts. Some coordination games may be played only once; Goeree and Holt (2001) report strong effort-cost effects in such games as well. A theoretical analysis of these effects (in the context of a logit equilibrium) can be found in Anderson, Goeree, and Holt (2001, 2002).

26.5 Extensions

For the minimum-effort games discussed in this chapter, the value of increasing the minimum was fixed. Brandts and Cooper (2006) report an interesting experiment in which a manager chooses this value, which is referred to as a "bonus" parameter. Workers, who are players in a coordination game, choose efforts simultaneously. The workers' wages depend on the product of the minimum effort and the bonus parameter announced by the employer. The employer's payoff is determined by the difference between revenue, price times the minimum effort, and the cost of bonuses paid. After each period, everybody observes the minimum effort but not individual efforts. In one treatment, there were no opportunities for communication, and in another, the manager could send a text message to all workers when the bonus for that period was announced. This one-way communication did not raise efforts significantly. Average efforts were higher in another treatment with two-way communication, which added the ability of each worker to send a text message to the manager at the same time the worker's effort was submitted for the period. The messages were coded, and the most effective messages for managers were to note the bonus amount, to suggest a specific level of effort, and to stress the mutual benefits of cooperation. Some sessions were run with student managers, and others were run with professional managers from an executive education program. In both cases, the workers were students. The professional managers were able to induce higher initial efforts, but this difference did not persist into later periods, where the performances of the student and professional managers were roughly comparable.

There is an interesting literature on factors that facilitate coordination on good outcomes in matrix games, e.g., Sefton (1999), Straub (1995), and Ochs (1995). In particular, notions of risk dominance and potential provide good predictions about behavior when there are multiple equilibria. Anderson, Goeree, and Holt (2001) introduce the more general notion of *stochastic potential* and use it to explain results of coordination game experiments. Models of learning and evolution have also been widely used in the study of coordination games, see Anderson, Goeree, and Holt (2004), Crawford (1991, 1995), Erev and Rapoport (1998), Van Huyck, Cook, and Battalio (1997), and the references in Ochs (1995).

There are numerous other applications of coordination games in economics. For example, Heal and Kunreuther (2005) analyze the policy implications of "interdependent security games" in which firms may decide whether or not to make a costly investment that enhances security. Even if a firm invests in security that lowers the chances of damage from a local breach, the firm may suffer the same damage due to a cross breach from another firm that did not invest. In this context, it may be profitable for a firm to invest in security when others do too, but when enough others do not, the benefits of local protection are diminished to the extent that it is no longer a best response for the firm to invest in security. In these games, there can be an equilibrium in which all invest, and another, low-payoff equilibrium in which none invest. See Hess, Holt, and Smith (2005) for an experimental study of factors that determine which equilibrium is more likely to be realized in these games.

Appendix: **An Analysis of Noisy Behavior in the Coordination Game**

The traveler's dilemma and the coordination game have similar payoff structures, so it is straightforward to modify the spreadsheet shown in Table 25.2 in Chapter 25 so that it applies to the coordination game. Here are the steps:

Step 1

Save the traveler's dilemma spreadsheet under a different name, e.g., cg.xls, before deleting all information in column L and farther to the right.

Step 2

The coordination experiment has fewer possible decisions, when restricted to $.10 increments: 110, 120, . . . , 170. Therefore, delete all material in rows 7–10, and in rows 18–20, leaving row 21 as it is. You will have to enter the possible effort levels in column A: **110** in **A11**, **120** in **A12**, and so on.

Step 3

There is no penalty/reward parameter in the coordination game, so enter a **0** in cell **B2**. Next put "**C =**" in cell **A3**, and enter a value of **0.75** in cell **B3**.

Step 4

The starting values for the cumulative column sums will have to be moved, so put values of **0** in cells **F10** and **H10**.

Step 5

To set the initial probabilities, change the entry in cell **D11** to **1**, and leave the other entries in that column 0.

Step 6

Next, the effort cost must be subtracted from the expected payoff formula in cell **I11**. The cost per unit effort in cell B3 must be multiplied by the effort in column A to calculate the total effort cost. Thus, you should *append* the term –**B3*$A11** to the end of the formula that is already in cell **I11**. Then this modified formula should be copied into rows 12–17 in this column.

Step 7

At this point, the numbers you have should be essentially the same as those shown in Table 26.5 (which have been truncated), with a new vector of probabilities in column K. To perform the first iteration, mark the block from **E10** to **K21**, copy, and place the cursor in cell **L10** before pasting. This same procedure can be repeated 10 times, so that the average effort after 10 iterations will be found on the far right side of the spreadsheet, in cell **BW21**.

The expected effort after one iteration, which is found in cell **L21**, is about 119. This rises to 125 by the fifth iteration. When the initial probabilities in column D are changed to put a probability of 1 for the highest effort and 0 for all other efforts, the iterations converge to about 125 by the 10th iteration. When the cost of effort is reduced from 0.75 to 0.25, the average claims converge to about 155 after several iterations. These average efforts are quite close to the levels for the two treatment averages in Figure 26.1 in the 10th round. As noted in Chapter 25, the convergence of iterated stochastic responses indicates an equilibrium in which a given set of beliefs about others' effort levels will produce a matching distribution of effort choice probabilities. The resulting effort averages are quite good predictors of behavior in the minimum-effort experiment when the error rate is set to 10. Even though any common effort is a Nash equilibrium, intuition suggests that lower effort costs may produce higher efforts. These spreadsheet calculations of the logit equilibrium

Table 26.5	Excel Spreadsheet for Coordination Game Logit Responses

	A	B	C	D	E	F	G	H	I	J	K
1	$\mu =$	10									
2	$R =$	0									
3	$C =$	0.75									
4											
5											
6	X	X	X	P	PX	$F(X)$	PX		π^e	$Exp(\pi^e/\mu)$	P
7											
8											
9											
10	100					0		0			
11	110	110	110	1	110	1	110	110	27.5	15.64	0.530
12	120	120	120	0	0	1	0	110	20	7.38	0.250
13	130	130	130	0	0	1	0	110	12.5	3.49	0.118
14	140	140	140	0	0	1	0	110	5	1.64	0.056
15	150	150	150	0	0	1	0	110	−2.5	0.77	0.026
16	160	160	160	0	0	1	0	110	−10	0.36	0.012
17	170	170	170	0	0	1	0	110	−17.5	0.17	0.006
18											
19											
20											
21				1	110					29.491	1

are consistent with this intuition; they explain why efforts are inversely correlated with effort costs. A lower error rate will push effort levels to one of the extremes, i.e., to 110 or 170 (see Question 3 at the end of the chapter).

QUESTIONS

1. Consider the game in the following table, and find all Nash equilibria in pure strategies. Is this a coordination game?

	Column Player			
Row Player	**Left (26%)**	**Middle (8%)**	**Non-Nash (68%)**	**Right (0%)**
Top (68%)	200, 50	0, 45	10, 30	20, −250
Bottom (32%)	0, −250	10, −100	30, 30	50, 40

2. The numbers under each decision label in the table above show the percentage of people who chose that strategy when the game was played only once (Goeree and Holt 2001). Why is the Column player's most commonly used strategy labeled as "Non-Nash" in the table? (*Note*: it was not given this label in the experiment.) Conjecture why the Non-Nash decision is selected so frequently by Column players.

3. Use the spreadsheet for the minimum-effort coordination game to fill in average efforts for the following table. Use initial belief probabilities of 1/7 (or 0.143) for each of the elements in column D between rows 11–17. Then discuss the effects of the error parameter on these predictions.

	Average Effort Predictions			
	$\mu = 1$	**$\mu = 5$**	**$\mu = 10$**	**$\mu = 20$**
High Cost ($C = 0.75$)				
Low Cost ($C = 0.25$)				

4. Consider the game shown below, which gives the Column player a safe decision, S. Row's payoffs depend on a parameter X that changes from one treatment to the other. Goeree and Holt (2001) report that the magnitude of X affects the frequency with which the Row player chooses Top, so the issue is whether this effect is predicted in theory. Find all Nash equilibria in pure and mixed strategies for $X = 0$, and for $X = 400$, under the assumption that each person is risk neutral.

	Column Player		
Row Player	**L**	**R**	**S**
Top	90, 90	0, 0	X, 40
Bottom	0, 0	180, 180	0 , 40

part 7

Individual Decision Experiments

Part 7 contains a series of chapters involving decision making when the payoffs cannot be known for sure. Uncertainty about outcomes is represented by probabilities, which can be used to calculate the expected value of a payoff or utility function. The notion of expected utility became widely accepted in economics after von Neumann and Morgenstern (1944) provided a set of plausible assumptions or axioms, which ensure that decisions will correspond to the maximization of the expected value of some utility function. This is, of course, an "as if" claim; sometimes you may see people calculate expected values, but it is rare to see a person actually multiplying out utilities and the associated probabilities. Today, expected utility is the standard in economics (and related areas like finance), despite some well-known situations where behavior is sensitive to biases and behavioral factors.

Chapter 27 pertains to the simplest two-way prediction task (e.g., rain or shine), when the underlying probabilities are fixed, but unknown in repeated rounds. Each new observation provides more information about the relative likelihood of the two events. The issue of probability matching concerns the relationship between the predictions and the underlying frequency of each event; it is shown that simple matching patterns typically represent deviations from optimal behavior. Probability matching experiments are also used to introduce some simple learning rules based on beliefs or reinforcements.

Anomalies in lottery-choice situations are discussed in Chapter 28 (e.g., the Allais paradox), which is a pattern of choices that cannot be explained by standard expected utility theory. There is also a discussion of prospect theory, which is the most widely suggested alternative.

All decision problems considered up to this point have been "static," i.e., without any time-dependent elements. Chapter 29 is organized around a dynamic situation involving costly search (e.g., for a high wage or a low price). Despite the complex nature of sequential search problems, observed behavior is often surprisingly consistent with search rules derived from an analysis of optimal decision making.

The decision problems introduced in Part 7 can be implemented with Web-based Veconlab programs, which allow log-in after hours from remote locations. Since these are individual decision problems, there is no need to coordinate login times.

chapter 27

Probability Matching

Perhaps the simplest prediction problem involves guessing which of two random events will occur. The probabilities of the two events are fixed but not known, so a person can learn about these probabilities by observing the relative frequencies of the two events. One of the earliest biases recorded in the psychology literature was the tendency for individuals to predict each event with a frequency that approximately matches the fraction of times that the event is observed. This bias, known as *probability matching*, has been widely accepted as being evidence of irrationality, despite Siegel's experiments in the 1960s, which tell a different story. These experiments provide an important methodological lesson for how experiments should be conducted. The results are also used to begin a discussion of learning models that may explain paths of adjustment to some steady state where systematic changes in behavior have ceased. Binary prediction tasks can be run by hand (see this chapter's Binary Prediction Game in the Class Experiments section) or by using the Veconlab Probability Matching program (listed under the Decisions menu).

27.1 Being Treated Like a Rat

Before the days of computers, the procedures for binary prediction tasks in psychology experiments sometimes seemed like a setup for rats or pigeons that had been scaled up for human subjects. In the setup used by Siegel and Goldstein (1959) the subject was seated at a desk with a plywood screen that separated the working area from the experimenter on the other side. The screen contained two light bulbs, one on the left and one on the right, and a third, smaller light in the center that was used to signal that the next decision must be made. When the signal light went on, the subject recorded a prediction by pressing one of two levers (left and right). Then one of the lights was illuminated, and the subject would receive reinforcement (if any) based on whether or not the prediction was correct. When the next trial was ready, the signal light would come on, and the process would be repeated, perhaps hundreds of times. No information was provided about the relative likelihood of the two events (Left and Right), although sometimes people were told how the events were generated, e.g., by using a printed list. In fact, one of the events would be set to occur more often, e.g., 75 percent of the time. The process generating these events was not always random, e.g., sometimes the events were rigged so that in each block of 20 trials, exactly 15 would result in the more likely event.

By the time of the Siegel and Goldstein experiments in the late 1950s, psychologists had already been studying probability matching behavior for over twenty years. The results indicated a curious pattern: the proportion of times that subjects predicted each event roughly matched the frequency with which the events occurred. For example, if Left occurred three-fourths of the time, then subjects would come to learn this by experience and then would tend to predict Left three-fourths of the time.

27.2 Are Rats Really More Rational Than Humans?

The astute reader may have figured out the best thing to do in such a situation, but a formal analysis will help ensure that the conclusion does not rely on hidden assumptions like risk neutrality. Let us assume that the events really were independent random realizations. Let U_C denote the utility of the reward for a correct prediction, and let U_I denote the utility of the reward for an incorrect prediction. The rewards could be "external" (money payments, food), "internal" (psychological self-reinforcement), or some combination. The only assumption is that there is some preference for making a correct prediction: $U_C > U_I$. These utilities may even change over time, depending on rewards already received; the only assumption is that an additional correct prediction is preferred.

Once a number of trials have passed, the person will have figured out which event is more likely, so let p denote the subjective probability that represents those beliefs, with $p > 1/2$. There are two decisions: predict the more likely event and predict the less likely event. Each decision yields a lottery:

Predict more likely event: U_C with probability p
U_I with probability $1 - p$

Predict less likely event: U_I with probability p
U_C with probability $1 - p$

Thus, the expected utility for predicting the more likely event is higher if

$$pU_C + (1 - p)U_I > pU_I + (1 - p)U_C$$

or equivalently,

$$(2p - 1)U_C > (2p - 1)U_I$$

which is always the case since $p > 1/2$ and $U_C > U_I$. Although animals may become satiated with food pellets and other physical rewards, economists have no trouble with a nonsatiation assumption for money rewards. Note that this argument does not depend on any assumption about risk attitudes, since the two possible payoffs are the same in each case, i.e., there is no more "spread" in one case than in the other. (With only two possible outcomes, the only role of probability is to determine whether the better outcome has a higher probability, so risk aversion does not matter. Another way to think about this is that if there are only two relevant points, then they essentially constitute a straight line.) Since the higher reward is for a correct prediction, the more likely event should always be predicted, i.e., with probability 1. In this sense, probability matching is irrational as long as there is no satiation: $U_C > U_I$.

Despite the clear prediction that one should predict the more likely event 100 percent of the time after it becomes clear which event that is, this behavior is often not observed in laboratory experiments. For example, in a summary of the probability matching literature, the psychologist Fantino (1998) concludes: "human subjects do not behave optimally. Instead they match the proportion of their choices to the probability of reinforcement. . . . This behavior is perplexing given that non-humans are quite adept at optimal behavior in this situation." As evidence for the higher degree of rational behavior in animals, he cites a 1996 study that reported choice frequencies for the more likely event to be well above the probability matching predictions in most treatments conducted with chicks and rats. Before concluding that the animal subjects are more rational than humans, it will be instructive to review a particularly well-designed probability matching experiment.

27.3 Siegel and Goldstein's Experiments

Sidney Siegel is perhaps the psychologist who has had the largest direct and indirect impact on experimental methods in economics. His early work provides a high standard of careful reporting and procedures, appropriate statistical techniques, and the use of financial incentives where appropriate. His experiments on probability matching are a good example of this work. In one experiment, 36 male Penn State students were allowed to make predictions for 100 trials, and then 12 of these students were brought back on a later day to make predictions in 200 more trials. The proportions of predictions for the more likely event are graphed in Figure 27.1, with each point being the average over 20 trials.

The 12 subjects in the "no-pay" treatment were simply told to "do your best" to predict which light bulb would be illuminated. These averages are plotted as the heavy dashed line, which begins at about 0.5 as would be expected in early trials with no information about which event is more likely. Notice that the proportion of predictions for the more likely event converges to the level of 0.75 (shown by a horizontal line on the right) predicted by probability matching, with a leveling off at about trial 100.

In the "pay-loss" treatment, 12 participants received $.05 for each correct prediction, and they lost $.05 for each incorrect decision. The 20-trial averages are plotted as the dark solid line in the figure. The line converges to a level of about 0.9. A third "pay" treatment offered a $.05 reward but no loss for an incorrect prediction, and the results (not shown)

Prediction Rate for
More Likely Event

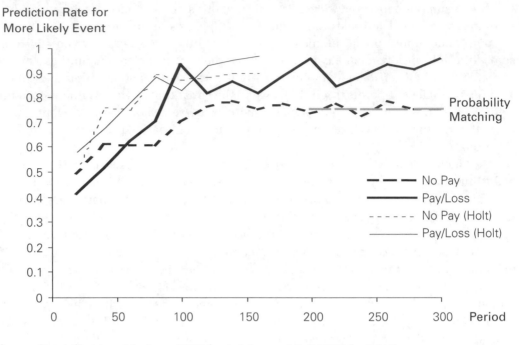

Source: Siegel, Siegel, and Andrews (1964) for dark lines and Holt (1992) for light lines

Figure 27.1 Prediction Proportions for the Event with Frequency 0.75

are between the other two treatments, and above 0.75. Clearly, incentives matter, and approximate probability matching is not observed with incentives in this context.

It would be misleading to conclude that incentives always matter, or that probability matching will be observed in no-pay treatments using different procedures. The two thin lines in Figure 27.1 show 20-trial averages for an experiment conducted by (Holt 1992) in which six University of Virginia students in no-pay and pay/loss treatments made decisions using computers, where the events were determined by a random number generator. The instructions matched those reported in Siegel, Siegel, and Andrews (1964), except that colored boxes on the screen were used instead of light bulbs. Notice that probability matching is not observed in either the pay/loss treatment (with a reward of $.10 and a penalty of $.10 shown by the thin solid line or the no-pay treatment shown by the thin dashed line). The results for a third treatment with a $.20 reward and no penalty (not shown) were similar. The reason that matching was not observed in the Holt no-pay treatment is unclear. One conjecture is that the computer interface makes the situation more anonymous and less like a matching pennies game. In the Siegel setup with the experimenter on one side of the screen, the subject might incorrectly perceive the situation as having some aspects of a game against the experimenter. Recall that the equilibrium in a matching pennies game involves equal probabilities for each decision. This might explain the lower choice percentages for the more likely event reported in the non-computerized setup, but this is only a guess.

Finally, note that Siegel's findings suggest a resolution to the paradoxical finding that rats are smarter than humans in binary prediction tasks. Since you cannot tell a rat to "do your best," animal experiments are always run with food or drink incentives on hungry or thirsty animals. As a result, the observed choice proportions are closer to those of financially motivated human subjects. In a survey of over fifty years of probability matching experiments, Vulkan (2000) concluded that probability matching is generally not observed in humans with real payoffs, although humans can be surprisingly slow learners in this simple setting.

27.4 | A Simple Model of Belief Learning

Probability matching experiments provide a useful data set for the study of learning behavior. Given the symmetry of the problem, a person's initial or prior beliefs ought to be that each event is equally likely, but the first observation should raise the probability associated with the event that was just observed. One way to model this learning process is to let initial beliefs for the probability of events L and R be calculated as shown in Equation (27.1):

$$\Pr(L) = \frac{\alpha}{\alpha+\alpha} \text{ and } \Pr(R) = \frac{\alpha}{\alpha+\alpha} \quad \text{(Prior beliefs)} \tag{27.1}$$

where α is a positive parameter to be explained below. Of course, α has no role yet, since both of the above probabilities are equal to 1/2.

If event L is observed, then $\Pr(L)$ should increase, so add 1 to the numerator for $\Pr(L)$. To make the two probabilities sum to 1, add 1 to the denominators for each probability expression, as shown in Equation (27.2).

$$\Pr(L) = \frac{\alpha+1}{\alpha+1+\alpha} \text{ and } \Pr(R) = \frac{\alpha}{\alpha+1+\alpha} \quad \text{(After observing L)} \tag{27.2}$$

Note that α determines how quickly the probabilities respond to the new information; a large value of α will keep these probabilities close to 1/2. Continuing to add 1 to the numerator of the probability for the event just observed, and to add 1 to the denominators, we have a formula for the probabilities after N_L observations of event L and N_R observations of event R. Let N be the total number of observations to date. Then the resulting probabilities are shown in Equation (27.3):

$$\Pr(L) = \frac{\alpha+N_L}{2\alpha+N} \text{ and } \Pr(R) = \frac{\alpha+N_R}{2\alpha+N} \quad \text{(After } N \text{ observations)}, \tag{27.3}$$

where $N = N_L + N_R$.

In the early periods, the totals, N_L and N_R might switch in terms of which one is higher, but the more likely event will soon dominate, and therefore Pr(L) will be greater than 1/2. The prediction of this learning model (and the earlier analysis of perfect rationality) is that all people will eventually start to predict the more likely event every time. Any unexpected prediction switches might be explained by adding some randomness to the decision-making, e.g., a logit choice function as discussed in Chapter 24.

An alternative approach would be to consider recency effects, which make probability assessments more sensitive to recently observed data. For example, recall that the sums of event observations in the belief-learning formula shown in Equation (27.3) weigh each observation equally. It may be reasonable to allow for "forgetting" in some contexts, so that the observation of an event like L in the most recent trial may carry more weight than something observed a long time ago. Of course, putting more weight on recent events would be optimal if the underlying probabilities were changing over time, which is not the case with probability matching, but people might be adapted to situations where probabilities do evolve, e.g., as food sources move. Regardless of the source, one approach is to replace sums with weighted sums. For example, if event L were observed three times, N_L in Equation (27.2) would be 3, which can be thought of as $1 + 1 + 1$. If the most recent observation (listed on the right in this sum) is twice as prominent as the one before it, then the prior event would get a weight of one-half, and the one before that would get a weight of one-fourth, and so on. A more flexible approach is to weight the most recent event by 1, the next most recent event by ρ, the observation before that by ρ^2, and so on. Then if ρ is estimated to be less than 1, this would indicate a *recency effect*.

27.5   Reinforcement Learning

In a psychology experiment, the rewards and punishments are referred to as "reinforcements." One prominent theory of learning associates changes in behavior to the reinforcements actually received. For example, suppose that the person earns a reinforcement of x for each correct prediction, nothing otherwise. If one predicts event L and is correct, then the probability of choosing L should increase, and the extent of the behavioral change may depend on the size of the reinforcement, x. One way to model this, as shown in Equation (27.4), is to let the choice probability be

$$\text{Pr(choose L)} = \frac{\alpha + x}{\alpha + x + \alpha} \quad \text{and Pr(choose R)} = \frac{\alpha}{\alpha + x + \alpha} \tag{27.4}$$

Despite the similarity with Equation (27.2), there are two important differences. The left side of Equation (27.4) is a choice probability, not a probability that represents beliefs. With reinforcement learning, beliefs are not explicitly modeled, as is the case for the "belief learning" models of the type discussed in Section 27.4. The second difference is that the x in Equation (27.4) represents a reinforcement, not an integer count as in Equation (27.2).

Of course, reinforcement is a broad term, which can include both physical things like food pellets given to rats, as well as psychological feelings associated with success or failure. One way to implement this model for experiments with money payments is to make the simplifying assumption that reinforcement is measured by earnings. Suppose that event L has been predicted N_L times and that the predictions have sometimes been correct and sometimes not. Then the total earnings for predicting L, denoted e_L, would be less than xN_L. Similarly, let e_R be the total earnings from the correct R predictions. The choice probabilities would then be as shown in Equation (27.5).

$$\text{Pr(choose L)} = \frac{\alpha + e_L}{2\alpha + e_L + e_R} \text{ and } \text{Pr(choose R)} = \frac{\alpha + e_R}{2\alpha + e_L + e_R} \tag{27.5}$$

Notice that the α parameters again have the role of determining how quickly learning responds to the stimulus, which in this case, is the money reinforcement.

This kind of model might also explain some aspects of behavior in probability matching experiments with financial incentives. The choice probabilities would be equal initially, but a prediction of the more likely event would be correct 75 percent of the time, the resulting asymmetries in reinforcement would tend to raise prediction probabilities for that event, and the total earnings for this event would tend to be larger than for the other event. Then e_L would be growing faster, so that e_R / e_L would tend to get smaller as e_L gets larger. Thus, the probability of choosing L in Equation (27.5) would tend to converge to 1. This convergence may be quite slow, as evidenced by some computer simulations reported by Goeree and Holt (2003a). (See Question 6 at the end of the chapter for some details on how such simulations might be structured.) Here, the simulations normalized the payoff x to be 1, and used a value of 5 for α. Figure 27.2 shows the 20-period averages for simulations run for 1,000 people, each making a series of 300 predictions. The simulated averages start somewhat above the observed averages for Siegel's subjects (more like the Holt data in Figure 27.1), but similar qualitative patterns are observed.

27.6 Extensions

Both of the learning models discussed here are somewhat simple, which is part of their appeal. The reinforcement model incorporates some randomness in behavior and has the appealing feature that incentives matter. But it has less of a cognitive element; there is no reinforcement for decisions not made. For example, suppose that a person chooses L three times in a row (by chance) and is wrong each time. Since no reinforcement is received, the choice probabilities stay at 0.5, which seems like an unreasonable prediction. Obviously, people learn something in the absence of previously received reinforcement, since they realize that making a good decision may result in higher earnings in the next round. Camerer and Ho (1999) have developed a generalization of reinforcement learning that contains some elements of belief learning. Roughly speaking, observed out-

Prediction Rate for
More Likely Event

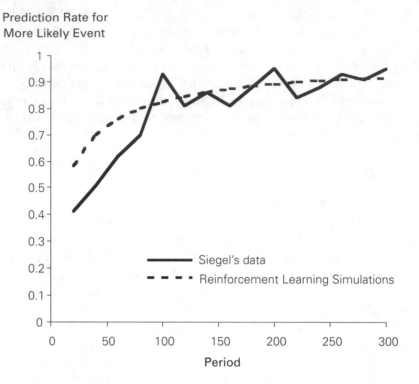

Source: For the simulated data, (Goeree and Holt 2003a)

| **Figure 27.2** | Simulated and Observed Prediction Proportions for the More Likely Event |

comes receive partial reinforcement even if nothing is earned. See Capra et al. (1999, 2002) for estimation results of belief learning models with recency effects, using data from game theory experiments.

QUESTIONS

1. The initial beliefs implied by Equation (27.1) are that each event is equally likely. How might this equation be altered in a situation where a person has some reason to believe that one event is more likely than another, even before any draws are observed?

2. A class experiment used the probability matching (PM) Veconlab software with payoffs of $.20 for each correct prediction, and in-class earnings averaged several dollars. There were six teams of 1–2 students, who made predictions for 20 trials only. (Participants were University of Virginia undergraduates in an experimental economics class

who had not read a draft of this chapter, but who had read drafts of the earlier chapters.) The more likely event was programmed to occur with probability 0.75. Calculate the expected earnings per trial for a team that follows perfect probability matching. How much more would a team earn per trial by being perfectly rational after learning which event is more likely?

3. Answer the two parts of Question 2 for the case where a correct answer results in a gain of $.10 and an incorrect answer results in a loss of $.10.

4. For the gain treatment described in Question 2, the more likely event actually occurred with probability 0.77 in the first 20 trials, averaged over all six teams. This event was predicted with a frequency of 0.88. Where would a data point representing this average be plotted in Figure 27.1?

5. For the gain/loss treatment described in Question 3, the more likely event was observed with a frequency of about 0.75 in the first 10 trials and 0.78 in the second 10 trials. Predictions were made by six teams of 1–2 students, and their earnings averaged about $.25 per team. (To cover losses, each team began with a cash balance of $1, as did the other six teams in the parallel gains treatment.) In the gain/loss treatment, the more likely event was predicted with a frequency of 0.58 in the first 10 trials and 0.70 in trials 11–20. To what extent do these results provide evidence in support of probability matching?

6. (A 10-sided die is required.) The discussion of long-run tendencies for the learning models was a little loose, since there are random elements in these models. One way to proceed is to simulate the learning processes implied by these models. Consider the reinforcement learning model, with initial choice probabilities of one-half each. You can simulate the initial choice by throwing the 10-sided die twice, where the first throw determines the "tens" digit and the second determines the "ones" digit. For example, throws of a 6 and a 2 would determine a 62. If the die is marked with numbers 0, 1, . . . , 9, then any integer from 0 to 99 is equally likely. The simulation could proceed by letting the person predict L if the throw is less than 50 (i.e., one of the 50 outcomes: 1, 2, 3, . . . , 49), which would occur with probability 0.5. The determination of the random event, L or R, could be done similarly, with the outcome being L if the next two throws determine a number that is less than 75. Given the prediction, the event, and the reward, say $.10, you can use the formula in Equation (27.4) to determine the choice probabilities for the next round. This whole process can be repeated for a number of rounds, and then one could start over with a new simulation, which can be thought of as a simulation of the decision pattern of a second person. Simulations of this type are easily done with computers, or even with the random number features of a spreadsheet program. However, if you choose to generate the random numbers, your task is to simulate the process for four rounds, showing the choice probabilities, the actual choice, the event observed, and the reinforcement for each round.

7. Consider a probability matching experiment in which each block of 20 trials is balanced to ensure that one of the events occurs in exactly 15 of the trials. Speculate on how this might change incentives for optimal prediction as the end of a block is approached. Herbert Simon, who later won a Nobel Prize for his work on bounded rationality, once remarked that data from experiments with these block designs suggest that the subjects may be smarter than the experimenters. What do you think he had in mind?

chapter 28

Lottery Choice Anomalies

Choices between lotteries with money payoffs may produce anxiety and other emotional reactions, especially if these choices result in significant monetary gains and losses. Expected utility theory implies that such choices, even the difficult and stressful ones, can be modeled as the maximization of a mathematical function (a sum of products of probabilities and utilities). As would be expected, actual decisions sometimes deviate from these mathematical predictions, and this chapter considers one of the more common anomalies: the Allais paradox. Other biases, such as the misperception of large and small probabilities are also discussed. This chapter's Lottery Choice Anomalies in the Class Experiments section is set up to evaluate the Allais paradox, loss aversion, and other anomalies. There are similar default settings for the Veconlab Pairwise Lottery Choice program, which can be run on the Web.

28.1 Introduction

The predominant approach to the study of individual decision-making in risky situations is based on expected utility, a model that was introduced in Chapter 4. Expected utility calculations are sums of probabilities times (possibly nonlinear) utility functions of the prize amounts. In contrast, the probabilities enter linearly, which precludes overweighting of low probabilities, for example. The nonlinearities in utility permit an explanation of risk aversion. This model, which dates to Bernoulli (1738), received a formal foundation in von Neumann and Morgenstern's (1944) book on game theory, which specified a set of assumptions ("axioms") that imply behavior consistent with the maximization of the expected value of a utility function.

Almost from the beginning, economists were concerned that behavior seemed to contradict some key predictions of this model. The most famous contradiction, the Allais paradox, is presented in the next section. Such anomalies have stimulated a lot of work on developing alternative models of choice under risk. Some aspects of the most commonly mentioned alternative, *prospect theory*, are discussed in the sections that follow.

A reader looking for a resolution of the key modeling issues will be disappointed; some progress has been made, but much of the evidence is mixed. The purpose of this chapter is to introduce the issues, and to help the reader interpret seemingly contradictory results obtained with different procedures. For example, it is not uncommon for the estimates of the environmental benefits of some policy to differ by a factor of 2, which may be attributed to the way the questions were asked and to a "willingness to pay/willingness to accept bias" that was discussed in Chapter 1. A familiarity with this and other biases is crucial for anyone interested in interpreting the results of experimental and survey studies of situations where the outcomes are unknown in advance.

28.2 The Allais Paradox

Consider a choice between a sure 3,000 and a 0.8 chance of winning 4,000. This choice can be thought of as a choice between two "lotteries" that yield random earnings.

A lottery is an economic item that can be owned, given, bought, or sold. People may prefer some lotteries to others, and economists assume that these preferences can be represented by a utility function, i.e., that there is some mathematical function with an expected value that is higher for the lottery selected than for the lottery not selected. This is not an assumption that people actually think about utility or do such calculations, but rather, that choices can be represented by (and are consistent with) rankings provided by the utility function.

The simplest utility function is the expected money value, which would represent the preferences of someone who is risk neutral. An expected payoff comparison would favor Lottery R in Table 28.1, since 0.8(4,000) = 3,200, which is higher than the 3,000 for the safe option. In this situation, Kahneman and Tversky reported that 80 percent of the subjects chose the safe option, which indicates some risk aversion (payoffs, in Israeli pounds, were hypothetical). A person who is not neutral to risk would have preferences represented by a utility function with some curvature. The decision of an expected utility maximizer who prefers the safe option could be represented by Equation (28.1):

$$U(3,000) > 0.8U(4,000) + 0.2U(0), \tag{28.1}$$

where the utility function represents preferences over money income.

Next, consider some simple mathematical operations that can be used to obtain a prediction for how such a person would choose in a different situation. For example, suppose that there is a three-fourths chance that all gains from either lottery will be confiscated, i.e., that is a 0.75 chance of earning $0 and only a 0.25 chance of obtaining the payoffs for the two lotteries in Table 28.1. To analyze this possibility, multiply the probabilities on both sides of Equation (28.1) by 0.25 to get Equation (28.2).

$$0.25U(3,000) > 0.2U(4,000) + 0.05U(0) \tag{28.2}$$

Table 28.1	A Lottery Choice Experiment (Kahneman and Tversky 1979)
Lottery S (Selected by 80%)	**Lottery R** (Selected by 20%)
3,000 with probability 1.0	4,000 with probability 0.8
	0 with probability 0.2

In order to make the probabilities on each side sum to 1, add the $0.75U(0)$ that corresponds to confiscation to both sides of Equation (28.2) to obtain Equation (28.3):

$$0.25U(3,000) + 0.75U(0) > 0.2U(4,000) + 0.8U(0), \tag{28.3}$$

where the direction of the inequality is unchanged by this equal addition to each side. This inequality implies that the same person (who initially preferred Lottery S to Lottery R in Table 28.1) would prefer a one-fourth chance of 3,000 to a one-fifth chance of 4,000. Any reversal of this preference pattern, e.g., preferring the sure 3,000 in the first choice and the 0.2 chance of 4,000 in the second choice would violate expected utility theory. A risk-neutral person, for example, would prefer the lottery with the possibility of winning 4,000 in both cases.

The intuition underlying these predictions can be seen by reexamining Equation (28.3). The left side is the expected utility of a one-fourth chance of 3,000 and a three-fourths chance of 0. Equivalently, we can think of the left side as a one-fourth chance of Lottery S (which gives 3,000) and a three-fourths chance of 0. Although it is not so transparent, the right side of Equation (28.3) can be expressed analogously as a one-fourth chance of Lottery R and a three-fourths chance of 0. To see this, note that Lottery R provides 4,000 with probability 0.8, and one-fourth of 0.8 is 0.2, as indicated on the right side of Equation (28.3). Thus, the implication of the inequality in Equation (28.3) is that a one-fourth chance of Lottery S is preferred to a one-fourth chance of Lottery R. The mathematics of expected utility implies that if you prefer Lottery S to Lottery R as in Equation (28.1), then you prefer a one-fourth chance of Lottery S to a one-fourth chance of Lottery R as in Equation (28.3). The intuition for this prediction is that an "extra" three-fourths chance of 0 is added to *both* sides of the equation in going from Equation (28.2) to Equation (28.3). This extra probability of 0 dilutes the chances of winning in both Lottery S and Lottery R, but this added probability of 0 is a common, and hence, "irrelevant" addition. Indeed, one of the basic axioms used to motivate the use of expected utility is the assumption of "independence with respect to irrelevant alternatives."

As intuitive as the argument in the previous paragraph may sound, a significant fraction of the Kahneman and Tversky subjects violated this prediction. Eighty percent chose Lottery S over Lottery R, but 65 percent chose the diluted version of Lottery R over the diluted version of Lottery S. This behavior is inconsistent with expected utility theory, and is known as an Allais paradox, named after the French economist, Allais (1953), who first proposed these types of paired lottery choice situations. In particular, this is the "common-ratio" version of the Allais paradox, since probabilities of positive payoffs for both lotteries are diluted by a common ratio. Anomalous behavior in Allais paradox situations has also been reported for experiments in which the money prizes were paid in cash (e.g., Starmer and Sugden, 1989, 1991). Battalio, Kagel, and MacDonald (1985) even observed similar choice patterns with rats that could choose between levers that provided food pellets randomly.

28.3 Prospect Theory: Probability Misperception

The Allais paradox results stimulated a large number of studies that were intended to develop alternatives to expected utility theory. The alternatives are typically more complicated to use, and none of them show a clear advantage over expected utility in terms of predictive ability. The possible exception to this conclusion is "prospect theory" proposed by Kahneman and Tversky (1979) and Tversky and Kahneman (1992). Prospect theory is really a collection of elements that specify how a person evaluates a risky prospect in relation to some status quo position for the individual. Roughly speaking, there is a reference point, e.g., current wealth, from which gains and losses are evaluated, and gains are treated differently from losses. People are assumed to be averse to losses, but when making choices where payoffs are all losses, they are thought to be risk seeking. On the other hand, when payoffs are all gains, in general, people are assumed to be risk averse. A final element is a notion that probabilities are not always correctly perceived, i.e., that low probabilities are over-weighted and high probabilities are under-weighted. These elements can be unbundled and evaluated one at a time, and modifications of expected utility theory that include one or more of these elements can be considered, which is the plan for the remainder of this chapter.

The possibility of probability misperception will be suggested by an experiment, reported in Chapter 30, in which people are provided some information and are asked to report the probability that some event has occurred. The incentives in this experiment are set so that subjects should report the truth, e.g., when the true probability is 0.75, they should report 0.75. In a graph with the true probability on the horizontal axis and the reported probability on the vertical axis, a 45-degree line would represent the correct report from which deviations could be observed. As will be seen, data shows a "reverse S" pattern to the deviations (over-weighting of low probabilities and under-weighting of high probabilities), although the biases there are somewhat small. Prospect theory predicts a probability weighting function with this general shape, starting at the origin, rising above the 45-degree line for low probabilities, falling below for high probabilities, and ending up on the 45-degree line in the upper-right corner, as shown in Figure 28.1. The notion that the probability weighting function should cross the 45-degree line at the upper-right corner is based on the intuition that it is difficult to misperceive a probability of one.

To see how prospect theory may explain the Allais paradox, note that Lottery S on the left side of Table 28.1 is a sure thing, so no misperception of probability is possible. The 0.8

Perceived
Probability

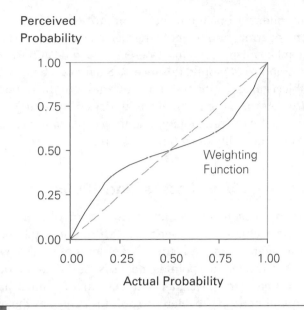

| Figure 28.1 | A Probability Weighting Function (Smooth Line) |

chance of a 4,000 payoff on the right, however, may be affected. Now reconsider Lottery R on the right side of Table 28.1, when the 0.8 probability of 4,000 is treated as if it were lower, say 0.7. This misperception would enhance the attractiveness of Lottery S, so that even a risk neutral person might prefer S if the probability was misperceived in this manner (see Question 2 at the end of the chapter). Next, consider the choice that results when both lotteries are diluted by a three-fourths chance of a 0 payoff. Note that the 0.25 probability of the 3,000 gain on the left side of Equation (28.3) is about the same as the 0.2 probability of the 4,000 on the right. In other words, 0.25 and 0.2 are located close to each other, so that a smooth probability weighting function will overweight them more or less by the same amount. Here a probability weighting function will have little effect, and a risk-neutral person will prefer the diluted version of Lottery R, even though the same person might prefer the undiluted version of Lottery S when the high probability of the 4,000 payoff for lottery R is under-weighted. Put differently, the certain payoff in the original Lottery S is not misperceived, but the 0.8 probability of 4,000 in Lottery R is under-weighted. So probability weighting tends to bias choices toward S. But the diluted S and R lotteries have probabilities in the same range (0.25 and 0.2) so no such bias would be introduced by a "smooth" probability weighting function.

This explanation of the Allais paradox is plausible, but it is not universally accepted. First, the evidence on probability weighting functions is mixed. Note that the reverse S pattern of deviations (raising low probabilities and lowering high probabilities) could also be due to the tendency for random errors in the elicitation process to spread out on the side where there is more room for error. A number of other recent studies have failed to find the reverse S pattern of probability misperceptions (Goeree, Holt, and Palfrey 2002, 2003). Harbaugh, Krause, and Vesterlund (2002) found this reverse S pattern when probabilities were elicited by asking for subjects to assign prices to the lotteries, but the opposite pattern (S-shaped) was observed when the probabilities were elicited by giving people choices between lotteries. As intuitive as the probability weighting explanation for the Allais paradox seems, the evidence on probability weighting itself is mixed.

28.4 Prospect Theory: Gains, Losses, and "Reflection Effects"

A second part of prospect theory pertains to the notion of a reference point from which gains and losses are evaluated. In experiments with money payments, the most obvious candidate for the reference point is the current level of wealth, which includes earnings up to the present. The reference point is the basis for the notion of loss aversion, which implies that losses are given more weight in choices with outcomes that involve both gains and losses. A second property of the reference point is known as the *reflection effect*, which pertains to cases where positive payoffs are multiplied by -1 in a manner that "reflects" them around 0. The reflection effect postulates that the risk aversion exhibited by choices when all outcomes are gains will be transformed into a preference for risk when all outcomes are losses.

A comparison of behavior in the gain and loss domains is difficult in a laboratory experiment for a number of reasons. First, the notion of a reference point is not precisely defined. For example, would "paper" earnings recorded up to the present point (but not actually paid) in cash be factored into the current wealth position? A second problem is that human subjects committees typically do not allow researchers to collect losses from subjects in an experiment, who cannot walk out with less money than they started with. One solution is to give people an initial stake of cash before they face losses, but it is not clear that this process will really change a person's reference point. The notion that an initial stake is treated differently than hard-earned cash is called the "house-money effect." There is some evidence that gifts (e.g., candy) tend to make people more willing to take risks in some contexts and less willing in others (Arkes et al. 1988, Arkes et al. 1994). It is at least possible that the warm glow of a house-money effect may cause people to appear risk seeking for losses when this may not ordinarily be the case with earned cash. One solution is to give people identical stakes before both gain and loss treatments, which holds the house-money effect constant. And making people earn the initial stake through a series of experimental tasks is probably more likely to change the reference point.

Kahneman and Tversky (1979) presented strong experimental evidence for a reflection effect. The design involved taking all gains in a choice pair like those shown in Table 28.1 and reflecting them around 0 to get losses, as shown in Table 28.2. Now the "safe" lottery, S*, involves a sure loss, whereas the risky lottery, R*, may yield a worse loss or no loss at all. The

Table 28.2	A Reflection Effect Experiment (Kahneman and Tversky 1979)

Lottery S* (selected by 8%)	Lottery R* (selected by 92%)
minus 3,000 with probability 1.0	*minus* 4,000 with probability 0.8
	0 with probability 0.2

choice pattern in Table 28.1, with 80 percent safe choices, is reversed in Table 28.2, with only 8 percent safe choices.

The Kahneman and Tversky experiments used hypothetical payoffs, which raises the issue of whether this reflection effect will persist with economic incentives. (Recall from Chapter 4 that risk aversion was strongly affected by the use of high economic incentives, as compared with hypothetical payoffs.) Holt and Laury (2003) evaluate the extent of the hypothetical bias in a reflection experiment. They took a menu of paired lottery choices similar to that shown in Table 4.1 and reflected all payoffs around 0. Recall that this menu has safe lotteries on one side and risky lotteries on the other, and that the probability of the higher payoff number increases as one moves down the menu. Risk aversion is inferred by looking at the number of safe choices relative to the number of safe choices that would be made by a risk-neutral person. All participants made decisions in both the gains menu and in the losses menu, with the order of menu presentation alternated in half of the sessions. In their hypothetical payoff treatment, subjects were paid a fixed amount $45 in exchange for participating in a series of tasks (search, public goods) in a different experiment, and afterward they were asked to indicate their decisions for the lottery choice menus with the understanding that all gains and losses would be hypothetical. When all payoffs were hypothetical gains, about half of the subjects were risk averse, and slightly more than 50 percent of those who showed risk aversion for gains were risk seeking for losses. The modal pattern in this treatment was reflection, although other patterns (e.g., risk aversion for gains and losses) were also observed with some frequency. The choice frequencies for the hypothetical choices are shown in the left panel of Figure 28.2. The modal pattern of reflection is represented by the tall spike in the back-right corner of the left panel.

The real-incentive treatments for gains and losses were run in a parallel manner with the same choice menus. Participants were allowed to build up earnings of about $45 in a different experiment using the same tasks used under the hypothetical treatment. In contrast with earlier results, the most common pattern with real incentives did not involve reflection; but rather it involved risk aversion for both gains and losses. The real-payoff choice frequencies are shown in the right panel of Figure 28.2. The modal pattern of risk aversion in both cases is represented by the spike in the back-left side of this panel. There is a little more risk aversion with real payoffs than with hypothetical payoffs; 60 percent of the subjects exhibit risk aversion in the gain condition, and of these only about one-fifth are risk seeking for losses. The rate of reflection with real payoffs is less than one-half of the reflection rate observed with hypothetical payoffs.

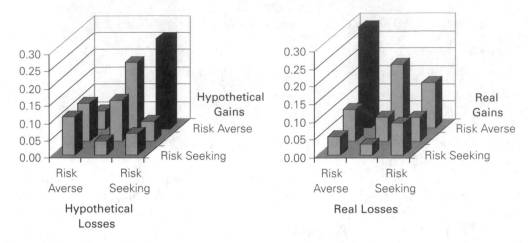

Source: (Holt and Laury 2003)

Figure 28.2   Inferred Risk Aversion for Hypothetical Payoffs (Left) and Real Payoffs (Right)

Despite the absence of a clear reflection effect, there is some evidence that gains and losses are treated differently. On average, people tend to be essentially risk neutral in the loss domain, but they are generally risk averse in the gain domain. This result provides some support for the notion of a reference point, around which gains and losses are evaluated, which suggests that laboratory data should be analyzed using utility as a function of earnings (gains and losses), not final wealth. In other words, if the net worth of a person's assets is w, and if a decision may produce earnings or losses of x, then the analysis of expected utility (with or without the probability weighting of prospect theory) should be expressed in terms of $U(x)$, not $U(w + x)$.

The absence of a clear reflection effect in the Holt and Laury data is a little surprising given the results of several other studies that found reflection with real money incentives (Camerer 1989; Battalio et al. 1990). One difference is that instead of holding initial wealth constant in both treatments (at a level high enough to cover losses), these prior studies provided a high initial stake in the loss treatment, so the final wealth position is constant across treatments. For example, a lottery over gains of 4,000 and 0 could be replaced with an initial payoff of 4,000 and a choice involving losses of 4,000 and 0. Each presentation or "frame" provides the same possible final wealth positions (0 or 4,000), but the framing is in terms of gains in one treatment and in terms of losses in the other. A setup like this is exactly what is needed to document a *framing effect*. Such an effect is present since both studies report a tendency for subjects to be risk averse in the gain frame and risk seeking in the loss frame. Whether these results indicate a reflection effect is less clear, since the higher stake provided in the loss treatment may itself have induced more risk seeking behavior, just as gifts of candy and money tend to increase risk seeking in experiments reported by psychologists.

28.5   Extensions

The dominant method of modeling choice under risk in economics and finance involves expected utility, either applied to gains and losses or to final wealth. The final wealth approach involves a stronger type of rationality in the sense that people can see past gains and losses and focus on the variable that determines consumption opportunities (final wealth). The Camerer (1989) and Battalio et al. (1990) experiments provide strong evidence that decisions are framed in terms of gains and losses, and that people do not integrate gains and losses into a final asset position. Indeed, there is little if any experimental evidence for such asset integration. Rabin (2000) and Rabin and Thaler (2001) also provide a theoretical argument against the use of expected utility as a function of final wealth; the argument being that the risk aversion needed to explain choices involving small amounts of money implies absurd levels of risk aversion for choices involving large amounts of money. Most analyses of risk aversion in laboratory experiments have, in fact, already been done in terms of gains and losses (Binswanger 1980; Kachelmeyer and Shehata 1992; Goeree, Holt, and Palfrey 2002, 2003).

Even if expected utility is modeled in terms of gains and losses, there is the issue of whether to incorporate other elements like nonlinear probability weighting. As noted above, the evidence on this method is mixed, as is the evidence for the reflection effect. Some, like Camerer (1995), have urged economists to give up on expected utility theory in favor of prospect theory and other alternatives. More recently, Rabin and Thaler (2001) have expressed the hope that they have written the final paper that discusses the expected utility hypothesis, referring to it as the "ex-hypothesis," with the same tone that is sometimes used in talking about an ex-spouse. Other economists, like Hey (1995), maintain that the expected utility model outperforms the alternatives, especially when decision errors are explicitly modeled in the process of estimation. In spite of this controversy, expected utility continues to be widely used, either implicitly by assuming risk neutrality or explicitly by modeling risk aversion in terms of either gains and losses or in terms of final wealth.

Some may find the mixed evidence on these issues to be worrisome, but to an experimentalist it provides an exciting area for new research. For example, there is a lot to be done in terms of finding out how people behave in high-stakes situations. One way to run such experiments is to go to countries where using high incentives would not be so expensive. For example, Binswanger (1980) studied the choices of farmers in Bangladesh when the prize amounts sometimes involved more than a month's salary. (He observed considerable risk aversion, which was more pronounced with very high stakes.) Similarly, Kachelmeier and Shehata (1992) performed lottery choice experiments in rural China.

They found that the method of asking the question has a large impact on the way people value lotteries. For example, if you ask for a selling price (the least amount of money you would accept to sell the lottery), people tend to give a high answer, which would seem to indicate a high value for the risky lottery, and hence, a preference for risk. But if you ask them for the most they would be willing to pay for a risky lottery, they tend to give a much lower number, which would seem to indicate risk aversion. The incentive structure was such that the optimal decision was to provide a "true" money value in both treatments (much as the instructions used in the Class Experiments section for Chapter 30 provide an incentive for people to tell the truth about their probabilities in a Bayes' rule experiment).

People seem to go into a bargaining mode when presented with a pricing task, demanding high selling prices and offering low buying prices. The nature of this willing-ness-to-pay/willingness-to-accept bias is not well known, at least beyond the simple bar-gaining mode intuition provided here (Coursey, Hovis, and Schulze 1987). Nevertheless, it is important for policymakers to be aware of the WTP/WTA bias, since studies of non-market goods (like air and water quality) may have estimates of environmental benefits that vary by 100 percent depending on how the question is asked. Given the strong nature of this WTP/WTA bias, it is usually advisable to avoid using pricing tasks to elicit valuations. For more discussion of this topic, see Shogren et al. (1994).

A number of additional biases have been documented in the psychology literature on judgment and decision-making. For example, there may be a tendency for people to be overconfident about their judgments. Some of the systematic types of judgmental errors have been discussed at length in earlier chapters, such as the winner's curse in auctions for prizes of unknown value. For further discussion of these and other anomalies, see Camerer (1995).

QUESTIONS

1. Show that a risk-neutral person would prefer a 0.8 chance of winning 4,000 to a sure payment of 3,000, and that the same person would prefer a 0.2 chance of winning 4,000 to a 0.25 chance of winning 3,000.

2. If the probability of the 4,000 payoff for Lottery R in Table 28.1 is replaced by 0.7, show that a risk-neutral person would prefer Lottery S.

chapter 29

ISO (in Search of . . .)

When you go out to make a purchase, you probably do not check prices at all possible loca-tions. In fact, you might stop searching as soon as you find an acceptable offer, even if you know that a better offer would probably turn up eventually. Such behavior may be optimal if the search process is costly, which makes it worthwhile to compare the costs and benefits of additional searching. The game discussed in this chapter is a search problem, where each additional offer costs a fixed amount of money. Observed behavior in such situations is often surprisingly rational, and the classroom game can be used to introduce a discus-sion of optimal search. As usual, the game can be done using 10-sided die to generate the random offers, following the instructions in this chapter's Search Game in the Class Experi-ments section, or it can be run on the Veconlab software (select Sequential Search from the Decisions menu).

29.1 Introduction

Many economists believed that the rise of e-commerce would lead to dramati-cally lower search costs and a consequent reduction in price levels and dispersion. Evi-dence to date, however, suggests that there is still a fair amount of price variability on the Internet, and most of us can attest to the time cost of searching for low prices.

Issues of search and price dispersion are central to the study of how markets promote efficiency by connecting buyers and sellers. Search is also important on a macroeconomic level, since much of what is called "frictional" unemployment is due to workers searching for an acceptable wage offer. This chapter presents a particularly simple search problem, in which a person pays a constant cost for obtaining each new observation (e.g., a wage offer or price quote). Observations are independent draws from a probability distribution that is known. From a methodological point of view, the search problem is interesting because it is dynamic, i.e., decisions are made in sequence.

29.2   Search from a Uniform Distribution

The setup used here is based on a particular probability framework, the uniform distribution. Many situations of interest involve equal probabilities for the relevant events. For example, consider an airport with continuously circulating buses numbered from 1 to 20, which all pass by a certain central pickup point. If there is no particular pattern, the next bus to pass might be modeled as a uniform random variable. The uniform distribution is easy to explain since all probabilities are equal, and the theoretical properties of models with uniform distributions are often quite simple. Therefore, the uniform distribution is used repeatedly in other parts of this book, for example, in the chapters on auctions.

A uniform distribution is easily generated with a random device, like drawing ping pong balls with different numbers written on them, so that each number is equally likely to be drawn. Besides being easy to explain and implement, the uniform distribution has the useful property that the expected value is the midpoint of the interval. This midpoint property is due to the absence of any asymmetry around the midpoint that would pull expected value in one direction or the other. To see this, consider the simple case of a bingo cage with nine balls labeled 1 to 9. The expected value is $(1/9)(1) + (1/9)(2) + . . . + (1/9) = 45/9 = 5$, which is the midpoint of the interval from 1 to 9.

The search instructions for the experiment discussed in this chapter present subjects with an opportunity to purchase draws from a distribution that is uniform on the interval from 0 to 90 (pennies). This distribution is generated by a computer random number generator for the Veconlab version, and it can be determined by the throws of dice by ignoring all outcomes above 90. Each draw costs $.05, and there is no limit on the number of draws. The subject may decline to search, thereby earning zero. If the first draw is D_1, then stopping at that point would result in earnings of $D_1 - 5$. Suppose that the second draw is D_2. Then the options are: 1) pay another nickel and search again, 2) stop and earn $D_2 - 10$, or if going back is allowed, 3) accept the first draw and earn $D_1 - 10$. We will say that there is "recall" if going back to take any previously rejected draw is permitted; otherwise we say that there is "no recall." Recall may not be possible in some situations, e.g., when going through the personal "in search of" (ISO) ads.

Some typical search sequences for one person are shown in Table 29.1. The round number is in the left column, and the draws are listed in sequence in the middle column, with the accepted draw shown in bold. The search cost was $.05, and the resulting earnings are shown in the right column. This person, who had no prior practice, seems to have stopped as soon as a draw of about $.45 or above was obtained.

The analysis of the optimal way to search is simplified if we assume that the person is risk neutral, which lets us determine a benchmark from which the effects of risk aversion can be evaluated. In addition, assume that the subject faces no cash constraint (wouldn't it be nice) on the number of nickels (well that's not so unreasonable) available to pay the search costs. In this case, the future always looks the same because the horizon is infinite and the payoff parameters (search cost, prize distribution) are fixed over time. Since the

Table 29.1	Individual Search with a $.05 Cost	
Round	**Draw Sequence (cents)**	**Earnings**
1	70	65
2	31, 43, **63**	48
3	21, 8, 43, 43, **51**	26
4	53	48
5	87	82
6	69	64
7	3, 8, 35, **43**	23
8	85	80
9	46	41
10	22, 12, **65**	50

future opportunities are the same regardless of how many draws have been rejected thus far, any draw rejected at one point in time should never be taken at a later point. Thus, each possible draw in the interval from 0 to 90 should either be always accepted or always rejected, and the boundary that separates the acceptable and unacceptable draws is a goal or *reservation value*. The person who made the choices shown in Table 29.1 seems to have a reservation value level of about $.45. It is useful to see a broader sample of how people behave in this situation before further analysis of the optimal manner of search.

29.3   Experimental Data

Figure 29.1 shows the results of a classroom experiment with different search cost treatments. Each search sequence was a series of draws made until the subject stopped and accepted a draw, and there were 10 such search sequences in each treatment. Consider the $.05 search cost treatments, shown on the far left and right sides of the figure, where the draw number is indicated on the horizontal axis. The solid dots indicate accepted draws, and the hollow circles indicate rejected draws. The horizontal lines show the predicted cutoff under risk neutrality (as developed in Section 29.4). There is also a light gray line that connects the empirical cutoffs for each round, with equal numbers of "errors" in each direction (rejections above and acceptances below). The divide between accepted and rejected draws for the $.05 cost treatment is in the $.45 range. In contrast, the dramatic increase in search cost to $.20 results in a much larger acceptance region, as shown in the middle third of the figure. With high search costs, there are fewer searches, and the actual

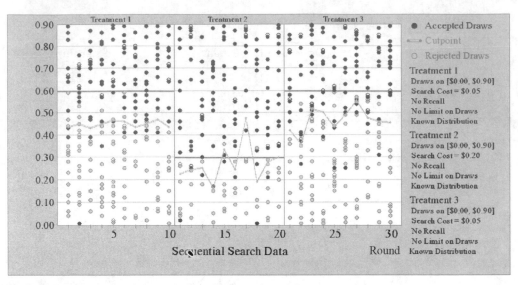

Key: Solid dots are accepted draws, hollow dots are rejected draws

---

Figure 29.1 | A Classroom Sequential Search Experiment with a Cost of $.05 for Rounds 1–10 and 21–30, and a Cost of $.20 for Rounds 11–20

divide between acceptances and rejections is between $.25 and $.30. The next step is to consider whether the observed divides can be explained with simple expected value calculations of benefits and costs.

29.4 Optimal Search

First, consider the low-search-cost treatment. There are 91 possible realizations: 0, 1, 2, . . . , 90. Any amount above 85 cents should be clearly accepted, since the potential gain from searching again is at most $.05 (if a very lucky draw of 90 is obtained) and the cost of the new draw is $.05. Thus, there is only a very low chance (1/91) that the new draw will cover the cost. At the opposite extreme, a low draw, say 0, would be rejected since the cost of another draw is only $.05 and the expected value of the next draw is $.45 (the midpoint of the distribution from 0 to 90). Notice the use of an expected value here, which is justified by the assumption of risk neutrality. To summarize, the benefits of further search exceed the cost when the best current draw is very low, and the cost exceeds the expected benefit when the best current draw is near the top of the range. The optimal reservation prize level is found by locating the point at which the expected benefits of another search are equal to the search cost.

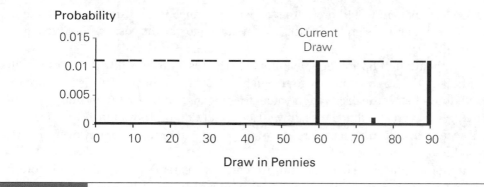

| Figure 29.2 | A Uniform Distribution on the Interval [0, 90] (with One-Third of the Probability to the Right of 60) |

Suppose that the best current draw is 60. There is essentially a 2/3 chance that the next draw is at 60 or below, in which case the net gain is 0. This situation is represented in Figure 29.2, where the horizontal dashed line represents the fact that each of the draws will be observed with the same probability. The area below this line represents probability. For example, two-thirds of the area below the dashed line is to the left of 60, and one-third is to the right of 60. In other words, starting from 60, there is a 1/3 chance of obtaining better draw.

Next, consider the expected gains from search when the best current draw is 60 (with recall and a $.05 search cost). A draw below 60 will not produce any gain, so the expected value of the gain will have a term that is the product: (2/3)0 = 0. The region of gain is to the right of the vertical line at 60 in Figure 29.2, and the area below the dashed line is one-third of the total area. Thus, there is essentially a 1/3 chance of an improvement, which on average will be half of the distance from 60 to 90, i.e., half of 30. The expected value of an improvement, therefore, is $.15. An improvement occurs with a probability about 1/3, so the expected improvement is approximately (1/3)(15) = $.05. Any current draw below 60 will produce an expected improvement from further search that is higher than the $.05 cost, and any current draw above 60 will produce a lower expected improvement. It follows that 60 is the reservation draw level for which the cost of another draw equals the expected improvement. The same reasoning applied to the $.20 search cost treatment implies that the optimal reservation draw is $.30 (see Question 2 at the end of the chapter).

The predicted reservation values of 60 and 30 are graphed as horizontal lines in Figure 29.1. There is a break between the solid dots indicating acceptance and the hollow dots indicating rejection, with little overlap. This break is somewhat below the 30 and 60 levels predicted for a risk-neutral person. Actually, adding risk aversion lowers the predicted cutoff. The intuition behind risk aversion effects is clear. While a risk-neutral person is approximately indifferent between searching again at a cost of $.05 and stopping with a draw of

60, a risk-averse person would prefer to stop with 60, since it is a sure thing. In contrast, drawing again entails the significant risk (2/3) of having to pay the cost without getting any improvement.

One implication of optimal behavior is that the reservation value is essentially the value of having the opportunity to go through this search process. This is because one rejects all draws below the reservation value, thereby indicating that the value of playing the search game is greater than those draws. Conversely, draws above the reservation draw level are accepted, indicating a preference for those sure amounts of money over a continuation of the search process.

To summarize, the value of continuing to search is greater than any number below the reservation value, and it is less than any number above the reservation value, so the value of continuing to search must be equal to the reservation value. This implication was tested by Schotter and Braunstein (1981), who elicited a price at which individuals would be willing to sell the option to search. In one of their treatments, the draws were from a uniform distribution on the interval from 0 to 200 with a search cost of $.05. The optimal reservation value for a risk neutral person is 155 (see Question 3 at the end of the chapter). This should be the value of being able to play the search game, assuming that there is no enjoyment derived from doing an additional search sequence after several have already been completed. The mean reported selling price was 157, and the average accepted draw was 170, which is about halfway between the theoretical reservation value of 155 and the upper bound of 200. These and other results lead to the conclusion that the observed behavior is roughly consistent with the predictions of optimal search theory in this experiment.

29.5   Extensions

The search game discussed here is simple, but it illustrates the main intuition behind the determination of the reservation draw level in a sequential search problem. There are many interesting and realistic variations of this problem. The planning horizon may not be infinite, e.g., when you have a deadline for finding a new apartment before you have to move out of the current one. In this case, the reservation value will tend to fall as the deadline nears and desperation takes over. In the Cox and Oaxaca (1989) experiments with a finite horizon, subjects stopped at the predicted point about three-fourths of the time, and the deviations were in the direction of stopping too soon, which would be consistent with risk aversion.

It is often unreasonable to assume that people know the probability distribution from which draws are being made. The implications of search models for macroeconomics and labor markets are often based on unpredicted changes in the distribution of wage draws. Generally speaking, an upward shift in the distribution should raise acceptance rates and reduce search intensity as draws tend to be above reservation levels that were based on the old draw distribution. This reduction in search might, however, be mitigated by learning.

Suppose, for example, that you think the draws will be in the range from 0 to 100, and you see a draw of 180. This would have been well above your reservation value if the draw distribution had an upper limit of 100, but now you realize that you do not know what the upper limit really is. In this case, a high draw may be rejected in order to find out whether even higher draws are possible (Cox and Oaxaca 2000).

Although the aggregate data from sequential search experiments are roughly consistent with theoretical predictions, this leaves the issue of how people learn to behave in this manner. They do not generally do any mathematical analysis. Hey (1981) has analyzed individual behavior in search of heuristics and adaptive patterns that may explain behavior at the individual level. Also, see Hey (1987), when he is "still searching." He specified a number of rules of thumb, such as:

- **One-Bounce Rule:** Buy at least two draws, and stop if a draw received is less than the previous draw.
- **Modified One-Bounce Rule:** Buy at least two draws, and stop if a draw received is less than the sum of the previous draw and the search cost.

With a search cost of $.05 and initial draws of 80 and 50, for example, the modified one-bounce rule would predict that the person would stop if the third draw turned out to be less than 55. The experiment involved treatments with and without recall, and with and without information about the distribution (a truncated normal distribution) from which draws were drawn. Behavior of some subjects in some rounds corresponded to one or more of these rules, but by far the most common pattern of behavior was to use a reservation draw level. In the fifth and final round, about three-fourths of the participants exhibited behavior that conformed to the optimal reservation-value rule alone.

QUESTIONS

1. The computerized experiments discussed in this chapter were set up so that draws were equally likely to be any amount on the interval from 0 to 90. When throwing 10-sided die with numbers from 0 to 9, the throws will be 0, 1, 2, . . . , 99. In order to truncate this distribution at 90, is it is convenient to ignore the first throw if it is a 9, so that all of the 90 integers from 0 through 89 are equally likely, i.e., each has a probability of 1/90. (This is the approach taken for the hand-run experiment instructions in this chapter's Search Game in the Class Experiments section.) If the current draw is 60, then the chances that the next draw will be as good or better are: a 1/90 chance of a draw of 60, for a gain of 0; a 1/90 chance of a draw of 61 for a gain of 0.01; a 1/90 chance of a draw of 62 for a gain of 2; and so on. Use a spreadsheet to find the expected value of the *gain* over 60 (not the expected value of the draw), and compare this with the search cost of $.05. Would a draw of 60 be rejected? Would a draw of 59 be rejected? *Hint*: make a column of integers from 60 up to 89, and then make a second column of gains over

the current draw (of either 59 or 60). Finally, weight each gain by the probability (1/90) of that draw, and add all of the weighted gains to get the expected gain, which can then be compared with the search cost of $.05.

2. With a search cost of $.20 per draw from a distribution that is uniform from 0 to 90, show that the person is approximately indifferent between searching again and stopping when the current best draw is 30.

3. With a search cost of $.05 for draws from a uniform distribution on the interval from 0 to 200, show that the reservation value is about 155.

4. Evaluate the data in Table 29.1 in terms of the One-Bounce Rule and the Modified One-Bounce Rule. Do these rules work well, and if not, what seems to be going wrong?

5. (Open-ended) Rules of thumb have more appeal in limited-information situations where rational behavior is less likely to be observed. Can you think of other rules of thumb that might be good when the distribution of draws is not known and the person searching has not had time to learn much about it?

6. Schotter and Braunstein (1981) used a willingness-to-pay question to obtain an estimate of 157 for the value of a search sequence in their experiment. What possible bias in the elicited value might be caused by the use of a "willingness-to-pay" elicitation method?

part 8

Information, Learning, and Signaling

I nformation specific to individuals is often unobserved by others. Such information may be conveyed at a cost, but misrepresentation and strategic non-revelation is sometimes a problem. Informational asymmetries yield rich economic models that may have multiple equilibria and unusual patterns of behavior.

Chapter 30 provides a closer look at exactly how new information is used to revise probabilistic beliefs (*Bayes' rule*). Chapter 31 pertains to a sequence of decisions made by different people. Those later in the sequence are able to learn from others' earlier decisions. This raises the possibility of a type of bandwagon effect, which is known as an "information cascade."

Statistical discrimination can arise if the employer uses past correlations between the fixed signal and worker productivity to make job assignment decisions. Biased expectations may be confirmed in equilibrium as workers of one type become discouraged and stop investing. The statistical discrimination model presented in Chapter 32 is implemented by assigning a color (purple or green) to each person in the worker role and then matching them with an employer who must make a job assignment on the basis of imperfect information. This exercise provides an excellent opportunity for informed and non-emotional class discussions of issues like race and gender discrimination.

Chapter 33 introduces the standard signaling game, where the proposer has a privately known attribute or "type." This actual type is not observed by the responder, who can only see a "signal" made by the proposer. For example, an employer may attempt to use an educational credential to infer something about a worker's productivity and energy. There are several different types of behavior that may emerge, depending on whether the signals effectively distinguish the different types of people. Signaling models have been widely applied to other situations in economics, politics, law, finance, and even a "stripped-down" version of poker that is also discussed.

Another topic considered is the ability of asset markets to aggregate diverse information held by partially informed traders to generate accurate predictions. Prediction markets have been used, for example, to predict the outcomes of events that span the range from corporate sales to presidential elections and political events in Iraq. These markets are discussed in the final chapter.

Bayes' Rule

Any careful study of human behavior has to deal with the issue of how people learn from new information. For example, an employer may have beliefs about a prospective employee's value to the firm based on prior experience with those of similar backgrounds. Then new information is provided by a job interview or a test, and the issue is how to combine initial prior beliefs with new information to form final posterior beliefs. This chapter uses simple frequency-based and "ball counting" heuristics from Hammerton (1973), Gigerenzer and Hoffrage (1995) and Anderson and Holt (1996a) to explain Bayes' rule, which is a mathematical formula for forming posterior beliefs. Actual behavior will never be perfectly described by a mathematical formula, and some typical patterns of deviation are discussed. This chapter's Bayes' Rule Class Experiment contains instructions for a game in which the participant sees draws of colored balls from one of two cups and has to form an opinion about which of the two cups is being used. This experiment can also be run with the Veconlab Probability Elicitation Game listed under the Decisions Menu. This Web-based experiment is quicker than hand-run versions, and it provides automatic calculations and a graph of average elicited probabilities as a function of the Bayes' prediction.

30.1 Introduction

Suppose that you have just received a test result indicating that you have a rare disease. The *base rate* or incidence of the disease for those in your socio-economic group is one-tenth of a percent (0.001). Unfortunately, the disease is life threatening, but you have some hope because the test is capable of producing a *false positive* reading. Your doctor tells you that if you do have the disease, the test will come back positive 100 percent of the time, but if you do not have the disease, there is a 1 percent chance of a false positive. The issue is to use this information to determine your chances of having the rare disease, given a positive test result. Please write down a guess here: _____ so that you do not forget.

Confronted with this problem, most people conclude that it is more likely than not that the person actually has the disease, but such a guess would be seriously incorrect. The 1 percent false positive rate means that testing 1,000 randomly selected people will generate about 10 positive results (1 percent), but on average only one person out of 1,000 actually has the disease and receives a true positive result. With 10 false positives and 1 true positive, the chances of having the disease after seeing a positive test result are only about 1/11, *even after you have tested positive with a test that is correct at least 99 times out of 100*. This example illustrates the dramatic effect of prior information about the base rate of some attribute in the population. This example also indicates how one might set up a simple frequency-based counting rule that will provide approximately correct probability calculations:

- Select a hypothetical sample of people (say 1,000).
- Use the base rate to determine how many of those, on average, would have the disease by multiplying the base rate and the sample size (e.g., $0.001 \times 1,000 = 1$).
- Next, calculate the expected number of positive test results that would come from someone who has the disease, i.e., true positives. (In the example, one person has the disease and the test would pick this up, so we have 1 positive from an infected person. If the test does not identify all cases of the disease, then this number would have to be scaled down – see Question 8 at the end of the chapter.)
- Subtract the number of infected people from the sample size to determine the number that are not infected ($1,000 - 1 = 999$).
- Estimate the number of positive test results that would come from people who are not infected. (The false positive rate is 1/100 in the example, so the number of positives from people who are not infected is 999/100, which is 9.99, or approximately 10.)
- Calculate the chances of having the disease given the positive test result by taking the ratio of the number of true positives to the total numbers of positives, i.e., the sum of true positives and false positives. For the example, this ratio is 1/(1 + 10), which is 1/11, or about 9 percent.

Calculations such as those given above are an example of the use of Bayes' rule. This chapter introduces this rule, which is an optimal procedure for using prior information, like a population base rate, together with new information, like a test result. As the incorrect answers to the disease question suggest, peoples' decisions and inferences in such situations may be seriously biased. A related issue is the extent to which people are able to correct for potential biases in market situations where the incentives are high and one is able to learn from past experience. And in some (but not all) situations, those who do not correct for biases lose business to those who do.

When acquiring new information, it is useful to think about the difference between the initial beliefs, the information obtained, and the new beliefs after seeing the information. If the initial (prior) beliefs are very strongly held, then the new (posterior) beliefs are not likely to change very much, unless the information is very good. For example, passing a lie detector test will not eliminate suspicion if the investigator is almost positive that the suspect is guilty. On the other hand, very good information may overwhelm prior beliefs, as would happen with the discovery of DNA evidence that clears a person who has already been convicted. Obviously, the final (posterior) beliefs will depend on the relative quality of the prior information and on the reliability of the test result. Bayes' rule provides a mathematical way of handling diverse sources of information. The Bayesian perspective is useful because it dictates how to evaluate different sources of information, based on their reliability. This perspective may even be valuable when it is undesirable or inappropriate to use some prior information, e.g., in the use of demographic information about crime rates in a jury trial. In such cases, knowing how such prior information would be used (by a Bayesian) may make it easier to guard against a bias derived from such information. Finally, Bayesian calculations provide a benchmark or baseline from which biases can be measured.

In terms of running experiments, there is an issue of how much context to supply. A description based on cups and colored marbles may seem abstract and distant from the kinds of problems that subjects face in their daily lives. But the alternative of supplying familiar context raises other problems. For example, Hammerton (1973) presented subjects with a rare disease example in which the medical test was not perfectly accurate, and subjects overestimated the probability of the disease, which was 0.5 based on the information provided. The assessed probability of the disease fell from about 0.8 to about 0.6 when the problem was presented to a different group of subjects in the context of a possible mechanical defect in a car that was evaluated by an auto mechanic. Here the context seems to have affected the subjects' perceptions of the reliability of the test. In economics, most experimental studies of probability assessment use situations with minimal context, or with an economic context that is designed to be neutral.

30.2   A Simple Example and a Counting Heuristic

The simplest informational problem is deciding which of two possible situations or "states of nature" is relevant, e.g., guilty or innocent, infected or not, defective or not, and so on. To be specific, suppose that there are two cups that contain equally sized Amber (**a**) and Blue (**b**) marbles, as shown in Figure 30.1. Cup A has two Ambers and one Blue, and cup B has one Amber and two Blues. We will use the flip of a fair coin to choose one of these cups. The cup selection is hidden, so your prior information is that each cup is equally likely. Then you are allowed to see several draws of marbles from the selected cup. Each time a draw is made and shown, it is then returned to the cup, so the draws are "with replacement" from a cup with contents that do not change.

Suppose the first draw is Amber and you are asked to report the probability that cup A is being used. An answer of 1/2 is sometimes encountered, since it can be justified by the argument that each cup was equally likely to be selected. But if each cup was equally likely

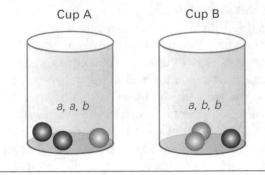

Figure 30.1   A Two-Cup Example

beforehand, what was learned from the draw? Another commonly reported probability for cup A following an Amber draw is 1/3, since this cup has a 1/2 chance of being used, and if used, there is a 2/3 chance of drawing an Amber. Then we multiply 1/2 and 2/3 to get 1/3 (a little math can be dangerous). This 1/3 probability is clearly wrong, since the cups were equally likely ex ante, and the Amber draw is more likely when cup A is used, so the probability of cup A should be greater than 1/2 after seeing an Amber draw. Another problem with this answer is that analogous reasoning requires the probability of cup B to be 1/2 times 1/3, or 1/6. This yields an inconsistency, since if the probability of cup A is 1/3 and the probability of cup B is 1/6, where does the rest of the probability go? These probabilities (1/3 and 1/6) sum to 1/2, so we should double them (to 2/3 and 1/3), which are the correct probabilities for cups A and B after the draw of one Amber marble. This kind of scaling up of probabilities will be seen later as a part of the mathematical formula for Bayes' rule.

A close look at where the Amber marbles are in Figure 30.1 makes it clear why the probability of cup A being used is 2/3 after the draw of an Amber marble. There are two *a* marbles on the left and one on the right. Why does this suggest that the right answer is 2/3? All six marbles are equally likely to be drawn before the die is thrown to select one of the cups. So, no Amber marble is more likely to be chosen than any other, and 2 of the 3 Amber marbles are in cup A. It follows that the posterior probability of cup A given an Amber draw is 2/3. In other words, there are two "true positive" *a* marbles (in the A cup) and one "false positive" *a* marble (in the B cup), so $Pr(A|a) = 2/3$.

The calculations in the previous paragraphs are a special case of Bayes' rule with equal prior probabilities for each cup. Now consider what can be done when the probabilities are not equal. In particular, suppose that the first marble drawn (Amber) is returned to the cup, and the decision-maker is told that a second draw is to be made from the *same* cup originally selected by the throw of the die. Having already seen an Amber, the person's beliefs before the second draw are that the probability of cup A is 2/3 and the probability of cup B is 1/3, so the person thinks that it is twice as likely that cup A is being used after observing one *a* draw.

The next step is to figure out how the previous paragraph's method of counting balls (when the two cups were initially equally likely) can be modified for the new situation where one cup is twice as likely as the other one. In order to create a situation that corresponds to the new beliefs, we want somehow to get twice as many possible draws as coming from the cup that is twice as likely. Even though the physical number of marbles in each cup has not changed, we can represent these beliefs by thinking of cup A as having twice as many marbles as cup B, *with each marble in either cup having the same chance of being drawn*. These posterior beliefs are represented in Figure 30.2, where the proportions of Amber and Blue marbles are the same as they were in cups A and B respectively. Even though the physical number of marbles is unchanged at six, the prior corresponds to a case in which the imagined marbles in Figure 30.2 are numbered from one to nine, with one of the nine marbles chosen randomly.

When the posterior beliefs after an Amber draw are represented in Figure 30.2, it is clear that a Blue on the second draw is equally likely to have come from either cup, since each cup contains two *b* marbles. Thus, the posterior probability for cup A after a Blue on the second draw is 1/2. This is consistent with intuition based on symmetry, since the prior probabilities for each cup were initially 1/2, and the draws of an Amber (first) and a Blue (second) are balanced. A mixed sample in the opposite order (Blue first, then Amber) would, of course, have the same effect.

Suppose instead that the two draws were Amber, with the two cups being equally likely to be used ex ante. As before, the posterior belief after the first Amber draw can be represented by the cups in Figure 30.2. Since four of the five (real or imagined) Amber marbles are in cup A, the posterior probability of cup A after seeing a second Amber draw is 4/5. After two Amber draws, cup A is, therefore, four times as likely as cup B, since 4/5 is four times as large as 1/5. To represent these posterior beliefs in terms of colored marbles that are equally likely to be drawn, we need to have four times as many rows on the cup A side of Figure 30.2 as there are on the cup B side. Thus, we would need to add two more imagined

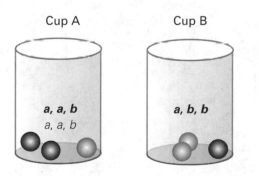

Cup A   Cup B

a, a, b
a, a, b

a, b, b

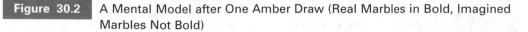

Figure 30.2   A Mental Model after One Amber Draw (Real Marbles in Bold, Imagined Marbles Not Bold)

rows of three marbles under cup A in Figure 30.2, holding the proportions of Amber and Blue marbles fixed. Doing this would provide the representation in Figure 30.3. To test your understanding, you might consider the probability of cup A after seeing two Ambers and a Blue (see Question 1 at the end of the chapter). Up to this point, the analysis has been intuitive, but it is now time to be a little more analytical.

30.3 Relating the Counting Heuristic to Bayes' Rule

To make the connection with Bayes' rule, we will need a little notation. Suppose there are N marbles in each cup. The marbles will be Amber or Blue, and we will use the letter C to represent a specific color, so C can be either Amber or Blue. What we want to know is the probability of cup A given the draw of a marble of color C. When C is Amber and the contents are shown in Table 30.1, we already know the answer (2/3), but our goal here is to find a general formula for the probability of cup A given a draw of a color C marble. This probability is denoted by Pr(A|C), which reads "the probability of A given C." This formula should be general enough to allow for different proportions of colored marbles, and for differences in the prior probability of each cup.

Consider Pr(C|A), which reverses the order of the A and the C from the order used in the previous paragraph. Note that Pr(C|A) is read as "the probability of color C given cup A." Thus, Pr(C|A) denotes the fraction of marbles in cup A that are of color C, where C is either Amber or Blue. Similarly, P(C|B) is the fraction of marbles in cup B that are of color C. For example, if there are 10 marbles in cup A and if Pr(C|A) = 0.6, then there must be six marbles of color C in the cup (calculated as 0.6 times 10). In general, there are a total of P(C|A)N marbles of color C in cup A, and there are P(C|B)N marbles of color C in cup B. If each cup is equally likely to be selected, then each of the 2N marbles in the two cups is equally likely to be drawn ex ante (before the cup is selected). Suppose the marble drawn is of color C. The posterior probability that a marble of color C was drawn from cup A, denoted Pr(A|C),

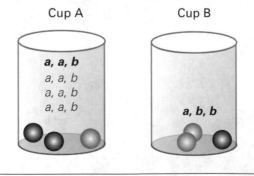

Figure 30.3   A Mental Model of the Situation after Two Amber Draws

is just the ratio of the number of color C marbles in cup A to the total number of marbles of this color in both cups, as shown in Equation (30.1):

$$\Pr(A|C) = \frac{\text{Number of color C marbles in cup A}}{\text{Number of color C marbles in both cups}}, \tag{30.1}$$

which can be expressed as shown in Equation (30.2).

$$\Pr(A|C) = \frac{\Pr(C|A)N}{\Pr(C|A)N + \Pr(C|B)N} \tag{30.2}$$

You can think of the numerator of Equation (30.2) as the number of true positives, and the sum in the denominator as being the total number of positives, true and false. It is worth emphasizing that this formula is only valid for the case of equal prior probabilities and equal numbers of marbles in each cup. Nothing is changed if we divide both numerator and denominator of the right side on Equation (30.2) by $2N$, which is the total number of balls in both cups. This division yields a formula shown in Equation (30.3) for calculating the posterior when the priors are $1/2$.

$$\Pr(A|C) = \frac{\Pr(C|A)(1/2)}{\Pr(C|A)(1/2) + \Pr(C|B)(1/2)} \quad \text{(For priors of } 1/2) \tag{30.3}$$

A person who has seen one or more draws may not have prior probabilities of $1/2$, so this formula must be generalized. This involves replacing the $(1/2)$ terms on the right side with the new prior probabilities, denoted $\Pr(A)$ and $\Pr(B)$. This is Bayes' rule, as shown in Equation (30.4).

$$\Pr(A|C) = \frac{\Pr(C|A)\,\Pr(A)}{\Pr(C|A)\,\Pr(A) + \Pr(C|B)\,\Pr(B)} \quad \text{(Bayes' rule)} \tag{30.4}$$

For the previous example with equal priors, $\Pr(A) = 1/2$, $\Pr(a|A) = 2/3$, and $\Pr(a|B) = 1/3$, so Equation (30.4) implies that the posterior probability following an Amber draw is as follows:

$$\Pr(A|a) = \frac{\dfrac{2}{3}\dfrac{1}{2}}{\dfrac{2}{3}\dfrac{1}{2} + \dfrac{1}{3}\dfrac{1}{2}} = \frac{\dfrac{1}{3}}{\dfrac{1}{2}} = \frac{2}{3}$$

Similarly, the probability of cup B is calculated: $\Pr(B|a) = (1/6)/(2/6 + 1/6) = 1/3$. Notice that the denominators in both of the previous calculations are $1/2$, so dividing by $1/2$ scales up the numerator by a factor of 2, which makes the probabilities add up to one.

To summarize, if there is a prior probability of $1/2$ that each cup is used and if the cups contain equal numbers of colored marbles, then the posterior probabilities can be calculated as ratios of numbers of marbles of the color drawn, as in Equation (30.1). If the marble drawn is of color C, then the posterior that the draw was from cup A is the number of color C marbles in cup A divided by the total number of color C marbles in both cups. When the prior probabilities or numbers of marbles in the cups are unequal, then the 1/2 terms in Equation (30.3) are replaced by the prior probabilities, as in Bayes' rule, as shown in Equation (30.4).

30.4   Experimental Results

Nobody would expect that something so noisy as the formation of beliefs would adhere strictly to a mathematical formula, and experiments have been directed toward finding the nature of systematic biases. The disease example mentioned earlier suggests that, in some contexts, people may underweight prior information based on population base rates.

This *base rate bias* was the motivation behind some experiments reported by Kahneman and Tversky (1973), who gave subjects lists of brief descriptions of people who were either lawyers or engineers. The subjects were told that the descriptions had been selected at random from a sample that contained 70 percent lawyers and 30 percent engineers. Subjects were asked to report the chances out of 100 that the description pertained to a lawyer. A second group was given some of the same descriptions, but with the information that the descriptions had been selected from a sample that contained 30 percent lawyers and 70 percent engineers. Respondents had no trouble with descriptions that obviously described one occupation or another, but some were intentionally neutral with phrases like "he is highly motivated" or "will be successful in his career." The modal response for such neutral descriptions involved probabilities of near one-half, regardless of the respondent's treatment group. This behavior is insensitive to the prior information about the proportions of each occupation, a type of base rate bias.

Grether (1980) pointed out several potential procedural problems with the Kahneman and Tversky experiment. There was deception to the extent that the descriptions had been made up, and even if people bought into the context, they would have no incentive to think about the problem carefully. Moreover, the information conveyed in the descriptions is hard to evaluate in terms of factors that comprise Bayes' rule formula. In other words, it is hard to determine an appropriate guess about the probability of a particular description conditional on the occupation. Grether based his experiments on cups with two types of balls as described. One of the biases that he considered is known as *representativeness bias*. In the two cup example discussed earlier, a sample of three draws that yields two Ambers and one Blue has the same proportions as cup A, and in this sense the sample looks representative of cup A. We saw that the probability of cup A after such a sample would be 2/3, and a person who reports a higher probability, say 80 percent, may be doing so due to representativeness bias.

Notice that a sample of two Ambers and one Blue makes cup A more likely. If you ask someone which cup is more likely, an answer of A cannot distinguish between Bayesian behavior and a strong representativeness bias, which also favors cup A. Grether cleverly got around this problem by introducing some asymmetries which make it possible for representativeness to indicate a cup that is less likely given Bayes' rule. In this manner, a sample of two Ambers and one Blue would look like the contents of cup A, but if the prior probability of A is small enough, the Bayesian probability of cup A would be less than one-half. In this manner, representativeness and Bayes' rule would have different predictions when a person is asked which cup is more likely.

A binary choice question about which cup is more likely makes it easy to provide incentives: simply offer a cash prize if the cup actually used turns out to be the one the person said is more likely. This is the procedure that Grether used, with a $15 prize for a correct prediction and a $5 prize otherwise. When representativeness and Bayesian calculations indicated the same answer, subjects tended to give the correct answer about 80 percent of the time (with some variation depending on the specific sample). This percentage fell to about 60 percent when representativeness and Bayes' rule suggested different answers.

30.5 Bayes' Rule with Elicited Probabilities

Sometimes it is useful to ask subjects to report a probability, instead of just saying which event is more likely. This can be phrased as a question about the "chances out of 100 that the cup used is A." The issue here is how to provide incentives for people to think carefully. The instructions in this chapter's Bayes' Rule Class Experiment provide one approach, which is complicated, but which is based on a simple idea. Suppose that you send your friends to purchase some fruit, and they ask you whether you prefer red or yellow tomatoes in case both are available. You would have no incentive to lie about your preference, since telling the truth allows your friends to make the best decision on your behalf. This chapter's Bayes' Rule Class Experiment describes a method of eliciting probabilities that is based on this intuition. Probability elicitation is useful when we need specific probability numbers to evaluate theoretical predictions, as opposed to the qualitative data obtained by asking which event is more likely. The disadvantage is that the elicitation process itself is not perfect in the sense that the measurements may contain more noise or measurement error than we get with binary comparisons.

Table 30.1 shows some elicited probabilities for a research experiment conducted with University of Virginia subjects, and prize amounts of $1 instead of $1,000. All earnings were paid in cash. The two cups, A and B, each contained three marbles with the contents as shown in Table 30.1. The experiment consisted of three parts. The first part was done largely to acquaint people with the complicated procedures. Then there were 10 rounds with asymmetric probabilities (a two-thirds chance of using cup A) and 10 rounds with symmetric probabilities (a one-half chance of using cup A). The order of the symmetric and asymmetric treatments was reversed with different groups of people.

The information and decisions for subjects 1 and 2 are shown in the table, for rounds 21–27 where the prior probability was 1/2 for each cup. First, consider subject 1 on the left.

Table 30.1	Elicited Probabilities for Two Subjects in a Bayes' Rule Experiment

| | Cup A: *a, a, b* | | | Cup B: *a, b, b* | |
| | Subject 1 | | | Subject 2 | |
Round	Draw (Bayes)	Elicited Probability	Round	Draw	Elicited Probability
21	None (0.50)	0.49	21	None (0.50)	0.50
22	*a* (0.67)	0.65	22	*b* (0.33)	0.30
23	*bb* (0.20)	0.18	23	*ba* (0.50)	0.60
24	*bab* (0.33)	**0.25**	24	*aba* (0.67)	0.70
25	*a* (0.67)	0.65	25	*a* (0.67)	0.65
26	*ab* (0.50)	0.49	26	*ab* (0.50)	0.30
27	*bba* (0.33)	0.33	27	*aab* (0.67)	**0.80**

In round 21, there were no draws, and the None (0.50) in the Draw column indicates that the correct Bayesian probability of cup A is 0.50. The subject's response in the Elicited Probability column was 0.49, as is also the case for this person in round 26 where the draws, AB, cancelled each other out. The other predictions can be derived using the counting heuristic or with Bayes' rule, as described above. In round 22, for example, there was only one draw, *a*, and the Bayesian probability of cup A is 0.67, since two of the three *a* balls from both cups are located in cup A. Subject 1 reported a probability 0.65, which is quite accurate. This person was unusually accurate, with the largest deviation from the theoretical prediction being in round 24, where the reported probability is a little too low, 0.25 versus 0.33.

Subject 2 was considerably less predictable. The *ab* and *ba* samples, which leave each cup being equally likely, resulted in answers of 0.60 and 0.30. The average of these answers is not far off, but the dispersion is atypically large for such an easy inference task, as compared with others in the sample. This person was fairly accurate with single draws of *b* (round 22) and of *a* (round 25), but the three-draw samples show behavior that is consistent with representativeness bias. In round 27, for example, the sample of *aab* looks like cup A, and the elicited probability of 0.80 for cup A is much higher than the actual probability of 0.67. Subject 1 also seems to fall prey to this bias in round 24, where the sample, *bab*, looks like cup B.

Figure 30.4 shows some aggregate results for the symmetric and asymmetric treatments, for all 22 subjects in the study. The horizontal axis plots the Bayesian probability of cup A, which varies from 0.05 for a sample of *bbbb* in the symmetric treatment (with equal priors) to 0.97 for a sample of *aaaa* in the asymmetric treatment (where the prior probability of cup A was 2/3). The elicited probabilities are shown in the vertical dimension. The 45-

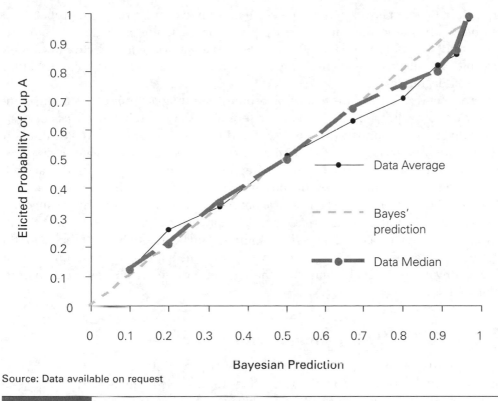

Source: Data available on request

Figure 30.4 Elicited Probabilities versus Bayes' Predictions

degree dotted line shows the Bayes' prediction, the solid line connects the average of the elicited probabilities, and the dashed line connects the medians.

In the aggregate, Bayes' rule does quite well. A slight upward bias on the left side of the figure and a slight downward bias on the right side might possibly be due to the fact that there is more room for random error in the upward direction on the left and in the downward direction on the right. This conjecture is motivated by the observation that the medians (thick dashed line) are generally closer to Bayesian predictions. For example, one person got confused and reported a probability of 0.01 for cup A after observing draws of *aa* in the symmetric treatment, which should lead to a posterior of 0.8. (The draws were of light and dark marbles, and were coded on the decision sheet as LL.) On the right side of the figure, there is more room for extreme errors in the downward direction. To see this, consider a vertical line above the point 0.8 on the horizontal axis of Figure 30.4. If you imagine some people with no clue who put marks more or less equally spaced on this vertical line, more of the marks will be below the 45-degree dashed line, since there is more room below. Random errors of this type will tend to pull average reported probabilities down below the 45-degree line on the right side of the figure, and the reverse effect (upward bias) would occur on the left side. Averages are much more sensitive to extreme errors than are medians, which may explain why the averages show more of a deviation from the 45-degree dashed line.

The averages graphed in the figure mask some interesting patterns of deviation. In the symmetric treatment, for example, there are several posterior probability levels that can result from different numbers of draws. A posterior of 0.67 can be achieved by draws of either *a* or *aab*. The average posterior for the *a* draw alone is 0.61, which a little too low relative to the Bayes' prediction of 0.67, and the "representativeness" pattern of *aab* is actually closer to the mark at 0.66. Similarly, the posterior of 0.33 can be reached by draw patterns of *b* or *bba*. The *b* pattern yielded an average of 0.42, whereas the *bba* pattern resulted in a lower average of 0.31. Representativeness would imply that the elicited probability should be lower than what is observed for the *bba* sample and higher than what is observed for the *aab* sample. It may be after several draws, some people are ignoring the prior information and reporting a probability that matches the sample average, which would be a natural type of heuristic.

30.6 A Follow-Up Experiment with a Rare Event

The data from the previous section involved prior probabilities in the 0.33 to 0.66 range, and in the aggregate, Bayes' rule provides reasonable predictions when subjects have a chance to make decisions and learn. This raises the issue of how subjects do when the prior probability of the event is low, as was the case for the rare disease example at the beginning of the chapter. For this test, a prior rate of 0.04 for the red cup was used, and the red cup only contained Red marbles. At this rate, in 100 trials there should be 4 Reds (true positives), and 96 times the Blue cup was used. In order to obtain a posterior of only 0.1 (as with the initial disease example), there would have to be 36 false positives from the 96 times the Blue cup was used, or a 36/96 = 3/8 false positive rate. Thus, the probability of a Red draw given the Blue cup was set to 3/8.

The payoffs and procedures were similar to those used in the hand-run experiments reported in Section 30.5, except that the computer permitted running more rounds, and the prior probability was maintained at the same level in all three sets of 20 decisions, to avoid sequence effects. Also, prize amounts were doubled to $2. As before, subjects saw either no draws, 1 draw, 2 draws, 3 draws, or 4 draws (with replacement) prior to reporting the chances of 100 that the Red cup is being used. The elicitation procedure (described in this chapter's Truthful Elicitation Appendix) was implemented with the Veconlab Bayes program, listed under the Decisions menu.

The posterior probability of the Red cup varies from 0 (if a Blue draw is ever observed) to 0.1 (one red draw), up to 0.68 (four red draws in a row). Figure 30.5 shows the means and

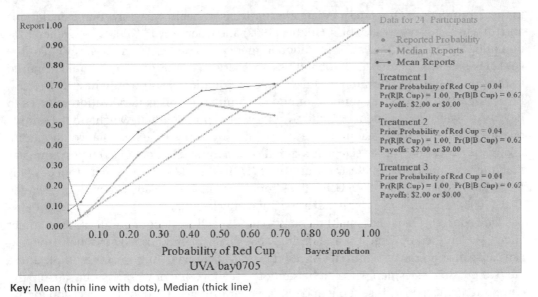

Key: Mean (thin line with dots), Median (thick line)

Source: Data available on request

Figure 30.5   Elicited Probabilities and Bayes' Predictions for a Low Probability Event

medians of all decisions made by the 24 subjects (60 decisions each). There is an upward bias, especially for the mean (thin line with connected dots), but the overall picture is surprisingly accurate. For example, consider the case of one red draw, which induces a posterior of 0.1 for red (as with the disease example at the start of the chapter, where the disease was rarer and the test was more accurate than the treatment used here). Looking vertically up from the 0.1 point on the horizontal axis of the graph, we see that the mean report was below 0.3 and the median was just slightly above the Bayes' prediction of 0.1.

30.7   Extensions

It is well known that elicited beliefs may deviate dramatically from Bayes' rule predictions, especially in extreme cases like the disease example discussed in Section 30.1. Instruction in the mathematics of conditional probability calculations may not help much, and such skills are probably quickly forgotten. On the other hand, the presentation of the problem in terms of frequencies and the use of counting heuristics help people make good probability assessments in new situations (Hoffrage and Gigerenzer 1998).

From a modeling perspective, the main issue is where to begin, i.e., whether to throw out Bayes' rule and begin fresh with something that has a more behavioral and less mathematical foundation. One intermediate alternative is to begin with Bayesian calculations and then to assess patterns of bias. Grether (1992) and Goeree et al. (2003) use a generalization of Bayes' rule that raises the conditional signal probabilities to a power, say β. For the case of two events, A and B, the probabilities of observing a draw of color C would be raised to the power, β, so the formula for Bayes' rule in Equation (30.4) would have the terms, $Pr(C|A)^\beta$ and $Pr(C|B)^\beta$ in the numerator and denominator. This generalization reduces to Bayes' rule when β = 1. When β < 1, this formula would put too much weight on the sample relative to the prior information. For example, if β = 1/2, then the formula would require taking the square root of the signal probabilities, and the square root of a fraction is greater than the fraction itself. (To illustrate, note that (1/2)(1/2) = 1/4, so the square root of 1/4 is 1/2, which is greater than 1/4.) Using data from information cascade experiments, Goeree et al. (2003) estimate values for β that are significantly less than 1.

One source of bias that might be hard to model is the effect of emotion. This "affect effect" is identified by Charness and Levin (2005) as a "win-stay, lose-switch" heuristic that can cause the optimal choice under Bayes' rule to "feel wrong." Suppose, for example, there are two possible salesmen who can be sent out on a job, one of whom is unavailable the current week. The other is sent out and his sales performance is good. The decision for the second week is whether to send the first salesman back out ("win-stay") or to switch. The reason that the win-stay approach is not necessarily the best is that the good performance of the first salesman could be due to good market conditions, and it may be the case that the other salesman has the experience to garner high sales under such good conditions. In this situation, the optimal decision could be to switch even though the first salesman was successful. The experiment design generated cases where the best decision was to switch after a good outcome and to stay with the initial decision after a bad outcome (see Question 9 at the end of the chapter). Roughly speaking, about half of the subjects' decisions were inconsistent with this optimal decision, with deviations being in the direction of what is implied by the win-stay, lose-switch heuristic. For other documented violations of Bayes' rule, see Zizzo et al. (2000) and Ouwersloot, Nijkam, and Rietveld (1998).

Although there are systematic deviations from the predictions of Bayes' rule, there is no widely accepted alternative model of how information is actually processed in a wide array of situations. Presently, economists tend to use Bayes' rule or parameterized generalizations to derive predictions, although there is some renewed interest in non-Bayesian models like that of reinforcement learning discussed in Chapter 27.

Appendix: **Truthful Elicitation**

Suppose that you have seen some draws (say Amber and Blue) and have concluded that the probability of cup A is 0.5. If you are promised a $1,000 payment if cup A is really used, then you essentially have a cup A lottery that pays $1,000 with probability one-half. The idea is to ask someone for the probability (in chances out of 100) that cup A is used, and to give them the incentive to tell the truth. This incentive will be provided by having the person running the experiment make a choice for the subject. In this context, the experimenter is like the friend going to the fruit stand; the subject needs to tell the truth about their preferences so that the experimenter will make the best choice on the subject's behalf. In order to set up the right incentives to tell the truth, we will have the experimenter choose between that cup A lottery and another one that is constructed randomly, by using throws of 10-sided die to get a number, N, between 0 and 100, in a manner which ensures that this die lottery pays \$1,000 with chances N out of 100. If the probability of cup A is 1/2, then this die lottery is preferred if $N > 50$, and the cup A lottery is preferred if $N < 50$. The subject should answer that the chances of cup A are 50 out of 100 so that the experimenter can make the right choice. This is really like the red and yellow tomato example previously discussed—the experimenter is choosing between two lotteries on the subject's behalf, and therefore needs to know the subject's true value of the cup A lottery to make the right decision.

To convince yourself that the subject is motivated to tell the truth in this situation, consider what might happen otherwise. Suppose that the subject incorrectly reports that the chances of cup A are 75 out of 100, when the person really believes that each cup is equally likely. Thus, the cup A lottery provides a one half chance of \$1,000. If the experimenter then throws a 7 and a 0, then $N = 70$, and the die lottery would yield a 70 percent chance of \$1,000, which is a much better prospect than the fifty-fifty chance based on the subject's (true) beliefs that each cup is equally likely. But since the subject incorrectly reported the chances for cup A to be 75 out of 100, the experimenter would reject the die lottery and base the subject's earnings on the cup A lottery, which gives a 20 percent lower chance of winning. A symmetric argument can be made for why it is bad to report that the chances of cup A are less than would be indicated by the subjects' true beliefs (see Question 3 at the end of the chapter). For a mathematical derivation of the result that it is optimal to reveal one's true probability, see Question 6 at the end of the chapter.

QUESTIONS

1. What would the mental model with imagined balls in Figure 30.3 look like after seeing two Amber draws and one Blue draw? What does this model imply that the posterior probability for cup A would be?

2. Answer Question 1 for a sample of three Amber draws, and check your answer using Bayes' rule. (*Hint*: the probability of getting three Amber draws from cup A is $(2/3)(2/3)(2/3) = 8/27$. You will also need to calculate the probability of getting three Amber draws from cup B.)

3. Suppose we are using the elicitation scheme described in this chapter's Truthful Elicitation Appendix, and that the subject believes that cups A and B are equally likely.

Show why it would be bad for the person to report that the chances for cup A are 25 out of 100.

4. In the asymmetric treatment discussed in Section 30.5, the prior probability of cup A is 2/3. Use the ball counting heuristic to calculate the probability of cup A after seeing a sample of *b*. What is the probability of cup A after a sample of *aaaa*?

5. Twenty-one University of Virginia students in an undergraduate Experimental Economics course participated in the Bayes' rule elicitation experiment, using the instructions for this chapter's Bayes' Rule Class Experiment, but with only seven rounds. The experiment lasted for about 20 minutes, and cash payments amounted to about $3–$4 per person, with all payments made in cash, despite the fact that this was a classroom experiment. Each cup was equally likely to be used. Participants claimed that they had time to do mathematical calculations. The draw sequences and the average elicited probabilities are shown in the table below.

   a. Calculate the Bayes' posterior for each case, and write it in the relevant box.

   b. How would you summarize the deviations from Bayesian predictions? Is there evidence for the representativeness bias in this context? Discuss briefly.

Mean and Median Elicited Probabilities for Cup A

Cup A = {L, L, D}   Cup B = {L, D, D}

Draw:	No Draws	L	D	DD	LD	LDD	DDD
Mean	0.5	0.68	0.33	0.24	0.47	0.28	0.13
Median	0.5	0.67	0.33	0.2	0.50	0.30	0.11
Bayes'							

6. (Advanced and tedious) The incentives for the method of eliciting probabilities discussed in this chapter's Truthful Elicitation Appendix can be evaluated with calculus. Let P denote the person's true probability of cup A, i.e., the probability that represents their beliefs after seeing the draws of colored marbles. Let R denote the reported probability. (To simplify notation, both R and P are fractions between 0 and 1, not numbers between 0 and 100 as required for the "chances out of 100" discussion in the text.)

   a. Explain why the following statement is true for the elicitation mechanism discussed in the appendix: "If the person reports R, then there is an R probability of ending up with the cup A lottery, which pays $1 with probability P."

   b. Explain why the following statement is true: "Similarly, there is a $1-R$ probability of ending up with the die lottery, which pays $1 with a probability $N/100$, where N is the outcome of the throw of the ten-sided die twice."

   c. We know that $N/100$ is greater than R, since the die lottery is only relevant if its probability of paying $1 is greater than the reported probability of cup A. Use these observations to express the expected payoff as $1/2 + PR - R^2/2$.

d. Then show that this quadratic expression is maximized when $R = P$, i.e., when the reported probability equals the probability that represents the person's beliefs. (*Hint*: Since the die lottery is only relevant if $N/100 > R$ and $N/100 < 1$, this die lottery has an expected value that is halfway between R and 1, i.e., $(1 + R)/2$.)

Comment: Probability elicitation methods of this type are sometimes called "scoring rules." The particular method being discussed is a "quadratic scoring rule" since the function being maximized, $1/2 + PR - R^2/2$, is quadratic.

7. (Fun for a change—this question was provided by Professor Brent Kreider.) Suppose that a cook produces three pancakes, one with one burnt side, one with two burnt sides, and one with no burnt sides. The cook throws a six-sided die and chooses the pancake at random, with each one having equal probability of the one being served. Then the cook flips the pancake high so that each side is equally likely to be the one that shows. All you know (besides the way the pancake was selected) is that the one on your plate is showing a burnt side on top. What is the probability that you have the pancake with only one burnt side? Explain with Bayes' rule or with the counting heuristic.

8. A 40-year old woman undergoes a routine screening for breast cancer, and the test comes back positive. The rate of previously undiagnosed breast cancer for a woman in this category is 0.01, or about 1 percent. The test is fairly accurate in the sense that if she has cancer, it will produce a positive result 80 percent of the time. For a woman who does not have cancer, the test will produce a positive result only 10 percent of the time. What is the probability that the patient actually has cancer? (In one study, 95 percent of physicians in Germany gave answers to this question that were not close to being correct, and the typical answer was off the mark by a factor of 10.)

9. Consider a decision-maker who has two decisions to make: one Moderate and one Extreme. The best decision depends on the unknown state of the world, which is equally likely to be "Good" or "Bad." Think of the particular combination of state and decision as a cup with six balls, marked H for high payoff or L for low payoff, as shown in the table below. For any given cup, one ball is drawn at random to determine the payoff. For example, if the Moderate decision is taken and the state is Good, then the chances are 4 out of 6 of getting a high payoff. Suppose that you are forced to choose Moderate and the outcome is H in the first round, and there is a second (and final) round in which the state will stay the same as in the first round. What is the probability that the state is Good? Is it best to stay with Moderate or switch to Extreme after getting the high payoff, H, in the first round? Explain using Bayes' rule.

	Good State (1/2)	Bad State (1/2)
Extreme Decision	H H H H H H	L L L L L L
Moderate Decision	H H H H L L	H H L L L L

chapter 31

Information Cascades

Suppose that individuals receive different information about some unknown event, like whether or not a newly patented drug will be effective. This information is then used in making a decision, like whether or not to invest in the company that developed the new drug. If decisions are made in sequence, then the second and subsequent decision-makers can observe and learn from earlier decisions. The *informational dilemma* occurs when one's private information suggests a decision that is different from what others have done before. An *information cascade* forms when people follow the consensus decision regardless of their own private information. This game could be implemented with draws from cups and throws of dice, as described in Anderson and Holt (1996b). Alternatively, the Veconlab Information Cascade Game is quite easy to administer.

31.1 "To Do Exactly as Your Neighbors Do Is the Only Sensible Rule."

Conformity is a common occurrence in social situations, as the section title implies (Emily Post 1927). People may follow others' decisions because they value conformity and fear social sanctions. For example, an economic forecaster may prefer the risk of being wrong along with others to the risk of having a deviant forecast that turns out to be inaccurate. Conversely, Keynes (1936) remarked: "Worldly wisdom teaches that it is better for reputation to fail conventionally than to succeed unconventionally."

People may be tempted to follow others' decisions because of the belief that there is some wisdom or experience implicit in an established pattern. The possible effects of collective wisdom may be amplified in a large group. For example, someone may prefer to buy a Honda or Toyota sedan thinking that the large market shares for those models signal significant customer satisfaction. This raises the possibility that a choice pattern started by a few individuals may set a precedent that results in a string of incorrect decisions. At any given moment, for example, there are certain classes of stocks that are considered good investments, and herd effects can be amplified by efforts of some to anticipate where the next fads will lead. Anyone who purchased tech stocks in the late 1990s can attest to the dangers of following the bulls.

A particularly interesting type of bandwagon effect can develop when individuals make decisions in a sequence and can observe others' prior decisions. For example, suppose that a person is applying for a job in an industry with a few employers who know each other well. If the applicant makes a bad impression in the first couple of interviews and is not hired, then the third employer who is approached may hesitate even if the applicant makes a good impression on the third try. This employer may reason: "Anyone may have an off day, but I wonder what the other two employers saw that I missed." If the joint information implied by the two previous decisions is deemed to be more informative than one's own information, it may be rational to follow the pattern set by others decisions, in spite of contradictory evidence. A chain reaction started in this manner may take on a life of its own as subsequent employers hesitate even more. This is why first impressions can be important in the workplace. The effect of information inferred from a sequential pattern of conforming decisions is referred to as an "information cascade" (Bikhchandani, Hirschleifer, and Welch 1992).

Since first impressions can be wrong, the interviews or tests that determine initial decisions may start an incorrect cascade that implies false information to those who follow. As John Dryden quipped: "Nor is the people's judgment always true, the most may err as grossly as the few." This chapter considers how cascades, incorrect or otherwise, may form even if individuals are good Bayesians in the way that they process information.

31.2   A Model of Rational Learning from Others' Decisions

The discussion of cascades will be based on a very stylized model in which the two events are referred to as cup A with contents a, a, b, and cup B with contents a, b, b. Think of these cups as containing Amber or Blue marbles, with the proportions being correlated with the cup label. Each cup is equally likely to be selected, with its contents then being emptied into an opaque container from which draws are made privately. Each person sees one randomly drawn marble from the selected cup, and then must guess which cup is being used. Decisions are made in a pre-specified sequence, so that the first person has nothing to go on but the color of the marble drawn. Draws are made with replacement, so the second person sees a draw from the unknown cup, and must make a decision based on two things: the first decision and the second (own) draw. Like the employers who cannot sit in on others' interviews, each person can see prior decisions but not the private information that may have affected those decisions. There is no external incentive to conform in the sense that one's payoff depends only on guessing the cup being used; there is no benefit in conforming to others' (prior or subsequent) decisions.

The first person in the sequence has only the observation, a or b, and the prior information that each cup is ex ante equally likely. Since two of the three a marbles are in cup A, the person should assess the probability of cup A to be 2/3 if an *a* is observed, and similarly for cup B. Thus, the first decision should reveal that person's information. In the experiments discussed below, about 95 percent of the people made the decision that corresponded to their information when they were first in the sequence.

The second person then sees a private draw, *a* or *b*, and faces an easy choice if the draw matches the previous choice. A conflict is more difficult to analyze. For example, if the first person predicts cup A, the second person who sees a *b* draw may reason: "The cups are now equally likely, since that was the initial situation and the *a* that I think the first person observed cancels out the *b* that I just saw." In such cases, the second person should be indifferent, and might choose each cup with equal probability. On the other hand, the second person may be a little cautious, being surer about what they just saw than about what they infer that the other person saw. Even a slight chance that the other person made a mistake (deliberate or not) would cause the second person to "go with their own information" in the event of a conflict. In the experiments, about 95 percent of the second decision-makers behaved in this manner in the experiment described below, and we will base the subsequent discussion on the assumption that this is the case.

Now the third person will have observed two decisions and one draw. There is no loss of generality in letting the first decision be labeled A, so the various possibilities are listed in Table 31.1. (An analogous table could be constructed when the first decision is B, and the same conclusions would apply.) In the top row of the table, all three pieces of information line up, and the standard Bayesian calculations would indicate that the probability of cup A is 0.89, making A the best choice (see Question 1 at the end of the chapter). The case in the second row is more interesting, since the person's *own* draw is at odds with the information inferred from others' decisions. When there are two others, who each receive independent draw "signals" that are just as informative as the person's own draw, it is rational to go with the decision implied by the others' decisions. The decision in the final two rows is less difficult because the preponderance of information favors the decision that corresponds to one's own information.

The pattern of following others' behavior (seen in the top two rows of Table 31.1) may have a domino effect: the next person would see three A decisions and would be tempted to

Table 31.1 | Possible Inferences Made by the Third Decision-Maker

Prior Decisions	Own Draw	Inferred Pr (Cup A)	Decision
A, A	*a*	0.89	A (no dilemma)
A, A	*b*	0.67	A (start cascade)
A, B	*a*	0.67	A
A, B	*b*	0.33	B

follow the crowd regardless of their own draw. This logic applies to all subsequent people, so an initial pair of matching decisions (AA or BB) can start an information cascade that will be followed by all others, regardless of their private information. If the first two decisions cancel each other out (AB or BA) and the next two form an imbalance (AA or BB), then this imbalance causes the fifth person to decide to follow the majority. An example of such a situation would be ABAA, in which case the fifth person should choose A even if the draw observed is b. Again, the intuition is that the first two decisions cancel each other and that the next two matching decisions are more informative than the fifth person's own draw.

Notice that there is nothing in this discussion that requires a cascade to provide a correct prediction. There is a 1/3 chance that the first person will see the odd marble drawn from the selected cup, and will guess incorrectly. There is a 1/3 chance that the same thing will happen to the second person, so in theory, there is a $(1/3)(1/3) = 1/9$ chance that both of the first two people will guess incorrectly and spark an incorrect cascade. Of course, cascades may initially fail to form and then may later form when the imbalance of draws is two or more in one direction or the other. In either case, the aggregate information inferred from others' decisions is greater than the information inherent in any single person's draw.

31.3   Experimental Evidence

Anderson and Holt (1997) used this setup in a laboratory experiment in which people earned $2 for a correct guess, nothing otherwise. Subjects were in isolated booths, so that they could not see others' draws. Decisions (but not subject ID numbers) were announced by a third person to avoid having confidence or doubts communicated by the decision-maker's tone of voice. The marbles were light or dark, with two lights and a dark in cup A, and with two darks and a light in cup B. The cup to be selected was determined by the throw of a six-sided die, with a 1, 2, or 3 determining cup A. The die was thrown by a monitor selected at random from among the participants at the start of the session. There were six other subjects in each session, so each prediction sequence consisted of six private draws and six public predictions. For each group of participants, there were 15 prediction sequences. The monitor used a random device to determine the order in which individuals saw their draws and made predictions. The monitor announced the cup that had actually been used at the end of the sequence, and all participants who had guessed correctly added $2 to their cumulative earnings. The monitor received a fixed payment, and all others were paid their earnings in cash. This "ball and cup" setup was designed to reduce or eliminate preferences for conformity that were not based on informational considerations.

It is possible that an imbalance of signals does not develop, e.g., alternating a and b draws, making a cascade unlikely. An imbalance occurred in about half of the prediction sequences, and cascades formed about 70 percent of the time in such cases. A typical cascade sequence is shown in Table 31.2.

Sometimes people deviate from the behavior that would be implied by a Bayesian analysis. For example, consider the sequence shown in Table 31.3.

Table 31.2	A Cascade					
	Subject					
	58	57	59	55	56	60
Draw	*b*	*b*	*a*	*b*	*a*	*a*
Prediction	B	B	B	B	B	B

Table 31.3	A Typical "Error"					
	Subject					
	8	9	12	10	11	7
Draw	*a*	*a*	*b*	*a*	*b*	*a*
Prediction	A	A	B	A	A	A

The decision of subject 12 in the third position is the most commonly observed type of error, i.e., basing a decision on one's own information even when it conflicts with the information implied by others' prior decisions. This type of error occurred in about one-fourth of the cases in which it was possible. Notice that the cascade starts later with subject 11 in the fifth position.

Once a cascade begins, the subsequent decisions convey no information about their signals (in theory), since these people are just following the crowd. In this sense, patterns of conformity are based on a few draws, and consequently, cascades may be very fragile. In particular, one person who breaks the pattern by revealing their own information may alter the decisions of those who follow.

Deviations almost always involve relying on one's own information, as is the case with the third person in the sequence in Table 31.3. This is because a deviation in that direction is less costly than a deviation away from both a cascade and from one's own signal information. This asymmetry in the direction of deviations is consistent with a model with small amounts of noisy behavior (Anderson and Holt 1997). Similarly, Goeree et al. (2003) explain the dynamic patterns of a cascade experiment with a model of mistakes and noisy behavior (quantal response equilibrium). They also consider a generalized version of Bayes' rule, which permits perfect Bayesian learning as a special case. As indicated in Chapter 30, their estimation results indicate that subjects tend to deviate from Bayes' rule in the direction of putting too much weight on their own signals and not enough on prior probabilities that could be constructed from prior decisions and the structure of the random draws. Celen and Kariv (2004) reach a similar conclusion from a cascade experiment with a direct elicitation of subjects' beliefs. Also, see Hück and Oechssler (2000) for a discussion of violations of Bayesian inference in a cascade context.

One interesting question is whether followers in a cascade realize that many of those ahead of them may also be followers who blindly ignore their own information. To address this issue, Kübler and Weizsäcker (2004) introduced a cost of information into the standard cascade model, so that each person could decide whether to purchase a signal after seeing prior decisions in the sequence, but not knowing whether or not the earlier people had purchased signals. The cost of the information was set high enough so that theoretically only the first person in the sequence should purchase information. In theory, the others should follow the initial decision, without any more information purchases. In the experiment, the first people in the sequence did not always purchase a signal, and those that followed tended to purchase too many signals, which could be justified if people do not trust those earlier in the sequence to make careful decisions. In a second treatment in which people could see whether those ahead of them had purchased signals (but not the signals themselves), people tended to purchase even more signals than in the baseline case where prior signal purchase decisions were not observed. It seems that people became nervous when they could actually see that those ahead of them were just following the crowd with no new information of their own. This raised signal purchase rates even higher above the theoretical predictions.

Since the signals received are noisy, it is possible that a cascade may form on the wrong event. Table 31.4 shows one such incorrect cascade for the Anderson and Holt setup. Cup B was actually being used, but the first two individuals were unfortunate and received misleading *a* signals, which could happen with probability $(1/3)(1/3) = 1/9$. The matching predictions of these two people caused the others to follow with a string of incorrect A predictions, which would have been frustrating given that these individuals had seen private draws that indicated the correct cup.

If the sequence in Table 31.4 had been longer, one wonders if the cascade would have been corrected. After all, two-thirds of those who follow will be seeing *b* signals that go against the others' predictions. Even a correct cascade can break and reform, as shown in Table 31.3. This type of breaking and reforming is even more apparent in the Goeree et al. (2003) data for very long decision sequences with groups of 20 and 40 people. Cascades invariably formed, but they were almost always broken at some point. Moreover, incorrect cascades tended to be corrected more often than not, and cascades later in the sequence were more likely to be correct than those that formed early in the sequence. Thus, the main

Table 31.4	An Incorrect Cascade (Cup B Was Used)					
			Subject			
	11	12	8	9	7	10
Draw	*a*	*a*	*b*	*b*	*b*	*b*
Prediction	A	A	A	A	A	A

point of the paper is conveyed well by the title: "Self-correcting Cascades." An article in the *Economist* about cascades mentioned the popular drug Prozac and asked: "Can 10 Million People Be Wrong?" The answer is probably not.

31.4 Extensions

The information cascade story is an important paradigm for social learning, and it has many applications. The model discussed in this chapter is based on Bikhchandani, Hirschleifer, and Welch (1992), which contains a rich array of examples. Hung and Plott (2001) discuss cascades in voting situations, e.g., when the payoff depends on whether the majority decision is correct. Some of the more interesting applications are in the area of finance. Keynes (1936) compared investment decisions with people in a guessing game who must predict which beauty contestant will receive the most votes. Each player in this game, therefore, must try to guess who is most attractive to the others, and on a deeper level, who the others think is most attractive to them. Similarly, investment decisions in the stock market may involve both an analysis of fundamentals and an attempt to guess what stocks will attract attention from other investors, and the result may be "herd effects" that that cause surges in prices and later corrections in the other direction. Some of these price movements are due to psychological considerations, which Keynes compared with "animal spirits," but herd effects may also result from attempts to infer information from others' decisions. In such situations, it may not be irrational to follow others' decisions during upswings and downswings in prices (Christie and Huang 1995). Bannerjee's (1992) model of herd behavior is motivated by an investment example. This model has been evaluated in the context of a laboratory experiment reported by Alsopp and Hey (2000). Other applications to finance are discussed in Devenow and Welch (1996) and Welch (1992).

A major difference between typical market settings and the cascade models is that information in markets is often conveyed by prices, which are continuous, as opposed to binary predictions made in cascade experiments. In some laboratory experiments, the prices are computed by a computerized "market maker" on the basis of past predictions (A or B) made by individuals who saw private signals and made predictions in sequence. A prediction in this case is a purchase of one of the two assets, A or B. The market maker's price adjustments were designed to incorporate the information content of all past purchase decisions, so that the best asset to purchase for the next person in a sequence is the asset that is indicated by that person's own signal. Thus, the prediction is that herding should not occur (assuming that prior decision-makers are rational and that the prices incorporate the information in their signals). Consider the standard two-event cascade design discussed in Section 31.3, and suppose that the first person sees a signal and predicts A. The market maker sets the prices of the A and B assets to 2/3 and 1/3, which are the probabilities calculated with Bayes' rule, assuming that the first person saw an *a* signal. If the next person in the sequence sees a *b* signal, that person would have a posterior of 1/2 for each event, so buying the B asset would make sense because it costs less. Thus each person should, in theory, "follow their own signal." In accordance with this prediction, cascades are not typically observed in these experiments with endogenous prices (Drehmann, Oechssler, and Roider 2005; Cipriani and Guarino 2005). There are, however, deviations from predicted behavior in other respects. For example, people sometimes ignore their signals to buy an asset that has a very low price. This trading against the market is called "contrarian behavior," and is consistent with the "favorite/longshot bias" observed in betting on horse races.

QUESTIONS

1. Use the ball-counting heuristic from Chapter 30 to verify the Bayesian probabilities in the right-hand column of Table 31.1 under the assumption that the first two decisions correctly reveal the draws seen.

2. (Advanced) The discussion in this chapter is based on the assumption that the second person in a sequence will make a decision that reveals their own information, even when this information differs from the draw inferred from the first decision. The result is that the third person will always follow the pattern set by two matching decisions, because the information implied by the first two decisions is greater than the informational content of the third person's draw. In this question, consider what happens if we alter the assumption that the second person always makes a decision that reveals the second draw. Suppose instead that the second person chooses randomly (with probabilities of 1/2) when the second draw does not match the draw inferred from the first decision. Use Bayes' rule to show that two matching decisions (AA or BB) should start a cascade even if the third draw does not match. (The intuition for this result is that the information implied by the first decision is just as good as the information implied by the third draw, so the second draw can break a tie if it contains at least some information.)

chapter 32

Statistical Discrimination

Economists and other social scientists have long speculated that discrimination based on observable traits (such as race or gender) could become self-perpetuating in a cycle of low expectations and low achievement. In such a case, the employers may be reacting rationally, without bias, to bad employment experiences with one type of worker. Workers of that "disadvantaged" type, in turn, may correctly perceive that job opportunities are diminished, and may reduce their investments in human capital. The result is a type of "statistical discrimination" that is based on observed data, not on any underlying bias. The game implemented by the Veconlab program sets up this kind of situation, with each worker being assigned a color, Purple or Green.

32.1 "Brown-Eyed People Are More Civilized"

As Jane Elliott approached her Riceville, Iowa, classroom one Friday in April 1968, she was thinking about the provocative experiment that she had planned the night before. Martin Luther King had been murdered in Memphis the day before, and she anticipated a lot of questions and confusion. She was desperate to do something that might make a difference. Her idea began to take shape when she recalled an argument with her father about racial prejudice that had caused his hazel eyes to flare.

As soon as her third grade class was seated, Ms. Elliott divided them into two groups based on eye color, as described in *A Class Divided* (Peters 1971). At first, brown-eyed people were designated as being superior, with the understanding that the roles would be reversed the next day. She began: "What I mean is that brown-eyed people are better than blue-eyed people. They are cleaner . . . more civilized. . . . And they are smarter than blue-eyed people." As the brown-eyed people were seated in the front of the room and allowed to drink from the water fountain without using paper cups, the blue-eyed students slumped in their chairs and exhibited other submissive types of behavior. Objections and complaints were transformed into rhetorical questions about whether blue-eyed children were impolite, and so on, which resulted in a chorus of enthusiastic replies from the brown-eyed people. When one student questioned Ms. Elliott about her own eye color (blue) and she tried to defend her intelligence, the reply was that she was not as smart as the brown-eyed teachers. What began as a role-playing exercise began to take on an uncanny reality of its own. These patterns were reversed when blue-eyed people were designated as superior on the following day.

Psychologists soon began conducting experiments under more controlled conditions (e.g., Tajfel 1970; Vaughan, Tajfel, and Williams 1981). A typical setup involved a task of skill like a trivia quiz or estimation of the lengths of some lines. The subjects would be told that they were being divided into groups on the basis of their skill, but in fact the assignments were random. Then the subjects would be asked to perform a task like division of money or candy that might indicate differential status (see the review in Anderson, Fryer, and Holt 2006). Such effects were often manifested as lower allocations to those with lower status. Moreover, people sometimes offered preferential treatment to those of their own group, which is known as an "in-group bias."

Economists are interested in whether group and status effects will carry over into market settings. For example, Ball et al. (2001) examined the effects of status assignments in double auctions where the demand and supply functions were "box" shapes with a large vertical overlap, which produced a range of market-clearing prices. In the earned-status treatment, traders on one side of the market (e.g., buyers) were told that they obtained a gold star as a result of their performance on a trivia quiz. The random-assignment treatment began with some people being selected to receive stars that were awarded in a special ceremony. The subjects were not told that the star recipients were selected at random. In each treatment, the people with stars were all on one side of the market (all buyers or all sellers). This seemingly trivial status permitted them to earn more of the total surplus, whether or not they were buyers or sellers.

Group differences were largely exogenous in the status experiments, but economists have long worried about the possibility that differences in endogenously acquired skills may develop and persist in a vicious circle of self-confirming differential expectations. Formal models of *experienced-based discrimination* were developed independently by Arrow (1973) and Phelps (1972), and have been refined by others. The intuition is that if some historical differences in opportunity cause employment possibilities for one group to be less attractive, then members of that group may rationally choose not to invest as much in human capital. In response, employers form lower expectations for members of that group. Expectations are based on statistics from past experience, so these have been called models of *statistical discrimination*.

The obvious question is why a member of the disadvantaged group cannot invest and break out of the cycle. This strategy may not work if the employer attributes a good impression made in an interview to random factors, and then bases a decision not to hire on past experience and the fear that the interview did not reveal potential problems. Think of the human capital being discussed as any aspect of productivity that is learned and that cannot be observed without error in the job application process. For example, the employer may be able to ascertain that a person attended a particular software class, but not the extent to which the person mastered the details of working with spreadsheets. Even if investment by members of the disadvantaged group results in good job placement some of the time, a lower success rate for people in this group will nevertheless result in a lower investment rate. After all, investment is costly in terms of lost income and lost opportunities to have children, and so on. These observations raise the disturbing possibility that two groups with ex ante identical abilities will be treated differently because of differential rates of investment in acquired skills. In such a situation, the employers need not be prejudiced in any way other than reacting rationally to their own experiences. It is, of course, easy to imagine how real prejudice might arise (or continue) and accentuate the economic forces that perpetuate discrimination.

32.2   Being Purple or Green

The focus in this chapter is on experiments in which some group aspects are exogenous (color) and some are endogenous (investments). The participants are assigned a role, employer or worker. Workers are also assigned a color: Purple or Green. Workers are given a chance to make a costly investment in skills that would be valuable to an employer, but only if they are hired. The employers can observe workers' colors and the results of an imperfect pre-employment test before making the hiring decision. Investment is costly for the worker, but it increases the chances of avoiding a bad result on the pre-employment test, and hence, of getting hired. The payoffs are such that the employers prefer to hire workers who invested, and not to hire those who did not.

This experimental setup, used by Fryer, Goeree, and Holt (2002), matches a theoretical model (Coate and Loury 1993) in which statistical discrimination is a possible outcome. The experiment consisted of a number of rounds with random pairings of employers and workers. Each round began with workers finding out their own (randomly determined) costs of making an investment in some skill. Investment costs were uniform on the range from $0.00 to $1.00, except as noted below. The employer could observe the worker's color, but not the investment decision. A test given to each worker provided noisy information about the worker's investment, and on the basis of this information the employer decided whether or not to hire the worker. The payoff numbers are summarized in Table 32.1.

Workers prefer to be hired, which yields a payoff of $1.50 per period, as opposed to the $0.00 payoff for not being hired. The investment cost (if any) is deducted from this payoff, whether or not the worker is hired. Investment is good in that it increases the probability of getting hired at $1.50. Thus, a risk-neutral worker would want to invest if the investment cost is less than the wage times the increase in the hire probability that results from investing. If the investment cost is C, then the decision rule is:

Worker decision: Invest if $C <$ ($1.50) (increase in hire probability).

Table 32.1	Experiment Parameters
Worker's Payoffs	$1.50 if hired
	$0.00 if not hired
Employer's Payoffs	$1.50 if the hired worker invested
	−$1.50 if the hired worker did not invest
	$0.50 if the worker is not hired

Employers prefer to hire a worker who invested, which yields a payoff of $1.50. Hiring someone who did not invest yields a payoff of −$1.50, which is worse than the $0.50 payoff the employer receives if no worker is hired. (Think of the $0.50 as what the manager can earn without any competent help.) The manager wishes to hire a worker as long as the probability of investment, p, is such that the expected payoff from hiring the worker, $p(1.50) + (1 − p)(−1.50)$, is greater than the $0.50 earnings from not hiring. It is straightforward to show that $p(1.50) + (1 − p)(−1.50) > 0.50$ when $p > 2/3$:

Employer decision: Hire when the probability of investment > 2/3.

The decision rules just derived, are of course, incomplete, since the probabilities of investment and being hired are determined by the interaction of worker and employer decisions.

The employer's beliefs about the probability that a worker invested are affected by a pre-employment test, which provides an informative but imperfect indication of the worker's decision. If the worker invests, then the employer sees two independent draws, with replacement, from the "invest cup" with 3 Blue marbles and 3 Red marbles, as shown on the left side of Figure 32.1. If the worker does not invest, the employer sees two draws with replacement from a cup with only 1 Blue and 5 Reds, as shown on the right side. Obviously, the Invest Cup provides three times as great a chance that each draw will be Blue (B), so Red (R) is considered a bad signal. If the decision is to invest (Inv), each color outcome is

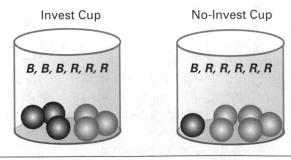

Invest Cup   No-Invest Cup

B, B, B, R, R, R   B, R, R, R, R, R

Figure 32.1   The Test Cups

equally likely, so the probabilities of the draw combinations are just products of $1/2$ for each outcome: $\Pr(BB|Inv) = (1/2)(1/2) = 1/4$, $\Pr(RR|Inv) = (1/2)(1/2) = 1/4$, and therefore, the residual probability of a mixed signal (RB or BR) is $1/2$. Similarly, the probabilities of the signal combinations for no investment (No) are: $\Pr(BB|No) = (1/6)(1/6) = 1/36$, $\Pr(RR|No) = (5/6)(5/6) = 25/36$, and $\Pr(RB \text{ or } BR) = 10/36$, which is the residual.

The signal combination probabilities just calculated can be used to determine whether or not it is worthwhile for a worker to invest, but we must know how employers react to signals. The discussion will pertain to an asymmetric equilibrium outcome in which one color gets preferential treatment in the hiring process. The theoretical question is whether asymmetric equilibria (with discriminatory hiring decisions) can exist, even if workers of each color have the same investment cost opportunities and payoffs. Consider the discriminatory hiring strategy, as shown in Equation (32.1):

Signal **BB**:	Hire both colors.
Signal **BR** or **RB**:	Hire Green, not hire Purple.
Signal **RR**:	Do not hire either color.

$$(32.1)$$

There are two steps to complete the analysis of this equilibrium: 1) to figure out the ranges of investment costs for which workers of each color will invest, given employer behavior in Equation (32.1) and 2) to verify that the conjectured hiring strategy in Equation (32.1) above is an optimal response for employers. The required arguments are developed in this chapter's Derivation of the Discriminatory Equilibrium Appendix, which shows that the discriminatory hiring strategy in Equation (32.1) is an equilibrium. It is also shown that there is a second, symmetric equilibrium in which workers of each color are treated equally and are hired whenever the signal is not RR.

32.3 **Data on Statistical Discrimination**

The advantage of running experiments is obvious in this case, since the model has both asymmetric and symmetric equilibria, and since exogenous sources of bias can be controlled. Moreover, the setup is sufficiently complex that behavior may not be drawn to any of the equilibria. Fryer, Goeree, and Holt (2002) have run a number of sessions using the statistical discrimination game. In some of the sessions there is little distinction between the way workers with different color designations are treated. This is not too surprising, given the symmetry of the model and the presence of a symmetric equilibrium.

Many field situations where unequal treatment is likely to persist have evolved from social situations where discrimination was either directly sanctioned or indirectly subsidized by legal rules and social norms. Therefore, we began some of the sessions with 10 rounds of unequal investment cost distributions. In particular, one color (e.g., Green) might be favored initially by drawing investment costs from a distribution that is uniform on [$0.00, $0.50], and Purple may draw from a distribution that is uniform on [$0.50, $1.00].

The vertical dashed line at round 10 in Figure 32.2 shows the round where these unequal cost opportunities ended. Subjects were not told of this cost difference; they were just told that all cost draws would be between $0.00 and $1.00, which was the case. All draws after round 10 were from a common uniform distribution on [$0.00, $1.00].

Figure 32.2 shows five-period average investment and hiring rates. Notice that the initial cost asymmetry works in the right direction; Greens start out investing at about twice the rate as Purples, as can be seen from the left panel. There is a slight crossover in rounds 10–15, which seems to have been caused by a "relative cost effect," i.e., the tendency for Purples to invest a lot when encountering costs that are lower than initially high levels that they were used to seeing. Similarly, investment rates for Greens fell briefly after period 10 when they began drawing from a higher cost distribution. As can be seen from the right panel in the figure, the employers seemed to notice the lower initial investment rates for Purples, and they continued hiring Greens at a higher rate. The inertia of this preference for Greens eventually caused the investment rates for Greens to rise above those for Purples again, and separation continued.

The color-based hiring preference was clear for a majority of the employers, although the separation was not as uniform as that predicted in Section 32.2 on equilibrium analysis. After an employer saw mixed signals (BR or RB), Greens were hired more frequently (96 percent versus 58 percent in the final 20 rounds). In fact, Greens were even hired more frequently after a negative RR signal (53 percent versus 0 percent in the final 20 rounds).

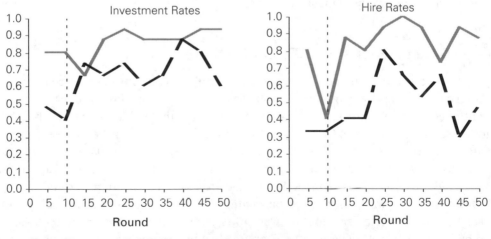

Source: (Fryer, Goeree, and Holt 2002)

Figure 32.2   A Separation Effect: Five-Period Average Investment and Hire Rates by Color (Green Is Solid, Purple Is Dashed) with Statistical Discrimination Induced by an Initial Investment Cost Asymmetry

The individual employer decisions for the final 15 rounds of this session are shown in Table 32.2. Most of the employers discriminated to some extent, either in the case of a mixed (RB or BR) signal, or in the case of a negative (RR) signal. Employers 1, 2, and 3 hired all

Table 32.2	Employer Information and Decisions for the Final 15 Rounds				
Round	Employer 1	Employer 2	Employer 3	Employer 4	Employer 5	Employer 6
36	Purple BB	Green BR	Green BR	Purple BR	Purple BR	Green BB
	Hire **Inv**	Hire **Inv**	Hire **Inv**	Hire **Inv**	Hire **Inv**	Hire **Inv**
37	Purple BR	Green RR	Green BB	Green BR	Purple BR	Purple BB
	Hire **Inv**	Hire **Inv**	Hire **Inv**	No Hire Inv	No Hire Inv	Hire **Inv**
38	Green BR	Purple BB	Purple RR	Green RR	Green RR	Purple BB
	Hire **No**	Hire **Inv**	No Hire No	No Hire Inv	No Hire Inv	Hire **Inv**
39	Purple RR	Green RR	Purple RR	Green RR	Green BR	Purple BR
	No Hire No	Hire **No**	No Hire Inv	No Hire Inv	Hire **Inv**	Hire **Inv**
40	Purple BR	Purple BB	Purple BB	Green BR	Green BR	Green BR
	No Hire Inv	Hire **Inv**	Hire **Inv**	Hire **Inv**	Hire **Inv**	Hire **Inv**
41	Purple RR	Green RR	Green BR	Green BR	Purple RR	Purple BR
	No Hire Inv	Hire **Inv**	Hire **No**	Hire **Inv**	No Hire Inv	Hire **No**
42	Purple BB	Purple BR	Green RR	Purple BR	Green BB	Green BB
	Hire **Inv**	No Hire Inv	Hire **Inv**	No Hire Inv	Hire **Inv**	Hire **Inv**
43	Purple BR	Purple RR	Green RR	Purple BR	Green BR	Green BB
	Hire **Inv**	No Hire Inv	Hire **Inv**	No Hire Inv	Hire **Inv**	Hire **Inv**
44	Purple BB	Green BB	Purple BR	Purple BR	Green BR	Green RR
	Hire **Inv**	Hire **Inv**	Hire **Inv**	No Hire Inv	Hire **Inv**	No Hire Inv
45	Green BR	Green BB	Purple BR	Purple BR	Green BR	Purple RR
	Hire **Inv**	Hire **Inv**	Hire **Inv**	No Hire No	Hire **Inv**	No Hire No
46	Purple RR	Purple BR	Green RR	Green BR	Green RR	Purple BR
	No Hire Inv	No Hire Inv	Hire **Inv**	Hire **Inv**	No Hire Inv	Hire **Inv**
47	Purple BB	Green RR	Green BR	Purple BB	Purple RR	Green BR
	Hire **No**	Hire **Inv**	Hire **Inv**	Hire **Inv**	No Hire No	Hire **Inv**
48	Purple RR	Green BB	Green BB	Green RR	Purple RR	Purple BR
	No Hire No	Hire **Inv**	Hire **Inv**	No Hire Inv	No Hire Inv	Hire **Inv**
49	Green BR	Green RR	Purple BB	Purple RR	Purple BR	Green BB
	Hire **Inv**	Hire **Inv**	Hire **Inv**	No Hire No	Hire **Inv**	Hire **Inv**
50	Purple RR	Green BB	Green RR	Purple BR	Green BR	Purple RR
	No Hire No	Hire **Inv**	Hire **No**	Hire **Inv**	Hire **Inv**	No Hire No

Key: Inv = investment observed ex post by employer.
  Inv = investment not observed ex post by employer.

Green workers encountered, even when the test result was RR. Employers 4 and 5 tended to discriminate after mixed signals, and employers 2 and 3 tended to discriminate after the negative signal. Employer 6 was essentially color-blind in the way workers were treated.

The experience of employer 2 indicates the problems facing Purple workers. All Purples encountered by this employer after round 40 had invested, but the employer was unable to spot this trend since no Purples were hired after round 40. (The investment decisions of the workers are shown in bold letters (**Inv** or **No**) when the worker was hired, and the unobserved investment decisions are shown in light gray when the worker was not hired.) Such differential treatment, when it occurs, is particularly interesting when the experiment is conducted in class for teaching purposes. One person in a classroom experiment remarked "Purple workers just can't be trusted . . . they won't invest." Another student remarked: "I invested every time, even when costs were high, because I felt confident that I would get the . . . job—because *I am Green.*"

The initial cost differences produced the same initial patterns in a second experiment, shown in Figure 32.3. The vertical dashed line again indicates the point after which the cost distributions became symmetric. Notice that the surge caused by the relative cost effect after 10 rounds carries over, causing a fascinating reverse separation where the initially disadvantaged group (Purple) ends up investing more for the remainder of the session. This differential investment rate seems to cause the hiring rates to diverge in the final 10 periods.

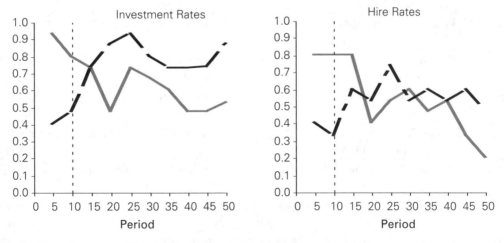

Source: (Fryer, Goeree, and Holt 2002)

Figure 32.3   A Cross-Over Effect: Five-Period Average Investment and Hire Rates by Color (Green Is Solid, Purple Is Dashed) with Reverse Statistical Discrimination Induced by an Initial Investment Cost Asymmetry

32.4 "Are Emily and Greg More Employable than Lakisha and Jamal?"

Many key elements of discrimination may be difficult to recreate in the lab, and field experiments can be quite informative. There is a small literature consisting of "audit studies" that measure discriminatory responses to fictitious job or housing applications that are tailored to be identical, except for gender or racial identifiers. Then these applications are mailed to employers or housing officials, who do not know that they are part of an experiment, and response rates are recorded. For example, Bertrand and Mullainathan (2004) infer that the response rate is about 50 percent higher for "white" names than for "black" names like Lakisha and Jamal, after controlling for quality. Some "black" names, like Ebony and Latonya, however, obtained response rates from employers that were similar to those for "white" names. The authors attributed this to the fact that these names were not necessarily indicative of lower income. This experiment highlights an advantage of a field experiment that permits an indirect measure of preferences, which are typically induced in a laboratory experiment. In addition, the participants in the field experiment are precisely the people making the employment or housing assignment decisions in naturally occurring markets.

Another category of field experiments looks at the ways that traders in a market are treated differently depending on demographics. For example, List (2004) recruited subjects to serve as buyers or sellers in a market for sports cards at a collectors' convention. The subjects were instructed to approach specific dealers to buy or sell sports cards of comparable value, and to record the initial and final offers received from the dealers. The subjects were provided with financial incentives to bargain seriously. For example, those with seller roles were told that they would earn the difference between the cost of the card provided and the price obtained from the dealer. The subjects did not know that the purpose of the experiment was to evaluate discrimination, and the dealers did not even know that they were in an experiment. Subjects who were members of minority groups, based on race, gender, and (old) age, received less favorable initial and final offers than the majority-group subjects. Interestingly, List concluded that this discrimination was *statistical* in nature, i.e., based on real or perceived statistical differences between groups. In particular, the less favorable offers given to minority groups were optimal responses to less aggressive bargaining strategies employed by these groups.

A clear argument for statistical discrimination in another field experiment is made by Gneezy and List (2006). The subjects drove a damaged car to auto body shops in the Chicago area to obtain repair estimates. In half of the cases, the subject was in a wheel chair. The average quote (for the same car) was about $500 for non-disabled drivers, which went up to about $595 for disabled drivers. This difference could either be due to the estimator's distaste for dealing with disabled car owners, which is a profit-reducing "animus." Alternatively, this discrimination could be due to (profit-maximizing) statistical discrimination, since it is natural to presume that it is more difficult for disabled drivers to go to a variety of shops for estimates. Clear evidence for the latter explanation is provided by a third treatment in which the disabled drivers began their interaction by saying "I'm going to get a few quotes." The average estimate for this treatment was slightly below the $500 level corresponding to the average quote received by non-disabled drivers. Note that discrimination is illegal in either case, but it helps from a scientific point of view to know the source. Finally, it is quite possible that discrimination would be primarily animus-based in some contexts and primarily statistical in others.

32.5   Extensions

There are a number of related theoretical models of statistical discrimination, which are presented with a uniform notation in Fryer (2001). Anderson, Fryer, and Holt (2006) survey experimental work in psychology and economics on discrimination-related issues. The classroom experiments mentioned in Section 32.4 are discussed in more detail in Fryer, Goeree, and Holt (2005). Anderson and Haupert (1999) describe a classroom experiment with exogenously determined worker skill levels. Davis (1987) provides an experimental test of the idea that perceptions about a group may be influenced by the highest skill level encountered in the past, which tends to benefit the majority group. Dickinson and Oaxaca (2005) study a type of discrimination that is based on variability, i.e., in which lower wages are paid to a group with a higher dispersion of abilities, even if the means are the same.

Experiments can also be used to evaluate policies designed to counter the effects of discrimination, e.g., affirmative action policies. For example, suppose that members of an "underrepresented" group in a particular market have higher costs, and that the policy solution is to provide them with a price preference that would make them more competitive with the low-cost providers. Obviously, this kind of preference will benefit members of the under-represented group and will tend to increase their participation in the market. What is not so obvious is that such a preference may make the market setting as a whole more competitive, which might also be a desired outcome. Corns and Schotter (1999) use a procurement auction setting to evaluate this possibility. Think of the bidders as being contractors who are bidding to supply a service, with the job going to the lowest bidder. Bidders' costs were randomly determined; four bidders drew from a low-cost distribution, and two others drew from a high-cost distribution. In some rounds, the high-cost bidders were given bid subsidies or "price preferences," which were subtracted from their bids before a winner was determined. In this design, small price preferences (in the 5 percent range) were effective at increasing minority win rates, and by making the auctions more competitive, these subsidies reduced the procurement costs for the buyer.

Appendix: **Derivation of the Discriminatory Equilibrium**

Step 1: Worker Investment Decisions

Recall that the worker will invest if the cost is less than the wage $1.50 times the increase in the probability of being hired due to a decision to invest. For the equilibrium in Equation (32.1), the Purple worker is only hired if both draws are blue, which happens with probability $(1/2)(1/2) = 1/4$ following investment and $(1/6)(1/6) = 1/36$ following no investment, so the increase in the probability of being hired is $1/4 - 1/36 = 9/36 - 1/36 = 8/36 = 2/9$. Hence $(2/9)\$1.50 = \$0.33$ is the expected net gain from investment, which is the optimal decision if the investment cost is less than $0.33. Since the costs are uniformly distributed between $0.00 and $1.00, the Purple workers will invest with probability $1/3$. In contrast, the favored Green workers are hired whenever the draw combination is not RR. So investment results in a hire with probability $1 - (1/2)(1/2) = 3/4$. Similarly, the probability of a Green worker being hired without investing is the probability of not getting two R draws from the No-Invest cup (BRRRRR), which is $1 - (5/6)(5/6) = 11/36$. The increase in the chances of getting a job due to investment is $3/4 - 11/36 = 27/36 - 11/36 = 16/36 = 4/9$. Hence, the expected net gain from investment by a Green worker is $(4/9)\$1.50 = \$0.67$, and Green workers invest with a $2/3$ probability. To summarize, given the hiring strategy that discriminates in favor of Green workers, the Green Workers are twice as likely to invest as the Purple workers. Thus, the discriminatory hiring rates induce more investment by the favored color.

Step 2: Employer Hiring Decisions

Recall that the employer's payoffs in Table 32.1 are such that it is better to hire whenever the probability that the worker invested is greater than $2/3$. Since Greens invest twice as often as Purples (a probability of $2/3$ versus $1/3$), the employer's posterior probability is that a worker invested will be higher for Green, regardless of the combination of draws. These posterior probabilities are calculated with Bayes' rule and are shown in Table 32.3.

Table 32.3	Probabilities That the Worker Invested Conditional on Test and Color: Decision Is to Hire if the Probability > 2/3	
	Green Workers	**Purple** Workers
Pr(worker invested | **BB**)	18/19 (hire Green)	9/11 (hire Purple)
Pr(worker invested | **BR** or **RB**)	18/23 (hire Green)	9/19 (not hire Purple)
Pr(worker invested | **RR**)	18/43 (not hire Green)	9/59 (not hire Purple)

For example, consider the top row of the Green column, which shows the probability that a Green worker with a BB signal invested. This probability, 18/19, is calculated by taking the ratio, with the Greens who invested and received the BB signal in the numerator and all Greens (who invested or not) who received the BB signal in the denominator. Since two-thirds of Greens invest and investment produces the BB signal with probability $(1/2)(1/2) = 1/4$, the numerator is $(2/3)(1/4)$. Since one-third of the Greens do not invest and no investment produces BB signal with probability $(1/6)(1/6) = 1/36$, the denominator also includes a term that is the product: $(1/3)(1/36)$. It follows that the probability of investment for a Green with the BB signal is: $(2/3)(1/4)$ divided by $(2/3)(1/4) + (1/3)(1/36)$, which reduces to 18/19, as shown in the table. The employer's optimal decision is to hire when the investment probability is greater than 2/3, so the Green worker with a BB test result should be hired. The other probabilities and hire decisions in the table are calculated in a similar manner (see Question 1 at the end of the chapter). A comparison of the middle and right columns of the table shows that these decisions discriminate against Purple in a manner that matches the original specification in Equation (32.1). It can be shown that there is also a symmetric equilibrium where both colors invest when the cost is less than $0.67 and both colors are treated like the employer treated Greens in Equation (32.1), i.e., always hire a worker of either color unless the test outcome is RR (see Question 2 at the end of the chapter).

QUESTIONS

1. Verify the Bayes' rule probability calculations for Purple workers in the right column of Table 32.3.

2. Consider a symmetric equilibrium where employers hire a worker regardless of color if the test result is BB, BR, or RB, and not otherwise. First show that workers of either color will invest as long as the cost is less than $0.67. Then calculate the probabilities of investment conditional on the test results, as in Table 32.3. Show that the employer's best response is to hire unless the test result is RR.

chapter 33

Signaling Games

When individuals have traits that cannot be directly observed by others, they may engage in costly activities in order to "signal" the presence of these traits. Many educational credentials, for example, are thought to provide signals of a prospective employee's productivity and enthusiasm. The simplest signaling game is one where the signals are not directly productive, but differential costs of signaling may allow people of one "type" to distinguish themselves from those of another type. Alternatively, there may be pooling equilibria in which both types of people send identical signals, so that the signal loses meaning. One example of pooling is in poker when people with weak hands bluff in an attempt to signal a strong hand. This chapter describes experiments that evaluate how these behavioral patterns emerge. The experiments, which include a "stripped-down" game of poker (Reiley, Urbancic and Walker 2005), can be run with playing cards or with the Veconlab Signaling Game, listed under the Information menu.

33.1 | *Real Men Don't Eat Quiche*

A typical college student has the opportunity to attend about 350 class periods per academic year. If you divide your annual tuition by the number of classes, the cost per class may seem high relative to what you think it might be worth to an employer. One explanation offered by economist Michael Spence (1973) is that education has value as a "signal" of high ability, since obtaining an education is easier and perhaps more enjoyable for high-ability workers. Signaling is pervasive, ranging from King Kong's chest beating to the use of high-quality paper for job market resumes. Some of the original work by game theorists on this topic was illustrated with a (somewhat less realistic) fable that was motivated by a popular book: *Real Men Don't Eat Quiche*. In this fable, one person wakes up feeling strong or weak, and decides whether to drink beer for breakfast or to eat quiche.

The second person observes the breakfast choice but not how the first person is feeling. The second person then decides whether or not to challenge the first to a duel, which would be a mistake if the first person turns out to be feeling strong. In this game, a *separating equilibrium* would be for strong types to drink beer, which they enjoy, and for weak types to eat quiche, which they prefer. But if being challenged to a duel is sufficiently bad for someone feeling weak, then that person would likely go for the beer breakfast in an effort to appear strong and avoid a duel.

Even seemingly wasteful signaling may serve a purpose. For example, the elaborate plumage of a peacock may hinder its movements, but at the same time it may signal strength to potential mates and rivals. In economics, signaling models have been used to evaluate why dominant firms might respond to entry in one market with aggressive pricing in order to deter entry in other markets. A widely cited and somewhat controversial theory of why firms pay dividends (even though they are treated unfavorably by U.S. tax law) is that dividend payments signal underlying value for the firm. Perhaps the most famous example of signaling in economics is due to Thorstein Veblin, who argued that the rich engage in "conspicuous consumption" of unneeded luxuries in order to signal their wealth.

33.2 Separating Equilibria

The idea behind the labor-market signaling model is illustrated by the extensive form game shown in Figure 33.1. Start in the center of the figure, where a random device determines whether a worker is of high or low ability. In this game, the probability of a high-ability worker is assumed to be 2/3, as indicated by the parenthetical expression in the upper part of the figure. Regardless of ability, a worker must choose whether or not to

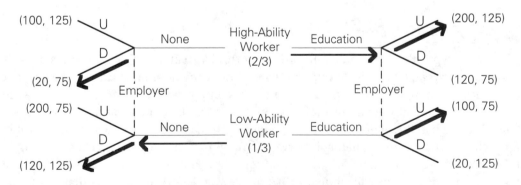

Key: (Worker Earnings, Employer Earnings)

Figure 33.1   A Labor Market Signaling Game with Separation Payoff

acquire an educational credential. For example, the Education decision is represented by a movement to the right. By assumption, the employer can observe the worker's decision (Education or None) but not the worker's ability (High or Low), so the employer's information set is represented by a dashed vertical line, on the right if the worker chooses Education, and on the left if the worker chooses None.

The employer then must make a job assignment, which we will call Up or Down, as represented by the upward (U) or downward (D) arrows from the employer's decision node. Think of Up as an upstairs administrative job, that is preferred by workers of either type. The employer's earnings, however, are higher if the low-ability worker is assigned to a Down job, and if a high-ability worker is assigned to an Up job. The payoffs at each terminal node show the worker's earnings on the left and the employer's earnings on the right.

For example, suppose that the employer observes an Education signal, so that the relevant information set is the vertical dashed line on the right side of Figure 33.1. The employer does not observe the worker's type, i.e., whether the relevant node is at the top of the dashed line or the bottom. If the employer could infer that the worker is in fact of high ability, then the Up decision provides the employer with 125, as compared with only 75 for the down arrow. The reverse is true in the bottom part of the figure, where the employer's best response is Down when the worker is of low ability.

Next, consider the worker's payoffs, which are listed on the left at each terminal node. For the low-ability worker, the worst outcome is to suffer through the educational process and still get the Down job, which results in a payoff of 20 for the worker, as shown in the lower-right part of the figure. From this point, getting reassigned to the Up job adds 80, and getting the preferred education (None) adds 100 to this worker's payoffs. Similarly, the high-ability worker's worst payoff of 20 is obtained when the valued education is missed and the job assignment is low. Switching to the preferred education raises this person's payoff by 100, and switching to the preferred job raises this person's payoff by 80.

In this game, each person's marginal value of 100 for the preferred education level is so high that it alone determines the best decision, i.e., the high-ability person obtains an education and the low-ability person does not. In equilibrium, therefore, the education signals the worker's ability, and the employer will respond by assigning those with an education to the Up job and others to the Down job, as indicated by the dark arrows in the figure. Notice that both arrows in a given information set point in the same direction, since the employer is not permitted to make one decision for the top node and a different decision for the bottom node. In this case, the signals reveal the unobserved worker types, which is known as a separating equilibrium. When checking to see if separation is a Nash equilibrium, you must consider whether either type would prefer to send the other signal and get treated like the other type. For example, a low-ability person might consider obtaining the costly education signal in order to obtain the Up job, but this person's payoff after the switch would be 100, which is lower than the 120 payoff obtained by this type in the separating equilibrium (lower-left corner of Figure 33.1).

33.3 Pooling

Now suppose that the value of the preferred education level is reduced from 100 to 40, which yields the game shown in Figure 33.2. In this case, a low-ability worker's payoff in the lower-left corner (None, Down) is only 60, so a deviation, getting an education (and the Up job) would raise this person's payoff to 100. This shows that separation is not an equilibrium, which raises the issue of whether it is an equilibrium for both types to get an education. Recall that two-thirds of the workers are of high ability, so the best response for an employer would be to assign all of those with educations to the Up job, since the employer's expected payoff in that case would be: (2/3)*125 + (1/3)*75, which is higher than the expected payoff for assigning the educated worker to the Down job (see Question 1 at the end of the chapter).

When both types choose the same signal, it is called a *pooling equilibrium*. To verify that it is a Nash equilibrium for both types to choose Education, one needs to check to be sure that neither worker type would want to deviate to the left side of the figure. The low-ability worker would be tempted to deviate to the left if an Up job assignment were anticipated, which would raise that person's payoff from 100 to 140. The way that this deviation is prevented is for the employer to assign the Down job to anyone with no education, as shown by the down arrows on the left side of the figure. This Down assignment, of course, would be the right decision for the employer if a decision of None was thought to have come from a low-ability worker. In equilibrium, this deviation never happens, so these are called "out-of-equilibrium beliefs," and are represented by the gray arrow to the left at the bottom of the figure.

Brandts and Holt (1992) used the payoff structure shown in Figure 33.2 in a laboratory experiment in which subjects were matched in a series of rounds, with first-movers in one room and second-movers in another. Participants were told that they would not be

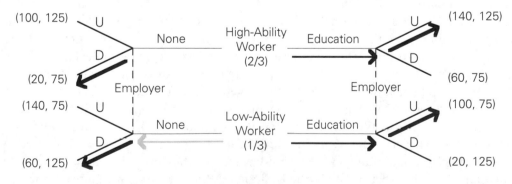

Key: (Worker Earnings, Employer Earnings)

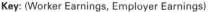

Figure 33.2   A Labor Market Signaling Game with Pooling Payoff

matched with the same person twice, nor would they be matched with anyone who had been matched with them previously. Roles were reversed after four rounds, and again after eight rounds, although this role reversal was not anticipated. One participant, selected initially at random, was the monitor who observed the matching process and threw the dice to determine the first-mover's type, a procedure that was intended to reduce any perception of deception. The instructions used neutral (non-labor market) terminology. Half of the sessions were run in the United States and half in Spain. Payoffs were in pennies or Spanish pesetas. (The only change in payoffs from those in Figure 33.2 was that the high-ability worker's earnings for the None/Up outcome were raised from 100 to 120, in order to equalize the worker's expected payoffs in the two pooling equilibria to be discussed.)

The initial data patterns showed strong separation for the game shown in Figure 33.2. The workers essentially separated in the first four rounds; 100 percent of the high-ability types chose the decisions corresponding to Education, and only 21 percent of the low-ability types chose that decision. By the last four rounds, all of the high-ability types continued to choose the Education signal, and 75 percent of the low-ability types switched over to that decision too. Virtually all of those who chose the Education signal obtained a response that corresponded to the Up job, whereas 60 percent of those who chose the None decision were given the less desirable (Down) response. Therefore, the final outcomes are best explained by the pooling equilibrium, and deviations are "punished" with the Down job more often than not. Even though these deviations were rare in the end, the second movers remembered that such deviations had tended to come from low-ability workers in the earlier rounds. *Thus, the "out-of-equilibrium beliefs" were probably shaped by actual experience during the process of adjustment.*

33.4   Unintuitive Beliefs and Reverse Type Dependence

There is another equilibrium for the game shown in Figure 33.2, and it also involves pooling, but with both types choosing "None." This equilibrium is represented by the dark arrows in Figure 33.3. With pooling, it is always in the interest of the employer to assign the Up job, since two-thirds of the workers will be of high ability. To prevent deviations from the no-education outcome, it must be the case that a deviant choosing Education will be punished with the Down job, since otherwise a high-ability person would want to deviate in order to obtain the preferred education level. This assignment of the Down job can only be optimal if the employer believes that the deviant is likely to be of low ability, as indicated by the light gray arrow in the lower-right part of the figure.

So the obvious question is whether an employer might reasonably interpret Education as a signal of low ability. First, note that the equilibrium payoffs on the left for the two worker types have been printed in bold. For the equilibrium shown in Figure 33.3, the low-ability type is earning the maximum possible amount, 140, since the cost of education is avoided and the Up job is obtained. There is no anticipated employer response that

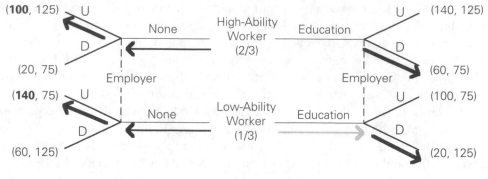

(**100**, 125)

(20, 75)

(**140**, 75)

(60, 125)

(140, 125)

(60, 75)

(100, 75)

(20, 125)

Key: (Worker Earnings, Employer Earnings)

Figure 33.3 A Labor Market Signaling Game with an "Unintuitive" Pooling Equilibrium Payoff

could entice the low-ability type to deviate from this equilibrium, and hence the "out-of-equilibrium beliefs" that support it are "unintuitive." Note that the high-ability type, who is earning 100 in this equilibrium, could conceivably do better with a deviation. This is the essence of the *equilibrium dominance* argument presented in Cho and Kreps (1987). The arguments essentially *start* from an equilibrium point, and then consider what the responder might infer from a deviation, i.e., whether one type or another could possibly gain from such a deviation. Beliefs that put high probability on a deviation by a type who could not conceivably benefit from the deviation are labeled as being unintuitive and are ruled out by this approach. Certainly, the experimental results just discussed are consistent with this prediction, since the preponderance of the observed outcomes are on the right side of the figure, with Education signals.

There is a subtle difference between the theoretical arguments of the previous paragraph and the intuition gained from the Brandts and Holt experiment. In the experiment, behavior in early rounds of the adjustment may have determined beliefs about which type is more likely to deviate, whereas the equilibrium dominance argument does not consider the process of adjustment, but rather, the thought process *begins* with the equilibrium payoffs and considers who might gain from a deviation from that point. These two approaches provide the same prediction for the signaling game under consideration, so the reader might wonder why this discussion is even taking place. One advantage of laboratory experiments is that it may be possible to construct an environment in which two alternative explanations do not yield the same prediction, and this was the goal of a subsequent Brandts and Holt (1992) experiment.

Consider the game shown in Figure 33.4. The labor-market terminology has been replaced by single-letter abbreviations (E or N for first-mover decisions), since the payoffs were not chosen to be realistic for this context. The equilibrium shown has the high type

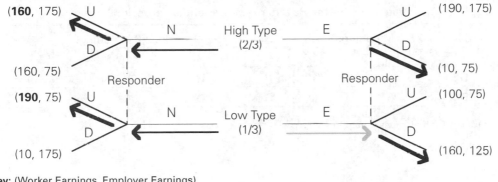

Key: (Worker Earnings, Employer Earnings)

Figure 33.4   A Signaling Game Designed to Induce Reverse Type Dependence Payoff

earning 160 and the low type earning 190, as indicated by the bold payoff numbers. The gray arrow on the right indicates that a deviant will be thought to be a low type. This out-of-equilibrium belief is unintuitive since the low type cannot conceivably earn more than the equilibrium payoff of 190 by deviating, but a deviation by the other type could possibly pay off. Hence, the equilibrium shown in Figure 33.4 is ruled out by an equilibrium dominance argument.

The experiment payoffs in Figure 33.4 were structured so that subjects of low type might start off going to the right (E) to obtain either 100 or 160, and the high types might go to the left (N) to get the sure 160 payoff. This creates what Brandts and Holt termed a "reverse type dependence" since (in the labor market interpretation) it is the low-ability workers who are initially getting an education and the high-ability workers who are not. This reverse type dependence, if it develops in the experiment, will then generate the beliefs that are ruled out by the equilibrium dominance arguments of the previous paragraph. Upon learning this pattern, the responder will choose U in response to N and will choose D in response to E, which in turn will induce the Low types to switch over to the N side, resulting in the unintuitive equilibrium shown in Figure 33.4.

Of course, the reverse type dependence sounds totally unrealistic for the labor market terminology, but remember that the equilibrium dominance arguments are based on comparisons of the payoff magnitudes, not on the way decisions are labeled. The experiment, which used neutral decision labels, was done with groups of 12 participants. There were 6 as first movers and 6 as second movers in a different room, and there was an unannounced role reversal after six rounds.

The data for the two sessions is shown in Table 33.1. In the first 6 matchings, about 60 percent of the high types chose N, and slightly more than half of the low types chose E. In the final 6 matchings, the N signal was sent 78 percent of the time (85 percent for high types and 62 percent for low types). Therefore, the overall pattern corresponded more

Table 33.1 | Outcomes for the Reverse Type Dependence Design

First 6 Matchings			Last 6 Matchings		
	N	**E**		**N**	**E**
U	(26, 9)	(12, 2)	**U**	(36, 13)	(3, 6)
D	(5, 1)	(8, 9)	**D**	(5, 2)	(4, 3)

Key: (Count for high types, Count for low types)

closely to the unintuitive equilibrium, since the N signal was predominant for both types. Next, note that in the final 6 matchings, deviations to the E signal are more likely to come from low types (7 of the deviations are from high types, 9 are from low types). Finally, sending the N signal results in the U response (preferred by both types) most of the time, deviating from the predominant pattern to the E signal results in the D "punishment" almost half of the time. To summarize, in the last half of the experiment, most of the proposers send the N signal, which is punished with a D response much less frequently than for those who send the "deviant" E signal.

In a follow-up experiment, Brandts and Holt (1993) report even stronger convergence to an unintuitive equilibrium, obtained by adding a third response that made reverse type dependence even sharper in early rounds. The bottom line is that for signaling games with multiple equilibria, an analysis of what beliefs are reasonable should be based on behavioral adjustment patterns toward equilibrium and not on equilibrium dominance arguments based on a deductive thought process that starts in equilibrium.

33.5 "Stripped Down Poker"

The curious reader might wonder what would happen in the pooling equilibrium signaling game shown in Figure 33.2 if the proportion of high-ability types is reduced from 2/3 to some level below 1/2. When the low-ability types are more numerous, the employer's best response to pooling is to make the Down job assignment, which would break the pooling equilibrium (see Question 6 at the end of the chapter). In this case, the Nash equilibrium would involve randomization. Sometimes students find randomization difficult to accept as a decision strategy, but the usefulness of a non-predictable approach becomes intuitively obvious in a game like poker, where bluffing with a weak hand is not uncommon. The game described in this section is known as "stripped down poker," and an easy way to run it in class is described in Reiley, Urbancic, and Walker (2005), who provide instructions. The game can also be implemented with the Veconlab Signaling program by selecting the Poker Terminology from the setup menu.

The two-person poker game begins with each person putting a stake of $1 on the table. There is a deck of four Kings and four Aces, which is shuffled. The informed person sees a single card drawn from the deck, which has been restored to equal numbers of Kings and Aces if a previous draw has been made. Knowing the card, the informed person decides whether to raise (by placing another dollar on the table) or fold, in which case the uninformed person gets the initial stake. If the informed person raises, then the uninformed person must decide whether to fold and lose their stake or to call by adding a second dollar so that each person has $2 on the table at this point. If the uninformed person chooses to call, then the card is revealed; the informed person wins ($2) if the card is an Ace, and the uninformed person wins ($2) if it is a King.

In a large class, the instructor can play the role of the informed person and play against volunteers from the class. Think about playing this with your professor. At first blush, you might conjecture that the professor will simply raise with an Ace (which always wins) and fold with a King (to avoid an embarrassing loss). If that is what you expect, then it would be best to fold whenever the professor raises. Suppose that you think about it some more and realize that if a professor who anticipates this reaction would try to sneak in a raise with a King, hoping that you will fold and lose your stake. So you decide to call a raise sometimes. If you call all of the time, then the professor would never raise with a King, and you would lose in those cases. So it is reasonable to expect that the professor would sometimes raise with a King, a "bluff," and that you would end up "calling the bluff" sometimes but not every time.

The rest of this section pertains to a Web-based experiment in which groups of 12 people were paired with the same partner in a sequence of 20 rounds of play. Player roles (informed or uninformed) did not change, and the program presented the game in terms of cards, with computer-generated random draws. Each person began with an initial capital amount of $20 to avoid negative cumulative earnings in this zero-sum game. The 5-period moving averages of the data, by round, are shown in Figure 33.5. The line at the top indicates that the informed person always chose raise with an Ace, as expected. The thick gray dashed line is the rate of bluffing (Raise|King). This bluff rate starts high and falls in response to having the bluff called a lot. The call rate (thin dashed line) starts high and goes up at first, probably in response to the frequent bluffing. Then the call rate declines as the bluff rate goes down. In the 10 final rounds, the call rate is about twice as high as the bluff rate.

The Nash equilibrium probabilities of calling and bluffing are indicated by the horizontal lines in the figure, at 0.67 and 0.33 respectively. To derive these predictions for risk-neutral players, let the Bluff rate be denoted by β, and let the call rate be denoted by γ (think β as B for bluff, and of γ as C for call). As noted earlier, the informed person will always raise with an Ace, since this card will win for sure if it is called.

First, consider the expected payoff for an informed person who draws a King. A person who decides to raise on a King will lose $2 with probability γ and will gain $1 with probability $(1 - \gamma)$, so the expected payoff is $-2\gamma + 1 - \gamma = 1 - 3\gamma$, which is no better or worse than fold-

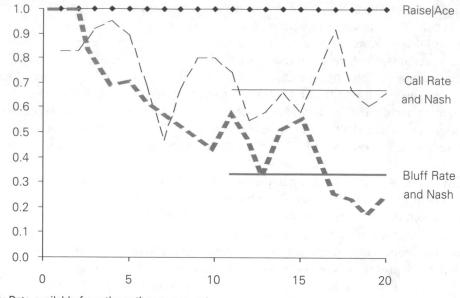

Figure 33.5   Bluff and Call Proportions for a "Stripped Down Poker" Experiment

ing and losing a dollar if $1 - 3\gamma = -1$, or if $\gamma = 2/3$. This call rate of $2/3$ is what it takes to make the informed person indifferent between raise and fold when they draw a King, and such indifference is needed for someone to be willing to decide randomly. The Nash prediction for the call rate is $2/3$, as shown by the thin horizontal line in the figure.

The analysis of the uninformed person's decision is a little more complicated, since that person must use Bayes' rule to make inferences about how likely it is that a person who raises really has an Ace. Think of it this way, half of the informed people have an Ace and raise, and a fraction β of the other half will raise on a King, so the proportion of Aces among those who raise is $1/(1+ \beta)$. The formal derivation with Bayes' rule is given in Equation (33.1), where Ace and King are abbreviated by A and K.

$$\Pr(A\,|\,Raise) = \frac{\Pr(Raise\,|\,A)\Pr(A)}{\Pr(Raise\,|\,A)\Pr(A) + \Pr(Raise\,|\,K)\Pr(K)} = \frac{1(0.5)}{1(0.5) + \beta(0.5)} = \frac{1}{1 + \beta} \quad (33.1)$$

Thus, the probability of a King given a raise is $1 - 1/(1 + \beta) = \beta/(1 + \beta)$. An uninformed person who sees a raise and decides to call, will lose \$2 with probability $1/(1 + \beta)$ and will win \$2 with probability $\beta/(1 + \beta)$. As shown in Equation (33.2), this uninformed person will, therefore, be indifferent between calling and folding (for a loss of \$1) if:

$$\frac{-2}{1 + \beta} + \frac{2\beta}{1 + \beta} = -1, \tag{33.2}$$

or equivalently, if $\beta = 1/3$.

These predictions, 0.67 for the call rate and 0.33 for the bluff rate, are quite close to the data averages for the last half of the experiment, where the observed call rate was 60 percent and the observed bluff rate was 33 percent.

33.6   Extensions: "Too Cool for School"

Miller and Plott (1985) investigated signaling in a rich market environment with both price and quality dimensions. Sellers would begin a market period by choosing an underlying quality level, "Regular" or "Super." The Supers were more costly to produce, but they were more valuable to buyers. Sellers could then add a number of "quality increments" to the product. The quality increments were observed by buyers, but the underlying grade (Regular or Super) was not observed. Separation was possible since it was less expensive for a seller of a Super to add quality increments. A typical pattern of separation would begin with sellers of Supers offering quality increments far in excess of what it would take to prevent sellers of Regulars from matching them, and then the quality increments for Supers would decline toward the minimum level that would prevent imitation by sellers of Regulars. The results were quite variable, with separation observed in some sessions and pooling observed in other sessions done with the same market parameters.

Jung, Kagel, and Levin (1994) also ran a series of signaling experiments in a market context, with an incumbent firm facing a series of potential entrants in Selten's chain store game. The incumbent's type was randomly determined to be either strong or weak, such that a weak firm would prefer not to contest entry in a single-period setting. With a string of potential entrants, however, a weak incumbent could contest entry in early periods to deter subsequent entry. This equilibrium, in which both strong and weak incumbents tend to contest entry in early periods, has elements of pooling.

With separation, the relationship between the unobserved type and the strength of the signal is monotonic for the games that have been considered, e.g., high-ability workers signal more. Sometimes the relationship between the signal and underlying type is not monotonic, for example the nouveau riche often spend more conspicuously than those with even larger amounts of "old money." Another example is when medium quality products are aggressively advertised to distinguish them from poor products, whereas high-quality products often rely largely on reputation. This tendency for those with very high types (ability, quality, money) to stop signaling is known as *counter-signaling*, and it is most likely when the type is partly or imperfectly observed, or observed with some noise. The notion of counter-signaling was introduced by Feltovich, Harbaugh, and To (2002) in an experimental economics paper subtitled "Too Cool for School?"— which says it all. A colleague of mine, Bill Johnson, even suggested that differences between unofficial faculty dress codes across university departments might be due to signaling and counter-signaling. A disheveled look may be a sign of real genius. Look at your professor today and decide for yourself.

QUESTIONS

1. For the pooling equilibrium shown in Figure 33.2, the expected payoff for an employer who responds to Education with the Up job is (2/3)*125 + (1/3)*75. Calculate the employer's expected payoff for the Down job assignment in this case and show that it is lower.

2. Consider the game with two players, a first-mover or "proposer," and a second mover or "responder." The proposer wakes up in the morning and realizes that he/she is either strong or weak. The ex ante probability of strong is 2/3. The proposer then decides whether to drink beer for breakfast, or to eat quiche. A strong proposer actually likes beer for breakfast, and a weak proposer prefers quiche. The responder can observe the proposer's breakfast but not the proposer's type. The responder would like to fight a weak proposer, and to flee from a strong proposer. The payoffs are:

Beer/Quiche Game: (Proposer Payoffs, Responder Payoffs)

	Flee	Fight
Beer (Strong type)	($2.80, $1.00)	($1.20, $0.50)
Quiche (Strong type)	($2.00, $1.00)	($0.40, $0.50)
Beer (Weak type)	($2.00, $0.50)	(($0.40, $1.00)
Quiche (Weak type)	($2.80, $0.50)	($1.20, $1.00)

Draw the extensive form of this game, using the same format as that of Figure 33.1 or 33.2, with Strong shown in the upper-half of the figure. Does the equilibrium involve separation, pooling, or both, and is there more than one Nash equilibrium? Explain.

3. Draw the extensive form and discuss the equilibrium for a beer/quiche game from Question 2, but with one payoff change (shown in bold):

Beer/Quiche Game: (Proposer Payoffs, Responder Payoffs)

	Flee	Fight
Beer (Strong type)	($2.80, $1.00)	($1.20, $0.50)
Quiche (Strong type)	($2.00, $1.00)	($0.40, $0.50)
Beer (Weak type)	($2.00, $0.50)	(($0.40, $1.00)
Quiche (Weak type)	($2.80, $0.50)	(**$2.20**, $1.00)

4. Describe an example of signaling in a context that is not discussed in the chapter. Does your example involve separation or pooling?

5. Consider a pooling equilibrium for the payoffs in Figure 33.4 with both types choosing the E decision. What "out-of-equilibrium beliefs" support this equilibrium, and can these beliefs be ruled out with an equilibrium dominance argument?

6. Suppose that the proportion of high-ability types for the game in Figure 33.2 is reduced from 2/3 to some level below one-half, say to 1/3. Show that pooling on either outcome (Education or None) is no longer a Nash equilibrium.

chapter 34

Prediction Markets

One of the central concepts in finance is the *efficient markets hypothesis*—that prices will (somehow) incorporate all relevant information. Given the widespread belief in the informational efficiency of markets, it is natural that economists and others have designed new trading institutions to generate price-based predictions about important events, e.g., sales outcomes and elections. This chapter considers information aggregation in laboratory markets and in parallel field settings that are popularly known as *prediction markets*. The Veconlab Political Event Market can be used to set up a Web-based trading exchange in the field, with payoffs that depend on the outcome of a subsequent event. Each student can then be given a trading account of hypothetical classroom dollars to use in this market, which can be cleared before class each day if after-hours trading is allowed. In the lab, the Limit Order program can implement an asset market experiment in which partially informed investors trade on the basis of their private information signals about the unknown common value of an asset.

34.1 The Rationale for Prediction Markets

The idea behind a prediction market is to create a tradable share or contract for each possible event. In the 2004 U.S. Presidential election, for example, one could buy and sell contracts for Bush, Kerry, and Nader using the Iowa Electronic Markets Web site, which is run by experimentalists in economics, accounting, and finance at the University of Iowa. In these types of markets, an initial investment of $1 provides the trader with a "market portfolio" of one contract for each major candidate, and one for "rest of field," so that all possible outcomes are covered. Each share has a cash payoff determined by how well that candidate performs in the subsequent election. In this manner, the transactions prices provide an indication of what investors expect.

The two main types of political event contracts are *winner-take-all* and *vote share*. In a vote share market, a contract associated with a particular candidate can be redeemed for an amount equal to the percentage of the vote subsequently obtained by that candidate. In 2004, Bush garnered about 51.5 percent of the vote, so shares of Bush were redeemed for about 51.5 cents each. (In some markets, all amounts are scaled up into dollars instead of pennies.) In contrast, there can be more risk in winner-take-all markets, since all shares have a 0 payoff, except for those of the winning candidate, which are redeemed for $1 each. In either type of market, a person who puts $1 in and then does not trade at all will have earnings of exactly $1, since the sum of the vote shares is 100 and there is only one winner.

It is possible to make money on arbitrage if prices in event markets are not aligned. For example, if bid prices sum to more than $1, then a trader can buy market portfolios for $1 each and sell them unbundled for a profit. Conversely, if the sum of asking prices is less than $1, a trader could purchase a market portfolio that offers a sure gain. Another opportunity for arbitrage would be if prices are lower in one exchange than in another, which provides an opportunity to buy in one and sell in another. These arbitrage opportunities are relatively minor. For example, Wolfers and Zitzewitz (2004) collected bid and ask prices every four hours for shares that would pay $100 if Arnold Schwarzenegger was elected Governor of California. There was considerable variation in these prices over time, but the TradeSports and World Sports Exchange prices shadowed each other closely to eliminate arbitrage opportunities quickly.

An individual might decide to trade in a vote share market on the basis of a hunch that the prices will go up (buy now) or down (sell now). If most people think that a candidate's shares are over-priced after some unexpected negative publicity, then that price will fall as traders try to sell, and conversely for price decreases. These buy and sell pressures push price to a point where supply equals demand, which would constitute a consensus about the vote share for that candidate. Thus, the trading prices in vote share markets convey information about the share of the vote that traders expect the candidate to obtain on election day.

In contrast, prices in winner-take-all markets are more closely related to probabilities. To see this, note that if a candidate has no chance of winning, then the winner-take-all price would be 0 since there will be no payout. Of course, a strong partisan might want to hold shares with no chance of a payout, but marginal traders should put intense downward pressure on the price if it were to rise much. In the 1988 U.S. Presidential election, for example, some traders wanted to "send a message for Jesse" by buying Jackson shares, but the resulting price increase was quickly reversed. Conversely, arbitrage would drive share prices for a sure winner up to $1. If a risk neutral person thinks that a candidate has a 50 percent chance of winning, then this person would be willing to pay any amount below $.50 and would want to sell shares for any amount above $.50. These somewhat loose arguments suggest that transactions prices are correlated with consensus win probabilities in these markets. There have been documented attempts to manipulate prices in political event markets, but these have not succeeded for very long (Wolfers and Zitzewitz 2005b).

To summarize, there is a strong connection between trading prices and consensus win probabilities in winner-take-all markets, and between consensus vote shares and trading prices in vote share markets. The intuition behind these connections is clear, although formal derivations of these connections are only available under special assumptions (Manski 2005; Gjerstad 2005; Wolfers and Zitzewitz 2005b).

The first step in setting up an event market is to define the events, which cover all possible outcomes. For example, a market designed to elicit information about sales forecasts could break down possible sales outcomes into categories, each being an event: sales below 100, between 100 and 110, and so on. These categories are analogous to candidates, so it is important that all possible outcomes are covered. Then a winner-take-all market would yield consensus probabilities associated with each of the events. Arbitrage pressures will force this collection of probabilities to sum to one. Therefore, the inferred event probabilities constitute a probability distribution over sales outcomes, which could be represented concisely as a bar graph for subsequent management use.

In addition, contracts can be defined for combinations of events. Such "compound event contracts" will pay off only if all of the listed events occur. During the 2004 U.S. Presidential election campaign, for example, one of the available contracts on the TradeSports site would pay off only if Bush won *and* if Osama Bin Laden was "neutralized" prior to election day. (This would have been a bad investment.) These compound event markets can be used to make inferences about more complicated events. For example, suppose that the desired information is how much Bush's chances of winning the election (event B) would have gone up if Osama Bin Laden had been neutralized (event O). So what we want to know is $Pr(B|O)$. A compound event market ("Bush wins *and* Osama loses") is denoted $P(B,O)$, and a separate single-market with contracts that pay if Bin Laden is neutralized would yield a forecast that is denoted by $Pr(O)$. It follows from the rules of conditional probability that $Pr(B,O) = Pr(B|O)Pr(O)$, since the only way to observe both events (left side) is for Bin Laden to be neutralized first, $Pr(O)$, and then for Bush to win afterward, $Pr(B|O)$, as shown on the right side of the conditional probability formula. Thus, $Pr(B|O) = Pr(B, O)/Pr(O)$, and markets for the single event and the compound event can be used to "back out" the conditional probability of a Bush win after Bin Laden is neutralized. In a similar manner, Davis and Holt (1994c) used simultaneous price data from contracts in nomination and general election event markets to infer that the front runner with intense partisan support in the Republican nomination market, Oliver North, would not have been as strong a candidate in the general election as the more centrist candidate, James Miller.

There is no requirement that the events be political; these markets are useful whenever traders have different sources of information to be aggregated. For example, health care workers only see people getting sick in their own areas, and simple counts of cases may not adequately convey the intensity of a disease or the speed with which it is spreading among family members and co-workers. A prediction market for flu cases was established in Iowa for the 2004 and 2005 flu seasons (Nelson, Polgreen, and Neumann 2006), a development that the *Economist* (October 13, 2005) termed "Trading in Flu-tures." Another example is the Hollywood Stock Exchange, a market that has generated forecasts of box office success and Oscar winners; these forecasts have compared favorably with those of industry experts (Pennock, Lawrence, Neilsen, and Giles 2001). The most infamous example of market-based forecasting was the Defense Advance Research Products Agency (DARPA) plan to allow trading in "terrorist futures," a plan that was quickly abandoned after negative press accounts.

Business applications of prediction markets have attracted a lot of attention recently, as major Internet companies are rumored to be developing them. For example, suppose that the traders are sales managers in differing geographic regions for a particular company, and each one sees local trends, worrisome signs when key clients hold back, and so on. Requests for sales forecasts may yield biased information, for example, if sales managers send in conservative predictions to make their subsequent performance look better. A market that collects and processes information from local sales managers could be quite valuable at the corporate headquarters where production decisions are made. One early business forecasting application involved Hewett-Packard printer sales. Chen and Plott (2002) report that the market-generated price forecasts were more accurate than those of internal experts. The most widely studied prediction markets, however, are based on political events, which is the next topic.

34.2   The Success of Political Event Markets

One advantage of prediction markets is that they operate on a 24×7 basis, so the effects of unforeseen events on share prices can be tracked quickly and inexpensively relative to polls. In the 1994 Virginia Senate race, for example, there was a fairly active IEM market for shares of the main candidates: incumbent Chuck Robb and the Republican challenger, Oliver North, and for two surprisingly strong independent candidates as well. Shares of Robb were selling above those for North throughout the month of August. The final debate on Labor Day weekend was held at Hampton Sidney College (North country), and in an effort to sound tough, Robb said that he would take food "out of the hands of widows and orphans" to control the growth of entitlement programs. The moderator gave him a chance to clarify, but he stood his ground. Most of the traders were college students in the area, and some of the Robb supporters expressed the view that he had won the debate, although North supporters strongly disagreed. Not surprisingly, this difference of opinion generated a high trading volume, and the price of North shares climbed overnight. The polls picked up North's lead in the days that followed, but there had been almost a month between the post-debate poll and the previous poll, so the market provided a quick estimate of the extent of North's surge that was not available otherwise. Several weeks later, there were newspaper accounts of bumper stickers that read "Widows and Orphans for North."

Another aspect of these markets is that, as with other financial markets, prices respond to *new* information, since old information is already incorporated. North's share prices had fallen in the spring campaign season when Ronald Reagan questioned the truthfulness of his statements on the Iran-Contra scandal, and soon stores were carrying "Oliver North Pack of Lies" playing cards, with one "lie" per card. But in September when Nancy Reagan repeated the charge, it had no effect on prices, despite wide press coverage. The North prices did fall that month, however, when he claimed that (then President) Clinton was not his commander-in-chief. As a result, North's aides launched the "stealth campaign," keeping him out of the spotlight. The press later reported that a motorcyclist caught up with the North motorcade at a stoplight and held up a sign reading "Clinton *is* your commander-in-chief, and Ronald Reagan doesn't even like you."

A typical pattern that showed up in this election market was that prices in the winner-take-all market were more volatile than vote share prices, which is explained by the fact that it only takes a relatively small margin to win. For example, North shares in the winner-take-all market doubled in price after the third debate, from about $.25 to about $.50, whereas prices in the vote share market changed by much less. Davis and Holt (1994c) estimated that each 1 percent change in the ratio of the vote share prices for the two leaders resulted in a 3.8 percent change in the ratio of the winner-take-all prices.

A final feature of vote share markets that is worth mentioning is that they are often less volatile than polls, and over the course of a long campaign, the prices are typically closer to the final election outcomes than the major polls (Berg et al. 2003). In the North-Robb campaign, the polls often bracketed the market price movements over the same time period. The intuitive reason for the relative stability of market predictions is that investors in the market are trying to guess what will ultimately happen on election day, i.e., to look past short-term events. In contrast, polls reflect individual voter's attitudes about candidates if the election were held that day. Another factor could be that investors are simultaneously considering multiple poll results, with subjective corrections for differing sample sizes and degrees of recency.

At their best, polls have the advantage of being based on representative samples, whereas investors in electronic markets are a self-selected group, with heavy representation of younger and better-educated voters. But pollsters have to make educated guesses about which of their respondents are likely voters. This correction can be quite large, and it usually means scaling down the Democratic percentages, making the results more subjective than is commonly thought. Most people express surprise at the possibility that markets composed of a relatively small group of traders can even come close to major polls in terms of predictive accuracy, but when you consider the variability across polls conducted at similar times, this does not seem too farfetched. Of course, comparisons are a little misleading since markets respond to polls. In the North-Robb race, for example, Robb's prices recovered to achieve parity with North's prices in the final days of the campaign, but only after the release of election eve poll results showing Robb to be in the lead.

A comparison of the IEM vote share prices and Gallup poll results of the last five U.S. presidential elections is tallied in Wolfers and Zitzewitz (2005). For the 13 candidates in these elections, the average absolute error for the final Gallup poll was 1.9 percentage points, as compared with 1.6 percentage points for the IEM markets. The most dramatic failure of the market forecasts came in 1996 when there was a major influx of new cash just prior to the election, but predictions based on the transactions-based average prices for the week prior to this election were quite accurate (Berg et al. 2003). The most dramatic success was for the 1988 U.S. presidential election, when the polls were all over the place, and the IEM prices were on target (Forsythe et al. 1991, 1992). In this election, George Bush (senior) won by 7.8 percent, which essentially matched the 8 percent Bush margin provided by the first vote share market run at Iowa. The election eve Gallup poll gave Bush a 12 percent edge, and both the Harris and the WSJ/CNN polls had Bush *losing* by about 5 percent. The resulting publicity surely put pressure on pollsters to refine their procedures, and it would not be surprising if the subjective use of data from other polls resulted in lower variance of forecasts in subsequent elections.

Considering all types of elections, the accuracy of vote share markets is increased when the election has high visibility (e.g., presidential elections), when there is a high trading volume, and when the number of possible contracts is smaller (Berg et al. 2003). An overall assessment is that the market-based forecasts are surprisingly accurate early in the campaigns, and that they do at least as well as polls in the final days. Moreover, political event markets sometimes attract a fair amount of trading activity in remote locations where polls are not available, e.g., in small local elections.

34.3 Information Aggregation and "Common Value Trading"

There is a parallel line of research with laboratory experiments in which the unknown event to be predicted is determined randomly, and each trader is provided with a randomly generated private "signal." In this case, it is possible to measure precisely what the relevant aggregate information is, and to see if this information is reflected in prices. The examples in this section are based on the Veconlab setup that provides traders with independent signals about an unknown final redemption value. The signals are analogous to bidders' signals in a common value auction; each person knows something about the final value, but nobody knows what it is exactly.

For example, suppose that an asset is traded for 20 periods, after which it will be redeemed for an unknown amount per share. You might think of period 20 as the time at which results of a drug patent approval decision will be made on the basis of ongoing clinical trials. Each trader may have different sources of information about the potential profitability of the drug relative to that of competing drugs, and trading prices for the asset may be affected by these different sources of information.

Suppose that the only information that one trader has is that the common redemption value is equally likely to be any amount between $25 and $75, and a second trader only knows that the redemption value is between $55 and $105. Since the first trader knows that the final value is no higher than $75 and the second trader knows that it will be at least $55, together they could reduce the range of possible final values to the $55–$75 range. In this example, each person's initial uncertainty was characterized by a $50 range, but their joint information narrowed the range to $20. It is easy to imagine that if additional traders have independent estimates of the unknown common value, their aggregate information may yield a much tighter range of possible values.

Bostian, Goeree, and Holt (2005) implemented this type of situation by providing each trader with a signal that is known to be within plus or minus $20 of the true redemption value. For example, if the true redemption value is $50, then with a range of plus or minus $20, individual signals would be between $30 and $70. A person with a relatively low signal of 35 would know that the value is between $15 and $55, and a person with a relatively high signal of 65 would know that the value is between $45 and $85. Traders were not told anything about the possible level of the redemption value, other then their own signals. A person with a signal of S, for example, was told that the final redemption value would be equally likely to be any amount between $S - \$20$ and $S + \$20$. In this case, the lowest of the signals puts an upper bound on the range of redemption values, and the highest of the signals puts a lower bound on this range. Therefore, the range will tend to be narrower in markets with more traders.

The asset did not pay dividends and there was no interest paid on cash, so the only information that might be revealed in the trading process would be something about others' beliefs about the final value. All sessions lasted for 20 periods, and each trader began with an initial portfolio of six shares and a signal as described above. In one treatment, traders were given low cash balances of $500, and in another treatment, they were given $1500. (Payoffs were made so that each $100 earned in the experiment resulted in a $1 cash payment.) The motivation for the high cash treatment was the observation of stronger price bubbles and crashes in the limit order asset markets discussed in Chapter 11. This information aggregation can be seen in Figure 34.1, which shows results for a high cash session. There is a slow, steady bubble that reached about $60 in period 13, before falling to the (unknown) true common value of about $50 in the final period, which is shown by the flat horizontal line. The range of possible common values for this session, based on the private information individual signals, was from $47.38 to $50.34. Despite the final period convergence, the results of these experiments offer mixed support for the accuracy of prediction markets, since price surges that are not based on fundamentals can occur.

Price bubbles were observed in all of the high-cash sessions, and with one exception, bubbles were not observed in the low-cash sessions. Regardless of whether or not a bubble formed, however, the final trading price in round 20 tended to be quite close to the narrow range implied by aggregating individuals' disparate information signals (again with one exception). Interestingly, each investor in the Iowa Electronic Markets are required to limit that person's total investment to $500. Moreover, the portfolio method of issuing contracts (with one contract for each candidate issued for each dollar invested) provides a balance that may diminish or eliminate bubbles. In particular, excess cash pressures to buy will tend to be balanced, since arbitrage will prevent the sum of the bid prices from exceeding 1.

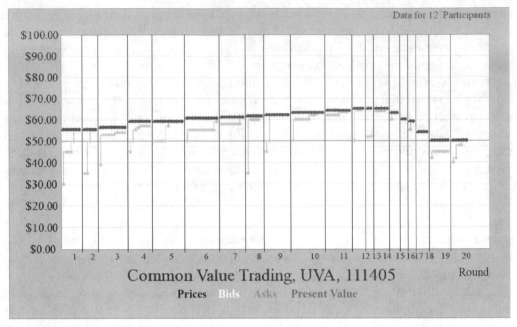

Source: (Bostian, Goeree, and Holt 2005)

| **Figure 34.1** | A Call Market with an Unknown Common Redemption Value (Dark Horizontal Line) |

Another setup option for the Veconlab Limit Order Market program is to provide signals to a subset of the traders, i.e., to designated "insiders," which focuses on whether insiders earn more than uninformed traders, and on whether the trading prices end up revealing the insiders' information. Plott and Sunder (1982) report an experiment with three possible "states" that determine final dividends. Some traders were told the actual state before trading began, although nobody knew identities of other insiders. Prices tended to adjust quickly to the level that would have been expected if all traders had been informed of insider information, i.e., to the price determined by the intersection of the supply and demand curves if all traders knew the true state. These information-aggregation predictions are known in the literature as "rational expectations" predictions. The adjustment to rational expectations predictions was so quick that the profits of insiders were not noticeably different from the profits of the uninformed traders. Watts (1992) reports a similar experiment in a different informational setting, and in this case, insiders tended to earn higher profits, although price convergence patterns were generally supportive of the information revelation ("rational expectations") predictions.

34.4 Extensions

Prediction markets are essentially betting mechanisms, and such mechanisms have arisen naturally in many forms. One example is the "pari-mutuel" betting structure used at racetracks. Under pari-mutuel betting, the purse (total amount bet, minus commissions) is divided among those who bet on the winner, in proportion to the amounts that they bet. Suppose, for example, that there are just two horses and equal dollar amounts are bet on each. Then the payout rates are the same, and the best decision is to bet on the horse that you think will win (which would then raise the price for the horse that you bet on). If instead there is twice as much cash being bet on one of the horses, then its payout rate is only half as high. If you do not think its chances of winning are two-thirds or more, then you should bet on the long shot. Even though the previous argument implicitly assumes risk neutrality, which is a bad assumption for bettors, the point is that the allocation of bets will tend to incorporate the diverse information that betters bring to the racetrack.

Plott, Wit, and Yang (1997) ran experiments motivated by pari-mutuel betting. There were six alternative assets, and only one of them had been selected at random to have a positive payout. The payout was divided equally among the investors in that asset. Each subject received a private signal with some information about which asset had been selected, but the order of decision-making was not exogenous as in the information cascade experiments discussed in Chapter 31. Individuals could observe others' decisions as they were made. In this manner, the information dispersed among the investors could become aggregated and incorporated into the prices of the six assets. In most cases, the asset prices ended up signaling which asset would actually produce a positive payout. In some cases, however, an initial surge of purchases for a particular asset stimulated others to follow, and the result was that the market price rose for an asset that had no payout in the end, as would be the case with an incorrect cascade.

QUESTIONS

1. In a vote share market, the shares for candidates are denoted D, R, I, and ROF for "rest of field." A dollar can be used to buy a market portfolio (one share of each), and the shares pay an amount in pennies that equals the percentage of the vote received by the candidate in the election. At any point in time, the market making software displays the highest bid prices (at which people are willing to buy) and the lowest ask prices (at which people are willing to sell). Explain whether each of the following sets of prices offer sure gains from arbitrage:

   a. Bid prices of 40, 40, 18, and 4 for D, R, I, and ROF respectively
   b. Ask prices of 40, 40, 18, and 4

    c. Bid prices of 40, 40, 18, and 0

    d. Ask prices of 40, 40, 18 and 0

2. Consider an election campaign for which the nominations are decided in June and the general election is in November. In the early spring, there are winner-take-all markets running simultaneously for the Republican nomination and for the general election. In the Republican nomination market, suppose that the prices are 67 cents for a strong partisan candidate, P, and 33 cents for a moderate, M. In the general election market, the winner-take-all prices for P and M are at 25 cents each, the the price is 50 for the other candidate, an incumbent Democrat who is sure to be nominated. The general feeling in the popular press is that the moderate Republican candidate, if nominated, might do better than the partisan candidate in the general election. What do the winner-take-all prices in these markets reveal about investor's assessments of how much better the moderate candidate would do in the general election (on the assumption that the Republican who loses the nomination will not run as an independent)?

References

Abdulkadiroglu, Atila, Parag A. Pathak, Alvin E. Roth, and Tayfun Sönmez (2006) "Changing the Boston School Choice Mechanism," Discussion Paper, Harvard University.

Akerlof, George A. (1970) "The Market for 'Lemons:' Quality Uncertainty and the Market Mechanism," *Quarterly Journal of Economics*, 84, 488–500.

Allais, M. (1953) "Le Comportement De L'homme Rationnel Devant Le Risque, Critique Des Postulates Et Axiomes De L'ecole Americaine," *Econometrica*, 21, 503–546.

Alsopp, L., and J. D. Hey (2000) "Two Experiments to Test a Model of Herd Behavior," *Experimental Economics*, 3, 121–136.

Andersen, Steffen, Glenn W. Harrison, Morten Lau, and E. E. Rustrom (2005) "Lost in State Space: Are Preferences Stable?" Discussion Paper, presented at the ESA Meetings in Tucson, October 2005.

Anderson, D. and M. Haupert (1999) "Employment and Statistical Discrimination: A Hands-On Experiment," *Journal of Econometrics*, 25(1) 85–102.

Anderson, L. R. (2001) "Payoff Effects in Information Cascade Experiments," *Economic Inquiry*, 39(4), 609 615.

Anderson, L. R., R. M. Fryer, and C. A. Holt (2006) "Experimental Studies of Discrimination," in the W. Rogers, ed., *Handbook on the Economics of Discrimination*, Northhampton, MA: Edward Elgar, 97–115.

Anderson, S. P., J. K. Goeree, and C. A. Holt (1998) "Rent Seeking with Bounded Rationality: An Analysis of the All Pay Auction," *Journal of Political Economy*, 106, 828–853.

—— (2001) "Minimum Effort Coordination Games: Stochastic Potential and Logit Equilibrium," *Games and Economic Behavior*, 34, 177–199.

—— (2002) "The Logit Equilibrium: A Unified Perspective on Intuitive Behavioral Anomalies in Games with Rank-based Payoffs," *Southern Economic Journal*, 68, 21–47.

—— (2004) "Noisy Directional Learning and the Logit Equilibrium," *Scandinavian Journal of Economics*, 106, 581–602.

Anderson, Lisa R. and Charles A. Holt (1996a) "Classroom Games: Understanding Bayes' Rule," *Journal of Economic Perspectives*, 10, 179–187.

—— (1996b) "Classroom Games: Information Cascades," *Journal of Economic Perspectives*, 10, 187–193.

—— (1997) "Information Cascades in the Laboratory," *American Economic Review*, 87, 847–862.

Anderson, Lisa R., Charles A. Holt, and David Reiley (2006) "Congestion and Social Welfare," forthcoming in *Experimental Methods, Environmental Economics*, T. L. Cherry, J. F. Shogren, and S. Kroll, eds., London: Routledge.

Anderson, Lisa R. and Sarah L. Stafford (2003) "An Experimental Analysis of Rent Seeking Under Varying Competitive Conditions," *Public Choice*, 115, 199–216.

Andreoni, J. (1993) "An Experimental Test of the Public Goods Crowding-out Hypothesis," *American Economic Review*, 83, 1317–1327.

Andreoni, J., M. Castillo, and R. Petrie (2003) "What Do Bargainers' Preferences Look Like? Experiments with a Convex Bargaining Game," *American Economic Review*, 93(3), 972–985.

Andreoni, J., W. Harbaugh, and L. Vesterlund (2003) "The Carrot or the Stick: Rewards, Punishments and Cooperation," *American Economic Review*, 93(3), 893–902.

Ansolabehere, Stephen, Shanto Iyengar, Adam Simon, and Nicholas Valentino (1994) "Does Attack Advertising Demobilize the Electorate?" *American Political Science Review* 88 (December): 829–838.

Aragones, Enriqueta and Thomas R. Palfrey (2004) "The Effect of Candidate Quality on Electoral Equilibrium: An Experimental Study," *American Political Science Review* 98 (February): 77–90.

Arkes, H. R., L. T. Herren, and A. M. Isen (1988) "The Role of Potential Loss in the Influence of Affect on Risk-Taking Behavior," *Organizational Behavior and Human Decision Processes*, 42, 191–193.

Arkes, H., C. Joyner, M. Pezzo, J. G. Nash, K. Siegel-Jacobs, and E. Stone (1994) "The Psychology of Windfall Gains," *Organizational Behavior and Human Decision Processes*, 59, 331–347.

Arrow, K. J. (1973) "The Theory of Discrimination" in *Discrimination in Labor Markets*. Orley Ashenfelter and Albert Rees, eds., Princeton, NJ: Princeton University Press.

Ausubel, L. M., P. Crampton, and P. Milgrom (2004) "The Clock-Proxy Auction: A Practical Combinatorial Auction Design," Discussion Paper, University of Maryland.

Avery, Christopher, Christine Jolls, Richard A. Posner, and Alvin E. Roth (2001) "The Market for Federal Judicial Law Clerks," *University of Chicago Law Review*, 68(3), 793–902.

Badasyan, N., J. K. Goeree, M. Hartmann, C. A. Holt, J. Morgan, T. Rosenblat, M. Servatka, and D. Yandell (2004) "Vertical Integration of Successive Monopolists: A Classroom Experiment," Discussion Paper, University of Virginia.

Ball, S. B., M. H. Bazerman, and J. S. Caroll (1990) "An Evaluation of Learning in the Bilateral Winner's Curse," *Organizational Behavior and Human Decision Processes*, 48, 1–22.

Ball, S. B. and C. A. Holt (1998) "Classroom Games: Bubbles in an Asset Market," *Journal of Economic Perspectives*, 12, 207–218.

Ball, S. B., C. C. Eckel, P. J. Grossman, and W. Zane (2001) "Status in Markets," *Quarterly Journal of Economics*, February, 161–188.

Bannerjee, A. V. (1992) "A Simple Model of Herd Behavior," *Quarterly Journal of Economics*, 107, 797–817.

Baron, David P. and John A. Ferejohn (1989) "Bargaining in Legislatures," *American Political Science Review* 83 (December): 1181–1206.

Barr, Abigail M. (2003) "Trust and Expected Trustworthiness: Experimental Evidence from Zimbabwean Villages," *Economic Journal*, 113, 614–630.

Basu, K. (1994) "The Traveler's Dilemma: Paradoxes of Rationality in Game Theory," *American Economic Review*, 84(2), 391–395.

Battalio, R. C., L. Green, and J. H. Kagel (1981) "Income-Leisure Tradeoffs of Animal Workers," *American Economic Review*, 71, 621–632.

Battalio, R. C., J. H. Kagel, and D. N. MacDonald (1985) "Animals' Choices over Uncertain Outcomes: Some Initial Experimental Results," *American Economic Review*, 75, 597–613.

Battalio, Raymond C., John H. Kagel, and Komain Jiranyakul (1990) "Testing Between Alternative Models of Choice Under Uncertainty: Some Initial Results," *Journal of Risk and Uncertainty*, 3(1), 25–50.

Bazerman, M. H. and W. F. Samuelson (1983) "I Won the Auction but Don't Want the Prize," *Journal of Conflict Resolution*, 27, 618–634.

Becker, Tilman, Michael Carter, and Jorg Naeve (2005) "Experts Playing the Traveler's Dilemma," Discussion Paper, Honhenheim University.

Berg, J. E., J. W. Dickhaut, and K. A. McCabe (1995) "Trust, Reciprocity, and Social History," *Games and Economic Behavior*, 10, 122–142.

Berg, Joyce, Robert Forsythe, Forrest Nelson, and Thomas Rietz (2003) "Results from a Dozen Years of Election Futures Markets Research," in C. Plott and V. Smith, eds., *The Handbook of Experimental Economics Results*, New York: Elsevier, forthcoming.

Bernoulli, D. (1738) "Specimen Theoriae Novae De Mensura Sortis (Exposition on a New Theory on the Measurement of Risk," *Comentarii Academiae Scientiarum Imperialis Petropolitanae*, 5, 175–192, translated by L. Sommer in *Econometrica*, 1954, 22, 23–36.

Bertrand, Marianne and Sendhil Mullainathan (2004) "Are Emily and Greg More Employable than Lakisha and Jamal? A Field Experiment on Labor Market Discrimination," *American Economic Review*, 94(4), 991–1013.

Bikhchandani, S., D. Hirschleifer, and I. Welch (1992) "A Theory of Fads, Fashion, Custom, and Cultural Change as Informational Cascades," *Journal of Political Economy*, 100, 992–1026.

Binswanger, H. P. (1980) "Attitudes toward Risk: Experimental Measurement in Rural India," *American Journal of Agricultural Economics*, 62, 395–407.

Bolton, G. E. and A. Ockenfels (2000) "ERC: A Theory of Equity, Reciprocity, and Competition," *American Economic Review*, 90(1), 166–193.

Bornstein, Gary and Ilan Yaniv (1998) "Individual and Group Behavior in the Ultimatum Game: Are Groups More 'Rational' than Individuals," *Experimental Economics*, 1, 101–108.

Bornstein, Gary, Tamar Kugler, and Anthony Ziegelmeyer (2004) "Individual and Group Decisions in the Centipede Game: Are Groups More "Rational" Players?" *Journal of Experimental Psychology*, 40, 599–605.

Bostian, A. J. and C. A. Holt (2005) "Price Bubbles in an Asset Market Experiment with a Flat Fundamental Value," Discussion Paper, University of Virginia.

Bostian, A. J., C. A. Holt, and A. Moore (2005) "An Experimental Analysis of the Newsvendor Problem: The Effects of Decision Frequency," Discussion Paper, University of Virginia.

Brams, S. J. and P. C. Fishburn (1978) "Approval Voting," *American Political Science Review*, 72, 831–847.

—— (1988) "Does Approval Voting Elect the Lowest Common Denominator?" *Political Science and Politics*, 21, 277–284.

Brandts, J. and C. A. Holt (1992) "An Experimental Test of Equilibrium Dominance in Signaling Games," *American Economic Review*, 82, 1350–1365.

—— (1993) "Adjustment Patterns and Equilibrium Selection in Experimental Signaling Games," *International Journal of Game Theory*, 22, 279–302.

Brunner, Christoph, Jacob K. Goeree, and Charles A. Holt (2005) "Bid Driven Versus Clock Driven Auctions with Package Bidding," Presentation at the Southern Economic Association Meetings in Washington, D.C., November 2005.

Brunner, Christoph, Jacob K. Goeree, Charles A. Holt, and John O. Ledyard (2006) "Combinational Auctioneering," Draft Discussion Paper, Caltech, May 2006.

Bryant, John (1983) "A Simple Rational Expectations Keynes-Type Model," *Quarterly Journal of Economics*, 98, 525–528.

Bykowsky, M., R. Cull, and J. Ledyard (2000) "Mutually Destructive Bidding: The FCC Auction Design Problem," *Journal of Regulatory Economics*, 17(3), 205–228.

Caginalp, G., D. Porter, and V. Smith (2001): "Financial Bubbles: Excess Cash, Momentum, and Incomplete Information," *Journal of Psychology and Financial Markets*, 2, 80–99.

Camerer, C. F. (1989) "An Experimental Test of Several Generalized Utility Theories," *Journal of Risk and Uncertainty*, 2, 61–104.

—— (1995) "Individual Decision Making," in *The Handbook of Experimental Economics*, J. H. Kagel, and A. E. Roth, eds., Princeton, NJ: Princeton University Press, 587–703.

—— (2003) *Behavioral Game Theory*, Princeton: Princeton University Press.

Camerer, C. F. and T.-H. Ho (1999) "Experience Weighted Attraction Learning in Normal-Form Games," *Econometrica*, 67, 827–874.

—— (2004) "A Cognitive Hierarchy Model of Games," Discussion Paper, Caltech.

Camerer, C. and D. Lovallo (1999) "Overconfidence and Excess Entry: An Experimental Approach," *American Economic Review*, 89, 306–318.

Capen, E. C., R. V. Clapp, and W. M. Campbell (1971) "Competitive Bidding in High-Risk Situations," *Journal of Petroleum Technology*, 23, 641–653.

Capra, C. M., J. K. Goeree, R. Gomez, and C. A. Holt (1999) "Anomalous Behavior in a Traveler's Dilemma?" *American Economic Review*, 89, 678–690.

—— (2000) "Predation, Asymmetric Information, and Strategic Behavior in the Classroom: An Experimental Approach to the Teaching of Industrial Organization," *International Journal of Industrial Organization*, 18, 205–225.

—— (2002) "Learning and Noisy Equilibrium Behavior in an Experimental Study of Imperfect Price Competition," *International Economic Review*, 43(3), 613–636.

Capra, C.M. and C. A. Holt (1999) "Coordination," *Southern Economic Journal*, 65, 630–636.

—— (2000) "Classroom Experiments: A Prisoner's Dilemma," *Journal of Economic Education*, 21(3), 229–236.

Cardenas, Juan Camilo (2003) "Real Wealth and Experimental Cooperation: Evidence from Field Experiments," *Journal of Development Economics*, 70(2), 263–289.

Cardenas, J.C., J. Stranlund, and C. Willis (2000) "Local Environmental Control and Institutional Crowding Out," *World Development*, 28(10), 1719–1733.

Cardenas, Juan Camilo, John K. Stranlund, and Cleve E. Willis (2002) "Economic Inequality and Burden-sharing in the Provision of Local Environmental Quality," *Ecological Economics*, 40, 379–395.

Carpenter, J., E. Verhoogen, and S. Burks (2005) "The Effect of Stakes in Distribution Experiments," *Economics Letters*, 86, 393–398.

Carpenter, J., S. Burks, and E. Verhoogen (2005) "Comparing Students to Workers: The Effects of Stakes, Social Context, and Demographics on Bargaining Outcomes," in J. Carpenter, G. Harrison, and J. List, eds., *Field Experiments in Economics*, JAI Press, 261–290.

Cason, T. N. (1992) "Call Market Efficiency with Simple Adaptive Learning," *Economics Letters*, 40, 27–32.

Cason, Timothy N. (1995) "Cheap Talk and Price Signaling in Laboratory Markets," *Information Economics and Policy*, 7, 183–204.

Cason, Timothy N. (2000) "The Opportunity for Conspiracy in Asset Markets Organized with Dealer Intermediaries," *The Review of Financial Studies*, 13(2), 385–416.

Cason, Timothy N. and Douglas D. Davis (1995) "Price Communications in Laboratory Markets: An Experimental Investigation," *Review of Industrial Organization*, 10, 769–787.

Cason, Timothy N. and Mui, Vai-Lam (2005) "Uncertainty and Resistance to Reform in Laboratory Participation Games," *European Journal of Political Economy*, 21(3), 708–737

Cason, T. N. and D. Friedman (1997) "Price Formation in Single Call Markets," *Econometrica*, 65, 311–345.

Celen, Bogachan and Shachar Kariv (2004) "Distinguishing Informational Cascades from Herd Behavior in the Laboratory," *American Economic Review*, 94(3), 484–497.

Chamberlin, E. H. (1948) "An Experimental Imperfect Market," *Journal of Political Economy*, 56, 95–108.

Charness, Gary and Dan Levin (2005) "When Optimal Choices Feel Wrong: A Laboratory Study of Bayesian Updating, Complexity, and Affect," *American Economic Review*, 95, 1300–1309.

Chen, Kay-Yut and Charles Plott (2002) "Information Aggregation Mechanisms: Concept, Design, and Field Implementation for a Sales Forecasting Problem," Social Science Working Paper 1131, California Institute of Technology.

Chen, Yan and C. R. Plott (1996) "The Groves-Ledyard Mechanism: An Experimental Study of Institutional Design," *Journal of Public Economics*, 59, 335–364.

Chen, Yan and Tayfun Sönmez (2004) "An Experimental Study of House Allocation Mechanisms," *Economics Letters*, 83(1), 137–140.

—— (2005) "School Choice: An Experimental Study," *Journal of Economic Theory*, forthcoming.

Cho, In-Koo and David M. Kreps (1987) "Signaling Games and Stable Equilibria," *Quarterly Journal of Economics*, 102, 179–221.

Christie, W. G. and R. D. Huang (1995) "Following the Pied Piper: Do Individual Returns Herd Around the Market?" *Financial Analysts Journal*, 51, 31–37.

Cipriani, Marco, and Antonio Guarino (2005) "Herd Behavior in a Laboratory Financial Market," *American Economic Review*, 95(5), 1227–1443.

Coate S. and G. Loury (1993) "Will Affirmative Action Eliminate Negative Sterotypes?" *American Economic Review*, 83(5) 1220–1240.

Cochard, F., N. Van Phu, and M. Willinger (2004) "Trust and Reciprocity in a Repeated Investment Game," *Journal of Economic Behavior and Organization*, 55(1), 31–44.

Cohen, Mark and David Scheffman (1989) "The Antitrust Sentencing Guidelines: Is the Punishment Worth the Cost," *Journal of Criminal Law*, 27, 330–336.

Composti, Jeanna (2003) "Asymmetric Payoffs in a Soccer Field Experiment," Distinguished Majors Thesis, University of Virginia.

Cooper, R., D. V. DeJong, R. Forsythe, and T. W. Ross (1996) "Cooperation without Reputation: Experimental Evidence from Prisoners' Dilemma Games," *Games and Economic Behavior*, 12(2) (February): 187–218.

Cooper, Russell and Andrew John (1988) "Coordinating Coordination Failures in Keynesian Models," *The Quarterly Journal of Economics*, 103, 441–464.

Coppinger, V. M., V. L. Smith, and J. A. Titus (1980) "Incentives and Behavior in English, Dutch and Sealed-Bid Auctions," *Economic Inquiry*, 18, 1–22.

Corns, Allan and Andrew Schotter (1999) "Can Affirmative Action Be Cost Effective? An Experimental Examination of Price Preference Auctions," *American Economic Review*, 89, 291–305.

Coursey, D. L., J. L. Hovis, and W. D. Schulze (1987) "The Disparity between Willingness to Accept and Willingness to Pay Measures of Value," *Quarterly Journal of Economics*, 102, 679–690.

Cox, J. C. and R. L. Oaxaca (1989) "Laboratory Experiments with a Finite Horizon Job Search Model," *Journal of Risk and Uncertainty, 2*, 301–329.

—— (2000) "Good News and Bad News: Search from Unknown Wage Offer Distributions," *Experimental Economics, 2*, 197–225.

Cox, J. C., B. Roberson, and V. L. Smith (1982) "Theory and Behavior of Single Object Auctions," in *Research in Experimental Economics*, Vol. 2, V. L. Smith, ed. Greenwich, CT: JAI Press, 1–43.

Cox, J. C., V. L. Smith, and J. M. Walker (1985) "Expected Revenue in Discriminative and Uniform Price Sealed-Bid Auctions," in *Research in Experimental Economics*, Vol. 3, V. L. Smith, ed. Greenwich, CT: JAI Press, 183–232.

—— (1988) "Theory and Individual Behavior of First-Price Auctions," *Journal of Risk and Uncertainty, 1*, 61–99.

Cox, J. C. and S. Vjollca (2001) "Risk Aversion and Expected Utility Theory: Coherence for Small and Large Scale Gambles," University of Arizona.

Cox, James (1999) "Trust and Reciprocity: Implications of Game Triads and Social Context," Working Paper, University of Arizona.

Crawford, V. P. (1991) "An 'Evolutionary' Interpretation of Van Huyck, Battalio, and Beil's Experimental Results on Coordination," *Games and Economic Behavior, 3*, 25–59.

Crawford, Vincent P. (1995) "Adaptive Dynamics in Coordination Games," *Econometrica, 63*, 103–144.

Croson, R. T. A. (1996) "Partners and Strangers Revisited," *Economics Letters, 53*, 25–32.

Croson, R. T. A. and M. Marks (2000) "Step Returns in Threshold Public Goods" A Meta- and Experimental Analysis," *Experimental Economics, 2*(3), 239–259.

Croson, Rachel and Karen Donohue (2002) "Experimental Economics and Supply-Chain Management," *Interfaces, 32*(5), 74–82.

—— (2003) "Impact of POS Data Sharing on Supply Chain Management: An Experimental Study," *Production and Operations Management, 12*(1), 1–11.

—— (2004) "Upstream Versus Downstream Information and Its Impact on the Bullwhip Effect," Discussion Paper, Carlson School, University of Minnesota.

—— (2005) "Behavioral Causes of the Bullwhip Effect and the Observed Value of Inventory Information," *Management Science*, forthcoming.

Cummings, R., C. A. Holt, and S. K. Laury (2004) "Using Laboratory Experiments for Policy Making: An Example from the Georgia Irrigation Reduction Auction," *Journal of Policy Analysis and Management, 3*(2), 241–263.

Cybernomics (2000), "An Experimental Comparison of the Simultaneous Multi-Round Auction and the CRA Combinatorial Auction," available at http://wireless.fcc.gov/auctions/conferences/combin2000/releases/98540191.pdf.

Darley, J. M. and B. Latane (1968) "Bystander Intervention in Emergencies: Diffusion of Responsibility," *Journal of Personality and Social Psychology, 8*, 377–383.

Davis, D. D. (1987) "Maximal Quality Selection and Discrimination in Employment," *Journal of Economic Behavior and Organization, 8*, 97–112.

Davis, D. D. and C. A. Holt (1992) "Capacity Constraints, Market Power, and Mergers in Markets with Posted Prices," *Investigaciones Economicas, 2*, 73–79.

—— (1993) *Experimental Economics*. Princeton, NJ: Princeton University Press.

—— (1994a) "Market Power and Mergers in Markets with Posted Prices," *RAND Journal of Economics, 25*, 467–487.

—— (1994b) "The 1994 Virginia Senate Market," unpublished draft, Virginia Commonwealth University.

—— (1998) "Conspiracies and Secret Price Discounts," *Economic Journal, 108*, 736–756.

—— (1996) "Price Rigidities and Institutional Variations in Markets with Posted Prices," *Economic Theory, 9*(1) 63–80.

Davis, D. D. and R. Reilly (1998) "Do Too Many Cooks Always Spoil the Stew? An Experimental Analysis of Rent Seeking and the Role of a Strategic Buyer," *Public Choice, 95*, 89–115.

Davis, D. D. and A. W. Williams (1991) "The Hayek Hypothesis in Experimental Auctions: Institutional Effects and Market Power," *Economic Inquiry, 29*, 261–274.

Davis, Douglas D. and Bart Wilson (1998) "The Effects of Synergies on the Exercise of Market Power," working paper, Middlebury College.

—— (2002) "Collusion in Procurement Auctions: An Experimental Examination," *Economic Inquiry*, 40(2), 213–230.

Dawes, R. M. (1980) "Social Dilemmas," *Annual Review of Psychology*, 31, 169–193.

DeJong, D. V., Robert Forsythe, and Russell Lundholm (1985) "Ripoffs, Lemons, and Reputation Formation in Agency Relationships: A Laboratory Market Study," *Journal of Finance*, 40, 809–820.

Devenow, A. and I. Welch (1996) Rational Herding in Financial Economics," *European Economic Review*, 40, 603–615.

Dickinson, D. L. and R. L. Oaxaca (2005) "Statistical Discrimination in Labor Markets: An Experimental Analysis," Discussion Paper, Appalachian State University.

Diekmann, A. (1985) "Volunteer's Dilemma," *Journal of Conflict Resolution*, 29, 605–610.

—— (1986) "Volunteer's Dilemma: A Social Trap without a Dominant Strategy and Some Empirical Results," in *Paradoxical Effects of Social Behavior: Essays in Honor of Anatol Rapoport*, A. Diekmann and P. Mitter, eds. Heidelberg: Physica-Verlag, 187–197.

—— (1993) "Cooperation in Asymmetric Volunteer's Dilemma Game: Theory and Experimental Evidence," *International Journal of Game Theory*, 22, 75–85.

Diekmann, A. and P. Mitter (1986) "Paradoxical Effects of Social Behavior: Essays in Honor of Anatol Rapoport," Heidelberg and Vienna: Physica-Verlag, 341.

Diermeier, D. and R. Morton (2005) "Experiments in Majoritarian Bargaining," in D. Austen-Smith and J. Duggan, eds., *Social Choice and Strategic Decisions*, Berlin: Springer.

Dohmen, T., A. Falk, D. Huffman, U. Sunde, J. Schupp, and G. Wagner (2005) "Individual Risk Attitudes: Evidence from a Large, Representative, Experimentally-Validated Survey," IZA Discussion Paper 1730, University of Bonn.

Dorsey, R. and L. Razzolini (2003) "Explaining Overbidding in First-Price Auctions Using Controlled Lotteries," *Experimental Economics*, 6, 123–140.

Drehmann, Mathias, Jörg Oechssler, and Andreas Roider (2005) "Herding and Contrarian Behavior in Financial Markets: An Internet Experiment," *American Economic Review*, 95(5), 1203–1426.

Dufwenberg, Martin, Tobias Lindqvist, and Evan Moore (2005) "Bubbles and Experience: An Experiment," *American Economic Review*, 95(5), 1731–1737.

Durham, Yvonne (2000) "An Experimental Examination of Double Marginalization and Vertical Relationships." *Journal of Economic Behavior and Organization*, 42(2) 207–229.

Eavey, C. L., and G. J. Miller (1984) "Fairness and Majority Rule Games with a Core," *American Journal of Political Science*, 28(3), 570–586.

Eckel, C. C. and P. Grossman (1998) "Are Women Less Selfish Than Men? Evidence from Dictator Games," *Economic Journal*, 108, 726–735.

—— (1999) "Differences in the Economic Decisions of Men and Women: Experimental Evidence," in *Handbook of Experimental Economics Results*, C. R. Plott and V. L. Smith, eds. New York: Elsevier, forthcoming.

Eckel, C. C. and C. A. Holt (1989) "Strategic Voting Behavior in Agenda-Controlled Committee Experiments," *American Economic Review*, 79, 763–773.

Engelbrecht-Wiggans, Richard, John A. List, and David H. Reiley (2005) "Demand Reduction in Multi-unit Auctions with Varying Numbers of Bidders: Theory and Field Experiments," forthcoming, *International Economic Review*.

Ensminger, Jean (2004) "Market Integration and Fairness: Evidence from Ultimatum, Dictator, and Public Goods Experiments in East Africa," in Henrich, Boyd, Bowles, Camerer, Fehr, and Gintis, eds., *Foundations of Human Sociality: Economic Experiments and Ethnographic Evidence from Fifteen Small-Scale Societies*, Oxford U.K.: Oxford University Press, 356–381.

Erev, I., and A. Rapoport (1998) "Coordination, "Magic," and Reinforcement Learning in a Market Entry Game," *Games and Economic Behavior*, 23, 146–175.

Falk, Armin (2004) "Charitable Giving as a Gift Exchange: Evidence from a Field Experiment," University of Bonn, IZA Discussion Paper 1148.

Falk, Armin and Ernst Fehr (2003) "Why Labour Market Experiments?" *Labour Economics*, 10, 399–406.

Falk, Armin and Ernst Fehr (2005) "The Hidden Costs of Control," University of Bonn, forthcoming in the *American Economic Review*.

Fantino, E (1998) "Behavior Analysis and Decision Making," *Journal of the Experimental Analysis of Behavior*, 69, 355–364.

Fehr, E. (2006) "Behavioral Effects of Minimum Wages," presentation at the 2006 ASSA Meetings.

Fehr, E., G. Kirchsteiger, and A. Riedl (1993) "Does Fairness Prevent Market Clearing? An Experimental Investigation," *Quarterly Journal of Economics*, 108, 437–459.

Fehr, E., Alexander Klein, and K. Schmidt (2001) "Fairness, Incentives, and Contractual Incompleteness," Working Paper 72, Institute of Empirical Research in Economics, University of Zurich.

Fehr, E. and J. List (2004) "The Hidden Costs and Returns of Incentives – Trust and Trustworthiness Among CEOs," *Journal of the European Economic Association*, 2(5), 743–771.

Fehr, E. and K. Schmidt (1999) "A Theory of Fairness, Competition, and Cooperation," *Quarterly Journal of Economics*, 114, 769–816.

—— (2003) "Theories of Fairness and Reciprocity – Evidence and Economic Applications," in M. Dewatripont, L. Hansen, and S. J. Turnovsky, eds., *Advances in Economics and Econometrics*, Cambridge: Cambridge University Press.

Feltovich, Nicholas J. (2005) "Slow Learning in the Market for Lemons: A Note on Reinforcement Learning and the Winner's Curse," forthcoming in *Computational Economics: A Perspective from Computational Intelligence*.

Feltovich, N., R. Harbaugh, and T. To (2002) "Too Cool for School? Signaling and Countersignaling," *Rand Journal of Economics*, 33, 630–649.

Fershtman, Chaim and Uri Gneezy (2001) "Discrimination in a Segmented Society: An Experimental Approach," *Quarterly Journal of Economics*, 116(1), 351–377.

Fey, M., Richard D. McKelvey, and Thomas R. Palfrey (1996) "An Experimental Study of Constant-Sum Centipede Games," *International Journal of Game Theory*, 25, 269–287.

Fiorina, M. P. and C. R. Plott (1978) "Committee Experiments Under Majority Rule: An Experimental Study," *American Political Science Review*, 72, 575–598.

Forrester, J. (1961) *Industrial Dynamics*, New York: MIT Press.

Forsythe, R., J. L. Horowitz, N. E. Savin, and M. Sefton (1988) "Fairness in Simple Bargaining Games," *Games and Economic Behavior*, 6, 347–369.

Forsythe, Robert, Roger Myerson, Thomas Rietz, and Robert Weber (1993) "An Experiment on Coordination in Multi-Candidate Elections: The Importance of Polls and Election Histories," *Social Choice and Welfare*, 10, 223–247.

—— (1996) "An Experimental Study of Voting Rules and Polls in Three-way Elections," *The International Journal of Game Theory*, 25, 355–383.

Forsythe, R., F. Nelson, G. R. Neumann, and J. Wright (1991) "Forecasting the 1988 Presidential Election: A Field Experiment," in *Research in Experimental Economics*, Vol. 4. Greenwich, CT: JAI Press, 1–44.

—— (1992) "Anatomy of an Experimental Political Stock Market," *American Economic Review*, 82, 1142–1161.

Fouraker, L. E. and S. Siegel (1963) *Bargaining Behavior*. New York: McGraw Hill.

Franzen, A. (1995) "Group Size and One Shot Collective Action," *Rationality and Society*, 7, 183–200.

Frechette, Guillaume R., John H. Kagel, and Steven F. Lehrer (2003) "Bargaining in Legislatures: An Experimental Investigation of Open versus Closed Amendment Rules," *American Political Science Review*, 97, 221–232.

Friedman, D. (1993) "How Trading Institutions Affect Financial Market Performance: Some Laboratory Evidence," *Economic Inquiry*, 31, 410–435.

Friedman, D. and S. Sunder (1994) *Experimental Methods*. Cambridge, U.K.: Cambridge University Press.

Friedman, M. and R. D. Friedman (1989) *Free to Choose*, New York: Harcourt Brace and Company.

Fryer, R. M. (2001) *Economists' Models of Discrimination: An Analytical Survey*, Unpublished Monograph, Chicago: University of Chicago Press.

Fryer, R. M., J. K. Goeree, and C. A. Holt (2002) "Experimenting with Discrimination," Discussion Paper, University of Virginia.

—— (2005) "Classroom Games: Experience-Based Discrimination," *Journal of Economic Education*, 36(2), 160–170.

Gale, David and Lloyd Shapley (1962) "College Admissions and the Stability of Marriage," *American Mathematical Monthly*, 69, 9–15.

Gerber, Alan S. and Donald P. Green (2000) "The Effects of Canvassing, Telephone Calls, and Direct Mail on Voter Turnout: A Field Experiment," *American Political Science Review*, 94, 653–663.

—— (2004) "Reclaiming the Experimental Tradition in Political Science," in I. Katznelson and H. Milnor, *State of the Discipline*, Vol. III, New York: Norton.

Gigerenzer G. and U. Hoffrage (1995) "How to Improve Bayesian Reasoning Without Instruction: Frequency Formats," *Psychological Review*, 102, 84–704.

—— (1998) "Using Natural Frequencies to Improve Diagnostic Inferences," *Academic Medicine*, 73, 538–540.

Gjerstad, Steve (2005) "Risk Aversion, Beliefs, and Prediction Market Equilibrium," Discussion Paper, Economic Science Laboratory, University of Arizona.

Gneezy, Uri and John List (2006) "Are the Physically Disabled Discriminated Against in Product Markets," Discussion Paper, University of Chicago.

Godby, Robert (2002) "Market Power in Emission Permit Double Auctions," *Research in Experimental Economics*, Vol. 7 (edited by C. A. Holt and R. M. Isaac), Greenwich, CT: JAI Press, 121–162.

Goeree, J. K. and C. A. Holt (1999a) "Rent Seeking and the Inefficiency of Non-Market Allocations," *Journal of Economic Perspectives*, 13, 217–226.

—— (1999b) "Stochastic Game Theory: For Playing Games, Not Just for Doing Theory," *Proceedings of the National Academy of Sciences*, 96, 10564–10567.

—— (2000) "Asymmetric Inequality Aversion and Noisy Behavior in Alternating-Offer Bargaining Games," *European Economic Review*, 1079–1089.

—— (2001) "Ten Little Treasures of Game Theory, and Ten Intuitive Contradictions," *American Economic Review*, 90(5), 1402–1422.

—— (2003a) "Learning in Economics Experiments," in L. Nadel, ed., *Encyclopedia of Cognitive Science*, Vol. 2, pp. 1060–1069. London: Nature Publishing Group, McMillan.

—— (2003b) "Coordination Games," in L. Nadel, ed., *Encyclopedia of Cognitive Science*, Vol. 2, 204–208. London: Nature Publishing Group, McMillan.

—— (2004) "A Model of Noisy Introspection," *Games and Economic Behavior*, 46(2), 281–294.

—— (2005a) "An Experimental Study of Costly Coordination," *Games and Economic Behavior*, 51(2), 349–364.

—— (2005b) "An Explanation of Anomalous Behavior in Models of Political Participation," *American Political Science Review*, 99(2), 201–213.

—— (2005c) "Comparing the FCC's Combinatorial and Non-Combinatorial Simultaneous Multiple Round Auctions: Experimental Design Report," Consulting Report submitted to the Federal Communications Commission, May 2005.

Goeree, J. K., C. A. Holt, and S. K. Laury (2002) "Private Costs and Public Benefits: Unraveling the Effects of Altruism and Noisy Behavior," *Journal of Public Economics*, 82, 257–278.

—— (2003) "Altruism and Error in Public Goods Experiments: Implications for the Environment," in J. List and A. de Zeeuw, eds. *Recent Advances in Environmental Economics*, Edward Elgar Publishing.

Goeree, J. K., C. A. Holt, and J.O. Ledyard (2006) "An Experimental Comparison of the FCC's Combinatorial and Non-Combinatorial Simultaneous Multiple Round Auctions," Report Prepared for the Wireless Telecommunications Bureau of the Federal Communications Commission.

Goeree, J. K., C. A. Holt, and T. R. Palfrey (2002) "Quantal Response Equilibrium and Overbidding in Private-Value Auctions," *Journal of Economic Theory*, 104(1), 247–272.

—— (2003) "Risk Averse Behavior in Asymmetric Matching Pennies Games," *Games and Economic Behavior*, 45, 97–113.

—— (2005) *Quantal Response Equilibrium*, forthcoming, Princeton, NJ: Princeton University Press.

—— (2006) "Regular Quantal Response Equilibrium," *Experimental Economics*, 8(4), 347–367.

Goeree, J. K., C. A. Holt, and A. M. Smith (2005) "An Experimental Examination of the Volunteer's Dilemma," Discussion Paper, University of Virginia.

Goeree, J. K., Theo Offerman, and Randolph Sloof (2005) "Demand Reduction and Preemptive Bidding in License Auctions," Discussion Paper, University of Amsterdam.

Goeree, J. K., T. R. Palfrey, B. W. Rogers, and R. D. McKelvey (2003) "Self-correcting Information Cascades," Discussion Paper, Caltech.

Goodfellow, Jessica and Charles R. Plott (1990) "An Experimental Examination of the Simultaneous Determination of Input Prices and Output Prices," *Southern Economic Journal*, 56, 969–983.

Grether, D. M. (1980) "Bayes' Rule as a Descriptive Model: The Representativeness Heuristic," *Quarterly Journal of Economics*, 95, 537–557.

—— (1992) "Testing Bayes' Rule and the Representativeness Heuristic: Some Experimental Evidence," *Journal of Economic Behavior and Organization*, 17, 31–57.

Grether, D. M. and C. R. Plott (1979) "Economic Theory of Choice and the Preference Reversal Phenomenon," *American Economic Review*, 69, 623–638.

—— (1984) "The Effects of Market Practices in Oligopolistic Markets: An Experimental Examination of the *Ethyl* Case," *Economic Inquiry*, 24, 479–507.

Grether, David M., Alan Schwartz, and Louis L. Wilde (1988) "Uncertainty and Shopping Behavior: An Experimental Analysis," *Review of Economic Studies*, 55, 323–342.

Grober, Jens and Arthur Schram (2004) "Neighborhood Information Exchange and Voter Participation: An Experimental Study," Discussion Paper, University of Cologne.

Guarnaschelli, Serena, Richard D. McKelvey, and Thomas R. Palfrey (2000) "An Experimental Study of Jury Decision Rules," *American Political Science Review*, 94, 407–423.

Guth, W., R. Schmittberger, and B. Schwarze (1982) "An Experimental Analysis of Ultimatum Bargaining," *Journal of Economic Behavior and Organization*, 3, 367–388.

Guyer, M. and A. Rapoport (1972) "2×2 Games Played Once," *Journal of Conflict Resolution*, 16, 409–431.

Guzik, Victor S. (2004) "Contextual Framing Effects in a Common Pool Resource Experiment," Economics Honors Thesis, Middlebury College.

Hammerton, M. (1973) "A Case of Radical Probability Estimation," *Journal of Experimental Psychology*, 101(2), 252–254.

Harbaugh, W. T., K. Krause, and L. Vesterlund (2002) "Risk Attitudes of Children and Adults: Choices Over Small and Large Probability Gains and Losses," *Experimental Economics*, 553–584.

Hardin, Garrett (1968) "The Tragedy of the Commons," *Science*, 162, 1243–1248.

Harper, D. G. C. (1982) "Competitive Foraging in Mallards: 'Ideal Free' Ducks," *Animal Behavior*, 30, 575–584.

Harrison, G. W., M. P. Lau, and E. E. Rutstrom (2005) "Estimating Risk Attitudes in Denmark: A Field Experiment," Discussion Paper, University of Central Florida.

Harrison, G. W., E. Johnson, M. M. McInnes, and E. Rutstrom (2005) "Risk Aversion and Incentive Effects: Comment," *American Economic Review*, 95(3), 897–901.

Haruvy, Ernan and Charles N. Noussair (2006) "The Effect of Short Selling on Bubbles and Crashes in Experimental Spot Asset Markets," *Journal of Finance*, forthcoming.

Hawkes, Kristen (1993) "Why Hunter-Gatherers Work," *Current Anthropology*, 34(4), 341–361 (with commentaries and author's reply).

Hay, George A. and Daniel Kelley (1974) "An Empirical Survey of Price Fixing Conspiracies," *Journal of Law and Economics*, 17, 13–38.

Hazlett, T. W. and R. J. Michaels (1993) "The Cost of Rent-Seeking: Evidence from Cellular Telephone License Lotteries," *Southern Economic Journal*, 59(3), 425–435.

Heal, Geoffrey and Howard Kunreuther (2005) "IDS Models of Airline Security," *Journal of Conflict Resolution*, 49(2), 201–217.

Henrich, J. et al. (2001) In Search of Homo Economicus: Behavioral Experiments in 15 Small-Scale Societies," *American Economic Review*, 91(2), 73–84.

Herrnstein, R. J. and D. Prelec (1991) "Melioration: A Theory of Distributed Choice," *Journal of Economic Perspectives*, 5, 137–156.

Hertwig, R. and A. Ortmann (2001) "Experimental Practices in Economics: A Methodological Challenge to Psychologists?" *Behavioral and Brain Sciences*, 24(3), 383–403.

Herzberg, R. Q. and R. K. Wilson (1988) "Results on Sophisticated Voting in an Experimental Setting," *Journal of Politics*, 50, 471–486.

Hess, R., C. Holt, and A. Smith (2005) "Coordination of Strategic Responses to Security Threats: Laboratory Evidence," Discussion Paper, University of Virginia.

Hewett, R., C. A. Holt, G. Kosmopoulou, C. Kymn, C. X. Long, S. Mousavi, and S. Sarangi (2005) "A Classroom Exercise: Voting by Ballots and Feet," *Southern Economic Journal*, 72(1), 252–263.

Hey, J. D. (1981) "Search for Rules of Search," *Journal of Economic Behavior and Organization*, 3, 65–81.

—— (1987) "Still Searching," *Journal of Economic Behavior and Organization*, 8, 137–144.

—— (1994) *Experimental Economics*, Heidelberg: Springer-Verlag.

—— (1995) "Experimental Investigations of Errors in Decision Making under Risk," *European Economic Review*, 39, 633–640.

Hillman, A. L. and D. Samet (1987) "Dissipation of Contestable Rents by Small Numbers of Contenders," *Public Choice*, 54(1), 63–82.

Ho, Teck-Hua and Juanjuan Zhang (2004) "Does Format of Pricing Contract Matter?" Discussion Paper, Haas School of Business, U. C. Berkeley.

Hoffman, E., K. McCabe, K. Shachat, and V. L. Smith (1994) "Preferences, Property Rights, and Anonymity in Bargaining Games," *Games and Economic Behavior*, 7, 346–380.

Hoffman, E., K. McCabe, and V. L. Smith (1996) "On Expectations and Monetary Stakes in Ultimatum Games," *International Journal of Game Theory*, 25(3), 289–301.

Hoffman, E., and M. Spitzer (1982) "The Coase Theorem: Some Experimental Tests," *Journal of Law and Economics*, 25, 73–98.

—— (1985) "Entitlements, Rights and Fairness: An Experimental Examination of Subjects' Concepts of Distributive Justice," *Journal of Legal Studies*, 14, 259–297.

Holt, C. A. (1985) "An Experimental Test of the Consistent-Conjectures Hypothesis," *American Economic Review*, 75, 314–325.

—— (1989) "The Exercise of Market Power in Laboratory Experiments," *Journal of Law and Economics*, 32, S107–S131.

—— (1992) "ISO Probability Matching," University of Virginia.

—— (1995) "Industrial Organization: A Survey of Laboratory Results," in *Handbook of Experimental Economics*, J. Kagel and A. Roth, eds. Princeton, NJ: Princeton University Press, 349–443.

—— (1996) "Classroom Games: Trading in a Pit Market," *Journal of Economic Perspectives*, 10, 193–203.

Holt, C. A. and L. R. Anderson (1999) "Agendas and Strategic Voting," *Southern Economic Journal*, 65, 622–629.

Holt, Charles A. and Douglas D. Davis (1990) "The Effects of Non-Binding Price Announcements on Posted Offer Markets," *Economics Letters*, 34, 307–310.

Holt, C. A., L. Langan, and A. Villamil (1986) "Market Power in Oral Double Auctions," *Economic Inquiry*, 24, 107–123.

Holt, C. A. and S. K. Laury (1997) "Classroom Games: Voluntary Provision of a Public Good," *Journal of Economic Perspectives*, 11, 209–215.

—— (1998) "Theoretical Explanations of Treatment Effects in Voluntary Contributions Experiments," in C. R. Plott and V. L. Smith, eds. *Handbook of Experimental Economics Results*. New York: Elsevier, forthcoming.

—— (2002) "Risk Aversion and Incentive Effects," *American Economic Review*, 92(5), 1644–1655.

—— (2003) "Further Reflections on Prospect Theory," Discussion Paper, University of Virginia.

—— (2005) "Risk Aversion and Incentive Effects: New Data without Order Effects," *American Economic Review*, 95(3), 902–912.

Holt, C. A., T. R. Palfrey, and A. M. Smith (2006) "Experimental Studies of Voting, Committees, and Elections," under preparation for the *New Palgrave Dictionary of Economics*.

Holt, C. A., and A E. Roth (2004) "The Nash Equilibrium: A Perspective," *Proceedings of the National Academy of Sciences, U.S.A.*, 101(12), 3999–4002.

Holt, C. A. and D. Scheffman (1987) "Facilitating Practices: The Effects of Advance Notice and Best-Price Policies," *RAND Journal of Economics*, 18, 187–197.

Holt, Charles A. and Roger Sherman (1990) "Advertising and Product Quality on Posted-Offer Experiments," *Economic Inquiry*, 28(3), 39–56.

—— (1994) "The Loser's Curse," *American Economic Review*, 84, 642–652.

—— (1999) "Classroom Games: A. Market for Lemons," *Journal of Economic Perspectives*, 13, 205–214.

—— (2000) "Risk Aversion and the Winner's Curse," Discussion Paper, University of Virginia.

Holt, Charles A. and Angela Smith (2006) "A Selective Survey of Experiments in Political Science," Discussion Paper, University of Virginia.

Holt, C. A. and F. Solis-Soberon (1992) "The Calculation of Equilibrium Mixed Strategies in Posted-Offer Auctions," in *Research in Experimental Economics*, Vol. 5, R. M. Isaac, ed. Greenwich, CT: JAI Press, 189–229.

Hück, Steffen, Hans-Theo Normann, and Jörg Oechssler (1999) "Learning in Cournot Oligopoly: an Experiment." *Economic Journal*, 109, 80–95.

Hück, Steffen and Jörg Oechssler (2000) "Information Cascades in the Laboratory: Do They Occur for the Right Reasons?" *Journal of Economic Psychology*, 21, 661–671.

Hung, A. A. and C. R. Plott (2001) "Information Cascades: Replication and an Extension to Majority Rule and Conformity Rewarding Institutions," *American Economic Review*, 91, 1508–1520.

Isaac, R. M. and C. R. Plott (1978) "Cooperative Game Models of the Influence of the Closed Rule in Three Person, Majority Rule Committees: Theory and Experiment," in P. C. Ordeshook, ed., *Game Theory and Political Science*, New York: New York University Press, 282–322.

—— (1981) "The Opportunity for Conspiracy in Restraint of Trade," *Journal of Economic Behavior and Organization*, 2, 1–30.

Isaac, R. Mark, Valerie Ramey, and Arlington Williams (1984) "The Effects of Market Organization on Conspiracies in Restraint of Trade," *Journal of Economic Behavior and Organization*, 5, 191–222.

Isaac, R. M. and S. Reynolds (1988) "Appropriability and Market Structure of a Stochastic Invention Model, *Quarterly Journal of Economics*, 4, 647–672.

Isaac, R. M. and J. M. Walker (1985) "Information and Conspiracy in Sealed Bid Auctions," *Journal of Economic Behavior and Organization*, 6, 139–159.

—— (1988a) "Communication and Free-Riding Behavior: The Voluntary Contributions Mechanism," *Economic Inquiry*, 26, 585–608.

—— (1988b) "Group Size Hypotheses of Public Goods Provision: The Voluntary Contributions Mechanism," *Quarterly Journal of Economics*, 103, 179–199.

Isaac, R. M., J. M. Walker, and A. W. Williams (1994) "Group Size and the Voluntary Provision of Public Goods: Experimental Evidence Utilizing Large Groups," *Journal of Public Economics*, 54, 1–36.

Jung, Y. J., J. H. Kagel, and D. Levin (1994) "On the Existence of Predatory Pricing: An Experimental Study of Reputation and Entry Deterrence in the Chain-Store Game," *Rand Journal of Economics*, 25, 72–93.

Kachelmeier, S. J. and M. Shehata (1992) "Examining Risk Preferences under High Monetary Incentives: Experimental Evidence from the People's Republic of China," *American Economic Review*, 82, 1120–1141.

Kagel, J. H. (1995) "Auctions: A Survey of Experimental Research," in *The Handbook of Experimental Economics*, J. H. Kagel and A. E. Roth, eds. Princeton: Princeton University Press, 501–585.

Kagel, J. H. and D. Levin (1986) "The Winner's Curse and Public Information in Common Value Auctions," *American Economic Review*, 76, 894–920.

—— (2002) *Common Value Auctions and the Winner's Curse*, Princeton: Princeton University Press.

—— (2004) "Multi-Unit Demand Auctions with Synergies: Behavior in Sealed-Bid versus Ascending-Bid Uniform-Price Auctions," Discussion Paper, Ohio State University, forthcoming in *Games and Economic Behavior*.

Kagel, J. H. and A. E. Roth (1995) *The Handbook of Experimental Economics*, Princeton: Princeton University Press.

—— (2000) "The Dynamics of Reorganization in Matching Markets: A Laboratory Experiment Motivated by a Natural Experiment," *Quarterly Journal of Economics*, 115, 201–237.

Kagel, J. H. and W. Vogt (1993) "The Buyers' Bid Double Auction: Preliminary Experimental Results," in D. Friedman and J. Rust, eds., *The Double Auction Market: Institutions, Theories, and Evidence*, Reading, MA: Addison-Wesley, 285–305.

Kahneman, Daniel (1988) "Experimental Economics: A Psychological Perspective," in *Bounded Rational Behavior in Experimental Games and Markets*, R. Tietz, W. Albers, and R. Selten, eds., New York: Springer-Verlag, 11–18.

Kahneman, D., J. L. Knetsch, and R. H. Thaler (1991) "The Endowment Effect, Loss Aversion, and Status Quo Bias: Anomalies," *Journal of Economic Perspectives*, 5, 193–206.

Kahneman, D., P. Slovic, and A. Tversky (1982) *Judgement under Uncertainty: Heuristics and Biases*, Cambridge: Cambridge University Press.

Kahneman, D. and A. Tversky (1973) "On the Psychology of Prediction," *Psychological Review*, 80, 237–251.

—— (1979) "Prospect Theory: An Analysis of Decision under Risk," *Econometrica*, 47, 263–291.

Karlan, Dean S. (2005) "Using Experimental Economics to Measure Social Capital and Predict Financial Decisions," *American Economic Review*, 95(5), 1688–1699.

Ketcham, J., V. L. Smith, and A. W. Williams (1984) "A Comparison of Posted-Offer and Double-Auction Pricing Institutions," *Review of Economic Studies*, 51, 595–614.

Keynes, J. M. (1936) *The General Theory of Employment, Interest, and Money*, London: Macmillan.

Kirstein, Roland and Annette Kirstein (2005) "Less Rationality, More Efficiency: a Laboratory Experiment on 'Lemons' Markets," *German Working Papers in Law and Economics*, Vol. 2005, Article 18. http://www.bepress.com/gwp/default/vol2005/iss1/art18.

Klemperer, Paul (2002) "What Really Matters in Auction Design," *Journal of Economic Perspectives*, 16(1), Winter, 169–189.

Knez, Marc and Colin Camerer (1994) "Creating Expectational Assets in the Laboratory: Coordination in 'Weakest-Link' Games," *Strategic Management Journal*, 15, 101–119.

Kosfeld, Michael, Markus Heinrichs, Paul J. Zak, Urs Fischbacher, and Ernst Fehr (2005) "Oxytocin Increases Trust in Humans," *Nature Letters*, 435(2), 673–677.

Kousser, J. M. (1984) "Origins of the Run-off Primary," *The Black Scholar*, 23–26.

Krueger, A. O. (1974) "The Political Economy of the Rent-seeking Society," *American Economic Review*, 64, 291–303.

Kruse, J. B., S. Rassenti, S. Reynolds, and V. Smith (1994) "Bertrand-Edgeworth Competition in Experimental Markets," *Econometrica*, 62, 343–372.

Kwasnica, A.M., J. O. Ledyard, D. Porter, and C. DeMartini, (2005) "A New and Improved Design for Multi-Object Iterative Auctions," *Management Science*, 51(3), March, 419–434.

Kübler, Dorothea and Georg Weizsäcker (2004) "Limited Depth of Reasoning and Failure of Cascade Formation in the Laboratory,' Discussion Paper, Humboldt University, Berlin.

Laury, S. K. and C. A. Holt (2000) "Voluntary Provision of Public Goods: Experimental Results with Interior Nash Equilibria," in C. R. Plott and V. L. Smith, eds. *Handbook of Experimental Economics Results*. New York: Elsevier, forthcoming.

Ledyard, J. O. (1995) "Public Goods: A Survey of Experimental Research," in *A Handbook of Experimental Economics*, A. Roth and J. Kagel, eds. Princeton: Princeton University Press, 111–194.

Ledyard, J. O., D. Porter, and R. Wessen (2000) "A Market-Based Mechanism for Allocating Space Shuttle Secondary Payload Priority," *Experimental Economics*, 2, 173–195.

Lee, H. L., V. Padmanabhan, and S. Whang (1997a) "Information Distortion in a Supply Chain: The Bullwhip Effect," *Management Science*, 43(4), 546–548.

—— (1997b) "The Bullwhip Effect in Supply Chains," *Sloan Management Review*, 38(3), 93–102.

Levine, D. and T. R. Palfrey (2005) "A Laboratory Test of the Rational Choice Theory of Voter Turnout," Discussion Paper, Princeton University.

Levine, M. E. and C. R. Plott (1977) "Agenda Influence and Its Implications," *Virginia Law Review*, 63, 561–604.

List, J. A. (2004) "The Nature and Extent of Discrimination in the Marketplace: Evidence from the Field," *Quarterly Journal of Economics*, 119, 49–89.

List, J. A. and T. L. Cherry (2000) "Learning to Accept in Ultimatum Games: Evidence from an Experimental Design That Generates Low Offers," *Experimental Economics*, 3, 11–29.

List, J. A. and D. Lucking-Reiley (2000) "Demand Reduction in Multi-Unit Auctions: Evidence from a Sportscard Field Experiment," *American Economic Review*, 90(4), 961–972.

—— (2002) "The Effects of Seed Money and Refunds on Charitable Giving: Experimental Evidence from a University Capital Campaign," *Journal of Political Economy*, 110(1), 215–233.

List, John A. and Michael K. Price (2005) "Conspiracies and Secret Price Discounts in the Marketplace: Evidence from a Field Experiment," *Rand Journal of Economics*, 36(3), 700–717.

Luce, R. D. (1959) *Individual Choice Behavior*, New York: John Wiley & Sons.

Lucking-Reiley, David (1999) "Using Field Experiments to Test Equivalence Between Auction Formats: Magic on the Internet." *American Economic Review*, 89(5), 1063–1080.

—— (2000) "Vickrey Auctions in Practice: From Nineteenth-Century Philately to Twenty-First Century E-Commerce," *Journal of Economic Perspectives*, 14(3), Summer, 183–192.

Lynch, M., R. M. Miller, C. R. Plott, and R. Porter (1986) "Product Quality, Consumer Information and 'Lemons' in Experimental Markets," in *Empirical Approaches to Consumer Protection Economics*, P. M. Ippolito and D. T. Scheffman, eds. Washington, D.C.: Federal Trade Commission, Bureau of Economics, 251–306.

Mackay, C. (1995) *Extraordinary Popular Delusions and the Madness of Crowds*, Hertfordshire, England: Wordsworth Editions Ltd. (originally 1841).

Malouf, M. W. K. and A. E. Roth (1981) "Disagreement in Bargaining: An Experimental Study," *Journal of Conflict Resolution*, 25, 329–348.

Manski, Charles (2005) "Interpreting the Predictions of Prediction Markets," *Economics Letters*, forthcoming.

Marwell, G. and R. E. Ames (1981) "Economists Free Ride, Does Anyone Else? Experiments on the Provision of Public Goods, IV," *Journal of Public Economics*, 15, 295–310.

McCabe, K. A., S. J. Rassenti, and V. L. Smith (1991) "Testing Vickrey's and Other Simultaneous Multiple Unit Versions of the English Auction," in R.M. Isaac, ed., *Research in Experimental Economics*, Vol. 4, Stamford, CT: JAI Press.

—— (1993) "Designing a Uniform-Price Double Auction, An Experimental Evaluation," in D. Friedman and J. Rust, eds., *The Double Auction Market: Institutions, Theory, and Evidence, SFI Studies in the Sciences of Complexity*, Proceedings, 15, Reading, MA: Addison-Wesley.

McDowell, R. (2003) "Going Once, Going Twice...," *GMDA News*, 2(2), 1.

McKelvey, R. D., and P. C. Ordeshook (1979) "An Experimental Test of Several Theories of Committee Decision-Making under Majority Rule," in *Applied Game Theory*, S. J. Brams, A. Schotter, and G. Schwodiauer, eds. Wurzburg: Physica Verlag.

McKelvey, R. D. and T. R. Palfrey (1992) "An Experimental Study of the Centipede Game," *Econometrica*, 60, 803–836.

—— (1995) "Quantal Response Equilibria for Normal Form Games," *Games and Economic Behavior*, 10, 6–38.

McKinney, C. Nicholas, Muriel Niederle, and Alvin E. Roth (2005) "The Collapse of a Medical Labor Clearinghouse (and Why Such Failures Are Rare)," *American Economic Review*, 95(3) 788–889.

Miller, R. M. and C. R. Plott (1985) "Product Quality Signaling in Experimental Markets," *Econometrica*, 53, 837–872.

Millner, E. L. and M. D. Pratt (1989) "An Experimental Investigation of Efficient Rent Seeking," *Public Choice*, 62 (August): 139–151.

—— (1991) "Risk Aversion and Rent Seeking: An Extension and Some Experimental Evidence," *Public Choice*, 69 (Feburary): 81–92.

Mitman, Kurt (2004) "An Experimental Analysis of Sellers' Reserve Price Decisions in Private Value Auctions," Distinguished Major's Thesis, University of Virginia.

Mongell, S., and Alvin E. Roth (1991) "Sorority Rush as a Two-Sided Matching Mechanism," *American Economic Review*, 81, 441–464.

Morgan, John and Martin Sefton (2002) "An Experimental Investigation of Unprofitable Games," *Games and Economic Behavior*, 40, 123–146.Morton, R. B. and T. A. Rietz (2004) "Majority Requirements and Voter Coordination," Discussion Paper, University of Iowa.

Nagel, Jack (1984) "A Debut for Approval Voting," *Political Science and Politics*, 17, 62–65.

Nagel, R. (1995) "Unraveling in Guessing Games: An Experimental Study," *American Economic Review*, 85, 1313–1326.

—— (1999) "A Survey of Experimental Beauty-Contest Games," in *Games and Human Behavior: Essays in Honor of Amnon Rapoport*, I. E. D. Budescu, I. Erev, and R. Zwick, eds. Hillside NJ: Erlbaum Association, 105–142.

Nagel, Rosmarie and Fang Fang Tang (1998) "Experimental Results on the Centipede Game in Normal Form: An Investigation of Learning," *Journal of Mathematical Psychology*, 42, 356–384.

Nalbanthian, Haig and Andrew Schotter (1995) "Matching and Efficiency in the Baseball Free Agent System: An Experimental Examination," *Journal of Labor Economics*, 13, 1–31.

Nash, J. (1950) "Equilibrium Points in N-Person Games," *Proceedings of the National Academy of Sciences, U.S.A.*, 36, 48–49.

Nelson, Forrest, George Neumann, and Philip Polgreen (2006) "Operating with Doctors: Results of the 2004 and 2005 Influenza Markets," Discussion Paper, University of Iowa.

Niemi, Richard G. and Larry M. Bartels (1984) "The Responsiveness of Approval Voting to Political Circumstances," *Political Science and Politics*, 17, 571–577.

Noussair, C. (2003) "Innovations in the Design of Bundled-Item Auctions," *Proceedings of the National Academy of Sciences*, 100(19), 10590–10591

Noussair, Charles N. and Steven Tucker (2003) "Futures Markets and Bubble Formation in Experimental Asset Markets," Discussion Paper, Emory University.

Ochs, J. (1994) "Games with Unique, Mixed Strategy Equilibria: An Experimental Study," *Games and Economic Behavior*, 10, 202–217.

—— (1995) "Coordination Problems," in *The Handbook of Experimental Economics*, J. H. Kagel and A. E. Roth, eds. Princeton, NJ: Princeton University Press, 195–249.

Olsen, Mark and David Porter (1994) "An Experimental Examination into Design of Decentralized Methods to Solve the Assignment Problem with and without Money," *Economic Theory*, 4, 11–40.

Ostrom, E. and R. Gardner (1993) "Coping with Asymmetries in the Commons: Self-Governing Irrigation Systems Can Work," *Journal of Economic Perspectives*, 7(4), 93–112.

Ostrom, E., R. Gardner, and J. K. Walker (1994) *Rules, Games, and Common-Pool Resources*. Ann Arbor: University of Michigan Press.

Ostrom, E. and J. K. Walker (1991) "Communication in a Commons: Cooperation without External Enforcement," in *Laboratory Research in Political Economy*, T. Palfrey, ed. Ann Arbor: University of Michigan Press, 289–322.

Ouwersloot, Hans, Peter Nijkam, and Piet Rietveld (1998) "Errors in Probability Updating Behaviour: Measurement and Impact Analysis," *Journal of Economic Psychology*, 19, 535–563.

Palfrey, T. R. (2005) "Laboratory Experiments in Political Economy," CEPS Discussion Paper, Princeton University.

Palfrey, T. R. and H. Rosenthal (1983) "A Strategic Calculus of Voting," *Public Choice*, 41, 7–53.

—— (1985) "Voter Participation and Strategic Uncertainty," *American Political Science Review*, 79, 62–78.

Pallais, Amanda (2005) "The Effect of Group Size on Ultimatum Bargaining," Discussion Paper, University of Virginia.

Parco, James E., Amnon Rapoport, and William E. Stein (2002) "Effects of Financial Incentives on the Breakdown of Mutual Trust" *Psychological Science*, 13, 292–297.

Pennock, David, Steve Lawrence, Finn Neilsen, and C. Lee Giles (2001) "Extracting Collective Probabilistic Success from Web Games," in *Proceedings of the Seventh ACM SIGKDD International Conference on Knowledge Discovery and Data Mining*, 174–183.

Peters, W. (1971) *A Class Divided*, New York: Doubleday and Company.

Petrie, R., S. Laury, and S. Hill (2004) "Crops, Water Usage, and Auction Experience in the 2002 Irrigation Reduction Auction," Water Policy Working Paper #2004–014.

Phelps, E. (1972) "The Statistical Theory of Racism and Sexism," *American Economic Review*, 62, 659–661.

Plott, C. R. (1979) "The Application of Laboratory Experimental Methods to the Public Choice," in C. S. Russell, ed., *Collective Decision Making: Applications from Public Choice Theory*, Baltimore: Johns Hopkins Press, 137–160.

—— (1983) "Externalities and Corrective Policies in Experimental Markets," *Economic Journal*, 93, 106–127.

—— (1986) "The Posted-Offer Trading Institution," *Science*, 232, 732–738.

—— (1989) "An Updated Review of Industrial Organization: Applications of Experimental Methods," in *Handbook of Industrial Organization*, Vol. II, R. Schmalensee and R. D. Willig, eds. Amsterdam: Elsevier Science, 1111–1176.

Plott, C. R. and M. E. Levine (1978) "A Model of Agenda Influence on Committee Decisions," *American Economic Review*, 68, 146–160.

Plott, C. R. and Jin Li (2005) "Tacit Collusion in Auctions and Conditions for Facilitation and Prevention: Equilibrium Selection in Laboratory Experimental Markets," Social Science Working Paper 1202, California Institute of Technology.

Plott, C. R. and S. Sunder (1982) "Efficiency of Experimental Security Markets with Insider Information: An Application of Rational-Expectations Models," *Journal of Political Economy*, 90(4), 663–698.

Plott, C. R., J. Wit, and W. C. Yang (1997) "Paramutuel Betting Markets as Information Aggregation Devices: Experimental Results," Working Paper, California Institute of Technology.

Ponti, G. (2002) "Cycles of Learning in the Centipede Game," *Games and Economic Behavior*, 30, 115–141.

Porter, David, Stephen Rassenti, Anil Roopnarine, and Vernon Smith (2003) "Combinatorial Auction Design," *Proceedings of the National Academy of Sciences*, 100(19), 11153–11157.

Porter, D., S. Rassenti, B. Shobe, V. Smith, and A. Winn (2005) "Virginia's NOx Allowance Auction," Discussion Paper presented at the 2005 ESA Meetings in Montreal.

Porter, David P. and Vernon L. Smith (1995) "Futures Contracting and Dividend Uncertainty in Experimental Asset Markets," *Journal of Business*, 68(4), 509–541.

Porter, Robert H. and J. Douglas Zona (1993) "Detection of Bid Rigging in Procurement Auctions," *Journal of Political Economy*, 101, 518–538.

Post, E. (1927) *Etiquette in Society, in Business, in Politics, and at Home*, New York: Funk and Wagnalls.

Potters, J., C. G. de Vries, and F. van Winden (1998) "An Experimental Examination of Rational Rent-Seeking," *European Journal of Political Economy*, 14, 783–800.

Rabin, M. (1993) "Incorporating Fairness into Game Theory and Economics," *American Economic Review*, 83, 1281–1302.

—— (2000) "Risk Aversion and Expected Utility Theory: A Calibration Theorem," *Econometrica*, 68, 1281–1292.

Rabin, M. and R. Thaler (2001) "Risk Aversion," *Journal of Economic Perspectives*, 15(1), 219–232.

Reiley, David (2005) "Experimental Evidence on the Endogenous Entry of Bidders in Internet Auctions," *Experimental Business Research, Volume 2: Economic and Managerial Perspectives*, A. Rapoport and R. Zwick, eds., Kluwer Academic Publishers: Norwell, MA, and Dordrect, The Netherlands.

—— (2006) "Field Experiments on the Effects of Reserve Prices in Auctions: More Magic on the Internet." forthcoming, *RAND Journal of Economics*.

Reiley, David H., Michael B. Urbancic, and Mark Walker (2005) "Stripped-down Poker: A Classroom Game to Illustrate Equilibrium Bluffing," Discussion Paper, University of Arizona.

Reynolds, Stanley S. and Bart J. Wilson (2005) "Market Power and Price Movements over the Business Cycle," *Journal of Industrial Economics*. 53(2), 145–174.

Romer, David (1996) *Advanced Macroeconomics*, New York: McGraw-Hill.

Rosenthal, R. W. (1982) "Games of Perfect Information, Predatory Pricing, and the Chain Store Paradox," *Journal of Economic Theory*, 25, 92–100.

Roth, A. E. (1984) "The Evolution of the Labor Market for Medical Interns and Residents: A Case Study in Game Theory," *Journal of Political Economy*, 92, 991–1016.

—— (1990) "New Physicians: A Natural Experiment in Market Organization," *Science*, 250, 1524–1528.

Roth, A. E. and M. W. K. Malouf (1979) "Game-Theoretic Models and the Role of Information in Bargaining," *Psychological Review*, 86, 574–594.

Roth, A. E., V. Prasnikar, M. Okuno-Fujiwara, and S. Zamir (1991) "Bargaining and Market Behavior in Jerusalem, Ljubljana, Pittsburgh, and Tokyo: An Experimental Study," *American Economic Review*, 81, 1068–1095.

Saijo, T., M. Une, and T. Yamaguchi (1996) "'Dango' Experiments," *Journal of the Japanese and International Economies*, 10, 1996, 1–11.

Samuelson, W. and R. Zeckhauser (1988) "Status Quo Bias in Decision Making," *Journal of Risk and Uncertainty*, 1, 7–59.

Santey, A. G., J. K. Rilling, J. A. Aronson, L. E. Nystrom, and J. D. Cohen (2003) "The Neural Basis of Economic Decision Making in the Ultimatum Game," *Science*, 300(13), 1755–1758.

Schechter, Laura (2006) "Traditional Trust Measurement and the Risk Confound: An Experiment in Rural Paraguay," *Journal of Economic Behavior and Organization*, forthcoming.

Schotter, A. and Y. M. Braunstein (1981) "Economic Search: An Experimental Study," *Economic Inquiry*, 19, 1–25.

Schotter, A. and K. Weigelt (1992) "Asymmetric Tournaments, Equal Opportunity Laws, and Affirmative Action: Some Experimental Results," *Quarterly Journal of Economics*, 107, 511–539.

Schram, A. and J. Sonnemans (1996a) "Voter Turnout as a Participation Game: An Experimental Investigation," *International Journal of Game Theory*, 25, 385–406.

—— (1996b) "Why People Vote: Experimental Evidence," *Journal of Economic Psychology*, 17, 417–442.

Schweitzer, Maurice and Gerard Cachon (2000) "Decision Bias in the Newsvendor Problem with a Known Demand Distribution: Experimental Evidence," *Management Science*, 46(3), 404–420.

Sefton, M. (1992) "Incentives in Simple Bargaining Games," *Journal of Economic Psychology*, 13, 263–276.

Sefton, M. (1999) "A Model of Behavior in Coordination Game Experiments," *Experimental Economics*, 2, 151–164.

Selten, Reinhard (1965) "Spieltheoretische Behandlung eines Oligopolmodells mit Nachfragetragheit," Parts I–II, *Zeitschrift für die Gesamte Staatswissenschaft*, 121, 301–324, and 667–689.

Selten, R. and J. Buchta (1999) "Experimental Sealed Bid First Price Auctions with Directly Observed Bid Functions," in *Games and Human Behavior: Essays in Honor of Amnon Rapoport*, I. E. D. Budescu, I. Erev, and R. Zwick, eds. Hillside NJ: Erlbaum Association, 101–116.

Selten, Reinhard, Michael Schreckenberg, Thomas Pitz, Thorsten Chmura, and Sebastian Kube (2002) "Experiments and Simulations on Day-to-Day Route Choice-Behaviour," Bonn Econ Discussion Papers, 35_2002, University of Bonn, Germany.

Sherstyuk, K. (1999) "Collusion without Conspiracy: An Experimental Study of One-Sided Auctions," *Experimental Economics*, 2, 59–75.

Shogren, J. F., S. Y. Shin, D. J. Hayes, and J. B. Kliebenstein (1994) "Resolving Differences in Willingness to Pay and Willingness to Accept," *American Economic Review*, 84, 255–270.

Siegel, S. (1956) *Nonparametric Statistics for the Behavioral Sciences*. New York: McGraw-Hill.

Siegel, S. and J. Castellan Jr. (1988) *Nonparametric Statistics for the Behavioral Sciences*. New York: McGraw-Hill.

Siegel, S. and D. A. Goldstein (1959) "Decision-Making Behavior in a Two-Choice Uncertain Outcome Situation," *Journal of Experimental Psychology*, 57, 37–42.

Siegel, S., A. Siegel, and J. Andrews (1964) *Choice, Strategy, and Utility*. New York: McGraw-Hill.

Slonim, R. and A. E. Roth (1998) "Learning in High Stakes Ultimatum Games: An Experiment in the Slovak Republic," *Econometrica*, 66, 569–596.

Smith, Adam (1976, originally 1776) *The Wealth of Nations*, E. Cannan, ed., Chicago: University of Chicago Press.

Smith, V. L. (1962) "An Experimental Study of Competitive Market Behavior," *Journal of Political Economy*, 70, 111–137.

—— (1964) "The Effect of Market Organization on Competitive Equilibrium," *Quarterly Journal of Economics*, 78, 181–201.

—— (1979) *Research in Experimental Economics*, Vol. 1. Greenwich, CT: JAI Press.

—— (1981) "An Empirical Study of Decentralized Institutions of Monopoly Restraint," in J. Quirk and G. Horwich, eds., *Essays in Contemporary Fields of Economics in Honor of E.T. Weiler, 1914–1979* (Purdue University Press, West Lafayette), 83–106.

—— (1982) "Markets as Economizers of Information: Experimental Examination of the 'Hayek Hypothesis,'" *Economic Inquiry*, 20, 165–179.

Smith, V. L., G. L. Suchanek, and A. W. Williams (1988) "Bubbles, Crashes, and Endogenous Expectations in Experimental Spot Asset Markets," *Econometrica*, 56, 1119–1151.

Smith, V. L. and J. M. Walker (1993) "Monetary Rewards and Decision Cost in Experimental Economics," *Economic Inquiry*, 31, 245–261.

Spence, Michael (1973) "Job Market Signaling," *Quarterly Journal of Economics*," 87, 355–374.

Stahl, D. O. and P. W. Wilson (1994) "Experimental Evidence on Players' Models of Other Players," *Journal of Economic Behavior and Organization*, 25, 309–327.

—— (1995) "On Players' Models of Other Players: Theory and Experimental Evidence, " *Games and Economic Behavior*, 10, 208–254.

Starmer, C. and R. Sugden (1989) "Violations of the Independence Axiom in Common Ratio Problems: An Experimental Test of Some Competing Hypotheses," *Annals of Operations Research*, 19, 79–102.

—— (1991) "Does the Random-Lottery Incentive System Elicit True Preferences? An Experimental Investigation," *American Economic Review*, 81, 971–978.

Steiglitz, Ken and Daniel Shapiro (1998) "Simulating the Madness of Crowds: Price Bubbles in an Auction-Mediated Robot Market," *Computational Economics*, 12, 35–59.

Sterman, John D. (1989) "Modeling Managerial Behavior: Misperceptions of Feedback in a Dynamic Decision Making Experiment," *Management Science*, 35(3), 321–339.

Straub, Paul G. (1995) "Risk Dominance and Coordination Failures in Static Games," *Quarterly Review of Economics and Finance*, 35(4), Winter 1995, 339–363.

Tajfel, H. (1970) Experiments in Inter-Group Discrimination," *Scientific American* (November): 96–102.

Thaler, R. H. (1988) "Anomalies: The Winner's Curse," *Journal of Economic Perspectives*, 2, 191–202.

—— (1989) "Anomalies: The Ultimatum Game," *Journal of Economic Perspectives*, 2, 195–206.

—— (1992) *The Winners Curse*. New York: Free Press.

Todorov, Alexander, Anesu N. Mandisodza, Amir Goren, and Crystal C. Hall (2005) "Inferences of Competence from Faces Predict Election Outcomes," *Science*, 308(5728), June 10, 1623–1626.

Tullock, G. (1967) "The Welfare Costs of Tariffs, Monopolies, and Thefts," *Western Economic Journal*, 5(3), 224–232.

Tversky, A. and D. Kahneman (1992) "Advances in Prospect Theory: Cumulative Representation of Uncertainty," *Journal of Risk and Uncertainty*, 5, 297–323.

Tversky, A. and R. H. Thaler (1990) "Anomalies: Preference Reversals," *Journal of Economic Perspectives*, 4, 201–211.

Van Boening, M., A. W. Williams, and S. Lamaster (1993) "Price Bubbles and Crashes in Experimental Call Markets," *Economics Letters*, 41, 179–185.

van Dijk, F., J. Sonnemans, and V. van Winden (2002) "Social Ties in a Public Good Experiment," *Journal of Public Economics*, 85(2), 275–299.

Van Huyck, J. B., R. C. Battalio, and R. O. Beil (1990) "Tacit Coordination Games, Strategic Uncertainty, and Coordination Failure," *American Economic Review*, 80, 234–248.

Van Huyck, J. B., J. P. Cook, and R. C. Battalio (1997) "Adaptive Behavior and Coordination Failure," *Journal of Economic Behavior and Organization*, 32, 483–503.

—— (1991) "Strategic Uncertainty, Equilibrium Selection, and Coordination Failure in Average Opinion Games," *Quarterly Journal of Economics*, 91, 885–910.

Vaughan, G. M., Tajfel, H., and J. Williams (1981) "Bias in Reward Allocation in an Intergroup and an Interpersonal Context," *Social Psychology Quarterly*, 44(1) 37–42.

Vickrey, W. (1961) "Counterspeculation and Competitive Sealed Tenders," *Journal of Finance*, 16(1), 8–37.

von Neumann, J. and O. Morgenstern (1944) *Theory of Games and Economic Behavior*. Princeton, NJ: Princeton University Press.

Vulkan, Nir (2000) "An Economist's Perspective on Probability Matching," *Journal of Economic Surveys*, 14(1), 101–118.

Walker, J. M., R. Gardner, and E. Ostrom (1990) "Rent Dissipation in a Limited-Access Common-Pool Resource: Experimental Evidence," *Journal of Environmental Economics and Management*, 19, 203–211.

Watts, Susan (1992) "Private Information, Prices, Asset Allocation, and Profits: Further Experimental Evidence," in R. M. Isaac, ed., *Research in Experimental Economics*, Vol. 5, Greenwich, CT: JAI Press, 81–117.

Weizsäcker, Georg (2003) "Ignoring the Rationality of Others: Evidence from Experimental Normal-Form Games," *Games and Economic Behavior*, XLIV, 145–171.

Welch, I. (1992) "Sequential Sales, Learning, and Cascades," *Journal of Finance*, 47, 695–732.

Werden, G. J. (1989) "Price-Fixing and Civil Damages: Setting the Record Straight," *The Antitrust Bulletin*, 24, 307–335.

Williams, A. W. (1980) "Computerized Double-Auction Markets: Some Initial Experimental Results," *Journal of Business*, 53, 235–258.

Wilson, R. B. (1969) "Competitive Bidding with Disparate Options," *Management Science*, 15, 446–448.

Wilson, R. K. (1988) "Forward and Backward Agenda Procedures: Committee Experiments on Structurally Induced Equilibrium," *Journal of Politics*, 48, 390–409.

—— (2005) "Classroom Experiments: Candidate Convergence," *Southern Economic Journal*, 71, 913–922.

Wolfers, Justin and Eric Zitzewitz (2004) "Prediction Markets," *Journal of Economic Perspectives*, 18(2). 107–126.

Wolfers, Justin and Eric Zitzewitz (2005a) "Five Open Questions About Prediction Markets," Discussion Paper, Stanford University.

Wolfers, Justin and Eric Zitzewitz (2005b) "Prediction Markets in Theory and Practice," Discussion Paper, Stanford University.

Xiao, Erte and Daniel Houser (2005) "Emotion Expression and Human Punishment Behavior," *Proceedings of the National Academy of Sciences*, 102(20), 7398–7401.

Yoder, R. D. (1986) "The Performance of Farmer-Managed Irrigation Systems in the Hills of Nepal," Ph.D. Dissertation, Cornell University.

Zauner, K. G. (1999) "A Payoff Uncertainty Explanation of Results in Experimental Centipede Games," *Games and Economic Behavior*, 26, 157–185.

Zizzo, Daniel J., Stephanie Stolarz-Fantino, Julie Wen, and Edmund Fantino (2000) "A Violation of the Monotonicity Axiom: Experimental Evidence on the Conjunction Fallacy," *Journal of Economic Behavior and Organization*, 41(3), 263–276.

Index

Class Experiments

Instructions

This final part of the book contains instructions for running key experiments in class, without the help of computers. There are 20 sets of instructions, which are organized by chapter. The setups often parallel those used in the research experiments described in the chapters, but the instructions are adapted for classroom use. In particular, there is often more context and social interaction than would be appropriate for research. Many of the experiments can be done with groups or with one-shot interactions, which conserves class time.

Some of the chapters in the book are based on experiments that have too much bookkeeping to be run by hand easily, e.g., the Limit-Order Asset Market in Chapter 11. Even without a computer classroom lab, this and similar games could be run with eight or so groups if there are that many students who can bring wireless laptops to class and serve as group communicators. In addition, many of the individual decision experiments and one-shot games can be run from home after hours if the instructor sets up the Veconlab game in advance. The Web-based experiments are available on the Companion Website for this book at http://www.aw-bc.com/holt.

For the experiments that are run by hand, there are several hints for making this process more useful:

- The class can often be divided into teams, or groups of 3–5 players. Such grouping makes it easier to collect and process decisions in a larger class and it may facilitate learning from group discussions. Teams are especially useful when decisions are made in sequence, which would slow down the process of collecting data from many different players, e.g., with the Quality-Choice Market game in Chapter 10.
- Some games, like the Pit Market, are hard to do with groups, but the decentralized nature of trading makes this market possible to run "by hand" for moderate-sized

classes. With very large classes, have teams send a representative to the trading floor to negotiate and report back between rounds.

- Most of the worksheets have enough space for recording decisions in 5–10 rounds of repeated play, but often the main point can be made quickly with just a round or two of decision-making, which helps prevent that *Ground Hog Day* feeling.

- For competitive markets and auctions, it is typically not necessary to provide cash or other motivations for participants. When incentives are desired, as in games involving bargaining and fairness issues, one option is for the instructor to select one person afterward at random and pay a small percentage of their earnings in cash, e.g., with the announcement that "each dollar equals one penny." Another option is to let earnings be converted into points that can be used as lottery tickets for a prize that is awarded in class every week or two.

- For some of the games, it is sufficient for the instructor to pick pairs of people and let them reveal their decisions, as the class observes. This may provide an important element of participatory learning, without necessarily calling on each student or doing lots of repetition. For example, the card-based games for Chapters 3 and 5 can be done this way, as can the Stripped Down Poker game described in Chapter 33 and in Reiley, Urbancic, and Walker (2005).

- Generally, it is best to have someone read the instructions out loud, so that there is common knowledge about procedures and so that everyone completes the instructions at the same time.

- Some of the experiments require playing cards and/or 10-sided dice, which are available from game stores. It makes sense to pick up one deck of cards for each 10 students in the class, along with some extra 10-sided dice to allow for an occasional loss.

Many of the instructions that follow are loosely adapted from those used in research and teaching experiments done with various coauthors. These include: Holt (1996) for the Pit Market experiment in Chapter 1, Capra and Holt (1999, 2000) for the Push-Pull and Battle of Colors experiments in Chapters 3 and 5, Laury and Holt (2002) for the Lottery Choice experiment in Chapter 4, Sherman and Holt (1999) for the Price/Quality Market experiment in Chapter 10, Holt and Laury (1997) for the Play or Keep game in Chapter 14, Goeree and Holt (1999a) for the Lobbying game in Chapter 17, Holt and Sherman (2000) for the Common Value Auction in Chapter 21, Cummings, Holt, and Laury (2004) for the Multi-Unit Auction in Chapter 22, and Goeree and Holt (2001) for the Claim Game instructions in Chapter 25.

Pit Market

We will set up a market in which the people on my right are buyers, and the people on my left are sellers. There will be equal numbers of buyers and sellers. Several assistants have been selected to help record prices. I will now give each buyer and seller a numbered playing card. Some cards have been removed from the deck(s), and all remaining cards have a number. Please hold your card so that others do not see the number. The sellers' cards are red (hearts or diamonds), and the buyers' cards are black (clubs or spades). Each card represents a "unit" of an unspecified commodity that can be bought by buyers or sold by sellers.

Trading. Buyers and sellers will meet in the center of the room (or other designated area) and negotiate during a 5-minute trading period. When a buyer and a seller agree on a price, they will come together to the front of the room to report the price, which will be announced to all. Then the buyer and the seller will turn in their cards, return to their original seats, and wait for the trading period to end. There will be several market periods.

Sellers. Each of you can sell a single unit of the commodity during a trading period. The number on your card is the dollar cost that you incur if you make a sale, and you will not be allowed to sell below this cost. Your earnings on the sale are calculated as the difference between the price that you negotiate and the cost number on the card. If you do not make a sale, you do not earn anything or incur any cost in that period. Think of it this way: it's as if you knew someone who would sell you the commodity for a price that equals your cost number, so you can keep the difference if you are able to resell the commodity for a price that is above the acquisition cost. Suppose that your card is a 2 of hearts and you negotiate a sale price of $3. Then you would earn: $3 - 2 = \$1$. You would not be allowed to sell at a price below $2 with this card (2 of hearts). If you mistakenly agree to a price that is below your cost, then the trade will be invalidated when you come to the front desk; your card will be returned and you can resume negotiations.

Buyers. Each of you can buy a single unit of the commodity during a trading period. The number on your card is the dollar value that you receive if you make a purchase, and you will not be allowed to buy at a price above this value. Your earnings on the purchase are calculated as the difference between the value number on the card and the price that you negotiate. If you do not make a purchase, you do not earn anything in the period. Think of it this way: it's as if you knew someone who would later buy the unit from you at a price that equals your value number, so you can keep the difference if you are able to buy the unit at a price that is below the resale value. Suppose that your card is a 9 of spades and you negotiate a purchase price of $4. Then you would earn: $9 - 4 = \$5$. You would not be allowed to buy at a price above $9 with this card (9 of spades). If you mistakenly agree to a price that is above your value, then the trade will be invalidated when you come to the front desk; your card will be returned and you can resume negotiations.

Recording Earnings. Some buyers and sellers may not be able to negotiate a trade, but do not be discouraged since new cards will be passed out at the beginning of the next period. Remember that earnings are 0 for any unit not bought or sold (sellers incur no cost and buyers receive no value). When the period ends, I will collect cards for the units not traded, and you can calculate your earnings while I shuffle and redistribute the cards. Your total earnings equal the sum of earnings for units traded in all periods; you can use the worksheet on the next page to keep track of your earnings. Sellers use the left side of the worksheet, and buyers use the right side. At this time, please draw a diagonal line through the side of the worksheet that you will *not* use. All earnings are hypothetical. Please do not talk with each other until the trading period begins. Are there any questions?

Final Observations. When a buyer and a seller agree on a price, both should come to the front *immediately* to turn in their cards together, so that we can verify that the price is neither lower than the seller's cost nor higher than the buyer's value. If there is a line, please wait together. After the price is verified, the assistant at the board will write the price and announce it loudly. Then, those two traders can return to their seats to calculate their earnings. The assistants should come to their positions in the front of the room. Buyers and sellers, please come to the central trading area *now*, and begin calling out prices at which you are willing to buy or sell. The market is open, and there are five minutes remaining.

class experiment worksheet · chapter 2

Pit Market

Seller Earnings				**Buyer Earnings**		
(Sellers use this side)				(Buyers use this side)		

− =	First Period	− =
(price) (cost) (earnings)		(value) (price) (earnings)

− =	Second Period	− =
(price) (cost) (earnings)		(value) (price) (earnings)

− =	Third Period	− =
(price) (cost) (earnings)		(value) (price) (earnings)

− =	Fourth Period	− =
(price) (cost) (earnings)		(value) (price) (earnings)

− =	Fifth Period	− =
(price) (cost) (earnings)		(value) (price) (earnings)

− =	Sixth Period	− =
(price) (cost) (earnings)		(value) (price) (earnings)

Total earnings
for all periods: _____

Total earnings
for all periods: _____

Push-Pull

We will play a card game in which everybody will be paired with someone on the opposite side of the room. I will now give each of you a pair of playing cards: one red card (hearts or diamonds) and one black card (clubs or spades). The numbers or faces on the cards will not matter, just the color. You will be asked to play one of these cards by holding it to your chest (so we can see that you have made your decision, but not what that decision is). Your earnings are determined by the cards played by you and by the person who is paired with you. If you play your red card, then your earnings in dollars will increase by $2, and the earnings of the person paired with you will not change. If you play your black card, your earnings will not change and the earnings of the person paired with you go up by $3. In other words, think of there being some dollar bills on the table between you and the other person. You can either "pull" $2 to yourself by playing the red card, or you can "push" $3 to the other person by playing the black card. If you each play the red card, you will each earn $2. If you each play the black card, you will each earn $3. If you play a black card and the other person plays a red card, then you earn 0 and the other person earns $5. If you play a red card and the other person plays a black card, then you earn $5, and the other person earns 0. Neither of you will be able to see what the other does (push or pull) until both decisions have been made. All earnings are hypothetical, except as noted below.

After you choose which card to play, hold it to your chest. I will then tell you who you are paired with, and you can each reveal the card that you played. Record your earnings on the worksheet. (*Optional*: After we finish all periods, I will pick one person with a random throw of dice and pay that person 10 percent of his or her total earnings, in cash. All earnings for everyone else are hypothetical. To make this easier, please write your identification number that I will give each of you at the top of the worksheet. Afterward, I will throw a 10-sided die twice, with the first throw determining the "tens" digit, until I obtain the ID number of one of you, who will then be paid 10 percent of his or her total earnings in cash.) Are there any questions?

Let's Begin.   I will proceed row by row, with each of the people on one side of the row being paired with someone on the other side. Would the people in the row that I designate please choose which card to play. Show that you have made your decision by picking up the card you want to play and holding it to your chest. Write the color of your card (R for Red, or B for Black) on the worksheet.

Has everyone finished? Now, I will pair you with another person, ask you to reveal your card, and write the color of the other person's card on the worksheet. Keep track of earnings in the last column of the worksheet.

You will be paired with a different person in round 2, and payoffs will change. In round 3 you will be paired with a different person and payoffs change again. You will be paired with the same person for rounds 3, 4, and 5.

Name: _____ ID: _____ Date: _____

Push Pull

Round	Payoffs	Your Card (R or B)	Other's Card (R or B)	Your Earnings
1	Red: pull $2 Black: push $3			
2	Red: pull $2 Black: push $8			
3	Red: pull $2 Black: push $3			
4	Red: pull $2 Black: push $3			
5	Red: pull $2 Black: push $3			

Lottery Choice

The Lottery Choice worksheet shows 10 decisions listed in the left column. Each decision is a paired choice between "Option A" and "Option B." You will make 10 choices and record these in the far-right column, but only one of them will be used in the end to determine your earnings. Before you start making your 10 choices, please let me explain how these choices will affect your earnings, which will be hypothetical unless otherwise indicated.

Here is a 10-sided die that will be used to determine payoffs; the faces are numbered from 1 to 10 (the "0" face of the die will serve as 10). After you have made all of your choices, we will throw this die twice, once to select one of the 10 decisions to be used, and a second time to determine what your payoff is for the option you chose (A or B), for the particular decision selected. Even though you will make 10 decisions, only one of them will affect your earnings, but you will not know in advance which decision will be used. Obviously, each decision has an equal chance of being used in the end.

Now, please look at Decision 1 at the top. Option A pays $2.00 if the throw of the 10-sided die is 1, and it pays $1.60 if the throw is 2–10. Option B yields $3.85 if the throw of the die is 1, and it pays $0.10 if the throw is 2–10. The other decisions are similar, except that the chances of the higher payoff for each option increase as you move down the table. For Decision 10 in the bottom row, the die will not be needed, since each option pays the highest payoff for sure, so your choice here is between $2.00 and $3.85.

To summarize, you will make 10 choices. You may choose A for some decision rows and B for other rows, and you may make your decisions in any order. When you are finished, I will come to your desk and throw the 10-sided die to select which of the 10 decisions will be used, i.e., which row in the table will be relevant. Then we will throw the die again to determine your money earnings for the option you chose for that decision. Earnings for this choice will be added to your previous earnings (if any).

Please look at the empty boxes on the right side of the worksheet. You will have to write a decision (A or B) in each of these boxes, and then the die throw will determine which one is going to count. We will look at the decision that you made for the choice that counts, and circle it, before throwing the die again to determine your earnings for this part. Then you will write your earnings at the bottom of the page. Are there any questions?

class experiment worksheet · chapter 4

Lottery Choice

	Option A	Option B	Your Choice A or B
Decision 1	$2.00 if throw of die is 1 $1.60 if throw of die is 2–10	$3.85 if throw of die is 1 $0.10 if throw of die is 2–10	
Decision 2	$2.00 if throw of die is 1–2 $1.60 if throw of die is 3–10	$3.85 if throw of die is 1–2 $0.10 if throw of die is 3–10	
Decision 3	$2.00 if throw of die is 1–3 $1.60 if throw of die is 4–10	$3.85 if throw of die is 1–3 $0.10 if throw of die is 4–10	
Decision 4	$2.00 if throw of die is 1–4 $1.60 if throw of die is 5–10	$3.85 if throw of die is 1–4 $0.10 if throw of die is 5–10	
Decision 5	$2.00 if throw of die is 1–5 $1.60 if throw of die is 6–10	$3.85 if throw of die is 1–5 $0.10 if throw of die is 6–10	
Decision 6	$2.00 if throw of die is 1–6 $1.60 if throw of die is 7–10	$3.85 if throw of die is 1–6 $0.10 if throw of die is 7–10	
Decision 7	$2.00 if throw of die is 1–7 $1.60 if throw of die is 8–10	$3.85 if throw of die is 1–7 $0.10 if throw of die is 8–10	
Decision 8	$2.00 if throw of die is 1–8 $1.60 if throw of die is 9–10	$3.85 if throw of die is 1–8 $0.10 if throw of die is 9–10	
Decision 9	$2.00 if throw of die is 1–9 $1.60 if throw of die is 10	$3.85 if throw of die is 1–9 $0.10 if throw of die is 10	
Decision 10	$2.00 if throw of die is 1–10	$3.85 if throw of die is 1–10	

Battle of Colors

We will play a card game in which everybody will be paired with someone on the opposite side of the room. I will give each of you a pair of playing cards, one red card (hearts or diamonds) and one black card (clubs or spades). (Optionally, these may be index cards with numbers written in red or black.) The people on the left side of the room have a red 8 and a black 2, whereas the people on the right side of the room have a red 2 and a black 8.

Left Side	Right Side
Red 8, Black 2	Red 2, Black 8

You will be asked to play one of these cards by holding it to your chest (so we can see that you have made your decision, but not what that decision is).

Your earnings are determined by the card that you play and by the card played by the person who is paired with you.

- If the colors of the cards *do not match* (red and black), you each earn nothing.
- If the colors *match*, earnings in dollars are equal to the number on your card.

After you choose which card to play, hold it to your chest. I will tell you who you are paired with, and you can each reveal the card that you played. Record your earnings on the next page. All earnings are hypothetical, except as noted below. (*Optional.* After we finish all rounds, I will pick one person with a random throw of dice and pay that person 10 percent of his or her total earnings, in cash. All earnings for everyone else are hypothetical. To make this easier, please write the identification number that I will give each of you at the top of the worksheet. Afterward, I will throw a 10-sided die twice, with the first throw determining the "tens" digit, until I obtain the ID number of one of you, who will then be paid 10 percent of his or her total earnings in cash.) Are there any questions?

Let's Begin. I will proceed by row, matching each person on one side of a row with someone on the other side. Would the people in the row that I designate please choose which card to play and write the color (R for red or B for black) in the "Your Card" column of the worksheet. Show that you have made your decision by picking up the card you want to play and holding it to your chest.

Everyone finished? Now, I will pair you with another person, ask you to reveal your card, and calculate your earnings. Remember to keep track of the other person's card and of your earnings on the worksheet.

In round 2 you will be paired with a different person, and a payoff change will be announced. In round 3 you will be paired with a different person and payoffs change again. You will be paired with the same person in rounds 3–8.

Game Payoffs

- Color key: R for red, B for black.
- If the cards match in color (RR or BB), you earn a dollar amount that is equal to the number on the card you played.
- If the cards do not match in color (RB or BR), you do not earn anything.
- Initial payoffs for round 1:

You play R, other plays R, you earn $_____.

You play B, other plays B, you earn $_____.

You play R, other plays B, you earn $0.00.

You play B, other plays R, you earn $0.00.

class experiment worksheet · chapter 5

Battle of Colors

Round	Payoffs	Your Card (R or B)	Other's Card (R or B)	Your Earnings
1	R card: $____ B card: $____			
2	R card: $____ B card: $____			
3	R card: $____ B card: $____			
4	R card: $____ B card: $____			
5	R card: $____ B card: $____			
6	R card: $____ B card: $____			
7	R card: $____ B card: $____			
8	R card: $____ B card: $____			

Quantity Choice Market

I will distribute one worksheet to each pair (or small group) of people in the class. In each market period (after the first one), your group will be paired with the same other group of students. The decisions made by your group and by the other group will determine the amounts earned by each group. (In the first period, your group will be the only seller in your market.)

At the beginning of a market period, your group will choose a quantity to produce and sell. Decisions will be made by writing the quantity on your worksheet. Your quantity may be any amount between and including 1 and 13 units. The other group will also select a quantity to produce. Each unit that you produce will cost your group $1, and similarly for the other group. The price at which you can sell all the units is determined by the total quantity, that is, the sum of your quantity and that of the other group, as shown in the table at the top of your worksheet. For example, if both of you select a quantity of 1, then the total is 2 and the price is 11. If both of you select 13, then the total is 26, and the price is 0, as will be the case whenever the total is greater than 12.

Example. Suppose that your quantity is 2 and the other group selects 1.

The price will be _____.
Your total sales revenue (price × your quantity) will be _____.
Your total cost ($1 × your quantity) will be _____.
Your profit (total revenue – total cost) will be _____.
You should have an answer of $18 in profit.

Please write your name on your worksheet. Going from left to right, you will see columns for the Period, Your Quantity, Other's Quantity, Market Price, Total Revenue, Your Cost, and Your Earnings. Your group begins by writing your own quantity in the appropriate column, for the current period only. As mentioned above, this quantity must be between (and including) 0 and 12. The units are indivisible, so please use only integer amounts (no fractions). After you find out the other group's quantity, fill out the information for the current period just as you did in the example. There will be a number of determined rounds.

At this time, make your decision for the first period. Note that the other group's quantity has been set to 0, i.e., your group will be the only seller in this first period. After that, you will be paired with the same other group in all remaining periods.

class experiment worksheet · chapter 6

Quantity Choice Market

Determination of Price As a Function of Total Quantity

Q	1	2	3	4	5	6	7	8	9	10	11	12	13+
Price	12	11	10	9	8	7	6	5	4	3	2	1	0

Period	Your Quantity	Other's Quantity	Market Price	Total Revenue	Your Cost	Your Earnings
1		0				
2						
3						
4						
5						
6						
7						
8						
9						
10						

Price/Quality Market

This market has four buyer teams and three seller teams, and each of you will be assigned to one of these teams. Each seller team will begin by choosing a price and a quality "grade." We will collect these decisions and write them on the blackboard. Then we will give buyer teams the chance to purchase from one of the sellers at the grade and price listed. The grade can be any number from 1 to 3. The grade is like a quality attribute; a higher grade costs more to produce and is worth more to buyers. The page that follows has a worksheet for a buyer and for a seller; cross out the part that you do not need. If you are a seller, the relevant table on your worksheet shows your costs of different grades. If you are a buyer, the relevant table shows your money values of different grades.

Each buyer team can buy only one "unit" of the commodity during a period. Each seller can sell up to two units, but the second unit costs $1 more to produce. If you are a seller, the top row of the table shows the cost of the first unit that you actually sell in a period (for the grade you choose); the second unit costs $1 more than the first unit. Unsold units are not produced and hence incur no cost.

Buyer teams earn money by making a purchase at a price that is below the value. The value to the buyer depends only on the grade, not on whether it is the seller's first or second unit in the period. A buyer's earnings are calculated as the difference between the value and the purchase price. If a buyer does not make a purchase, the buyer earns $0 for the period.

Seller teams earn money by making one or more sales at a price that is above the cost of the unit (determined from the table shown on the worksheet). A seller's earnings are calculated as the sum of the earnings on the units actually sold, and such earnings are calculated as the difference between the sale price and the cost of the grade produced. A seller who does not make a sale in a period will earn $0.

When all sellers have finished choosing their prices and grades for the period, we will collect the worksheets and write the prices and grades on the blackboard under the seller numbers. Then I will randomly select a buyer number, and that buyer can purchase a unit from one of the sellers or choose not to purchase. The remaining buyers are selected in order; if buyer 2 goes first, then buyer 3 is second, . . . and buyer 1 is last. Once a seller has sold a unit, the second unit costs $1 more, so the seller will be asked whether he or she wishes to sell a second unit at the advertised price and grade. If a second unit is sold, it must be at the same price and grade as the first unit. If a seller refuses to sell or sells both units in a period, I will draw a line through that seller's price on the blackboard.

You can use the table shown on the worksheet to calculate (hypothetical) earnings. Are there any questions? We will begin by having each seller team choose a price and a grade for period 1, which you should write in the top two rows of your worksheet.

Name: _____ ID: _____ Date: _____

Price/Quality Market

Seller Worksheet

Seller Number: ____

	Grade 1	Grade 2	Grade 3
Seller cost of first unit	$1.40	$4.60	$11.00
Seller cost of second unit	$2.40	$5.60	$12.00

	Period 1	Period 2	Period 3	Period 4	Period 5
1. Grade for current period					
2. Price for current period					
3. Sales price on first unit					
4. Cost of first unit					
5. Profit on first unit: (3)–(4)					
6. Sales price on second unit					
7. Cost of second unit					
8. Profit on second unit: (6)–(7)					
9. Total profit: (5)+(8)					
10. Cumulative profit					

Buyer Worksheet

Buyer Number: _____

	Grade 1	Grade 2	Grade 3
Buyer value	$4.00	$8.80	$13.60

	Period 1	Period 2	Period 3	Period 4	Period 5
1. ID of seller of product					
2. Grade of product					
3. Value to you (from table)					
4. Purchase price					
5. Earnings: (3)–(4)					
6. Cumulative earnings					

Bargaining

I have $10 to split. Those in the front of the room are "responders," and those in the back are "proposers." There are 11 ways that the $10 can be divided between two people in even dollar amounts (see the options shown on the worksheet). The proposer must suggest one of these by selecting one (and only one) of the listed options. The worksheets will then be collected and shuffled. One of the sheets will be given to each responder, who must either accept or reject the proposal by checking the appropriate box on the worksheet. If the responder accepts, then the proposal is enacted. If the responder rejects, then the money is not divided and each person, proposer and responder, will earn nothing. Then I will collect the worksheets and use the throw of a 10-sided die to select one of the proposer numbers, and the earnings (if any) determined by the decisions on that sheet will actually be paid to the proposer and responder who made those decisions. This payment will be in cash. At this time I will assign an ID number to each person. Please write down your number so that you will remember it after I collect the worksheets.

Bargaining

Proposer Number: _____

Check one and only one of the following boxes.

❏ $0 for the proposer, $10 for the responder
❏ $1 for the proposer, $9 for the responder
❏ $2 for the proposer, $8 for the responder
❏ $3 for the proposer, $7 for the responder
❏ $4 for the proposer, $6 for the responder
❏ $5 for the proposer, $5 for the responder
❏ $6 for the proposer, $4 for the responder
❏ $7 for the proposer, $3 for the responder
❏ $8 for the proposer, $2 for the responder
❏ $9 for the proposer, $1 for the responder
❏ $10 for the proposer, $0 for the responder

Responder Number: _____

Check one and only one of the following boxes.

❏ I accept, and earnings will be determined by the proposal.
❏ I reject, and both of us will earn nothing.

14

Play-or-Keep

Each of you will be given four playing cards, two of which are red (hearts or diamonds), and two of which are black (clubs or spades). All of your cards will be the same number.

The experiment will consist of a number of rounds. At the start of a round, I will come to each of you in order, and you will play *two* of your four cards by placing them face down on top of the stack in my hand.

Your earnings in dollars are determined by what you do with your red cards. For each red card that you keep in a round you will earn $4 for the round, and for each black card that you keep you will earn nothing. Red cards that are placed on the stack affect everyone's earnings in the following manner. I will count the total number of red cards in the stack, and everyone will earn this number of dollars. Black cards placed on the stack have no effect on the count. When the cards are counted, I will not reveal who made which decisions. To summarize, your earnings for the round will be calculated as follows:

Your Earnings = $4 × the number of red cards you kept
+ $1 × the total number of red cards I collect.

At the end of the round I will return your own cards to you by coming to each of you in reverse order and giving you the top two cards, face down, off of the stack in my hand. Thus, you begin the next round with two cards of each color, regardless of which cards you just played.

After the fifth round (or perhaps sooner), I will announce a change in the earnings for each red card you keep. Even though the value of red cards kept will change, red cards placed on the stack will always earn $1 for each person.

Use the worksheet to record your decisions, earnings, and cumulative earnings. (*Optional*: At the end of the game, one person will be selected at random and will be paid ____ percent of his or her actual earnings, in cash.) All earnings are hypothetical for everyone else. Are there any questions?

Play-or-Keep

Earnings from Each Red Card Collected = $1

Round	Number of Red Cards Kept	Value of Each Red Card Kept	Earnings from Red Cards Kept	Earnings from Red Cards Collected	Total Earnings	Cumulative Earnings
1		$4				
2		$4				
3		$4				
4		$4				
5		$4				
6		$2				
7		$2				
8		$2				
9		$2				
10		$2				

15

Volunteer's Dilemma Game

Each of you will be given two playing cards, one red (hearts or diamonds), and one black (clubs or spades). At the start of a round, I will ask each of you to play one of your cards by picking it up and holding it against your chest with the color hidden until I ask everyone to reveal which card they played.

After the card decisions have been made, but before they have been revealed, I will select one or more people to be in your group and will ask all of you to reveal your cards at the same time. Your earnings in dollars are determined by the card that you play and by the cards played by the others in your group. Think of playing a red card as a decision to volunteer to perform some task. Volunteering has a cost for you ($0.25), but everyone in the group will benefit (by receiving $2.00) if at least one person volunteers. There is no additional benefit if there is more than one volunteer in your group. The payoffs are as follows:

- Payoff if there is no volunteer: $0.00
- Payoff if there is at least one volunteer and you *do not* volunteer: $2.00
- Payoff if there is at least one volunteer and you *do* volunteer: $1.75

We will begin with groups of two for the first rounds, so when I point to you and to another randomly selected person in the room, show your cards, return your card to your desk, and calculate your earnings. The people who have not yet been paired should keep holding their cards to their chests so that I can continue to match people until nobody remains to be paired. Then the next round will begin. Each person will decide which card to play for that round by holding that card against their chest until they are paired. After several rounds, I will divide people into groups of four, and you will have to record the new group size in the relevant column of the worksheet. Before beginning, I will select one person to record all decisions.

All earnings are hypothetical. (*Optional:* At the end of the game, one person will be selected at random and will be paid _____ percent of his or her actual earnings, in cash.) Are there any questions?

Volunteer's Dilemma Game

Round	Group Size	Card Played (R or B)	Red Cards Played in Your Group	Your Earnings	Cumulative Earnings
1	2				
2					
3					
4					
5					
6					
7					
8					
9					
10					

Payoff:

- If there is *no volunteer*: $0.00
- Payoff if there is at least one volunteer and you *do not* volunteer: $2.00
- Payoff if there is at least one volunteer and you *do* volunteer: $1.75

Lobbying Game

This is a simple card game. Each person has been assigned to a team of investors bidding for a local government communications license that is worth $16,000. The government will allocate the license by choosing randomly from the applications received. The paperwork and legal fees associated with each application will cost your team $3,000, regardless of whether you obtain the license or not. (Think of this $3,000 as the opportunity cost of the time and materials used in completing the required paperwork.) Each team is permitted to submit any number of applications, up to a limit of 13 per team. Each team begins with a working capital of $100,000.

There will be four teams competing for each license, each of which is provided with 13 cards of the same suit. Your team will play any number of these cards by placing them in an envelope provided. Each card you play is like a lottery ticket in a drawing for a prize of $16,000. All cards that are played by your team and the other three teams will be placed on a stack and shuffled. Then one card will be drawn from the deck. If that card is of your suit, then your team will win $16,000. Otherwise you receive nothing from the lottery. Whether or not you win, your earnings will decrease by $3,000 for each card that you play. To summarize, your earnings are calculated:

> Earnings = $16,000 if you win the lottery
> − $3,000 × the number of cards you play (win or lose).

Earnings are negative for the teams that do not win the lottery, and negative earnings are indicated with a minus sign on the worksheet under round 1. The cumulative earnings column on the right begins with $100,000, reflecting your initial financial capital. Earnings are hypothetical, and should be added to or subtracted from this amount. Are there any questions?

Round 2 is for a second license. Your team begins again with 13 cards, but the cost of each card played is reduced to $1,000, due to a government efficiency move that requires less paperwork for each application. This license is worth $16,000 as before, whether or not your team already acquired a license.

In round 3, the value of the license may differ from team to team. Your team begins again with 13 cards, and the cost of each card played remains at $1,000. You will be informed of the license value, which you should write in the appropriate place on the worksheet. These values are determined by adding 10 to the outcome of the throw of the 10-sided die (the die will be thrown for each team), so the value will be between $10,000 and $19,000.

In round 4, the license will be worth the same to you as it was in the third round, but there is no lottery and no application fee. Instead, I will conduct an auction by starting with a low price of $8,000 and calling out successively higher prices until there is only one team actively bidding. The winning team will have to pay the amount of its final bid. The losing teams do not have to pay anything for the license that they did not purchase; the winning team earns an amount that equals its license value minus the price paid. The revenue from the auction will be divided equally among the teams.

Lobbying Game

Round	Number Cards Played	Cost per Card Played	Total Cost	License Value	Your Earnings	Cumulative Earnings $100,000
1		$3,000		$16,000		
2		$1,000		$16,000		
3		$1,000				
4* bid =						

*In round 4, your earnings amount is equal to your license value minus your bid if you win; $0 otherwise.

Private Value Auction

We will conduct a series of auctions in which the highest bidder obtains the "prize." In each auction, you will be paired with another randomly selected member of the class. The value of the prize will be determined by throws of 10-sided dice. Prior to the auction, I will come to each of you and throw the 10-sided die two times: the first throw determines the dimes digit, and the final throw determines the pennies digit. These two throws determine the prize value to you if you win. The other person will also see two throws of the dice that will determine his or her prize value, so the prize will generally be worth different amounts to each of you. You will make your bid decision after seeing your value, but without knowledge of the other person's value or the other person's bid. The higher bidder wins the prize and earns the difference between their own prize value and their own bid amount. The low bidder earns nothing. You will be paired with another person in the classroom in each period. This other person will be selected at random, unless indicated otherwise.

The worksheet should be used to keep track of your decisions. The ID number will be used to match you with another bidder each period. The period number is shown on the left side of each row. At the beginning of the period, I will come to your desk to throw the dice that determine your prize value, which can be recorded in column (1). After recording this number, you should decide on a bid for the period, which will be entered in column (2). Do this when you make your bid, before you hear what the other person's bid is. Then I will match you with someone else in the class, and you will each call out your bids. You should use column (3) to record the other person's bid. If you had the higher bid, your earnings will be the value (1) minus your bid in (2). If you had the lower bid, your earnings will be 0 for the period. Ties will be decided by the flip of a coin. Earnings are entered in column (4). Are there any questions?

Instructions for Part B

This part will be the same as before, with values determined by the throws of 10-sided dice and with the high bidder being the winner. The only difference is that the winning bidder only has to pay the *second-highest bid price*. The high bidder earns the difference between his or her own value and the other person's bid, and the low bidder earns nothing. For example, if your value is 2 and you bid X and the other person bids Y, then you win with a bid of X but you only have to pay Y, so you earn $2 - Y$.

Private Value Auction

Part A

Period	(1) Your Value	(2) Your Bid	(3) Other Bid	(4) Your Earnings	(5) Cumulative Earnings
1					
2					
3					
4					
5					

Part B

Period	(1) Your Value	(2) Your Bid	(3) Other Bid	(4) Your Earnings	(5) Cumulative Earnings
6					
7					
8					
9					
10					

Takeover Game

I will divide the class into two-person teams. Half of the teams will be buyers and half will be sellers in a market. I will choose teams and indicate your role: buyer or seller. Each team should have a single copy of these instructions and a single worksheet, with the role assignment, buyer or seller, indicated on the worksheet.

Each seller team is the owner of a business. The money value of the business to the seller is only known by the seller. Each of the buyers will be paired with one of the sellers. The buyer will make a single bid to buy the business. The buyer does not know the value of the business to the seller, but the buyer is a better manager and knows that he or she can increase the profits to 1.5 times the current level. After receiving the buyer's bid, the seller must decide whether or not to accept it. The seller will earn the value of the business if it is not sold, and the seller will earn the amount of the accepted bid if the business is sold. The buyer will earn nothing if the bid is rejected. If the buyer's bid is accepted, the buyer will earn 1.5 times the seller's value, minus the bid amount.

A 10-sided die will be thrown twice to determine the value to the seller, in thousands of dollars. This will be done for each seller individually. The die is numbered from 0 to 9; the first throw determines the tens digit and the second determines the ones digit, so the seller value is equally likely to be any integer number of thousands of dollars, from 0 to 99 thousand dollars. If the business is purchased by the buyer, it will be worth 1.5 times the seller value, so the value to the buyer will be between 0 and 148.5 thousand dollars.

The worksheet can be used to record the outcomes. For simplicity, records will be in thousands of dollars; i.e., a 50 means 50 thousand. I will begin by coming to each seller's desk to throw the 10-sided die twice, and you can record the resulting seller value in column (1). Then each buyer, not knowing the seller's value, will decide on a bid and record it in column (2). Then I will pair the buyers and sellers randomly, and each buyer will communicate the bid to the corresponding seller, who will say yes (accept) or no (reject). The seller's decision is recorded in column (3). If the bid is accepted, then the seller will communicate the seller's value to the buyer, who will multiply it by 1.5 and enter the sum in column (4). Finally, buyers and sellers calculate their earnings in the appropriate column (5) or (6). The buyer earns either 0 (if no purchase) or the difference between the buyer value (4) and the accepted bid. The seller either earns the seller value (if no sale) or the amount of the accepted bid. Each of you will begin with an initial cash balance of $500,000; gains are added to this amount and losses are subtracted. You can keep track of your cumulative cash balance in column (7), and all earnings are hypothetical. Are there any questions?

Now I will come around to the desks of sellers and throw the dice to determine the seller values. While I am doing this, those of you who are buyers should now decide on a bid and enter it in column (2). For those of you who are buyers, the seller value column (1) is blank. You only find out the seller value after you announce your bid. Those of you who are sellers have no decision to make at this time. When you hear the buyer's bid, you must choose between keeping the value of the business (determined by the dice throws) or giving it up in exchange for the buyer bid amount. Please only write in the first row of the table at this time. (After everyone has been paired and has calculated their earnings for the first set of decisions, you will switch roles, with buyers becoming sellers, and vice versa. The second set of decisions will be recorded in the bottom row.)

class experiment worksheet · chapter 20

Takeover Game

Role:

- ❏ Buyer
- ❏ Seller

Round	(1) Seller's Value	(2) Buyer's Bid	(3) Seller's Decision	(4) Value to Buyer 1.5*(1)	(5) Seller's Earnings (1) or (2)	(6) Buyer's Earnings (4) – (2) or 0	(7) Cash Balance 500 (thousand)
1			❏ Accept ❏ Reject				
2			❏ Accept ❏ Reject				

Common Value Auction

We will conduct a series of auctions in which the highest bidder obtains the "prize." In each auction, you will be paired with another randomly selected member of the class. You and the person you are paired with will each see half of the prize value. The value of the prize will be determined by throws of 10-sided dice. Prior to the auction, I will come to each of you and throw the 10-sided die two times: the first throw determines the dimes digit, and the final throw determines the pennies digit. These two throws determine your value component, which is equally likely to be any penny amount from $0.00 to $0.99. The other person will see two throws of the dice that will determine his/her value component in exactly the same manner. The value of the prize is just the sum of the two value components, so the prize value will be no less than $0.00 and no greater than $1.98. You will make your bid decision after seeing your value component, but without knowledge of the other person's value component or the other person's bid. The higher bidder wins the prize and earns the difference between the prize value (sum of the two value components) and the bid amount. This will be a gain if the bid is lower than the prize value, and this will be a loss if the bid is higher than the prize value. The low bidder earns nothing. You will be randomly paired with another person in the classroom in each period, so you only bid against one other person, but that person will generally be different in each successive auction "period."

The worksheet should be used to keep track of your decisions. The ID number will be used to match you with another bidder in each period. The period number is shown on the left side of each row. At the beginning of the period, I will come to your desk to throw the dice to determine your value component, which can be recorded in column (1). After recording this number, you should decide on a bid for the period, which will be entered in column (2). Do this when you make your bid, before you hear what the other person's bid is. Then I will randomly match you with someone else in the class, and you will each call out your bids. You should use column (3) to record the other person's bid. At this time, you will know whether you won the auction or not, but you will not yet know the prize value. Finally, each person will announce their value components, so that you can record the other person's value component in column (4) and calculate the sum of the components in column (5). If you have the higher bid, your earnings will be the value sum in (5) minus your bid in (2). If you have the lower bid, your earnings will be 0 for the period. Earnings are entered in column (6). You begin the first period with an initial cash balance of $5.00; gains are added to this and losses are subtracted. You can keep track of your cumulative cash balance in column (7). Are there any questions?

class experiment worksheet · chapter 21

Common Value Auction

Period	(1) Value Component	(2) Your Bid	(3) Other Bid	(4) Value Component	(5) Sum of Values	(6) Your Earnings	(7) Cumulative Earnings $5.00
1							
2							
3							
4							

Multi-Unit Auction

The instructor will need a box of ballpoint pens or some other items to be repurchased at auction, and a little cash for the repurchase. If the quantity is limited, the class can be divided so that each group receives one item. The discriminatory auction instructions can be given to half of the class, and the uniform price instructions that follow can be given to the other half. The instructions can be read once, stressing the italicized auction rule that differs for the two auction types.

A Discriminatory Auction

Each person has been given a pen. This is yours to keep, unless you decide to sell it back. I have an amount of money that is sufficient to purchase _____ pens. I will let each of you write down an offer to sell your pen, using the Discriminatory Auction form on the worksheet.

Please write your name and offer (between $0.00 and $1.00) in the boxes. After you have turned in your offer, all offers will be ranked from low to high, regardless of pen color, and the _ __ lowest offers will be accepted. *Each person with an accepted offer will receive an amount that equals that person's own offer amount, and they must, in turn, give up their pens.* People with rejected offers will keep their pens.

For example, if the quantity goal is two pens and the bids are $.10, $.13, $.15, and $.20, then two bids ($.10 and $.13) will be accepted because we start with the lowest bid and stop when the quantity goal is reached. *The people with accepted offers get reimbursed an amount that equals their own offer, which means that one person receives $.10 and the other receives $.13.* Both of these people must then give up their pens. The others keep their pens and receive no payment. In the actual auction, the quantity goal will be _____ pens instead of the two pens used in this example.

A Uniform Price Auction

Each person has been given a pen. This is yours to keep, unless you decide to sell it back. I have an amount of money that is sufficient to purchase _____ of these pens. I will let each of you write down an offer to sell your pen, using the Uniform Price Auction form on the worksheet.

Please write your name and offer (between $0.00 and $1.00) on Uniform Price Action table on the worksheet. After you have turned in your offer, all offers will be ranked from low to high, regardless of pen color, and the _____ lowest offers will be accepted. *Each person with an accepted offer will receive an amount that equals the lowest rejected offer, and they must, in turn, give up their pens.* People with rejected offers will keep their pens.

For example, if the quantity goal is two pens and the bids are $.10, $.13, $.15, and $.20, then two bids ($.10 and $.13) will be accepted because we start with the lowest bid and stop when the quantity goal is reached. *The people with accepted offers get reimbursed an amount that equals the lowest rejected bid, which is $.15 in this case, so the people who bid $.10 and $.13 will each receive $.15.* Both people must then each give up their pens. The others keep their pens and receive no payment. In the actual auction, the quantity goal will be _____ pens instead of the two pens used in this example.

Name: _____ ID: _____ Date: _____

Multi-Unit Auction

Discriminatory Auction

Your Name: _____

Sale Offer Price (between $0.00 and $1.00): _____

Uniform Price Auction

Your Name: _____

Sale Offer Price (between $0.00 and $1.00): _____

Claim Game

I will distribute one worksheet to each pair (or small group) of people in the class. In each period, your group will be randomly paired with another group of students. The decisions made by your group and by the other group will determine the amounts earned by each group.

Imagine that you have suffered a loss of money and that only you know the amount that you lost. You will choose a number or "claim." Claims must be integer dollar amounts (no pennies!). Your claim amount may be any dollar amount between and including $25 and $100. The other group will have suffered an equivalent loss, and they will make a claim between and including $25 and $100. If the claims are equal, then your group and the other group each receive the amount claimed. If the claims are not equal, I will pay each of you the lower of the two claims. In addition, the group making the lower claim will earn a reward of $2, and the group making the higher claim will have a penalty of $2 deducted from the reimbursement. Thus, your group will earn an amount that equals the lower of the two claims, plus a $2 reward if you made the lower claim, or minus a $2 penalty if you made the higher claim. There is no penalty or reward if the two claims are exactly equal, in which case each group receives what they claimed, as long as it is in the range from $25 to $100.

Example. Suppose that your claim is X and the other claim is Y.

- If X = Y, you get X, and the other gets Y.
- If X > Y, you get Y minus $2, and the other gets Y plus $2.
- If X < Y, you get X plus $2, and the other gets X minus $2.

Please write your name and assigned ID number on your worksheet. Going from left to right, you will see columns for "Your Claim," "Other Claim," "Minimum Claim," "Penalty Paid or Reward Received," and "Your Earnings." Your group begins by writing down your own claim in the first column, for the current period only. As mentioned above, this claim must be greater than or equal to $25 and less than or equal to $100, and the claim may be any amount in this range (no pennies).

After you record your claim, hold your paper up to your chest, and I will designate two groups and ask them to announce their decisions. When you find out the other group's claim, please write it in the third column, followed by the minimum, the penalty or reward (if the claims are not equal), and your earnings. Then leave your paper on your desk so that I will know which people have not been paired yet. The process may be repeated with a different penalty reward amount in the second period.

Claim Game

	Penalty/ Reward	Your Claim (between $25 and $100)	Other Claim	Minimum Claim	Penalty Paid or Reward Received	Your Earnings
Period 1	$2					
Period 2	$25					

Effort Game

I will distribute one worksheet to each of you. Please write your name or ID number on the worksheet. In each round of this experiment, you will begin by choosing a number or "effort" that can be 1, 2, 3, 4, 5, 6, or 7. Efforts will be made by writing the number you choose in the second column of your worksheet, for the current round only. When everyone is finished, the sheets will be collected. Then I will call out the numbers and ask one of you to write them on the board.

Your payoff will depend on your effort choice and on the minimum of all efforts, including your own. After we write all efforts on the blackboard, the lowest one will be circled. The second lowest effort will be marked with an asterisk. Your payoff will be determined in one of two ways:

- If your effort is not the lowest, then the circled number will determine the relevant column of the payoff table below, and your effort determines the row. The number in the cell that corresponds to the intersection of this row and column will be your earnings in cents.
- If your effort is the lowest, then the lowest of the other efforts is the number marked with an asterisk, and that number determines the column, while your number determines the row as before.

Your Effort	Minimum of Other Efforts						
	1	2	3	4	5	6	7
7	10	30	50	70	90	110	130
6	20	40	60	80	100	120	120
5	30	50	70	90	110	110	110
4	40	60	80	100	100	100	100
3	50	70	90	90	90	90	90
2	60	80	80	80	80	80	80
1	70	70	70	70	70	70	70

Once you know the minimum of the other efforts and have determined your earnings, please write them in the relevant columns, and we will begin the next round.

Name: _____ ID: _____ Date: _____

Effort Game

Round	Your Effort	Minimum of All Other Efforts	Your Earnings
1			
2			
3			
4			
5			

Binary Prediction Game

This is an exercise in prediction. You will be asked which of two random events will occur. The events will be called L (left) and R (right). I will throw the dice to determine which event will occur in each period. Please look at the worksheet. The number of the round is on the left, and you will use the second column to record your prediction, L or R. You begin by recording your prediction *for round 1 only*, leaving all remaining rows blank. After everyone has written their prediction for round 1 in the top row, we will throw the dice in the front of the room to determine the event, L or R. The throwing of the dice will be done behind a screen so that you cannot see what method is being used. The dice throw will be compared with a fixed cutoff, which will determine whether the event is L or R. You will not be told this cutoff; all you know is that this cutoff will remain unchanged. The main thing to remember is that the person throwing the dice will not know your predictions, so these decisions cannot affect the chances that one event or the other will be observed in future rounds. When we announce the event (L or R) for the current period, please write in your earnings: +$1 if you were correct, and −$1 if you were incorrect. Then you can proceed to record your decision for the following round. You can keep track of your cumulative earnings in the final column. Earnings may be hypothetical or one person will be selected at random to be paid a fraction of earnings. To summarize, each period consists of (1) the prediction stage, (2) the throwing of the dice to determine the event, (3) the announcement of the event and the calculation of results. Are there any questions?

Name: _____ ID: _____ Date: _____

Binary Prediction Game

Round	Your Prediction (L or R)	Observed Event (L or R)	Your Earnings	Total Earnings
1				
2				
3				
4				
5				
6				
7				
8				
9				
10				
11				
12				
13				
14				
15				
16				
17				
18				
19				
20				

Paired Lottery Choices

Your worksheet shows 10 decisions listed on the left, which are labeled 0, 1, 2, . . . , 9. Each decision is a paired choice between a randomly determined payoff described on the left and another one described on the right. You will make 10 choices and record these in the final column, but in the end only one of them will be used to determine your earnings. Before you start making your 10 choices, I'll explain how these choices will affect your earnings. Unless otherwise indicated, all earnings are hypothetical.

Here is a 10-sided die that will be used to determine payoffs; the faces are numbered from 0 to 9. After you have made all of your choices, I will throw this die three times, once to select one of the 10 decisions to be used, and then two more times to determine what your payoff is for the option you chose (on the left side or on the right side) for the particular decision selected. Even though you will make 10 decisions, only one of them will end up affecting your earnings, but you will not know in advance which decision will be used. Obviously, each decision has an equal chance of being used.

Now, please look at Decision 0 at the top. If this were the decision that we ended up using, I would throw the 10-sided die two more times. The two throws will determine a number from 0 to 99, with the first throw determining the tens digit and the second one determining the ones digit. The option on the left side pays $6.00 if the throw of the 10-sided die is 0–99, and it pays $0.00 otherwise. Since all throws are between 0 and 99, this option provides a sure $6.00. The option on the right pays $8.00 if the throw of the die is 0–79, and it pays $0.00 otherwise. Thus, the option on the right side of Decision 0 provides 80 chances out of 100 (a four-fifths probability) of getting $8.00. The left and right options for the other decision rows are similar, but with different payoffs and chances of getting each payoff. In addition, you will receive $10.00 for participating, so any earnings will be added to this amount. Some of the decisions involve losses, indicated by minus signs. If the decision selected ends up with a loss, this loss will be subtracted from the initial $10.00 payment to determine your final earnings.

To summarize, you will make 10 choices: for each decision row you will have to choose between the option on the left and the option on the right. Make your choice by putting a check by the option you prefer. If you change your mind, cross out the check and put it on the other side. Thus, there should be one check mark in each row. You may make your decisions in any order. When you are finished, mark your final choices, L for left or R for right, in the far-right column, and I will come to your desk and throw the 10-sided die to select which of the 10 decisions will be used. We will circle that decision before throwing the die again to determine your money earnings for the option you chose for that decision.

Note that different people may make different choices for the same decision, in the same manner that one person may purchase a sweater that differs from that purchased by someone else. We are interested in *your* preferences, i.e., which option you prefer, so please think carefully about each decision, and please do not talk with others in the room. Are there any questions?

Paired Lottery Choices

Decision	Left Side	Right Side	Your Choice L or R
Decision 0	$6.00 if throw of die is 0–99	$8.00 if throw of die is 0–79 $0.00 if throw of die is 80–99	
Decision 1	$2.00 if throw of die is 0–99	$4.00 if throw of die is 0–79 –$4.00 if throw of die is 80–99	
Decision 2	$6.00 if throw of die is 0–24 $0.00 if throw of die is 25–99	$8.00 if throw of die is 0–19 $0.00 if throw of die is 20–99	
Decision 3	$30.00 if throw of die is 0–99	$40.00 if throw of die is 0–79 $0.00 if throw of die is 80–99	
Decision 4	$4.00 if throw of die is 0–49 $3.20 if throw of die is 50–99	$7.70 if throw of die is 1–49 $0.20 if throw of die is 50–99	
Decision 5	–$6.00 if throw of die is 0–99	–$8.00 if throw of die is 0–79 –$0.00 if throw of die is 80–99	
Decision 6	$2.00 if throw of die is 0–49 $1.20 if throw of die is 50–99	$5.70 if throw of die is 1–49 –$1.80 if throw of die is 50–99	
Decision 7	–$6.00 if throw of die is 0–24 –$0.00 if throw of die is 25–99	–$8.00 if throw of die is 0–19 –$0.00 if throw of die is 20–99	
Decision 8	–$4.00 if throw of die is 0–49 –$3.20 if throw of die is 50–99	–$7.70 if throw of die is 1–49 –$0.20 if throw of die is 50–99	
Decision 9	$30.00 if throw of die is 0–24 $0.00 if throw of die is 25–99	$40.00 if throw of die is 0–19 $0.00 if throw of die is 20-99	

Search Game

In this game, we will use throws of dice to determine a series of money amounts, and you will choose which amount to accept, with the understanding that each additional throw entails a cost that will be deducted from the money amount that you finally accept.

Please look at this 10 sided die. The sides are marked from 0 to 9, so if I throw it twice and use the first throw for the tens digit, I will determine a number from $0 to $.99. By ignoring the first draw if it is a 9 (and throwing again for a new first number, I will obtain a number between (and including) $0 and $.89. A number of pennies determined in this way will be yours to keep, but there is a cost of obtaining this amount.

In particular, if you pay a cost of $.05, I will throw the dice for you, and you can either keep the amount determined, or you can decide to pay another $.05 and I'll throw the dice again to get a second number in the range from $0 to $.89. (If the throw for the tens digit is a 9, I will throw the die again.) You can do this as many times as you wish (with no limit), but you have to pay $.05 for each new number. When you decide to stop, you can use the highest two-digit number that you have received up to that point, and your earnings will be that number minus the total cost of the search process, which is $.05 times the number of times that you asked me to throw the dice. There is no limit on the number of times you can pay the $.05 cost in search of a higher number.

Use the worksheet to keep records; use another sheet if you need additional space. Each new two-digit number will be called an "offer." For the first offer that you pay to obtain, look at the "1st" column. After I throw the dice, write the number in the top row for "Value of current offer." The highest offer received up to now is written in the second row. (At first, the current offer is also the highest offer.) Moving down to the next row, the total search cost is the number of draws times $.05. The "Earnings if you stop" are calculated by subtracting the total search cost from the highest draw so far. After calculating these earnings, you can decide whether to stop or to pay and search again. Write "S" for stop or "C" for continue. When you stop, please circle your earnings at that point and stop recording the new numbers. I will keep throwing the dice and announcing numbers until everyone has decided to stop. Then the whole process will be repeated, for another "search sequence," and so on.

All earnings are hypothetical unless otherwise indicated. Are there any questions?

I will do this again with a search cost of $.20, but there is a maximum of three offers, which are equally likely to be any amount between $0 and $.89. You can stop before the first draw and earn 0, or you can pay $.20 for the first offer, stop or pay $.20 more for a second, and stop with the higher of the two or pay $.20 more for a third, and take the highest of the three. Before doing this, please decide how high the first offer must be for you to stop after only one time, and how high the best of the two initial offers must be for you to stop after only two times. You may want to discuss this with your neighbor. Please record your decisions below.

- On the first draw, I will stop if it is at least _____ .
- On the second draw, I will stop if the higher of the first two offers is at least

    _____.

Now I will throw the dice for the first offer, and so on, and you can record your earnings on the worksheet.

Search Game

Record of the First Search Sequence

Order of offer	1st	2nd	3rd	4th	5th	6th	7th	8th	9th	10th
Value of current offer (in cents)										
Highest offer so far										
Total search cost (5 for each search)	5	10	15	20	25	30	35	40	45	50
Earnings if you stop (use—for losses)										
Will you stop now? (S=Stop/C=Continue)										

Record of the Second Search Sequence

Order of offer	1st	2nd	3rd	4th	5th	6th	7th	8th	9th	10th
Value of current offer (in cents)										
Highest offer so far										
Total search cost (5 for each search)	5	10	15	20	25	30	35	40	45	50
Earnings if you stop (use—for losses)										
Will you stop now? (S=Stop/C=Continue)										

Record of the Third Search Sequence

Order of offer	1st	2nd	3rd	4th	5th	6th	7th	8th	9th	10th
Value of current offer (in cents)										
Highest offer so far										
Total search cost (20 for each search)	20	40	60	80	100	120	140	160	180	200
Earnings if you stop (use—for losses)										
Will you stop now? (S=Stop/C=Continue)										

Record of the Fourth Search Sequence

Order of offer	1st	2nd	3rd	4th	5th	6th	7th	8th	9th	10th
Value of current offer (in cents)										
Highest offer so far										
Total search cost (20 for each search)	20	40	60	80	100	120	140	160	180	200
Earnings if you stop (use—for losses)										
Will you stop now? (S=Stop/C=Continue)										

Bayes' Rule

The setup requires a 6-sided die, a 10-sided die, three light marbles, three dark marbles, a plastic cup for making draws, two paper envelopes marked A and B, and a way to hide the cup selection process from view. The reading of the instructions and the experiment itself can be done in about 25 minutes.

In this experiment, you will observe balls (colored marbles) drawn from one of two possible cups. You will see the balls drawn, but you will not know for sure which cup is being used. Then you will be asked to indicate your beliefs about which cup is being used. I will begin by choosing someone to serve as a monitor to assist in setting things up and drawing the marbles.

The two cups will be called cup A and cup B. Cup A contains two light balls and one dark ball, and cup B contains one light ball and two dark balls. The cup will be chosen by the throw of a 6-sided die: cup A is used if the roll of the die yields a 1, 2, or 3, and cup B is used if the roll of the die yields a 4, 5, or 6. Thus, it is equally likely that either cup will be selected.

Cup A (used if the die is 1, 2, or 3)	Cup B (used if the die is 4, 5, or 6)
2 light balls	1 light ball
1 dark ball	2 dark balls

Once a cup is determined by the roll of the die, we will empty the contents of that cup into a container. The container is always the same, regardless of which cup is being used, so you cannot guess the cup by looking at the container. Then we will draw one or more balls from the container. (If more than one draw is to be made, then the first ball drawn will be put back into the container, which is then shaken before a second draw is made, and so on.)

Recording Your Beliefs

After the draw has been made, I will ask you to tell us your beliefs about the chances that cup A is being used. You will indicate a number between 0 and 100, which we will call P, such that the chances that cup A is being used are "P out of 100." If you are sure that cup A is being used, you should choose $P = 100$ to indicate that the chances are "100 out of 100" that cup A is being used. If you are sure that cup A is not being used, you should choose $P = 0$ to indicate that the chances are "0 out of 100" that cup A is being used. Thus, the magnitude of P corresponds to the chances that cup A is being used. For example, if the manner in which the cup is selected and the balls that you see drawn cause you to think that cup A is just as likely as cup B, then you should choose $P = 50$, indicating that the chances of A are "50 out of 100."

Use the worksheet to record your information and decisions. At the start of each period, the monitor will throw a 6-sided die to select the cup (A if the throw is 1, 2, or 3 and B if the throw is 4, 5, or 6). The monitor will then place the three balls for that cup in the plastic container from which we make the draws. The period number is shown in column (1) of the worksheet. The results of the draws are to be recorded in column (2). Please look at the worksheet for periods 1–10. In the first period, there will be no draws, as indicated in column (2), so the only information that you have is the information about how the cup is selected.

In subsequent periods, you will see one or more draws, and you can use column (2) to record the draw(s). Write L (for light) or D (for dark) in this column at the time the draw is made. In periods 2–4, there will be only a single draw. In periods 5–7, there will be two draws from the same cup (with replacement after the first draw). In periods 8–10, there will be three draws (with each ball drawn being put back into the cup before the next draw is made).

After seeing the draw(s), if any, for the period, you will be asked to indicate the chances that cup A is being used by writing a number, P, between 0 and 100 in column (3).

Earnings

Next, let me describe a procedure that will help you make your decision. The procedure is complicated, but the underlying idea is simple. It's as if you send your friend to a fruit stand for tomatoes, and they ask you what to do if there are both red and yellow tomatoes. You should tell them the truth about your preference so that they can make the best choice for you. We'll set up the incentives so that your report about the chances of cup A will enable us to choose a lottery that gives you the highest chance of winning a $1 prize.

Suppose that, after seeing the draw or draws from the unknown cup, you think the chances are P out of 100 that cup A is being used. If you were to receive $1 in the event that the cup actually used was A, then this determines a "P lottery" which pays $1 with chances of P out of 100, nothing otherwise.

After you write down the number *P* that represents your beliefs about likelihood of cup A, we will use a 10-sided die to determine a second lottery, the "dice lottery." To do this, we throw the die twice, with the first throw giving the tens digit (0, 1, . . . , 9) and the second throw giving the ones digit (0, 1, . . . 9). Thus, the random number will be between 0 and 99. If the number is *N*, then the "dice lottery" will give you an *N* out of 100 chance of earning $1. (To play the dice lottery for a given value of *N*, we would throw the 10-sided die two more times to get a number that is equally likely to be 0, 1, . . . , 99, and you would earn $1 if this second throw is less than *N*.)

Up to this point, you will have written down a number *P* for what you think are the chances out of 100 that cup A is being used. The resulting *P* lottery will pay $1 if cup A is used. Then we will have used a throw of dice to determine a dice lottery that will pay $1 with chance *N* out of 100. Which would you rather have? It is better to have the dice lottery if *N* is greater than *P*, and it is better to have the *P* lottery otherwise. We'll give you the one that is best for you.

Case 1: *P* < *N*

If you write down a number *P* and the number *N* determined subsequently by the dice throws is greater, you will get to play the dice lottery (throwing the dice again to see if you get the $1, i.e., when the number determined by the second throw is less than *N*.)

Case 2: *P* ≥ *N*

If you write down a number *P* that is greater than or equal to the number *N* determined subsequently by the dice throw, then your earnings are determined by the *P* lottery, i.e., you will get $1 if the cup used turns out to be cup A.